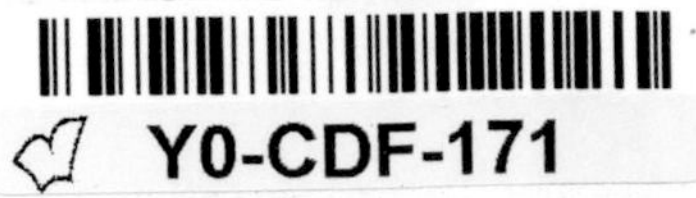

Third Edition

MARKETING RESEARCH ESSENTIALS

Carl McDaniel, Jr.
University of Texas at Arlington

Roger Gates
DSS Research

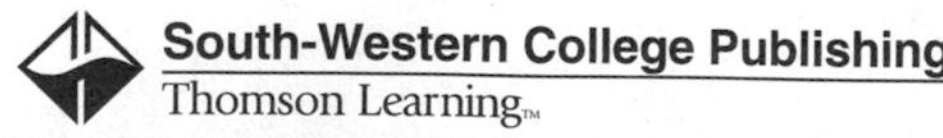
South-Western College Publishing
Thomson Learning™

Australia • Canada • Denmark • Japan • Mexico • New Zealand • Philippines
Puerto Rico • Singapore • South Africa • Spain • United Kingdom • United States

Marketing Research Essentials, Third Edition by Carl McDaniel, Jr. and Roger Gates

Publisher: Dave Shaut
Acquisitions Editor: Pamela M. Person
Developmental Editor: Bryant Editorial Development
Executive Marketing Director: Steve Scoble
Production Editor: Tamborah E. Moore
Manufacturing Coordinator: Sandee Milewski
Media Production Editor: Robin K. Browning

Cover and Internal Design: Liz Harasymczuk Design, Toronto
Internal Design Illustrations: Harvey Chan, Toronto
Photo Manager: Cary Benbow
Production House: The Left Coast Group
Compositor: The Left Coast Group
Printer: West Group

Photo Credits follow index.

Printed in the United States of America
2 3 4 5 03 02 01 00

For more information contact South-Western College Publishing, 5101 Madison Road, Cincinnati, Ohio, 45227 or find us on the Internet at http://www.swcollege.com

For permission to use material from this text or product, contact us by
- **telephone: 1-800-730-2214**
- **fax: 1-800-730-2215**
- **web: http://www.thomsonrights.com**

Library of Congress Cataloging-in-Publication Data

McDaniel, Carl D.
Marketing Research Essentials/Carl McDaniel, Roger Gates.
p. cm.
Includes bibliographical references and index.
ISBN 0-324-02317-0 (package: book & CD)
ISBN 0-324-02840-7 (book only)
ISBN 0-324-03713-9 (CD only)
1. Marketing research. I. Gates, Roger H., 1942- II. Title.

HF5415.2.M3825 2000
658.8'3—dc21

00-036524

This book is printed on acid-free paper.

To Our Children

Chelley, Mark, Raphaël, Michèle, and Sèbastien

CARL McDANIEL

Stephanie, Lara, and Jordan

ROGER GATES

CONTENTS IN BRIEF

CONTENTS

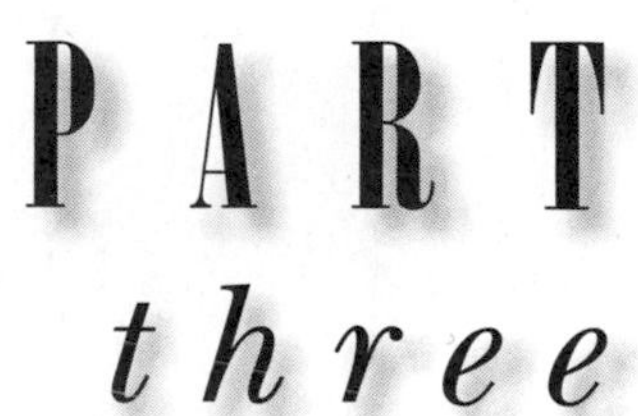

PART
three

PREFACE

A basic tenet of this text is that marketers must understand their clients and then do their best to deliver outstanding value and service to them. We have tried hard to follow this important principle in writing about what we believe are the essentials of doing marketing research. In today's rapidly changing global marketplace, cost-effective, accurate, and timely marketing decision making is critical. The practice of marketing research, in turn, is undergoing profound changes in technology and methodology to meet the information demands of key decision makers. One way we attempt to present you with a valuable text is by incorporating such cutting-edge changes in the practice of marketing research into this third edition.

This book will seem familiar and comfortable to you in many ways, and fresh and exciting in others. As always, it acknowledges the necessity of a solid research foundation by continuing to provide thorough coverage of fundamental research methods and traditional quantitative tools. It features the real-world applications of marketing research that the authors have learned in their years of working in the research industry. Simply stated, in today's business climate—and in this edition—*what* decision makers do with the research is as important as *how* they do the research.

Carl McDaniel is chairman of the Marketing Department at the University of Texas at Arlington. A distinguished author of a multitude of articles and books in marketing research, McDaniel was also the co-owner and manager of a marketing research firm for 12 years.

Roger Gates is the president of a major marketing research firm. Being active in the industry every day, he sees changes as they occur and trends as they develop. Thus, this text not only has the most current academic research in marketing, but also unmatched industry perspective, straight from the marketing research firing line.

The Internet Has Profoundly Changed Marketing Research . . . and We Describe Its Influence Throughout the Third Edition

Since the first survey was taken over 120 years ago in the United States, nothing has impacted the marketing research industry like the Internet. The third edition captures the profound changes in marketing research resulting from this phenomenal technology. For example, the Internet is now used to disseminate requests for proposals (RFPs), to respond to RFPs, to view focus groups on line anywhere in the world, to conduct focus groups and survey research, and to disseminate final reports. The entire process of gathering secondary data is now significantly faster and at much lower cost due to the Web. All these topics are covered in detail throughout the text. The end of each chapter includes a section called "Working the Net." Here you will find guided exercises designed to allow students to further understand the material covered in the chapter by investigating Internet resources.

Internet coverage is not limited to the textbook. On-line resources include a website specifically for this text at mcdaniel.swcollege.com and a marketing research discipline website at mktresearch.swcollege.com. There is also a student supplement called *Using Alternate Media for Marketing Research.* This item is available as a text or as an on-line service that can help your students begin to use the Internet and other resources to conduct marketing research.

Other New Features

- **An Increased Emphasis on Global Marketing Research.** We have included more "Global Issues" boxed features than before. These popular features give students insight into research practices in different countries around the world and offer tips on conducting research in the global marketplace. We also present a new section entitled "Trends in Global Research" in Chapter Three.
- **The Chapter on "Communicating the Research Results" Has Been Completely Rewritten.** In today's fast-moving world of management decision making, time has become a precious commodity. The thick, highly detailed reports that made reading them a laborious task are virtually extinct. The new, lively, cut-to-the-heart-of-the-matter report is today's standard. We canvassed over 50 top marketing research executives and used their experience with research reports, plus our own, to remake this chapter. Like the remainder of the third edition, this chapter represents today's contemporary marketing research.
- **New Chapter-Opening Vignettes.** We maintain the contemporary edge by creating vignettes that focus on the most up-to-date topics and research conducted in marketing research today. We address the problems and solutions companies discover when launching their products into the marketplace.
- **The Latest in Marketing Research Techniques.** The latest marketing research techniques and practices are examined in the boxed feature "In Practice." This popular feature from the second edition has been upgraded to include many new marketing stories.
- **New End-of-Chapter Cases.** Virtually all of the end-of-chapter cases have been replaced. Examples of new end-of-chapter cases include: Chilton Research, Yamaha, and the U.S. sports car market.

- **All Chapters Thoroughly Revised.** We carefully reviewed each chapter and incorporated the latest trends and ideas. The following chapter descriptions highlight some of these changes.
  - **Chapter One.** "The Role of Marketing Research in Management Decision Making"—New material on identifying target markets and researching the marketing mix. A new section on introduction to marketing research and the Internet.
  - **Chapter Two.** "The Marketing Research Process and the Management of Marketing Research"—A complete rewrite of the "problem/opportunity identification and formulation" stage of the research process. Distinctions are made between the marketing research problem, the marketing research objective, and the management decision problem. The section on creating the research design has been rewritten and there is an all-new section on managing research. This section addresses the question "What do clients want from a research department or research supplier?" along with issues of data quality and cost control.
  - **Chapter Three.** "The Marketing Research Industry and Research Ethics"—A new section on the users of marketing research. A new section on internal and external clients. New material on trends in global research suppliers. The chapter concludes with a succinct discussion of research ethics from the perspectives of client, supplier, and consumer.
  - **Chapter Four.** "Secondary Data, Databases, the Internet, and Decision Support Systems"—A new section on finding secondary data on the Internet, plus one on secondary data for marketing researchers on the Web. A new section on search operators for the Internet. A new section on using discussion groups and special interest groups on the Internet as sources of secondary data. And a new section on information management.
  - **Chapter Five.** "Qualitative Research"—New material on selecting a focus group moderator and on helping research users (observers) get more out of the focus groups. Also, new material on the special problems of conducting global focus groups. New material on Internet focus groups.
  - **Chapter Six.** "Primary Data Collection: Observation"—New material on emerging survey research methods. A new section on Internet surveys, Internet samples, and conducting Internet surveys. A new international survey research appendix.
  - **Chapter Seven.** "Primary Data Collection: Survey Research"—The section on mystery shoppers was completely rewritten. A new section on shopper patterns and shopper behavior research. A new tool called the Rapid Analysis Measurement System is described. The people meter controversy is updated. A new section on Information Resources, Inc. software.
  - **Chapter Eight.** "Primary Data Collection: Experimentation"—New examples to demonstrate causality. New material on simulated test marketing.
  - **Chapter Nine.** "The Concepts of Measurement and Attitude Scales"—A new example on ordinal scales.

- **Chapter Ten.** "Questionnaire Design"—New material on scale labels and the number of points on the scale. A new section on Internet questionnaires. A new section on the questionnaire's role in a research firm's costs and profitability.
- **Chapter Eleven.** "Basic Sampling Issues"—New material on unlisted telephone numbers. New material on convenience samples. New material on Internet samples.
- **Chapter Twelve.** "Sample Size Determination"—A new section on statistical power.
- **Chapter Thirteen.** "Data Processing, Basic Data Analysis, and the Statistical Testing of Differences"—New material on data entry with instantaneous results. New material on statistical packages available on the Internet. A new discussion on the insistence of many researchers on the .05 level for *p*-values.
- **Chapter Fourteen.** "Correlation and Regression Analysis"—New material on spurious correlations. New material comparing Spearman's rank-order correlation and Pearson's product moment correlation.
- **Chapter Fifteen.** "Communicating the Research Results"—This chapter was completely rewritten to reflect the expectations of today's clients, as previously described.

We Have Retained the Two Key Features that Made the Second Edition a Best-Seller

There is probably no greater hindrance to learning than a dull textbook. With this in mind, we have strived to make *Marketing Research Essentials,* Third Edition, a truly pleasurable and captivating reading experience by:

- *Writing in a lively, informal style developed over the years by two highly experienced and successful authors.* Careful attention to language and sentence structure and the use of hundreds of real-world examples make *Marketing Research Essentials,* Third Edition, engrossing while at the same time rigorous.
- *Implementing a research user's orientation.* A number of features have been incorporated into the text to aid future managers in effectively using marketing research.

Classroom-tested Pedagogy Puts Students in the Know

The pedagogy for the third edition has been developed in response to what you have told us delivers value to you and your students. These refined learning tools strengthen student learning while making the book more enjoyable and easy to read.

Learning Objectives

These challenge the student to explain, discuss, understand, and clarify the concepts to be presented.

Opening Vignettes

Each chapter opens with a case-type synopsis of a real marketing research situation. Your students will recognize many of the companies profiled, and will be surprised by some of the successes, failures, and challenges described.

In-Chapter Boxes

Typically, boxed items can interrupt the flow of the text and impede student understanding by creating a disjointed reading experience. For that reason, we have been conscientious not only in the placement of boxed material, but also in the design elements used to differentiate it from the body of the text. Two types of boxes are included in this edition: "In Practice" and "Global Issues." Each was previously described.

Clear, Concise Chapter Summaries

Concise summaries present the core concepts that underpin each chapter. Although the summary is located at the end of the chapter, students can read it and the opening vignette together as a prereading exercise before diving into the rest of the chapter.

Key Terms and Definitions

Key terms appear in boldface in the text, with definitions in the margins, making it easy for students to check their understanding. A complete list of key terms and definitions appears at the end of each chapter as a study checklist. Students will find a full glossary of all key terms at the end of the text.

Questions for Review and Critical Thinking

Our society has an enormous capacity for generating data, but our ability to use the data to make good decisions has lagged behind. In the hope of better preparing the next generation of business leaders, many educators are beginning to place greater emphasis on developing critical-thinking skills. Accordingly, we have added a number of critical-thinking questions at the end of each chapter. Review questions are also offered to direct students to the core concepts of the chapter.

Working the Net

We send students to URLs related to chapter materials. Not only does this amplify and update concepts discussed in the text, but it also helps them use the Internet as a marketing researcher would. Links to the URLs mentioned are available on our website at mcdaniel.swcollege.com.

Real-Life Marketing Research Minicases

Over half of the cases are new to this edition. These cases help students to synthesize chapter concepts by focusing on real marketing research problems.

A Supplement Package to Keep Your Planning Simple

Instructor Manual with Test Bank, Video Guide, and Power Notes

We have created a comprehensive teaching resource to accompany the third edition. The *Instructor Resource Manual* has everything you need to create your syllabus and plan your lectures. Testing material includes multiple-choice and true/false questions, and poses essay questions or problems for every chapter. Thorough teaching notes give you an overview of the objectives for the chapter, the terminology covered, and a detailed outline of the chapter content, with additional examples for you to use to supplement your presentation. Solutions for all end-of-chapter materials are also provided.

Video teaching notes help you to incorporate video into your classroom without sacrificing the presentation of critical content. Teaching suggestions are provided for every segment.

ExamView Testing Software

ExamView software allows you to customize your tests to reflect the material you have covered in class. Rearrange existing questions or add your own to create a perfectly tailored test that evaluates your students' mastery of the material.

Videos

The third edition has a complete video package to dynamically support text content. A segment on how to prepare for a focus group reinforces the material in Chapter Five. Students will then see how the theory translates into practice when they watch two real focus group discussions: one on deodorant and one on women's shoes. Additional segments include company profiles on industry leaders Chilton Research Services and ACNielsen. A new segment on Burke Marketing Research, Inc. highlights the activities of this top research firm.

PowerPoint Makes Lectures Easy

Over 300 PowerPoint slides have been developed for the third edition. Each slide shows pertinent information from a chapter in a visually organized manner. Students using the PowerPoints to create PowerNotes will have an easy time organizing the material in their minds. Both a projection presentation and an overhead presentation are downloadable from the mcdaniel.swcollege.com website.

Mcdaniel.swcollege.com

Capitalizing on the strength of *Contemporary Marketing Research,* Fourth Edition, the third edition boasts a content-rich website. Numerous resources and extra text material are posted, as well as on-line quizzing to help your students review. In addition, exercises found only at mcdaniel.swcollege.com help your students understand the increasing role that Internet technology is playing in the marketing research industry.

Supplements to Help Your Students Learn

All-New Student CD-ROM

Each student text comes with a CD-ROM full of extra learning opportunities. Ethical dilemmas give students the chance to evaluate various situations from an ethical perspective and to appreciate how ethics comes into play when conducting and using marketing research. Cross-functional exercises help students see how marketing research is not confined to a single department. The new Burke Marketing Research video segment is included so that students can review it periodically throughout the term, gaining new insights as they master more concepts. A copy of the full PowerPoint presentation is included as PowerNotes to help students review for quizzes, tests, and exams. A comprehensive case with a complete data set is also included. Toward the end of the term, students will have enough understanding to work the case and present a research report.

Mcdaniel.swcollege.com

The resources on our website aren't just for instructors. Students can expand their view of the marketing research industry and check their comprehension by taking advantage of the numerous opportunities at mcdaniel.swcollege.com.

A Special Thanks

We would like to extend special thanks to the many people who made this text and its supplement package a reality. Tom Quirk (Webster University) compiled the wonderfully detailed teaching notes and testing material; E. Charles Pflanz (Scottsdale Community College) created the full PowerPoint presentation that visually organizes even the most difficult content.

We would also like to thank our reviewers, who help keep us on the cutting edge of content and pedagogy.

Judy Berkowitz, Emerson College
Eileen Bridges, Kent State University
John Cox, University of Texas Pan American
Charles Duke, Clemson University
Richard E. Fetter, Butler University
Andrew Forman, Hofstra University
Gopala Ganesh, University of North Texas
John Gwin, University of Virginia
Carol Himeloch, Cleary College
Linda Morris, University of Idaho
Joseph Orsini, CSU, Sacramento
Jan Owens, University of Wisconsin
Gordon Patzer, University of Northern Iowa
James Roberts, Baylor University
Peter Sanchez, Villanova University
Bruce Stern, Portland State University
Gail Tom, California State University, Sacremento
Michael Wood, Hunter College, CUNY

MARKETING RESEARCH ESSENTIALS

Third Edition

PART one

An Introduction to Marketing Research

Check it out!

Remember to visit http://mcdaniel.swcollege.com for information to help you with the material in Part One. MR Online in the Resource Center of http://marketing.swcollege.com can also help you review for your final exam!

The Role of Marketing Research in Management Decision Making

Learning Objectives

1 *To review the marketing concept and the marketing mix*

2 *To comprehend the marketing environment within which managers must make decisions*

3 *To define marketing research*

4 *To understand the importance of marketing research in shaping marketing decisions*

5 *To learn when marketing research should and should not be conducted*

CHAPTER *one*

Forget American Express. Some businesspeople don't leave home without their teddy bears. That was one of the surprising facts Courtyard by Marriott found when it commissioned research on its customer base. At Courtyard, market research is "very important to us to understand the wants and needs of our customers. We can't find out if we don't ask," said Geary Campbell, director of national public relations at Marriott. Surveys also serve as a marketing tool "to tell the media and customers what our customers do while they are on the road," Campbell said, "and to get greater recognition for the Courtyard brand."

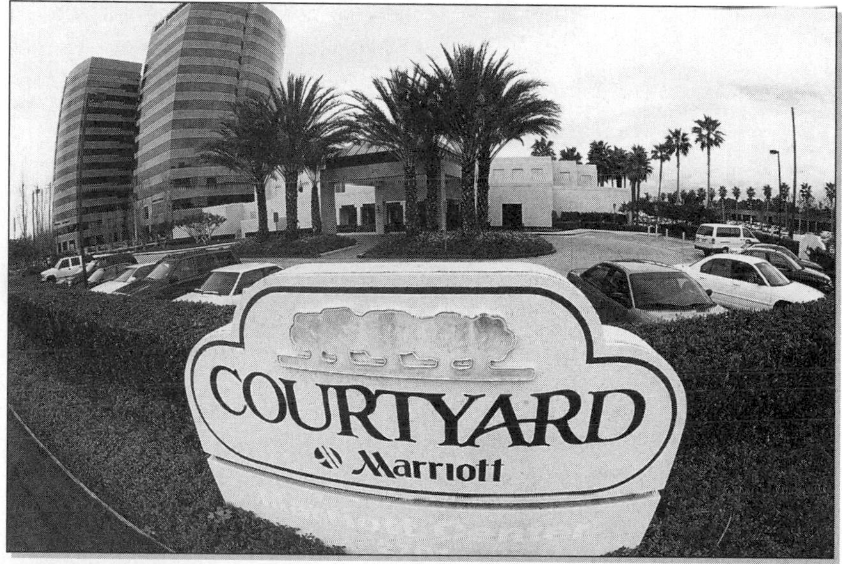

By conducting marketing research, Courtyard was able to identify the needs and wants of its business travelers and to create services that would keep them coming back.

The Courtyard by Marriott Business Traveler Profile of 300 business travelers who had taken at least six work-related trips in the previous 12 months was conducted by D. K. Shifflet & Associates of McLean, Virginia. The 30-question telephone survey focused on how travelers communicate with their homes and offices, as well as what they do or what they bring with them to make life on the road feel more like home. "We also wanted to find out quirky things," Campbell said, "such as their travel behaviors."

Marriott predicted some of the results ahead of time. For example, the survey found that 58 percent of business travelers bring along a laptop computer. Other findings came as a surprise: 70 percent of those with laptops said they have games on their computer, and 7 percent of business travelers admitted that they travel with a teddy bear or other type of stuffed animal.

Armed with these data, Courtyard has made some changes in its marketing approach. Aware that many business travelers have laptop PCs and access to the Net, for example, Marriott's website provides information for business travelers, such as maps to hotel sites and Courtyard-sponsored promotions. Because the survey indicated that many business travelers like to have time to relax, Courtyard promotes its quiet lounges, which don't have music or TV noise to distract guests.

Survey results confirmed that business travelers want "more than a friendly face" greeting them at the front desk, Campbell said. Business travelers who are on the road want the opportunity to purchase breakfast in advance and efficient

Find out more about Courtyard's commitment to business travelers by clicking on What's New at

http://www.courtyard.com

check-ins and check-outs. Because business travel is hectic, Courtyard strives to make the travelers' stays as hassle-free and consistent as possible. "Whether they are staying at a Courtyard in Washington, D.C., or Seattle, Washington, they will have the same experience, and they will know what to expect," she said.

Marriott launched its Courtyard brand in 1983, after two years of research conducted on guests of their full-service hotels, asking what features they would want in a moderately priced hotel. Courtyard's main customer base is the business traveler, Campbell said.[1]

Marriott uses marketing research both to design new products—the Courtyard brand—and to build brand equity by altering its products to meet the ever-changing needs of the marketplace. What exactly is marketing research? How important is marketing research to shaping marketing decisions? When should marketing research be conducted? These are some of the issues we will discuss in Chapter 1. ■

The Nature of Marketing

Marketing The process of planning and executing the conception, pricing, promotion, and distribution of ideas, goods, and services to create exchanges that satisfy individual and organizational objectives.

Marketing is the process of planning and executing the conception, pricing, promotion, and distribution of ideas, goods, and services to create exchanges that satisfy individual and organizational objectives. The potential for exchange exists when there are at least two parties, and each has something of potential value to the other. When the two parties can communicate and deliver the desired goods or services, exchange can take place. How do marketing managers attempt to stimulate exchange? They follow the "right principle." They attempt to get the right goods or services to the right people at the right place at the right time at the right price using the right promotion techniques. This principle tells you that marketing managers control many factors that ultimately determine marketing success. To make the right decisions, management must have timely decision-making information. Marketing research is a primary channel for providing that information.

Marketing concept A business philosophy based on consumer orientation, goal orientation, and systems orientation.

Consumer orientation Identifying and focusing on the people or firms most likely to buy a product and producing a good or service that will meet their needs more effectively.

Goal orientation Focusing on the accomplishment of corporate goals with a limit set on consumer orientation.

The Marketing Concept

To efficiently accomplish their goals, firms today have adopted the **marketing concept,** which requires (1) a consumer orientation, (2) a goal orientation, and (3) a systems orientation. A **consumer orientation** means striving to identify the people or firms that are the most likely to buy a product (the target market) and to produce a good or offer a service that will meet the needs of target customers more effectively in the face of competition.

The second tenet of the marketing concept is a **goal orientation,** meaning that a firm is consumer oriented only to the extent that it also accomplishes corporate goals. In profit-making firms these goals usually center on financial criteria, such as a 15 percent return on investment.

The third component of the marketing concept is a **systems orientation.** A system is an organized whole—or a group of diverse units that form an integrated whole—functioning or operating in unison. It is one thing for a firm to say it is consumer oriented and another actually to be consumer oriented. Systems must be established first to find out what consumers want and to identify market opportunities. As you will see later, identifying target market needs and market opportunities is the task of marketing research. Next, this information must be fed back to the firm. Without feedback from the marketplace, a firm cannot be truly consumer oriented.

Systems orientation Creating systems to monitor the external environment and deliver the marketing mix to the target market.

Identifying Target Markets and Researching the Marketing Mix: The Opportunistic Nature of Marketing Research

Marriott's marketing research uncovered an opportunity to create a new hotel chain that would primarily serve business travelers, with homey surroundings at moderate prices. Marriott used marketing research to identify marketing opportunities. The Courtyard concept was aimed at a new target market for Marriott.

After identifying the target market, a **marketing mix** had to be created. A marketing mix is the unique blend of product/service, pricing, promotion, offerings, and distribution strategies designed to reach a specific target market. Marriott spent two years creating the marketing mix for Courtyard. Research identified the best sites for Courtyard units (distribution), prices to be charged in various locations, how to position the product in the marketplace, and what features to promote. Marriott also used research to determine the size of the rooms and what features and amenities most business travelers desired(product/service offering). Marketing research identified an opportunity, which then enabled Marriott to use further research to create a successful addition to its product line: Courtyard by Marriott.

Marketing mix The unique blend of product/service, pricing, promotion, offerings, and distribution designed to meet the needs of a specific group of consumers.

The External Marketing Environment

Over time, a marketing mix must be altered because of changes in the environment in which consumers and businesses live, work, compete, and make purchasing decisions. This means that some new consumers and businesses will become part of the target market, just as others will drop out, and the new mix may have different tastes, needs, incomes, lifestyles, and purchasing habits than the original target consumers.

Although managers can control the marketing mix, they cannot control elements in the external environment that continually mold and reshape the target market. Unless management understands the external environment, a firm cannot intelligently plan its future. An organization is often unaware of the forces that influence its future. Marketing research is a key means for understanding the environment. Knowledge of the environment helps a firm not only to alter its present marketing mix, but also to identify new opportunities. For example, Goodyear's environmental scanning marketing research found that drivers were becoming more and more concerned about safety. Part of this concern was driving in bad weather. A needs analysis research program determined that consumers wanted a tire that would be stable on wet roads. Goodyear took this information to its engineers, who created a design system that removed water from the tire as it rolled down the road. The Goodyear Aquatread was born. Target consumers for this product are 10 times as likely to mention Aquatread than any other tire brand.[2]

The Role of Marketing Research in Decision Making

Marketing research plays two key roles in the marketing system. First, it is part of the marketing intelligence feedback process. It provides decision makers with data on the effectiveness of the current marketing mix and provides insights for necessary changes. Second, marketing research is the primary tool for exploring new opportunities in the marketplace. Segmentation research and new product research help identify the most lucrative opportunities for marketing managers.

Marketing Research Defined

Now that you have an understanding of how marketing research fits into an overall marketing system, we can proceed with a formal definition of the term as specified by the American Marketing Association:

> Marketing research is the function which links the consumer, customer, and public to the marketer through information—information used to identify and define marketing opportunities and problems; generate, refine, and evaluate marketing actions; monitor marketing performance; and improve understanding of marketing as a process. Marketing research specifies the information required to address these issues; designs the method for collecting information; manages and implements the data collection process; analyzes the results; and communicates the findings and their implications.[3]

Marketing research The planning, collection, and analysis of data relevant to marketing decision making and the communication of the results of this analysis to management.

We like a shorter definition: **Marketing research** is the planning, collection, and analysis of data relevant to marketing decision making and the communication of the results of this analysis to management.

The Importance of Marketing Research to Management

Descriptive function Gathering and presenting statements of fact.

Marketing research can be viewed as playing three functional roles: descriptive, diagnostic, and predictive. Its **descriptive function** includes gathering and presenting statements of fact. For example, what is the historic sales trend in the industry? What are consumers' attitudes toward a product and its advertising? The second role of research is the **diagnostic function,** wherein data or actions are explained. What was the impact on sales when we changed the design on the package? In other words, how can we alter our product/service offerings to better serve customers and potential customers? The final role of research is the **predictive function.** How can we best take advantage of opportunities as they arise in the ever-changing marketplace?

Diagnostic function Explaining data or actions.

Predictive function Specifying how to use descriptive and diagnostic research to predict the results of a planned marketing decision.

The Unrelenting Drive for Quality and Customer Satisfaction

Quality and customer satisfaction have become the key competitive weapons of the new century. Few organizations will prosper in today's environment without a focus on quality, continual improvement, and customer satisfaction. Corporations across the globe have implemented quality improvement and satisfaction programs in an effort to reduce costs, retain customers, increase market share, and, last but not least, improve the bottom line.

When total quality management swept through corporate America in the late 1980s, the emphasis was strictly on product improvement. But product improvement per se wasn't the answer. Consider the case of Varian Associates, Inc., a manufacturer of scientific equipment. The company put 1,000 of its managers through a four-day course on quality. The company's Silicon Valley headquarters buzzed with quality-speak. Talk of work teams and cycle times replaced discussion of electrons and X rays. Varian went about virtually reinventing the way it did business—with what seemed to be stunning results. A unit that makes vacuum systems for computer clean rooms boosted on-time delivery from 42 percent to 92 percent. The semiconductor unit cut the time it took to put out new designs by 14 days. However, producing quality products wasn't enough. Obsessed with meeting production schedules, the staff in that vacuum-equipped unit didn't return customers' phone calls, and the operation ended up losing market share. Radiation repair people were so rushed to meet deadlines that they left before explaining their work to customers. "All of the quality-based charts went up and to the right, but everything else went down," says Richard M. Levy, executive vice president for quality. The company actually lost money in the late 1980s.[4]

The drive for quality, as demonstrated by Varian, was often a production-oriented, mechanistic exercise that proved meaningless to customers. Quality that means little to customers usually doesn't produce a payoff in improved sales, profits, or market share. It's wasted effort and expense. Today the new mantra is **return on quality.** This means two things: (1) that the quality being delivered is the quality desired by the target market and (2) that added quality must have a positive impact on profitability. Today, for example, banking giant NationsBank Corporation measures every improvement in service, from adding more tellers to offering new mortgage products, in terms of added profitability.

Return on quality A management objective based on the principles that the quality being delivered is the quality desired by the target market and that quality must have a positive impact on profitability.

The key to making return on quality work is marketing research. It is the mechanism that enables organizations to determine what types and forms of quality are important to a target market. Marketing research can sometimes force companies to abandon cherished beliefs. United Parcel Service, Inc., for example, had always assumed that on-time delivery was the paramount concern of its customers. Everything else came second. Before long, UPS's

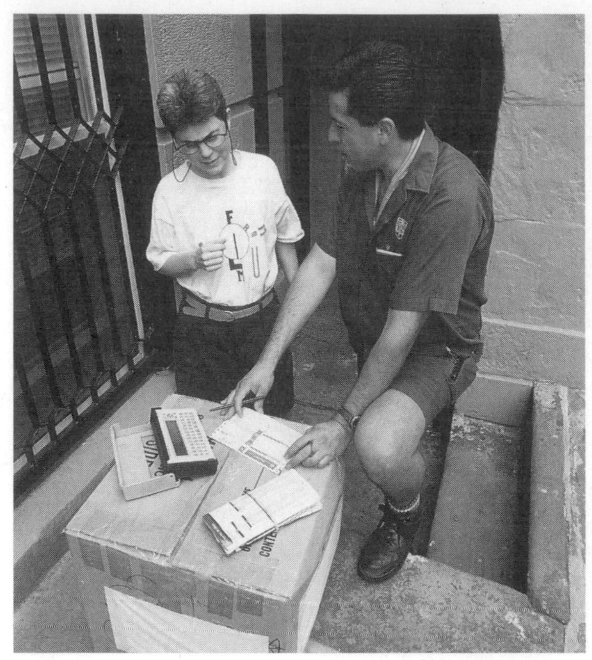

UPS was forced to rethink its definition of quality service when the results of marketing research surveys revealed that customers wanted more interaction with the drivers. Go to the Services folder at http://www.ups.com to see how UPS may have used part of these results on its Web page.

definition of quality centered almost exclusively on the results of time-and-motion studies. Knowing the average time it took elevator doors to open on a certain city block and figuring how long it took people to answer their doorbells were critical parts of the quality equation. So was pushing drivers to meet exacting schedules. The problem was that UPS's marketing research was asking the wrong questions. Its survey asked customers if they were pleased with delivery time and whether they thought delivery should be even faster.

When UPS recently began asking broader questions about how it could improve service, it discovered that clients weren't as obsessed with on-time delivery as the company had previously thought. The biggest surprise to UPS management: Customers wanted more interaction with drivers—the only face-to-face contact any of them had with the company. If drivers were less harried and more willing to chat, customers could get some practical advice on shipping. "We've discovered that the highest rated element we have is our drivers," says Lawrence E. Farrel, UPS's service quality manager.

In a sharp departure from company policy, UPS is encouraging its 62,000 delivery drivers to get out of their trucks and visit customers, sometimes accompanied by salespeople. It also allows drivers an additional 30 minutes a week to spend at their discretion to strengthen ties with customers and perhaps bring in new sales.[5]

The Paramount Importance of Keeping Existing Customers

An inextricable link exists between customer satisfaction and customer loyalty. Long-term relationships don't just happen; they are grounded in the delivery of services and good value. Customer retention pays big dividends for organizations. Powered by repeat sales and referrals, revenues and market share grow. Costs fall because firms spend fewer funds and energy attempting to replace customers who defect. Steady customers are easy to serve because they understand the company's modus operandi and make fewer demands on employees' time. Increased customer retention also drives job satisfaction and pride, which leads to higher employee retention. In turn, the knowledge employees acquire as they stay longer increases productivity. A Bain & Company study estimates that a 5 percent decrease in the customer defection rate can boost profits by 25 percent to 95 percent.[6]

The ability to retain customers is based on an intimate understanding of their needs. This knowledge comes primarily from marketing research. For example, British Airways recast its first-class transatlantic service because of detailed marketing research. Most airlines stress top-of-the-line service in their transatlantic first-class cabins. British Airways research found that most first-class passengers simply wanted to sleep. British Airways now gives premium flyers the option of dinner on the ground, before takeoff, in the first-class lounge. Once on board, they can slip into British Airways pajamas, put their heads on real pillows, slip under blankets, and then enjoy an interruption-free flight. On arrival, first-class passengers can have breakfast, use comfortable dressing rooms and showers, and even have their clothes pressed before they set off for business. These changes in British Airway's first-class service were driven strictly by marketing research.[7]

Managers Must Understand the Ever-Changing Marketplace

Marketing research helps managers understand what is going on in the marketplace and take advantage of opportunities. Marketing research has been practiced for as long as marketing has existed. The early Phoenicians carried out market demand studies as they traded in the various ports of the Mediterranean Sea. Marco Polo's diary indicates that he was performing a marketing research function in his travels to China. There is even evidence that the Spanish systematically conducted "market surveys" as they explored the New World, and there are examples of marketing research conducted during the Renaissance.

Marketing will continue to have a place in commerce. Today, a marketing manager might, for example, consider offering coupons with the introduction of a new frozen pastry. The coupon will be used along with network television advertising to induce people to try the new pastry. The question is, who should receive the coupons? The sales promotion expenditure will be more effective if coupons are mailed to those households most likely to redeem them. Previous experience with frozen pastry coupon redemptions suggests that heavy coupon users in general are most likely to redeem the new pastry coupons. The next logical question for the marketing manager to ask is, "Are there any identifiable demographic characteristics of heavy coupon users versus light users?" If market research reveals that the only statistically significant difference is that the female head of household is not employed full time (see Table 1.1), then the marketing manager would specify this characteristic when purchasing the mailing list for the new frozen pastry coupons.

Table 1.1

Demographics of Coupon Users

	Heavy User (top 20%)	Medium to Light User	Nonuser
Average household size	3.6	3.2	3.4
Average age of female head	43.1	45.2	41.9
Household income ($ in thousands)	$30.9	$29.1	$28.7
Female head attended college	51%	50%	52%
Average monthly grocery bill	$334	$292	$303
Female head does not work outside or works part time	65%	61%	55%

Understanding the marketplace is not just a U.S. or industrialized market phenomenon. Managers all over the world must understand the ever-changing marketplace and their customers. The Global Issues box illustrates this point.

The Proactive Role of Marketing Research

Understanding the nature of the marketing system is a necessity for a successful marketing orientation. By having a thorough knowledge of factors that have an impact on the target market and the marketing mix, management can be proactive rather than reactive. A proactive management alters the marketing mix to fit newly emerging patterns in economic, social, and competitive environments, whereas a reactive management waits for change to have a major impact on the firm before deciding to take action. It is the difference between viewing the turbulent marketing environment as a threat (a reactive stance) or an opportunity (a proactive stance). For example, two large U.S. department store chains, Sears and JC Penney, have largely been reactive to retailing on the Internet. A proactive position would have been to becomc cutting-edge Internet marketers. Marketing research plays a key role in proactive management by anticipating changes in the market and customer desires and then designing goods and services to meet those needs.

The proactive manager continually seeks new opportunities in the ever-changing marketplace, both with existing customers and potential new customers. For example, even in today's slow-growth economy, some new consumers enter while others leave. The characteristics of new consumers vary widely by product category, but two groups are particularly important for a wide range of products: young people and immigrants (see Figure 1.1). Both groups are forming their preferences for numerous products and services, and both will support the marketplace for numerous products and services for decades after they make their initial choices.

Figure 1.1

Emergent Markets

Source: David W. Stewart, "Advertising in a Slow Growth Economy," by *American Demographics,* September 1994, p. 42. Reprinted from *American Demographics* magazine, courtesy of Intertec Publishing Corp., Stamford, Connecticut. All Rights Resevered.

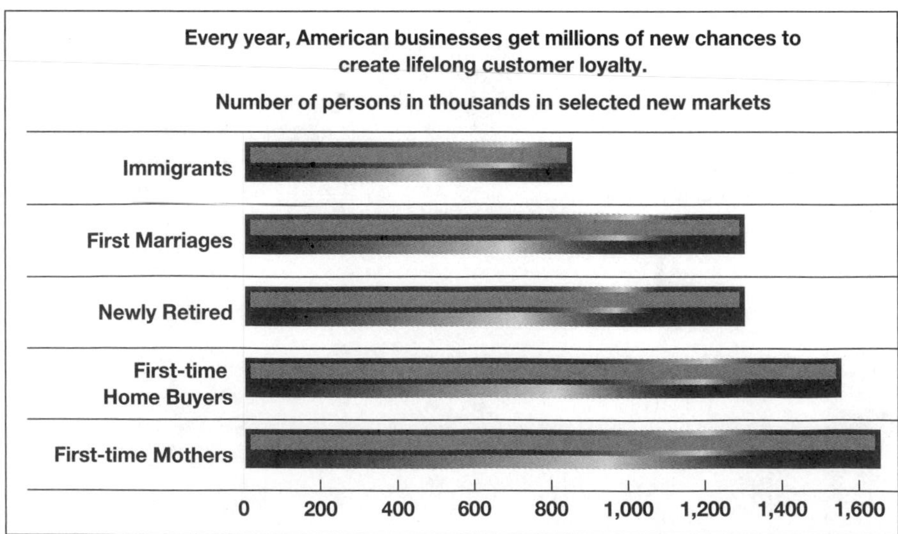

Global ISSUES

FOREIGN COMPANIES HAVE DISCOVERED JAPAN'S BEST MARKETING BELLWETHER: THE TEENAGE GIRL. As Japanese companies have long known, the nation's highschool girls have an uncanny ability to predict which products will be hits with consumers of all age groups. What's more, a select pool of these teens can create a buzz that turns a new product into a nationwide smash.

"A fad that catches on among teenage girls often becomes a big trend throughout the country and among consumers in general," says Etsuko Katsube, a Coca-Cola Company marketing executive who used teenage girls to market a now-popular soft drink made with fermented milk.

Girl guides are taken very seriously in Japan. Food makers like Calbee Foods Co. and Meiji Seika Kaisha Ltd. frequently round up schoolgirls from Tokyo's streets to sample potato-chip recipes or chocolate bars. Asahi Broadcasting Corporation surveys high school girls to fine-tune story lines for higher ratings on the television network's prime-time dramas. Other companies pay girls to keep diaries of what they buy.

Boom, one of a group of Tokyo research firms that specialize[s] in teen surveys, offers a portfolio of several thousand Tokyo-area high school girls that includes, it says, 500 girls deemed to be "trend setters." Boom's clients include giants such as 7-Eleven Japan Company and Shiseido Company.

On a recent afternoon, a trio of Tokyo high school girls sat in a Boom interview room poking at blobs of fruit gelatin. They were helping Meiji Milk Products Company narrow down a list of six flavors to four that Meiji Milk will sell in 7,300 Japanese convenience stores. Swallowing a spoonful of apple gelatin, 15-year-old Kanako Yonemura cocked her head and proclaim[ed], "This is too sweet." The interviewer listened intently. The girl added: "And I'd like to know how many calories it has per serving."

Shiseido says that by tapping teen insights it unexpectedly hit on a broad market for a low-priced line of nail polishes. The cosmetics maker had named the line Chopi; the girls preferred another name, Neuve. They also persuaded Shiseido to change the container's color from the usual black, white, or silver to beige.

"Just about all the basic ideas for Neuve came from high school girls," says Masaru Miyagawa, a Shiseido marketing director. The company credits the girls with the fact that a product originally aimed at teens proved appealing to women of all ages. Over the past year, Neuve sales totaled 20 million units. Annual sales of 1 million units is considered a marketing success in Japan.[8] ■

In 1990, 24 million Americans were between the ages of 13 and 19. By 2040, this population will grow to nearly 34 million, according to Census Bureau projections. Eight percent of the U.S. population is foreign-born, and 24 percent of the foreign-born have entered the United States since 1985. The Census Bureau estimates that immigration will account for more than one-third of U.S. population growth over the next 50 years. This huge

Thousands of foreign-born consumers move to the United States each year creating new markets.

number of new consumers will need to become acquainted with brands, retail outlets, and service providers. The best way for a proactive company to get its share of these new consumers is to understand their needs and wants. This means marketing research.

A proactive manager not only examines emerging markets, but also seeks, through strategic planning, to develop a long-term marketing strategy for the firm. It is **marketing strategy** that guides the long-term use of a firm's resources based on the firm's existing and projected internal capabilities and on projected changes in the external environment. A good strategic plan is based on good marketing research and helps the firm meet long-term profit and market-share goals. Poor strategic planning can threaten a company's survival. For example, Wards, floundering for almost a decade because of inadequate planning and a lack of understanding of the marketplace, had to give up its once-dominant catalog sales division. Good strategic planning would have enabled Wards to remain a market leader.

Marketing strategy Guiding the long-term use of a firm's resources based on its existing and projected capabilities and on projected changes in the external environment.

Applied Research Versus Basic Research

Applied research Research aimed at solving a specific pragmatic problem—a better understanding of the marketplace, a determination of why a strategy or tactic failed, a reduction of uncertainty in management decision making.

Basic or pure research Research aimed at expanding the frontiers of knowledge rather than solving a specific pragmatic problem.

Virtually all marketing research is conducted to better understand the market, to find out why a strategy failed, or to reduce uncertainty in management decision making. All research conducted for these purposes is called **applied research.** For example, should the price of frozen dinners be raised 40 cents? What name should Ford select for a new sedan? Which commercial has the highest level of recall: A or B? On the other hand, **basic or pure research** attempts to expand the frontiers of knowledge; it is research not aimed at a specific pragmatic problem. Basic research hopes to provide further confirmation to an existing theory or to learn more about a concept or phenomenon. For example, basic research might test a hypothesis on high-involvement decision making or consumer information processing. In the long run, basic research helps us understand more about the world in which we live. Usually, basic research findings cannot be implemented by managers in the short term. Most basic research is now conducted in universities. The findings are reported in such publications as *The Journal of Marketing Research* and *The Journal of Marketing.* In contrast, most research undertaken by businesses is applied research because it must be cost-effective and of demonstrable value to the decision maker.

Deciding Whether to Conduct Market Research

A manager who is faced with several alternative solutions to a particular problem should not instinctively call for applied marketing research. In fact, the first decision to be made is whether to conduct marketing research at all. In a number of situations, it is best not to conduct marketing research.

A lack of resources. There are two situations when a lack of resources should preclude marketing research from being undertaken. First, an organization may lack the funds to do the research properly. If a project calls for a sample of 800 respondents but the budget allows for only 50 interviews, the quality of the information would be highly suspect. Second, funds may be available to do the research properly but insufficient to implement any decisions resulting from the research. Sometimes small organizations in particular lack the necessary resources to create an effective marketing mix. In one case, for example, the director of a performing arts guild was in complete agreement with the recommendations that resulted from a market research project. However, two years after the project was completed, nothing had been done because the money to implement then was not available.

Research results would not be useful. Some types of marketing research studies measure lifestyle and personality factors of customers and potential customers. Assume that a study finds that introverted men with a poor self-concept but a high need for achievement are the most likely to patronize a discount brokerage service. The management of Charles Schwab discount brokerage might be hard-pressed to use this information.

Poor timing in the marketplace. Marketing research should not be undertaken if the opportunity for successful entry into a market has already passed. If a product is in the late maturity or decline stage of the products life cycle, such as record turntables or console black-and-white television sets, it would be foolish to do research for a new product entry. The same is true for markets rapidly approaching saturation, such as super premium ice cream; that is, Häagen-Dazs, Ben and Jerry's, Schrafft's, and Blue Bell. For products already in the market, however, research is needed to modify then as tastes, competition, and other factors change.

The decision has already been made. In the real world of management decision making and company politics, marketing research has sometimes been used improperly. Several years ago, a large marketing research study was conducted for a bank with over $300 million in deposits. The purpose of the research project was to guide top management in mapping a strategic direction for the bank during the next five years. After presenting the report to the president, he said, "I fully agree with your recommendations because that was what I was going to do anyway! I'm going to use your study tomorrow when I present my strategic plan to the board of directors." The researcher then asked, "What if my recommendations had been counter to your decision?" The bank president laughed and said, "They would have never known that I had conducted a marketing research study!" Not only was the project a waste of money, but it also raised a number of ethical questions in the researcher's mind.

When managers cannot agree on what they need to know to make a decision. Although it may seem obvious that research should not be undertaken until objectives are specified, it sometimes happens. Although preliminary or exploratory studies are commonly done to better understand the nature of a problem, a large, major research project should not be. It is faulty logic to say, "Well, let's just go ahead and do the study and then we will better understand the problem and know what steps to take." The wrong phenomena may be studied or key elements needed for management decision making may not be included.

When decision-making information already exists. Some companies have been conducting research in certain markets for many years. They understand the characteristics of target customers and what they like and dislike about existing products. Under these circumstances, further research would be redundant and a waste of money. Procter & Gamble, for example, has extensive knowledge of the coffee market. After it conducted initial taste tests, P&G went into national distribution with Folger's Instant Coffee without further research. The Sara Lee Corporation did the same thing with its frozen croissants, as did Quaker Oats with Chewy Granola Bars. This tactic, however, does not always work. P&G thought it understood the pain reliever market thoroughly, so it bypassed market research for Encaprin encapsulated aspirin. The product failed because it lacked a distinct competitive advantage over existing products and was withdrawn from the market.

When the costs of conducting research outweigh the benefits. There is rarely a situation in which a manager has such tremendous confidence in his or her judgment that additional information relative to a pending decision would not be accepted if it were available and free. But the manager might be unwilling to pay much for it or wait long to receive it. The willingness to acquire additional decision-making information depends on a manager's perception of its quality, price, and timing. The manager would be willing to pay more for perfect information—data that leaves no doubt about which alternative to follow—than for information that leaves uncertainty about what to do. Research should be undertaken only when the expected value of the information is greater than the cost of obtaining it.

Generally speaking, potential new products with large profit margins benefit more from marketing research than products with small profit margins, assuming that both items have the same sales potential. Similarly, new product opportunities in large markets offer greater potential benefits than those in small markets, if the competitive intensity is the same in both markets (see Table 1.2). The decision of whether to conduct marketing research depends on whether the perceived cost is

Table 1.2

Deciding Whether to Conduct Market Research

Market Size	Small Profit Margin	Large Profit Margin
Small	Costs are likely to be greater than benefits, such as for eyeglass replacement screws, or tire valve extensions. Don't conduct marketing research.	Benefits are possibly greater than costs, such as for ultra-expensive Lamborgini-type sportswear; large specialized industrial equipment; or computer-aided metal stamping machines. Perhaps conduct marketing research. Learn all you can from existing information prior to making the decision to conduct research.
Large	Benefits are likely to be greater than costs, such as for Stouffer's frozen entrees or Crest's tartar control toothpastes. Perhaps conduct marketing research. Learn all you can from existing information prior to making the decision to conduct research.	Benefits are probably greater than costs, such as for medical equipment like CAT scanners and Toshiba's high-definition television. Conduct marketing research.

greater than the perceived benefit. Two important determinants of potential benefits are profit margins and market size.

It is difficult to tell precisely where research will go in the future, but it is safe to predict that marketing research will greatly expand, both quantitatively and qualitatively. More studies will be conducted and costs will definitely rise. At the same time, increasingly more sophisticated approaches will be adopted and refined. (Some of these trends will be highlighted in subsequent chapters, as the topics come up.) There will be a greater emphasis on scanner-based research, database marketing, and customer satisfaction research, to name a few. Of greatest significance, however, is the fact that marketing research activities will grow in scope and extend into other arenas, such as nonprofit organizations and government services. Also, fewer companies will be without formal market research departments. Perhaps the greatest impact on the future of marketing research will be the Internet. The marketing research industry faces many challenges, such as integrating the Internet into the research process and the declining willingness of people to participate in survey research. These challenges are covered in detail throughout the text. A quick glimpse of how the Internet impacts marketing research is described in the Going On-Line box on page 16.

Going ON-LINE

Ways to Use the Internet in Marketing Research

BECAUSE THE INTERNET IS BECOMING SUCH A POWERFUL tool for marketing researchers, we have included Internet discussions throughout the text.

Major areas of Internet use in marketing research include:

- *Secondary source material.* The virtual replacement of libraries and various printed materials as sources of secondary data. On their website, the Bureau of the Census (http://www.census.gov) indicates that they plan to gradually make the Internet the major means of distributing census data. The same is true for a number of other government agencies. Information is available on the user's desktop or notebook PC almost instantaneously.
- *Data collection.* The Web is already being used to collect survey data from various respondent groups. At the present time this use is limited in a number of ways and there are many problems. However, it is being used very successfully for certain applications. Probably the most ambitious project related to using the Web for data collection is the joint venture between The MARC Group and America Online. They have formed an organization known as the Digital Marketing Group in Dallas. Their system is running on America Online, and you can go to it by entering the keywords rewards town. Consumer response to the site has exceeded all expectations.
- *Project management.* E-mail, delivered via the Internet, along with tools such as Lotus Notes, are being widely used as project management tools by research clients and marketing research suppliers. The Internet is being widely used to distribute project status reports, topline reports, and other project management communications. These types of applications have grown dramatically over the past few years as more and more client firms are using external e-mail.
- *Report distribution.* Reports can be published directly to the Web from programs such as PowerPoint and all the latest versions of leading word processing, spreadsheet, and presentation software packages. This means that results are available to appropriate managers worldwide on an almost instantaneous basis. Reports can be searched for content of interest using the same Web browser used to view the report.
- *General communication.* Team members in marketing research firms can communicate more efficiently and effectively with each other and with individuals in client organizations using the Internet to deliver their communications. ■

Summary

Marketing is a process of planning and executing the conception, pricing, promotion, and distribution of ideas, goods, and services to create exchanges that satisfy individual and organizational objectives. Marketing managers attempt to get the right goods or services to the right people at the right place at the right time at the right price, using the right promotion technique. This can be accomplished by following a marketing concept. The marketing concept is based on consumer orientation, goal orientation, and systems orientation.

The marketing manager must work within an internal environment of the organization and understand the external environment over which he or she has little, if any, control. The primary variables over which the marketing manager has control are place, price, promotion, and product decisions. The unique combination of these four variables is called the marketing mix.

Marketing research plays a key part in providing the information for managers to shape the marketing mix. Marketing research has grown in importance because of management's focus on customer satisfaction and retention. It is also a key tool in proactive management. Marketing research should be undertaken only when the perceived benefits are greater than the costs.

Marketing researchers have begun to use the Internet extensively. The Internet affects the marketing research industry in the following ways: It can virtually replace libraries and various printed materials as sources of secondary data; it serves as a vehicle for data collection; it aids in project management; it can be used to distribute reports; and team members working on a project can use it to communicate with each other.

Key Terms & Definitions

Marketing The process of planning and executing the conception, pricing, promotion, and distribution of ideas, goods, and services to create exchanges that satisfy individual and organizational objectives.

Marketing concept A business philosophy based on consumer orientation, goal orientation, and systems orientation.

Consumer orientation Identifying and focusing on the people or firms most likely to buy a product and producing a good or service that will meet their needs more effectively.

Goal orientation Focusing on the accomplishment of corporate goals with a limit set on consumer orientation.

Systems orientation Creating systems to monitor the external environment and deliver the marketing mix to the target market.

Marketing mix The unique blend of product/service, pricing, promotion, offerings, and distribution designed to meet the needs of a specific group of consumers.

Marketing research The planning, collection, and analysis of data relevant to marketing decision making and the communication of the results of this analysis to management.

Descriptive function Gathering and presenting statements of fact.

Diagnostic function Explaining data or actions.

Predictive function Specifying how to use descriptive and diagnostic research to predict the results of a planned marketing decision.

Return on quality A management objective based on the principles that the quality being delivered is the quality desired by the target market and that quality must have a positive impact on profitability.

Marketing strategy Guiding the long-term use of a firm's resources based on its existing and projected capabilities and on projected changes in the external environment.

Applied research Research aimed at solving a specific pragmatic problem—a better understanding of the marketplace, a determination of why a strategy or tactic failed, a reduction of uncertainty in management decision making.

Basic or pure research Research aimed at expanding the frontiers of knowledge rather than solving a specific pragmatic problem.

Questions for Review & Critical Thinking

1. The role of marketing is to create exchanges. What role might marketing research play in facilitating the exchange process?
2. Marketing research has traditionally been associated with manufacturers of consumer goods. Today, an increasing number of organizations, both profit making and nonprofit, are using marketing research. Why do you think this trend exists? Give some examples.
3. Explain the relationship between marketing research and the marketing concept.
4. Name two consumer goods, two services, and two nonprofit concepts that might have logically been developed with marketing research.
5. Comment on the following statement: "I own a restaurant in the downtown area. I see customers every day whom I know on a first-name basis. I understand their likes and dislikes. If I put something on the menu and it doesn't sell, I know that they didn't like it. I also read the magazine *Modern Restaurants,* so I know what the trends are in the industry. This is all of the marketing research I need to do."
6. Why is marketing research important to marketing executives? Give several reasons.
7. How do you think marketing research might differ between (a) a retailer, (b) a consumer goods manufacturer, (c) an industrial goods manufacturer, and (d) a charitable organization?
8. Ralph Moran is planning to invest $1.5 million in a new restaurant in Saint Louis. When Ralph applied for a construction financing loan, the bank officer asked whether he had conducted any research. Ralph replied, "I checked on research, and a marketing research company wanted $20,000 to do the work. I decided that with all the other expenses of opening a new business, research was a luxury that I could do without." Comment.
9. What is meant by "return on quality"? Why do you think the concept evolved? Give an example.

10. Give a personal example in which a company either retained your business or lost you as a customer because of service delivery.
11. Describe three situations in which marketing research should not be undertaken. Explain why this is true.
12. Give an example of (a) the descriptive role of marketing research, (b) the diagnostic role of marketing research, and (c) the predictive function of marketing research.

Working the Net

Using the Internet and a Web browser, visit a search engine such as Lycos or Yahoo! and type in marketing research. You will then have thousands of options. Pick a website that you find interesting and report on its content to the class.

Real-Life Research

"Got Milk?" and More

Researchers are always striving to uncover consumer purchase motivations. Striving to better understand consumer psyches has led to some rather offbeat techniques. The success of the "Got Milk?" advertising campaign has been attributed to an "outside-the-box" technique. The ads were inspired by an exercise in consumer deprivation. Goodby, Silverstein & Partners, a unit of the Omnicom Group, asked dozens of people to skip milk for a week and record their feelings in a diary. By the fifth day, one man said he was so desperate he was looking in his cat's bowl. The San Francisco agency recreated the scene in a TV spot, complete with a cat meowing fiercely in the background.

Another unusual technique is called "naked behavior," or unguarded reactions. Researchers from Greenfield Consulting Group in Westport, Connecticut, for example, regularly sidle up to shoppers in stores, mumbling, "Gosh, I don't understand, there are so many brands." Ideally, unsuspecting consumers will offer to share their impressions of products far more candidly than they would tell a survey taker.

Then there's the early morning ambush. Leo Burnett, the Chicago agency that creates Kellogg ads, has sent researchers out to knock on test subjects' doors at sunrise, to discover "what drives a dynamic choice at 7:30 A.M.," says Catherine DeThorne, Burnett's director of planning.[9]

Questions

1. Does this type of research qualify as marketing research?
2. Do you think that the elements of a firm's marketing mix should be modified after receiving results from these methods?
3. Could these techniques be used to evaluate service quality?

The Marketing Research Process and the Management of Marketing Research

Learning Objectives

1. *To learn the steps involved in the marketing research process*

2. *To understand the components of the research request*

3. *To learn the advantages and disadvantages of survey, observation, and experimental research techniques*

4. *To become familiar with the nature of research management*

CHAPTER *two*

The National Cattlemen's Beef Association and the National Pork Producers Council are very concerned about what we eat. For these groups, the fewer the number of vegetarians, the better. Both groups, in fact, try very hard to get you to eat more of their type of meat. Remember, for example, [the slogans] that pork is "the other white meat" and "Beef: it's what's for dinner." Both organizations use marketing research to measure their success. Recently, both have been quite pleased with their efforts.

A small core of the public remains true to vegetarianism: 1 percent describe themselves as "strict vegetarians" and 4 percent as "pretty much vegetarians," about the same as [in] the past. But, in another sign of relaxing/rethinking diets, there's been a decline in Americans saying they're "careful about how much" meat they eat (20%, down 5% since 1992). In turn, more say they eat meat "quite often and regularly" (73%, up 5%). The results suggest that the predicted shift to quasi-vegetarianism as the population ages has been put on hold; apparently, Americans plan to eat meat as long as they can.

Those who are careful about meat eating or are vegetarians have relaxed their diets: Most still avoid red meat (61%, down marginally from 1994). But far smaller percentages avoid eggs (22%, down 18%) and dairy products (13%, down 6%).

Why eat a vegetarian diet? Increasingly, vegetarians and those who watch how much meat they eat respond that it's "better for your health" (72%, up 7% from 1992 and up 28% from 1978), rather than that it's "a lot more economical" (10%, down 9% from 1992 and down 12% from 1978). Relatively few cite animal welfare (14%) or world hunger (12%).[1]

Gathering data about meat eaters versus vegetarians (or any other subject) requires marketing research. Conducting marketing research requires a series of logical steps. What are the steps in the marketing research process? How is marketing research managed? These are the issues we will address in Chapter 2. ■

Find out more about research conducted by the Cattlemen's Beef Association and the Pork Producers Council at

http://www.beef.org and http://www.nppc.org

The Research Process

The research process builds a foundation for the remainder of the text. Every subsequent chapter examines a specific aspect of this procedure. The marketing research process is shown in Figure 2.1.

Step One: Identifying and Formulating the Research Problem/Opportunity

The research process begins with the recognition of a marketing problem or opportunity. As changes occur in a firm's external environment, marketing managers are faced with the questions "Should we change the existing marketing mix?" and, if so, "How?" Marketing research may be used to evaluate product, promotion, distribution, or pricing alternatives. In addition, it is used to find and evaluate new market opportunities.

For example, over 30 million babies have been born in the United States since 1990. It is the largest generation since the baby boomers. More impressive than their numbers, though, is their wealth. The increase in single-parent and dual-earner households means that children are making shopping decisions once left to moms and dads. Combining allowance, earnings, and gifts, children ages 14 and under directly spend an estimated $20 billion a year and influence purchasers spending another $200 billion.[2]

Figure 2.1

The Marketing Research Process

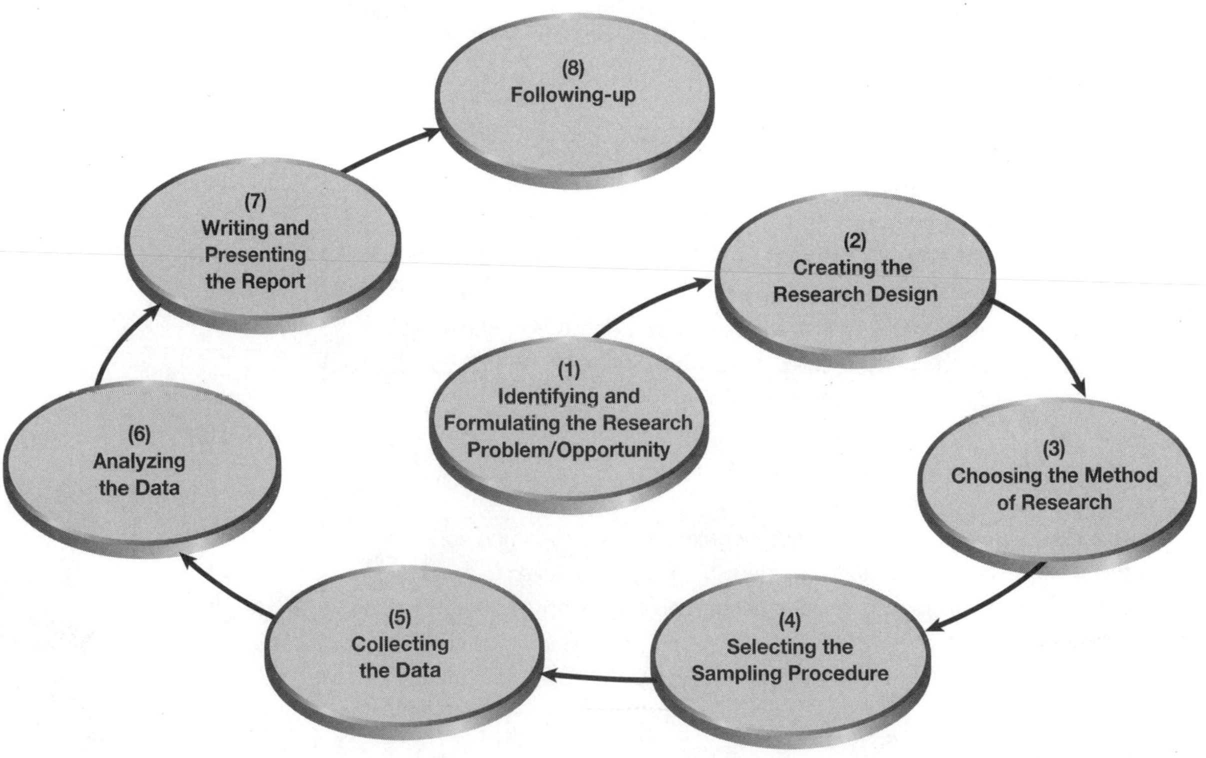

For savvy marketers, these statistics represent opportunity. Marketing research can hone in and clarify where the best opportunities lie. Disney, for example, is launching a 24-hour children's radio network based on its marketing research. Sometimes research can lead to unexpected results requiring creative uses of the marketing mix. General Motors recently completed an analysis of "backseat consumers," that is, children between 5 and 15 years of age. Marketing research discovered that parents often let their children play a tie-breaking role in deciding which car to purchase. Marketing managers, armed with this information, launched several programs. GM purchased the inside cover of *Sports Illustrated for Kids,* a magazine for boys from 8 to 14 years old. The ad featured a brightly colored two-page spread for the Chevy Venture minivan, a vehicle targeted at young families. GM also sent the minivan into malls and showed Disney movies on a VCR inside the van.

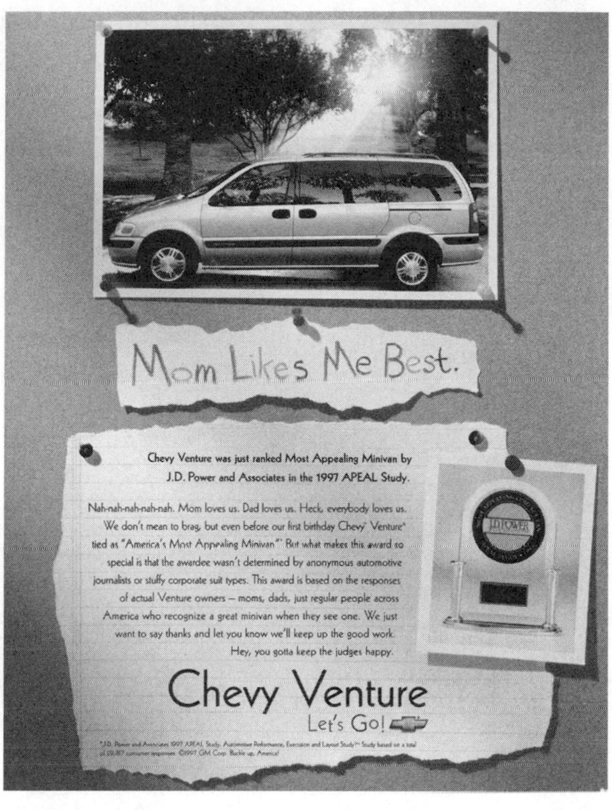

Marketing research uncovered the fact that children often play a "tie-breaker" role in deciding whether or not to purchase a Chevy Venture minivan.

Source: Copyright General Motors Corp., used with permission.

The GM story illustrates an important point about defining a problem/opportunity. The **marketing research problem** is information oriented. It involves determining what information is needed and how that information can be obtained efficiently and effectively. The **marketing research objective,** then, is to provide insightful decision-making information. Specific pieces of information are needed to answer the marketing research problem. Managers must combine this information with their own experience and other information to make a proper decision. In the GM scenario, the marketing research objective was to determine what role, if any, backseat consumers play in a family's decision to purchase an automobile.

Marketing research problem A statement of the specific information needed by a decision maker to help solve a management decision problem.

Marketing research objective The specific information needed to solve a marketing research problem.

Management decision problem The managerial action required to solve a marketing research problem.

In contrast, the **management decision problem** is action oriented. Management problems tend to be broad in scope and general, whereas marketing research problems must be narrowly defined and specific for the research effort to be successful. Sometimes several research studies must be conducted to solve a broad management problem. Once GM determined that children within its target market played a tie-breaker role, the question became, "What should be done to influence the tie-breakers?" GM used marketing research to determine that direct advertising to children in the target market and mall visits would be the best forms of promotion.

In the In Practice feature on page 24, Paul Conner, president of Application, a St. Louis-based marketing research firm, discusses the steps that must be taken to define marketing research objectives that will be management-action oriented.

Once a problem or opportunity has been sensed, the marketing researcher comes into the picture. The first responsibility of the researcher, whether from internal staff or outside an consulting firm, is to work with the

In PRACTICE

Management-Oriented Applications of Marketing Research

Management-oriented applications represent the decisions that will be made on the basis of the research. Objectives, or information objectives, represent the data that will be needed to support the applications. The key is developing information objectives that relate to the applications. The steps in the applications and objectives process are as follows:

1. *Applications.* Clearly list the decisions you want to make or actions you want to take on the basis of the research.
2. *Application options.* For each decision or action, delineate all clearly existing decision or action options (for some decisions the options may not clearly exist).
3. *Application criteria.* For each decision or decision option, make a statement of the criteria upon which the decision will be based. Don't forget to include who you need the information from to direct the sampling procedures.
4. *Information objectives.* The decision criteria will directly or indirectly contain the information needed to support the decisions to be made or actions to be taken. Extract and list needed information from the decision criteria.

An example: A product manager for a bank needed to decide whether to use a humorous or serious ad approach for a new product targeting senior citizens. Here's how he proceeded.

1. *Application.* Decide what type of ad approach to use for the new product.
2. *Application options.* Use humor or use a serious approach.
3. *Application criteria.* Use the approach that, among senior citizens, generates the highest amount of interest in using the new bank product while communicating the name of the bank to at least 75 percent of the target [market].
4. *Information objectives.* To support the applications through their criteria, the research will need to collect the following information from senior citizens about their reactions to the two ad approaches: how interested they are in using the product on the basis of each ad approach and whether they recall the name of the bank in each approach.[3] ■

marketing manager to clearly articulate the management decision problems whose symptoms have been observed and then to define precisely the marketing research problem. Certainly, no area of marketing research requires more insight and creativity than the process of defining the marketing research problem. It is not only the first step in arriving at a solution, it is also the most critical part of the marketing research process. Properly defining a marketing research question provides guidance and direction for the entire research process. A well-defined marketing research problem is half the battle of conducting research.

Anthony Miles, vice president of the Boston Consulting Group, discusses three key questions he always seeks to answer at the problem/opportunity definition stage:

1. Why is the information being sought?
2. Does this information already exist?
3. Can the question really be answered?

Find Out Why the Information Is Being Sought Large amounts of money, effort, and time are wasted because requests for marketing information are poorly formulated or misunderstood. For example, managers may not have a clear idea of what they want or may not phrase the question properly. The following activities may help to focus on the question:

- Discuss what the information is to be used for and what decisions might be made as a result. Go through examples in detail.
- Try to get the client or manager to set priorities among the questions. This helps sort out the central questions from incidental ones.
- Rephrase the questions in several slightly different forms and discuss the differences.
- Create sample data and ask if they would help answer the questions. Simulate the decision process.

Remember that the more clear-cut you think the questions are and the more quickly you come to feel that the question is straightforward, the more you should doubt that you have understood the real need.

Determine Whether the Information Already Exists It often seems easier and more interesting to develop new information than to delve through old reports and data files to see whether it already exists. There is a tendency to assume that current data are superior to data collected in the past. Yet existing data can save managers time and money if they solve the research question.

On the other hand, current data may have a better "fix" on today's perspectives. With fresh data, a researcher can gain more control over the format and more comprehensiveness, and can be easier to work with.

Determine Whether the Question Can Really Be Answered When marketing researchers promise more than they can deliver, it hurts the credibility of marketing research. It is extremely important to avoid being impelled by overeagerness to please or by managerial macho into an effort that one knows has a limited probability of success. In most cases, it is possible to discern in advance the likelihood of success by identifying:

- instances in which you know for certain that information of the type required exists or can be readily obtained.
- situations in which you are fairly sure, but not fully certain, that the information can be gathered, based on similar prior experiences.
- cases in which you know you are trying something quite new and in which there is a real risk of drawing a complete blank.

Using Exploratory Research to Define the Problem/Opportunity

Once a problem/opportunity is recognized, it is extremely important for the researcher to understand exactly what needs to be examined. Nickelodeon, for example, is well aware of the new baby boom, but what does it mean for the network? Exploratory research uncovered that a long-held assumption about children's attitudes was not accurate. The belief that female images generally work with girls but alienates boys in TV programming seemed to be changing. This tidbit was uncovered through exploratory research. **Exploratory research** is usually small-scale research undertaken to define the exact nature of a problem and to gain a better understanding of the environment within which a problem has occurred. Exploratory research for Nickelodeon consisted of a small-scale pilot study on the Internet and small groups of children brought together to discuss their attitudes toward television. These groups are called focus groups and are fully discussed in Chapter 5. Exploratory research tends to be highly flexible, with researchers following ideas, clues, and hunches as long as time and money constraints permit. Often ideas and clues can be obtained from so-called experts in the field. Nickelodeon, for example, could have spoken with child psychologists.

Exploratory research
Preliminary research to clarify the exact nature of the problem to be solved.

As a researcher moves through the exploratory research process, he or she should develop a list of marketing research problems and subproblems. The investigator should discern all the factors that seem to be related to the problem area. These are probable research topics. This stage of problem definition requires a brainstorming-type approach, but one guided by the previous stage's findings. All possibilities should be listed without regard to the feasibility of addressing them via research. Nickelodeon ultimately decided to define the marketing research problem as the determination of whether a live-action show with girls as the protagonists would appeal to both sexes. Marketing research results showed that such a program would have dual appeal. Managerial action taken as a result was "The Secret World of Alex Mack." The stars are female, but the audience is 53 percent male.[4]

Unfortunately, given the natural desire of managers to get research going and the typically short time frame available for marketing research projects, the marketing research problem-definition phase of the project is often not given proper attention. In many instances, this phase can be time-consuming and seem to be heading nowhere. The tendency to short-circuit problem definition is unfortunate, for it can be very costly. The value of this phase of the research process lies in getting efforts off on the right track. A considerable amount of time and effort can be wasted in pursuit of the wrong problem.

Definition of Research Objectives The culmination of the problem/opportunity formulation process is a statement of the research objectives. These objectives are stated in terms of the precise information necessary to answer the marketing research problem/opportunity. Well-formulated objectives serve as a road map in developing the research project. They also serve as a standard that enables managers to evaluate the quality and value of the work. Were the objectives met and do the recommendations flow logically from the objectives and the research findings?

Objectives must be as specific and unambiguous as possible. Remember that the entire research effort in terms of time and money is geared toward achieving the objectives. When the marketing researcher meets with a committee to learn the goals of a particular project, committee members may not fully agree on what is needed. We have learned from experience to go back to a committee (or the individual in charge) with a written list of research objectives. The researcher should then ask the manager, "If we accomplish the objectives on this list, will you have enough information to make your decisions about the problem?" If the reply is "Yes," the manager should then be asked to sign off on the objectives. Then the marketing researcher should give the manager a copy and keep a copy for the research files. Putting the agreed-upon objectives in writing avoids the problem later on of a manager saying, "Hey, this is not the information I wanted." In a busy and hectic corporate environment, misunderstandings like this happen more frequently than one might be imagined.

Research Objectives Must Avoid the "Nice-to-Know" Syndrome

Even after conducting exploratory research, managers often tend to discuss research objectives in terms of broad areas of ignorance. They say, in effect, "Here are some things I don't know." General Motors' management might say, "I wonder if the target consumers are thinking about having larger families." Managers are implicitly thinking, "When the research results come in, it will be nice to know more about the target market's trend in family size. Once I have more knowledge, then I can make some decisions." Unfortunately, this scenario usually leads to disappointment. There is nothing wrong with interesting findings, but they must also be actionable. That is, the findings must provide decision-making information.

Accomplishing a research objective must do more than reduce management's level of ignorance. Unless all the research is exploratory, it should lead to a decision. Perhaps the best way to assure actionable research is to determine how the research results will be implemented. In the case of General Motors, assume that exploratory research uncovered a number of reports on middle-class families with children (the primary target market). One such report described a satellite global positioning system now available on some cars in Japan. The system essentially guides the driver from point A to point B using video maps. Other reports noted that families taking a vacation by car tend to bring "a lot of stuff" for over-the-road entertainment and consumption. This could have implications for storage space (perhaps either hot or cold), vehicle electronics and plug-ins, food holders, and so forth.

Management Decisions and Research Objectives The research objectives for this study are basically a restatement in research terms of what management needs to know to make a decision. In the General Motors case, the research objectives are to determine

1. the percentage of families who get lost at least once on a family driving vacation.
2. the receptiveness of minivan owners to a satellite video mapping system at alternative price levels.

3. the demand for a food warmer in the minivan.
4. the demand for a refrigerator in the minivan.
5. the demand for a built-in VCR player in the minivan.
6. the need for additional food/drink holders throughout the vehicle.

Hypothesis A conjectural statement about a relationship between two or more variables that can be tested with empirical data.

Research Objectives Stated as Hypotheses Often researchers state research objectives in the form of a hypothesis. A **hypothesis** is a conjectural statement about a relationship between two or more variables that can be tested with empirical data. Hypotheses are tentative statements that are considered to be plausible given the available information. A good hypothesis will contain clear implications for testing stated relationships. For example, based on exploratory research, a researcher might hypothesize that the addition of a satellite video mapping system as an exclusive General Motors Venture minivan option, at a price of $2,000, will increase GM's minivan market by 4 percent. A second hypothesis might be that new Venture minivan customers will predominately be families with adult heads of the household between 28 and 45 years of age, with two children living at home, and with a total family income of $55,000 to $90,000 annually. The development of research hypotheses sets the stage for creating the research design.

Step Two: Creating the Research Design

Research design The plan to be followed to answer the marketing research objectives; the structure or framework to solve a specific problem.

The **research design** is the plan to be followed to answer the research objectives or hypotheses. In essence, the researcher develops a structure or framework to answer a specific research problem/opportunity. There is no single, best research design. Instead, the investigator faces an array of choices, each with certain advantages and disadvantages. Ultimately, trade-offs are typically involved. A common trade-off is between research costs and the quality of the decision-making information provided. Generally speaking, the more precise and error-free the information obtained, the higher the cost. Another common trade-off is between time constraints and the type of research design selected. The researcher must attempt to provide management with the best information possible, subject to the various constraints under which he or she must operate.

Descriptive studies Studies that answer the questions who, what, when, where, and how.

Descriptive Studies The researcher's first task is to decide whether the research will be descriptive or causal. **Descriptive studies** are conducted to answer who, what, when, where, and how questions. Implicit in descriptive research is the fact that management already knows or understands the underlying relationships of the problem area. Returning to our General Motors example, it is assumed, based on the exploratory research, that if Americans on vacation by car get lost with some degree of regularity or would like to know where hotels, motels, and restaurants are located, they would be interested in a satellite video mapping system. Without knowledge of relationships, descriptive research would have little value for decision makers. For example, it would make no sense to do a research study in the northeastern sector of the United States that provided the age, income, family size, and educational levels of various geographic segments if GM had no idea what relationship, if any, these variables had on the demand for a Venture minivan.

Causal Studies A **variable** is simply a symbol or concept that can assume any one of a set of values. In **causal studies** the researcher investigates whether one variable causes or determines the value of another variable. Experiments (the subject of Chapter 5) can be used to measure causality. A **dependent variable** is a variable that is expected to be predicted or explained. An **independent variable** is a variable in an experiment that the market researcher can, to some extent, manipulate, change, or alter. An independent variable in a research project is the presumed cause of the dependent variable, the presumed effect. For example, does the level of advertising (independent variable) determine the level of sales (dependent variable) for General Motors?

Variable A symbol or concept that can assume any one of a set of values.

Causal studies These studies examine whether one variable causes or determines the value of another variable.

Dependent variable A symbol or concept that is expected to be explained or caused by the independent variable.

Descriptive research can tell us that two variables seem to be somehow associated, such as advertising and sales, but it cannot provide convincing proof that high levels of advertising cause high sales. Because descriptive research can shed light on associations or relationships, it helps the researcher in selecting the variables for a causal study. For example, without descriptive data, a GM researcher wouldn't know whether to examine age, occupation, income, or a host of other variables.

Independent variable A symbol or concept over which the researcher has some control or can manipulate to some extent and that is hypothesized to cause or influence the dependent variable.

A causal study for General Motors might involve changing one independent variable (for example, the number of direct mailings over a six-month period to target customers) and then observing the effect when the number of promotional mailings is increased. There is an appropriate causal order of events—the effect follows closely the hypothesized cause. This sequence of events is called **temporal sequence** and is one criterion for causality that must be met.

Temporal sequence Appropriate causal order of events.

A second criterion for causality is **concomitant variation:** the degree to which a presumed cause (direct-mail promotions) and presumed effect (minivan sales) occur together or vary together. If direct-mail promotions are considered a cause of increased minivan sales, then when the number of direct-mail promotions goes up, minivan sales should go up, and when the number of promotions falls, sales should fall. If, however, an increase in direct-mail promotions does not result in an increase in minivan sales, the researcher must conclude that the hypothesis about the relationship between the increase in direct-mail promotions and minivan sales is not supported.

Concomitant variation The degree to which a presumed cause and presumed effect occur or vary together.

An ideal situation would be one in which sales of minivans increased markedly every time General Motors increased its direct-mail promotions (up to a saturation level). But, alas, we live in a world where perfection is rarely achieved. One additional mailing might bring in a small increase in sales and the next mailing a larger increment, or vice versa. In another six-month period, an increase in direct-mail promotions might produce no increase or even a decline in sales. Remember, even perfect concomitant variation does not prove that A causes B. All that the researcher can say is that the association makes the hypothesis more likely.

The third issue of causality is to recognize the possibility of **spurious association.** This means that other variables might possibly cause changes in the dependent variable. The ideal situation is one in which the researcher demonstrates that there is a total absence of other causal factors. In the real world of marketing research, it is difficult to identify and control all potential causal factors. Think for a moment of all the variables that could cause the sales of General Motors minivans to increase or decrease.

Spurious association A relationship between a presumed cause and a presumed effect that occurs as a result of an unexamined variable or set of variables.

The researcher may lower spurious associations by holding constant other factors that could influence sales of minivans, for example, prices, newspaper and television advertising, coupons, discounts, and dealer inventory levels. Alternatively, the researcher may look at changes in sales in similar socioeconomic areas.

Step Three: Choosing a Basic Method of Research

A research design, either descriptive or causal, is chosen according to a project's objectives. The next step is to select a means of gathering data. There are three basic research methods: (1) survey, (2) observation, and (3) experiment. Survey research is often descriptive in nature, but can be causal. Experiments are almost always causal, and observation research is typically descriptive.

Survey research Research in which an interviewer interacts with respondents to obtain facts, opinions, and attitudes.

Survey **Survey research** involves an interviewer (except in mail surveys) interacting with respondents to obtain facts, opinions, and attitudes. A questionnaire is used to provide an orderly and structured approach to data gathering. Face-to-face interviews may take place within the respondent's home, in a shopping mall, or at a place of business.

Observation research Descriptive research that monitors respondents' actions without direct interaction.

Observation **Observation research** is research that monitors respondents' actions without direct interaction. The fastest-growing form of observation research involves the use of check-out terminals with scanners, which read tags with bar codes to identify the item being purchased. The future of observation research is somewhat mind-boggling. For example, ACNielsen has been using black boxes for years on television sets to silently siphon off information on a family's viewing habits. But what if the set is on and no one is in the room? To overcome that problem, infrared passive "people meters" have been invented that will identify the faces of family members watching the television set. Thus, if the set is on and no one is watching, these data will be duly recorded.

Experiments Research to measure causality in which one or more variables are changed by the researcher while observing the effect of the change(s) on another variable.

Experiments **Experiments** are the third method researchers use to gather data. An experiment is distinguished by the researcher's changing one or more variables—price, package, design, shelf space, advertising theme, or advertising expenditures—while observing the effects of those changes on another variable (usually sales). The objective of experiments is to measure causality. The best experiments are those in which all factors are held constant except the ones being manipulated. This enables the researcher to infer with confidence that changes in sales, for example, are caused by changes in the amount of money spent on advertising. Holding all other factors constant in the external environment is a monumental and costly, if not impossible, task. Factors such as competitors' actions in various markets, weather, and economic conditions are beyond the control of the researcher.

One way researchers attempt to control factors that might influence a dependent variable is to use a laboratory experiment—an experiment conducted in a test facility rather than in the natural environment.

Researchers sometimes create simulated supermarket environments, give consumers scrip (play money), and then ask them to shop as they normally would for groceries. By varying package design or color over several time periods, for example, a researcher can determine which package is most likely to stimulate sales. Although laboratory techniques can provide valuable information, how consumers act in a unnatural environment may differ from an actual shopping situation. Experiments are discussed in detail in Chapter 8.

Step Four: Selecting the Sampling Procedure

While the sample is actually part of the research design, it is a still separate step in the research process. A sample is a subset from a larger population. Several questions must be answered before a sampling plan can be selected. First, the population or universe of interest must be defined. This is the group from which the sample will be drawn. It should include all the people whose opinions, behavior, preferences, and attitudes will yield information for answering the research problem. An example would be all the people who eat Mexican food at least once every 60 days. After population has been defined, the next question is whether to use a probability sample or a nonprobability sample.

Probability Versus Nonprobability Samples

A **probability sample** is characterized by every element in the population having a known nonzero probability of being selected. Such samples allow the researcher to estimate how much sampling error is present in a given study. **Nonprobability samples** include all samples that cannot be considered probability samples. Specifically, any sample in which little or no attempt is made to ensure that a representative cross section of the population is obtained can be considered a nonprobability sample. The researchers cannot statistically calculate the reliability of a nonprobability sample; that is, they cannot determine the degree of sampling error that can be expected. Sampling is the topic of Chapters 11 and 12.

Probability samples Subsets of a population that ensure a representative cross section by giving every element in the population a known nonzero chance of being selected.

Nonprobability samples Subsets of a population in which little or no attempt is made to ensure a representative cross section.

Step Five: Collecting the Data

Most data collection is done by marketing research field services. Field service firms, found throughout the country, specialize in providing personal and telephone interviewing for data collection on a subcontract basis. A typical research study involves data collection in several cities and requires working with a comparable number of field service firms. To ensure that all subcontractors do everything in exactly the same way, detailed field instructions should be developed for every job. Nothing should be left to chance; no interpretations of procedures should be left to the subcontractors.

Besides interviewing, field service firms provide group research facilities, mall intercept locations, test product storage, and kitchen facilities to prepare test food products. They may also conduct retail audits (counting the amount of a product sold from retail shelves). After an in-home interview has been completed, field service supervisors typically validate the survey by recontacting about 15 percent of the respondents to make sure that prescribed procedures were followed and the persons were actually interviewed.

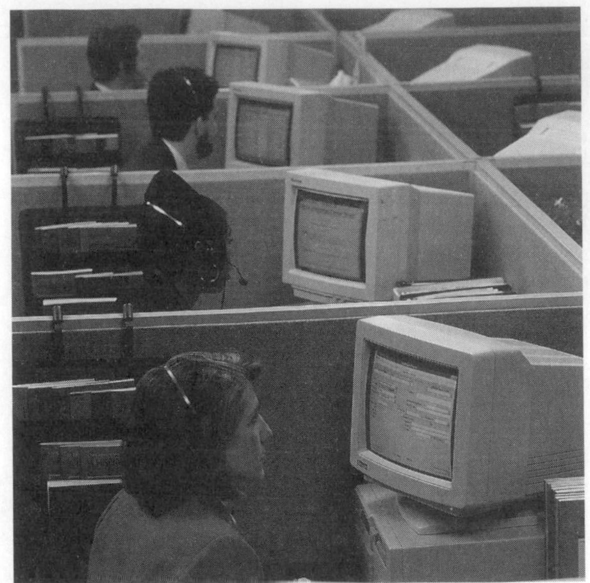

Field service firms establish clear and uniform instructions for their interviewers to ensure that the data is collected accurately. Inconsistencies in approach can invalidate the survey results.

Step Six: Analyzing the Data

After the data have been collected, the next step in the research process is data analysis. The purpose of this analysis is to interpret and draw conclusions from the mass of collected data. The marketing researcher may use techniques beginning with simple frequency analysis and ultimately culminating in complex multivariate techniques. Data analysis is discussed in Chapters 13 and 14.

Step Seven: Preparing and Writing the Report

After data analysis is completed, the researcher must prepare a report and communicate the conclusions and recommendations to management. This is a key step in the process because a marketing researcher who wants conclusions acted upon must convince the manager that the results are credible and justified by the data collected.

The researcher will ordinarily be required to present both written and oral reports on the project. The nature of the audience must be kept in mind when these reports are being prepared and presented. An oral report should begin with a clear statement of the research objectives and be followed by an outline of the methodology. A summary of major findings should come next. The report should end with a presentation of conclusions and recommendations for management. In today's fast-paced world of marketing research, long, elaborate written reports are virtually a thing of the past. Today, decision makers typically only want a copy of the PowerPoint presentation.

Because most people who enter marketing become research users rather than research suppliers, it is important to know what to look for in a research report. Evaluating research is likely to be of greater importance in a marketing job than other aspects of marketing research. Like many other items purchased, quality is not always readily apparent. Nor does a high price for the project necessarily guarantee superior quality. The basis for measuring quality is to return to the research proposal. Did the report meet the objectives established in the proposal? Was the methodology outlined in the proposal followed? Are the conclusions based on logical deductions from the data analysis? Do the recommendations seem prudent, given the conclusions?

Step Eight: Following Up

After a company has spent a considerable amount of effort and money conducting marketing research and preparing a report, it is important that the findings be used. It is the role of management to determine whether the recommendations are followed and if not, why not. One way to help ensure that the research will be used is to minimize conflict between the marketing research department and other departments.

Putting Research Reports on the Web

Going ON-LINE

IT IS BECOMING INCREASINGLY COMMONPLACE FOR RESEARCH suppliers and clients to publish research reports on the Web.

All the latest versions of major word-processing, spreadsheet, and presentation packages have the capability of producing Web-ready material. This simplifies the process of putting reports on the Web. Some companies, such as Texas Instruments, are doing this today. This material is ordinarily not located in public areas but in areas on corporate intranets or in password-protected locations on publicly accessible websites. Publishing reports on the Web has a number of advantages:

- Reports become immediately accessible to managers and other authorized and interested parties worldwide.
- Reports can incorporate a full multimedia presentation, including text, graphs, various types of animation, audio comments, and video clips.
- Reports are fully searchable. A manager, for example, might be interested in any material relating to advertising in a long and detailed report. Instead of manually scanning the report for these mentions, he or she can search the report for those comments relating to advertising. ■

The Research Request

Before conducting the research project, General Motors might require approval of a formal **research request.** Moderate- and large-sized retailers, manufacturers, and nonprofit organizations often use the research request as a basis for determining which projects will be funded. Typically, in large organizations there are far more requests by managers for marketing research information than monies available to conduct such research. The research request step is a formalized approach to allocating scarce research dollars.

Research request A document that describes a potential research project, its benefits to the organization, and estimated costs. In many organizations, a project cannot begin until the research request has been formally approved.

It is important for the brand manager, new product specialist, or whoever is in need of research information to clearly state in the formal research request why the desired information is critical to the organization. Otherwise, the person with approval authority may fail to see why the research expenditure is necessary.

In small organizations, the communication link between brand managers and market researchers is much closer. Day-to-day contact often removes the need for a formal research request. Instead, decisions to fund research are made ad hoc by the marketing manager or the director of marketing research.

Completion and approval of the request represents a disciplined approach to identifying research problems and obtaining funding to solve them. The degree of effort expended at this step in the research process will be reflected in the quality of information the researcher ultimately provides to the decision maker, because it will guide the design, data gathering, analysis, and reporting of the research toward a highly focused objective. The components of a formal research request should be as follows:

1. *Action.* The decision maker must describe the action to be taken on the basis of the research. This will help the decision maker focus on what information makes sense and guide the researcher in creating the research design and in analyzing the results.
2. *Origin.* This is a statement of the events that led to a need for a decision to act. It helps the researcher understand more deeply the nature of the management decision problem.
3. *Information.* The decision maker must list the questions that he or she needs to have answered before taking action. Carefully considering this area improves the efficiency of the research and ensures that the questions make sense in light of the action to be taken.
4. *Use.* This section explains how each piece of information will be used to help make the actual decision. It gives logical reasons for each piece of the research and ensures that the questions make sense in light of the action to be taken.
5. *Targets and subgroups.* This section describes from whom the information must be gathered to address the research problem. This helps the researcher design the sample for the research project.
6. *Logistics.* Time and budget constraints always affect the research technique that is chosen for a project. For this reason, approximations of the amount of money required and the amount of time that exists before results are needed must be stated as a part of the research request.
7. *Comments.* Any other comments relevant to the research project must be stated so that, once again, the researcher can fully understand the nature of the problem.

Managing Marketing Research

Successful marketing research requires meeting the needs and expectations of the decision maker. This, then, becomes the ultimate objective of marketing research management. The logical follow-up question is "What exactly do decision makers want?"

What Decision Makers Want from Marketing Research

Market Directions, a Kansas City marketing research firm, asked marketing research clients around the United States to rate the importance of several statements about research companies and research departments. It received replies from a wide range of industries, resulting in the following top-10 list:

1. maintains client confidentiality
2. is honest
3. is punctual
4. is flexible
5. delivers according to project specifications
6. provides high quality output
7. is responsive to the client's needs
8. has high quality-control standards
9. is customer oriented in interactions with client
10. keeps the client informed throughout a project[5]

The two most important factors, confidentiality and honesty, are ethical issues covered in the next chapter. The remaining issues relate to managing the research function and maintaining good communication.

Good Communication Is a Necessity

Referring again to the top-10 list, "is flexible," "is responsive to the client's needs," "is customer oriented," and "keeps the client informed" are all about good communication. A successful marketing research firm or department requires good communication both within the research company and with clients. How important is communication? Consider this: Managers spend at least 80 percent of every working day in direct communication with others. In other words, 48 minutes of every hour is spent in meetings, on the telephone, or talking informally while walking around. The other 20 percent of a typical manager's time is spent doing desk work, most of which is also communication in the forms of reading and writing. Communication permeates every aspect of managing the marketing research function.[6]

The Nature of the Decision-Making Information Depends on the Type of Research Conducted

Marketing research studies can be classified in three broad categories: programmatic, selective, or evaluative. **Programmatic research** is done to develop marketing options through market segmentation, market opportunity analysis, or consumer attitude and product usage studies. **Selective research** is used to test decision alternatives. Some examples are testing concepts for new products, testing advertising copy, and test marketing. **Evaluative research** is done to assess program performance. Illustrations include tracking advertising recall, organizational image studies, and examining customer attitudes on the quality of service that a firm is providing.

Programmatic research Research done to develop marketing options through market segmentation, market opportunity analysis, or consumer attitude and product usage studies.

Selective research Research to choose among several viable alternatives identified by programmatic research.

Evaluative research Research to determine the effectiveness and efficiency of specific programs.

Programmatic decision problems arise from management's need to obtain periodic market overviews. This is usually prompted by a feeling that the market is continually changing or by new marketing plans that call for the introduction of new products, ad campaigns, or packaging. Perhaps product management is concerned that the existing market information base is inadequate or outdated for present decision making. Current information is needed to develop viable marketing options. Some typical questions are:

- Does the market exhibit any segmentation opportunities?
- If so, what are the profiles of the various segments?
- Do some segments appear to be more likely candidates than others for the company's marketing efforts?
- What new product opportunities are in the various segments?
- What marketing program options should be considered in light of the segmentation analysis?

The marketing research department's role is to suggest a research program that will answer these questions within a firm's budgetary constraints.

Selective decision problems arise after several viable options have been identified by programmatic research. If no alternative is clearly superior to the others, product management will normally want to test several alternatives. Selective research may be required at the concept stage or any other stage in the marketing process, such as when developing advertising copy, evaluating various product formulations, or assessing an entire marketing program, as in test marketing.

Evaluative decision problems arise when the effectiveness and efficiency of programs need evaluation. Evaluative research is closely related to programmatic research, and is often a precursor to programmatic research when there is a demand for program changes or entirely new options because of dissatisfaction with present performance. The response of the marketing research department to the need for evaluative information is often to conduct tracking studies.

Managing the Research Process

Research management has three important goals beyond excellent communication: assurance of data quality, cost control, and adherence to time schedules.

Data Quality

Marketing research managers can help assure high quality data by attempting to minimize sources of error. The various types of error are covered in detail in Chapter 7.

Managers must have procedures that require the careful proofing of all text, charts, and graphs in written reports and other communication provided to the client. Mistakes may mislead the client into making the wrong decision. If the data suggest purchase intent at 25 percent and the report reverses the digits to 52 percent, it could easily lead to an incorrect decision. If the client finds even small mistakes, the credibility of the researcher and all of the findings of the research may be brought into serious question. The rule of thumb is never to provide information to a client unless it has been carefully checked.

Managers must have policies and procedures in place to minimize sources of error. Once they are in place, management will have gone a long way toward assuring data quality.

Managing Costs

In comparison to data quality management, cost management is straightforward and requires only adherence to good business practices. The research firm must have good cost tracking and control processes and procedures in place. In particular, procedures for cost control should include these following elements:

- systems that accurately capture data collection and other costs associated with the project on a daily basis.
- daily reporting of costs to project managers; ideally, reports should show actual costs in relation to budget.
- policies and practices in the research organization that require project managers to communicate the budget picture to clients and to senior managers at the research company.
- policies and practices that quickly identify overbudget situations and then identify causes and seek solutions.

If a project is over budget and if the reason can be attributed to reliance on information provided by the client that has proven to be erroneous (such as, incidence rate or interview length), then it is imperative that the client be offered options early in the process, such as budgeting for higher costs, allowing a smaller sample size, or planning a shorter interview, or some combination of options. By waiting until a project is completed to communicate this type of problem to a client, the client is likely to say, "You should have told me sooner—there is nothing I can do now." In this situation, the firm will likely have to swallow the cost overrun.

Time Management

A third requirement of research management is to keep the project on schedule. Time schedules are always important in marketing research because clients often have specified a time schedule that they must meet. For example, it may be absolutely imperative that the research results be available on March 1st so they can be presented at the quarterly meeting of the New Products Committee. At this meeting, the committee will decide if a certain test product will receive additional funding for development.

The project manager must have early information about whether or not it appears that the project can be completed on time. If a problem exists, the manager must determine whether there is anything that can be done to speed up the process. Possibilities might include additional interviewer training to see if certain sections of the survey can be expedited or the ability to devote more interviewers to the project. Second, the researcher must communicate with the client and inform the client when it appears that the project is going to take longer than expected. Then the researcher can explore with the client whether it is possible to get a time extension or what changes the client might be willing to make to get the project completed according to the original time schedule. For example, the client might be willing to reduce the total sample size or the length of the interview by eliminating questions that are judged to be less critical. The important point is that the system must be structured so that both the researcher and the client are alerted to potential problems within the first few days of the project.

Time management, like cost controls, requires that systems be put in place to tell management whether the project is on schedule or not. Policies and procedures must be established to efficiently and quickly solve behind-schedule problems, and must include prompt notification of the client about the problem and potential solutions.

Good Research Management Motivates Decision Makers to Use Research Information

When research managers communicate effectively, generate quality data, control costs, and deliver information on time, they increase the probability that decision makers will use the research information. Yet academic research shows that political factors and preconceptions can also influence whether research information is used. Specifically, the determinants of whether or not a manager used research data were: (1) conformity to prior expectations (2) clarity of presentation (3) research quality (4) political acceptability within the firm; and (5) lack of challenge to the status quo.[7] Managers and researchers both agree that technical quality is the most important determinant of research use. However, managers are less likely to use research that does not conform to preconceived notions or is not politically acceptable.[8] This does not mean that researchers should alter their findings to meet management's preconceived notions. Marketing managers in industrial firms tend to use research findings more than do their counterparts in consumer goods organizations.[9] This finding is attributed to a greater exploratory objective in information collection, a greater degree of formalization of organizational structure, and a lesser degree of surprise in the information collected.

Summary

The steps in the market research process are

1. identifying and formulating of the problem/opportunity.
2. creating the research design.
3. choosing the method of research.
4. selecting the sampling procedure.
5. collecting data.
6. analyzing data.
7. preparing the research report.
8. following up.

In larger organizations, it is common to have a research request prepared after the research objectives have been defined. The research request generally describes the action to be taken on the basis of the research, the reason for the need for the information, how the information will be used, the target groups from whom the information should be gathered, the amount of time and money needed to complete the research project, and any other information pertinent to the request.

In specifying a research design, the researcher must determine whether the research will be descriptive or causal. Descriptive studies are conducted to answer who, what, when, where, and how questions. Causal studies are those in which the researcher investigates whether one variable (independent) causes or determines the value of another variable (dependent). The next step in creating a research design is to select a research method: survey, observation, or experiment. Survey research involves an interviewer interacting with a respondent to obtain facts, opinions, and attitudes. Observation research, in contrast, does not rely on direct interaction with people. An experiment takes place where a researcher changes one or more variables while observing the effects of the change or changes on another variable (usually sales). The objective of most experiments is to measure causality.

A sample is a subset of a large population. A probability sample is characterized by every element in the population having a known nonzero probability of being selected. Nonprobability samples include all samples that cannot be considered probability samples. Any sample in which little or no attempt is made to ensure that a representative cross section of the population is obtained can be considered a nonprobability sample.

Good communication is the foundation of research management and in getting decision makers to use research information. The information communicated to a decision maker depends on the type of research being conducted. A marketing research study can be described as programmatic, selective, or evaluative. Programmatic research is done to develop marketing options through market segmentation, market opportunity analysis, or attitude and usage studies. Selective research is used to test decisional alternatives. Evaluative research is done to assess program performance.

Managing the research process has three important goals beyond excellent communication: assurance of data quality, cost control, and adherence to time schedules. Marketing research managers can help assure high quality data by attempting to minimize sources of error. Cost management requires good cost tracking and control processes and procedures. Time management also requires a system to notify management of potential problems and policies to efficiently and quickly solve behind-schedule problems.

Key Terms & Definitions

Marketing research problem A statement of the specific information needed by a decision maker to help solve a management decision problem.

Marketing research objective The specific information needed to solve a marketing research problem.

Management decision problem The managerial action required to solve a marketing research problem.

Exploratory research Preliminary research to clarify the exact nature of the problem to be solved.

Hypothesis A conjectural statement about a relationship between two or more variables that can be tested with empirical data.

Research design The plan to be followed to answer the marketing research objectives; the structure or framework to solve a specific problem.

Descriptive studies Studies that answer the questions who, what, when, where, and how.

Variable A symbol or concept that can assume any one of a set of values.

Causal studies These studies examine whether one variable causes or determines the value of another variable.

Dependent variable A symbol or concept that is expected to be explained or caused by the independent variable.

Independent variable A symbol or concept over which the researcher has some control or can manipulate to some extent and that is hypothesized to cause or influence the dependent variable.

Temporal sequence Appropriate causal order of events.

Concomitant variation The degree to which a presumed cause and presumed effect occur or vary together.

Spurious association A relationship between a presumed cause and a presumed effect that occurs as a result of an unexamined variable or set of variables.

Survey research Research in which an interviewer interacts with respondents to obtain facts, opinions, and attitudes.

Observation research Descriptive research that monitors respondents' actions without direct interaction.

Experiments Research to measure causality in which one or more variables are changed by the researcher while observing the effect of the change(s) on another variable.

Probability samples Subsets of a population that ensure a representative cross section by giving every element in the population a known nonzero chance of being selected.

Nonprobability samples Subsets of a population in which little or no attempt is made to ensure a representative cross section.

Research request A document that describes a potential research project, its benefits to the organization, and estimated costs. In many organizations, a project cannot begin until the research request has been formally approved.

Programmatic research Research done to develop marketing options through market segmentation, market opportunity analysis, or consumer attitude and product usage studies.

Selective research Research to choose among several viable alternatives identified by programmatic research.

Evaluative research Research to determine the effectiveness and efficiency of specific programs.

Questions for Review & Critical Thinking

1. The definition of the research problem is one of the most critical steps in the research process. Why? Who should be involved in this process?
2. What role does exploratory research play in the market research process? How does exploratory research differ from other forms of market research?
3. In the absence of company problems, is there any need to conduct marketing research?
4. Are there any situations in which it would be better to take a census of the population rather than a sample? Give several examples.
5. Critique the following methodologies and suggest more appropriate alternatives:
   - A supermarket was interested in determining its image. It dropped a short questionnaire in each customer's grocery bag prior to sacking the groceries.
   - To assess the extent of its trade area, a shopping mall stationed interviewers in the parking lot every Monday and Friday evening. Interviewers walked up to people after they had parked their cars and asked them for their ZIP codes.
   - To assess the potential for new horror movies starring alien robots, a major studio invited people to call a 900 number and vote "yes" if they would like to see such movies or "no" if they would not. Each caller was billed $2.
6. You have been charged with determining how to attract more business majors to your school. Outline the steps you would take, including the sampling procedures, to accomplish this task.
7. What are some sources of conflict between marketing researchers and other managers? How can they be minimized?
8. What are the conditions for causality? Discuss the criteria.
9. Do you think marketing researchers should always use probability samples? Why or why not?
10. What can researchers do to increase the chances that decision makers will use the marketing research information generated?

Working the Net

1. Go to the Internet and search on the words intranet + future. Report your findings to the class.
2. Describe how putting research reports on the Web can benefit managers.

Real-Life Research

Twentysomething Women Take Charge

Although millions of baby-boomer women rejected the June Cleaver role model, the majority are still locked into traditional roles when making purchasing decisions. Today, while most household purchasing decisions are made jointly, the latest MlleMeter report from *Mademoiselle* magazine and Roper Starch Worldwide, Inc. finds that twentysomething women are more likely than their baby-boomer counterparts to declare themselves the primary decision makers for cars, computers, and electronics—everything except grocery products.[10]

Do you or your spouse/partner have the most say in household consumer decision making? (Asked of women with spouse/partner)

	Percentage of Women Ages 18–29			Percentage of Women Ages 30–49		
	Me	Spouse/ Partner	Both Equally	Me	Spouse/ Partner	Both Equally
Make of new car	10%	27%	58%	6%	24%	68%
Computer products	13	19	20	11	17	35
Make of home electronics	15	37	44	12	31	56
Household savings/investments	16	17	66	10	17	71
Vacation plans	15	11	68	10	7	81
Brand of nonprescription drugs	67	4	28	51	7	39
Selection of house/residence	13	9	75	14	6	87
Home furnishings	45	5	50	33	8	58
Interior home design	50	4	40	44	6	48
New kitchen appliances	23	24	50	20	10	66
Brands of grocery products	53	5	40	61	6	32
Type of food for household	51	9	41	57	4	39

Questions

1. Is this an exploratory study? If not, what are the research questions?
2. Do you think this research is causal or descriptive? Defend your answer.
3. In terms of decision-making information, is this research programmatic, selective, or evaluative? Why?
4. Explain how this information might be of value to managers at the following firms:

   General Motors
   Sony
   Black & Decker
   Procter & Gamble

   Give examples to reinforce your answer.

CD Opportunity

Learn more about the marketing research process by watching the video segment on your CD. The segment profiles Burke Marketing Research, one of the top 20 marketing research firms in the United States.

The Marketing Research Industry and Research Ethics

Learning Objectives

1. *To appreciate the structure of the marketing research industry*
2. *To comprehend the nature of corporate marketing research departments*
3. *To learn about the various types of firms and their functions in the market research industry*
4. *To learn who uses marketing research*
5. *To understand the growing importance of strategic partnering*
6. *To appreciate the trends in global marketing research*
7. *To review contemporary ethics in the marketing research industry*
8. *To discover methods by which the level of professionalism in marketing research can be raised*

CHAPTER *three*

The blue and white car banking the Daytona International Speedway track at 165 miles per hour on February 13 was not sponsored by one of the circuit's usual suspects. Alltel—the cellular, Internet, and local phone service provider—was the name fans saw emblazoned across the roof and side of the car each time it pulled into the lead position in the season's first NASCAR Busch Series Grand National race. Though the driver wiped out in the 65th lap, Alltel is still elated with its choice to back the team, and the following week sponsored an entire race, the Alltel 200.

Alltel is no anomaly among NASCAR sponsors. It is just one of several high-tech companies, including Lycos, Philips, 3M, and Bell-South, that have woken up to the power of NASCAR, particularly to the attractive demographics of its fans.

Fan demographics have changed dramatically since the mid-'90s, as new racetracks have opened outside of the sport's traditional stronghold in the Southeast, television networks have expanded their race coverage, and drivers like Jeff Gordon—who are slicker, less down-home, and more media-savvy—have joined the NASCAR ranks. And car-racing fans are more educated than in the past: Those with at least a college degree comprised 22 percent of the pool in 1998, an increase of 18 percent from 1995. Female fans have grown 5 percent since 1995, currently comprising almost 40 percent of NASCAR enthusiasts, a greater percentage of women than in any other sport.

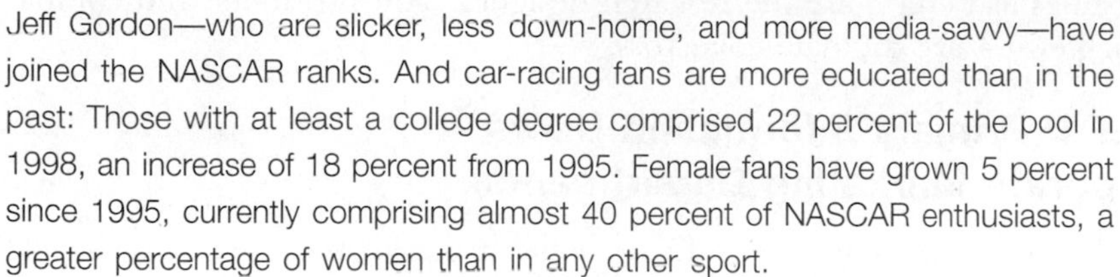

As the demographics have grown, so too has the sponsor list. Alltel got in and on the car two years ago when it learned that 71 percent of the households in its wireless service areas are also fans of the sport. Half of NASCAR devotees now use a cell phone, according to Performance Research in Newport, Rhode Island. That's 10 percent higher than the average U.S. citizen, according to a study by NFO Worldwide Research. Lycos, too, is sponsoring a team for the second season in a row. "It allows for a tremendous amount of pure brand exposure on television," says Jim Hoenscheid, Lycos's director of brand marketing and promotions. And, he adds, "NASCAR fans are an extremely loyal and wired audience."[1]

Find out more about NASCAR sponsers at

http://nascar.com

Lycos and Alltel are marketing research users. Performance Research and NFO Worldwide Research are their research suppliers. What are the various types of marketing research suppliers and users? What are the basic characteristics of the research industry today? What are the ethical standards that have developed in the marketing research industry? We will examine these questions in this chapter. ■

The Evolving Structure of the Marketing Research Industry

Today, over $11 billion a year is spent on marketing, advertising, and public opinion research services around the world.[2] U.S. spending on marketing research is $6.4 billion.[3] During the past two decades, the marketing research industry has become highly concentrated. About 54 percent is held by the 50 largest worldwide organizations.[4] The other half is shared literally by a thousand or more small research firms. This concentration is even more pronounced in the United States, where the 10 largest firms account for 77 percent of the total U.S. spending for marketing, advertising, and public opinion research.[5]

The various types of organizations encountered in the research industry are summarized in Table 3.1. The structure of the marketing research industry is summarized in Figure 3.1 on page 48, which shows the process for survey-based research operating at four levels. The diagram depicts companies at Levels 1 and 2 as the ultimate consumers of marketing research data: the information users. The information they need rests with individual consumers and those who make business purchase decisions: the respondents. Companies at Level 3 are the research designers and providers, and companies at Level 4 are the data collectors.

Level 1: Primary Information Users (Corporate Marketing Departments)

Level 1 organizations are the ultimate users of marketing research data provided by their marketing research departments. Their primary business is the sale of products and services. They use marketing research data to support the marketing decision-making process. They need marketing research data on an ongoing basis to

1. determine how various target groups will react to alternative marketing mixes.
2. evaluate the success of operational marketing strategies.
3. assess changes in the external or uncontrollable environment and their implications for product or service strategies.
4. identify new target markets.
5. create new marketing mixes for new target markets.

Table 3.1

General Categories of Institutions Involved in Marketing Research

Level	Institution	Activities, Functions, and Services
1	Corporate marketing departments	Marketing departments in firms such as Kraft General Foods or Procter & Gamble.
2	Ad agencies	Advertising agencies such as J. Walter Thompson, Young & Rubicam, or Foote, Cone & Belding.
3	Syndicated service firms	Marketing research data-gathering and reporting firms such as ACNielsen, Arbitron, or Information Resources, which collect data of general interest to many firms but for no one firm in particular. Anyone can buy the data they collect; they are prominent in the media audience field and retail sales data.
3	Custom or ad hoc research firms	Marketing research consulting firms such as Market Facts, Data Development, or MARC, which do customized marketing research projects addressing specific problems for individual clients.
4	Field service firms	Collect data only, on a subcontract basis, for corporate marketing research departments, ad agency research departments, custom research firms, or syndicated research firms.
*	Specialized service firms	Provide specialized support service to the marketing research industry, such as SDR in Atlanta, which provides sophisticated quantitative analysis.
*	Others	Government agencies, university research bureaus, individual university professors, database providers, and others.

*These organizations typically operate at Levels 1, 2, or 3.

Figure 3.1 shows that these companies, and their marketing research departments, may work with a combination of custom and syndicated research firms, go directly to ad agencies, or use all or some combination of these alternatives to satisfy their many marketing research needs.

Level 2: Secondary Information Users (Ad Agencies)

Ad agencies (Level 2) are also in the position of serving corporate clients, but they may also be the ultimate consumers of marketing research data. Their main business is the development and execution of ad campaigns. To properly fulfill this role, they often need marketing research data. They may obtain data from custom and syndicated research firms or from field service firms, or they may use some combination of these alternatives.

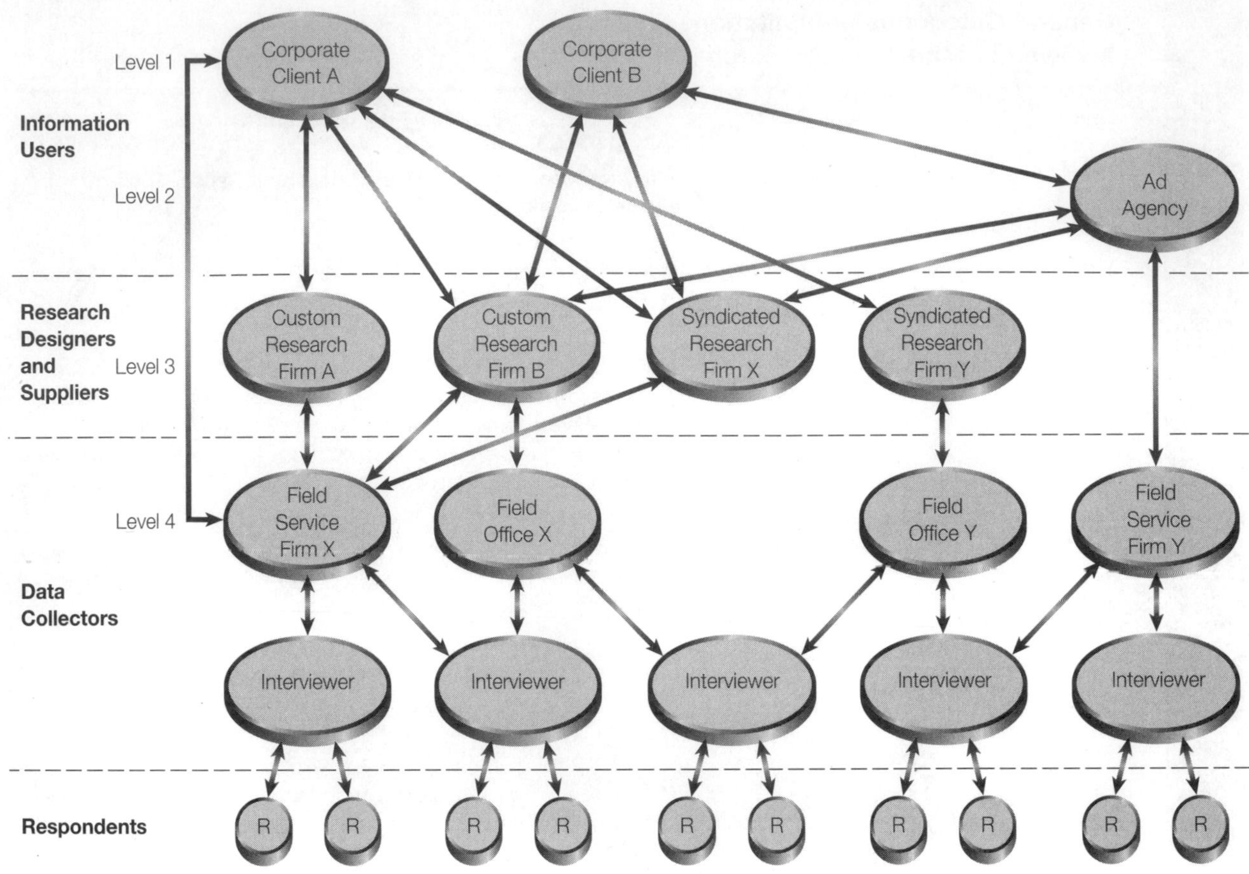

Figure 3.1

The Marketing Research Industry

Level 3: Research Designers and Suppliers

Custom and syndicated marketing research firms (Level 3) represent the front line of the research industry. They sell research services, design research studies, analyze the results, and make recommendations to their clients. They design research, manage its execution, and buy data collection and other services from firms down the line.

Level 4: Data Collectors

Field service firms (Level 4) collect data for syndicated research firms, custom research firms, ad agencies, and corporations. Field offices are data collection operations run by custom or syndicated research firms; however, they are rare today. Most custom and many syndicated research firms depend on field services for their survey data collection needs.

At Level 4 are the interviewers who actually collect the data. They typically work on a part-time, as-needed basis and may work for several different field service firms, depending on the amount of business the various field services have at any given time.

Measurement of the opinions, intentions, and behavior of respondents or potential buyers is the goal of the research process. What potential buyers feel, think, do, and intend to do are the focus of the entire marketing research industry.

Corporate Marketing Research Departments

Because corporations are the final consumers and initiators of most marketing research, they are the logical starting point in developing an understanding of how the research industry operates. Most large corporations have a marketing research department. Some companies have merged marketing research with strategic planning, whereas others have combined marketing research with the customer satisfaction department. Virtually all consumer packaged-goods manufacturers of any size have a marketing research department.

The average size of marketing research departments is quite small. One recent study found that only 15 percent of service companies such as Federal Express and Delta Airlines had marketing research departments with more than 10 employees.[6] Twenty-three percent of manufacturers' research departments had more than 10 employees. The size of research departments has been trending downward because of mergers and reengineering. Few research managers expect staff reduction to continue. On another encouraging note, about half the research managers expect their budgets to continue to grow.[7] As marketing research departments shrink in size and budgets continue to grow, the implication is clear: Companies are conducting less research internally and are outsourcing more to research suppliers. Often persons in small corporate marketing research departments act as a intermediaries between internal research users and outside suppliers.

Because we cannot deal with all types of marketing research departments, we will devote our attention to those found in the more sophisticated, larger companies. In these companies, "research" is a staff department and the director of the department likely reports to the top marketing executive. Although the research manager reports to a high-level marketing executive, most of the work of the department is with product or brand managers, new product development managers, and other frontline managers. With the possible exception of various recurring studies that may be programmed into the firm's marketing information system, the marketing research department typically does not initiate studies. In fact, the research director may control little or no actual budget. Instead, line managers have funds in their budgets earmarked for research. When brand managers perceive that they have a problem that requires research, they go to the marketing research department for help. Working with the marketing research manager or a senior analyst, they go through a series of steps that may lead to the design and execution of a marketing research project.

The Marketing Research Industry

Level 3: The Big Marketing Research Companies

Although the marketing research industry is characterized by hundreds of small firms, there are some giants in the industry. Table 3.2 shows sales for the 30 largest marketing research firms. The four largest firms in the industry—namely ACNielsen Corporation, IMS Health, Inc., Information Resources, Inc., and Nielsen Media Research, Inc.—are all (or largely) syndicated service firms. Most of the remaining firms are either primarily custom research firms or combination firms offering some syndicated services along with their custom research services.

ACNielsen Corporation has about 20,700 full-time employees in offices in 80 countries and customers in more than 100 countries. Nielsen's retail measurement services provides continuous tracking of consumer purchases at the point of sale via scanning and in-store audits in food, drug, and other retail outlets in more than 80 countries. Information includes actual purchases, market shares, distribution, pricing, merchandising, and promotional activities. For the motion picture industry, ACNielsen provides continuous tracking of box office receipts from more than 45,000 movie screens in 11 countries. Nielsen's consumer panel services tracks the buying behavior and demographics of more than 126,000 households through purchase panels in 18 countries. In the United States, a panel of 52,000 households uses in-home scanners to record buying behavior and shopping patterns from a variety of outlets, including warehouse clubs, convenience stores, supermarkets, independent drugstores, mass merchandisers, and bookstores.

IMS Health Inc., the number-two research firm, has about 8,000 employees with offices in 74 countries, and provides services in 94 countries. IMS's market research products include pharmacy and hospital audits, plus the measurement of disease and treatment patterns.

Information Resources, Inc. (IRI) has about 4,100 employees. Its two main products are InfoScan and BehaviorScan. InfoScan is a syndicated market tracking service that provides weekly sales, price, and store condition information on products sold in a sample of food, drug, and mass merchandise stores. BehaviorScan, an electronic test marketing service, enables marketers to test new products or new marketing programs. BehaviorScan targets TV commercials in a controlled environment to specific households and tracks the effectiveness of those ads in six smaller markets.

Nielsen Media Research, Inc. (NMR), the fourth largest research firm, has 2,500 full-time employees. NMR's core business is providing audience measurement information on the television industry for broadcast and cable network and station providers, program developers and distributors, and advertisers and their agencies in the United States and Canada. The Nielsen TV ratings are the currency for transactions between buyers and sellers of television time—more than $43 billion per year in the United States and Canada.

Table 3.2

The 30 Largest Marketing Research Firms

Rank	Organization	Headquarters	Total Research Revenues (millions)
1	ACNielsen Corp.	Stamford, Conn.	$1,425.4
2	IMS Health, Inc.	Westport, Conn.	1,084.0
3	Information Resources, Inc.	Chicago	511.3
4	Nielsen Media Research, Inc.	New York	401.9
5	NFO Worldwide, Inc.	Greenwich, Conn.	275.4
6	Westat, Inc.	Rockville, Md.	205.4
7	The Arbitron Co.	New York	194.5
8	Maritz Marketing Research, Inc.	St. Louis	169.1
9	The Kantar Group Ltd.	London	150.6
10	The NPD Group, Inc.	Port Washington, N.Y.	138.5
11	Market Facts, Inc.	Arlington Heights, Ill.	136.5
12	Taylor Nelson Sofres Intersearch	Horsham, Pa.	68.9
13	J. D. Power and Associates	Agoura Hills, Calif.	64.8
14	United Information Group	New York	59.0
15	Audits & Surveys Worldwide, Inc.	New York	58.3
16	Opinion Research Corp. Int.	Princeton, N.J.	58.2
17	Burke, Inc.	Cincinnati	52.4
18	Roper Starch Worldwide, Inc.	Harrison, N.Y.	51.3
19	Macro International, Inc.	Calverton, Md.	48.7
20	Abt Associates, Inc.	Cambridge, Mass.	45.8
21	MORPACE International, Inc.	Farmington, Mich.	45.1
22	The MARC Group, Inc.	Irving, Tex.	39.8
23	Wirthlin Worldwide	McLean, Va.	38.7
24	Total Research Corp.	Princeton, N.J.	36.8
25	Diagnostic Research Int., Inc.	Los Angeles	35.5
26	Lieberman Research Worldwide	Los Angeles	34.8
27	C&R Research Services, Inc.	Chicago	34.5
28	Elrick & Lavidge Marketing Research	Tucker, Ga.	32.7
29	Market Strategies, Inc.	Southfield, Mich.	30.6
30	Ipsos–ASI, Inc.	Norwalk, Conn.	30.5

Source: Jack Honomichl, "Top 50 U.S. Research Organizations," *Marketing News* (June 7, 1999), p. 144. Reprinted with permission from *Marketing News*, published by the American Marketing Association.

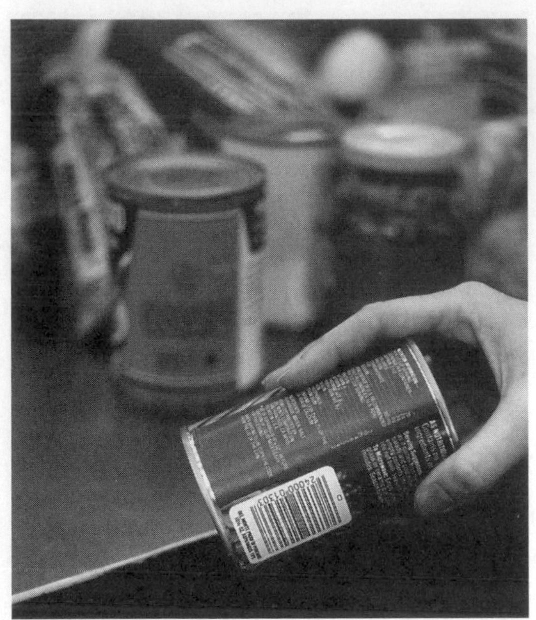

ACNielsen's ScanTrack provides marketing decision-makiers with sales, market share, and price information on consumer-packaged goods.

Level 3: Custom or Ad Hoc Marketing Research Firms

Custom or ad hoc, marketing research firms, are primarily in the business of executing custom, one-of-a-kind marketing research projects for corporate clients. If a corporation has a new product or service idea, packaging idea, ad concept, pricing strategy, product reformulation, or other related marketing problem or opportunity, the place to go for research help is a custom research firm.

There are thousands of custom marketing research firms in this country. The overwhelming majority of these firms are small, with billings of less than $1 million and less than 10 employees. They may serve clients only in their local areas. They may or may not specialize by type of industry or type of research. Examples of large custom research firms include Market Facts, Inc., The MARC Group, Opinion Research Corporation International, Elrick & Lavidge, Burke, Inc., and Wirthlin Worldwide.

Level 3: Syndicated Service Firms

In sharp contrast to custom research companies, **syndicated service research firms** collect and sell the same marketing research data to many firms. Anyone willing to pay the price can buy the data these firms collect, package, and sell. There are relatively few syndicated service firms and, in comparison to custom research firms, they are relatively large. They deal primarily with media audience and product movement data and are based on serving the information needs that many companies have in common. For example, many companies advertise on network television. A typical problem is to select these shows that reach their target customers the most efficiently. They need information on the size and demographic composition of the audiences for different television programs. It would be extremely inefficient for these data to be collected for individual companies.

Approximately 31 percent of all research monies are spent on syndicated research; the remainder is spent for custom research. Half of all research dollars are spent on custom quantitative studies and 19 percent is on custom qualitative research.[8] Table 3.3 gives a list of some syndicated research firms and their offerings.

Custom, or ad hoc, marketing research firms Research companies that carry out customized marketing research to address specific projects for corporate clients.

Syndicated service research firms Companies that collect, package, and sell the same general market research data to many firms.

Field service firms Companies that only collect survey data for corporate clients or research firms.

Level 4: Field Service Firms

A true **field service firm** does nothing but collect survey data—no research design, no analysis. Field service firms are run by data collection specialists who collect data on a subcontract basis for corporate marketing research departments, custom research firms, and ad agency research departments. The following description of the sequence of activities undertaken by a typical field service company provides a good idea of how these firms operate:

Client contact A client custom research firm, syndicated research firm, a corporate or ad agency research department alerts field service firm that it has a particular type of study (telephone interview, mail interview, etc.).

Table 3.3

Syndicated Service Research Firms

Company	Location	Syndicated Services
ACNielsen	Stamford, Conn.	Television ratings; scanner-based data; wholesale/retail audits
Audits and Surveys Worldwide	New York, N.Y.	Retail sales; product/service distribution
Connect Consultants International	Minneapolis, Minn.	Web-based surveys
FIND/SVP	New York, N.Y.	Large variety of industry/product studies
Kadence Ltd.	London, England	European marketing studies
Maritz Marketing Research	Fenton, Mo.	Customer satisfaction studies
Roper Starge Worldwide	New York, N.Y.	Public opinion surveys; lifestyle research; media/advertising effectiveness
Information Resources, Inc.	Chicago, Ill.	Scanner-based data

Interviewer training The day the job is to begin, a briefing or training session is held to acquaint interviewers with the requirements of the particular job or questionnaire.

Interviewing status reports Daily reports are made to the client regarding progress, number of interviews completed, and costs, which permit the client to determine whether the job is on schedule and within budget. The field service also advises its client of problems in any areas.

Quality control Interviewers bring in their completed assignments and the interviews are edited and validated (editing refers to checking interviews to see that they were completed correctly; validation entails calling a certain percentage of each interviewer's respondents to determine whether the interview took place and was done in the prescribed manner).

Ship to client Finally, the completed, edited, and validated interviews are shipped to the client.

A field service provides what its name suggests—interviewing and supervisory services in the field. Most custom research firms rely on field services because it is not cost-effective for them to handle the work themselves. There are too many cities to cover, and it is uncertain which cities' data will be needed over time. Field service firms in various cities maintain a steady work flow by having many research firms and corporate and ad agency research departments as their clients.

Until about 20 years ago, most field service firms were operated by women out of their homes. Their major asset was typically a pool of a dozen or so interviewers available for assignments. Although small field service firms of this type still exist, the trend is toward larger, more professional, and better equipped organizations. The major field service firm of today has a permanent office. It probably has one or more permanent mall test centers, focus group facilities, a centralized telephone interviewing facility, other specialized facilities and equipment, and possibly even WATS (wide area telephone service) lines for interviewing throughout the country from a single location. An emerging trend in the field service business is multicity operations.

Specialized Service or Support Firms

A number of specialized service or support firms provide various types of support services to marketing research and other firms.

Sample Generation One realm where specialized service firms are found is in the sample generation area. Firms such as Survey Sampling, Inc., of Westport, Connecticut, provide samples of households and businesses to their clients. They maintain databases with information on millions of households and businesses from which they generate samples to their clients' specifications.

Going ON-LINE

Using the Net

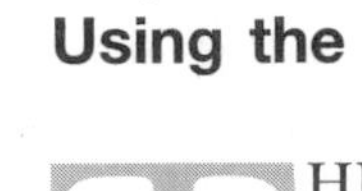

THE INTERNET IS A POWERFUL TOOL FOR IDENTIFYING research suppliers that provide particular types of services and for doing a preliminary review of these firms. Most research firm sites have e-mail, so, after research buyers have identified likely candidates through a preliminary research and evaluation, they can send e-mail to those organizations requesting additional information. A few firms even include RFP (request for proposal) form on their sites permitting research buyers to submit an RFP by e-mail.

One way to access information on hundreds of marketing research firms worldwide is to follow these steps:

- Using your Web browser, go to the Yahoo search engine site at http://www.yahoo.com.
- On the opening menu click on Business & Economy.
- On the Business and Economy menu, click on Marketing and Advertising.
- On the Marketing and Advertising menu, click on Companies@.
- On the Companies@ menu, click on Market Research.
- On the Market Research menu, scroll down the page and you will find a list of hundreds of marketing research firms with listings on the Web. Find DSS Research and click on it.
- This will take you to the home page for DSS Research and permit you to review the services offered by this marketing research firm. You can go through this same process for any of the hundreds of other marketing research firms to find out more about their offerings. ■

Secondary Data

Another area of specialized service to the research industry is provided by firms providing access to specialized databases via computer. For example, no company needs to purchase all of the U.S. census tapes when it needs a demographic profile of a single metropolitan area. A secondary data firm can provide access to the data via on-line computer networks, or provide the desired data on disks or CDs so that their clients can process it on their own PCs.

Statistical Analysis

With the growing use of sophisticated statistical techniques, a new type of marketing research support firm, the data analysis specialist, has emerged. Firms such as Sophisticated Data Research in Atlanta provide sophisticated consulting services to marketing research firms and corporate marketing research departments regarding the selection and use of various statistical techniques for the analysis of marketing research data.

Other Organizations and Individuals

Although not actually part of the marketing research industry, various other organizations and individuals, make a special contribution to it. Included are various government agencies at the federal, state, and local levels; university bureaus of business and economic research; individual university professors that serve as marketing research consultants; and research units associated with various industry groups. Except for the university professors, these institutions serve primarily as sources of valuable and useful data for the marketing research industry. University professors, primarily those in marketing departments, and who also act as marketing research consultants, provide a pool of sophisticated talent that is tapped on an as-needed basis by corporate marketing research departments, companies with no internal marketing research capabilities, and custom research firms.

Government agencies usually provide of secondary data. Examples of agencies and the types of data they provide are presented and discussed in Chapter 4.

Users of Marketing Research

Now that you know who provides marketing research, let's look at who uses it. It is likely that, as a businessperson, the future encounters you have with marketing research will be as a research user. The variety and types of customers for marketing research are shown in Figure 3.2 on page 56. Despite the importance of research to nonmarketing internal customers, some marketing research departments or firms pay little attention to the specific marketing information this group needs. As you might expect, these poorly served customers have also demonstrated little interest in marketing research information. It has been our experience that the most successful marketing research departments/firms are those which are committed to the complete

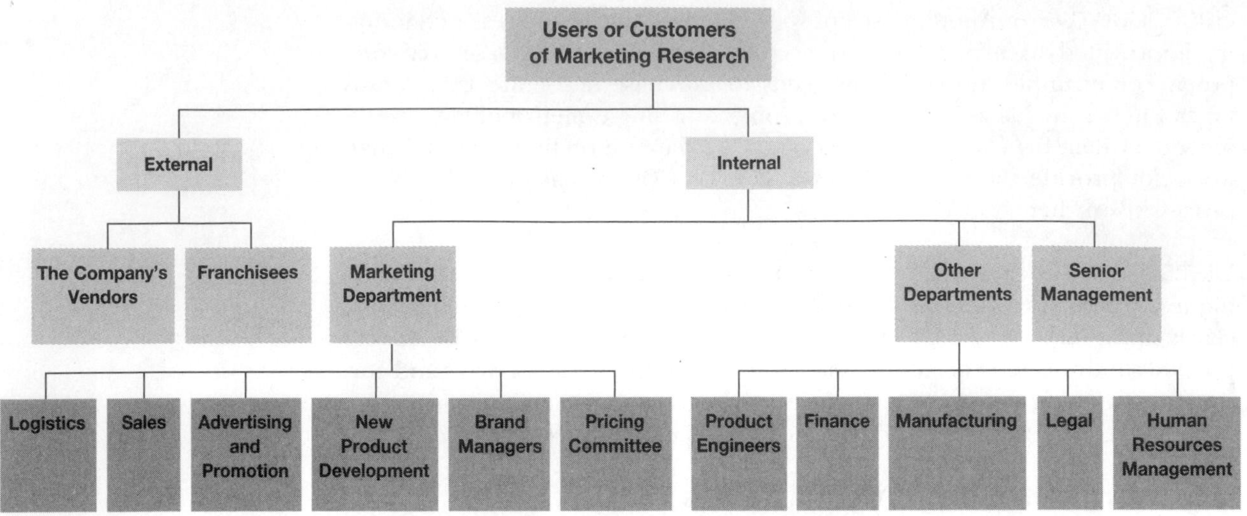

Figure 3.2

Marketing Research Customers

satisfaction of all of their clients. Let's take a closer look at what types of information these various customers need and use.

External Clients

Because marketing research can be a valuable source of new or improved competitive advantages and because it is often very expensive to gather, its circulation outside of the company is usually limited. Many firms do not provide any information to outsiders. However, those that do usually find it is to their mutual benefit.

Vendors Manufacturers are moving into strategic partnerships with their vendors as the only way to implement just-in-time manufacturing. Strategic partnerships are based upon fully integrated manufacturer-supplier logistics systems. These systems are designed to get the components to the assembly line just when they are needed. The result is little or no raw materials inventory and significantly reduced carrying costs. The backbone of this system is shared information. Large retailers such as Wal-Mart have this type of relationship with their major vendors.

Marketing research information is fed back to a manufacturer's suppliers when consumers have voiced opinions about a component on the manufacturer's customer satisfaction surveys. For example, if Pioneer is supplying radios to Honda and customers are complaining about how difficult a certain model is to program, this research information would be shared with Pioneer. Or, another example, a major retail chain commissions a study on changes in customer preferences for Christmas-related items such as gift wrap, cards, artificial trees, and ornaments to help its suppliers of production materials understand the importance of making specific product changes and to provide guidance in making those changes.

Franchisees Most major franchisers of consumer goods and services provide marketing research data to their franchisees. Perhaps the most common data are from mystery shoppers. A mystery shopper poses as a customer and observes how long it takes to receive an order, how courteous the counter clerks are, cleanliness, and whether the order was properly prepared. Mystery shopping is discussed in detail in Chapter 6.

Franchisers also share marketing research information with their franchisees to help reinforce why they are taking certain actions. When McDonald's suggests to a franchisee that a store be remodeled in a particular style, it will show research data pointing out that the store is perceived as out of date or old-fashioned. Other data will reveal which new theme or style its current customers are likely to prefer. And, when Burger King launches a major new promotional campaign, research data may be shared with franchisees showing that the selected campaign theme was preferred by customers and noncustomers over alternative themes.

Internal Clients

Virtually every manager within an organization will, at some point, use marketing research information. Marketing managers use research data more than anyone else. Recall that the marketing mix consists of decisions about products, promotions, distribution, and pricing. Marketing research helps decision makers in each of these areas make better decisions. Product managers, for example, use research to define their target market. Sometimes, managers use research to target the heavy users of their product within a target market. Marketing research revealed that heavy users of Miracle Whip consume 550 servings, or 17 pounds, of the product a year.[9] These data were used to target a $30 million promotional campaign to core users telling them not to "skip the zip." As a result, Miracle Whip's market share went up 2.1 percent to $305 million in annual sales.[10] The ad campaign was thoroughly tested for effectiveness by marketing research before it was launched.

New product development managers are among the heaviest users of marketing research. Beginning with qualitative research techniques that often generate product ideas, to concept testing, product prototype testing, and 10 test marketing, marketing research is the key to creating a new product. For example, Post's research had always shown that bananas are America's favorite cereal fruit. Therefore, why not a banana-flavored cereal? Post's new product manager concocted cereals with dried banana pieces, but they failed marketing research taste tests. The researcher didn't understand why. Then further research uncovered that consumers felt there was no reason to buy a cereal with preserved bananas. "Bananas are available year-round. They're fresh and they're cheap." If consumers wanted a banana cereal, they'd peel a banana and make one on the spot. One day the manager had an inspiration. Consumers had told her that they liked banana nut bread. It conjured up thoughts of something wonderful tasting that grandma used to make. Using this notion, she had Post's labs create a new cereal for test marketing in consumers' homes. The new product received very high consumer test scores. Thus, Banana Nut Crunch, Post's hottest new cereal, was born.[11] It is

Marketing research not only reveals consumer opinion about existing product and services, but it can also shape opportunities into successful new products offerings. Banana Nut Crunch won the American Marketing Association's award for Best New Product in 1993.

solely a product of marketing research, created from the initial concept of a product manager.

Marketing research also plays an important role in the distribution function. Research is used to choose locations for new stores and to test consumer reactions to internal store design fixtures and features. Banana Republic, for example, has relied on marketing research to create the right atmosphere in its stores. The stores are trendy and fast-paced, with a young, energetic sales staff.

In large organizations, pricing decisions are usually made by committees with representatives from marketing, finance, production, and perhaps other departments. A recent marketing research study conducted by Ford Motor Company took a look at some of the new ideas generated by their engineers to determine whether target customers were interested in a particular feature and, if the concept had appeal, whether consumers would pay the suggested retail price. Qualitative research (see Chapter 5) was conducted in both the United States and the United Kingdom. Twenty-eight new technology features were evaluated to clarify customer likes and dislikes (see Table 3.4). Personal interviews were conducted with the aid of desktop computers. Video descriptions were integrated with a computerized quantitative questionnaire for all feature evaluations. Qualitative research (see Chapter 5) was conducted in the United States and in the United Kingdom to clarify customer likes and dislikes on specific features. Some concepts were perceived as a bit "gimmicky" or just "something else to break." For example, Fingerprint Passive Entry was not perceived as a benefit over remote keyless entry systems. On the other hand, features that were inexpensive but offered high utility were desirable, for example, the Sun Tracking Visor and the Infinite Door Check. As might be expected, consumers overestimated the manufacturer's target retail price for some items and underestimated it for others. Correspondingly, consumers were willing to pay the manufacturer's suggested retail price for some features but not for others.[12]

Top Management's Use of Marketing Research Senior management uses strategic marketing research to help plan the strategic vision, mission, and long-term allocation of resources for the organization. Sears steadily lost market share and profits during the 1980s and till the mid-1990s. Sears had lost sight of its customers. "We didn't know who we wanted to serve,"

Table 3.4

Marketing Research Is Used by Ford Motor Company to Assess Demand and Prices for New Technology Created by Its Engineers

Sample features are shown below:

Fingerprint Passive Entry (U.S. $980, reg. power locks—$350/U.K. £504, central locks—£280)

Finger Print Passive Entry allows the driver to gain access to vehicles equipped with power locks, without the use of a key. The driver's own finger print is used as a unique identification to lock and unlock the vehicle. The vehicle recognizes the driver's finger print through the use of a touch pad. To lock the driver's door or all the vehicle's doors, simply touch the pad for half a second. (U.K. VERSION) Finger Print Passive Entry is also available for easy truck or liftgate access. The vehicle can still be locked or unlocked with a key.

Night Vision System (U.S. $2,100/U.K. £1,400)

The Night Vision System enhances driver visibility at night without causing glare to oncoming drivers. The system uses infrared headlamps to illuminate the road ahead. Sensors form an image of the road on a transparent display which lowers into the driver's view. An enhanced image of the road ahead is displayed on the screen, improving visibility.

Sun Tracking Visor (U.S. $42/U.K. £35)

The Sun Tracking Visor slides along a track from the inside rearview mirror to the edge of both front side doors, providing more accurate coverage. This feature is easy to use and provides a wide range of coverage.

Front Impact Warning

Indicator Light and Tone (U.S. $420/U.K. £210)
Indicator Light and Voice (U.S. $420/U.K. £210)
Indicator Light and Brake Tap (U.S. $490/U.K. £252)
The Front Impact Warning System alerts drivers when approaching another vehicle or object. Sensors located in the bumper detect obstacles in front of the vehicle. The Front Impact Warning System combines an indicator light and audible tone to alert the driver: A combined indicator light and voice warning, or a combined indicator light and automatic brake tap.

Infinite Door Check (U.S. $35/U.K. £14)

The Infinite Door Check holds the door at any open position selected. When in a cramped parking space or on an inclined surface, the door can be stopped at any position without bumping the vehicle next to you.

Skin Temperature Sensor (U.S. $28, reg. ATC—$245/U.K. £14, reg. ATC—£420)

The Skin Temperature Sensor can be added to vehicles equipped with automatic temperature control to automatically cool the temperature inside the vehicle. The Skin Temperature Sensor uses an interior infrared sensor to measure a face's skin temperature. The sensor adjusts the fan and air conditioning to cool the vehicle's interior, until the skin temperature is within a normal range.

Source: Courtesy of Ford Motor Company, 1997. Prices are not actual.

concedes CEO Arthur C. Martinez. "That was a huge hole in our strategy. It was also not clear on what basis we thought we could win against the competition."[13] A major strategic overhaul led to the disposal of nonretail assets and a renewed focus on Sears' core business. Martinez renovated dowdy stores, upgraded women's apparel, and launched a new ad campaign to engineer a major turnaround of the department store giant. Then he had to prove he can make the business grow, a tough assignment since Sears was still locked into relatively cramped mall-based stores. So in 1996 Martinez enlisted Slywotsky's Corporate Decisions to help Sears create a new future. "What I liked most about them is that they came at it from a customer perspective," says Martinez. "Strategy can sometimes be this inside-out, self-absorbed self-examination process. But they have an outside-in view of strategy. I was mightily taken with that, because one of the things that got the company in trouble was its lack of focus on the customer."

Extensive customer research discovered high levels of brand loyalty to Sears' hardware lines. The research also suggested that by segmenting the do-it-yourself market and focusing on home projects with a low degree of complexity, such as papering a bathroom or installing a dimmer switch, Sears could avoid a major competitive collision with Home Depot and other home improvement giants. Customers, the Sears research showed, desired convenience more than the breadth of available items in hardware stores.

After successfully testing the concept of hardware outlets, Martinez is now making a billion-dollar capital bet that Sears can gain growth in this new market. He hopes to have 1,000 freestanding, 20,000-square-foot hardware stores built in five years.[14]

Other Internal Users of Marketing Research

From time to time, other individuals besides marketing and top management find a need for marketing research. For example, Ford engineers sometimes invent new items for which demand must be assessed. Ford marketing research, however, feeds engineering management a steady stream of consumer desires and dislikes. Manufacturing also receives continual feedback from customer satisfaction surveys about loose-fitting door panels, unwieldy sunroof openers, and the like.

The finance department uses test market data to forecast revenue streams for one to three years. Similarly, repositioning research helps financial managers to forecast revenue spurts from older products. Originally, Gatorade was promoted as a drink for competitive athletes. Marketing research found that its main users were men aged 19 to 44, who understood the product, had a good perception of what it did, and knew when to drink it. The product was repositioned toward physical activity enthusiasts as a drink that would quench their thirst and replenish the minerals they had lost during exercise better than other beverages did. The new positioning dramatically increased sales.

Human resource managers may call on marketing research to survey employees about a variety of topics. Offering quality customer service depends upon employees having a good, positive image of the company. Firms like Southwest Airlines and NationsBank monitor employee attitudes through survey research.

Legal departments are relying more than ever before on marketing research to win over juries. Recently, a San Francisco jury ruled against Kendall–Jackson Winery in its case against E. & J. Gallo Winery. Kendall–Jackson claimed that Gallo copied its Vintner's Reserve label, which features a grape leaf with fall colors, by using a similarly styled logo on the Gallo Turning Leaf line of varietal wines (see Figure 3.3). After a two-week trial and several days of deliberation, the jury found that Gallo had not infringed upon Kendall–Jackson's bottle design or trade dress. It also ruled that Gallo had not tried to palm off its wine as a Kendall–Jackson product. Kendall–Jackson was asking for $30 million in damages, but the jury awarded none.[15] Marketing research plays a major role in trials such as this by supporting or disproving consumer confusion between brands. When customer attitudes and impressions are important in deciding a court case, lawyers are increasingly turning to marketing research to prove their positions.

Figure 3.3

Despite the similarity of these two labels, a San Francisco jury ruled against Kendall–Jackson because the marketing research did not support the claim of consumer confusion. For more detailed information about the case, visit http://www.ipmag.com/moskin.html.

Source: (top) © E. & J. Gallo Winery, Modesto, Calif. TURNING LEAF and the leaf label design are registered trademarks of E. & J. Gallo Winery. All rights reserved. Reprinted by permission. (bottom) Reproduced with permission of Kendall–Jackson Wine Estates, Ltd., all rights reserved.

The Growing Role of Strategic Partnering and Global Research

Strategic partnering Two or more marketing research firms with unique skills and resources form an alliance to offer a new service for clients, provide strategic support for each firm, or in some other manner create mutual benefits.

Marketing research is now often a team effort between supplier and client/user. Under pressure from clients and the cost of increasingly sophisticated technology, research companies form strategic alliances and sharing data or capabilities as a cost-effective way to grow. This trend toward **strategic partnering**—even with competitors—will continue, industry executives say.

"The '90s is the decade of the strategic alliance agreement," said Tom Daley, president of Spectra Marketing, Chicago. "The technology is so expensive and leadership positions so vulnerable that it's the way business has to go. It used to be that when you introduced a new [research] product or service, it was two or three years before everyone matched it. Now Nielsen can have it in the marketplace next week. So everyone's asking, 'How can I get smarter faster?' And strategic alliances are the answer."[16]

Spectra, a geodemographic research company founded in 1988, has been built through a series of strategic alliances. It has deals with several major companies, including Information Resources, Incorporated (IRI), Claritas Corporation, Market Facts, Inc., and Donnelly Marketing's Carol Wright unit. IRI has been one of the most active in forming alliances, having set deals with Arbitron Company, Citicorp, VideOCart, and Simmons Marketing Research. The latter partnership combines IRI's data on who buys what in the United States with Simmons magazine readership data. The combination enables the partnership to develop indices about what products appeal to magazine readers. "In 1979, we introduced BehaviorScan for an investment of a few million dollars. You couldn't even begin to think of duplicating that system for anywhere near that cost," said former IRI Chairman and CEO Gian Fulgoni. "The cost of doing business and the complexity of the business are driving the trend to strategic alliances."[17]

In a strategic partnership, the client and research firm work together on a forward-looking and ongoing basis. A partnering relationship establishes a defined set of activities for which a research firm provides services without bidding project by project. Services provided may include data collection, product or customer tracking systems, or any research activity for which the firm may have special expertise or capability.

About half of all large marketing research departments engage in strategic partnering with research suppliers.[18] Partnering is most common in service companies and consumer packaged-goods manufacturers. The advantages of this type of partnering are twofold: It allows for better coordination of effort and increased productivity as the supplier develops an intimate knowledge of the research user's needs and its customers. The research firm, in turn, can concentrate resources directly on the client's projects rather than on selling and making proposals.

Global Marketing Research Trends

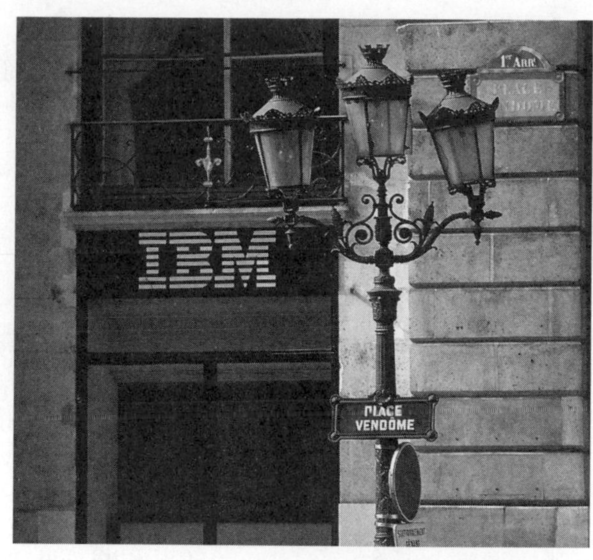

The largest users of global marketing research are big multinational organizations like IBM.

Strategic partnering is not just a phenomenon in the United States, but is occurring all around the globe. The predominant buyers of global marketing research are the world's large multinational companies. As their organizations and strategies become increasingly global, they will require ongoing strategic counseling relationships, rather than a string of individual projects. Research suppliers that hope to capitalize on global strategic partnerships will have to have offices in a number of countries, or at least have a local presence. Suppliers must also have the personnel and expertise to conduct global research studies, combined with a high level of technical expertise in the home office. Finally, a global marketing research supplier must have thorough knowledge of global marketing. Philip Barnard, chairman of Research International, the second largest marketing research firm in the world, with offices in over 40 countries, discusses several trends he foresees in the Global Issues feature.

Global ISSUES

International Marketing Research is Changing

MARKETING RESEARCH PRACTICE IS EVOLVING AND MATURING AROUND THE GLOBE.

In this period of change, there are new opportunities both for those in research companies and for corporate researchers. A few hundred multinational corporations probably account for around 70 percent of worldwide research expenditures through work commissioned at national, regional, and corporate (global) levels. It is estimated that U.S. corporations alone are still responsible for more than half [of] the global spending.

Structurally, the global market is split roughly into 30 percent continuous research and 70 percent custom survey/ad hoc research. "Continuous" refers mainly to syndicated market and media measurement services involving panels of households, stores, and doctors, etc. The use of scanner technology, massive computing power, database management/decision support systems, and the costly recruitment and maintenance of panels (or data acquisition from store chains) means that this sector of the research business demands a high investment. Barriers to entry are therefore high, as are rewards when market dominance is achieved. However, technological development

and intense (price) competition between research leviathans have seen margins fall or disappear in recent years and several players forced out of the market following major losses, involving tens or even hundreds of millions of dollars.

Trends in Research Demand

There have been a number of developments in client demand in recent decades. Some of the most significant are identified in this section.

1. *Broadening the user base.* The buying and using of marketing research is no longer dominated by consumer packaged goods companies, although they remain the largest single category. Growth in recent years has been particularly strong in the consumer services sector (especially financial services) and in the area of utilities/public sector/regulated industries. Privatization programs throughout the world have accelerated this trend.
2. *Widening of market research boundaries.* No longer does product and communication research, together with usership and attitude studies, dominate the custom/ad hoc sector. There has been much growth in the measurement of such areas of information as customer satisfaction, service quality/business performance, brand equity and strategic positioning—stimulated in some cases by the disciplines of total quality management programs.
3. *Internationalization.* This dramatic trend has many manifestations. First the corporate globalization and development and roll-out of regional/international brands has brought the world "out there" much closer to the daily lives of corporate marketers and researchers—even to a growing degree in the U.S., where "domestic" and "international" have traditionally been well separated.

Many major multinational corporations have moved to establish head office guidelines for marketing research and to standardize and harmonize globally the approaches and techniques they use. It is then but a small step to nominate preferred research suppliers (or, a stage further, global partners) to conduct such work worldwide. This process works in reverse, too, with international research companies being invited to establish or refine a portfolio of global techniques for their clients.

This internationalization trend has also been enhanced by the opening up of previously closed economies, particularly in central and eastern Europe and Asia, together with the rapid growth of emerging economies in Latin America and Asia-Pacific. Such global and regional trade agreements as GATT/WTO, NAFTA, Mercosur, EU, and ASEAN have added further impetus.

Trends in Global Research Supply

To a considerable degree, these trends reflect the changing priorities in demand, but some supply trends stem from increased recognition of marketing research as a growth sector within the business/professional services market and one seemingly less affected by recession than some others.

1. *Concentration of ownership.* Although the marketing research industry remains highly fragmented, with over 3,000 serious research companies worldwide, mergers and acquisitions in the 1980s and [1990s] have created a small num-

ber of large global and regional businesses at the top end. The top 25 account for around 55 percent of the total market, with D&B Marketing Information (Nielsen, IMS, SRG), alone representing nearly one-quarter of the worldwide research business. The top four research companies operate primarily in the syndicated "continuous" research sector of the market.

2. *Heterogeneity of supply.* What has emerged in the past decade or so is an industry structure that includes a small number of public companies or subsidiaries thereof, some of them small multinationals themselves (for example, ACNielsen in syndicated services, Research International in custom research), together with many privately owned businesses. Traditional cottage industry firms compete alongside specialist boutiques, consultants, and number-crunching data supermarkets. There are few truly global research businesses, but several strong regional ones and a few global networks, as well as many companies that have licensed their techniques or franchised their services abroad. The range and variety of research companies offer clients a tremendous choice of supply.
3. *Specialization.* Client demand has led large research companies to reorganize on a specialized divisional basis as well as encouraging the growth of specialist suppliers. The fastest growing research firms in recent years have been specialist businesses such as Millward Brown.
4. *Internationalization.* Many research companies now coordinate multicountry studies for their clients, working through affiliates, networks, or preferred suppliers throughout the world. International franchising and research technique licensing agreements have also spread widely.[19] ■

Making Ethical Decisions in Marketing Research

The foundation of global marketing research alliances and strategic partnering is mutual trust. Trust exists when an organization develops and practices high ethical standards. Today's business ethics are actually a subset of the values held by society as a whole. The values used by marketing people to make decisions have been acquired through family, educational, and religious institutions, as well as social movements (such as the antinuclear movement and women's rights). A marketing researcher with a mature set of ethical values accepts personal responsibility for decisions that affect the entire community, including responsibility for

1. employees' needs and desires and the long-range best interests of the organization.

2. people directly affected by company activities and their long-range goodwill and best interests (this creates good publicity for the firm).
3. social values and conditions for society at large that provide values, sanctions, and a social structure that enable the company to exist.

A high standard of ethics and professionalism go hand in hand. Good ethics provides a solid foundation for professionalism, and striving for a lofty level of professionalism necessitates proper ethics on the part of researchers.

Indications of a Lack of Professionalism in the Research Industry

Push polling A style of research gathering in which zealous political supporters deride one candidate to lead voters to support the other candidate.

Push Polls

There are numerous signs that professionalism has not reached a desired level in the marketing research industry. One example is **push polling,** where zealous political supporters make derogatory and damaging statements about one candidate to lead voters to support the other candidate. In contrast to legitimate political polls that may be 10 or more minutes long, include a range of questions, and have a statistical sample of 500 or so respondents, push poll calls are of short duration (often 30 seconds), with one or two questions or statements, and usually target many thousands of people, with no statistical sampling involved.

The National Council on Public Polls (NCPP) and the American Association of Political Consultants (AAPC) have both issued statements to the public and the press warning about push polling. California passed a law in 1996 requiring that calls "that advocate support of, or opposition to, a candidate, ballot measure, or both" must announce "during the course of the call that it has been paid for or furnished by the candidate, committee, or other organization." The interpretive language accompanying this bill specifically states that legitimate political polling is not meant to be affected by this legislation.[20]

Sales Pitches Disguised as Research

Another serious problem is when sales pitches are disguised as marketing research. Although this problem is usually caused by people outside the research industry, it still casts a negative light on legitimate researchers.

The Council of American Survey Research Organizations (CASRO), a trade association representing approximately 130 full-service marketing research firms, has been fighting firms who use sales pitches disguised as marketing research. Because some firms that conduct marketing research and other organizations that conduct survey research realized that more needed to be done, in 1992 the Council for Marketing and Opinion Research (CMOR) was created. It is sponsored by CASRO, the Marketing Research Association, and the Advertising Research Foundation. CMOR is an umbrella organization for survey research companies, and is designed to act as a unified voice to respondents, legislators, and regulators. CMOR's objectives are to protect the research industry against unnecessarily restrictive legislation, deal with waning respondent cooperation, and fight sales pitches disguised as research. CMOR, for example, has asked "sugging marketers" (firms selling under the guise of research) to use more forthright and honest marketing techniques. Another problem is "frugging," which is fundraising under the guise of research. The Sierra Club used frugging, and, after a call from CMOR, agreed not to use the technique again.

The Better Business Bureau has issued a memorandum describing legitimate marketing research, stating that "real" marketing research does not sell. The U.S. Postal Service has issued cease-and-desist orders to two companies that conducted fraudulent operations under the guise of research.[21]

Fostering Professionalism

Because of the specialized knowledge and expertise they possess, members of a profession have influence and power over those for whom they provide the service. Just as no layperson can use the tools of a doctor or lawyer, so does the marketing profession guard its knowledge and control who has access to it. Marketing does not have a credentialing process or high entry barriers. Even so, marketing researchers and marketers wield power and influence over their customers, and the society at large. The argument can be made that the group of marketers that most need to think and behave as professionals are those in marketing research.

A recent study measured the level of professionalism in marketing research. The distinction between a "profession" and "professionalism" is important because it suggests that a profession and membership to it are objectively determined, similar to taking medical board exams. Professionalism is more personal and subjective. The study found that marketing researchers had autonomy in their jobs and were permitted to exercise their own judgment. They also had a high level of expertise and an ability to work independently.[22] These are all characteristics of professionalism. However, most researchers did not readily identify the contribution that marketing makes to society. And, most firms did not tend to reward staff participation in professional organizations. These are not indicators of an emphasis on high levels of professionalism.

The Efforts of CASRO

Several positive steps have been taken recently to improve the level of professionalism in the marketing research industry. CASRO has sponsored several symposia that deal with ethical issues in survey research. It also has created a code of ethics that has been widely disseminated to research professionals. The CASRO board has worked with other groups such as the Marketing Research Association to provide input to legislatures considering antimarketing research legislation.

The Creation of CMOR

In January 1992, research industry leaders decided to band together to address the critical issues of government affairs and respondent cooperation because no existing association could adequately move forward on addressing them alone. These issues required broad industry support and involvement, along with substantial funding. It became evident that the marketing and opinion research industry needed to take action to protect itself from unreasonable government prohibitions, bolster its image among the public and legislators, promote self-regulation, and develop a means to differentiate the research industry from other similarly appearing industries.

The January 1992 meeting of research professionals led to the creation of the Council for Marketing and Public Opinion Research (CMOR). Since its founding, the organization has undertaken a number of actions concerning respondent cooperation; it has

- compiled a list of possible responses to sugging (selling under the guise of research) and frugging (fundraising under the guise of research) efforts, and created a series of letters to respond to suggers and fruggers.
- prepared a consumer brochure and a thank-you card to help educate consumers about legitimate marketing and opinion research.
- established an 800 telephone number to give consumers a forum for asking questions and seeking information about specific interviews or surveys in general.
- developed and disseminated the "Respondent Bill of Rights," which describes principles governing a researcher's responsibilities to a respondent.
- reviewed data and literature on respondent cooperation and cooperation improvement campaigns, including public education, media efforts, and internal controls.[23]

Jay Wilson, chairman and CEO of Roper Starch Worldwide, Inc. and CMOR board chairman, says, "The basic value and integrity of what we do is very much a function of our ability to satisfy our respondent customers—I tend to look at them as customers. We have a lot to do as an industry to make them happy about the research process and more willing to be interviewed."[24]

CMOR has also been active in the area of government affairs. Specifically, it has

- established a computerized monitoring program of all federal and state legislation.
- monitored and responded to well over 10,000 pieces of state and federal legislation on such issues as electronic monitoring, unsolicited telephone calls, data privacy, use of lists, and research abuses.
- reviewed the rule-making of the federal Telephone Consumer Protection Act of 1991.
- worked to defeat the federal electronic monitoring bill in the House and Senate.
- helped to outlaw sugging by drafting an amendment now included in the telemarketing fraud law that requires telemarketers to state promptly that they are selling something, what the product is, and how much it costs.
- secured an exemption to the federal crime bill that allows continued access to DMV records for automotive research and other legitimate research uses.
- compiled a list of existing federal and state laws in the area of telecommunications and privacy.

- amended Illinois law to allow marketing and opinion research companies to monitor telephone interviewing for quality control and validation purposes.
- supported legislation to prohibit push polling while protecting the legitimate political polling process.[25]

Is There a Need for Researcher Certification?

Today it is far too easy to begin practicing marketing research. We have seen several "fast-talkers" convince unwary clients that they are qualified researchers. Unfortunately, relying on poor information to make major decisions has resulted in the loss of market share, profits, and, in some cases, bankruptcy.

Certification has generated a great deal of debate among members of the marketing research industry. Note that certification is not licensing. Licensing is a mandatory procedure administered by a government body that allows someone to practice a profession. Certification is a voluntary program administered by a nongovernment body that provides a credential for the purpose of differentiation in the marketplace. The issue of certification is sensitive because it directly affects marketing researchers' ability to practice their profession freely. The arguments can be summed up as follows:

CON: There is no single criterion on which to judge a researcher. The profession is too diverse, so the exam would have to be very basic.

PRO: It is not necessary to test every competency for every type of research. Other diverse groups, such as the American Society of Interior Design, have a successful certification program.

CON: Politics would play a big part in the process, it would be expensive and time-consuming, and there isn't a viable organization to oversee the process.

PRO: Organizations are composed of members; members use their collective voice to create a certification program. Researchers could be certified through continuing education programs and phased listing.

CON: Because certification is voluntary, there is no guarantee that poor researchers wouldn't continue to operate. Certification, therefore, would not legitimize the profession. Also, a certification program probably would require grandfathering in many current researchers. Thus some incompetent researchers probably would be certified.

PRO: Certification would help to establish marketing research as a true profession. It demonstrates to government regulators that the industry is concerned about competency. The certification process would provide a forum for discussing what is considered to be professional behavior.

CON: There is no evidence that certification would create higher quality research.

PRO: Certification would help the public distinguish between legitimate surveys and those done with a built-in bias. (Certified researchers would not conduct biased polls.) Certified researchers would be held more accountable through such things as mandatory methodology disclosures.

CON: Because certification is voluntary, it never resolves ethical issues.

PRO: Current organizational ethical codes have not been effective in preventing abuses. Self-regulation may forestall governmental regulation.

CON: Certification can't guarantee competence.

PRO: Certification would help protect consumers and clients because the research profession now suffers a multitude of poorly trained and inexperienced practitioners. Certification would at least provide research users with some assurance of knowledge, experience, and commitment to the profession.[26]

As you can see, the issues of certification are complex and emotional. Not surprisingly, there is great diversity of opinion within the research industry. A recent study of almost 300 marketing research professionals found 17 percent strongly in favor of certification, 20 percent strongly opposed, and the remainder somewhere in the middle.[27] To date, no organization has taken action to begin a certification program.

Summary

This chapter focuses on the types of firms that form the marketing research industry and the functions they perform. The research industry may be categorized as follows:

Level 1. Corporate marketing departments—marketing departments in major firms such as Kraft General Foods and Ralston Purina.
Level 2. Ad agencies—advertising agencies such as J. Walter Thompson and Grey Advertising.
Level 3. Custom or ad hoc research firms—firms that handle customized marketing research projects addressing specific problems for individual clients. Syndicated service firms—firms that collect data of general interest; anyone can purchase the information. These companies are prominent in the media audience field and scanner data research.
Level 4. Field service firms—data collection firms.

The structure of the research industry may be viewed as having four levels: the users of research data, ad agencies, custom and syndicated marketing research firms, and field service firms. Users of marketing research can be further categorized as external or internal to a firm. External users include company vendors and franchisees. Internal users include the marketing department for logistics, sales, promotion, new product development, brand management, and pricing decision-making information. Other groups and departments using research are product engineering, finance, manufacturing, human resources, legal, and senior management.

A key trend in the research industry today is strategic partnering.

Today's business ethics are a subset of the values held by society as a whole. A marketing researcher with mature ethical values assumes responsibility for employees' needs and desires, people directly affected by company activities, and social values and conditions for society at large.

The level of professionalism in the marketing research industry has been raised by the efforts of CASRO and CMOR. CMOR is primarily concerned with respondent cooperation and with legislation that curtails or prohibits various forms of survey research. Researcher certification continues to be a highly controversial and emotional issue within the research community.

Key Terms & Definitions

Custom, or ad hoc, marketing research firms Research companies that carry out customized marketing research to address specific projects for corporate clients.

Syndicated service research firms Companies that collect, package, and sell the same general market research data to many firms.

Field service firms Companies that only collect survey data for corporate clients or research firms.

Strategic partnering Two or more marketing research firms with unique skills and resources form an alliance to offer a new service for clients, provide strategic support for each firm, or in some other manner create mutual benefits.

Push polling A style of research gathering in which zealous political supporters deride one candidate to lead voters to support the other candidate.

Questions for Review & Critical Thinking

1. Compare and contrast custom and syndicated marketing research firms.
2. What is the role of field services in marketing research?
3. Discuss several types of support service firms in the research industry.
4. Describe the levels of the marketing research industry.
5. List several key characteristics of corporate marketing research departments.
6. Discuss the different product offerings of syndicated service firms.
7. Define strategic partnering. Why has it become so prominent in the marketing research industry?
8. What do you foresee as the role of a code of ethics within an organization? What can be done to ensure that employees follow this code of ethics?
9. Who would you say has the greatest responsibility within the marketing research industry to raise the standards of ethics—marketing research suppliers, marketing research clients, or field services?
10. What role should the federal government play in establishing ethical standards for the marketing research industry? How might they be enforced?
11. If respondents agree or consent to interviews after being told they will be paid $20 for their opinions, do they forfeit all respondent rights? If so, what rights have they forfeited?

Working the Net

1. Using the Internet, go to http://www.dssresearch.com and then go to http://www.burke.com. Compare the offerings of the two marketing research firms DSS Research and Burke, Inc.
2. Research International is part of the Kantar Group, Ltd. (see Table 3.2) and is one of the world's most global marketing research firms, with offices in 54 countries. Go to its website, http://www.research-int.com and report on its international research capabilities.
3. Go to http://www.worldopinion.com and report to the class on the number and description of research firms listed at this site. Also, inform the class about events coming up in the research industry. Finally, use this site to report on job openings in the marketing research industry.

Real-Life Research

Maritz Marketing Research Goes Global

Maritz Marketing Research, Inc., Fenton, Missouri, recently announced partnerships with six European research firms. Going global is a "defensive strategy at this point," said Ron Lipovsky, company president. Bigger research companies, and Maritz is one of them, know that if they can't provide their clients with data from around the world that's comparable to what they're getting in the United States, those clients will find a company that can.

In the past, Maritz had lined up partners on a project-by-project basis, said Lipovsky. "The benefit [of the new partnerships] for clients is that we've established good, strong working relationships with these companies. That should reduce the number of communication problems" and ensure that "common practices are followed all the way through."

All of the partners are expected to adhere to a common code of ethics and protocols. In many areas, for example, single entry of data is acceptable, but because Maritz believes the error rate is too high, companies will be required to employ a double-entry system. Maritz is reviewing research companies in Latin America and the Asia-Pacific area and hopes to have partnerships established soon.[28]

Questions

1. Do you think that strategic partnering is the best way for U.S. research firms to go global?
2. What problems can arise from strategic partnering?
3. Do you think that it is important for a U.S. firm to be the dominant partner in a strategic partnering relationship? Why or why not?

CD Opportunity

1. Review the Burke video segment on your CD for new insights into the marketing research industry.
2. The Ethical Dilemmas and Marketing Research Across the Organization exercises found on your CD will help you understand the role and responsibility of marketing research in society and the firm.

PART *two*

Creating a Research Design

Check it out!

Remember to visit http://mcdaniel.swcollege.com for information to help you with the material in Part Two. MR Online in the Resource Center of http://marketing.swcollege.com can also help you review for your final exam!

Secondary Data, Databases, the Internet, and Decision Support Systems

CHAPTER *four*

Learning Objectives

1. *To understand how firms create an internal database*

2. *To become familiar with the growing popularity of firms using their websites to build a database*

3. *To learn about data mining*

4. *To distinguish between primary and secondary data and understand the advantages and disadvantages of each*

5. *To understand the role of the Internet in obtaining secondary data*

6. *To learn the nature of decision support systems*

To understand how Wal-Mart Stores, Inc. makes sense of the zillions of pieces of information it has on the thousands of purchases it rings up, think about bananas. Bananas, according to Wal-Mart's research, are the most common item in America's grocery carts—more common even than milk or bread. So even though Wal-Mart Supercenters sell bananas in the produce section, they also crop up in the cereal aisle to help sell a few more corn flakes.

Wal-Mart's banana placement skills were put to the test when it opened its first Wal-Mart Neighborhood Market near the retailer's headquarters in Bentonville, Arkansas. The suburban-style supermarket is the first. If Wal-Mart expands the concept—nicknamed Small Mart—on a large scale, it will put the giant retailer in head-to-head competition with Kroger Company, Safeway, Inc., and other seasoned grocery rivals.

Many retailers talk a good game when it comes to mining data collected at cash registers as a way to build sales. Wal-Mart, the nation's largest retailer, has been doing it since about 1990. Now, it is sitting on an information trove so vast and detailed that it far exceeds what many manufacturers know about their own products.

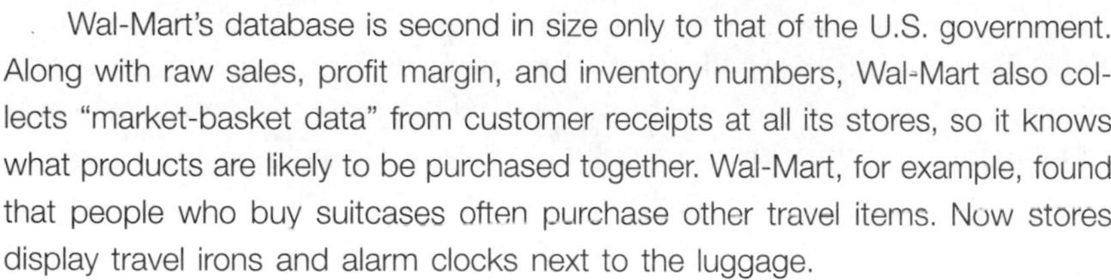

Wal-Mart's database is second in size only to that of the U.S. government. Along with raw sales, profit margin, and inventory numbers, Wal-Mart also collects "market-basket data" from customer receipts at all its stores, so it knows what products are likely to be purchased together. Wal-Mart, for example, found that people who buy suitcases often purchase other travel items. Now stores display travel irons and alarm clocks next to the luggage.

At 192,000 square feet, Wal-Mart Supercenters are about the size of four football fields. Wal-Mart quickly found customers have trouble navigating them. To address customers' frustrations, Wal-Mart dug through heaps of purchase data from its supercenters and unearthed lots of ways to help people find things they didn't even know they needed. Kleenex tissues are in the paper-goods aisle and also mixed in with the cold medicine. Measuring spoons are in housewares and also hanging next to Crisco shortening.

Another interesting tactic is the way transaction data help Wal-Mart lead shoppers out of low-margin merchandise and into more profitable sections. At the supercenters, mops and brooms—two "hard goods" used in the kitchen—turn

Find out more about Wal-Mart's data collection by reading a presentation by the company's chief information officer posted to

 **http://www.cio.com/CIO/101497_mott.html**

out to be a good segue between low-margin food and higher-margin household items like gardening tools. Then, it is on to electronics and clothes. Wal-Mart also sprinkles high-margin products in with the staples: Wal-Mart's baby aisle now often features baby food, formula, and diapers along with infant clothes and children's medicines.[1]

Wal-Mart's huge database has been created from secondary data. What is secondary data? What are the pros and cons of secondary data? How is the Internet enabling firms to build valuable and effective databases? What role does the Internet play in secondary research? These are some of the questions we will answer in Chapter 4. ■

The Nature of Secondary Data

Secondary data Data that have previously been gathered.

Primary data New data gathered to help solve the problem at hand.

Secondary data include information that has been gathered and that only might be relevant to the problem at hand. **Primary data,** in contrast, are survey, observation, or experiment data collected to solve the particular problem under investigation. In other words, it is highly unlikely that any marketing research problem is entirely unique or has never occurred before. It is also probable that someone else has investigated this problem or one similar to it in the past. There are two basic sources of secondary data: the company itself (internal databases) and other organizations or persons (external databases).

Creating an Internal Database

Internal database A database developed from data within an organization.

For many companies, a computerized **internal database** containing information about customers and prospects has become an essential marketing tool. A database is simply a collection of related information. A firm's website can be an excellent way to create an internal database. A traditional starting point for creating an internal secondary database has been to pull information from the firm's sales or inquiry processing and tracking system. Typically, such a system is built on a salesperson's "call report." Call reports provide a blueprint of a salesperson's daily activities. A report details the number of calls made; characteristics of each firm visited; sales activity resulting from a call; and information picked up about competitors, such as price changes, new products, credit term modifications, and new features stressed by competitors.

Creating an internal marketing secondary database built on sales results and customer preferences can be a powerful marketing tool. Catalog companies such as Speigel's and L. L. Bean have become masters at building and using internal databases. The story of how Cabela's, a major fishing tackle and outdoor products company, uses its database is presented in the In Practice feature.

The Database and Customer Information

In PRACTICE

Cabela's depends on its database to control the distribution costs of its four-color catalogs. In a typical year, Cabela's sends out at least nine mailings of between 300,000 and 3 million catalogs each.

Cabela's constantly winnows out the people who do not respond. It also sends specific kinds of catalogs to buyers based on their purchasing patterns, says marketing director Sharon Robison. The company divides customers into 10 major categories, from the buyers of footwear to buyers of gifts and fishing and bow-hunting equipment. Cabela's gathers new names by sharing its mailing list with similar catalog companies, such as Gander Mountain, by renting address lists from magazines, by advertising in hunting and fishing publications, and by soliciting new names from current catalog recipients.[2] ■

The Growing Importance of Internal Database Marketing

Internal Databases as Collective Memory Banks

Perhaps the fastest-growing use of an internal database is database marketing. Database marketing is the creation of a large computerized file of the profiles and purchase patterns of customers and potential customers.

In the 1950s, network television enabled advertisers to "get the same message to everyone simultaneously." Database marketing can get a customized, individual message to everyone simultaneously through direct mail. This is why database marketing is sometimes called "micromarketing." Database marketing can create a computerized form of the old-fashioned relationship that people used to have with the corner grocer, butcher, or baker. "A database is sort of a collective memory," says Richard G. Barlow, president of Frequency Marketing, Inc., a Cincinnati-based consulting firm. "It deals with you in the same personalized way as a mom-and-pop grocery store, where they knew customers by name and stocked what they wanted.[3]

The size of some databases is impressive: Ford Motor Company's is about 50 million names; Kraft General Foods, 30 million; Citicorp, 30 million; and Kimberly Clark, maker of Huggies diapers, 10 million new mothers. American Express can pull from its database all cardholders who made purchases at golf pro shops in the past six months, or who attended symphony concerts, or who traveled to Europe more than once in the past year, or the few people who did all three activities.

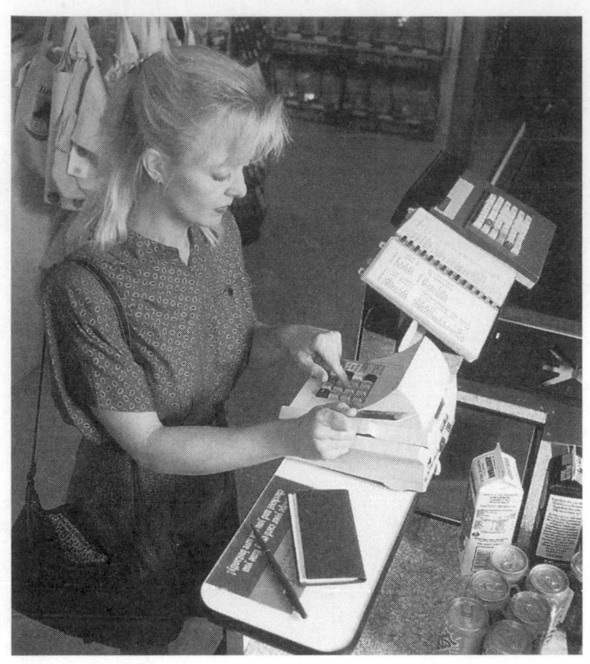

By using their VonsClub check-approval card at the register, customers are providing the supermarket, food processors, and manufactures information about their grocery buying habits.

A technique of growing popularity for building a database is the creation of "customer clubs." Kraft, for example, has been inviting kids to join the Cheese & Macaroni Club. For three proofs of purchase, $2.95, and a completed membership form with the child's (and, of course, the parents') address, Kraft will send a painter's cap, a bracelet, shoelaces, a book of stickers, and other goodies.[4] By requiring customers who respond to offers of free shirts, sleeping bags, or other merchandise to fill out detailed questionnaires, Philip Morris has built a database of about 26 million smokers.

Blockbuster Entertainment Corporation is using its database of 36 million households and 2 million daily transactions to help its video rental customers select movies and steer them to other Blockbuster subsidiaries. In Richmond, Virginia, the company is testing a computerized system that recommends 10 movie titles based on a customer's prior rentals. The suggestions are printed on a card that also offers targeted promotions. Customers who have rented children's films, for example, might get a discount at Discovery Zone, Blockbuster's play-center subsidiary.

Vons Company, Southern California's largest supermarket chain, and ninth largest in America, has upgraded its check approval card into a Vons Club card. The card was a foundation for creating a database that gave automatic discounts on items selected for promotion. Vons' objective was to build a comprehensive database of exactly what is in shoppers' baskets each time they leave the store. Using that data, Vons can understand consumer behavior better and send a monthly mailing of individually laser-printed discount coupons to each VonsClub member. Even food processors and manufacturers benefit from Vons' database.

Beech-Nut, a maker of baby foods, has used the VonsClub mailer to identify every household that has purchased a baby product for the first time in the preceding eight weeks. Susan Widham, vice president of marketing at Beech-Nut, says that this program enables her to target offers specifically to consumers based on the type and quantity of the products they buy, the frequency with which they buy them, and whether they buy Beech-Nut products or a competitor's. The company is considering, a 50-cents-off coupon to hold on to Beech-Nut customers and a $1-off coupon for Gerber's customers, to get them to switch brands.[5]

Internal Databases Can Even Be Created from Conversations

"Your call may be monitored to ensure quality." This disclaimer crops up all the time these days. People are especially likely to hear it when they call various help desks to ask about product warranties, software problems, travel arrangements, medical services, or dozens of other issues. At many companies, the monitoring isn't done by supervisors but by digital recorders. As a result, companies are accumulating mammoth databases of audio files.

In PRACTICE

Database Design and Implementation

With an undergraduate degree in computer science and an MBA, Mike Foytik, senior vice president for information science for DSS Research, exemplifies the new breed of managers in marketing service jobs with strong backgrounds in computers.

He is a strong proponent of the use of "relational databases." He has designed dozens for DSS clients in direct marketing and retailing. He notes that there are many advantages to using a relational database compared with the traditional database approach, sometimes referred to as the *flat-file method.* In a relational database, data are stored in several small structures or files rather than in a single large one. Each of the small files in a relational database contains key information that allows individual records in the database to be linked to associated data in other individual files that make up the entire database structure.

For example, a customer database might contain one file that includes customer information, such as name, mailing address, and Social Security number. This information needs to be updated occasionally. Products purchased by each customer would go into another file that is updated frequently (every time the customer buys something). The two files might be linked by the customer's Social Security number. With each new order, a record will be created that includes the product purchased, the price, other relevant information concerning the purchase, and the buyer's Social Security number. Under the traditional flat-file approach, all this information (the product purchase information and the buyer's personal information) would have to be entered with each product purchase. Relational databases have a number of distinct advantages:

- *Less data storage space required.* There is very little redundant information in a relational database. Data such as addresses are stored only once for each customer, rather than being stored with every new purchase that is added. Foytik notes that "we have achieved 75 percent storage space reductions for some of our clients."
- *More flexible.* Relational databases offer much greater flexibility and efficiency regarding changes in the data to be stored and the way data are used in the future. With flat-file databases, every time a new data field is added to the database, the database must be recreated so that the new data field is added to every record in the database. With a relational database, new information would be stored in a new file and, therefore, has no effect on existing data in other files in the database.
- *Easier to restrict access to sensitive information.* Relational databases can be easily designed to restrict user access to certain areas of the database via the use of special passwords or codes, while still allowing more general access to less sensitive areas. In flat-file databases, this sort of restricted access

to some parts of the database is all but impossible. Users must have either total access or no access.

- *The database can easily be designed to accommodate many users.* Foytik notes that "most of our clients have a number of different departments with very different informational needs accessing customer data." With flat-files, separate copies of the database must be created and modified to meet the needs of different users. With relational databases, the physical data remain unchanged while the data or reports seen by the different user groups (sometimes called the logical data) can be varied.

Finally, he notes, all these advantages come at some cost. First, relational databases require much more sophisticated software and more sophisticated people to program it. Second, relational databases require much more up-front planning if the company is to reap the full benefits of this type of data. Finally, relational databases tend to require more processor horsepower. This is becoming less of an issue with the price/performance ratio of computers constantly improving.[6] ■

Dragon Systems, Inc. in Newton, Massachusetts, offers computer-based tools to help analyze conversations for insights on customer satisfaction, shifts in buying patterns, and other trends. Using the same speech-recognition technology that is employed in Dragon's NaturallySpeaking dictation software, the new program can create word indexes from reams of recorded speech. The indexes allow managers to move quickly to the locations on the tape where the key words and phrases occur.

Users can also query the database about the frequency with which a certain word is used in phone conversations. Managers can find out, for example, how many calls on a given day made reference to a particular glitch in the software.[7]

Website Databases—A Marketer's Dream

Web Retailing If a person were opening, say, a wine shop today, which one gives the owner the best opportunity to build a database—a traditional store or a Web retailer like Virtual Vineyards, Inc.? The Web retailer wins, hands down.

A Web merchant like Virtual Vineyards has access to data about its clients that would make its physical-world counterparts cry. A customer's conduit to an on-line store is a two-way electronic link, allowing an on-line merchant to gather all sorts of information, particularly if that customer has shopped with that merchant before.

Getting the customer's name, address, and purchasing history are only the beginning, however. A Web merchant can record that customer's actions as she moves through the merchant's site, taking note not only of purchases but also of window shopping. The end result is a file that allows the merchant to determine what that customer is most likely to purchase next—and then offer inducements to make it happen.

Meanwhile, back in the physical world, the wine store owner sits behind his busy register, eyeing the anonymous customer who just went out empty-handed. Had he been here before? If he had, what did he buy? Did he even see the new chardonnay that just came in? Unfortunately, he was too busy to ask those questions (and the customer would have been offended if he had). Maybe the customer will come back—maybe he won't.[8]

Web Advertising Preview Travel, Inc. is an on-line travel agency based in San Francisco that determined that Las Vegas, Orlando, and Cancun were the top three vacation spots among its customers. The firm responded by purchasing keywords for the three destinations on several Internet directory sites; when a Web surfer searched for any of the three vacation spots, a Preview Travel advertising banner would accompany the list of results.

Karen Askey, senior vice president of consumer marketing at Preview Travel, says traditional travel agencies could employ the same promotional tactics, but adds that she doubts they could spot top destinations as quickly. "The speed at which you can get that data is basically instantaneous," she says.[9]

Using Cookies Once a Web surfer starts clicking around the virtual aisles of an on-line store, merchants can monitor their every move. The best known method involves a technology called a **cookie,** a text file that sits on a user's computer to identify when the user revisits a website.

Cookie A text file placed on a user's computer in order to identify the user when he or she revisits the website.

Even some privacy advocates admit cookies have beneficial uses: For instance, they can store passwords, sparing users the hassle of having to identify themselves every time they go to a website, and they make on-line shopping carts work. Despite what some Net users believe, a site can only read the cookies that that site previously put on a user's system, not any other cookies the user has collected around the Web.

Cookies are a powerful device for monitoring a user's behavior within a site, one that can tell a merchant whether the user lingers in the lingerie department or wants to buy lawn chairs. "What it's like," says Nick Donatiello, president of Odyssey, a market research firm based in San Francisco, "is if every time you walk into Macy's, they put a little tracker on you that follows you everywhere you go, how long you look at perfume and blue jeans."[10]

Cookies give Web merchants an advantage over their competitors in traditional retailing. They can follow window shoppers, then use the information to target promotions at them on return visits. And, unlike their physical counterparts, an on-line merchant can rearrange the entire layout of a store in real time, sticking in an advertisement for, say, parkas on the front door when an avid skier comes calling.

Data Mining American Express is using a neural network to examine the hundreds of millions of entries in its database that tell how and where individual cardholders transact business. A **neural network** is a computer program that mimics the processes of the human brain that are capable of learning from examples to find patterns in data. The result is a set of "purchase propensity scores" for each cardholder. Based on these scores, AmEx matches offers from affiliated merchants to the purchase histories of individual cardholders

Neural network A computer program that mimics the processes of the human brain that are capable of learning from examples to find patterns in data.

and encloses these offers with their monthly statements. The benefits are reduced expenses for AmEx and information of higher value for its cardholders. American Express is engaged in data mining.

Data mining The use of statistical and other advanced software to discover non-obvious patterns hidden in a database.

Data mining is the use of statistical and other advanced software to discover nonobvious patterns hidden in a database. The objective is to identify patterns that marketers can use in creating new strategies and tactics to increase a firm's profitability. Camelot Music Holdings used data mining to identify a group of high-spending, 65-plus members of the store's frequent shopper club who were buying lots of classical music, jazz, and movies. However, a large percentage were also buying rap and alternative music. Data mining revealed that these were grandparents buying for the grandchildren. Now, Camelot tells the senior citizens what's hot in rap and alternative music, as in well as traditional music.[11]

Data mining is searching for interesting patterns and following the data trail wherever it leads. The discovery process often involves sifting through massive quantities of data. Electronic point-of-sale transactions, inventory records, and on-line customer orders matched with demographics can easily use up hundreds of gigabytes of data storage. The use of probability sampling, descriptive statistics programs, and multivariate statistics are all tools of data mining that make the task manageable. These techniques are all discussed later in the text. Other, more advanced data mining tools, such as neural networks, genetic algorithms, and case-based reasoning systems must be left for an advanced text on research methodology.

Data mining has many potential uses in marketing. Four of these with the widest application are:

- *Customer acquisition.* In the first stage of a two-stage process, direct marketers apply data-mining methods to discover attributes that predict customer responses to offers and communication programs such as catalogs. In the second stage, the attributes of customers that the model says are most likely to respond are matched to the corresponding attributes applied to rented lists of noncustomers, so that only the noncustomer households most likely to respond to a new offer or communication are selected.
- *Customer retention.* In a typical marketing application, data mining identifies those customers who contribute to the company's bottom line but who are likely to leave and go to a competitor. With this information, the company can target the vulnerable customers for special offers and other inducements not available to non-vulnerable customers.
- *Customer abandonment.* Some customers cost more than they contribute and should be encouraged to take their business elsewhere. At FedEx, customers who spend a lot with little service and marketing investment get different treatment than those who spend just as much but cost more to keep. "Good" customers can expect a phone call if their shipping volume falters, in the hopes of heading off defections before they occur. As for "bad" customers—those who spend but are expensive to the company—FedEx is turning them into profitable customers in many cases by charging higher shipping prices. And the "ugly"?—those customers who

spend little and show few signs of spending more in the future? They can catch the TV ads. "We just don't market to them anymore," says Sharanjit Singh, managing director for marketing analysis at FedEx. "That automatically brings our costs down."[12]

- *Market-basket analysis.* By identifying the associations between product purchases in point-of-sale transactions, retailers and direct marketers can spot product affinities and develop focused promotion strategies that work more effectively than traditional "one-size-fits-all" approaches. The American Express selective envelope-stuffing strategy discussed earlier is an example of how market-basket analysis can be employed to increase marketing efficiency.[13]

Published Secondary Data

Internal Secondary Data

Published secondary information originating within the company includes documents such as annual reports, reports to stockholders, product testing results perhaps made available to the news media, and house periodicals composed by the company's personnel department for communication to employees, customers, or others. Often this information is incorporated into a company's internal database.

External Secondary Data

Innumerable outside sources of secondary information also exist, principally in the forms of government (federal, state, and local) departments and agencies that compile and publish summaries of business data. Trade and industry associations also provide published secondary data. Still more data are business periodicals and other news media that regularly publish studies and articles on the economy, specific industries, and even individual companies. The unpublished summarized secondary information from these sources corresponds to internal reports, memos, or special-purpose analyses with limited circulation. Economic considerations or priorities in the organization may preclude publication of these summaries. Finally, it is conceivable that pockets of raw data may reside in these organizations, just as they occur in the marketing researcher's own (client) firm. It should be evident that each type of secondary information requires that unique tasks be performed to render it useful to the researcher.

Advantages of Secondary Data

Marketing researchers use secondary information because it can be obtained at a fraction of the cost, time, and inconvenience of doing primary data collection. Additional advantages for using secondary information include the following:

1. Secondary information may help to clarify or redefine the definition of the problem as part of the exploratory research process. As you learned in Chapter 2, secondary data play a key role in exploratory research. A local YMCA was concerned about its stagnant level of membership and the lack of participation in many traditional YMCA programs. It decided to survey members and nonmembers. Secondary data revealed a tremendous influx of young, single persons into the target market, while the number of "traditional families" remained constant. The problem was redefined to examine how the YMCA could attract a significant share of the young, single-adult market while maintaining its traditional family base.
2. Secondary information may actually provide a solution to the problem. It is highly unlikely that a problem faced by a manager and communicated to a marketing researcher will never before have been encountered; there is always the possibility that someone else has addressed the identical problem or a similar one. Someone may have collected the precise information desired but not for the same purpose as the problem faced by the manager.

   Many states publish a directory of manufacturers that contains information on the location, markets, product lines, number of plants, names of key personnel, number of employees, and sales levels of companies. For example, a consulting company specializing in long-range strategic planning for members of the semiconductor industry desired a regional profile of its potential clients. Individual state directories were used to compile the profile. No primary data collection was necessary.
3. Secondary information may provide primary data research method alternatives. Each primary research endeavor is custom-designed for the situation at hand; consequently, the marketing researcher should always be open to information that offers research alternatives. For example, we conducted a research project for a large southwestern city's convention and visitor's bureau. We obtained a research report prepared by *Meeting and Convention Planners* magazine before designing the questionnaire. The secondary report published by the magazine contained the original questionnaire that used a series of scaling questions. Not only were the scales well designed, but also results from the study could be compared with the magazine's data.
4. Secondary information may alert the marketing researcher to potential problems or difficulties. Apart from alternatives, secondary information may divulge potential dangers. Unpopular collection methods, sample selection difficulties, or respondent hostility may be uncovered. For example, an examination of a study of anesthesiologists by a researcher planning to conduct a study to measure the level of satisfaction with certain existing drugs used in the profession uncovered a high refusal rate in a telephone survey. The researcher had also planned a telephone study, but switched to a mail questionnaire with a response incentive.

5. Secondary information may provide necessary background information and build creativity for the research report. Secondary information can often provide a wealth of background data for planning a research project. It may offer a profile of potential buyers versus nonbuyers, industry data, language used by purchasers to describe the industry, existing products and their advantages and disadvantages, and desired new product features. Language used by target consumers can aid in phrasing questions that respondents will understand correctly and be meaningful. Background data can also often meet some research objectives, eliminating the need to ask certain questions in a present study. Shorter questionnaires typically have higher completion rates. Secondary data can sometimes enrich research findings by providing additional insights into what the data mean or by corroborating current findings. Finally, secondary data can serve as a reference base for subsequent research projects.

Limitations of Secondary Data

Despite the many advantages of secondary data, they also pose some dangers and pitfalls. The disadvantages are lack of availability, lack of relevance, inaccuracy, and insufficiency.[14]

Lack of Availability

For some research questions there are simply no available data. If Kraft General Foods wants to evaluate the taste, texture, and color of three new gourmet brownie mixes, there are no secondary data that would answer these questions. Consumers must try each mix and then evaluate it. If McDonald's wants to evaluate its image in Phoenix, Arizona, it must gather primary data. If Ford wants to know the reaction of college students to a new two-seater sports car design, it must show prototypes to the students and evaluate their opinions. Secondary data, however, may have played a major role in the engineer's design plan for the car.

Lack of Relevance

It is common for secondary data to be expressed in units or measures that cannot be used by the researcher. For example, Joan Dermott is a retailer of oriental rugs who determined that the primary customers for her wares are families with total household incomes of $40,000 to $80,000. Consumers with higher incomes tend to purchase rugs beyond the price range Dermott carries. In attempting to decide whether to open a store in another Florida city, she could not find useful income data. One source offered class breakdowns from $30,000 to $50,000, $50,000 to $70,000, $70,000 to $90,000, and so forth. Another secondary source broke down incomes as less than $15,000, $15,000 to $30,000, and more than $30,000. Even if the income brackets had met Dermott's needs, she encountered another problem: lack of publication currency. One study was conducted in 1980 and the other in 1982. In Florida's dynamic markets, the percentages were probably were no longer relevant. This is often the case with U.S. census data, which are historically nearly two years old before they become available in publications. However, computer disks for the 1990 census were available much sooner.

Inaccuracy Users of secondary data should always assess the accuracy of the data. There are a number of potential sources of error when a researcher gathers, codes, analyzes, and presents data. Any report that does not mention possible sources of error and ranges of error should be suspect.

Using secondary data does not relieve the researcher from attempting to assess their accuracy.[15] The following list offers a few guidelines for determining secondary data accuracy.

1. *Who gathered the data?* The source of the secondary data is a key to accuracy. Federal agencies, most state agencies, and large commercial market research firms can generally be counted on to have conducted their research as professionally as possible. One should always be on guard when examining data in which a hidden agenda might be present. A chamber of commerce, for instance, is always going to put its best foot forward. Similarly, trade associations often advocate one position or another.
2. *What was the purpose of the study?* Data are always collected for some reason. Understanding the motivation for the research can provide clues in assessing the quality of the data. A chamber of commerce study conducted to provide data that can be used to attract new industry to the area should be viewed with a great deal of scrutiny and caution. There have been situations in which advertising agencies were hired by their clients to assess the impact of their advertising programs. In other words, advertising agencies were asked to evaluate the quality of the job they were doing for their own clients!
3. *What information was collected?* A researcher should always identify exactly what information was gathered. For example, in a dog food study, were purchasers of canned, dry, and semi-moist food interviewed, or were just one or two types of dog food purchasers surveyed? In a voters' survey, were only Democrats or Republicans interviewed? What method assured that respondents were registered voters? Was any attempt made to ascertain respondents' likelihood of voting in the next election? Were self-reported data used to infer actual behavior?
4. *When was the information collected?* A shopping mall study that surveyed shoppers only on weekends would not reflect the typical mall patrons. A telephone survey conducted from 9:00 A.M. to 5:00 P.M. would vastly underrepresent working persons. A survey of Florida visitors conducted during the summer would probably reveal different motivations and interests from winter visitors.
5. *How was the information collected?* Were the data collected by mail, telephone, or personal interview? Each of these techniques offers advantages and disadvantages. What was the refusal rate? Were decision makers interviewed or representatives of decision makers? In short, the researcher must attempt to discern the amount of bias injected into the data by the information-gathering process. A mail survey with a 1-percent response rate (where only 1 percent of those who received the survey mailed it back) probably contains a lot of self-selection bias.

6. *Is the information consistent with other information?* A lack of consistency between secondary data sets should serve as a cautionary sign. The researcher should delve into possible causes of the discrepancy. A different sample frame, time factor, sampling methodology, questionnaire structure, and other factors can lead to variations in studies. If possible, the researcher should assess the reliability of the studies as a basis of determining which, if any, study should be used for decision making.

Insufficient Data A researcher may determine that data are available, relevant, and accurate, but they may still not be sufficient to make a decision or bring complete closure to a problem. A manager for Wal-Mart discount stores may have sufficient secondary data on incomes, family sizes, number of competitors, and growth potential to determine, in which one of five Iowa towns with a population of under 20,000 it wishes to locate its next store. However, since no traffic counts exist for the selected town, primary data will have to be gathered to select a specific site for the store.

The New Age of Secondary Information: The Internet and the World Wide Web

While gathering secondary data is necessary in almost any research project, it has traditionally been a tedious and boring job. The researcher often had to write to government agencies, trade associations, or other secondary data providers and then wait days or weeks for a reply that might never come. Often the researcher made one or more trips to the library, only to find that needed reports were checked out or missing. In the last few years, the rapid development of the Internet and the World Wide Web promise to eliminate the drudgery associated with the collection of secondary data.

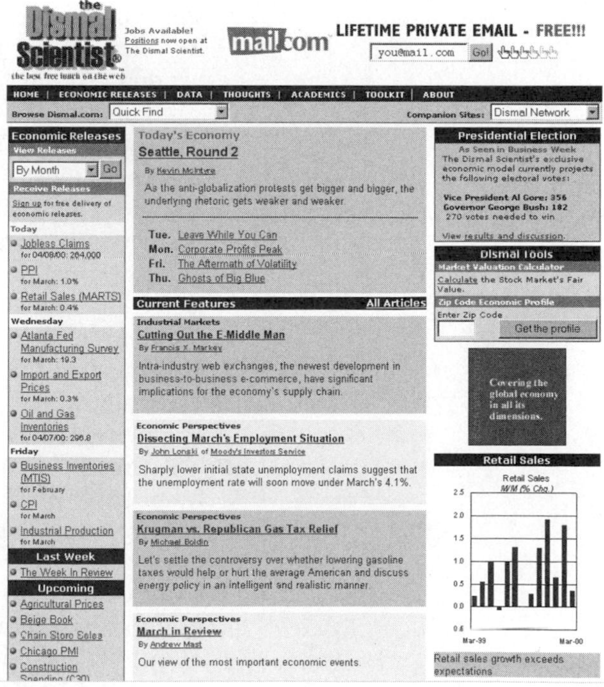

Finding Secondary Data on the Internet

If you know the address of a particular website that contains the secondary data you are searching for, you can type a description of what you are looking for into your Web browser (Netscape Navigator or Microsoft Internet Explorer are the dominant browsers). A Web address or URL (uniform reference locator) is similar to a street address in that it identifies a particular location (Web server and file on that server) on the Web.

Search Engines

Sites such as Yahoo!, AltaVista, Excite, and HotBot have become popular destinations for Web users looking for information on the Web. Each of these search engines contains collections of links to documents throughout the world, and each uses its own indexing system to help you locate the information you are looking for. All of them allow you to enter one or more keywords and search their databases of websites for all occurrences of those words. They then return listings that you can click on to go immediately to the site described. URLs and other information on some of the popular search engines are provided in Table 4.1.

Finding the information that you need on the Web can be very easy, or it can require some work and some trial and error. Your Web connection provides access to over 100 million websites throughout the world, more information than any library can offer. It doesn't matter where you are, whether you are in New York City or Whitefish, Montana, or any other place on the globe. As long as you have an Internet connection, you have access to all this information. There are basically two ways to find the information you need. First, as mentioned above, if you know the URL of the site where the information you need is located, you can simply enter the URL for that site in the Search window of your Web browser and go directly to that site. A list of some of the websites that have useful information for marketing researchers is provided in Table 4.2.

The second way of finding the information you need is to use a search engine to find it. If, for example, you are looking for information on population estimates, then you would need to go through several steps:

- First, you would use your Web browser to go to one of the search engine sites on the Web (see Table 4.1). You visit a search engine site by entering the URL for the search engine that you want to go to in the Search window of your Web browser. If you want to visit the Yahoo! site, then you enter the URL for that site, http://www.yahoo.com, to go there.
- After you get to the search engine site, you enter a search request in the Search window provided. Different search engines use slightly different rules for controlling the parameters of your search. Some commonly used operators for controlling Web searches are summarized in Table 4.3.
- You must then click on a Search button, provided for all search engines, after you enter your search request. The search engine then searches the entire Web or a subset of the Web to locate sites that include information meeting the requirements you entered.
- Normally, in less than a minute (sometimes several minutes), the search engine returns a list of sites that have information meeting your criteria.
- The first thing you should do is look at the number of sites located. This number is typically printed at the top of a list of qualifying sites on the output returned by the engine. If your search is too broad, then you may have far too much extraneous information, and you can save yourself a great deal of trouble by starting over and narrowing your search. For example, a search on the term "population" with AltaVista returned a list of over 900,000 sites with some mention of population. If you are actually

looking for Texas population estimates, then you should narrow your search. Changing the search request to "Texas population estimates" reduces the number of sites located to approximately 200.

Table 4.1

Major Search Engines

Search Site	URL	Comments
AltaVista	http://www.altavista.com	Probably the biggest and fastest search engine around.
DejaNews	http://www.deja.com	Most powerful Usenet search engine.
Excite	http://www.excite.com	Cutting-edge, fast, big, with site reviews and travel guides.
HotBot	http://www.hotbot.lycos.com	Uses Inktomi search engine technology, which makes it very fast.
Infoseek	http://www.infoseek.go.com	Easy-to-use search engine, plus Web directory with site reviews. Good place to start for new user.
Lycos	http://www.lycos.com	An old standard. Good data in comparison to some of the new search engines.
Magellan	http://www.magellan.excite.com	Family-oriented Web directory and search engine.
SavvySearch	http://www.savvysearch.com	Search consolidator that submits your query to several search engines at the same time.
World Wide Web Virtual Library	http://vlib.org/Overview.html	A volunteer effort to organize the World Wide Web by subject.
Yahoo!	http://www.yahoo.com	Very organized and easy to use. Another good place to start for the new user.
Looksmart	http://www.looksmart.com	Provides excellent category breakdowns to facilitate your search. Very easy to use.
Dogpile	http://www.dogpile.com	Excellent megasearch capabilities. Allows you to enter search engines for more listings or continue checking other engines.
google	http://www.google.com	Default search engine for Netscape search.
Ask Jeeves	http://www.ask.com	Very good research consolidator, including nine search engine indexes.

Table 4.2

Sources of Secondary Data for Marketing Researchers on the Web

Organization	URL	Description
American Demographics/ Marketing Tools	http://www.demographics.com	Searches the full text of all of American Demographics and Marketing Tools.
American Marketing Association	http://www.ama.org	Enables you to search all of the AMA's publications by uaing keywords.
BLS Consumer Expenditure Surveys	http://stats.bls.gov/csxprod.htm	Provides information on the buying habits of consumers, including data on their expenditures, income, and consumer credit.
Bureau of Economic Analysis	http://www.bea.doc.gov	Wide range of economic statistics.
Bureau of Transportation Statistics	http://www.bts.gov	Comprehensive source for a wide range of statistics on transportation.
CACI	http://www.demographics.caci.com	On CACI Marketing Systems' site, users can type in their ZIP codes to get a snapshot of the dominant profile type in their town. Population figures are available for the ZIPs, as are percentages for race and sex. Median household income, average home values, and average rent are also presented.
The Dismal Scientist	http://www.dismal.com	The Dismal Scientist is an authoritative site for timely economic information, with comprehensive data and analysis at the metro, state, and national levels. There's also data and analyses of global issues, including situations facing Asia, South America, and Europe. Visitors can rank states and metropolitan areas on more than 100 economic, socioeconomic, and demographic categories.
Easy Analytic Software	http://www.easidemographics.com	Easy Analytic Software, Inc., a New York City-based developer and marketer of demographic data, offers demographic site reports, or three-ring studies, including current estimates for population and households. Each three-ring study offers census estimates for race, ethnicity, age distribution, income distribution, and weather data. The site also offers one million pages of demographic reports for all ZIP codes, counties, metropolitan areas, cities, regional centers, television markets, states, and other geographical areas.

continued

Table 4.2

Sources of Secondary Data for Marketing Researchers on the Web (*continued*)

Organization	URL	Description
Economic Research Service, Department of Agriculture	http://www.econ.ag.gov	Wide range of agricultural statistics.
Equifax National Decision Systems	http://www.ends.com	Provides access to wide range of secondary data on many topics. Most must be purchased.
Find/SVP	http://www.findsvp.com	Offers consulting and research services. Claims to offer access to the largest private information center in the U.S.
Mediamark Research	http://www.mediamark.com/mri/docs/toplinereports.html	Marketers and researchers looking for demographic data on magazines, cable TV, or 53 different product or service categories can find it at Top-Line Reports site. Top-Line Reports breaks down cable TV networks according to viewers' age, sex, median age, and income. Magazines are listed by total audience, circulation, readers per copy, median age, and income.
Office of Research & Statistics, SSA	http://www.ssa.gov/policy	Another source of a range of government statistics.
PCensus for Windows	http://www.tetrad.com	Provides detailed information about the population of metropolitan areas.
Population Reference Bureau	http://www.prb.org/	Source of demographic information on population issues.
Strategic Mapping	http://www.stratmap.com	Offers extensive selection of geographic files, includes detailed geography for entire U.S.
U.S. Census Bureau	http://www.census.gov	Very useful source of virtually all census data.
U.S. Demography	http://www.ciesin.org	Excellent source of demographic information concerning the U.S.
USA Data	http://www.usdata.com	Provides access to consumer lifestyle data on a local, regional, or national basis.
World Opinion	http://www.worldopinion.com	Perhaps the premier site for the marketing research industry. Thousands of marketing research reports available.

Table 4.3

Operators for Use with Search Engines to Control Your Search

Operator	Purpose	Example
+ (plus sign)	Indicates words that must appear in each webpage of the query results list. With no plus sign, the word is considered a request and not a requirement.	The query "+florida gators football" will return only pages mentioning florida—and some of those may include the words gators and/or football.
– (minus sign)	Identifies words that cannot appear on any webpage on the results list.	The query "horned frog–tcu" will return pages about horned frogs, but not tcu.
" " (quotation marks)	Indicates exact multiword phrases you want to search for. If a phrase is not enclosed in quotation marks, the search engine will treat it as a list of separate query terms.	The phrase "king of the hill" will return a list of webpages containing that exact phrase. However, the query "king of the hill" will return pages with the words king, of, the, and hill in any order.
OR	Use to connect two or more words, at least one of which must appear on each webpage identified by the query.	Can be used to find synonyms or alternate spellings. An example would be the query "geography OR geographic."
NOT	Purpose is similar to that of the minus sign to exclude words. It must be used with AND or OR.	The query "freestyle AND NOT skiing" finds webpages containing references to freestyle that do mention skiing.
( ) (parenthesis)	Used to group sets of advanced operators together.	The query "analysis AND (regression or discriminant)" will find webpages about one or both statistical techniques.
* (wild card)	Stands for any number of letters or numbers on most search engines.	The query "eco*" will locate pages that include economy, econometrics, ecology, economical, etc.

Finding Federal Government Data on the Internet

Several sites for finding government statistics are listed in Table 4.2. However, there are some 70 federal agencies that publish data, and diligent searchers are hard-pressed to wade through all the results. In the past two years, federal agencies have posted a rich array of current information on the Internet, from the latest press releases to a wide range of historical results. The issue is finding what you need.

Several new hubs have been created to help solve the problems. The Statistical Universe was created by the Congressional Information Services (CIS) and is available to the public from Lexis–Nexis. The Statistical Universe is available either as a Web-based service (http://www.cispubs.com) or through the Lexis–Nexis STATIS library.

Statistical Universe builds on the CIS American Statistics Index (ASI), which researchers have used for decades. But unlike the ASI, which is a catalog of materials, the Statistical Universe displays the actual results from about 60 percent of the reports available. Earlier material, dating back to the 1970s, is catalogued, but only about 2,000 of these reports from 1995 to 1997 can be accessed directly.

Using the Statistical Universe is like having a library card catalog that gets inside the books to take you to the page or table you are looking for. Once there, users can display the specific material or download the entire report. Statistical Universe provides the most comprehensive and fully indexed source for federal stats online. Users looking for a particular recent report or those who know which agency issued the data they are looking for might be better served by first checking with the free government websites.

A good place to start is FEDSTATS (http://www.fedstats.gov), which has links to the 70 federal agencies recognized by the Office of Management and Budget as issuing statistical data. This site's search engine covers reports from the 14 major statistical agencies, including the U.S. Census Bureau, Department of Commerce, and Bureau of Labor Statistics, and provides links to all the other agencies.

If you're looking for information related to subjects in the news, try the White House Briefing Room (http://www.whitehouse.gov/WH/html/briefroom.html). The latest Federal Government Statistics section of the page contains two interesting links: one for economic issues (http://www.whitehouse.gov/fsbr/esbr.html) and one for social issues and statistics (http://www.whitehouse.gov/fsbr/ssbr.html). These sites provide an overview of the most newsworthy trends.[16]

Internet Discussion Groups and Special Interest Groups as Sources of Secondary Data

A primary means of communicating with other professionals and special interest groups on the Internet is through newsgroups. With an Internet connection and newsreader software, you can visit any newsgroup supported by your service provider. If your service provider does not offer newsgroups or does not carry the group in which you are interested, you can find one of the publicly available newsgroup servers that does carry the group you'd like to read.

Newsgroups function much like bulletin boards for a particular topic or interest. A newsgroup is established to focus on a particular topic. Readers stop by that newsgroup to read messages left by other people, post responses to others' questions, and send rebuttals to comments with which they disagree. Generally, there is some management of the messages to keep discussions within the topic area and to remove offensive material. However, readers of a newsgroup are free to discuss any issue and communicate with anyone in the world that visits that newsgroup. Images and data files can be exchanged in newsgroups, just as they can be exchanged via e-mail.

Newsgroups Internet sites devoted to a specific topic where people can read and post messages.

With over 250,000 newsgroups currently in existence and more being added every day, there is a newsgroup for nearly every hobby, profession, and lifestyle. Both Netscape Navigator and Microsoft Internet Explorer, as well as other browsers, come with newsgroup readers. If you do not already have a newsgroup reader, you can go to one of the search engines and search for one of the freeware or shareware newsgroup readers. These newsgroup readers function much like e-mail programs. To find a particular newsgroup:

- Connect to the Internet in your usual way.
- Open your newsreader program.
- Search for the topic of interest. Most newsreaders allow you to search the names of the newsgroups for any keywords or topics you are interested in. Some newsreaders, like Microsoft Internet Explorer, also allow you to search the brief descriptions that accompany most newsgroups.
- Select the newsgroup in which you are interested.
- Begin scanning messages. The title of each message generally gives an indication about the subject matter.

Newsgroup messages look like e-mail messages. They contain a subject title, an author, and a message body. Unlike normal e-mail messages, newsgroup messages are threaded discussions. This means that any reply to a previous message will appear linked to that message. Therefore, you can follow a discussion between two or more people by starting at the original message and following the links (or threads) to each successive reply. You can send images, sound files, and video clips attached to your message for anyone to download and examine.

Databases on CD-ROM

A number of companies offer database packages on CD-ROM for personal computers. For example, the Claritas Corporation has created a package called Compass/Agency designed for advertising agencies and Compass/Newspapers for newspapers to do segmentation and demographic studies and mapping. Claritas recently added Arbitron ratings, along with data from both Simmons Marketing Research Bureau and Mediamark on product usage, to Compass/Agency. The Compass/Newspaper system contains more than 200 preformatted reports and maps. Users can also import data on subscribers, readership, or advertisers and display them as reports and maps, or export data into other standard software packages, such as spreadsheets, word processing programs, and graphics applications.[17]

InfoUSA, a large secondary information provider, offers the following on CD-ROM:

BusinessUSA. Covers 10 million businesses in the United States. Search by company, business classification code, major industry, employee size, sales volume, headquarters/branch, and more. Package includes CD-ROM and printed directory.

HouseholdsUSA. CD-ROM provides key information on 100 million U.S. households: names, addresses, estimated home value, length of residence, homeowner versus apartment dweller information, and estimated household income.

Physicians & Surgeons. Search by name of physician, specialty, or even computer use. Listings include over 575,000 physicians in 105 specialties. Package includes CD-ROM and printed directory.

Big Businesses. Printed directory and CD-ROM include information about 177,000 top firms and 581,000 key executives. You can search by executive name, plus, you'll find fax numbers.

Manufacturers. All 612,000 manufacturers are broken down by the 6-digit SIC code. Printed directory lists all manufacturers with 25 or more employees.

Small Business Owners. Over 4.5 million businesses with fewer than 100 employees are listed on this CD-ROM and the compatible directory lists over 1 million successful entrepreneurs. Search by owner or company name, business size, or geographic area.[18]

Geographic Information Systems

Geographic information system (GIS) Computer-based system that takes secondary or primary data to generate maps that visually display answers to research questions.

A **geographic information system (GIS)** typically includes a demographic database, digitized maps, a computer, and software that enables the user to add corporate data to the mix. Utilities, oil companies, large retailers, and government agencies have long used these systems to display and analyze various types of data geographically. Today the technology accounts for $2.1 billion a year in hardware, software, and consulting sales.[19] The big change is that the cost of a GIS has fallen so dramatically in recent years that the GIS is now one of the hottest business information tools. Companies as diverse as Cigna, Sears, SuperValu, the Gap, and Isuzu have embraced mapping as an easy and powerful way to interpret data that previously would have been presented in the form of mind-numbing printouts, spreadsheets, and charts. Maps offer researchers, managers, and clients an intuitive way to organize data and to see relationships and patterns.

Geographers talk about lines, points, and areas, while marketing researchers talk about roads, stores, and sales territories. But thinking in terms of lines, points, and areas is a good way to sort out the business uses of geovisual databases. Applications involving lines include finding the quickest truck routes for long-haul freight companies to calculating the shortest routes for local delivery trucks. Applications involving points include finding the best potential sites for retail bank branches and devising the best strategy for a network of miniwarehouses. Applications involving areas range from finding the best markets for hardware sales to identifying the best location for a new Taco Bell. GIS can also answer more detailed marketing questions. If a marketing researcher for Target wants to know how many of the company's high sales performance stores have trading areas that overlap by at least 50 percent with the trading areas for Wal-Mart, a geovisual system will perform a function geographers call *spatial querying* to answer it.

The following example shows one way a GIS can be applied. Aftermarket auto repair is a highly competitive $90 billion-a-year business, and dealerships continue to improve their aftermarket services and marketshare. To stay ahead of the competition, Meineke Discount Muffler Shops has turned to GIS. Each week Meineke's 900 franchisees send detailed customer and service records back to Meineke headquarters in Charlotte, North Carolina. Records include the customer's name and home address; vehicle make, model, and year; work performed; and payment method. It also explains how the customer learned about Meineke, such as through the Yellow Pages, a friend, or a TV commercial featuring George Foreman.

Meineke processes 5,000 records a week through MapMarker, a GIS from MapInfo Corporation of Troy, New York. MapMarker cleanses the data, such as eliminating post office boxes and assigning "north" or "south" to addresses, and pinpoints each location on a map. Meineke can then map its stores, competitors, and other retail outlets in relation to its customer base.

By using MapMarker, Meineke can gauge the effectiveness of an advertising campaign by mapping all of the households in a particular market that visited an outlet because of a local radio or TV commercial. The geocoding tool can also detect potential sites for new Meineke outlets (see Figure 4.1).

Meineke can customize trade areas as it sees fit. If market research shows that some customers don't cross a river or a state boundary to get to the

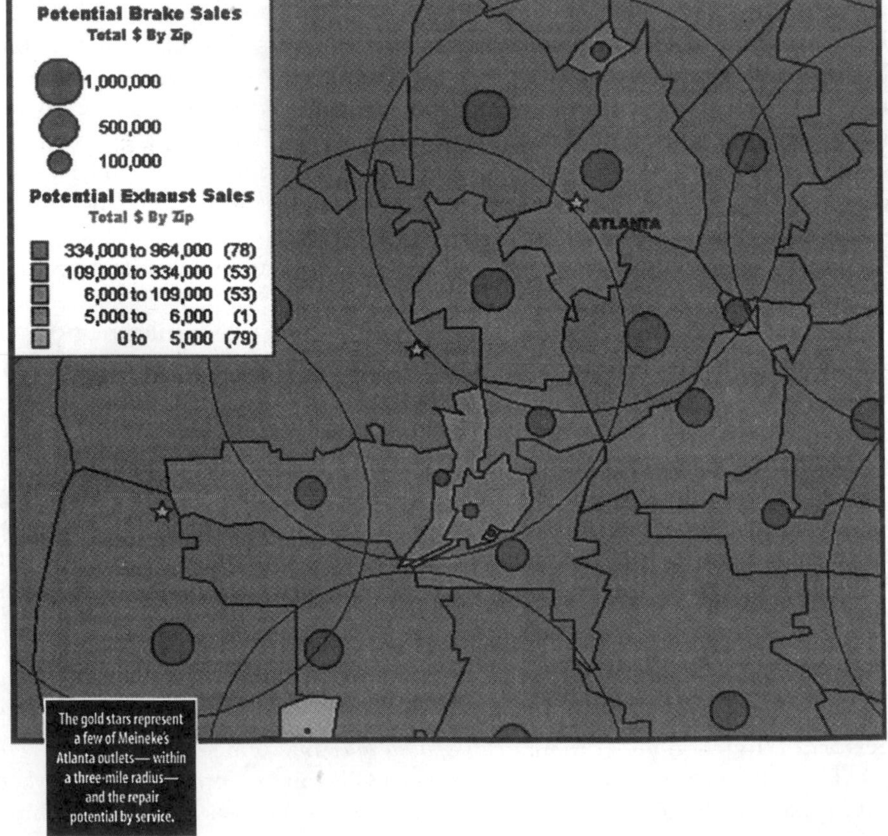

Figure 4.1

A GIS Map Created for Meineke Discount Muffler Shops in Atlanta

Source: Meineke Discount Muffler Shops, Inc.

nearest outlet, but will drive 2 miles farther to another Meineke franchise in a different ZIP code, the company can use MapMarker to create a map that reflects those shopping patterns. Then it can overlay demographic data onto the map to determine the region's overall sales potential. "We can see what our share of the market is instantly," says Stacey Monroe, an analyst at Meineke.[20]

Information Management

Computerized databases, published secondary data, the Internet, and internal databases are important parts of an organization's information system. Intelligent decision making is always predicated on having good information. The problem today is how to manage all the information available. According to David Shenk, sometime after the middle of this century and for the first time in human history, we began to produce information faster than we could process it. Shenk notes that various innovations—computers, microwave transmissions, television, satellites, and the like—have pushed us from a state of information scarcity to a state of information surplus in a very short time. To make better decisions, the emphasis needs to move from the problems of data acquisition to the problems of effectively managing and utilizing the vast sea of data available to us. Everyone who has been faced with a decision recognizes that information is the single most important influence on the quality of that decision. You need information to define the problem, to determine its scope and magnitude, and to generate and evaluate alternatives. Poor decisions are usually the result of using incorrect information, invalid assumptions, or inappropriate analysis of the information available.[21]

Today, most managers in large- and medium-sized organizations and progressive small ones are bombarded with information. The concern at large firms such as American Airlines, Parke–Davis Pharmaceuticals, and Citicorp has shifted from the generation of information to the shaping and evaluation of information to make it useful to decision makers.

Information management is the development of a system for capturing, processing, and storing this information so that it can be readily found and retrieved when needed for management decision making. In other words, some type of marketing information system is needed. American Airlines foresees in the near future information systems that will drive the transition from corporate hierarchies to networks. Companies will become collections of experts who form teams to solve specific business problems and then disband. Information technology will blur distinctions between centralization and decentralization; senior managers will be able to contribute expertise without exercising authority.

An information system will allow senior executives to make their presence felt more deeply without requiring more day-to-day control. Eventually, executives should be able to practice selective intervention. The information system, by virtue of its comprehensiveness, will alert senior managers to pockets of excellence or trouble, and allow them to take appropriate action more quickly. Over time, the role of management will change from oversight and control to resolving important problems and transferring the best practices throughout the organization.[22]

Decision Support Systems

Decision support system (DSS) An interactive, personalized mapping information system, designed to be initiated and controlled by individual decision makers.

Decision support systems (DSS) began coming into vogue during the late 1970s. A single DSS is designed from an individual decision maker's perspective. In theory, a DSS represents something close to the ultimate in data management. We say, "in theory" because, for the most part, the ideal textbook DSS has not been realized in practice. Some notable exceptions have provided glimpses into how a DSS can truly support the decision-making process. A DSS must be designed to support the needs and styles of individual decision makers. Characteristics of a true DSS are as follows:

1. *Interactive.* The manager gives simple instructions and sees results generated on the spot. The process is under the manager's direct control; no computer programmer is needed and no need to wait for scheduled reports.
2. *Flexible.* The system can sort, regroup, total, average, and manipulate the data in a variety of ways. It will shift gears as the user changes topics, matching information to the problem at hand. For example, the chief executive can see highly aggregated figures, while the marketing analyst can view very detailed breakouts.
3. *Discovery oriented.* It helps managers probe for trends, isolate problems, and ask new questions.
4. *Easy to learn and use.* Managers need not be particularly computer-savvy. Novice users should be able to elect a standard, or default method of using the system, bypassing optional features to work with the basic system immediately and gradually learning its possibilities. This minimizes the frustration that frequently accompanies new computer software.

Managers can use a DSS to conduct sales analyses, forecast sales, evaluate advertising, analyze product lines, and keep tabs on market trends and competitors' actions. A DSS not only allows managers to ask "what if" questions, but also enables them to slice the data any way they want to (see Figure 4.2).

Using DSS

A hypothetical example of using DSS is provided by Bill Boswell, manager of new products for Central Corporation.

> To evaluate sales of a recently introduced new product, [the VP] can "call up" sales by the week, then by the month, breaking them out at his option by, say, customer segments. As he works at his terminal, his inquiries could go in several directions depending on the decision at hand. If his train of thought raises questions about monthly sales last quarter compared to forecasts, he wants his decision support system to follow along and give him answers immediately.
>
> He might see that his new product's sales were significantly below forecast. Forecasts too optimistic? He compares other products' sales to his forecasts and finds that the targets were very accurate. Something wrong with the product? Maybe his sales department is getting insufficient leads or is not putting leads to good use. Thinking a minute about how to examine that question, he checks ratios of leads converted to sales, product by product. The results disturb him. Only 5 percent of the new product's leads generate orders, compared to the company's 12 percent all-product average. Why? He

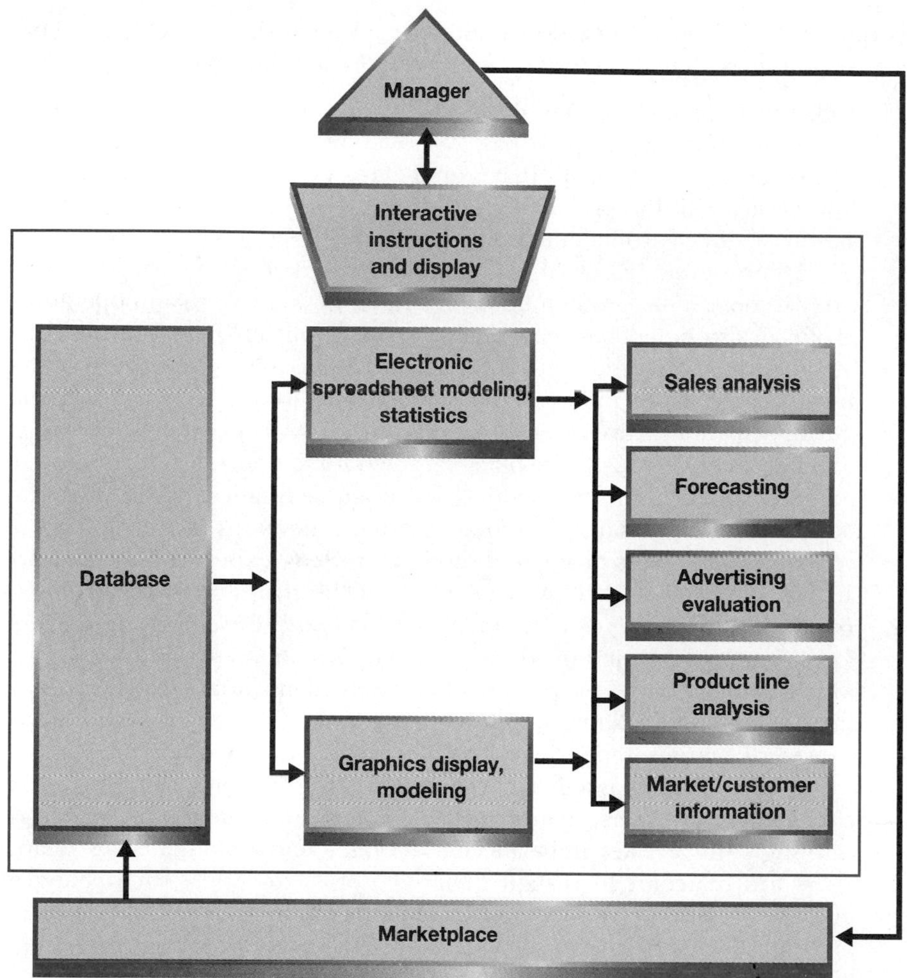

Figure 4.2

A Decision Support System

Source: Adapted from Michael Dressler, Ronald Beall, and Joquin Ives Brant, "Decision Support Systems," *Industrial Marketing* (March 1983), p. 54. Reprinted by permission.

guesses that the sales force is not supporting the new product vigorously enough. Quantitative information from the DSS perhaps could provide more evidence to back that suspicion. But already having enough quantitative knowledge to satisfy himself, the VP acts on his intuition and experience, and decides to have a chat with his sales manager.[23]

At Quaker Oats more than 400 marketing professionals use the company DSS daily. System usage can be grouped into three major categories: reporting and tracking (including running the standard reports), marketing planning (how Quaker Oats automates the brand planning and budgeting process by adding "what if" analysis and marketing capabilities), and ad hoc queries that elicit immediate answers to spontaneous marketing-based questions. Consider the examples in the In Practice feature.

The Move Toward DSS Today thousands of small businesses have information systems more sophisticated than those that America's largest corporations had just a decade earlier. The advantages of an effective DSS can be immense, and can include any or all of the following:

1. *Substantial cost savings.* One direct-mail insurance company developed a simple method to compare past response rates of various market segments, and saved $40,000 that would have been wasted by mailing to households with low probabilities of response. Similarly, other companies can draw direct profitability from their DSS.

   A DSS developed by Coca-Cola enables marketing managers interactively to determine profit and loss by brand, gross margin, and operating profit; it also helps managers analyze gross profit changes, and marketing and sales expense fluctuations. This DSS also allows interactive analysis of various profit-and-loss situations with differing performance levels through its interactive interrogation features. As DSS models are built, other areas of Coca Cola are being targeted for support. Company-owned bottlers benefit from using models that evaluate financial alternatives for bottler plant expansions. Corporate planning develops models to review company sales, gross profit, and direct marketing expenses, as well as to analyze company and competitor shares of the market and advertising.
2. *Increased understanding of the decision environment.* Development of DSS forces managers to view the decision and information environment within which they operate. This process often leads them to face decision areas that they previously shoved under the rug and to recognize relationships between decisions and information flows that they never noticed before.

   A sales territory is a dynamic environment, constantly being swept by changes in customers, competitors, products, and sales force turnover. Although this creates imbalanced workloads and potential sales, managers are reluctant to realign their territories to reflect such changes because of the time and tedious calculations required. Merrell Dow Pharmaceuticals put an end to such reluctance with a DSS. A manager enters his or her own criteria, such as potential and actual sales, doctor and pharmacy counts, and travel time. The DSS combines this business data with geographic features, road networks, and five-digit ZIP codes to come up with the optimal territory alignment.

   The program was especially helpful when the company replaced its single sales force with two sales forces to get broader product coverage. A Merrell Dow sales force promotes prescription pharmaceuticals, and a Lakeside sales force sells over-the-counter drugs. In all, the United States had to be redrawn to create 400 Merrell Dow sales territories and 250 Lakeside territories.
3. *Upgraded decision-making effectiveness.* Many companies can now retrieve and utilize information that was never accessible before. This substitution of facts for intuition in the decision-making process has led to more effective decision making than in

Use of SURF data can help apparel manufacturers identify consumer reaction to the merchandise. Liz Claiborne's website, http://www.lizclaiborne.com, also enables the company to gauge consumer reaction to designs in its LizMatch page, which also links to retail outlets that carry certain lines.

In PRACTICE

DSS and Brand Planning

Nancy Bydalek, brand manager for Quaker's Van de Camp products, uses the DSS to compile information needed for brand planning. "By running what if? scenarios and marketing spreadsheets based on such considerations as forecasted volume, prices, and advertising spending," she says, "I get a national view of my business compared to the competition, so I can identify geographical areas that are doing well and not so well."

The system also helps Quaker sharpen its promotions. "When we plan a specific promotion," explains Greg Peterson, marketing manager of the Cornmeal brand, "we go back in time and see the bottom-line effect that different promotional events had on sales. We then plug in the cost of a planned promotion and see what the final effect is going to be on the brand's volume and profit."

Like Quaker Oats, other companies' successful use of DSS has resulted in a growing popularity of the systems. Kmart, Northwestern Mutual Life, and 3M now find that their DSS provide an invaluable competitive advantage. Companies such as Federal Express, Avis, Otis Elevator, and Frito-Lay have increased the efficiency of gathering field reports by providing their employees with hand-held computers.

Frito-Lay, for instance, has given hand-held computers to all of its 11,000 delivery people. The data they collect feed a system that helps the company manage production, monitor sales, and guide promotional strategy. A delivery person can enter orders at each store in a minute or two, running through a programmed product list complete with prices. The machine plugs into a printer in the delivery truck to produce an itemized invoice. At day's end, it generates a sales report and, through a hookup in the local warehouse, transmits it in seconds to company headquarters in Dallas.[24] ■

the past. Jerome Chazen, executive vice president of Liz Claiborne, Inc., notes that the firm's DSS has improved management decision making. Systematic updated retail feedback (SURF) reports come in daily from 16 stores that represent a cross section of store sizes and geographical locations.

Computer programs take the SURF data and "play with it in dozens of different ways to get a feeling for how the consumer is reacting to the merchandise we're shipping," Chazen says. "Most apparel manufacturers tend to identify the best-selling items in the line with how they're purchased by the retailer. We've discovered that there's often no relationship between what the retailer thinks and what the consumer buys."[25]

4. *Improved value of information.* Proper implementation of a DSS means that managers will have relevant, reliable, and timely information that they didn't have before.

Summary

Secondary data is any information previously gathered but that only might be relevant to the problem at hand. Primary data is survey, observation, or experimental data collected to solve the particular problem under investigation. Secondary data can come from sources internal to the organization or external to it. A database is a collection of related data. A traditional type of marketing internal database is founded on customer information. For example, a customer database may have demographic and perhaps psychographic information about existing customers and such purchase data as when the goods and services were bought, the types of merchandise procured, the dollar sales amount, and any promotional information associated with the sales. A database can even be created from recorded conversations. An internal database may also contain competitive intelligence, such as new products offered by competitors, price changes, and changes in competitors' service policies.

Website databases can prove to be very insightful. A Web merchant can track a person as he or she clicks through a site. The merchant can examine what the customer looked at and bought. The screen the customer will see first on the next visit to the site can be tailored to the customer's past purchase and browsing behavior. "Cookies" are an important tool for monitoring a user's behavior within a site.

Data mining has dramatically increased the effectiveness of getting insightful information out of databases. Data mining can be used to acquire new customers, retain existing customers, abandon noncost-effective accounts, and engage in market based analysis.

There are several advantages to secondary data. First, secondary data may help to clarify or redefine the definition of the problem as part of the exploratory research process. Second, secondary information may actually provide a solution to the problem. Third, secondary information may provide primary data research method alternatives. Fourth, secondary data may alert the marketing researcher to potential problems and difficulties. And finally, secondary information may provide necessary background data and build credibility for the research report. The disadvantages of secondary data can be the lack of needed information, lack of relevance, inaccurate data, and insufficient information for decision making.

The Internet has in many ways revolutionized the gathering of secondary data. Now, rather than waiting for replies from government agencies or other sources, millions of pieces of information can be found on the Internet. Trips to the library may become a thing of the past for some researchers. Search engines like Yahoo! and AltaVista contain links to millions of documents throughout the world. Special interest groups on the Internet can also be sources of secondary data.

Besides the Internet, CD-ROM database packages from firms like Claritas Corporation and InfoUSA can leverage the value of primary data by marrying it with the secondary information found in the database packages. One application, for example, is using demographic data from a primary study to ascertain lifestyle information from secondary databases owned by Claritas or Equifax. Geographic information systems that consist of a demographic database, digitized maps, and software, also enable primary data from a current study (or corporate secondary data) to be added to the mix. The result is computer-generated maps that can reveal a variety of strategic findings for marketing managers; for example, a map may indicate an optimal location for a new retail store.

Decision support systems are designed from the individual decision maker's perspective. A DSS system is interactive, flexible, discovery oriented, and easy to learn. A good DSS offers many benefits to small and large firms alike.

Key Terms & Definitions

Secondary data Data that have previously been gathered.

Primary data New data gathered to help solve the problem at hand.

Internal database A database developed from data within an organization.

Cookie A text file placed on a user's computer in order to identify the user when he or she revisits the website.

Neural network A computer program that mimics the processes of the human brain that are capable of learning from examples to find patterns in data.

Data mining The use of statistical and other advanced software to discover nonobvious patterns hidden in a database.

Newsgroups Internet sites devoted to a specific topic where people can read and post messages.

Geographic information system (GIS) Computer-based system that takes secondary or primary data to generate maps that visually display answers to research questions.

Decision support system (DSS) An interactive, personalized mapping information system, designed to be initiated and controlled by individual decision makers.

Questions for Review & Critical Thinking

1. Why should companies consider creating a marketing internal database? Name some types of information that might be found in this database and some sources of this information.
2. Why should vendors' websites be a desirable tool for creating internal databases?
3. Why has data mining become so popular with firms like United Airlines, American Express, and Ford Motor Company?
4. What are some of the keys to ensuring the success of an internal database?
5. Why is secondary data often preferred to primary data?
6. What pitfalls might a researcher encounter in using secondary data?
7. Why has the Internet been of such great value to researchers seeking secondary data?
8. In the absence of company problems, is there any need to conduct marketing research? Develop a decision support system.

Working the Net

1. Go to http://www.yankelovich.com. Explain to the class the nature and scope of the Yankelovich MONITOR. How can marketing researchers use the data from this research?
2. Go to http://www.icpsr.umich.edu/gss. What is the General Social Survey? Compare and contrast its usefulness to marketing researchers with the Yankelovich MONITOR.
3. You are interested in home-building trends in the United States because the company you work for, Whirlpool, is a major supplier of kitchen appliances. Go to http://www.nahb.com and describe what types of information at this site might be of interest to Whirlpool.
4. Go to http://www.sbponline.com. Describe the types of secondary data available at this site.
5. For more detailed information on maneuvering around the Internet, see the appendix for this chapter located at http://mcdaniel.swcollege.com.

Real-Life Research

U.S. Sports Car Market

Jack Marquardt recently received his MSMR (Master of Science in Marketing Research) degree from the University of Texas at Arlington. He accepted a position with Nissan USA and is a marketing researcher assigned to work with a product management group. The product management group is in the midst of a crash program to evaluate its current product portfolio for the U.S. market and make recommendations to senior management about auto product requirements for this market for the next 10 years.

Phase I in the process is to do background research on various broad segments of the market (sports utility vehicles, sports cars, economy cars, luxury cars, etc.). Different members of the marketing research team have been assigned to do the background research on individual segments. Jack has been assigned to analyze the sports car segment of the market. He needs to have his preliminary work completed by the next morning in order to present his analysis and preliminary conclusions about the future potential and trends in this segment.

Given the short time frame available, Jack knows his only hope is to find the information he needs for assembling his report in time for the meeting the next day. His first step is to connect to the Internet and go to the HotBot site at http://www.hotbot.lycos.com. This brings him to the opening page of the HotBot search engine site. He enters "sports car sales" in the search phrase box and clicks on Exact phrase in the box just above. Then he clicks on the Search button to the right.

Repeat the above steps. Review the sites returned, go to the sites that appear to have relevant information, follow appropriate links from those sites to other sites, and conduct additional searches using other phrases in the same manner that you conducted the initial search. Also, go to other search engines and conduct similar searches.

Questions

Write a two-page report covering the following points:

1. the current size of the U.S. sports car market
2. market growth trends
3. leading brands in the market today
4. demographic trends that will affect the market over the next 10 years
5. other points you think are relevant to the questions above
6. whether this is a good time or a bad time for Jack's company to establish a larger presence in this market.

CHAPTER *five*

Qualitative Research

Learning Objectives

1 *To define qualitative research*

2 *To explore the popularity of qualitative research*

3 *To understand why qualitative research is not held in high esteem by some practitioners and academicians*

4 *To learn about focus groups and their tremendous popularity*

5 *To gain insight into conducting and analyzing a focus group*

6 *To study other forms of qualitative research*

Judith Langer Associates Inc., New York, is a well-respected qualitative research firm. Recently Ms. Langer conducted qualitative research on consumer attitudes toward brands and presented the results to the Advertising Research Foundation.

A three-hour focus group with men and women 35 to 65 years old was conducted in New York. That was followed by 20 telephone in-depth interviews, 30 to 40 minutes long, with men and women nationwide who were 25 to 60 years old.

Nostalgia influences brand loyalty strongly, especially in food, drinks, and cleaning products. "Campbell's tomato soup is the only one that will do," one woman explained. "It's like a cozy, comforting thing. It tastes good mainly because you associate it with what it did for you when you were a kid. Maybe it doesn't even taste that good, but somehow it works on a level beyond just your taste buds."

Qualitative research can provide clues and insights about a product or service. Does Volvo use its website to conduct any informal qualitative research? Go to http://www.volvocars.com to find out.

"Pinnacle brands" are icons. They include Rolex, BMW, Mercedes-Benz, and Giorgio Armani. The longing to buy these brands can start in childhood. Buying them becomes the fulfillment of a fantasy. "I would consider myself more successful being able to afford those," one respondent said.

There are some lower-ticket pinnacle brands, such as Godiva chocolates and *Vogue* magazine. Chanel cosmetics can provide the pleasure of feeling rich, while a Chanel suit is out of reach.

"Premium brands" include Nike, Donna Karan, Microsoft, Chivas Regal, and Lexus. These are respected, somewhat elite, high-priced for their category, but not considered overpriced. A more balanced mix of high- and lower-ticket items, the premium level is an affordable luxury for many. Consumers recognize they are paying more but feel justified because of quality and brand image.

While premium brands are not considered as pricey as those in the pinnacle category, there are consumers who steer clear of this level. They resent paying for the name rather than the product. Some don't want the pressure of living up to this level.

A woman who would like a Canon camera but has not bought one said the reason is "price, but also the feeling of obligation it would bring. If you have a little camera, all you have to do is take a little snapshot. But if you get one

Find out more about the Advertising Research Foundation and its activities at

http://www.arfsite.org

that's more sophisticated, you kind of feel that you have to rise to the occasion to do it justice."[1]

Judith Langer specializes in qualitative research. What is qualitative research? How is it conducted? Is one form of qualitative research more popular than others? What makes qualitative research so controversial? These are some of the issues we will explore in Chapter 5. ■

The Nature of Qualitative Research

Qualitative Research Defined

Qualitative research
Research data not subject to quantification or quantitative analysis.

Quantitative research
Studies that use mathematical analysis.

Qualitative research is a loosely used term. It means that the research findings are not subject to quantification or quantitative analysis. A quantitative study's findings may determine that a heavy user of a brand of tequila is 21 to 35 years of age with an annual income of $18,000 to $25,000. **Quantitative research** can reveal statistically significant differences between heavy and light users. In contrast, qualitative research can be used to examine the attitudes, feelings, and motivations of a heavy user. Advertising agencies planning a campaign for tequila might employ qualitative techniques to learn how heavy users express themselves, what language they use, and, essentially, how to communicate with them.

The qualitative approach flows from the work of the mid-18th-century historian Giambattista Vico. Vico wrote that only people can understand people and that they do this through a faculty called intuitive understanding. In sociology and other social sciences, the concept of Verstehen, or the intuitive experiment, and the use of empathy have been associated with major discoveries (and disputes) within the field.

The Qualitative Versus Quantitative Controversy

Table 5.1 compares qualitative and quantitative research on several levels. Perhaps most significant to managers is that qualitative research is typically characterized by small samples, which is a focal point for the criticism of all qualitative techniques. Many managers are reluctant to base important strategy decisions on small-sample research because it relies so greatly on the subjectivity and interpretation of the researcher. They strongly prefer a large sample with computer analysis, summarized into tables. Large samples and statistical significance levels are aspects of marketing research with which these managers feel comfortable because the data are generated in a rigorous and scientific manner.

The Popularity of Qualitative Research

The popularity of qualitative research continues to grow unabated. Several reasons tend to account for its popularity. First, qualitative research is usually

Table 5.1

Qualitative Versus Quantitative Research

Comparison Dimension	Qualitative Research	Quantitative Research
Types of questions	Probing	Limited probing
Sample size	Small	Large
Information per respondent	Much	Varies
Administration	Requires interviewer with special skills	Fewer special skills required
Type of analysis	Subjective, interpretive	Statistical, summarization
Hardware	Tape recorders, projection devices, video, pictures, discussion guides	Questionnaires, computers, printouts
Ability to replicate	Low	High
Researcher training	Psychology, sociology, social psychology, consumer behavior, marketing, marketing research	Statistics, decision models, decision support systems, computer programming, marketing, marketing research
Type of research	Exploratory	Descriptive or causal

much cheaper than quantitative research. Second, there is no better way than qualitative research to understand in-depth the motivations and feelings of consumers. Because product managers often unobtrusively conduct a popular form of qualitative research by observing groups from behind a one-way mirror, they obtain firsthand experiences with "flesh-and-blood" consumers. Rather than read a computer printout containing countless tables of numbers or a consultant's report that digests reams of numbers, the product manager and other marketing personnel observe consumers' reactions to concepts and hear them discuss the manufacturer's and competitors' products at length in their own words. Sitting behind a one-way mirror can be a humbling experience to a new product development manager when consumers begin to tear apart product concepts that were months in development in the sterile laboratory environment.

A third reason that qualitative research is popular is that it can improve the efficiency of quantitative research. Volvo of America Corporation was concerned that the U.S. automotive market was undergoing vast changes that could affect its market share. Volvo decided that it needed to do a major research study to gain an appreciation of the changing marketplace. The project involved both a quantitative and a qualitative phase. The first phase of the project enabled researchers to conduct a quantitative study that was both more insightful and less expensive because of a shorter questionnaire. Among the insights gained in the next qualitative phase were the following:

1. Potential buyers considered Volvo in a number of different ways. Some considered Volvo very seriously and narrowed the choice of cars to Volvo and one other make. Others considered Volvo seriously, but it was not among the cars that survived the final decision.

2. Some considered Volvo seriously without ever visiting a showroom.
3. Despite Volvo's small share of the U.S. market, the qualitative information hinted at several important subsegments within the Volvo market.

It is becoming more common for marketing researchers to combine qualitative and quantitative research into a single study or series of studies. The Volvo example shows how qualitative research can be used subsequent to quantitative research; in other research designs, the reverse order may be used. The patterns displayed in quantitative research can be enriched with the addition of qualitative information about the reasons and motivations of consumers. For example, a major insurance company conducted a quantitative study in which respondents were asked to rank the importance of 50 service characteristics. Later, focus groups were conducted in which participants were asked to define and expound upon the top-10 characteristics found in the quantitative study. Most of the top 10 dealt with client–insurance agent interaction. The researchers found from these focus groups that "agent responds quickly" meant both virtually instant response and response within a reasonable time. In the qualitative focus groups, the criteria were "about 24 hours for routine matters" and "as soon as is humanly possible for emergencies." The researchers commented that had they not conducted focus groups after the quantitative study had been completed, they could only have theorized about what "agent responds quickly" meant to customers.[2]

In the final analysis, all research is undertaken to increase the effectiveness of marketing decision making. Qualitative research blends with quantitative measures by providing a more thorough understanding of consumer demand. Qualitative techniques involve open-ended questioning and probing. The data are rich, human, subtle, and often very revealing.

Limitations of Qualitative Research

Qualitative research can, and does, produce helpful and useful information. Yet it is held in disdain by many researchers. The first limitation relates to the fact that many times marketing successes and failures are based on small differences in the marketing mix. Qualitative research does not distinguish these small differences as well as large-scale quantitative research does. However, qualitative research is sometimes superior in detecting problems that may escape notice in a quantitative study. For example, a major manufacturer of household cleaners conducted a large quantitative study in an effort to learn why its bathroom cleanser had lackluster sales. The manufacturer knew that the chemical compound was more effective than those used by leading competitors. The quantitative study provided no clear-cut answer. The frustrated product manager then turned to qualitative research, which quickly uncovered that the muted pastel colors on the package did not connote "cleansing strength" to shoppers. Also, a number of people were using old toothbrushes to clean between the bathroom tiles. The package was redesigned with brighter colors and included a brush built into the top.

A second limitation of qualitative studies is that they do not necessarily represent the population that is of interest to the researcher. It would be inaccurate to expect that a group of 10 college students is representative of all college students, of college students at a particular university, of business majors at that university, or even of marketing majors! Small sample sizes and free-flowing discussion can lead qualitative research projects down many paths. People who are subjects of qualitative research often feel free to tell the researcher only what interests them. A dominant individual in a group discussion can lead a group into areas of only tangential interest to the study. It takes a highly skilled researcher to get the discussion back on track without stifling the group's interest, enthusiasm, and willingness to speak out.

A final concern about qualitative research is the multitude of individuals who, without formal training, profess to be experts in the field. Because there is no certification body in marketing research, anyone can call himself or herself a qualitative expert. Unfortunately, it is often difficult for the unsuspecting client to discern the researcher's qualifications or the quality of the research. On the other hand, to conduct a sophisticated quantitative study requires extensive training. It is extremely difficult, if not impossible, to bluff one's way through this type of project.

The Growing Role of Focus Groups

Focus Groups Defined

Focus groups had their beginnings in group therapy used by psychiatrists. Today, a **focus group** consists of 8 to 12 participants who are led by a moderator in an in-depth discussion on one particular topic or concept. The goal of focus group research is to learn and understand what people have to say and why. The emphasis is on getting people talking at length and in detail about the subject at hand. The intent is to find out how they feel about a product, concept, idea, or organization; how it fits into their lives; and their emotional involvement with it.

Focus group A group of 8 to 12 participants who are led by a moderator in an in-depth discussion on one particular topic or concept.

Focus groups are much more than merely question-and-answer interviews. There is a distinction between group dynamics and group interviewing. The interaction provided in **group dynamics** is essential to the success of focus group research; this interaction is the reason for conducting group rather than individual research. One of the essential postulates of using group sessions is the idea that a response from one person may become a stimulus for another, thereby generating an interplay of responses that may yield more than if the same number of people had contributed independently.

Group dynamics The interaction among people in a group.

The idea for group dynamics research in marketing came from the field of social psychology, where studies indicated that, unknown to themselves, people of all walks of life and in all occupations will tell us more about a topic and do so in greater depth if they are encouraged to act spontaneously instead of reacting to questions. Normally then, in group dynamics, direct questions are avoided. In their place are indirect inquiries that stimulate free and spontaneous discussion. The result is a much richer base of information of a kind impossible to obtain by direct interviews.

The Popularity of Focus Groups

Qualitative research and focus groups are often used as synonyms by marketing research practitioners. Popular writings abound with examples of researchers referring to qualitative research in one breath and focus groups in the next, even though focus groups are but one aspect of qualitative research. Yet the overwhelming popularity of the focus group technique has overshadowed other qualitative tools.

How popular are focus groups? Most marketing research firms, advertising agencies, and consumer goods manufacturers use the technique. Today, more than $378 million a year is spent on focus group research by client firms. Leo Burnett Company, for example, conducts more than 350 focus groups each year for clients. Focus groups tend to be used more extensively by consumer goods companies than by industrial goods organizations. The low incidence of use is understandable because industrial groups pose a host of problems not found in consumer research. For example, it is usually quite easy to assemble a group of 12 homemakers. However, putting together a group of 10 engineers, sales managers, or financial analysts is far more costly and time-consuming.

Bausch & Lomb was in the process of exploring various interim packaging alternatives for its soft contact lens solutions. In focus groups conducted for the firm, product arrays were used to explore consumer reactions to current Bausch & Lomb and competitors' products.

> Reactions to four proposed logos and seven proposed package designs were examined against a background of response to current packaging. Among the design elements analyzed were:
>
> - A white Bausch & Lomb logo (reverse type) on blue and green background colors. (Maintaining this reverse type and current colors was preferred and has the best brand association.)
> - Color coding of the product types in the line was deemed more important than secondary brand names.
> - Use of the "product type" color for package print.
> - The use of numbers to designate heat (thermal) versus chemical (cold) systems was found to be inadequate and confusing.[3] *The specific words were chosen instead.*

The focus group information guided the package designers in creating new designs for test marketing.

Lewis Stone, former manager of Colgate–Palmolive's Research and Development Division, claims:

> If it weren't for focus groups, Colgate–Palmolive Company might never know that some women squeeze their bottles of dishwashing soap, others squeeeeeze them, and still others squeeeeeeeeze out the desired amount.

Then there are the ones who use the soap "neat." That is, they put the product directly on a sponge or washcloth and wash the dishes under running water until the suds run out. Then they apply more detergent.[4]

In focus groups a researcher can experience the reactions of flesh-and-blood consumers. Stone, for example, could observe how women demonstrated their use of dishwashing soap. Reality in the kitchen or supermarket differs drastically from that of most corporate offices. In focus groups a researcher can observe the emotional framework in which a product is being used. In a sense, the researcher can go into people's lives and relive with them the satisfactions, dissatisfactions, rewards, and frustrations experienced when a product is taken home.

Conducting Focus Groups

Now that you understand the concept of focus groups, let us proceed to the process of conducting focus groups (see Figure 5.1). The space devoted to this topic is considerable because there is much potential for researcher error when conducting focus groups.

Preparing for a Focus Group

The Setting Focus groups are usually held in a **focus group facility.** The setting is normally conference-room style with a large one-way mirror in one wall. Microphones are placed in an unobtrusive location (usually the ceiling) to record the discussion. Behind the mirror is the viewing room, which consists of chairs and note-taking benches or tables for the clients. The viewing room also houses the recording or videotape equipment. Figure 5.2 on page 114 is an advertisement for a focus group facility and shows clients viewing a focus group behind a one-way mirror.

Focus group facility A facility consisting of a conference-room or living-room setting and a separate observation room. The facility also has audiovisual recording equipment.

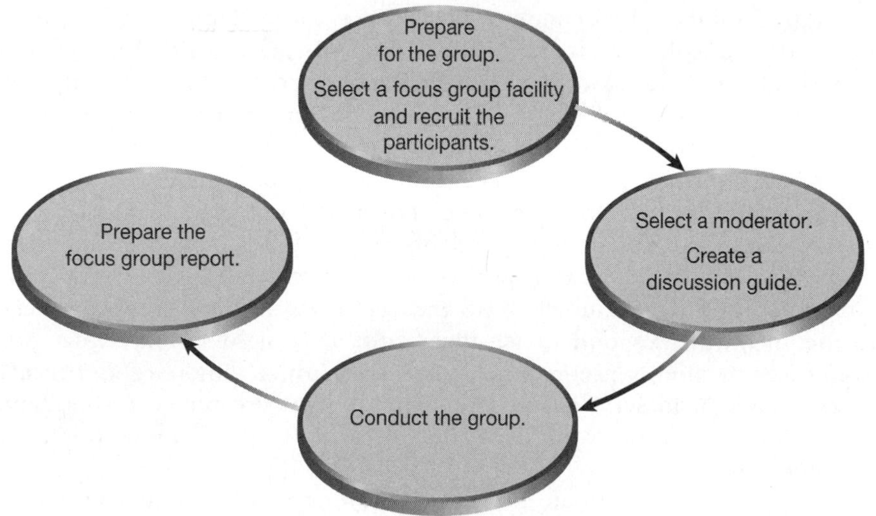

Figure 5.1

Steps in Conducting a Focus Group

Figure 5.2

Since qualitative research involves in-depth interviews or discussions, focus groups can be an ideal way for researchers to get clues about the underlying motivation of consumers. For an on-line directory of qualitative suppliers, visit http://www.focusgroups.com.

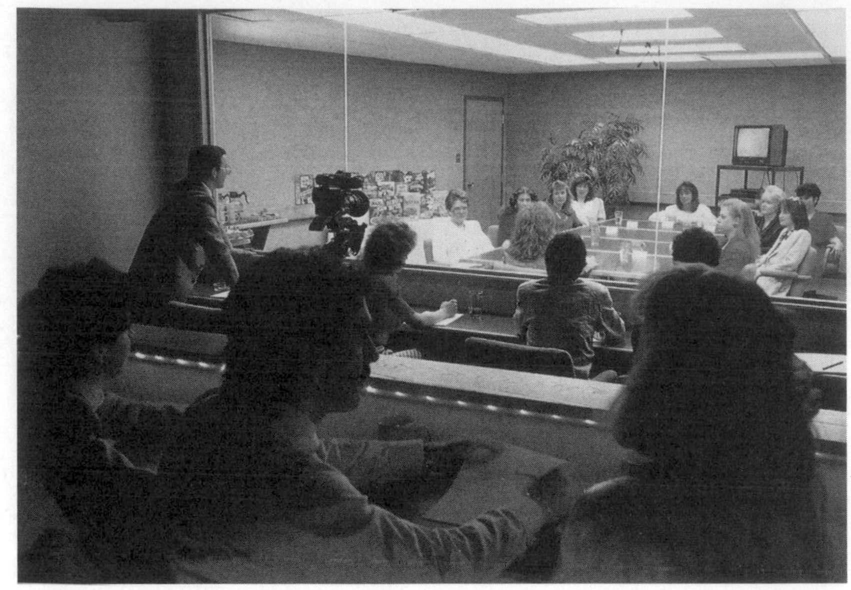

Some research firms offer a living-room setting as an alternative to the conference room. It is presumed that the informality of the living room will make the participants more at ease, as in a typical homelike setting. Another variation is not to use a one-way mirror but to televise the proceedings to a remote viewing room. This approach offers the advantage of clients being able to move around and speak in a normal tone of voice without being heard through the wall. On more than one occasion, a client has lit a cigarette while viewing a group, resulting in the flash being seen through the mirror.

Recruiting Participants

Participants are recruited for focus groups from a variety of sources. Two common procedures are mall-intercept interviews and random telephone screening. (Both methods are described in detail in the next chapter.) Researchers normally establish criteria for the group participants. For example, if Quaker Oats is researching a new cereal, it might request mothers with children ranging in age from 7 to 12 years old who had served cold cereal, perhaps a specific brand, in the past three weeks.

Usually researchers strive to avoid repeat or "professional" respondents in focus groups. Professional respondents are viewed by many researchers as actors, or at least persons who provide less than candid answers. And what motivates people to continually go to group sessions anyway? Are they lonely? Do they need the respondent fee that badly? It is highly unlikely that professional respondents are representative of many, if any, target markets. Unfortunately, field services find it much easier to use repeat respondents than to recruit a fresh group each time. Most participate simply to get the respondent fee.

Moderators can eliminate professional respondents by requiring participants to show their driver's license or other photo ID at the beginning of the session. Also, the information on the driver's license can then be checked against the information on the screening form. Another solution to the professional respondent problem is to require participants to complete a second screener questionnaire when they arrive at the facility. This screener can be compared with the one obtained when respondents were initially recruited.

A typical group contains eight participants. If the group contains 10 people, there is little time for group members to express their opinions. Rarely will a group last more than two hours, and an hour and a half more is common. The first 10 minutes is spent on introductions and an explanation of procedures. This leaves about 80 useful minutes in the session, of which 25 percent is taken by the moderator. With 10 people in the group, this leaves an average of only 6 minutes per individual for actual discussion; with 8 participants, each can speak about 7½ minutes. Yet there is no ideal number of participants. If the topic is quite interesting or of a technical nature, fewer respondents are needed.

Why do people agree to participate in focus groups? One study showed that the number-one reason is money. Other motivations, in rank order, were:

- The topic is interesting.
- It was a convenient time.
- Focus groups are fun.
- Knows a lot about the product.
- Curiosity.
- Offers an opportunity to express opinions.

The study also found that participants who come only for the money are less committed to research and tend to fulfill their roles more perfunctorily.[5]

Selecting the Moderator

Having qualified respondents and a good **focus group moderator** are the keys to successful focus groups. A moderator needs two sets of skills. First, the moderator must be able to conduct a group properly. Second, the moderator must have good business skills to effectively interact with the client.

Focus group moderator The person hired by the client to lead the focus group. This person may need a background in psychology or sociology or, at least, marketing.

Key attributes and skills for conducting a focus group include:

1. A genuine interest in people, their behavior, emotions, lifestyles, passions, and opinions.
2. Acceptance and appreciation for the differences in people, especially those whose lives vary greatly from your own—what Henderson refers to as unconditional positive regard.
3. Good listening skills: the ability to hear both what is being said and to identify what is not being said.
4. Good observation skills: the ability to see in detail what is happening or not happening and to interpret body language.
5. Interest in a wide range of topics and the ability to immerse yourself in the topic and learn the necessary knowledge and language quickly.
6. Good oral and written communication skills: the ability to clearly express yourself and to do so confidently in groups of all types and sizes.
7. Objectivity: the ability to set your personal ideas and feelings aside and remain open to the ideas and feelings of others.

8. Sound knowledge of the basic principles, foundations, and applications of research, marketing, and advertising.
9. Flexibility, ability to live with uncertainty, make fast decisions, and think on your feet (or the part of your anatomy that is seated in the moderator's chair).
10. Good attention to detail and organizational ability.[6]

In addition to the above, a moderator needs the following client-focused skills:

1. An ability to understand the client's business in more than just a cursory fashion, to become an integral part of the project team, and to have credibility with senior management.
2. The ability to provide the strategic leadership in both the planning and the execution phases of a project in order to improve the overall research design and to provide more relevant information on which to base decisions.
3. Providing feedback to and being a sounding board for the client at every stage of the research process, including before, during, and after the groups. This includes being able to turn the research findings into strategically-sound implications for the client at the end of the project.
4. Reliability, responsiveness, trustworthiness, independence, and a dogged determination to remove obstacles in order to get the job done.
5. A personal style that is a comfortable match with the client.[7]

In the past few years there has been an increase in the number of formal moderator training courses offered by manufacturers with large market research departments, advertising agencies, and research firms. Most programs are strictly for employees, but a few are open to anyone.

The second school of thought on moderator training maintains a different posture. It emphasizes personality, empathy, sensitivity, and good instincts. It assumes that some people just have a "feel" for conducting groups. Individuals who observe long enough and have these innate abilities can become good group moderators. Here, training consists of observing an established moderator conduct a few groups and then finding themselves in a room with 8 or 10 people. Emerging an hour and a half later, they realize that they have conducted their first focus group.

Not only is it important for the moderator to be well trained and prepared, but the client must also be prepared when observing a group behind a mirror. A series of suggestions are offered in the In Practice box to help ensure that the client gets the maximum out of each session.

Developing the Discussion Guide

Discussion guide A written outline of topics to cover during a focus group discussion.

Regardless of the type of training and personality a moderator possesses, a successful focus group requires a well-planned discussion guide. A **discussion guide** is an outline of the topics to be covered during the session. Usually the guide is generated by the moderator based on the research objectives and client information needs. It serves as a checklist to make certain that all

In PRACTICE

How Clients Can Get the Most Out of Focus Groups

The following series of suggestions will help client/focus group observers get more information and better insights out of each focus group.

First, the client must be totally familiar with the discussion guide before the groups begin. This guide reveals the specific types of information the moderator is after and the relative emphasis that will be placed on each before the discussion begins. As a result, the client can concentrate on the discussion in front of the mirror rather than looking at a copy of the discussion guide to figure out whether the moderator will be covering some topic of interest later on in the session.

Second, the client must decide how to communicate with the moderator during the group session. There are many ways to do this, and different moderators have preferences as to what works best for them. For example, many moderators would prefer to come to the back room during a group to talk with the observers, as they find this less distracting than receiving notes during the session. The important thing is that the clients get a chance to talk with the moderator a few times during the session to share ideas about the input from the participants and to suggest new topics or new ways to approach a subject.

Third, before the group starts, the client should write down the three to five most important things he or she would like to learn from the participants. Then, while the group is in progress, the client should make certain that the moderator is adequately covering these topics. A client should take one page for each topic and jot down thoughts and feelings that emerge from the groups about each topic as they are mentioned by the participants.

Fourth, the client must be disciplined to focus on the big picture rather than the comments of the minority during the discussion. A client should take care not to listen only to the one or two people who are the most dominant, the most positive, or the most negative about the subject being discussed. It is very easy to walk away from a group with a false sense of the group feeling due to the aggressive behavior of one or two participants. The best way to focus on the input from the full group is to jot down brief notes on the comments made regarding a particular topic by each of the participants.

Fifth, at the conclusion of each focus group, the client writes a brief summary statement that indicates the following three thoughts:

- the most important things learned during the group.
- things not learned that need to be covered in subsequent sessions.
- suggestions for changes in the discussion guide relative to future focus group sessions that will result in more helpful input.[8] ■

salient topics are covered and in the proper sequence. For example, an outline might begin with attitudes and feelings toward eating out, then move to fast foods, and conclude with a discussion of the food and decor of a particular chain. It is important for the research director and other client observers, such as a brand manager, to agree that the topics listed on the guide are the most important ones to be covered. Often a team approach is used in generating a discussion guide.

The moderator's guide also tends to flow through three stages. In the first stage, rapport is established, the rules of group interaction are explained, and objectives are given. The second stage is characterized by the moderator attempting to provoke intensive discussion. The final stage concerns summarizing significant conclusions and testing limits of belief and commitment.

Table 5.2 shows an actual discussion guide (although more detailed than many guides) used by a moderator to explore the credit card usage of college students, their reactions to different tabletop concepts or displays that might be used in student unions to entice students to sign up for cards, their reactions to different product concepts for credit cards, and, finally, their reactions to different designs for credit cards. The displays and offers were built around three concepts:

- *CDs.* A free CD to be chosen from a list when someone signs up. Earn points toward free CDs via card usage.
- *Environment.* Card issuer donates money to plant a certain number of trees based on card usage. Money is given to an internationally recognized environmental organization.
- *Credit education.* Educational material on credit use and abuse provided periodically. Credit reports provided free of charge once per year. Gold card provided after graduation if credit history is good.

The groups were conducted in several areas of the country with students from a variety of universities and colleges. In general, the educational approach was not attractive. Participants were split between preferring the CD or the environmental donation. However, none of the concepts tested really well.

Preparing the Focus Group Report

Typically, after the final group in a series is completed, there will be a moderator debriefing, sometimes called an *instant analysis.* There are both pros and cons to this tradition. Arguments for employing instant analysis include the idea that it provides a forum for combining the knowledge of the marketing specialists who viewed the group with that of the moderator, getting an initial hearing of and reaction to the moderator's top-of-mind perceptions, and using the heightened awareness and excitement of the moment to generate new ideas and implications in a brainstorming environment.

The shortcomings include biasing future analysis on the part of the moderator; engaging in "hip-shooting commentary" without leaving time for reflecting on what transpired; recency, selective recall, and other factors associated with limited memory capabilities; and not being able to hear all that

Table 5.2

Discussion Guide for College Student Credit-Card Concepts Groups

I. Warm-Up Explanation of Focus Group and Rules (10–12 minutes)

A. Explain focus groups.
B. No correct answers—only your opinions. You are speaking for many other people like yourself.
C. Need to hear from everyone.
D. Some of my associates are watching behind mirror. They are very interested in your opinions.
E. Audiotapes—because I want to concentrate on what you have to say—so I don't have to take notes. Video, too.
F. Please—only one person talking at a time. No side discussions—I'm afraid I'll miss some important comments.
G. Don't ask me questions because what I know and what I think are not important—it's what you think and how you feel that are important. That's way we're here.
H. Don't feel bad if you don't know much about some of the things we'll be talking about—that's OK and important for us to know. If your view is different from that of others in the group, that's important for us to know. Don't be afraid to be different. We're not looking for everyone to agree on something unless they really do.
I. We need to cover a series of topics, so I'll need to move the discussion along at times. Please don't be offended.
J. *Any questions?*

II. Credit Card History (15 minutes)

First of all, I am interested in your attitudes toward, and usage of, credit cards.

A. How many have a major credit card? Which credit card/cards do you have? When did you acquire these cards?
B. Why/how did you get that credit card/cards?
C. Which credit card do you use most often? Why do you use that credit card most often? For what purpose/purposes do you use your credit card/cards most often?
D. Is it difficult for college students to get credit cards? Are some cards easier to get? Which ones? Is it difficult for college students to get a "good" or "desirable" credit card?
E. What is your current attitude toward credit cards and their use? Have your attitudes toward credit cards changed since you got one? How have they changed?

III. Tabletop Concepts (15 minutes)

Now I am going to show you several concepts for tabletop displays for credit cards that might be set up on campus in places where students congregate, such as student union and student activities buildings. Each display would be one of several displays for different products and services. I am interested in your reactions to the different displays. After I show you each display, I would like for you to write down your initial reactions on this form *(show and pass out form).* I am interested in your initial reactions. After we take a minute for you to write down your reactions, we will discuss each concept in more detail.

A. SHOW FIRST CONCEPT.
   1. HAVE THEM WRITE FIRST REACTION.
   2. DISCUSSION.
      a. What was your first reaction to this tabletop display? What, if anything, do you particularly *like* about this display?
      b. Would you stop to find out more? Are you drawn to this display? Why? Why not? What, if anything, is interesting about it?
      c. What is your reaction to ENVIRONMENTAL/EDUCATION/MUSIC OFFER? Likes/dislikes?
B. REPEAT FOR SECOND CONCEPT.
C. REPEAT FOR THIRD CONCEPT.
D. SHOW ALL THREE CONCEPTS.
   1. Which of these concepts, if any, would be *most likely* to attract your attention? Get you to stop for more information? Why?
   2. Which one would be *least likely* to attract your attention? Get you to stop for more information? Why?

continued

Table 5.2

Discussion Guide for College Student Credit-Card Concepts Groups (*continued*)

IV. Brochures and Offers (25 minutes)

Now I would like for you to see the credit card offers that might go with each of the displays we just discussed. First of all, I will show you a sample brochure and offer. Next, I would like for you to indicate your first reaction to the offer on the sheet provided. Finally, we will discuss your reactions to each offer.

A. SHOW FIRST BROCHURE AND OFFER.
   1. ASK THEM TO RECORD THEIR FIRST REACTION.
   2. DISCUSSION.
      a. What was your first reaction to this offer?
      b. What, if anything, do you particularly *like* about this offer? What, if anything, do you particularly *dislike* about this offer?
      c. Do you understand the offer?
      d. Do you feel it is an important benefit?
      e. Would you sign up for this offer? Why?
      f. Would this card displace an existing card?
      g. Would this be your card of choice?
      h. Would you continue to use this product after college?
      i. How does this card, described in this offer, compare with the card you use most frequently?
      j. How likely would you be to apply for this card? Why/why not? Would you plan to actually use this card, or just have it? Would you plan to keep it after college?

B. REPEAT FOR SECOND BROCHURE AND OFFER.

C. REPEAT FOR THIRD BROCHURE AND OFFER.

D. SHOW ALL THREE BROCHURES AND OFFERS.
   1. Which of these is the best offer? Why do you say that?
   2. Which, if any, of the cards described in these offers would you apply for? Why?

V. Designs (10 minutes)

Finally, I would like for you to see three alternative designs for the credit card that would go with the environmental offer. As with the two previous sections of the discussion, I will show each design, ask for you to write down your initial reaction to the design, and then we will discuss each design. Please use the form provided earlier to write down your initial reactions.

A. SHOW FIRST DESIGN.
   1. ASK THEM TO WRITE DOWN FIRST REACTION.
   2. DISCUSSION.
      a. What is your first reaction to this design? Is there anything you particularly *like* about this design? *Dislike* about it?
      b. Is there anything about this design that would make you uncomfortable about using it while you are in college? How about after you get out of college?

B. REPEAT FOR SECOND DESIGN.

C. REPEAT FOR THIRD DESIGN.

D. SHOW ALL THREE DESIGNS.
   1. Which, if any, of these cards would you use? Prefer?
   2. Are there any of these cards you would not use? Why?

Thanks for your participation.

was said in a less than highly involved and anxious state. There is nothing wrong with a moderator debriefing as long as the moderator explicitly reserves the right to change his or her opinion after reviewing the tapes.

Written reports tend to follow several different patterns, depending on the client's needs, the researcher's style, and the terms of the research proposal. The investigator can prepare a brief, subjective summary of the principal findings, relying mainly on memory. This form of report is most likely used with a client for which the primary goal is to get an impression of flesh-and-blood consumers. The client often retains the tape recordings of the sessions and listens to the groups several times to become immersed in what the consumers are saying.

Another approach is often called the *cut-and-paste technique.* It lacks the in-depth psychological analysis of the clinical report, but still requires considerable skill and insight on the part of the researcher. The first step is to have the group sessions transcribed. Next, the researcher reviews the transcripts looking for common threads or trends in response patterns. Similar patterns are then cut apart and matched between the groups. The researcher then ends up with folders containing relevant material by subject matter.

The last report to write is the formal one. It normally begins with an introduction describing the purpose of the research, the major questions the researcher sought to answer, the nature and characteristics of the group members, and how they were recruited. Next, it is common to present a two- or three-page summary of findings and recommendations and conclude with the main body of findings. If the group members' conversations have been well segmented and sorted, preparing the main body of the report will not be difficult. The first major topic is introduced and major points of the topic are summarized and then driven home with liberal use of actual respondents' remarks ("verbatims"). Subsequent topics are then covered in similar fashion.

Advantages and Disadvantages of Focus Groups

The advantages and disadvantages of qualitative research in general also apply to focus groups. But focus groups themselves have some unique pros and cons that deserve mention.

Advantages of Focus Groups

The interaction among respondents can stimulate new ideas and thoughts that might not arise during one-on-one interviews. And group pressure can help challenge respondents to keep their thinking realistic. The energetic interaction among respondents also means that a group usually provides firsthand consumer information to the client observers in a shorter amount of time and in a more interesting way than do individual interviews.

Another advantage focus groups offer is the opportunity to observe customers or prospective customers from behind a one-way mirror. In fact, there is growing use of focus groups to expose a broad range of employees to customer comments and views. "We have found that the only way to get people to really understand what customers want is to let them see customers, but there are few people who actually come in contact with customers," says Bonnie Keith, corporate market research manager at Digital Equipment Corporation. "Right now, we are getting people from our manufacturing and engineering operations to attend and observe focus groups," says Keith.

Another advantage focus groups offer is that they can often be executed more quickly than many other research techniques. Too, findings from groups tend to be easier to understand and have a compelling immediacy and excitement. "I can get up and show a client all the charts and graphs in the world, but it has nowhere near the impact of showing 8 or 10 customers sitting around a table and saying that the company's service isn't good," says Jean–Anne Mutter, director of marketing research at Ketchum Advertising.[9]

Disadvantages of Focus Groups

Unfortunately, some of the very strengths of focus groups can also become disadvantages. For example, the immediacy and apparent understandability of focus group findings can mislead instead of inform. Jean–Anne Mutter says, "Even though you're only getting a very small slice, a focus group gives you a sense that you really understand the situation." She adds that focus groups can strongly appeal to "people's desire for quick, simple answers to problems, and I see a decreasing willingness to go with complexity and to put forth the effort needed to really think through the complex data that will be yielded by a quantitative study."[10]

The preceding sentiment is echoed by Gary Willets, director of marketing research for NCR Corporation. He notes, "What can happen is that you will do the focus group, and you will find out all of these details, and someone will say, 'Okay, we've found out all that we need to know.' The problem is that what is said in a focus group may not be all that typical. What you really want to do is a qualitative study on the front end and follow it up with a quantitative study."[11] Focus groups, and qualitative research in general, are essentially inductive in their approach. The research is data-driven, with findings and conclusions being drawn directly from the information provided. In contrast, quantitative studies follow a deductive approach in which formulated ideas and hypotheses are tested, with data collected specifically for these purposes.

Other disadvantages relate to the focus group mix and interview environment. For example, focus group recruiting is a problem if the type of person recruited responds differently to the issues being discussed than do other target segments. White middle-class individuals, for example, seem to participate in qualitative research in numbers that are disproportionate to their presence in the marketplace. Also, some focus group facilities create an impersonal feeling, making honest conversation unlikely. Corporate or formal decor with large boardroom tables and unattractive, plain, or gray decor may make it difficult for respondents to relax and share their feelings.

The greatest potential for distorting focus group research is during the group interview itself. The moderator is part of the social interaction and must take care not to behave in ways that prejudice responses. The moderator's style may contribute to bias. For example, an aggressive, confronting style may systematically lead respondents to say whatever they think the moderator wants them to say as a way of avoiding attack. "Playing dumb" by the moderator may create perceptions that the moderator is insincere or phony, which may cause respondents to withdraw.

Respondents' personalities can also inhibit group interaction. Some individuals are introverted and do not like to speak out in group settings. Other people may attempt to dominate the discussion. These are people who know it all, or think they do, and who invariably answer every question first and do not give others a chance to speak. A dominating participant may succeed in swaying other group members. If a moderator is abrupt with a respondent, it can send the wrong message to other group members: "You'd better be cautious or I will do the same thing to you." A good moderator can stifle a dominant group member without inhibiting the rest of the group. Simple techniques moderators use include avoiding eye contact with a dominant person; reminding the group that "we want to give everyone a chance to talk," saying "Let's have someone else go first"; and if someone else is speaking and the dominant person interrupts, looking at the initial speaker and saying, "Sorry, I cannot hear you."

Conducting focus groups in an international setting raises a number of issues, as the Global Issues box on page 124 explains.

Trends in Focus Groups

A number of fads have come and gone in focus group research in the past decade. No longer do we hear much about replicated groups, mega groups, multivariate groups, videothematic apperception test groups, or sensitivity groups. What we are seeing instead is a continued growth in the use of focus groups. Although no reliable data exist, we estimate that more than 50,000 focus groups are conducted in the United States annually. Commensurate with this volume is the expanding number (more than 700) and quality of focus group facilities in the United States. Most cities with a population of more than 100,000 have at least one group facility. Tiny viewing rooms with small one-way mirrors are rapidly disappearing. Instead, field services are installing plush two-tiered observation areas that wrap around the conference room to provide an unobstructed view of all respondents. Built-in counters for taking notes, padded chairs, and a fully stocked refreshment center are becoming commonplace (the latter can create problems).

Videoconferenced Focus Groups

One trend is videoconferenced focus groups. Why send a group of staffers to a distant city—and pay for their airfare, lodging, and meals—to observe a group when you can shuttle them to a local focus group facility or into a conference room down the hall to watch the groups on a TV monitor?[12]

Global ISSUES

Japanese Focus Groups Are Different

INTERNATIONAL FOCUS GROUP WORK DEMANDS SPECIAL AWARENESS AND ADAPTATIONS. THE MAJOR issues that confront the project manager on the international front can be reduced to four basic categories:

- sociocultural differences
- linguistic differences
- differences in business practices
- world events and economic differences.

Japan will be used as an example. Some countries might be a challenge on one or two fronts, but Japan is a challenge on all of them! How are Japanese research companies different? There are relatively few research companies to choose from, even in cities the size of Tokyo. This creates booking problems, especially when you realize that the facilities are very tiny by American standards.

The cultural and linguistic differences between the United States and Japan require that your discussion guide and other materials be translated by your host organization and then translated back to English by an independent source to make sure that the correct nuances are getting across. This takes time. Often, direct translation is impossible, and you have to rely on interpretation—getting the general idea across without word-for-word equivalence.

Another time constraint is that you can really only accomplish one group per evening instead of the two to which we are accustomed. The Japanese in urban areas like Tokyo must commute from one to three hours home.

The cost of doing foreign focus groups is invariably higher than similar work undertaken domestically. As a general rule you can expect a project to cost 2 to 2½ times more in Europe than it would in the United States, and 4 to 6 times more in Japan. Higher real estate costs and salaries make the cost of doing business in Japan very high for your subcontractors.

Japanese consumers still display a deference to seniority, power, and status as defined by their culture. Within moments of arrival, everyone in the group will know where they stand and will tend to defer to the most powerful person. As a result, the moderator has a daunting task with many groups. Female executives and decision makers are still rare in Japan. In most groups, it is best not to mix women and men because the women may just sit and smile nervously and defer to the men.[13] ■

While rates and capabilities vary, the services that specialize in serving the research market, such as the VideoConferencing Alliance Network (VCAN), FocusVision, VideoFocus Direct, and Direct Window, allow clients the ability to view groups remotely. Some clients view the groups on their own equipment; some buy or lease from the services.

At its Basking Ridge, New Jersey, offices, AT&T uses GroupNet, a service provided by VCAN, a network of research firms that provides facilities for videoconferencing focus groups in 20 U.S. markets, using Picture Tel equipment. AT&T has set up viewing rooms at its offices and at the offices of its ad agency partners in New York.

For Nancy Canali Lucas, vice president of research for TBS Superstation, Atlanta, using videoconferencing has helped expose more TBS staffers to the live research process.

> It allows us to get a larger audience of people who don't normally attend focus groups, people like the head of the network, for example, or the head of the entertainment division, who may not be interested in the micro-issues that we deal with but who can step in and take a look at the group because it's being shown right here.[14]

On-line Focus Groups Perhaps the hottest controversy in qualitative research today is the rapidly growing popularity of on-line focus groups. Many marketing researchers, such as Greenfield Online, NFO Interactive, Harris Black International and others, believe that Internet focus groups can replace face-to-face focus groups, although they acknowledge that on-line research has limitations. Others that are moving aggressively into on-line market research, such as Millward Brown International and Digital Marketing Services, are avoiding on-line focus groups.

Advantages of On-line Focus Groups But marketers that have used on-line focus groups and the marketing researchers conducting them, say benefits far outweigh limitations. Those benefits include no geographic barriers, much lower costs (about half as much), faster turnaround time, and intangibles such as respondents being more open without an interviewer staring them in the face.

> "I think [the panelists] were more definite about things they didn't like [on a new Web site] than they'd be in front of a moderator," said Lisa Crane, vice president for sales and marketing for Universal Studios Online, which used on-line focus groups to test a redesigned site it is developing for Captain Morgan Original Spiced Rum, a brand of its parent company Seagram Company. Rudy Nadilo, president and CEO of Greenfield Online, which conducted the on-line focus group for Universal, said they are meant "to complement, not replace" traditional panels.[15]

> Greenfield product manager Susan Roth said she received 2,700 responses within one day of sending out a so-called screener e-mail to approximately 6,000 users in Greenfield's database of 500,000 Internet homes. She then formed two groups of eight panelists each for the client, which needed to make sure respondents were over 21 and had certain drinking preferences.
>
> During the on-line focus groups, each held in a private chat room on Greenfield's site, a moderator fields questions and answers on one side of a split screen, while clients made suggestions—instantly by typing—on the left side of the screen. "I loved the way I was able to influence what the moderator said instantly," said Ms. Crane. Greenfield charges about $6,000 plus incentives for this type of two-group project. A conventional two-group package costs about $10,000.[16]

Not only are the costs for the focus groups less, but there are substantial travel savings for the client as well. Round-trip airline tickets to distant cities, meals, hotels, and taxis are avoided. Clients merely log on in their own office, or even at home, to observe the research in progress.

Another advantage of on-line groups lies in getting to a hard-to-reach target population. On line it is possible to access populations that are traditionally inaccessible due to time or professional constraints—groups such as physicians, lawyers, senior business executives, and other professionals. Chances are higher they will be available to participate, since they do not need to take time from their busy schedules to visit a focus group facility, but rather can participate from the privacy of their own homes.

On-line focus group advocates claim that not seeing a focus group participant does not necessarily mean that an observer cannot sense emotion. Because it is not yet easily possible to see people as they are participating on line, certain nonverbal cues (the way one is sitting, leaning, smirking, etc.)

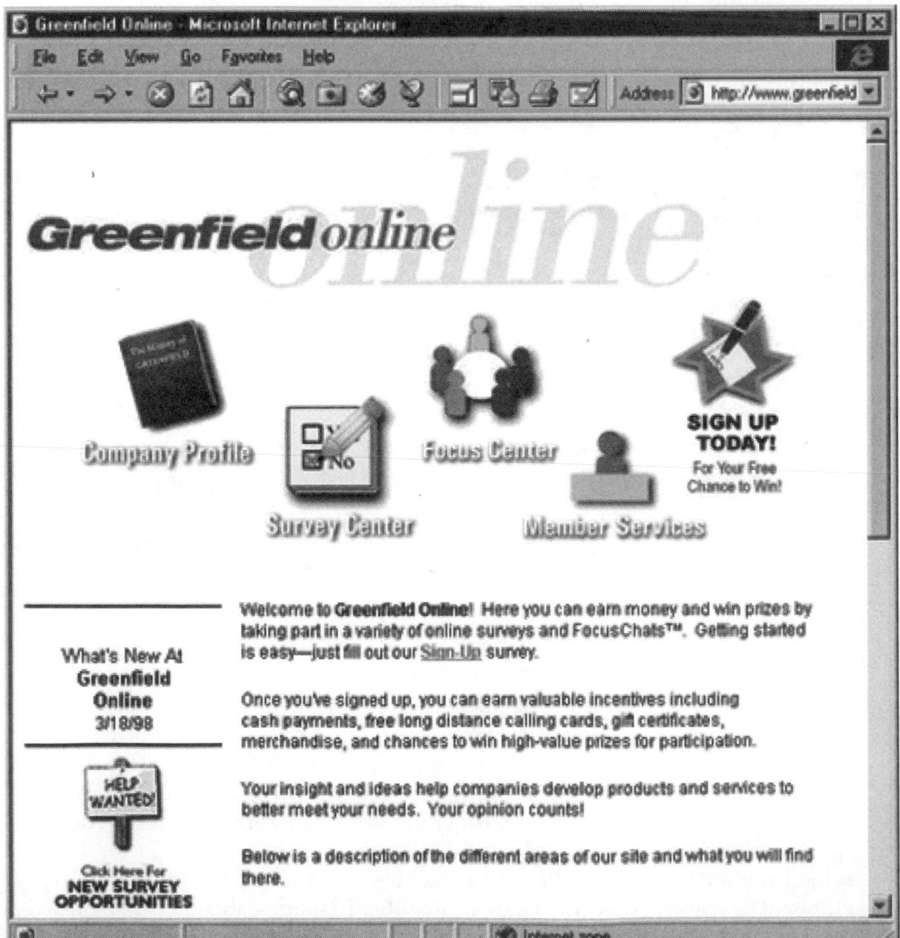

Source: From the Greenfield Online website http://www.greenfieldonline.com Greenfield Online is a Westport, Connecticut-based on-line marketing research company. Reprinted with permission

are sacrificed. Nevertheless, numerous nonverbal cues do occur in an on-line chat environment. These "emoticons," as they are called by on-line users, are text-based "pictures" that result from combining punctuation marks so that they look somewhat like expression-bearing faces. In addition to emoticons, on-line focus group respondents tend to rely more on words and complete sentences (rather than hand movements or expressions) to express their thoughts, and on expressing their thoughts concisely—without depending on the pauses and hesitations that occur during spoken communications.[17]

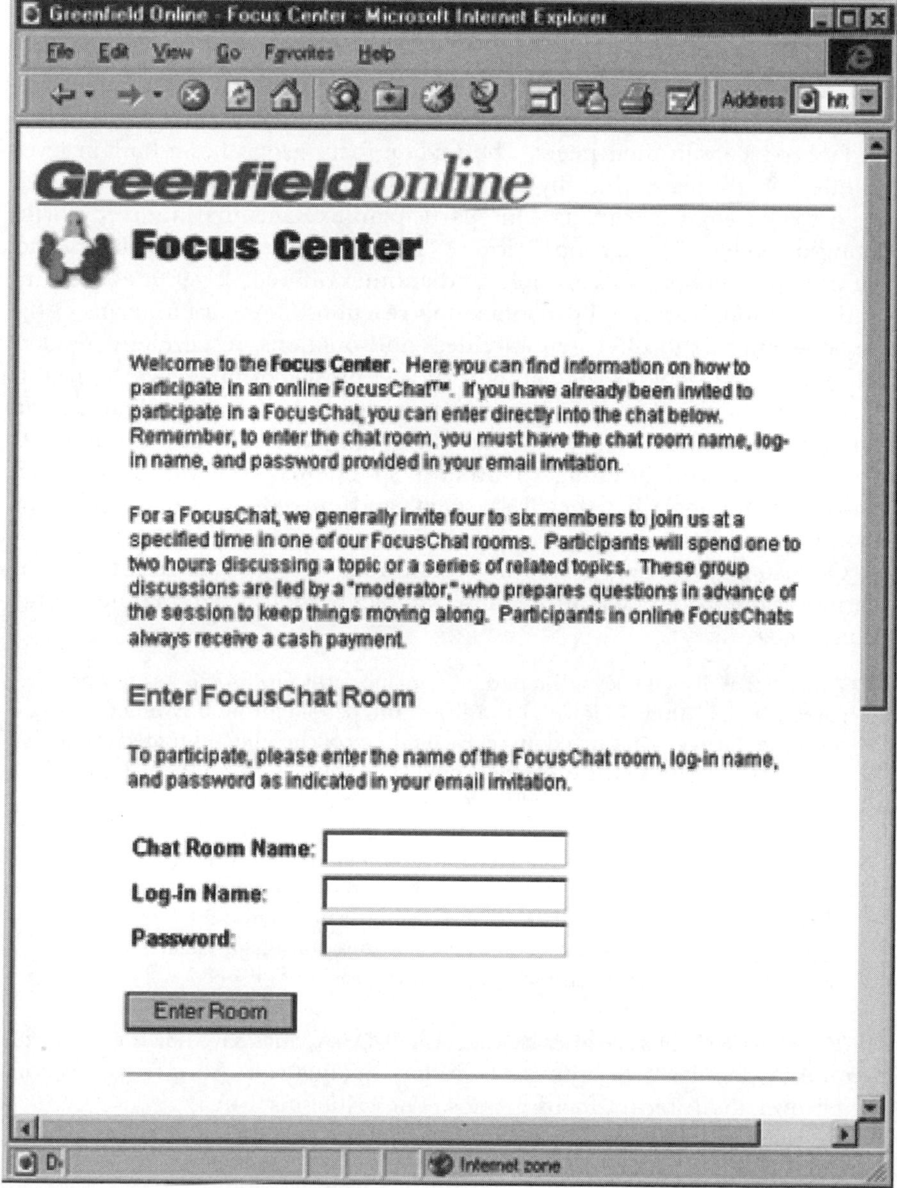

Source: From the Greenfield Online website http://www.greenfieldonline.com Greenfield Online is a Westport, Connecticut-based on-line marketing research company. Reprinted with permission

Efficient moderator-client interaction is another advantage claimed for on-line focus groups. During a traditional focus group, the client observes the discussion from behind a one-way glass; communication with the moderator is impossible without interfering with the discussion. An on-line focus group, though, offers two-way interaction between the moderator and client. The remarkable opportunity for the client to interact directly with the moderator while the moderator conducts the group has become a necessity to operating a fully effective focus group discussion. Rather than sneaking into the room with a note scribbled on a piece of paper, the client can address the moderator directly, clearly, efficiently, and without interrupting the flow of the group dynamic.[18]

In traditional focus groups there are always the "natural talkers" who dominate the discussion, despite a good moderator's attempt to equalize participant contributions. Similarly, there are others who are less comfortable voicing opinions in a group and who will express themselves more freely when not face-to-face with their peers. The on-line focus group has a built-in leveling effect in the sense that shy participants can express themselves as freely as more outgoing participants. One participant explains that he liked participating in on-line focus groups because "I can be honest without the face-to-face peer pressure of focus groups," and another offered, "I get to express my opinion without having to hear someone's reaction."[19] At least in terms of the honest willingness to offer genuine ideas and opinions, respondents tend to feel more comfortable participating from the privacy of their own homes.

In fact, the likelihood for distraction is lessened when participants focus on reading a computer screen instead of sitting in a focus group room watching the moderator, listening to other respondents, thinking about their answers, wondering what they'll say next, and envisioning what's going on behind the one-way mirror.

Occasionally, natural talkers in off-line focus groups can become domineering or obnoxious. The problem sometimes worsens when people are not sitting face-to-face.

> When Jeff Walkowski began moderating on-line focus groups, he was not prepared for the "Animal House" behavior of the people involved. Women in a detergent focus group ganged up on each other; college students traded crude comments. "I didn't realize people would sling mud at each other on line," said Mr. Walkowski, president of the group moderator service QualCore.com, who has moderated off line and on-line focus groups for such clients as American Honda Motor Company's Acura Division, PowerBar, and Procter & Gamble Company. "They'd be more civil in a face-to-face environment, he says. Then he found the Virtual Research Room, called Vrroom (http://www.vrroom.com), which has an instant ejection feature for unruly participants. He hasn't used that feature yet, but likes to know it is there if needed.[20]

Disadvantages of On-line Focus Groups Critics say that the research community does itself an injustice by calling qualitative research sessions conducted over the Internet focus groups. The criticisms are:

- *Group dynamics.* One of the key reasons to use traditional focus groups is to benefit from the interactions between group participants, as they can provide excellent insights. In cyberspace, it is difficult, if not impossible, to create any real group dynamics, since the participants are reading from computer screens rather than interacting verbally.
- *Nonverbal inputs.* Experienced moderators will use nonverbal input from the participants while moderating and analyzing sessions. It is not possible to duplicate the nonverbal input in an on-line environment.
- *Client involvement.* Many organizations use the focus group methodology because it gives client personnel an opportunity to experience some direct interface with consumers in an objective environment. Nothing can replace the impact of watching focus groups from behind a one way mirror, no matter how good the videotapes, remote broadcast facilities, or reports written by moderators. With on-line focus groups, the client personnel only can monitor written responses on a computer screen.
- *Security.* When conducting focus groups, you know who is in the room, assuming appropriate screening has been conducted. With on-line groups, there is no way to be sure who is sitting at the computer. If you cannot see the person, how do you know who he or she really is?
- *Attention to the topic.* Another important benefit of the traditional focus group process is that the participants in the group understand that they are expected to stay in the room for the full two hours of the session and contribute to the discussion. It is difficult for participants in a well-moderated focus group to be distracted from the proceedings. However, in an on-line environment, the moderator never knows if the participants are watching TV, reading a book, or eating dinner while the session is proceeding.
- *Exposure to external stimuli.* A key use of focus groups is to present advertising copy, new product concepts, prototypes, or other stimuli to the participants to get their reactions. In an on-line chat situation, it is almost impossible to duplicate the live focus group environment relative to the participant exposure to external stimuli. As a result, the input received may not be as valuable as it would in a live environment.
- *Role and skill of moderator.* Most marketing professionals agree that the quality of traditional focus group research depends on the skill of the moderator. Experienced moderators have developed techniques that involve more than simply asking questions of participants. A good moderator understands ways to draw out quiet or shy participants, energize a slow group, and use innovative techniques that will delve a little deeper into the minds of the participants. The techniques available to the moderator sitting at the computer are much more limited due to the lack of face-to-face involvement with the participants.[21]

Table 5.3 on page 130 summarizes the advantages of and disadvantages of traditional versus on-line focus groups.

Table 5.3

Advantages and Disadvantages of On-line Versus Traditional Focus Groups

Characteristics	Traditional Focus Group	On-line Focus Group
Basic cost	Typically \$2,000+. More expensive.	\$2,000 or more. Less expensive.
Participants		
Geographic factors	Participants are local due to travel time and expense.	Anyone in the world with a computer and modem.
Time commitment	Approximately 3½-hour time commitment. Busy respondents less available.	No driving to facility, approximately 1-hour time commitment. Busy respondents more likely to be available.
Respondent openness	Some respondents are intimidated in a face-to-face group setting.	Lack of face-to-face contact may lead to expressing true feelings in writing.
Group dynamics	What one person says and does (gestures and expressions) leads to others reacting.	None, according to critics.
Nonverbal communication	Can observe body language.	Cannot observe body language; participants can use emoticons to enhance communication.
Transcripts	Transcript time-consuming and expensive to obtain. Often not in complete sentences or thoughts.	Word-for-word transcripts available almost immediately. Usually in complete sentences or thoughts.
Respondent recruiting	Difficult to recruit certain types of respondents, e.g., physicians, top managers.	Easier to obtain all types of respondents.
Client travel costs	Can be very expensive when going to several cities for one or two days each.	None.
Communication with moderator	Observers send notes into focus group room.	Can communicate privately with a split screen.
Respondents		
Security	Participants accurately identified.	More difficult to be certain who is participating.
Attention to topic	Can observe respondents' attentiveness.	Respondents may be engaged in other activities.
Client involvement	Client can observe "flesh-and-blood" consumers interacting.	Client can read transcripts.
Exposure to external stimuli	Can show package designs, advertising copy, product prototypes with demonstrations.	Currently only limited ability to show stimuli.

Other Qualitative Methodologies

Most of this chapter has been devoted to focus groups because of their pervasive use in marketing research. However, several other qualitative techniques are used in research, albeit on a much more limited basis.

Depth Interviews

The term **depth interviews** has historically meant a relatively unstructured one-on-one interview. The interviewer is thoroughly trained in the skill of probing and eliciting detailed answers to each question. Sometimes psychologists are used as depth interviewers. They use clinical nondirective techniques to uncover hidden motivations.

Depth interviews One-on-one interviews that probe and elicit detailed answers to questions, often using nondirective techniques to uncover hidden motivations.

The direction of a depth interview is guided by the responses of the interviewee. As the interview unfolds, the interviewer thoroughly probes each answer and uses the replies as a basis for further questioning. For example, a depth interview might begin with a discussion of snack foods. Each answer might follow with, "Can you tell me more?" "Would you elaborate on that?" "Is that all?" The interview might then move into the pros and cons of various ingredients, such as corn, wheat, potatoes. The next phase could delve into the sociability of snack foods. Are Fritos, for example, eaten alone or in a crowd? Are Wheat Thins usually reserved for parties? When should you serve Ritz crackers?

The advantages of depth interviews relative to focus groups are as follows:

1. Group pressure is eliminated so that each respondent reveals more honest feelings, not necessarily those considered the most acceptable among peers.
2. The personal one-to-one situation gives the respondent the feeling of being the focus of attention, whose personal thoughts and feelings are important and truly wanted.
3. The respondent attains a heightened state of awareness in a personal interview because he or she is in constant rapport with the interviewer and there are no group members to hide behind.
4. The longer time devoted to an individual respondent encourages the revelation of new information.
5. A respondent can be probed at length to reveal the feelings and motivations that underlie statements.
6. Without the restrictions of cultivating a group process, new directions of questioning can be improvised more easily. Individual interviews allow greater flexibility in exploring casual remarks and tangential issues, which may provide critical insights into the main issue.
7. The closeness of the one-to-one relationship allows the interviewer to become more sensitive to nonverbal feedback.
8. Depth interviews may be the only viable technique for certain situations in which competitors might otherwise be placed in the same room. For example, it might be difficult to do a focus group on certain topics (say, systems for preventing bad checks) with managers from competing department stores or restaurants present.

The disadvantages of depth interviews relative to focus groups are as follows:

1. Depth interviews are much more expensive than groups, particularly when viewed on a per interview basis.
2. Depth interviews do not generally get the same degree of client involvement as focus groups. If one of the objectives is for a client to view the research so that it benefits firsthand from the information, it is difficult to convince most client personnel to sit through multiple hours of depth interviews.
3. Depth interviews are physically exhausting for the moderator, so it is difficult to cover as much ground in one day as it is with groups. Most moderators will not do more than four or five interviews in a day, yet in two focus groups they will cover 20 people.
4. Focus groups give the moderator an ability to leverage the dynamics of the group to obtain reactions from individuals that might not otherwise be generated in a one-on-one session.[22]

The success of any depth interview depends entirely on the interviewer. Good depth interviewers, whether psychologists or not, are hard to find and expensive. A second factor that determines the success of depth research is proper interpretation. The unstructured nature of the interview and the clinical nature of the analysis increase the complexity of the analysis. Small sample sizes, unstructured interviews that make comparisons difficult, interpretation that is subject to the nuances and frame of reference of the researcher, and high costs have all contributed to the lack of popularity of depth interviewing.

A few firms have found that depth interviews have an important role to play in qualitative research. N. W. Ayer, one of the nation's largest advertising agencies, had conducted several market segmentation studies of "baby boomers," but still felt that it lacked a good understanding of these consumers. Ayer's research director decided to conduct depth interviews.

The depth interviews generated four market segments: Satisfied Selves, who are optimistic and achievement oriented; Contented Traditionalists, who are home oriented and socially very conservative; Worried Traditionalists, anticipating disaster on all fronts; and '60s in the '90s, people who are aimless, unfulfilled, and have no direction in life.

Behavioral differences translated down to brand use. Using the category of alcohol, for example, Satisfied Selves use upscale brands and are the target for imported wine. Contented Traditionalists consume little alcohol, but when they drink they favor brown liquors, such as whiskey. Worried Traditionalists drink at an average level, but their consumption amount is very different from the other segments. For each type of liquor there was a dual brand-use pattern; people in this segment reported using an upscale brand as well as a lower-priced one. "Maybe they have one brand on hand for when they entertain guests, the socially visible brands, and a cheaper brand they consume when home alone," the research director said. The members of the '60s in the '90s segment are heavy liquor consumers, especially of vodka and beer.[23]

Projective Techniques

Projective techniques are sometimes incorporated into depth interviews. The origins of projective techniques lie in the field of clinical psychology. In essence, the objective of any projective test is to delve below surface responses to obtain true feelings, meanings, or motivations. The rationale behind projective tests comes from the knowledge that people are often reluctant or cannot reveal their deepest feelings. In other instances, they are unaware of those feelings because of psychological defense mechanisms.

Projective techniques Ways of tapping respondents' deepest feelings by having them "project" those feelings into an unstructured situation.

Projective tests are techniques for penetrating people's defense mechanisms and allowing true feelings and attitudes to emerge. In general, subjects are presented with an unstructured and nebulous situation and asked to respond. Because the situation is ill defined and has no true meaning, respondents must use their own frame of reference to answer the question. In theory, the respondents "project" their feelings onto the unstructured stimulus. Because the subjects are not talking directly about themselves, defense mechanisms are purportedly bypassed. The interviewees are talking about something else or someone else, yet revealing their inner feelings.

Use of Projective Tests

Most projective tests are easy to administer and are tabulated like any other open-ended question. They are often used in conjunction with nonprojective open- and closed-ended questions. Projective tests serve as a basis for gathering "richer" and perhaps more revealing data than standard questioning techniques. Projective techniques are often intermingled with image questionnaires, concept tests, and occasionally advertising pretests. It is also common to apply several projective techniques during a depth interview.

Types of Projective Tests

The most common forms of projective tests used in marketing research are word association, sentence and story completion, cartoon test, photo sorts, consumer drawings, and third-person techniques. Other techniques such as psychodrama tests and true TATs (thematic apperception tests) have been popular in treating psychological disorders but have been of less help in marketing research.

Word Association Tests

Word association tests are among the most practical and effective projective tools for marketing researchers. An interviewer reads a word to a respondent and asks him or her to mention the first thing that comes to mind. Usually the consumer will respond with a synonym or an antonym. The list is read in quick succession to avoid time for defense mechanisms to come into play. If the respondent fails to answer within 3 seconds, some emotional involvement with the word is assumed.

Word association tests Tests in which the interviewer says a word and respondents must mention the first thing that comes to mind.

Word association tests are used to select brand names, advertising campaign themes, and slogans. For example, a cosmetics manufacturer might ask consumers to respond to the following potential names for a new perfume:

Infinity	Flame	Precious
Encounter	Desire	Erotic

One of these words or a synonym suggested by the consumers might then be selected as the brand name.

Sentence and story completion tests Tests in which respondents complete sentences or stories in their own words.

Sentence and Story Completion **Sentence and story completion tests** can be used in conjunction with word association tests. The respondent is furnished with an incomplete story or group of sentences and asked to complete them. A few examples follow:

1. Marshall Fields is . . .
2. The people who shop at Marshall Fields are . . .
3. Marshall Fields should really . . .
4. I don't understand why Marshall Fields doesn't . . .
5. Sally Jones just moved to Chicago from Los Angeles, where she had been a salesperson for IBM. She is now a district manager for the Chicago area. Her neighbor, Rhonda Smith, has just come over to Sally's apartment to welcome her to Chicago. A discussion of where to shop ensues. Sally notes, "You know, I've heard some things about Marshall Fields. . . ." What is Rhonda's reply?

As you can see, story completion simply provides a more structured and detailed scenario for respondents. Again, the objective is for the interviewees to project themselves into the imaginary person mentioned in the scenario. Sentence completion and story techniques have been considered by some researchers to be the most useful and reliable of all the projective tests.

Cartoon tests Tests in which respondents fill in the dialogue of one character in a cartoon.

Cartoon Tests **Cartoon tests** create a highly projective mechanism by means of cartoon figures or strips similar to those seen in comic books. The typical cartoon test consists of two characters—one balloon is filled with dialogue and the other balloon is blank. The respondent is then asked to fill in the blank balloon, such as the example shown in Figure 5.3. Note that the figures are vague and without expression. This is done so that the respondent

Figure 5.3

Cartoon Test

is not given "clues" suggesting a certain type of response. The ambiguity is designed to make is easier for the respondent to project onto the cartoon.

Cartoon tests are extremely versatile. They can be used to obtain differential attitudes toward two businesses of the same type, e.g., two department stores, and the congruity or lack of congruity between these establishments and a particular product. They can be used to measure the strength of an attitude toward a particular product or brand. They also can be used to ascertain what function is being performed by a given attitude.

Photo Sorts

BBDO Worldwide, one of the country's largest advertising agencies, has developed a trademarked technique called Photosort. In **photo sorts,** consumers express their feelings about brands through a specially developed photo deck showing pictures of different types of people, from business executives to college students. Respondents connect the people with the brands they think they use. A photo sort conducted for General Electric found that consumers thought the brand attracted conservative, older business types. To change that image, GE adopted the "Bring Good Things to Life" campaign. Another photo sort for Visa found the card had a wholesome, female, middle-of-the-road image in customers' minds. The "Everywhere You Want to Be" campaign was devised to interest more high-income men.[24]

Photo sorts Respondents sort photos of different types of people, identifying those photos they feel would use the specified product or service.

BBDO interviewed 100 consumers who are the primary target market for beer: men ages 21 to 49 who drink at least six beers a week. Using Photosort, researchers showed each respondent 98 photographs and asked him to match each picture with the brand of beer that the photo subject probably drank. A Bud drinker, as viewed by the respondents, was not exactly the corporate type: He appeared tough, grizzled, blue-collar. The Miller drinker, in contrast, came off as light blue-collar, civilized, and friendly looking. Coors had a somewhat more feminine image—not necessarily a plus in a business in which 80 percent of the product is consumed by men.[25]

Another photo-sort technique was created by Grey Advertising, also a large New York advertising agency, entitled the Pictured Aspirations Technique (PAT). The device attempts to uncover how a product fits into a consumer's aspirations. Consumers sort a deck of photos according to how well the pictures describe their aspirations. In research done for Playtex's 18-hour bra, this technique revealed that the product was out of sync with the aspirations of potential customers. The respondents chose a set of pictures that expressed the "me they want to be" as energetic, slim, youthful, and vigorous. But the pictures they used to express their sense of the product were a little more old-fashioned, a little stouter, less vital and energetic looking. Out went the "Good News for Full-Figured Gals" campaign with Jane Russell as spokesperson, and in came the more sexy, fashionable concept "Great Curves Deserve 18 Hours."

Consumer Drawings

Researchers sometimes ask consumers to draw what they are feeling or how they perceive an object. Sometimes **consumer drawings** can unlock motivations or express perceptions. For example, McCann–Erickson advertising agency wanted to find out why Raid roach spray outsold Combat insecticide disks in certain markets. In interviews, most users

Consumer drawings Respondents draw what they are feeling or how they perceive an object.

agreed that Combat is a better product because it kills roaches without users expending any effort. So the agency asked the heaviest users of roach spray—low-income southern women—to draw pictures of their prey (see Figure 5.4). The goal was to get at their underlying feelings about this dirty job.

Figure 5.4

An Example of Consumer Drawings. McCann-Erickson advertising agency asked users of roach spray to create drawings of their prey. From the drawings, the agency determined that roach spray sold better than insecticide disks, since the users wanted control, and spray allowed them to actively kill the roaches. Combat disks and other traps were too passive.

Source: Courtesy of McCann–Erickson, New York.

"One night I just couldn't take the horror of these bugs sneaking around in the dark. They are always crawling when you can't see them. I had to do something. I thought wouldn't it be wonderful if when I switch on the light the roaches would shrink up and die like vampires to sunlight. So I did, but they just all scattered. But I was ready with my spray so it wasn't a total loss. I got quite a few . . . continued tomorrow night when nighttime falls."

"A man likes a free meal you cook for him; as long as there is food he will stay."

"I tiptoed quietly into the kitchen, perhaps he wasn't around. I stretched my arm up to turn on the light. I hoped I'd be alone when the light went on. Perhaps he is sitting on the table I thought. You think that's impossible? Nothing is impossible with that guy. He might not even be alone. He'll run when the light goes on I thought. But what's worse is for him to slip out of sight. No, it would be better to confront him before he takes control and 'invites a companion'."

All of the 100 women who participated in the agency's interviews portrayed roaches as men. "A lot of their feelings about the roach were very similar to the feelings that they had about the men in their lives," said Paula Drillman, executive vice-president at McCann–Erickson. Many of the women were in common-law relationships. They said that the roach, like the man in their life, "only comes around when he wants food." The act of spraying roaches and seeing them die was satisfying to this frustrated, powerless group. Setting out Combat disks may have been less trouble, but it just didn't give them the same feeling. "These women wanted control," Drillman said. "They used the spray because it allowed them to participate in the kill."[26]

Story Telling

Story telling is, as the name implies, asking consumers to tell stories about their experiences. It is a search for subtle insights into consumer behavior. Gerald Zaltman, a Harvard Business School professor, has created a metaphor laboratory to facilitate the story-telling process. Metaphors are a definition of one thing in terms of another, and people can use them to represent thoughts that are tacit, implicit, and unspoken.

Story telling Respondents tell stories to describe their experiences.

Zaltman draws metaphors out of consumers by asking them to spend several weeks thinking about how they would visually represent their experiences with a company. He asks them to cut pictures from magazines that somehow convey those experiences. Then consumers come to his lab and spend several hours telling stories about all of the images they chose and the connections between them.

One metaphor study was conducted on pantyhose. "Women in focus groups have always said that they wear them because they have to, and they hate it," says Glenda Green, a marketing research manager at DuPont, which supplies the raw material for many pantyhose manufacturers. "We didn't think we had a completely accurate picture of their feelings, but we hadn't come up with a good way to test them." DuPont turned to the metaphor lab for better insights. Someone brought a picture of a spilled ice-cream sundae, capturing the rage she feels when she spots a run in her hose. Another arrived with a picture of a beautiful woman with baskets of fruit. Other photos depicted a Mercedes and Queen Elizabeth. "As we kept probing into the emotions behind the choice of these photos, the women finally began admitting that hose made them feel sensual, sexy, and more attractive to men," says Green. "There's no way anyone would admit that in a focus group." Several stocking manufacturers used this information to alter the advertising and package design.[27]

Third-person Technique

Perhaps the easiest projective technique to apply, other than word association, is the **third-person technique**. Rather than asking people directly what they think, questions are couched as "your neighbor" or "most people" or some other third party. Rather than asking people why they typically do not provide a nutritionally balanced breakfast to their children, a researcher might ask, "Why don't many people provide their families with nutritionally balanced breakfasts?" The third-person technique is often used to avoid issues that might be embarrassing or evoke hostility if answered directly by respondents.

Third-person technique Ways of learning respondents' feelings by asking them to answer for a third party, such as "your neighbor" or "most people."

The Future of Qualitative Research

The rationale behind qualitative research tests is as follows:

1. The criteria employed and the evaluations made in most buying and usage decisions have emotional and subconscious content.
2. This emotional and subconscious content is an important determinant of buying and usage decisions.
3. Such content is not adequately or accurately verbalized by respondents through direct communicative techniques.
4. Such content is adequately and accurately verbalized by respondents through indirect communicative techniques.[28]

To the extent that these tenets remain true or even partially correct, the demand for qualitative applications in marketing research will continue. But the problems of small sample sizes and subjective interpretation will also continue to plague some forms of qualitative research. The inability to validate and replicate qualitative research will further deter its growth.

On the positive side, the use of on-line focus groups will continue to grow. Focus group research can provide data and insight not available through any other techniques. The low cost and ease of application will provide an even greater impetus for focus group use in the twenty-first century. Clearly the qualitative-quantitative split will begin to close as adaptations and innovations are made to the techniques of both sides, allowing researchers to enjoy the advantages of both approaches simultaneously.

Summary

Qualitative research refers to research findings not subject to quantification or quantitative analysis. It is often used to examine attitudes, feelings, and motivations. Qualitative research, particularly focus groups, continues to grow in popularity, for several reasons. First, qualitative research is usually less expensive to conduct than quantitative studies. Second, it is an excellent means to understand in depth the motivation and feelings of consumers. Third, it can improve the efficiency of quantitative research.

Qualitative research has its disadvantages. One problem is that qualitative research sometimes does not distinguish small differences in attitudes or opinions as well as in large-scale quantitative studies. Also, the respondents in qualitative studies are not necessarily representative of the population that is of interest to the researcher. Third, a number of individuals lack formal training yet profess to be experts in the field.

Focus groups typically consist of 8 to 12 participants who are led by a moderator in an in-depth discussion on a particular topic or concept. The goal of the focus group is to learn and understand what people have to say and why. The emphasis is on getting people to talk at length and in detail about the subject at hand. The interaction provided by group dynamics is essential to the success of focus group research. The idea is that a response from one person may become a stimulus for another, thereby generating an interplay of responses that may yield more information than if the same number of people had contributed independently to the discussion. Focus groups are the most popular type of qualitative research.

Most focus groups are held in a group facility, which is typically set up conference-room style with a large one-way mirror in one wall. Microphones are placed in unobtrusive locations to record the discussion. Behind the mirror is a viewing room. Respondents are paid to participate. The moderator plays a critical role in determining the success or failure of the group. More and more focus groups are being conducted on line because they are fast and cost-effective. However, a number of problems are associated with on-line focus groups.

A number of other qualitative research methodologies are used, but much more infrequently. One technique is depth interviews. Depth interviews are historically unstructured. The interviewer is thoroughly trained in the skill of probing and eliciting detailed answers to each question. He or she often uses clinical, nondirective techniques to uncover hidden motivations. Projective techniques are another form of qualitative research. The objective of any projective test is to delve below the surface responses to obtain true feelings, meanings, or motivations. Some common forms of projective tests are word association tests, sentence and story completion tests, cartoon tests, photo sorts, consumer drawings, and third-person techniques.

Key Terms & Definitions

Qualitative research Research data not subject to quantification or quantitative analysis.

Quantitative research Studies that use mathematical analysis.

Focus group A group of 8 to 12 participants who are led by a moderator in an in-depth discussion on one particular topic or concept.

Group dynamics The interaction among people in a group.

Focus group facility A facility consisting of a conference-room or living-room setting and a separate observation room. The facility also has audiovisual recording equipment.

Focus group moderator The person hired by the client to lead the focus group. This person may need a background in psychology or sociology or, at least, marketing.

Discussion guide A written outline of topics to cover during a focus group discussion.

Depth interviews One-on-one interviews that probe and elicit detailed answers to questions, often using nondirective techniques to uncover hidden motivations.

Projective techniques Ways of tapping respondents' deepest feelings by having them "project" those feelings into an unstructured situation.

Word association tests Tests in which the interviewer says a word and respondents must mention the first thing that comes to mind.

Sentence and story completion tests Tests in which respondents complete sentences or stories in their own words.

Cartoon tests Tests in which respondents fill in the dialogue of one character in a cartoon.

Photo sorts Respondents sort photos of different types of people, identifying those photos they feel would use the specified product or service.

Consumer drawings Respondents draw what they are feeling or how they perceive an object.

Story telling Respondents tell stories to describe their experiences.

Third-person technique Way of learning respondents' feelings by asking them to answer for a third party, such as "your neighbor" or "most people."

Questions for Review & Critical Thinking

1. What are the major differences between quantitative and qualitative research?
2. What are some of the possible disadvantages of using focus groups?
3. What are some of the trends in focus group research? Why do you think these trends have evolved?
4. What can the client do to get more out of focus groups?
5. What is the purpose of projective techniques? What major factors should be considered in conducting a projective test?
6. Conduct a focus group in your class on one of the following three topics:
   a. student experiences at your student union.
   b. the quality of frozen dinners and snacks, and new items that would be desirable.
   c. how students spend their entertainment dollars and what additional entertainment opportunities they would like to see offered.
7. What are some major issues in conducting international focus groups?
8. Compare and contrast nominal group sessions and focus groups.
9. What are cyberfocus groups? Explain the process.
10. Consumer drawing tests may ask study participants to draw the kind of person that would be consuming a particular product. Draw a typical Pepsi drinker and a typical Coke drinker. What do the drawn images suggest about the participants' perceptions of Coke and Pepsi drinkers?
11. Use the metaphor technique to tell a story about going to the supermarket.

Working the Net

Go to http://www.researchconnections.com and look at the information on Focus Connect. Report your findings to the class.

Cahners Business Information Learns On Line that DOOM and MYST Rule

Real-Life Research

Cahners Business Information organized an on-line panel through a proprietary bulletin board operated by the company. Cahners collected data on the general area of technology and media from teens (aged 11 to 18, living at home). The aim of the on-line panel was to collect qualitative data that were nationally projectable. Researchers recognized that this panel would be comprised of teens of a special kind, that is, teens who owned computers with modems. Still, if the panel of teens was representative of modem-owning teens in general and could provide interesting qualitative data, it would meet Cahners criteria for success.

At the start of this project, Cahners was fortunate enough to have a national sample of households with teens drawn from their omnibus surveys. The firm had, also fortunately, conducted an interview with an adult in the household, so it had household data going into the study. From this sample, interviewers conducted a telephone survey with 750 teenagers and collected data on their media and technology usage, along with general attitudes and demographics.

The company also put in place validation checks to ensure that the teens on line were the same teens interviewers had spoken to over the telephone. This meant that the sample could not snowball into a much larger, but unidentifiable, group.

Initial results were encouraging: Over 50 teens signed onto the bulletin board within a month and the discussions were lively. Teens posted messages constantly through a bulletin board-style service, and more teens, with additional reminder notes, began to join. However, after a few months, researchers noticed a sharp drop-off.

The drop-off in itself was not alarming; all panels need refreshing. But this one differed from normal panel attrition. Here, it was the dynamics of the on-line panel itself that made teens drop: Certain teens were "discriminated against" because they didn't fit in. Typically, panel designs don't rely on respondents to get along with one another, but because Cahners had created an on-line community, the panel design demanded that respondents communicate with each other. This was very different from a focus group. These teens had to live with one another on line.

Researchers expected from the outset that on-line/Internet panels would favor respondents who enjoyed writing. However, they underestimated the effect of assertiveness. Girls, initially enthusiastic, began to lose interest because boys were more assertive verbally, often making nasty comments and making cyber life less fun for girls. In five months, Cahners had a small cohort of articulate, opinionated teens, mostly boys. The company had lost many girls and also those teenagers who were more timid.

With this change, the diversity of opinions that initially had existed on line withered. So, after all the care the researchers took to create a nationally projectable group, it ended up with a select group instead. Cahners then had to work to bring back those who had left by sending them private messages by e-mail or traditional mail. When looking at data derived from Usenet groups and websites, it is important to keep this bias in mind.

Even with all of the caveats discussed above, on-line data collection offers some genuine advantages. Computer games and on-line gaming was a perfect kind of market to explore through the panel. Cahners had highly sophisticated teens who had modems, liked using computers, and liked expressing their opinions to one another. If researchers wanted to learn about how teens responded to CD-ROM games, these teens were excellent candidates. Furthermore, the researchers knew at the outset that teens' involvement in games was intense, so it seemed that on-line panels could shed light on the nature of that experience.

Because the on-line panel was a kind of minicommunity, the teens started to treat each other as friends with whom they would exchange advice and/or recommendations. Therefore, Cahners could see how teens developed a word-of-mouth system about games and gaming. Teens liked to recommend not only specific games, but also branches of games like MYST. Teens asked pals on line if they had heard of specific games, like Full Throttle and ROTT, and what they thought of them. The researchers could monitor and overhear these recommendations. Teens were savvy about gaming, and they were also pretty thrifty. When one teen asked if he should buy Ultimate Doom, he was quickly warned, "I've played Ultimate Doom, and it's not really all it's cracked up to be. Why spend $50 for the game when you can get a patch off the Internet for free? Anyway, the fourth episode is okay, it just doesn't really keep the Doom spirit."

Questions

1. Would you call this an on-line focus group? Why or why not?
2. What disadvantages do you see to qualitative on-line research? What advantages are there?
3. Go to http://www.cahners.com and determine what other types of research Cahners is conducting. Report your findings to the class.

CHAPTER six

Primary Data Collection: Observation

Learning Objectives

1 *To develop a basic understanding of observation research*

2 *To learn the approaches to observation research*

3 *To understand the advantages and disadvantages of observation research*

4 *To explore the types of human observation*

5 *To describe the types of machine observation and their advantages and disadvantages*

6 *To explore the tremendous impact scanner research has had on the marketing research industry in the past few years*

As a manufacturer of top-quality loudspeakers and other audio equipment, Bose Corporation has a reputation for excellence.Thanks to the firm's strong belief in R&D, audiophiles and the general public alike know that the Bose name is synonymous with technological innovation and great sound.

To make sure employees extend the pursuit of excellence to the retail setting, Bose has been using mystery shopping since 1995 to monitor performance of salespeople at its factory stores—which sell new and factory-renewed products—and at its Bose showcase stores—which sell new merchandise. Mystery shops are also conducted at department stores and electronics superstores where Bose products are sold. . . .

The Bose store mystery shops are two-part. They begin with a phone call, in which the shopper calls to ask questions on specific products. Shoppers indicate if the employee performed tasks such as answering questions clearly. Employees are also rated on their friendliness, helpfulness, etc., using a excellent-satisfactory-unsatisfactory scale. Finally, shoppers have space to write about their interaction and support the ratings they gave the employee.

"We ask our shoppers specifically what we could have done to improve. We have a lot of yes/no questions so that it can be as objective as possible but we also want them to express in their own words how we did and what we could do to make them feel more welcome," Pazol says. [Lisa Pazol, manager, customer experience, retail direct group, Bose Corp.]

For the in-person visit, shoppers describe how/if they were greeted, their evaluation of the employee in charge of the theater presentation (Bose stores contain a theater for presenting a short audiovisual show which highlights Bose equipment), the employee's selling and closing skills and exploration of customer needs (Did the employee use language which helped you picture having the product in your home?), product demonstration and knowledge (Did the employee describe and demonstrate the benefits?), and overall impressions (Did the Bose representative make you feel important, provide a comfortable environment?). At the factory stores, shoppers must note if the employee volunteered an explanation of factory-renewed products during their visit. . . .

Find out more about Bose's commitment to its customers at

http://www.bose.com 

Each store receives a quarterly summary showing the staff's overall performance. "The district and store managers also get copies of the mystery shopping trips. The stores use the mystery shopping data as a tool to bring awareness of where they're doing well and where there are opportunities to do better. . . ."

Depending on each store's overall performance, the employee team, including managers, are awarded a customer satisfaction bonus. Outstanding mystery shopping reports are often posted at the individual stores so employees can celebrate. Individual employees are noted only for outstanding service (they're not singled out if they perform poorly) and can win points in the Bose employee recognition program.[1]

The opening story describes a form of observation research. What is observation research? What are its advantages and limitations? Are other mechanical devices used in observation research? These are some of the questions we will answer in Chapter 6. ■

The Nature of Observation Research

Observation Research Defined

Instead of asking people questions, as in a survey, observation depends on watching what people do. **Observation research** can be defined as the systematic process of recording the behavioral patterns of people, objects, and occurrences without questioning or communicating with them. A market researcher using the observation technique witnesses and records information as events occur or compiles evidence from records of past events. Carried a step further, observation may involve watching people or phenomena and may be conducted by human observers or machines. Examples of these various observational situations are shown in Table 6.1.

Observation research Recording behavioral patterns without verbal communication.

Conditions for Using Observation

Three conditions must be met before observation can be successfully used as a data collection tool for marketing research. First, the needed information must be observable or inferable from observable behavior. For example, if a researcher wants to know why an individual purchased a new Jeep Cherokee rather than a Ford Explorer, observation research will not provide the answer. Second, the behavior of interest must be repetitive, frequent, or predictable in some manner. Otherwise, the costs of observation make the approach prohibitively expensive. An observer can't wait around until an individual decides to buy a new vehicle. Finally, the behavior of interest must be of relatively short duration. Observation of the entire decision-making process for purchasing a new home, which might take several weeks or months, is not feasible.

Table 6.1

Observation Situations

Situation	Example
People watching people	Observers stationed in supermarkets watch consumers select frozen Mexican dinners. The purpose is to see how much comparison shopping people do at the point of purchase.
People watching phenomena	Observer stationed at an intersection counts traffic moving in various directions.
Machines watching people	Movie or videotape cameras record behavior as in people-watching-people example.
Machines watching phenomena	Traffic-counting machines monitor traffic flow.

Approaches to Observation Research

The researcher has a variety of observational approaches to choose from. The question is one of choosing the most effective approach from the standpoint of cost and data quality for a particular research problem. The five dimensions along which observational approaches vary are

- natural versus contrived situations
- disguised versus undisguised situations
- structured versus unstructured observation
- human versus machine observers
- direct versus indirect observation.

Natural Versus Contrived Situations

Counting how many people use the drive-in window at a particular bank during certain hours is a good example of a completely natural situation. The observer is playing no role in the behavior being monitored. Those being observed should have no idea they are under observation. At the other extreme, a researcher might recruit people to do their shopping in a simulated supermarket—rows of stocked shelves set up in a market research field service's mall facility are commonly used—and carefully observe their behavior. In this case, the recruited people will have at least some idea that they are participating in a study. The participants might be given grocery carts and asked to browse the shelves and pick out items that they might normally use. The researcher might use alternative point-of-purchase displays for several products under study. The observers would note how long shoppers paused in front of the test displays and how often the product was actually selected, thus getting an idea of the effectiveness of the various displays.

A contrived environment better enables the researcher to control extraneous influences that might have an impact on people's behavior or the interpretation of that behavior. Also, a simulated environment tends to speed up the observation data-gathering process. The researcher does not have to wait for natural events to occur, but instead instructs the participants to perform certain actions. Because more observations can be collected in the same length of time, the result will either be a larger sample or a target sample size that is collected faster. The latter should lower the costs of the project.

The primary disadvantage of a contrived setting is that it is artificial and the observed behavior may be different from what would occur in a real-world situation. The more natural the setting, the more likely the behavior will be normal for the individuals being observed.

Open Versus Disguised Observation

Do the people being observed know they are being observed? It is well known that the presence of an observer may have an influence on the phenomena being observed.[2] Two mechanisms can work to bias the data. First, if people know they are being observed (as in **open observation**), they may behave differently. Second, the appearance and behavior of the observer offers a potential for bias similar to that associated with the presence of an interviewer in survey research.

Open observation The process of monitoring people who know they are being watched.

Disguised observation is the process of monitoring people who do not know they are being watched. A common form of disguised observation is observing behavior behind a one-way mirror. For example, a product manager may observe respondent reactions to alternative package designs behind a one-way mirror during a focus group discussion.

Disguised observation The process of monitoring people who do not know they are being watched.

Structured Versus Unstructured

Observation can be structured or unstructured much in the same way surveys are. In a **structured observation,** the observer fills out a form similar to a questionnaire on each person observed. In an **unstructured observation,** the observer simply makes notes on the behavior being observed. In general, the same considerations that determine whether a survey should be structured or unstructured also determine the format an observation takes. If you already know a good deal about the behavior to be studied, it probably makes more sense to do structured observations. If you know little, unstructured observation is the proper method, at least as a preliminary approach.

Structured observation A study in which the observer fills out a questionnairelike form or counts the number of times an activity occurs.

Unstructured observation A study in which the observer simply makes notes on the behavior being observed.

Structured observation often consists of simply counting the number of times a particular activity occurs. For example, a researcher may be interested in testing two sets of instructions on a new cake mix recipe. To develop a baseline of behavior, the researcher could have the participants prepare their own favorite recipes using the cake mix. One-half of the group would get one set of instructions, and the other half, the other set. Activities counted might be things such as the number of times the instructions are read, the number of trips to the cabinet to retrieve bowls and utensils, and the number of strokes that the mix is beaten.

Human Versus Machine Observers

In some situations it may be possible and even desirable to replace human observers with machines. In certain situations machines may do the job less expensively, more accurately, or more readily. Traffic-counting devices are probably more accurate, are definitely less expensive, and are certainly more willing than human observers. It would not be feasible, for example, for ACNielsen to have human observers in people's homes to record television viewing habits. Movie cameras and audiovisual equipment record behavior much more objectively and in greater detail than human observers ever could. The electronic scanners found in a growing number of retail stores provide more accurate and timely data on product movement than human observers ever could.

Indirect observation Making a record of past behavior.

Direct Versus Indirect Observation Most of the observation done in marketing research is direct observation, that is, the process of directly observing current behavior. However, in some cases past behavior must be observed. To take advantage of **indirect observation** it is necessary to make some record of the behavior. Archaeologists dig up sites of old settlements and attempt to determine the nature of life in old civilizations from the physical evidence they find. Garbologists sort through people's garbage to analyze household consumption patterns. Marketing research is usually much more mundane. In a product prototype test it may be important to know how much of the test product was actually used. The most accurate way to find out is to have respondents return the unused product so that the researcher can measure how much is left. If a laundry soil-and-stain remover was tested in the home, it would be important to know how much of the product respondents applied. The answers to other questions would be considered from this usage perspective.

Advantages of Observation Research

Watching what people actually do rather than depending on their reports of what they did has a significant and obvious advantage: Observers see what people actually do rather than having to rely on what they say they did. This approach can avoid much of the biasing factors caused by the interviewer-and-question structure associated with the survey approach. The researcher is not subject to problems associated with the willingness and ability of respondents to answer questions. Also, some forms of data are gathered more quickly and accurately by observation. Rather than ask people to enumerate every item in their grocery bags, it is more efficient to let a scanner record it. Alternatively, rather than asking young children which toys they like, the major toy manufacturers invite target groups of children into a large playroom and observe via a one-way mirror which toys they choose and how long their choices hold their attention.

Disadvantages of Observation Research

The primary disadvantage of observation research is that usually only behaviors and physical and personal characteristics can be examined. The researcher does not learn about motives, attitudes, intentions, or feelings. Also, only public behavior is observed; private behavior, such as dressing for work, committee decision making, and family activities at home are beyond the researcher's scope. A second problem is that present observed behavior may not be projectable to the future. Although purchasing a certain brand of milk after examining several alternatives may accurately reflect a purchasing decision today, it cannot account for tomorrow's purchasing decision.

Observation research can be time-consuming and costly if the observed behavior occurs infrequently. For example, if an observer in a supermarket is waiting to record the purchase behavior of shoppers selecting Lava soap, it may be a long wait. If the observed consumers are selected in a biased pattern (for example, those who grocery shop after 5:00 P.M.), distorted data may be obtained.

Human Observation

As noted in Table 6.1, people can be used to watch other people or certain phenomena. For example, people can take the roles of mystery shoppers, observers behind one-way mirrors, or recorders of shopper traffic and behavior patterns. Researchers also conduct retail and wholesale audits and do content analysis, which are other types of observation research.

Mystery Shoppers

Mystery shoppers are used to gather observational data about a store (are the shelves neatly stocked?) and to collect data about customer/employee interactions. In the latter case, of course, communication must take place between the mystery shopper and the employee. The mystery shopper may ask, "How much is this item?" or "Do you have this in blue?" or "Can you deliver this by Friday?" The interaction is not an interview, and communication occurs only so that the mystery shopper can observe the employee's actions and comments. Mystery shopping is, therefore, classified as an observational marketing research method, even though communication is often involved.

Mystery shoppers People employed to pose as consumers and shop at an employer's competitors or their own stores to compare prices, displays, and the like.

> . . . There are basically four variations on the mystery shopping concept. Each offers choices in the depth and type of information collected.
>
> *Level 1.* The mystery shopper conducts a mystery telephone call. Here, the mystery shopper calls the client location and evaluates the level of service received over the phone, following a scripted conversation.
>
> *Level 2.* The mystery shopper visits an establishment and makes a quick purchase; little or no customer employee interaction is required. For example, in a Level 2 mystery shop, a mystery shopper purchases an item (e.g., gas, a hamburger, or a lottery ticket) and evaluates the transaction and image of the facility.
>
> *Level 3.* The mystery shopper visits an establishment and, using a script or scenario, initiates a conversation with a service and/or sales representative. Level 3 mystery shopping usually does not involve an actual purchase. Examples include discussing different cellular telephone packages with a sales representative [and] reviewing services provided during an oil change.
>
> *Level 4.* The mystery shopper performs a visit that requires excellent communication skills and knowledge of the product. Discussing a home loan, the process for purchasing a new car, or visiting apartment complexes serve as examples. . . . [3]

Service affects sales, customer satisfaction, and ultimately customer loyalty, and that affects a company's profits. Mystery shopping improves how the universe of consumers (both purchasers and nonpurchasers) are treated by the staff, customer service representatives, and telephone service representatives. It tells management whether the "front line" is treating consumers consistently and in a manner that adheres to company standards. More specifically, mystery shopping measures whether the staff is knowledgeable, efficient, helpful, and courteous. Conducted on a continuous basis, mystery shopping can motivate and recognize service performance.

Used as a benchmark, mystery shopping can pinpoint strengths and weaknesses for training operations and policy refinements. A benchmark can also reveal how a firm measures up against the competition. In addition, it can identify the competition's best and worst practices and present the client company with opportunities to improve. In the end, mystery shopping helps build greater customer satisfaction, deeper product usage, and higher customer retention, which spells increased profits.[4]

Assume that a national bookstore chain, such as Barnes & Noble, has created service policies stating that when a customer enters the store a floor employee should (1) ask questions to determine the customer's area of interest, (2) take the customer to the appropriate section of the store, (3) show the customer several alternative titles, (4) help the customer decide which one(s) to buy, and (5) ask if there is something else he or she can do to help the customer. A sample mystery shopper evaluation form is shown in Figure 6.1.[5]

Costs for mystery shopping can vary considerably. The cost depends on the level of shopping, as described above, the difficulty in shopping, the frequency and amount of shopping, and the depth of the reports. The costs

Figure 6.1

Excerpt from a Mystery Shopper Scoring Sheet

Source: Dan Prince, "How to Ensure an Objective Mystery Shop," *Quirk's Marketing Research Review,* January 1996, p. 42. Reprinted by permission of *Quirk's Marketing Research Review.*

BOOKSTORE EVALUATION

Store ______________________ Date ______________

Employee ______________________ Shopper ______________
(describe if no name tag visible)

Time entered store ______________ Time exited store ______________

Time spent waiting for employee ______________ minutes 1 2 3 4 5

Asks questions (must do all three to score a 5)

__________ Greets customer with a smile

__________ Asks "Is there something in particular I can help you with today?"

__________ Asks at least one additional follow-up question to assist customer

No ____ Yes ____ Takes customer to appropriate section

No ____ Yes ____ Shows customer two more titles

generally range from $25 to $125 to the client, with an average fee of $65 per shopping event.[6]

One-way Mirror Observations

In the discussion of focus groups in Chapter 5 we noted that focus group facilities almost always include an observation room with a **one-way mirror.** This allows clients to observe the group discussion as it unfolds. New product development managers, for example, can note consumers' reactions to various package prototypes as they are demonstrated by the moderator. The clients can also observe the degree of emotion exhibited by consumers as they speak. One-way mirror observations are sometimes used by child psychologists and toy designers to watch children at play. One researcher spent 200 hours watching mothers change diapers to help with the redesign of disposable diapers.

One-way mirror observation The practice of watching unseen from behind a one-way mirror.

To properly use an observation room, the lighting level must be very dim relative to the lighting in the focus group room. Otherwise, the focus group participants can see into the observation room. Several years ago, the authors were conducting a focus group using orthopedic surgeons in St. Louis. One physician arrived approximately 20 minutes early and was ushered into the group room. A young assistant product manager for the pharmaceutical manufacturer was already seated in the observation room. The physician, being alone in the group room, decided to take advantage of the large framed mirror on the wall for some last-minute grooming. He walked over to the mirror and began combing his hair, at the same time the assistant product manager, sitting about a foot away on the other side of the mirror, decided to light a cigarette. As the doctor combed his hair, there was suddenly a bright flash of light and another face appeared through the mirror. What happened next goes beyond the scope of this text. In recent years, the trend has been to inform participants of the one-way mirror and to explain who is in the other room watching and why.

Shopper Patterns and Behavior

Shopper pattern studies are used by retailers to trace the flow of shoppers through a store. Normally, the researcher uses a diagram of the aisles and traces the footsteps of a shopper with a pen. By comparing the flows of a representative sample of shoppers, store managers can determine where best to place such items as impulse goods. Or the store can change layouts over time to see how they modify shopping patterns. Retailers want shoppers to be exposed to as much merchandise as possible while in the store. Supermarkets, for example, typically place necessities toward the rear of the store, hoping that shoppers will place more items in their basket on impulse as they move down the aisle to reach the milk, bread, or eggs.

Shopper patterns Drawings that record the footsteps of a shopper through a store.

Shopper behavior research involves observing, or perhaps filming and then watching the film of, shoppers or consumers in a variety of shopping settings. Starbucks, Anheuser–Busch, McDonald's, and Procter & Gamble, among others, hire Envirosell, a marketing research firm, to observe shopper behavior. The company creates about 15,000 hours of videotapes of shoppers

Shopper behavior research A study involving observing, either in person or on videotape, shoppers or consumers in a variety of shopping settings.

each year. The videos are then analyzed for behavioral tendencies. Some of Envirosell's findings include:

- Installing ledges for customers' pocketbooks cut a store's checkout time by 15 percent.
- Pedestrians can take 25 feet to slow down, so a store just past an establishment without visual appeal may be missed.
- Special displays just inside stores will be seen by more people if moved back, near the end of the "decompression zone," where customers adjust to light and surroundings.
- Old people tend to shop in couples or groups, and should have access to chairs in stores and something to look at while their more active friends browse.
- Large toy stores have ignored a wealth of potential business from grandparents who will not shop there because they cannot find good advice on what toys are popular and appropriate for various age groups.
- The average number of times a product is handled by shoppers before it is bought is: lipsticks, 6; towels, 6.6; compact discs and toys, 11.[7]

Masten/ImageNet specializes in marketing research with the youthful ultracool segment. It recently sent three researchers with cameras to a San Francisco rock and folk music concert dedicated to freeing Tibet. It was observation research such as this that helped Reebok decide to introduce new sneakers in soft, pastel colors. In the same vein, Mountain Dew learned that pagers were still "in" with its youthful target market. It created a promotion that offered customers a low-priced pager if they consumed enough of the drink.[8]

Content Analysis

Content analysis A technique used to analyze written material (usually advertising copy) by breaking it into meaningful units using carefully applied rules.

Content analysis is an observation technique used to analyze written material (usually advertising copy) into meaningful units using carefully applied rules.[9] It is an objective, systematic description of the content of a communication. Communication can be analyzed at many levels, such as image, words, or roles depicted. A researcher using content analysis attempts to determine what is being communicated to a target audience.

One study, for example, noted that the Federal Trade Commission had adopted an advertising substantiation program. The goals of the program were for ads to provide information that might aid consumers in making rational choices and for ads to provide evidence that would enhance competition by encouraging competitors to challenge advertising claims. Content analysis was used to measure the change in the content of advertisements before and after the substantiation program. The researchers looked at product attributes and claims, the level of verifiability in the ads, and how informative the ads were. The study found that the number of claims in the ads had declined, while the level of verifiable information had increased. The general level of informativeness, however, did not change.[10]

Another study hypothesized that because of the growing number of elderly Americans, advertisers were using more elderly models in their promotions. The researchers found that there had, in fact, been a significant increase in the use of the elderly in advertisements over the past three decades. The research also found that the older people were often portrayed in relatively prestigious work situations and that older men were used much more frequently in ads than were older women.[11]

Humanistic Inquiry

A controversial research method that is new to marketing and that relies heavily on observation is **humanistic inquiry.** The humanistic approach advocates immersing the researcher in the system or group under study, rather than following the traditional scientific method in which the researcher stands apart from the system or group being studied. Thus, a traditional researcher would conduct a large-scale survey or experiment to test a hypothesis, whereas a humanist would engage in "investigator immersion" by becoming part of the group he or she plans to study.

Humanistic inquiry A research method in which the researcher is immersed in the system or group under study.

One humanistic researcher was interested in interpreting the consumption values and lifestyles of old-line white, Anglo-Saxon Protestant (WASP) consumers. For 18 months the researcher engaged in field visits to Richmond, Virginia; Charleston, South Carolina; Wilton, Connecticut; and Kennebunkport, Maine. She participated in organizations and observed WASP consumers working, playing, eating dinner, attending church, discussing politics, and shopping in department stores and supermarkets.

Throughout the immersion process, the humanistic researcher maintains two diaries or logs. One is a **theory-construction diary** that documents in detail the thoughts, premises, hypotheses, and revisions in thinking developed by the researcher. The theory-construction diary is vital to humanistic inquiry because it shows the process by which the researcher has come to understand the phenomenon under study.

Theory-construction diary A journal that documents in detail the thoughts, premises, hypotheses, and revisions in thinking of a humanistic researcher.

The second set of notes maintained by the humanistic researcher is a **methodological log.** In it are kept detailed and time-sequenced notes on the investigative techniques used during the inquiry, with special attention to biases or distortions a given technique may have introduced. The investigative techniques almost always include participant observation and may be supplemented by audiotape or videotape recordings, artifacts (such as shopping lists, garbage), and supplemental documentation (such as magazine articles, health records, survey data, census reports).

Methodological log A journal of detailed and time-sequenced notes on the investigative techniques used during a humanistic inquiry, with special attention to biases or distortions a given technique may have introduced.

To assess whether the interpretation is drawn in a logical and unprejudiced manner from the data gathered and the rationale employed, humanistic inquiry relies on the judgment of one or more outside auditors. These individuals should be researchers themselves, familiar with the phenomena under study. Their task is to review the documentation, field notes, methodological diary, and other supportive evidence gathered by the investigator to confirm (or not confirm) that the conclusions reached flow from the information collected.[12]

Audits

Audits are another category of human observation research. An **audit** is the examination and verification of the sale of a product. Audits usually fall into two categories: retail audits that measure sales to final consumers and

Audits The examination and verification of the sale of a product.

Global ISSUES

Observation Research Is Used Sparingly in Many Countries

OBSERVATION RESEARCH IS USED EXTENSIVELY IN THE UNITED STATES AND JAPAN, BUT LESS SO in Europe. For example, little observation research is conducted in Ireland. Where it is used, it tends to be as a generalized technique to get a research idea or to help the researcher decide what aspects of the problem are worth researching. It may be used as a check on other research techniques. Many researchers avoid using the method due to its inability to observe such factors as attitudes, motivations, and plans.

There is a reluctance on the part of Irish businesses to allow the researcher to come on site and observe behaviors over a period of time. Many Irish researchers would question the reliability of what they are observing. There is a tendency for many people to act differently than they would otherwise. Most of the observation that is used is of the natural, direct, and unobtrusive type.[13] ■

wholesale audits that determine the amount of product movement from warehouses to retailers. Wholesalers and retailers allow auditors into their stockrooms and stores and allow them to examine the company's sales and order records to verify product flows. In turn, they receive cash compensation and basic reports about their operations from the audit firms.

Because of the availability of scanner-based data (discussed later in the chapter), physical audits for the retail market may someday all but disappear. Already the largest nonscanner-based wholesale audit company, SAMI, is out of business. Its client list was sold to Information Resources, Inc. (IRI), a company that specializes in providing scanner data. ACNielsen, the largest retail audit organization, no longer uses auditors in grocery stores; the data are entirely scanner based. Nielsen still uses both auditors and scanners in other types of retail outlets, but will probably shift to scanners only once the majority of retailers within a store category (such as hardware stores, drugstores) installs scanners.

Machine Observation

The observation methods discussed so far have involved people watching consumers (observation) or things (audits). Now we turn our attention to machines observing people and things.

Traffic Counters

Traffic counters are perhaps the most common and popular form of machine-based observation research (other than scanners). As the name implies, **traffic counters** are machines used to measure vehicular flow over a particular stretch of roadway. Outdoor advertisers rely on traffic counts to determine the number of exposures per day to a specific billboard. Retailers use the information to ascertain where to place a particular type of store. Convenience stores, for example, require a moderately high traffic volume to reach target levels of profitability.

Traffic counters Machines used to measure vehicular flow over a particular stretch of roadway.

Physiological Measurement

When an individual is aroused or feels inner tension or alertness, this condition is referred to as *activation*. Activation is stimulated via a subcortical unit called the reticular activation system (RAS), which is located in the human brain stem. The sight of a product or advertisement, for example, can activate the RAS. As a result of directly provoking arousal processes in the RAS, there is an increase in the processing of information.[14] Researchers have used a number of devices to measure the level of a person's activation.

EEG The **electroencephalogram (EEG)** is a machine that measures rhythmic fluctuations in the electric potential of the brain. It is probably the most versatile and sensitive procedure for detecting activation, but involves expensive equipment, a laboratory environment, and complex data analysis using special software programs. Researchers claim that EEG measures can be used to assess, among other effects, viewers' attention to an advertisement at specific points in time, the intensity of the emotional reactions elicited by specific aspects of the ad, and their comprehension and attention to the ad.[15] Other researchers have disputed the value of EEG for marketing research because of the cost of the equipment and the special environment required.[16]

Electroencephalogram (EEG) A machine that measures rhythmic fluctuations in the electrical potential of the brain.

GSR The **galvanic skin response (GSR),** also known as the electrodermal response, measures changes in the electric resistance of the skin associated with activation responses. A small electric current of constant intensity is sent into the skin through electrodes attached to the palmar side of the fingers. The changes in voltage observed between the electrodes indicate the level of stimulation. Because the equipment is portable and not expensive, the GSR is the most popular device for measuring activation. The GSR is used primarily to measure stimulus responses to advertisements, but is sometimes used in packaging research.

Galvanic skin response (GSR) The measurement of changes in the electric resistance of the skin associated with activation responses.

Inner Response, Inc. uses the GSR to evaluate commercials. In one Eastman Kodak Company film-processing ad, Inner Response determined that the viewers' interest level built slowly in the opening scenes, rose when a snapshot of an attractive young woman was shown, but spiked highest when a picture appeared of a smiling, pigtailed girl. Kodak then knew which scenes had the highest impact, and could retain them when making changes in the spot or cutting it to 15 seconds from 30.[17]

Pupilometer A machine that measures changes in pupil dilation.

Pupilometer The **pupilometer** measures changes in pupil dilation. The basic assumption is that increased pupil size reflects positive attitudes, interest, and activation in an advertisement. The subjects view an advertisement while brightness and distance from the screen are held constant. The pupilometer has fallen from favor among many researchers because pupil dilation appears to measure some combination of arousal, mental effort, processing load, and anxiety.[18] Arousal alone is much better measured by means of the GSR.

Voice pitch analysis The study of changes in the relative vibration frequency of the human voice to measure emotion.

Voice Pitch Analysis **Voice pitch analysis** examines changes in the relative vibration frequency of the human voice to measure emotion. In voice analysis, the normal or baseline pitch of an individual's speaking voice is charted by engaging the subject in an unemotional conversation. Supposedly, the greater the deviation from the baseline, the greater is the emotional intensity of the person's reaction to a stimulus, such as a question. Voice pitch analysis has several advantages over other forms of physiological measurement:

- It records without physically connecting wires and sensors to the subject.
- The subject need not be aware of the record and analysis.
- The nonlaboratory setting overcomes the weaknesses of an artificial environment.
- It provides instantaneous evaluation of answers and comments.[19]

Voice pitch analysis has been used in package research, to predict consumer brand preference for dog food, and to determine which consumers from a target group would be most predisposed to try a new product.[20] Other research has applied voice analysis to measure consumers' emotional responses to advertising.[21] The validity of such studies have been subject to serious question.[22]

The devices just discussed are used to measure involuntary changes in an individual's physiological makeup. Arousal produces adrenaline, which enhances the activation process via a faster heart rate, increased blood flow, higher skin temperature, increased perspiration, pupil dilation, and increased brain-wave frequency. Researchers often impute information about attitudes and feelings based on these measures.

Opinion and Behavior Measurement

People Reader A machine that simultaneously records the respondent's reading material and eye reactions.

People Reader The Pretesting Company has invented a device called the **People Reader.** The machine looks like a lamp and is designed so that when respondents sit in front of it they are not aware that it is simultaneously recording both the reading material and their eyes. The self-contained unit is totally automatic and can record any respondent—with or without glasses—without the use of attachments, chin rests, helmets, or special optics. It allows respondents to read any size magazine or newspaper, and lets them spend as much time as they need to go back and forth through the publication. With the use of the People Reader and specially designed hidden cameras, the Pretesting Company has been able to document a number of pieces of information concerning both reading habits and the results of different-sized ads in terms of stopping power and brand-name recall. The company's research has found the following:

- Nearly 40 percent of all readers start from the back of a magazine or fan a magazine for interesting articles and ads. Fewer than half the readers start from the very first page of a magazine.
- Rarely does a double-page ad provide more than 15 percent additional top-of-mind awareness than a single-page ad. Usually, the benefits of a double-page spread are additional involvement and communication, not top-of-mind awareness.
- In the typical magazine, nearly 35 percent of each of the ads receives less than two seconds' worth of voluntary examination.
- The strongest involvement power recorded for ads has been three or more successive single-page ads on the right-hand side of a magazine.
- Because most ads "hide" the name of the advertisers and do not show a close-up view of the product package, brand-name confusion is greater than 50 percent on many products, such as cosmetics and clothing.
- A strong ad that is above average in stopping power and communication will work, regardless of which section in the magazine it is placed. It will also work well in any type of ad or editorial environment. However, an ad that is below average in stopping power and involvement will be seriously affected by the surrounding environment.[23]

Rapid Analysis Measurement System (RAMS) A machine that allows respondents to record how they are feeling by turning a dial.

Rapid Analysis Measurement System (RAMS)

A **Rapid Analysis Measurement System (RAMS)** is a hand-held device, about the size of a portable telephone, with a dial in the center. Respondents turn the dial to the right when they are feeling more favorable toward a subject, and vice versa. Best Western is the world's largest hotel system. Its image, however, was that of a mom and pop motel along the highway. The company was afraid that its existing "Best Places . . . Best Bet" advertising campaign was not communicating the notion that Best Western is a global chain with hotels in nice locations. So an audience was equipped with RAMS equipment and shown commercials for Holiday Inn, Ramada, and Best Western. RAMS scores were highest for Best Western commercials, resulting in the firm's keeping its "Best Places . . . Best Bet" campaign. The company estimates that it saved as much as $750,000 by staying with the old campaign instead of developing a new one.[24]

The People Meter Controversy

Several years ago, ACNielsen announced that it would use its people meter to measure the size of television audiences. The system is a microwave computerized rating system that transmits demographic information overnight to measure national TV audiences. It replaces the 30-year-old National Audience Composition (NAC) diary system used to record this information. The **people meter** provides information on what TV shows are being watched, the number of households watching, and which family members are watching. The type of activity is recorded automatically; household members merely have to indicate their presence by pressing a button.

People meter A microwave computerized rating system that transmits demographic information overnight to measure national TV audiences.

The people meter changeover has created intense controversy in the television industry. For example, in 1996 Nielsen said that 1.2 million fewer 18 to 34 year olds were watching prime time at any given minute, compared with the same time a year earlier. This translated into $100 million in lost advertising revenue for the networks.[25] The controversy became so intense that CBS, ABC, NBC, and 14 global advertising agencies decided to fund a competing system to the Nielsen people meter. The result is a methodology called SMART, created by Statistical Research Inc. (SRI). SMART's methodology differs from Nielsen's approach in a few key ways. Nielsen wires its meters directly to the tuners in the TVs and VCRs of each sample household and makes a telephone connection to gather return data. SMART's people meters have sensors that can take the signals from the air, requiring no wire connection. Existing household electrical wiring is used to transmit return data.

SMART is also designed to read the new universal television program codes (UTPCs), which are embedded in some program signals. Use of such codes is expected to grow as the broadcast industry moves to digital technology. A decoder attached to the back of the TV, along with the meter, will be able to record the UTPC, identifying the program being viewed.

A further distinction between the two systems comes when respondents log in. In the traditional Nielsen approach to the people meter, members of the household are instructed to log in when they intend to watch TV. With the SRI system, anyone who enters a room where a TV set is turned on is instructed to log in, whether they intend to watch or not.

George Hooper, SRI senior associate, says that SRI's approach is a reflection of the way people use television today. Often people find themselves in a room with the television switched to a program selected by another family member. If people are in a position to pick up information, even if they are not giving the TV their undivided attention, SRI maintains they should be counted. Nielsen counters that this methodology artificially inflates the audience size.

In 1998, Nielsen began testing a new metering system called active/passive (A/P) technology. Like SMART people meters, Nielsen's A/P meters are unintrusive, located outside each TV set with no wire connection. In the active mode, the sensors will read any codes embedded in the TV programs or commercials. Unlike SMART technology, which only identifies programming that has been coded, Nielsen's system can produce ratings even if no codes are present. If no code is sensed, the A/P meter automatically extracts audio and video samples from the unknown program and creates unique digital signatures. These signatures are downloaded to Nielsen's operations center, where they are matched to a library of signatures captured by a national network of media monitoring sites covering all 211 TV markets nationwide.[26]

Scanner-based Research

Scanners Devices that read the UPC codes on products and produce instantaneous information on sales.

Two electronic monitoring tools create the scanner-based research system: television meters and laser **scanners,** which "read" the universal product codes (UPCs) on products and produce instantaneous information on sales. Each monitoring device provides marketers with current information on the advertising audience and on sales and inventories of products. Together, television meters and scanners measure the impact of marketing. Has scanner-based research been of much benefit to marketers? The top executive of one manufacturer estimates that one-third to one-half of its gains in profitability in the past several years can be attributed to scanner-based research.[27]

The marriage of scanners, database management, telecommunications, artificial intelligence, and computing gives hope for a "brave new world" of marketing. Discussions of this potential new world are presented in the following In Practice feature.

In PRACTICE

Real-Time Marketing Is on the Way

Walker Smith, vice president of Marketing Spectrum, Atlanta, sees the marriage described in the text as leading to "real-time marketing." As the gap in time between marketplace activity and marketplace response shrinks and disappears, marketing will become a real-time activity, no longer constrained to wait for batches of data before actions can be taken. Improvements in marketing strategy and tactics will be initiated the instant any weaknesses or opportunities become apparent and, in this world, the advantage will accrue to firms with superior and more secure communications networks and to those with better ways of instantly evaluating, verifying, testing, and acting on marketplace data.

This scenario is not as far-fetched as it may seem. Already on Wall Street, real-time marketing is being implemented under the guise of program trading (an observation owed to Doug Haley of Yankelovich Clancy Shulman). In industries more dependent on physical distribution and delivery systems (as opposed to the electronic transfers possible in the financial industry), developments like just-in-time inventory are overcoming the barriers to real-time marketing.

Blair Peters, group research manager of Kraft General Foods Marketing Information Department, sees the future this way:

It does not take much imagination to weave a future scenario in which businesses base most of their decisions on robust and self-calibrating models. Such models will be robust in that the information takes into account every aspect of human behavior (e.g., purchasing, media) and product movement through the company's distribution channel (from plant, to warehouse, to store takeaway). The models will be self-calibrating because of expert systems powered by artificial intelligence. This futuristic scenario is both exciting and frightening. It is exciting in that it represents a world that every information professional has dreamed about. Most problems could be analyzed. However, the scenario is frightening in that many people will be left behind in the wake of these changes. Professionals will have to retool in terms of their mindset and technical skills or become obsolete.[28] ■

The two major scanner-based research suppliers are Information Resources, Inc. (IRI) and ACNielsen; each has about half the market. To gain an appreciation of scanner-based research, we will examine IRI in more detail.

BehaviorScan A scanner-based research system that maintains a panel of approximately 3,000 households to record consumer purchases based on manipulation of the marketing mix.

BehaviorScan

IRI is the founder of scanner-based research. Its first product, called **BehaviorScan**, consists of a household panel in each of seven markets. The BehaviorScan markets are in geographically dispersed cities: Pittsfield, Mass.; Eau Claire, Wisc.; Cedar Rapids, Iowa; Grand Junction, Colo.; Midland, Tex.; and Visalia, Calif. (see Figure 6.2).

Panel members shop with an ID card, which is presented at checkout in supermarkets, drugstores, and mass merchandisers, allowing IRI to electronically track each household's purchases, item by item, over time. With such a measure of household purchasing, it is possible to manipulate marketing variables, such as TV advertising or consumer promotions, or to introduce a new product and analyze real changes in consumer buying behavior.

For strategic tests of alternative marketing plans, the BehaviorScan household panels are split into two or more subgroups, balanced on past purchasing, demographics, and stores shopped. For advertising issues, commercials can be substituted at the individual household level, allowing one subgroup to view a test commercial, the other a control ad. This is done over the cable network without the consumer realizing that the commercial is only a test ad. This makes BehaviorScan the most effective means of evaluating

Figure 6.2

BehaviorScan Market Map

Source: Courtesy of Information Resources, Inc.

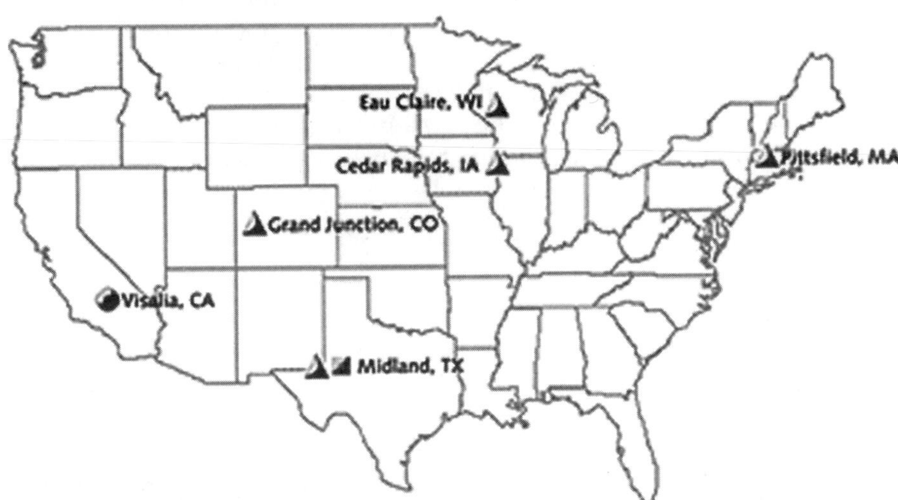

changes in advertising. In each market, IRI maintains permanent warehouse facilities and staff to control distribution, price, and promotions. Competitive activity is monitored and a record of pricing, displays, and features permits an assessment of the responsiveness to a brand promotion.

For testing consumer promotions such as coupons, sampling, or refund offers, balanced panel subsamples are created within each market. Then through direct mail or split newspaper-route targeting, a different treatment is delivered to each group. Both sales and profits are analyzed.

In-store variables may also be tested. Within the markets, split groups of stores are used to read the effect on sales of a change in packaging, shelf placement, or pricing. Tests are analyzed primarily on a store movement basis, but analysis of purchasing by panel shoppers in the test and control stores is also possible. With the BehaviorScan system, it is possible to test alternative advertising levels while simultaneously varying in-store prices or consumer promotions, thereby testing a completely integrated marketing plan.

In summary, BehaviorScan allows marketing managers to answer critical marketing questions such as

- What is the impact of our new advertising program?
- How can we minimize incremental media costs?
- What happens to sales if we change the ad frequency or daypart?
- How many units of our new product will we sell in a year?
- How many units will be cannibalized from existing products by the new product?
- What is the effectiveness of each marketing mix element in driving trial and repeat purchasing?
- What is the impact of an alternative marketing program on results?

InfoScan A scanner-based tracking service for consumer packaged goods.

InfoScan Tracking Service

InfoScan is an all-store, census scanner data system that collects data weekly from more than 31,000 supermarkets, drug stores, and mass merchandisers. Coverage is now being expanded to convenience stores and liquor stores. IRI maintains the largest multi-outlet consumer panel in America with 55,000 households (see Figure 6.3) on page 162.

The continual collection of huge amounts of scanner panel data has created a mammoth secondary database. The database can be used to examine the impact of each element of the marketing mix on sales. It can also be used to discern consumer consumption trends. For example, Joe Durrett, Chairman and CEO of IRI, discussed seven recent consumer trends that have created significant growth opportunities for astute consumer package goods marketers:

1. *Convenience and portability*—products such as bottled water, moist towelettes, and lunch kits, saw average sales increases of 98 percent since 1994.
2. *Ready-to-eat consumption*—over $4 billion of growth in categories such as frozen pizza and appetizers, refrigerated dinners, and fresh salad kits in past five years.
3. *Natural/organic foods*—an ever-growing number of products bear nutritional claims, and natural/organic products accounted for $9.4 billion in 1999.

UPCs for each grocery item are scanned at checkout. Information is sent from store to chain and on to IRI via telecommunication systems.

Household panel members present an identification card at that checkout which identifies and assigns items purchased to that household. Coupons are collected and matched to the appropriate UPC. Information is electronically communicated to IRI computers.

IRI field personnel visually surveys stores and all print media to record retailers' merchandising efforts, displays, and ad features. Field personnel also survey retail stores for a variety of custom applications (e.g., average number of units per display, space allocated to specific sections, and number of facings). Results are electronically communicated to IRI computers.

Household panel members are selected for television monitoring and equipped with meters that automatically record the set's status every five seconds. Information is relayed back to IRI's computers.

Information is received at IRI and processed through the Neural Network (Artificial Intelligence) Quality Control System. The system approves the more than 35 million records obtained weekly for further data processing and identifies records that require further verification.

Completed databases are converted to the required client format, transferred to appropriate recording mediums . . . hard copy, mag tape, PC diskette, etc. . . . and sent to the subscriber.

Figure 6.3

How InfoScan Works

Source: Courtesy of Information Resources, Inc.

4. *Functional foods*—high-protein meals, energy bars, and herbal-enhanced products grew in excess of 75 percent since 1994.
5. *Health and self-care*—nine categories, including hair growth and hair-coloring products, nutritional supplements, antacids, and antismoking products grew from $3.5 billion in 1994 to nearly $7 billion in 1999.
6. *Extra care and indulgence rewards*—sales of premium ice creams and premium-priced toothbrushes are growing rapidly; aromatherapy helped boost candle sales to $833 million.
7. *Female influence*—with 60 percent of adult females working outside the home, sales of many beauty categories are up over 55 percent; conversely, hosiery sales have declined in today's casual workplace.

InfoScan Tracking The InfoScan Tracking Service includes total outlet information used to benchmark retailer performance against other retailers in the same trading area. Figure 6.4 shows a supermarket retailer's cookie category performance in Chicago versus total supermarket sales in the Chicago market. Based on the retailer's share of the total Chicago market,

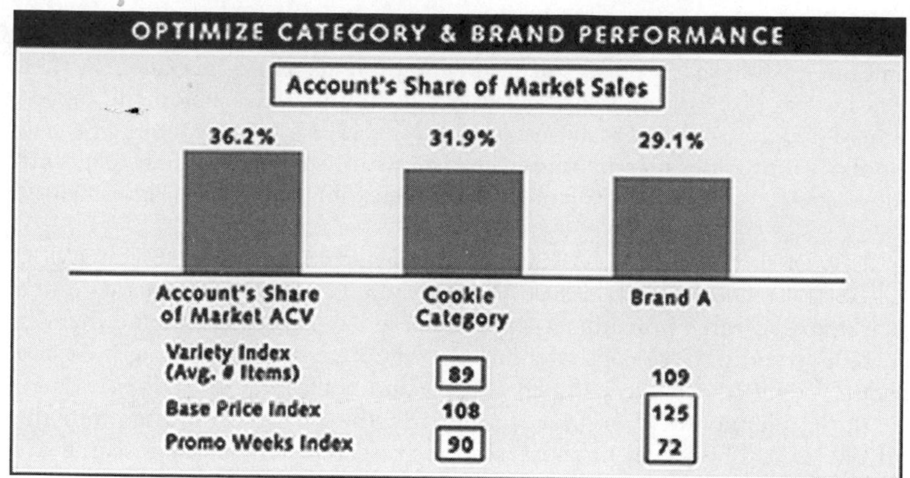

Figure 6.4

Optimizing product category and brand performance using the InfoScan Tracking Service

Source: Courtesy of Information Resources, Inc.

the account is not getting its fair share of sales for the cookie category or for Brand A. This topline analysis suggests the problems could stem from a number of factors, including low category item assortment (index of 89), higher price for Brand A (index of 125), and fewer weeks of promotion support (indices of 90 and 72).

InfoScan Reviews InfoScan Reviews® is a syndicated data service that offers a common source of retail scanner-based information for manufacturers, retailers, and brokers. The Reviews provide aggregate data on 266 InfoScan consumer package goods product categories. The data can help a researcher monitor trends across categories, products, and competitive factors. The Reviews enable one to analyze historical sales and promotion trends and identify market opportunities as well.

Shoppers' Hotline

The Shoppers' Hotline multi-outlet panel is comprised of 55,000 households. Using IRI's proprietary ScanKey in-home scanner, each member household records its purchase information on an ongoing basis. By combining this information with demographic data on each panel household, Shoppers' Hotline panel monitors consumer purchase behavior. It answers consumer questions such as who buys what, when, and why. Shoppers' Hotline panel households are also available for attitudinal surveys. Combining survey and panel data adds even more depth to consumer understanding.

IRI's Software Managers want decision-making information, not data. The key to IRI's success is not the millions of new scanner records it obtains each week, but rather the useful information derived from those records. Useful information for management is gleaned from powerful software. For example, IRI's Apollo Space Management software helps answer one of the most fundamental questions faced by manufacturers and retailers: What is the most optimal use of retail shelf space—the most valuable asset in any store?

Apollo analyzes scanner data from the InfoScan database to review the amount of shelf space, price, and profit components of product category shelf sets such as dishwashing soaps or cereals. It then provides actionable suggestions for optimizing shelf allocations for each item in the section. The new Apollo 7.0 provides merchandising realism with 3-D shelving views. The software produces color-coded planograms and custom reports (see Figure 6.5).[29]

Behavioral Research Versus Attitude Research—the Growing Chasm in Marketing Research The authors and a number of noted marketing research practitioners have observed a growing, and somewhat disturbing, trend in large consumer-packaged goods marketing research departments.[30] The controversy between attitude and behavioral research is not new in the academic world, but has surfaced in the research industry with the advent of scanner data. In short, scanner research and survey research are not just two separate sets of research tools, they are becoming two separate sets of people. The scanner researchers (behavioralists) have a strong quantitative bent and are often mathematical modelers or statisticians. They spend their time interacting with the scanner data supplier, and rarely, if ever, perform traditional survey research. The same is true in reverse for survey researchers (attitude researchers).

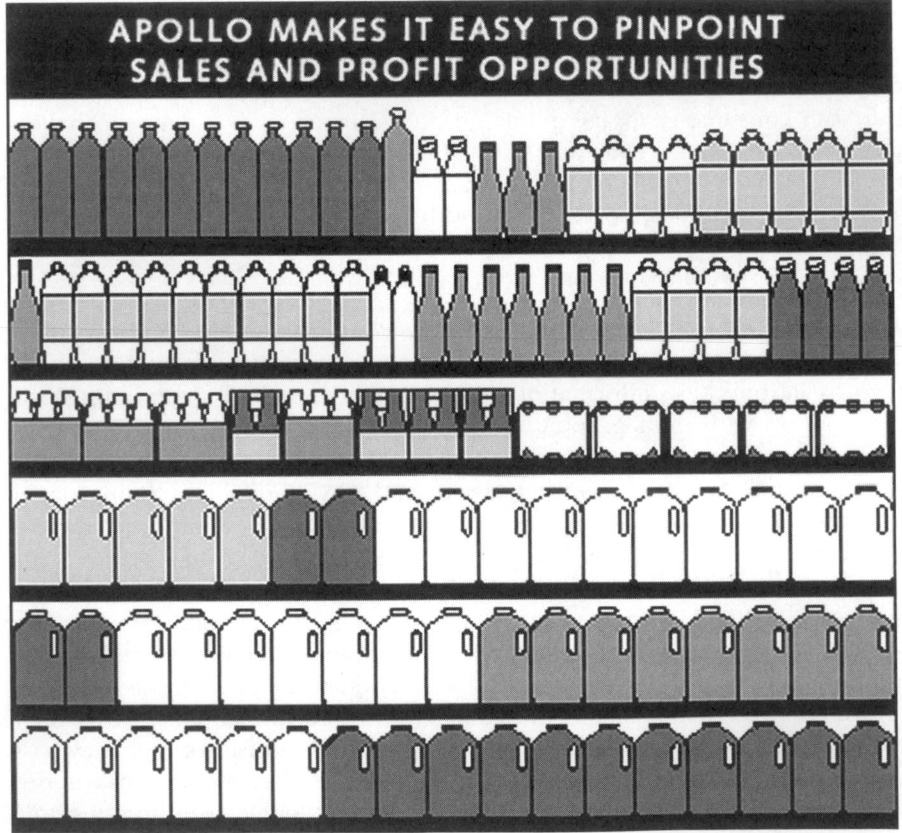

Figure 6.5

Color-coded planograms help retailers pinpoint sales and profit opportunities with optimal shelf plans

Source: Courtesy of Information Resources, Inc.

Behavioralists are interested in what consumers actually do. This can be measured by the scanner data. To the attitude researchers they point out that "just because people tell you they are going to do something does not mean they will." Also, people do not always know or are not always willing to tell an interviewer what their motivations and feelings really are. The attitude researcher replies to the behavioralist that "scanner data are so sterile. You do not know feelings, how the products are used in their homes, or attitudes toward products, brands, or leading retailers. In fact, scanner research is like driving a car down the street but sitting backward in the driver's seat looking out the rear window. Regardless of how current, the scanner data look at past behavior while you (the company) attempt to move forward."

Marketing researchers need to be marketing oriented and not in one camp or another. The goal is to provide decision-making information to management. This means both types of data are needed.

The Future of Scanning The next generation of scanners, known as Scanner Plus, will have abilities far beyond those of today's machines. These scanners will be able to communicate with personal computers in homes. One function could be to analyze an individual household's consumption based on its prior purchase patterns and offer menu projections or product-use suggestions with an associated shopping list. To encourage the use of that shopping list, special offers may be made on certain listed items. These special offers can be designed for each household rather than offering everyone the same promotion.

Scanner Plus may also keep track of each household's coupons and other special offers received directly from advertisers. These offers will simply be entered into the household's electronic account in both the household's personal computer as well as its "promotion" bank in Scanner Plus.

An example of a similar system already in use is the Vision Value card offered by Big Bear Supermarkets in Ohio. It combines scanning with the computerized equivalent of Green Stamps to provide consumers with coupons for products they actually use.

How will this new development affect marketing research? Advertisers will want to test what has previously been untestable, namely, how is a product's acceptance affected by a household's menu, or what is the optimum menu scenario for a product's particular set of attributes? Advertisers will want to test promotional values as a function of menu mix and repeat consumption, rather than use today's criteria of covering the cost of the promotion.[31]

Summary

Observation research is the systematic process of recording people's behavioral patterns without questioning or communicating with them. To be successful, the needed information must be observable and the behavior of interest must be repetitive, frequent, or predictable in some manner. The behavior under study should also be of a relatively short duration. There are five dimensions along which observational approaches vary: (1) natural versus contrived situations, (2) disguised versus undisguised situations, (3) structured versus unstructured observation, (4) human versus machine observers, and (5) direct versus indirect observation.

The biggest advantage of observation research is that we can see what people actually do rather than having to rely on what they say they did. Some forms of data are more quickly and accurately gathered by observation. The primary disadvantage of this type of research is that the researcher learns nothing about motives, attitudes, intentions, or feelings.

People watching people can take the form of mystery shoppers; one-way mirror observations, such as child psychologists watching children play with toys; studies of shopper patterns and behavior; content analysis; humanistic inquiry; and audits.

Machine observation includes traffic counters, physiological measurement devices, the People Reader, people meters, the Rapid Analysis Measurement System (RAMS), and scanners. The use of scanners in carefully controlled experimental settings enables the marketing researcher to accurately and objectively measure the direct causal relationship between different kinds of marketing efforts and actual sales. The leaders in this scanner-based research are Information Resources, Inc. and ACNielsen.

In the future, scanners will be able to communicate with personal computers in homes. One function may be to offer menu and product-use suggestions.

Key Terms & Definitions

Observation research Recording behavioral patterns without verbal communication.

Open observation The process of monitoring people who know they are being watched.

Disguised observation The process of monitoring people who do not know they are being watched.

Structured observation A study in which the observer fills out a questionnairelike form or counts the number of times an activity occurs.

Unstructured observation A study in which the observer simply makes notes on the behavior being observed.

Indirect observation Making a record of past behavior.

Mystery shoppers People employed to pose as consumers and shop at an employer's competitors or their own stores to compare prices, displays, and the like.

One-way mirror observation The practice of watching unseen from behind a one-way mirror.

Shopper patterns Drawings that record the footsteps of a shopper through a store.

Shopper behavior research A study involving observing, either in person or on videotape, shoppers or consumers in a variety of shopping settings.

Content analysis A technique used to analyze written material (usually advertising copy) by breaking it into meaningful units using carefully applied rules.

Humanistic inquiry A research method in which the researcher is immersed in the system or group under study.

Theory-construction diary A journal that documents in detail the thoughts, premises, hypotheses, and revisions in thinking of a humanistic researcher.

Methodological log A journal of detailed and time-sequenced notes on the investigative techniques used during a humanistic inquiry, with special attention to biases or distortions a given technique may have introduced.

Audits The examination and verification of the sale of a product.

Traffic counters Machines used to measure vehicular flow over a particular stretch of roadway.

Electroencephalogram (EEG) A machine that measures rhythmic fluctuations in the electrical potential of the brain.

Galvanic skin response (GSR) The measurement of changes in the electric resistance of the skin associated with activation responses.

Pupilometer A machine that measures changes in pupil dilation.

Voice pitch analysis The study of changes in the relative vibration frequency of the human voice to measure emotion.

People Reader A machine that simultaneously records the respondent's reading material and eye reactions.

Rapid Analysis Measurement System (RAMS) A machine that allows respondents to record how they are feeling by turning a dial.

People meter A microwave computerized rating system that transmits demographic information overnight to measure national TV audiences.

Scanners Devices that read the UPC codes on products and produce instantaneous information on sales.

BehaviorScan A scanner-based research system that maintains a panel of approximately 3,000 households to record consumer purchases based on manipulation of the marketing mix.

InfoScan A scanner-based tracking service for consumer packaged goods.

Questions for Review & Critical Thinking

1. You are charged with the responsibility of determining whether men are brand-conscious when shopping for racquetball equipment. Outline an observation research procedure for making that determination.
2. Fisher–Price has asked you to develop a research procedure for determining which of its prototype toys is most appealing to four and five year olds. Suggest a methodology for making this determination.
3. What are the biggest drawbacks of observation research?
4. Compare and contrast the advantages and disadvantages of observation research versus survey research.
5. It has been said that "people buy things not for what they do but for what they mean." Discuss this statement in relation to observation research.

6. You are a manufacturer of a premium brand of ice cream. You want to know more about your market share, competitors' pricing, and types of outlets where your product is selling best. What kind of observational research data would you purchase? Why?
7. How might a mystery shopper be valuable to the following organizations: Delta Airlines, Marshall Field's, H&R Block?
8. Why do you think that the research method of humanistic inquiry has caused such a controversy among social scientists? How does it differ from the traditional scientific method?
9. Why has scanner-based research been seen as "the ultimate answer"? Do you see any disadvantages of this methodology?
10. Explain the attitudinal versus behavioralist controversy in the marketing research industry. Where do you stand?

Working the Net

Go to http://www.acnielsen.com and http://www.infores.com and determine what ACNielsen and IRI are saying on the Web about their latest scanner based technology.

Real-Life Research

Mystery Shopping for Yamaha Digital Pianos

For most marketers, mystery shopping means sending consumers to a retail outlet to check on service issues like employee attitude and store appearance. But mystery shopping can be used for many other purposes, including boosting product awareness. For example, Yamaha Corporation of America, a Buena Park, California, maker of musical instruments, uses a mystery shopping program to stimulate interest in and sales of its line of Clavinova digital pianos.

When the product was introduced in 1985 it was an innovation, an electronic piano with weighted keys and digitally sampled sounds to match the feel and tone of a real piano.

As a leader in the new piano market, Yamaha saw the Clavinova line as a way to grab a share of the much larger used piano market while not competing against itself for new piano customers. The digital piano's reasonable price points make it an option for consumers who may be seeking a used piano because they think a new one is unaffordable.

"The market for new pianos is approximately 100,000 pianos a year," says Jim Lynch, assistant general manager of the Keyboard Division of Yamaha. "The used piano market is 500,000 per year. Not all of those are sold—some are passed between family members—but a lot of retail stores get customers who say they're interested in a used piano. We felt if we could get those customers to look at a Clavinova, we'd sell a lot of product, so that's how the secret shopper program started."

The gist of Yamaha's secret shopper program is simple. The shopper enters the music store and tells the salesperson that he or she would like to see a good used piano. The salesperson is free to show them a used piano—that is, after all, ostensibly why they're there—but if the first new piano they demonstrate for the customer is a Clavinova they are immediately given a check for $100 and told that they've "won."

If the salesperson doesn't show the shopper a Clavinova, the shopper is instructed to terminate the interaction quickly, without revealing his or her identity as a secret shopper. "If the salesperson doesn't win, the shopper doesn't say anything. They've taken up the salesperson's time and we don't want to have a negative impact by having them spend time on a sale that's not real," Lynch says.

In cases where salespeople don't win, one of Yamaha's 14 regional general managers will talk to them, to reinforce in a positive way that they missed an opportunity. That positive approach is key to handling store personnel who don't perform well in the mystery shop, says Hughes. "For manufacturers, talking to store management and employees is a way to say, 'Here's where you can improve the sales of our products by following these guidelines and using the sales tools that we provide you. If you follow these you probably would see a sales increase.' It's not a way of catching somebody doing something wrong, it's a way of catching somebody doing it right and promoting it."[32]

Questions

1. Is the Yahama program really mystery shopping? If not, what would have to be done to change it to a traditional program?
2. What other marketing research methods might be helpful to Yamaha in fine-tuning their marketing mix?
3. Would you say that mystery shopping is essentially a negative activity—that is, trying to catch an employee doing something wrong?
4. Look up mystery shopping on the Web. Report your general findings to the class.

CHAPTER *seven*

Primary Data Collection: Survey Research

Learning Objectives

1. *To understand the reasons for the popularity of surveys*

2. *To learn the types of error in survey research*

3. *To describe the types of surveys*

4. *To gain insight into the factors that determine the choice of particular survey methods*

5. *To realize the importance of the marketing research interviewer*

6. *To appreciate the differences between domestic and international survey research*

7. *To discover the advantages and disadvantages of Internet survey research*

As the Age of the Individual Investor rolls on, fueled by a seemingly bullet-proof economy and fears that Social Security is now a misnomer, money keeps pouring into mutual funds. To monitor their portfolios and seek out other investment vehicles, many mutual fund shareholders are turning to the Internet.

Mutual fund companies have been quick to pick up on this, adding a host of services to their websites, from on-line prospectuses to portfolio tracking. But will the mutual fund companies see a payoff from their investment in on-line information provision?

Having launched its own website, American Century Investments, a Kansas City, Missouri, mutual fund company (which includes the Twentieth Century Group, American Century Group, and Benham Group of mutual funds), conducted an Investor Internet Adoption Study. The objectives of the study were to:

- gauge mutual fund investor access to the Internet and on-line services
- understand mutual fund website usage
- identify desired mutual fund services on the Internet
- capture concerns related to Internet investment activity.

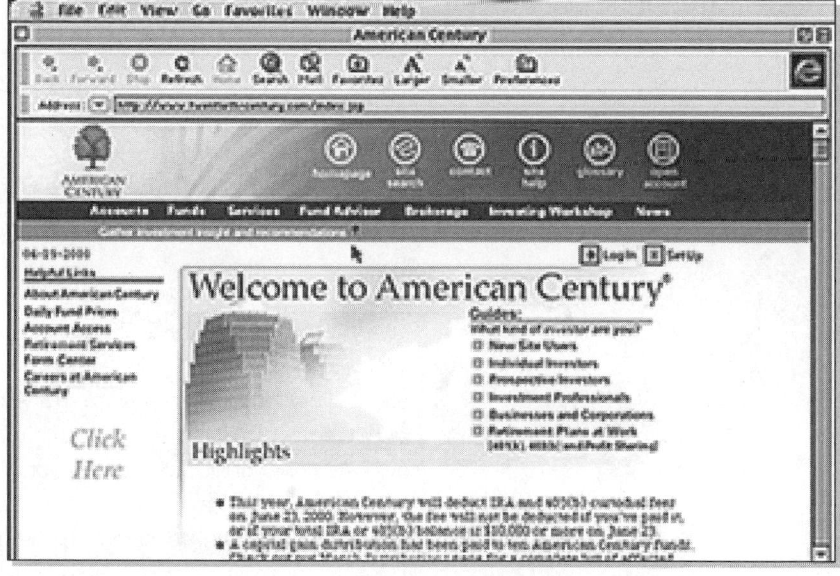

Source: Courtesy of American Century Services Corporation.

With the help of Elrick and Lavidge, an Atlanta-based research firm, American Century contacted almost 1,400 mutual fund owners by telephone to identify 250 respondents (18%) who currently access the Internet. "We wanted to get an idea of how quickly the technology was being adopted by investors," says Angela Murray, senior marketing research analyst, American Century Investments. "Beyond that, what types of things are they doing on line? Are they making transactions? Are they interested in having account access on the Internet?"

The study found that mutual fund investors are in the early stages of discovering and using mutual fund websites. The most frequently mentioned reasons for using the Internet are for research and information or e-mail. Financial services ranks fifth at 32 percent of respondents. This is comparable to the 28 percent who reported having ever visited a mutual fund website.

Find more out about the on-line services offered by American Century Investments at:

http://www.twentieth-century.com/index.jsp

Reasons for Using the Internet	
Research/Information	79%
E-mail	60%
Entertainment	45%
News	43%
Financial services	32%
Bulletin boards	28%

The research suggests that there is still a large gap between what investors can do and what they want to do on the Internet. The most common actions taken at a mutual fund website are checking fund share prices and reading/downloading prospectuses. Other website activities occur at much lower rates. In fact, 13 percent of investors who have visited a fund site have done so to check account balances, an action not readily available on many fund websites.

Only 10 to 11 percent indicated being likely to buy shares, move shares, or sell shares on line. However, the likelihood of using transaction services on the Internet is double for those who have already made some type of purchase on-line.[1]

Survey research is the use of a questionnaire to gather facts, opinions, and attitudes. It is the most popular way to gather primary data. What are the various types of survey research? The American Century survey could have been conducted on the Internet. What are some of the pros and cons of Internet surveys? As noted previously, not everyone is willing to participate in a survey. What kind of error problems does that create? What are the other types of errors encountered in survey research? These questions are answered in Chapter 7. ■

Reasons for the Popularity of Surveys

Some 126 million Americans have been interviewed at some point in their lives. Each year about 70 million people are interviewed in the United States, which is the equivalent of over 15 minutes per adult per year. Surveys have a high rate of usage in marketing research compared to other means of collecting primary data, for some very good reasons.

1. *The need to know why.* In marketing research there is generally a critical need to have some idea about why people do or do not do something. For example, why did they buy or not buy our brand? What did they like or dislike about it? Who or what influenced them? We do not mean to imply that surveys can prove causation, only that they can be used to develop some idea of the causal forces at work.

2. *The need to know how.* At the same time, the marketing researcher often finds it necessary to understand the process consumers go through before taking some action. How did they make the decision? What time period passed? What did they examine or consider? When and where was the decision made? What do they plan to do next?
3. *The need to know who.* The marketing researcher also needs to know who the person is from a demographic or lifestyle perspective. Information on age, income, occupation, marital status, stage in the family life cycle, education, and other factors is necessary to the identification and definition of market segments.

Types of Error in Survey Research

When assessing the quality of information obtained from survey research, the manager must make some determination of the accuracy of those results. This requires careful consideration of the research methodology employed in relation to the various types of error that might result. The various types of error that might be encountered in a survey are shown in Figure 7.1 on page 174.

Sampling Error

Two major types of error may be encountered in connection with the sampling process. They are random error and systematic error, sometimes referred to as *bias.*

Surveys often attempt to obtain information from a representative cross section of a target population. The goal is to make inferences about the total population based on the responses given by the respondents sampled. Even if all aspects of the sample are executed properly, the results are still subject to a certain amount of error (**random error** or **random sampling error**) because of chance variation. *Chance variation* is the difference between the sample value and the true value of the population mean. This error cannot be avoided, only reduced by increasing the sample size. It is possible to estimate the range of random error at a particular level of confidence. Random error and the procedures for estimating it are discussed in detail in Chapters 11 and 12.

Random error or random sampling error Error that results from chance variation.

Systematic Error

Systematic error or **bias** results from mistakes or problems in the research design or from flaws in the execution of the sample design. Systematic error, also called systematic bias, exists in the results of a sample if those results show a consistent tendency to vary in one direction (consistently higher or consistently lower) from the true value of the population parameter being estimated. Systematic error includes all sources of error except those introduced

Systematic error or bias Error that results from research design or execution.

by the random sampling process. Therefore, systematic errors or bias are sometimes called *nonsampling errors*. The types of nonsampling error that can systematically influence survey answers can be categorized as sample design error and measurement error. Sample design error is systematic error that results from an error in the sample design or sampling procedures, and can be biased for a number of reasons.

Frame error Error resulting from an inaccurate or incomplete sample frame.

Frame Error

The sampling frame is the list of population elements or members from which units to be sampled are selected. **Frame error** results from using an incomplete or inaccurate sampling frame. The problem is that a sample drawn from a list that includes frame error may not be a true cross section of the target population. A common example of a situation that is likely to include frame error in marketing research involves the use of a published telephone directory as a sample frame for a telephone survey. Many

Figure 7.1

Total Survey Error and Its Components

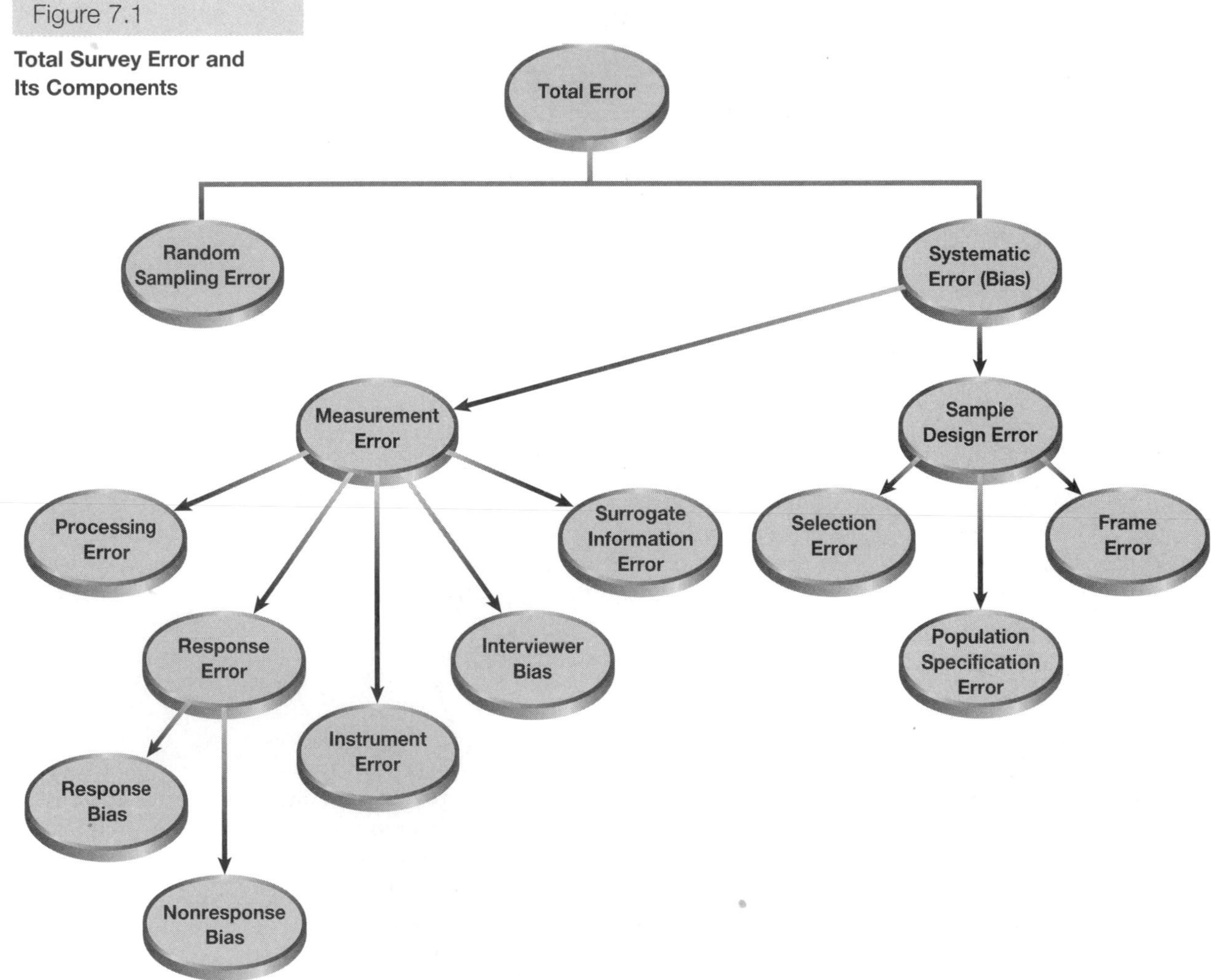

households are not listed or not listed accurately in the current telephone book because they do not want to be listed or because they have recently moved or changed their telephone number. Research has shown that those people who are listed in telephone directories are systematically different from those who are not listed in certain important ways.[2] This means that any study purporting to represent the opinions of all households in a particular area that is drawn from the current telephone directory will be subject to frame error.

Population Specification Error

Population specification error results from an incorrect definition of the population or universe from which the sample is selected. For example, we might define the population or universe for a study as people over the age of 35. It might later be determined that younger individuals should have been included and that the population should have been defined as those people 20 years of age or older. If those younger people who were excluded are significantly different in the variables of interest, then the sample results will be biased.

Population specification error Error that results from incorrectly defining the population or universe from which a sample is chosen.

Selection Error

Selection error can occur even when the analyst has a proper sample frame and has defined the population correctly. **Selection error** occurs when sampling procedures are incomplete or improper or when appropriate selection procedures are not properly followed. For example, door-to-door interviewers might decide to avoid houses that do not look neat and tidy because they think the people who live there will not be "pleasant." If people who live in houses that are not neat and tidy are systematically different from those in tidy houses, then selection error will be introduced into the results of the survey. Selection error is a serious problem in connection with nonprobability samples, a subject discussed in Chapter 11.

Selection error Error that results from following incomplete or improper sampling procedures or not following proper ones.

Measurement Error

Measurement error is often a much more serious threat to survey accuracy than random error. Frequently in the media, when the results of public opinion polls are quoted, and in professional marketing research reports, an error figure is reported (say, plus or minus 5%). The television viewer or the user of a marketing research study is left with the impression that this figure refers to total survey error. Unfortunately, this is not the case. This figure refers only to random sampling error. It does not include sample design error and speaks in no way to the measurement error that may exist in the research results. **Measurement error** occurs when there is a variation between the information being sought (true value) and the information actually obtained by the measurement process. Our main concern is with systematic measurement error. A number of types of error may be caused by various deficiencies in the measurement process.

Measurement error Error that results from a variation between the information being sought and what is actually obtained by the measurement process.

Surrogate Information Error

Surrogate information error occurs when there is a discrepancy between the information actually required to solve a problem and the information being sought by the researcher. It relates to general problems in the research design, particularly failure to properly

Surrogate information error Error that results from a discrepancy between the information needed to solve a problem and that sought by the researcher.

In PRACTICE

Americans Are Aging and This Affects Survey Research

One of the significant demographic changes in recent years has been the shift from a youth-oriented population to one oriented to people middle aged or older. Not only are more Americans living longer, but they are also living better. The 65-and-older population controls 50 percent of the discretionary income in the United States. This segment of thc market is being courted increasingly by marketers. Marketing research plays an important role in understanding the desires, lifestyles, and values of this group. However, the research methods, tasks, and techniques must be carefully adapted to accommodate the characteristics of this market.

There are numerous physiological, cognitive, and social changes that take place during the aging process, which have marketing research implications. Farsightedness and other vision changes mean larger type on printed materials, additional lighting, or perhaps the use of contrasting colors. Diminished hearing means that special adjustments must be made for telephone and personal interview[er]s to speak clearly and slowly, using interviewers with deep voices, or paying special attention to the delivery of the questions. To compensate for the diminished perception, learning, and information processing, questionnaire design should be simple and concise. Visual aids should be used when possible. Mail questionnaires may be better because respondents can control the pace. If a telephone survey is selected, it could be used in conjunction with a paper questionnaire.

Interviewer training for personal interviews and telephone surveys is important. Data collection takes longer and involves more social interaction, so interviewers must be patient and as helpful as possible without biasing the results.

Changes in data collection methods may be necessary. In particular, pretesting is extremely important. Personal interviews are less stressful for older respondents and have higher response rates but also higher costs. Because of the abuses of direct marketers, older people are more likely to refuse to participate. Mail surveys are appropriate because they rely only on vision and they allow self-pacing. However, because of low response rates it is necessary to use a precontact letter, a personalized cover letter, a self-addressed and stamped return envelope, and a reminder card. Mall intercepts have many advantages, but the special needs of older respondents must be taken into consideration. If focus groups are used, times as well as special transportation needs must be factored into the research design.[3] ■

define the problem. A classic and well-known situation that involved surrogate information error was the New Coke fiasco. Apparently the research for New Coke focused on the taste of the product and failed to consider the attitudes of consumers toward a change in the product. The resulting failure of New Coke strongly suggests, as the producers of Coke should understand, that people purchase Coke for many reasons other than taste.

Interviewer error or bias Error that results from the interviewer consciously or unconsciously influencing the respondent.

Interviewer Error **Interviewer error,** or **interviewer bias,** is due to the interaction between an interviewer and a respondent. The interviewer may, consciously or unconsciously, influence a respondent to give untrue or inaccurate answers. The interviewer's dress, age, sex, facial expressions, body language, or tone of voice may influence the answers given by some or all respondents. This type of error is caused by problems in the selection and training of interviewers or by the failure of interviewers to follow instructions. Interviewers must be properly trained and supervised to appear neutral at all times. Another type of interviewer error is when deliberate cheating takes place. This can be a particular problem in connection with door-to-door interviewing, where interviewers may be tempted to falsify interviews and get paid for work they did not actually do. The procedures developed by the researcher must include safeguards to make sure this problem will be detected (see Chapter 13).

Measurement instrument bias Error that results from the design of the questionnaire or measurement instrument.

Measurement Instrument Bias **Measurement instrument bias** results from problems with the measurement instrument or questionnaire (see Chapter 9). Examples are leading questions or elements of the questionnaire design that make recording responses difficult or prone to recording errors (see Chapter 10). Problems of this type can be avoided by careful attention to detail in the questionnaire design phase of the research and by using questionnaire pretests before field interviewing begins.

Processing error Error that results from the incorrect transfer of information from a document to the computer.

Processing Error **Processing errors** are primarily due to mistakes that occur when entering information from survey documents into the computer. For example, a data-entry operator might enter the wrong response to a particular question. Errors of this type are avoided by developing and strictly adhering to quality control procedures when processing survey results. This process is discussed in detail in Chapter 13.

Nonresponse bias Error that results from a systematic difference between those who do and do not respond to a measurement instrument.

Nonresponse Bias Ideally, if we select a sample of 400 people from a particular population, all 400 of those individuals should be interviewed. As a practical matter, this will never happen. Response rates of 5 percent or less are common in mail surveys. The question is, "Are those who did respond to the survey systematically different in some important way from those who did not respond?" Such differences are called **nonresponse bias.** The authors recently examined the results of a study conducted among customers of a large savings and loan association. The response rate to the questionnaire, included in customer monthly statements, was slightly under 1 percent. Analysis of the occupations of those who responded revealed that the percentage of retired people among respondents was 20 times higher than in the local metropolitan area. This overrepresentation of retired individuals raised serious doubts about the accuracy of the results.

Yet this experience may be the exception rather than the rule. One researcher reviewed 14 studies in which differences between respondents and nonrespondents (or earlier or later respondents) to mail surveys were reportedly found.[4] When the raw data were recalculated to address the question of whether differences between respondents and the entire sample were large enough to be meaningful, the less complete returns were found to closely approximate the more complete returns. Of all the studies that have looked for such differences, none has been reported that found meaningful, practical differences between respondents and the entire sample or between early respondents and respondents as a whole.

Obviously, the higher the response rate, the less the possible impact of nonresponse, because nonrespondents then represent a smaller subset of the overall picture. If the decrease in bias associated with improved response rates is trivial, then allocating resources to obtain higher response rates might be wasteful in studies in which resources could be used for better purposes.

Thomas Danbury, chairman of Survey Sampling, reports that his firm conducted one study in which 65,000 telephone interviews were completed. Interviewers made up to seven attempts over a four-week period to reach each household and then up to seven more to interview a randomly selected adult. At the end of the project, the researchers looked at what they would have found if only one attempt had been made, or two, all the way to seven. Danbury noted, "To our surprise, the results would have been very similar had we made no callbacks at all!"[5] Table 7.1 shows the incidence of several demographic characteristics measured by one attempt versus seven attempts. Despite these findings, Danbury still recommends three callback attempts.

Nonresponse error occurs when

- a person cannot be reached at a particular time
- a potential respondent is reached but cannot or will not participate at that time (for example, receiving a telephone request to participate in a survey just as the family sits down to dinner)
- a person is reached but refuses to participate in the survey. This is the most serious problem because it may be possible to achieve future participation in the first two circumstances.

Today the refusal rate is at its highest rate ever, running at close to 40 percent. Fortunately, most people do not refuse all of the time. In fact, 84 percent of those who refused to participate in at least one study did participate in another study or studies. The three main reasons people first refused to participate were

inconvenience	64%
uninteresting subject matter	22%
fear of a sales pitch	13%[6]

Other research on refusal rates suggests that the type of survey may influence whether individuals participate. For example, consumers had a more

Table 7.1

Differences in Demographic Characteristics Based on One Callback Attempt Versus Seven in a Survey of 65,000 Adults

Demographic Characteristic	One Call	Seven Calls
Income $50,000+	45%	47%
Some college +	47%	49%
Employed full time	76%	78%
Married	65%	63%
Unlisted number	35%	37%
1- to 2-person household	52%	52%
Rent home	29%	30%
Moved in 5 years	48%	50%
Male	45%	46%

Source: Courtesy Survey Sampling, Inc. © Copyright 1999 Survey Sampling, Inc.

favorable attitude toward participating in door-to-door surveys or mall interviews than other types of surveys.[7]

Response bias Error that results from the tendency of people to answer a question incorrectly, through deliberate misrepresentation or unconscious falsification.

Response Bias If there is a tendency for people to answer a particular question in a certain way, then there is **response bias.** Response bias can occur in two basic forms: deliberate falsification or unconscious misrepresentation. Deliberate falsification occurs when people purposefully give untrue answers to questions. There are many reasons why people might knowingly misrepresent information in a survey. They may wish to appear intelligent, not reveal information they feel is embarrassing, or conceal information that they consider to be personal. For example, in a survey about fast-food behavior, the respondents may have a fairly good idea of how many times they visited a fast-food restaurant in the past month. However, they may not remember which fast-food restaurants they visited or how many times they visited each restaurant. Rather than answering "Don't know" in response to the question regarding which restaurants they visited, the respondents may simply guess.

Unconscious misrepresentation occurs when the respondent is legitimately trying to be truthful and accurate, but gives an inaccurate response. This type of bias may occur because of question format, question content, or various other reasons. Types of error and strategies for minimizing them are summarized in Table 7.2 on page 180.

Table 7.2

Types of Error and Strategies for Minimizing Error

Random error can only be reduced by increasing sample size.

Systematic error can only be reduced by minimizing sample design and measurement errors.

Sample Design Errors	
Frame error	This error can be minimized by getting the best frame possible and doing preliminary quality control checks to evaluate the accuracy and completeness of the frame.
Population specification error	This error results from flaws in research design (for example, incorrect defining the population of interest). It can be reduced or minimized only by means of more careful consideration and definition of the population of interest.
Selection error	This error results from the use of incomplete or improper sampling procedures or when appropriate procedures are not followed. It can occur even when there is a good sample frame and an appropriate specification of the population. It is minimized by developing selection procedures that ensure randomness by developing quality control checks to make sure that these procedures are being followed in the field.
Measurement Errors	
Surrogate information error	This error results from seeking and basing decisions on the wrong information (as in the New Coke example cited in the text). It results from poor design and can be minimized only by paying more careful attention to specifying the types of information required to fulfill the objectives of the research.
Interviewer error	This error occurs due to interaction between interviewer and respondent that affect the responses given. It is minimized by careful interviewer selection and training. In addition, quality control checks should be employed that involve unobtrusively monitoring interviewers to ascertain whether prescribed behavior is being adhered to.
Measurement instrument bias	Also referred to as *questionnaire bias,* this error is minimized only by careful questionnaire design and pretesting.
Nonresponse bias	This error results from the fact that people chosen for the sample who actually respond are systematically different from those who are chosen and do not respond. It is particularly serious in connection with mail surveys. It is minimized by doing everything possible (shortening the questionnaire, making the questionnaire more respondent-friendly, callbacks, incentives, contacting people when they are most likely to be at home, etc.) to encourage those chosen for the sample to respond.
Response bias	Response bias occurs when something about a question leads people to answer it in a particular way. This type of error can be minimized by paying special attention to the questionnaire design. In particular, the researcher should avoid questions that are hard to answer, might make respondents appear uninformed if they cannot answer, or deal with sensitive issues. Questions should be modified to deal with these problems (see Chapter 10).
Processing error	This error can occur during the process of transferring data from the questionnaires to the computer. It is minimized by developing and following rigid procedures for transferring data and supporting quality control checks.

Types of Surveys

Asking people questions is the essence of the survey approach. But what type of survey is "best" for a given situation? The survey alternatives discussed in this chapter are summarized in Table 7.3. Emerging approaches are summarized in Table 7.4 on page 182.

Table 7.3

Different Survey Approaches Commonly Used in Marketing Research

Type of Interview	Description
Door-to-door interviews	Interviewer completes survey in respondent's home.
Executive interviews	Interview industrial product user (e.g., engineer, architect, doctor, executive) or decision maker at place of business regarding industrial product.
Mall-intercept interviews	Interviewer interviews consumer in shopping mall or other high-traffic location. Interviews may be done in public areas of the mall or the respondent may be taken to a private test area.
Central-location telephone interviews	Interviewing is conducted from a telephone facility set up for that purpose. These facilities typically have equipment that permits the supervisor to unobtrusively monitor the interviewing while it is taking place. Many of these facilities do national sampling from a single location. An increasing number have computer-assisted interviewing capabilities. At these locations the interviewer sits in front of a computer terminal attached to a mainframe or a personal computer. The questionnaire is programmed into the computer. The interviewer enters responses directly.
Self-administered questionnaires	Most frequently employed at high-traffic locations such as shopping malls or in captive audience situations such as classrooms and airplanes. Respondents are given general information on how to fill out the questionnaire and are left to fill it out on their own. Computers are being used in this area by sending software-driven questionnaires on diskettes to individuals who have personal computers.
Ad hoc (one-shot) mail surveys	Questionnaires are mailed to a sample of consumers or industrial users. Instructions are included. Respondents are asked to fill out the questionnaire and return it via mail. Sometimes a gift or monetary incentive is provided. The same comment regarding computers under self-administered questionnaires applies here.
Mail panels	Several companies, including Market Facts, NPD Research, and National Family Opinion Research operate large (more than 100,000 households) consumer panels. There are several important differences between mail panels and ad hoc mail surveys. First, people in the panel have been precontacted. The panel concept has been explained to them. They have agreed to participate for some period of time. In addition, participants are offered gratuities to participate in mail panels. Mail panels typically generate much higher response rates than ad hoc mail surveys.

Door-to-Door Interviewing

Door-to-door interviews
Interviews conducted face-to-face with consumers in their homes.

Door-to-door interviewing, where consumers are interviewed in person in their homes, was at one time thought of as the best survey method. This conclusion was based on a number of factors. First, the door-to-door interview is a personal, face-to-face interview with all the attendant advantages—feedback from the respondent, the ability to explain complicated tasks, the ability to use special questionnaire techniques that require visual contact to speed up the interview or improve data quality, the ability to show the respondent product concepts and other stimuli for evaluation, and so on. Second, the participant is at ease in a familiar, comfortable, secure environment.

Table 7.4

Emerging Survey Approaches

Approach	Description and Comments
Point-of-service touch screen	Kiosks equipped with touch-screen monitors provide a new way to capture information from individuals in stores, health clinics, and other shopping or service environments. This approach is currently being used on a limited basis, and little is known definitively about its advantages and disadvantages.[8]
Fax	This technique has emerged as a viable way to collect data from business firms in recent years. It has many of the same features of mail surveys. The major advantage is the speed with which information can be obtained in that the time required to get the survey in the hands of target respondents and to get it back from them is greatly reduced. There is some evidence that response rates are higher than with mail surveys of comparable length.[9]
Internet	This type of survey is the fastest-growing form of survey research. As the number of individuals connected to the Internet increases, this approach will become increasingly attractive.
E-mail	There are a few reported instances of surveys being done via e-mail. Texas Instruments has used this approach for a number of employees. Current technology limits the types and complexity of information that can be obtained.
Voice mail	Sophisticated IVR (interactive voice response) systems make it possible to complete automated surveys over the telephone. Respondents dial local or 800 numbers and respond to voice prompts (multiple-choice questions) by using the buttons on their touch-tone telephones. This approach has not been widely used. However, it has been successfully used with physicians and some other difficult-to-reach populations. Respondents can call when it is convenient for them, 24 hours per day, 365 days per year.
Computer disk by mail	The computer disk-by-mail survey medium basically has all the advantages and disadvantages of a typical mail survey. An additional advantage is that a disk survey can incorporate skip patterns into the survey. For example, a question might ask "Do you own a cat?" If the answer is no, then all questions related to cat ownership are skipped automatically. A disk survey can also use respondent-generated words in questions throughout the survey. Also, a disk survey can easily display a variety of graphics and directly relate them to questions. Finally, a disk survey eliminates the need to encode data from paper surveys. The primary disadvantage is that respondents must have access to and be willing to use a computer.[10]

This approach to interviewing has a number of drawbacks that explain its virtual disappearance. Jerry Rosenkranz, chairman of Data Development, a large New York-based custom research firm, lists the disadvantages of door-to-door interviewing:

- The growth of the two-adult working family and other changes in family composition mean less availability of potential respondents.
- Although response rates for in-home interviews were historically higher than for other approaches, they are gradually deteriorating.
- Unsafe (high-crime) areas, distance, and lack of accessibility sometimes negate reaching the desired sample.
- The drop in qualified interviewing personnel, whether because of a drop in education or the increase in other options with better pay, has become a factor over time.
- The special characteristics required of a field interviewer, that is, the "chutzpah to make a cold call," limit the potential pool of interviews.
- The client and field service's unease due to the lack of "hands-on" control of a field force that is out there somewhere (in direct comparison to a permanent workforce in a centralized location under supervision—clocking in 9 to 5).
- The lack of communication between the home office, the field office, and the interviewing staff (except at the end of day) is a serious handicap if one wishes to execute questionnaire changes, examine incidence rate, or hasten data retrieval.
- The effects of such old bugaboos as weather (too good or too bad), car problems, broken-in [to] cars, sickness, etc.
- Cheating, fudging, or shortcutting by the interviewers, interviewing the wrong respondent, etc., promote low levels of validation. This postfield check may be too late to permit us to replace the necessary data. In any case, it is very costly to go back for it.[11]

The door-to-door approach to survey data collection is not likely to disappear from the marketing research scene; it is still the only viable data collection alternative in a number of situations. On the other hand, it is also unlikely that this type of interviewing will ever regain the prominence it once enjoyed. Less than 10 percent of all interviews today are personal interviews.

Mall-Intercept Interviewing

Mall-intercept interviewing is a popular survey method consisting of around one-third of all personal interviews. This survey approach is relatively simple. Shoppers are intercepted in the public areas of shopping malls and either interviewed on the spot or asked to come to a permanent interviewing facility in the mall. Approximately 500 malls throughout the country have permanent survey facilities operated by marketing research firms. An equal or greater number of malls permit marketing researchers to interview on a daily basis. Many malls do not permit marketing research interviewing because they view it as an unnecessary nuisance to shoppers.

Mall-intercept interviews
Interviews conducted in public areas of malls by intercepting shoppers and interviewing them face to face.

Mall interviewing is of relatively recent origin. The earliest permanent facilities date back to less than 30 years ago; the greatest growth in the use of this technique occurred in the 1970s. The mall-intercept interview is a low-cost substitute for the door-to-door interview. In fact, this approach has probably grown primarily at the expense of door-to-door interviewing.

Mall surveys are less expensive than door-to-door interviews because respondents come to the interviewer rather than the other way around. Interviewers spend more of their time actually interviewing and less of their time hunting for someone to interview. Also, mall interviewers do not have the substantial travel time and mileage expenses associated with door-to-door interviewing. In addition to low cost, mall interviews have many of the advantages associated with door-to-door interviews in that respondents can be shown various stimuli for their reactions and special questionnaire techniques can be used.

However, a number of serious disadvantages are associated with mall interviewing. First, it is virtually impossible to get a sample representative of a large metropolitan area from shoppers at a particular mall. Even though malls may be large, most of them draw shoppers from a relatively small local area. In addition, malls tend to attract certain types of people based on the stores they contain. Studies also show that some people shop more frequently and therefore have a greater chance of being selected than others. Finally, many people refuse mall interviews. One study found that over half of those approached refused to cooperate, either on initial contact or after they had been qualified for an interview.[12] By *qualified* we mean that responses to screening questions indicate that an individual falls into a group in which the researcher is interested. In summary, mall interviewing cannot produce a good or representative sample except in the rare case in which the population of interest is coincident with or is a subset of the population who shops at a particular mall.

Second, the mall environment is not the comfortable home environment associated with the door-to-door interview. Respondents may be ill at ease, in a hurry, or preoccupied by various distractions outside the researcher's control. These factors may adversely affect the quality of the data obtained. Even with all its problems, the popularity of mall-intercept interviews has held steady in recent years.[13]

Executive Interviewing

Executive interviews The industrial equivalent of door-to-door interviewing.

Executive interviewing is used by marketing researchers as the industrial equivalent of door-to-door interviewing. This type of survey involves interviewing business people at their offices concerning industrial products or services. For example, if Hewlett–Packard wanted information about user preferences for different features that might be offered in a new line of computer printers, it would need to interview prospective user-purchasers of the printers. It would thus be appropriate to locate and interview these people at their offices.

This type of interviewing is expensive. First, individuals involved in the purchasing decision for the product in question must be identified and located. Sometimes lists can be obtained from various sources, but more frequently screening must be conducted over the telephone. A particular company may indeed have individuals of the type being sought, but locating them within a large organization can be expensive and time-consuming. Once a qualified person is located, the next step is to get that person to agree to be interviewed and to set a time for the interview. This is not usually as hard as it might seem, because most professionals seem to enjoy talking about topics related to their work.

Finally, an interviewer must go to the particular place at the appointed time. Long waits are frequent; cancellations are common. This type of survey requires the very best interviewers because they are frequently interviewing on topics they know little about. Executive interviewing has essentially the same advantages and disadvantages as door-to-door interviewing.

Telephone Interviewing

Until 1990 telephone surveys were the most popular form of survey. The advantages of telephone interviewing are compelling. First, the telephone is a relatively inexpensive way to collect survey data. The major reason is that interviewer travel time and mileage are eliminated. A second advantage of the telephone interview is that it has the potential to produce a high-quality sample. If proper sampling and callback procedures are employed, the telephone approach probably produces a better sample than any other survey procedure.[14] Random-digit sampling or random-digit dialing is a frequently used sampling approach (see Chapter 11). The basic idea is simple: Instead of drawing the sample from the phone book or other directory, telephone numbers are generated via a random-number procedure. This approach ensures that people with unlisted numbers and those who have moved or otherwise changed their telephone numbers since the last published phone book are included in the sample in correct proportion.

The telephone survey approach has several inherent disadvantages. First, in the typical telephone interview of today, respondents cannot be shown anything. This shortcoming ordinarily eliminates the telephone survey as an alternative in situations that require respondents to comment on visual product concepts, advertisements, and the like.

Some critics have suggested that the telephone interview does not permit interviewers to make various judgments and evaluations that can be made by in-home interviewers—such as those concerning respondent income, based on the home lived in and other outward signs of economic status. Granted, interviewers do not have these cues in a telephone situation, but in reality, marketing research interviewers are almost never called upon to make such judgments. The reasons are spelled out in the section at the end of this chapter on marketing research interviewers.

A third disadvantage of the telephone interview is that it is more limited in the quantity and types of information that can be obtained than the door-to-door interview. Some evidence suggests that telephone interviews should be shorter than door-to-door interviews. Respondent patience wears thin more easily over the phone, and it is certainly easier to hang up the phone than throw an interviewer out of the living room. The telephone is also a poor vehicle for conducting a depth interview or a long interview with many open-ended questions.

A fourth disadvantage of telephone interviewing is the increased use of screening devices, such as Caller ID, and screening via answering machines.

Approximately 40 million U.S. households are equipped with telephone answering machines, and more than half of them screen their calls at least some of the time. Call screening increases the nonresponse rate. Nonresponse rates are continuing to rise for telephone interviewing primarily because of telemarketing. A major survey found that 86 percent of respondents would be more likely to participate in a telephone survey if they knew the call was to conduct a legitimate telephone survey rather than to sell them something.[15]

Central-Location Telephone Interviewing

Central-location telephone interviews Interviews conducted by calls to respondents from a centrally located marketing research facility.

Central-location telephone interviewing is conducted from a facility set up for that purpose. Nearly all telephone interviews are conducted in this type of environment today.

The reasons for the prominence of central-location phone interviews are fairly straightforward. In a single word, the main reason is control. First, the interviewing process can be monitored; most central-location telephone interviewing facilities have unobtrusive monitoring equipment that permits supervisors to listen in on interviews as they are being conducted. Interviewers who are not doing the interview properly can be corrected and those who are incapable of conducting a proper interview can be eliminated. One supervisor can monitor from 10 to 20 interviewers. Ordinarily each interviewer is monitored at least once per shift. Second, completed interviews are edited on the spot as a further quality control check. Interviewers can be immediately informed of any deficiencies in their work. Finally, there is control over the hours that interviewers work. Interviewers report in and out and work regular hours.

Most national studies are conducted from a single facility. Without this capability, a study requiring, for example, 150 telephone interviews in Dallas, 150 in Washington, D.C., and 150 in Sacramento, California, would require the use of a field service firm in each of the three cities to conduct the interviewing. Sample data from such a study are shown in Table 7.5. The researcher analyzing the data must decide whether differences in results for the three cities represent real differences or differences in the way the survey was administered in the three cities. If the interviewing had been conducted from a single facility, there would be no question. The analyst could feel relatively certain that consumers in Sacramento and Washington really liked the product better than did consumers in Dallas.

Computer-Assisted Telephone Interviewing (CATI)

Computer-assisted telephone interviews (CATI) Central-location telephone interviews in which interviewers enter answers directly into a computer.

Most research firms have computerized the central-location telephone interviewing process. In **computer-assisted telephone interviewing (CATI),** each interviewer is seated in front of a computer terminal or a personal computer. When a qualified respondent gets on the line, the interviewer starts the interview by pressing a key or series of keys on the keyboard. The questions and multiple-choice answers appear on the screen one at a time. The interviewer reads the question and enters the response, and the computer skips ahead to the appropriate next question. For example, the interviewer might ask

Table 7.5

Data from a Three-City Product Concept Test

	Total	Dallas	Sacramento	Washington
Total	151 (100%)	50 (100%)	51 (100%)	50 (100%)
Will definitely purchase	39 (26%)	11 (22%)	15 (29%)	13 (26%)
Will probably purchase	40 (26%)	8 (16%)	15 (29%)	177 (34%)
Is uncertain about purchase	37 (25%)	13 (26%)	9 (18%)	15 (30%)
Will probably not purchase	19 (13%)	10 (20%)	5 (10%)	4 (8%)
Will definitely not purchase	16 (11%)	8 (16%)	7 (14%)	1 (8%)

Note: All percentages are computed with the column total as the base.

whether a person has a dog. If the answer is "Yes," there might be a series of questions regarding what type of dog food the person buys. If the answer is "No," those questions would be inappropriate. The computer takes into account the answer to the dog ownership question and skips ahead to the next appropriate question.

In addition, the computer can help customize questionnaires. For example, in the early part of a long interview, a respondent is asked the years, makes, and models of all the cars he or she owns. Later in the interview, questions might be asked about each specific car owned. The question might come up on the interviewer's screen as follows: "You said you own a 1997 GMC truck. Which family member drives this vehicle most often?" Other questions about this vehicle and others owned would appear in similar fashion. Questions like this can be handled in a traditional pencil-and-paper interview, but they are handled much more efficiently in the computerized version.

This approach eliminates the need for separate editing and data-entry steps. There is no editing because there are no questionnaires. More to the point, in most computer systems it is not possible to enter an "impossible" answer. For example, if a question has three possible answers with the codes A, B, and C, and the interviewer enters D, the computer will not accept it. It will ask that the answer be reentered. If a combination or pattern of answers is impossible, the computer will not accept the answer, and so on. Keying in completed questionnaires is eliminated because data are entered into the computer as interviews are completed.

Another advantage of computer interviewing is that computer tabulations can be run at any point in the study—after 200 people have been interviewed, after 400, or after any number. This luxury is not available with the pencil-and-paper interview. With the traditional interview, there may be a wait of a week or more after completing all interviews before detailed tabulations of the results are available. Instantaneous results available with computer-assisted telephone interviewing systems provide some real advantages. Based on preliminary tabulations, certain questions might be dropped, saving time and money in subsequent interviewing. If, for example, 98.3 percent of those interviewed answer a particular question in the same manner, there is probably no need to continue asking the question. Tabulations may also suggest the need to add questions to the survey. If an unexpected pattern of product use is uncovered in the early stages of interviewing, questions can be added that delve further into this behavior. Finally, management may find the early reporting of survey results useful in preliminary planning and strategy development.

Self-Administered Interviewing

Self-administered questionnaires Questionnaires filled out by respondents with no interviewer present.

The self-administered and mail survey methods discussed in this section have one thing in common: They differ from the other survey methods discussed in that no interviewer—human or computer—is involved. The major disadvantage of the **self-administered questionnaire** approach is that no one is present to explain things to the respondents and clarify responses to open-end questions. For example, if someone was asked via an open-ended question why he or she does not buy a particular brand of soft drink, a typical answer would be something like "Because I don't like it." From a managerial perspective this answer is useless. It provides no information that can be used to alter the marketing mix and thereby make the product more attractive. If the survey was being conducted by an interviewer, however, he or she would "probe" for a response. This would mean that, after receiving and recording the useless response, the interviewer would ask the respondent what it was he or she did not like about the product. The interviewee might then indicate a dislike for the taste. The interviewer would then ask what it was about the taste that the person did not like. Here the interviewer might finally get something useful, with the respondent indicating that the product in question was, for example, too sweet. If many people gave a similar response, management might elect to reduce the sweetness of the drink. The point is that without probing, there would only the useless first response.

Some have argued that the absence of an interviewer is an advantage in that it eliminates one source of bias. There is no interviewer whose appearance, dress, manner of speaking, failure to follow instructions, and so on may influence respondents' answers to questions.

Self-administered interviews are often used in malls or other central locations where the researcher has access to a captive audience. Airlines, for example, often have programs in which questionnaires are administered during the flight. Passengers are asked to rate various aspects of the airline's services and the results are used to track passenger perceptions of service over time. Many hotels, restaurants, and other service businesses provide brief questionnaires to patrons to find out how they feel about the quality of service provided.

A recent development in the area of direct computer interviewing is kiosk-based computer interviewing. Kiosks are developed with multimedia, touch-screen computers contained in freestanding cabinets. These computers can be programmed to administer complex surveys, show full-color scanned images (products, store layouts), and play sound and video clips. The kiosks have been used successfully at trade shows and conventions, and are now being tried in retail environments where they have many applications. From a research standpoint, kiosk-based interviewing can be used in place of exit interviews to capture data on recent experiences. This form of interviewing tends to be less expensive. Kiosks have other definite advantages: People tend to give more honest answers than they would to a human interviewer, and internal control is higher because the survey is preprogrammed.

Mail Surveys

Two general types of mail surveys are used in marketing research: ad hoc mail surveys and mail panels. In **ad hoc,** or one-shot, **mail surveys,** the researcher selects a sample of names and addresses from an appropriate source and mails questionnaires to the people selected. Ordinarily there is no prior contact, and the sample is used only for a single project. However, the same questionnaire may be sent to nonrespondents several times to increase the overall response rate. In contrast, **mail panels** operate in the following manner:

Ad hoc mail surveys Questionnaires for a particular project sent to selected names and addresses with no prior contact by the researcher.

Mail panels Precontacted and screened participants who are periodically sent questionnaires.

1. A sample of people is precontacted by letter. In this initial contact the purpose of participating in the panel is explained. People are usually offered a gratuity for participating in a panel for a period of time.
2. As part of the initial contact, consumers are asked to fill out a background data questionnaire on the number of family members, ages, education, income, types of pets, types of vehicles and ages, types of appliances, and so forth.
3. After the initial contact, panel participants are sent questionnaires from time to time. The background data collected on initial contact enable researchers to send questionnaires only to appropriate households. For example, a survey about dog food usage and preferences would be sent only to dog owners.

A mail panel is a type of longitudinal study. A **longitudinal study** is one that questions the same respondents at different points in time.

Longitudinal study Study in which the same respondents are resampled over time.

On first consideration, mail appears to be an attractive way to collect survey data. There are no interviewers to recruit, train, monitor, and pay. The entire study can be sent out and administered from a single location. Hard-to-reach respondents can be readily surveyed. Mail surveys appear to be convenient, efficient, and inexpensive.

Mail surveys of both types encounter the same problems associated with not having an interviewer present, which were discussed in the section on self-administered questionnaires. As with self-administered surveys, no one is there to assist respondents. In particular, no one is there to probe responses to open-ended questions, a real constraint on the types of information that can be sought. Usually the number of questions and consequently the quantity of obtainable information is more limited in mail surveys than in surveys involving interviewers.

The ad hoc mail survey suffers from a high rate of nonresponse and the attendant systematic error. Nonresponse in mail surveys is not a problem as long as everyone has an equal probability of not responding. However, numerous studies have shown that certain types of people—people with more education, high-level occupations, women, those less interested in the topic, students, and others—have a greater probability of not responding.[16] Other types of people—in general the opposite of those just named—have a greater probability of responding. Response rates in ad hoc mail surveys may run anywhere from less than 5 percent to more than 50 percent, depending on the length of the questionnaire, content, the group surveyed, the incentives employed, and other factors.[17] Those who operate mail panels claim response rates in the vicinity of 70 percent.

To deal with the problem of low response rates to mail surveys, many strategies designed to enhance response rate have been developed. Some of the more common ones are summarized in Table 7.6. The question must always be, "Is the cost of the particular strategy worth the increased response rate generated?" Unfortunately, there is no clear answer to this question that can be applied to all procedures in all situations.

Even with its shortcomings, mail remains a popular survey data collection technique in commercial marketing research. In fact, more people participate in mail surveys than in any other type of survey research.

Table 7.6

Tactics Employed to Increase Mail Survey Response Rates

- advance postcard or telephone call alerting respondent of survey
- follow-up postcard or phone call
- monetary incentives (nickel, dime, quarter, half-dollar)
- premiums (pencil, pen, keychain, etc.)
- postage stamps rather than metered envelopes
- self-addressed, stamped return envelope
- personalized address and well-written cover letter
- promise of contribution to favorite charity
- entry into drawings for prizes
- emotional appeals
- affiliation with universities or research institutions
- personally signed cover letter
- multiple mailings of the questionnaire
- bids for sympathy
- reminder that respondent participated in previous studies.

Internet Surveys

Developments in mid to late 1999 have signaled the fact that Internet interviewing is moving into the mainstream. Gordon Black, chairman of Harris Black International, has noted that "all research is going to migrate to the Internet." He believes that Internet interviewing will all but eliminate telephone polling in the future. Though many researchers still condemn Web surveys as flawed, the movement toward the Internet appears to be inevitable. A long list of leading marketing research firms are currently testing various approaches to Internet surveys. The results of these endeavors will begin to appear in 2000. Currently, Harris Black has a database of 3 million Internet users. By agreeing to take part in periodic Harris poll on-line surveys, subjects are offered the chance to win various prizes and cash awards. For each survey, the company sends e-mail to target individuals inviting them to visit the Harris poll website and answer questions. Target individuals are given unique passwords to ensure that they respond to the survey one time only. The company hopes to have 5 million potential respondents in its database by the end of 2000.[18]

Tools for Implementing Internet Surveys

Large research organizations have their own internal proprietary tools for implementing Internet surveys, from data collection through tabulation and analysis. Fortunately for smaller organizations, a number of emerging Web software companies are offering complete solutions for Web survey implementation and execution. One of these organization is WebSurveyor. The offering can be found at http://www.websurveyor.com. WebSurveyor offers a complete solution that you can test from its site with a free five-day trial account. This system permits a researcher to create a new survey, enter questions (a library of questions is also available), arrange questions, preview the survey and make final edits, publish the survey, analyze the results, and even generate a report that you can output to your printer or to a series of html pages for Web publication. The emergence of these integrated Web surveying tools will permit even the smallest organizations to participate in the growth of Web interviewing.

Advantages of Internet Surveys

The popularity of Internet surveys surged in the late 1990s. There are several reasons for this trend. First is the speed with which a questionnaire can be created, distributed to respondents, and the data returned. Because printing, mailing, and data-entry delays are eliminated, you can have data in hand within hours of writing a questionnaire. Data are obtained in electronic form, so statistical analysis software can be programmed to process standard questionnaires and return statistical summaries and charts automatically.

A second reason to consider Internet surveys is cost. Printing, mailing, data-entry, and interviewer costs are eliminated, and the incremental costs of each respondent are typically low, so studies with large numbers of respondents can be done at substantial savings compared to mail or telephone surveys.

Another reason is that, with the creation of respondent panels on the Internet, the researcher can create longitudinal studies by tracking attitudes, behavior, and perceptions over time. Sophisticated panel-tracking software can tailor follow-up questions in the next survey, based on responses from a previous survey. Also, missing answers can be filled in.

A fourth reason is that it typically is not worthwhile to conduct a phone survey to ask two or three questions. But on the Internet, a survey component can unobtrusively be included within a general site that is used for marketing or business transactions. For example, people who accesses a banking

In PRACTICE

Nickelodeon Goes On Line to Gather Data

How to find out what kids are thinking? This was the problem facing Karen Flischel, Nickelodeon's vice president of research. The programmers and marketers at the cable television network for kids wanted information from their young viewers that traditionally had been gathered via time-consuming focus groups and one-on-one interviews. It was the advent of e-mail that gave Flischel the idea to put kids on line.

Nickelodeon put 70 viewers on line via CompuServe. The kids use personal computers and modems to talk with Nickelodeon and with one another about a variety of topics. They can post notes on the computer bulletin board, and three times a week they log on for scheduled meetings. During these meetings, network researchers lead discussion on various topics. Specific network programs are discussed about a third of the time.

The kids who participate are, of course, CompuServe users. They range in age from 8 to 12 and represent households with incomes ranging from $30,000 to $100,000. Half are minorities. The estimated annual maintenance for the system is $80,000 to $100,000, a fraction of what traditional research methods would cost.

Nickelodeon now gets more detailed data faster and cheaper than it could through traditional research methods. The kids provide instant feedback on programs. Other data come from responses to survey questions.

There are some who view this approach with skepticism and point out that it may be biased in favor of garrulous kids. Flischel points out that this system is a qualitative tool, and, as with any other qualitative research, the results cannot be projected to the national level.[19] ■

home page and then go to the Credit Card link, can be asked a few questions about the features of a credit card they find most important before moving along to the information component.

Yet another benefit of using the Internet for research is the ability to reach large numbers of people. It is hard to imagine another medium that can provide so much potential while remaining so economically feasible. The Internet is an international arena in which many barriers to communication have been erased. The Graphics, Visualization and Usability Center (GVU) and the Georgia Institute of Technology, which reportedly conduct "the oldest and largest public service Web-based surveys" (http://www.cc.gatech.edu/gvu/user_surveys), are currently experimenting with surveys in French, German, Spanish, and Japanese.

And last, Internet questionnaires delivered via the Web have some other unique advantages. They can be made visually pleasing with attractive fonts and graphics. The graphical and hypertext features of the Web can be used to present products for reaction or to explain service offerings. For respondents with current versions of Netscape or Internet Explorer, the two most popular Web browsers, audio and video can be added to the questionnaire. This multimedia ability of Web-delivered questionnaires is unique.[20]

There are some populations, such as computer products purchasers and users of Internet services, that are ideal for Internet surveys. Business and professional users of Internet services are also an excellent population to reach with Internet surveys. More businesses than ever before have Internet connections, and that number will only continue to increase through the 21st century.

Disadvantages of Internet Surveys

Despite the advantages of Internet surveys, there are still many drawbacks. Perhaps the largest problem is that Internet users do not represent the population as a whole. However, this is changing rapidly with almost 45 percent of the population using the Internet at home, work, school, or other locations. The CommerceNet/Nielsen Internet Demographics Study (http://www.nielsenmedia.com) is a World Wide Web survey done in conjunction with a phone survey to assess the bias inherent in Web data. As the discrepancy between the two survey formats decreases, the Web can become more of a mass market vehicle. This may be quite a few years away, but in this age of rapid change and widespread adoption of new technologies, many are betting on it happening sooner rather than later.[21]

A second problem is security on the Internet. Users today are quite understandably worried about privacy issues. This fear has been fueled by sensational media accounts of "cyberstalkers" and con artists who prey on Internet users. A solution to the security issue already exists in the form of **SSL (secure socket layer) technology.** Most responsible organizations collecting sensitive information over the Internet use this technology. The major problem is that consumers do not understand that this type of 128-bit encryption provides an extremely high level of security for all their sensitive information. It is up to the industry to communicate this fact to potential users.

SSL (secure socket layer) technology A computer encryption system that secures sensitive information.

Unrestricted Internet sample A survey set up on the Internet and accessible to anyone who desires to complete it.

A third problem is when an **unrestricted Internet sample** is set up on the Internet. This means anyone who wishes to complete the questionnaire can do so. It is fully self-selecting and probably representative of no one except Web surfers. The problem gets worse if the same Internet user can access the questionnaire over and over. For example, *InfoWorld,* a computer user magazine, decided to conduct its 1997 Readers Choice survey for the first time on the Internet. The results were so skewed by repeat voting for one product that the entire survey was publicly abandoned and the editor asked for readers' help to avoid the problem again.[22] All responsible organizations conducting surveys over the Internet easily guard against this problem by providing unique passwords to those individuals they invite to participate. These passwords permit one-time access to the survey.

Internet Samples

Screened Internet sample A survey set up on the Internet that restricts respondents by imposing quotas based on some desired sample characteristics.

Internet samples are classified as unrestricted, screened, or recruited.[23] We discussed unrestricted samples above. **Screened Internet samples** adjust for the unrepresentativeness of the self-selected respondents by imposing quotas based on some desired sample characteristics. These are often demographic characteristics, such as gender, income, and geographic region; or product-related criteria, such as past purchase behavior, job responsibilities, or current product use. The applications for screened samples are generally similar to those for unrestricted samples.

Screened sample questionnaires typically use a branching or skip pattern for asking screening questions to determine whether or not the full questionnaire should be presented to respondents. Some Web survey systems can make immediate market segment calculations that assign a respondent to a particular segment based on screening questions, then select the appropriate questionnaire to match the respondent's segment.

Alternatively, some Internet research providers maintain a "panel house" that recruits respondents who fill out a preliminary classification questionnaire. This information is used to classify respondents into demographic segments. Clients specify the desired segments, and the respondents who match the desired demographics are permitted to fill out the questionnaires of all clients who specify that segment.

Recruited Internet sample A controlled survey set up on the Internet that is used for target populations.

Recruited Internet samples are used for target populations in surveys that require more control over the makeup of the sample. Respondents are recruited by telephone, mail, e-mail, or in person. After qualification, they are sent the questionnaire by e-mail or are directed to a website that contains a link to the questionnaire. At websites, passwords are normally used to restrict access to the questionnaire only to recruited sample members. Since the makeup of the sample is known, completions can be monitored and, to improve the participation rate, follow-up messages can be sent to those who have not completed the questionnaire.

Recruited samples are ideal in applications that already have a database from which to recruit the sample. For example, a good application would be a survey that used a customer database to recruit respondents for a purchaser satisfaction study.

Determining the Choice of Particular Survey Methods

A number of factors may affect the choice of a survey method in a given situation.[24] The researcher should choose the survey method that will provide data of the desired types, quality, and quantity at the lowest cost. The major considerations in the selection of a survey method are summarized in Table 7.7 and discussed here.

Table 7.7

Factors that Determine the Selection of a Particular Survey Method

Factor	Comment
Sampling precision	How accurate do the study results need to be? If the need for accuracy is not great, less rigorous and less expensive sampling procedures may be appropriate.
Budget available	How much money is available for the interviewing portion of the study?
Need to expose respondent to various stimuli	Taste tests, product concept and prototype tests, ad tests and the like, require face-to-face contact, etc.
Quality of data required	How accurate do the results of the study need to be?
Length of questionnaire	Long questionnaires are difficult to do by mail, over the phone, in a mall, etc.
Necessity of having respondent perform certain specialized tasks	Card sorts, certain visual scaling methods, and the like, require face-to-face contact.
Incidence rate	Are you looking for people who make up 1 percent of the total population or 50 percent of the population? If you are looking for a needle in a haystack, you need an inexpensive way to find it.
Degree of structure of questionnaire	Highly unstructured questionnaires may require data collection by the door-to-door approach.
Time available to complete survey	Might not be able to use mail because you do not have time to wait for response.

Sampling Precision Required

The required level of sampling precision is an important factor in determining which survey method is appropriate in a given situation. Some projects by their very nature require a high level of sampling accuracy, whereas in others this may not be a critical consideration. If sampling accuracy were the only criterion, the appropriate data collection technique would probably be central-location telephone interviewing. The appropriate survey method for a project not requiring a high level of sampling accuracy might be the mail approach.

The trade-off between these two methods in regard to sampling precision is one of cost versus accuracy. The central-location telephone survey method employing a random-digit dialing sampling procedure will probably produce a better sample than the mail survey method. However, the mail survey will most likely cost less.

Mall surveys, as noted earlier, often produce poor samples. Other methods, such as door-to-door interviewing, have the potential to produce good samples if the interviewing process is carefully monitored and controlled.

Budget Available

The commercial marketing researcher frequently encounters situations in which the budget available for a study has a strong influence on the survey method used. Actually, budget is usually not the only impact on the choice of a survey method, but rather budget in combination with other considerations. For example, assume that for a particular study the budgetary constraint for interviewing is $10,000 and the sample size required for the necessary accuracy is 1,000. If we estimate that administering the questionnaire on a door-to-door basis would be $27.50 per interview and the cost of administering it via central-location telephone interview would be $9.50 per interview, the choice is fairly clear. This assumes that nothing about the survey would absolutely require face-to-face contact.

Need to Expose Respondents to Various Stimuli

In many studies the marketing researcher needs to get respondent reactions to various marketing stimuli–product concepts, product components, and advertisements. In most cases the need to get respondent reactions to stimuli implies personal contact between interviewer and respondent.

Non-face-to-face interviewing methods are generally out of the question for studies of this type. There are exceptions to this general rule that highlight the creativity of some researchers. Belden and Associates of Dallas developed a procedure built around sending respondents an envelope inside an envelope. The outer envelope contained an explanation of the study and a request that the inner envelope not be opened until the respondent was called on the phone by an interviewer. Researchers wanted to control respondent access to the stimuli so that they could get top-of-mind responses and be sure that all respondents had spent an equal amount of time examining the materials. When people who received envelopes were called on the telephone, they were asked to open the inner envelope, and the interviewer recorded their reactions to the stimuli (product concepts, ads, etc.).

The options are more limited for taste tests, TV ad tests, and other similar types of tests. Taste tests typically require food preparation. This preparation must be done under controlled conditions so that the researcher can be certain that each person interviewed is responding to the same stimulus. The only viable survey alternative for tests of this type is the mall-intercept approach or some variant. One variant, for example, is recruiting people to come to properly equipped central locations such as church community centers to sample products and be interviewed. For similar reasons, much TV ad testing is done via mall intercept. TV ad testing depends on the use of videotaped prototypes of commercials. The equipment needed to show these tapes is expensive and not readily portable. Interviewing, therefore, must be conducted at malls and other central locations where the equipment can be set up.

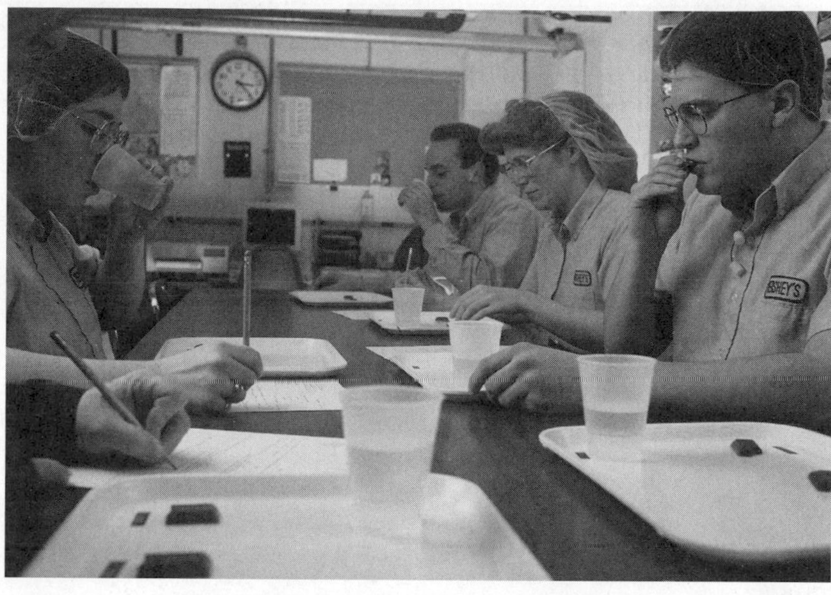

There are few alternatives to focus groups when researchers want to conduct taste tests. Do you think a mall-intercept survey would work for Hershey's? Go to http://www.hersheys.com to see if they do internet surveys.

Quality of Data Required

The quality of data required is an important determinant of which survey method to use. Data quality refers to the validity and reliability of the resulting data. These two concepts are discussed in detail in Chapter 9. Validity refers to the degree to which a measure reflects the characteristic of interest. In other words, a valid measure provides an accurate reading of the thing the researcher is trying to measure. Reliability refers to the consistency with which a measure produces the same results with the same or comparable populations.

Many factors other than the interviewing method affect data quality. Sampling methods, questionnaire design, specific scaling methods, and interviewer training are a few of them. However, the various interviewing methods each have certain inherent strengths and weaknesses for producing quality data. These strengths and weaknesses are summarized in Table 7.8 on page 198.

The point is that the issue of data quality may override other considerations such as cost. For example, the researcher might estimate that it would be less expensive to conduct a long questionnaire with many open-ended questions via mall intercept. However, the data obtained by conducting

Table 7.8

Strengths and Weaknesses of Various Data Collection Techniques in Terms of Quality of Data Produced

Method	Strength	Weakness
Door-to-door interview	Respondent is at ease and secure in home; face-to-face contact; interviewer can observe respondent's home, etc.; interviewer can show, explain, probe, etc.	Cannot readily monitor interviewing process; may have distractions from other family members, telephone, etc.; greater chance for interviewer bias; sampling problems.
Mall-intercept interview	Interviewer can show, explain, probe, as in door-to-door method.	May have many distractions inherent in mall environment; respondent may be in a hurry, not in proper frame of mind; more chance for interviewer bias; nonprobability sampling problems.
Central-location telephone interview	Can monitor the interviewing process readily; can have excellent sample; interviewer can explain and probe.	Respondent may be distracted by things going on at the location; problems in long interviews and interviews with many open-ended questions.
Self-administered questionnaire	Elimination of interviewer and associated biases; respondent can complete the questionnaire when convenient; respondent also can look up certain information and work at own pace.	No interviewer to show, explain, or probe; poor sample because of nonresponse; no control of who actually completes the questionnaire.
Mail questionnaire	Same as for self-administered method.	Same as for self-administered questionnaire; sample quality is better with mall panel.
Internet questionnaire	Inexpensive to administer; respondent can be shown stimuli, data can be quickly gathered.	Population skewed toward young, educated, above-average income males; if site not secured respondent can answer questionnaire multiple times; unrestricted sample is a simple convenience sample.

the study by this method might be so biased, due to respondent fatigue, distraction, carelessness, and so on, that it would be worthless at best and misleading at worst. From a quality-of-information perspective, the study should be conducted door to door.

Length of Questionnaire

The length of the questionnaire—the amount of time that it takes the average respondent to complete the survey—is an important determinant of the appropriate survey method to use. If the questionnaire for a particular study takes an hour to complete, the choices of survey method are extremely limited. Telephone, mall intercept, and just about all other types of surveys except door-to-door interviews will not work. People shopping at a mall ordinarily do not have an hour to spend being interviewed. Terminations increase

Levi's Uses CATI to Interview Children

Survey research methods are becoming more creative, making them more adaptable to companies' specific needs. After tracking fashion trends in the youth market for a period of time, the Youthwear Division of Levi Strauss & Company found that the interview was becoming more comprehensive and time consuming. The problem was how to administer a 30- to 45-minute interview and still maintain the accuracy and integrity of the data as well as the attention and involvement of the boys who were ages 9 to 14. Additionally, the company wanted to do the interviews in mall facilities across the country.

In conjunction with Touchstone Research, Brandon, Connecticut, and Analytical Computer Software (ACS), Levi Strauss designed a system involving an interviewer and a child. The interview format had a segment in which an interviewer entered data and a segment in which the children interacted with the computer. The system also included a videotape with explanations and instructions. Colors, sounds, and practice questions were included in the system to make it "kid friendly." There were also brief entertainment sections to give the boys a break during the questioning.

The computer-assisted interviewing was successful for several reasons. The boys seemed to be more comfortable interacting with the computer and were, therefore, more open and honest about their feelings. When interviews are done in several different markets, there is a risk that the differences in the quality of interviewing at the different locations will affect the accuracy of the data. The computer-assisted system provided continuity across markets.

The system simplified the interviewing process for the interviewers as well. A handbook was developed, which made the system relatively fail-safe for the interviewers. The software greatly reduced the number of tasks and the amount of paperwork interviewers had to handle.

This new technology is certainly not appropriate for all research situations, but it does have many applications. In particular, it seems to have many benefits in children's research, especially in tracking situations, concept testing, and similar situations where complex information must be presented to the respondent and the measurements will be repeated.[25] ■

In PRACTICE

Learn more about survey research in the international market by checking out the Internet appendix to this chapter at http://mcdaniel.swcollege.com

Source: Levi's® logo courtesy of Levi Strauss & Company

and tempers flare when trying to keep respondents on the phone for an hour. Response rates plummet when people receive through the mail questionnaires that take an hour or more to complete. The trick is to match the survey technique to the length of the questionnaire.

Necessity of Having Respondents Perform Certain Specialized Tasks

Some surveys require face-to-face interviewing because of the use of special measurement techniques or the need to obtain specialized forms of information. The tasks are so complex that the interviewer must be available to explain the task and to ascertain whether the respondents understand what is required of them.

Incidence Rate

Incidence rate Percentage of people or households in the general population that fit the qualifications to be sampled.

Incidence rate refers to the percentage of people or households out of the general population that fit the qualifications for interviewees in a particular study. For example, assume that you are doing a taste test for a new stovetop stuffing mix. It has been decided that only those who have purchased a stovetop stuffing mix in the last 30 days should be interviewed. It is estimated that out of the general population, only 5 percent of all adults fall into this category. The incidence rate for this study is 5 percent. In marketing research it is typical to seek people with a 5 percent or lower incidence rate.

Search costs, which represent the time spent trying to locate qualified respondents, frequently exceed the costs of the time spent actually interviewing. In situations where the researcher expects incidence rates to be low and search costs high, it is important that an interviewing method or combination of methods be employed that will provide the desired survey results at a reasonable cost.

Doing a low-incidence rate study on a door-to-door basis would be very expensive. This approach should be taken only if there is some compelling reason for doing so—a long depth interview, for example. The lowest-cost survey alternative for the low-incidence study is probably the mail panel, assuming that this approach meets the other data collection requirements of the study. This is particularly true if the panel can be prescreened—asked a number of questions, usually including some on product usage, when the panel is set up. For example, if panel members had been asked if anyone in their household participated in downhill or Alpine snow skiing, the mail panel operator could pull out only those households with one or more skiers for a survey of Alpine skiers at very low cost.

Telephone interviewing offers the next most efficient device to screen for low-incidence consumers. Sometimes two or more survey methods may be combined to deal more efficiently with the problem of locating them. For example, a researcher might screen for people who meet the study qualifications over the telephone and then send someone out to interview them in person. This approach can dramatically reduce costs in comparison to doing the study totally on a door-to-door basis.

Degree of Structure of the Questionnaire

In addition to the length of the questionnaire, the degree of structure required in the questionnaire may be a factor in determining which survey method is most appropriate for a given study. By *structure* we mean the extent to which the questionnaire follows a set sequence or order, follows a set wording of questions, and relies primarily on closed-end (multiple-choice) questions. A questionnaire that does all these things would be structured; one that deviates from these set patterns would be considered unstructured. A questionnaire with little structure is likely to require a face-to-face interview. Very brief, highly structured questionnaires do not ordinarily require face-to-face contact between interviewer and respondent. For studies of this type, mail, telephone, and self-administered questionnaires become viable options.

The Marketing Research Interviewer

No discussion of survey research in marketing can be considered complete without at least taking a look at the person who actually does the interviewing. As noted in Chapter 3, most marketing research interviewing is done under the direct supervision of field service firms. The actual interviewing is conducted, to a large extent, by individuals who work part-time for relatively low wages. The brand new, totally inexperienced interviewer works at a rate somewhere between minimum wage and minimum wage plus 20 percent. It is unusual to find even the most experienced interviewers earning more than minimum wage plus 50 percent. The pay is not good, and fringe benefits are usually nonexistent—no retirement benefits, no insurance, no extras.

Prospective interviewers are ordinarily sent on assignment with only a minimum of training. There is a high failure rate among first-time interviewers. It is strictly a "survival-of-the-fittest" system. Somehow, this system produces a core of competent and dedicated interviewers. Questionnaires should be designed with the presumption that the capabilities of those who will administer them are limited. In general, the interviewer is treated as an automaton—ask questions exactly as written, record exactly what the respondent said, and so on. In general, questionnaires and interviewer instructions are set up with this principle in mind. Little or no discretion is left to the interviewer. The sample interviewer instructions and questionnaire shown in Chapter 10 illustrate these points.

Ordinarily, an interviewer's involvement with an interviewing assignment begins when he or she is asked to work on a particular job by a supervisor at a field service firm. If the interviewer accepts the assignment, he or she will be given a date and time for a briefing or training session about the job. At the briefing, the questionnaire for the study and all deadlines and requirements for the job are discussed. Interviewers may be asked to bring in their first day's work (if interviewing is being conducted off the premises) to make sure there have been no misunderstandings and that everything is being done correctly. Ultimately, all interviews are checked, and a certain percentage, usually 10 to 20 percent, of the people interviewed by each interviewer are recontacted to make certain they were actually interviewed before the completed questionnaires are sent to the client.

It would appear, given the above discussion, that interviewers do not play a major role in the marketing research process. However, interviewers are typically the main interface with consumers and are, therefore, a vital link to consumer cooperation. This is an area of concern now being addressed by the Marketing Research Association. They suggest several steps that should be used to develop and strengthen interviewers' consumer interaction skills: good training programs that include consumer rapport elements and a basic understanding of "cooperation turning points," frequent monitoring of interviewers' interaction skills to evaluate their impact on consumer cooperation, and feedback on monitoring results.[26]

The importance of interviewers has been echoed by industry leaders. According to Howard Gershowitz, senior vice-president of MKTG, "Companies that are succeeding right now realize that the interviewers are the key to their success."[27]

Summary

Surveys are popular for several reasons. First, managers need to know why people do or do not do something. Second, managers need to know how decisions are made. Third, managers need to know what kind of person, from a demographic or lifestyle perspective, is making the decision to buy or not buy a product.

There are two major categories of error in survey research: random sampling error and systematic error or bias. Systematic error can be further broken down into measurement error and sample design error. Sample design error is composed of frame, population specification, and selection error. Frame error results from the use of an incomplete or inaccurate sampling frame. Population specification error results from an incorrect definition of the universe or population from which the sample is to be selected. Selection error results from using incomplete or improper sampling procedures or from not properly following appropriate selection procedures.

The second major category of systematic error is measurement error. Measurement error occurs when there is a discrepancy between the information being sought (the true value) and the information obtained by the measurement process. Measurement error can be created by a number of factors, including surrogate information error, interviewer error, measurement instrument bias, processing error, nonresponse bias, or response bias. Surrogate information error results from a discrepancy between the information actually required to solve a problem and the information sought by the researcher. Interviewer error occurs because of interactions between the interviewer and the respondents. Measurement instrument bias is caused by problems within the questionnaire. Processing error results from mistakes in the transfer of information from survey documents to the computer. Nonresponse bias occurs when a particular individual in a sample cannot be reached or refuses to participate in the survey. Response bias means that interviewees answer questions in a particular way. It may be deliberate falsification or unconscious misrepresentation.

There are several types of surveys. Mall-intercept interviewing is contacting shoppers in public areas of shopping malls, then either interviewing them in the mall or asking them to come to a permanent interviewing facility within the mall. Executive interviewing is the industrial equivalent of door-to-door interviewing; it involves interviewing professional people at their offices, typically concerning industrial products or services. Central-location telephone interviewing is interviewing from a facility set up for the specific purpose of conducting telephone survey research. Computer-assisted telephone interviewing (CATI) is associated with the central-location interviewing process. Each interviewer is seated in front of a computer terminal or personal computer. The computer guides the interviewer and the interviewing process by delivering the appropriate questions on the computer screen. The data are entered into the computer as the interview takes place. A self-administered interview is a survey questionnaire filled out by the respondent. The big disadvantage of this approach is that probes cannot be used to clarify responses. Mail surveys can be divided into ad hoc, or one-shot, surveys and mail panels. In ad hoc mail surveys, questionnaires are mailed to potential respondents without prior contact. The sample is used only for s single survey project. In a mail panel, consumers are precontacted by letter and are offered an incentive for participating in the panel for a period of time. If they agree, they fill out a background data questionnaire. Then periodically panel participants are sent questionnaires. Today, Internet surveys are beginning to move into the mainstream. They offer many of the same advantages and disadvantages as mail surveys.

The factors that determine which survey method will be used include sampling precision, budget availability, the need to expose respondents to various stimuli, the quality of data required, the length of the questionnaire, the necessity of having respondents perform certain specialized tasks, the incident rate sought, the degree of structure of the questionnaire, and the time available to complete the survey.

The key individual in survey research is the marketing research interviewer. For the most part, interviewing is conducted by individuals who work part-time for relatively low wages. The job not only is low paying, but also is devoid of fringe benefits. Interviewers are often provided only minimal training. Also, because of the high failure rate, it is a survival-of-the-fittest system. Yet, somehow this system tends to produce a core of competent and dedicated interviewers.

International survey research faces many of the same problems and opportunities as domestic research. In addition, international research faces cultural differences that may lower the participation rate and language and comprehension problems. In spite of these barriers, the cost of conducting international survey research is usually less than the benefits.

Key Terms & Definitions

Random error or random sampling error Error that results from chance variation.

Systematic error or bias Error that results from research design or execution.

Frame error Error resulting from an inaccurate or incomplete sample frame.

Population specification error Error that results from incorrectly defining the population or universe from which a sample is chosen.

Selection error Error that results from following incomplete or improper sampling procedures or not following proper ones.

Measurement error Error that results from a variation between the information being sought and what is actually obtained by the measurement process.

Surrogate information error Error that results from a discrepancy between the information needed to solve a problem and that sought by the researcher.

Interviewer error or bias Error that results from the interviewer consciously or unconsciously influencing the respondent.

Measurement instrument bias Error that results from the design of the questionnaire or measurement instrument.

Processing error Error that results from the incorrect transfer of information from a document to the computer.

Nonresponse bias Error that results from a systematic difference between those who do and do not respond to a measurement instrument.

Response bias Error that results from the tendency of people to answer a question incorrectly, through deliberate misrepresentation or unconscious falsification.

Door-to-door interviews Interviews conducted face-to-face with consumers in their homes.

Mall-intercept interviews Interviews conducted in public areas of malls by intercepting shoppers and interviewing them face to face.

Executive interviews The industrial equivalent of door-to-door interviewing.

Central-location telephone interviews Interviews conducted by calls to respondents from a centrally located marketing research facility.

Computer-assisted telephone interviews (CATI) Central-location telephone interviews in which interviewers enter answers directly into a computer.

Self-administered questionnaires Questionnaires filled out by respondents with no interviewer present.

Ad hoc mail surveys Questionnaires for a particular project sent to selected names and addresses with no prior contact by the researcher.

Mail panels Precontacted and screened participants who are periodically sent questionnaires.

Longitudinal study Study in which the same respondents are resampled over time.

SSL (secure socket layer) technology A computer encryption system that secures sensitive information.

Unrestricted Internet sample A survey set up on the Internet and accessible to anyone who desires to complete it.

Screened Internet sample A survey set up on the Internet that restricts respondents by imposing quotas based on some desired sample characteristics.

Recruited Internet sample A controlled survey set up on the Internet that is used for target populations.

Incidence rate Percentage of people or households in the general population that fit the qualifications to be sampled.

Questions for Review & Critical Thinking

1. The owner of a hardware store in Eureka, California, is interested in determining the demographic characteristics of people who shop at his store versus competing stores. He also wants to know what his image is relative to competing hardware stores. He would like to have the information within three weeks and is working on a limited budget. Which survey method would you recommend? Why?
2. Your supervisor has asked you to recommend which type of telephone interviewing your company should purchase from a survey research organization. Which would you recommend? Why?
3. The critical function within the survey research process is performed by the interviewer. Yet interviewers are typically paid a low wage. If interviewers are so important, why is this true? What do you think should be done to raise the quality of survey research?
4. "A mall-intercept interview is representative only of people who shop in that particular mall. Therefore, only surveys that relate to shopping patterns of consumers within that mall should be conducted in a mall-intercept interview." Discuss.
5. A colleague is arguing that the best way to conduct a study of attitudes toward city government in your community is through a mail survey because it is cheapest. How would you respond to your colleague? If time were not a critical factor in your decision, would this change your response? Why?
6. Discuss the various sources of sample design error and give examples of each.
7. Why is it important to consider measurement error in survey research? Why is this typically not discussed in professional market research reports?
8. What types of error might be associated with the following situations?
   a. Conducting a survey about attitudes toward city government, using the telephone directory as a sample frame.
   b. Interviewing respondents only between 8:00 A.M. and 5:00 P.M. on features they would like to see in a new condominium development.

c. Asking people if they have visited the public library in the past two months.
d. Asking people how many tubes of toothpaste they used in the past year.
e. Telling interviewers they can probe using any particular example they wish to make up.

9. What are the advantages and disadvantages of conducting surveys on the Internet?
10. Explain the three types of Internet samples and discuss why a researcher might choose one over the other.

Working the Net

1. Go to http://www.websurveyor.com/home_intro.asp and explain how the company's software lets you distribute questionnaires over the Internet.
2. Go to http://www.acop.com and tell the class about the site and what type of Internet sample is being drawn. Also, describe the types of surveys being taken.
3. Go to http://www.autonomy.com/company/index.html and explain what type of marketing research resources are offered at the site.
4. Participate in a survey at one of the following URLs and report your experience to the class:

   Personality test:
   http://www.users.interport.net/~zang/personality.html

   Emotional intelligence test:
   http://www.utne.com/azEQ.tmpl

   Values and Lifestyles (VALS) test:
   http://future.sri.com/vals/valsindex.shtml

   Various on-line surveys on topics such as politics and consumer trends:
   http://www.survey.net

   Prudential Securities Investment Personality Quiz:
   http://www.prusec.com/financial_concerns/quiz.htm

   Various surveys:
   http://www.dssresearch.com/mainsite/surveys.htm

5. Go to http://ukweb.quantime.co.uk/son/Tour0.html and explain how this organization can help a company conduct Internet surveys.

Real-Life Research

Yahoo!'s Audience Analysis Research

Yahoo! Inc. is an Internet media company that offers a network of globally branded properties, specialized programming, and aggregated content distributed primarily on the Web, serving business professionals and consumers. As the first on-line navigational guide to the Web, http://www.yahoo.com is the single largest guide in terms of traffic, advertising and household reach, and is one of the most recognized brands associated with the Internet.

For Yahoo! the Web was an obvious means of surveying customers. As an electronic medium, the company was already in a position to supply exact traffic figures to companies advertising with it. But as a sales-driven business model, its ideal was to empower its advertisers with more accurate statistics as to who is visiting Yahoo!'s sites, and provide detailed profiles of the individuals who actually make up its audience.

Yahoo!'s European sites welcomed 70 advertisers during the first quarter of 1997, and Yahoo! Inc. recently announced that IBM Corporation, one of the top three Web advertisers, has selected the Yahoo! Network to launch the world's first global multilingual Internet advertising program. Other major European advertisers with Yahoo! include British Airways, Opal, Nescafé, Peugeot, and Karstadt.

Yahoo! commissioned the U.K.-based marketing research company Continental Research to do an analysis of users of Yahoo! sites in Germany, France, and the United Kingdom. Continental, in turn, partnered with Quantime Corporation, a New York-based provider of survey research software and support services. Continental and Quantime developed a two-stage research program. Stage One provided data on business and consumer users visiting Yahoo! France, Germany, and United States and to measure motivation for usage and point of primary Internet access. It was essential to Yahoo! that the survey and any direct correspondence was carried out in the respondent's own language.

Stage One: Collecting the Data

The first of the Yahoo! surveys consisted of 10 questions that probed respondents about their media preferences, education, age, and expenditure patterns. Our major design objective in developing the Web software used in the Yahoo! survey was to maintain compatibility with the existing CATI package, Quancept. Since the same scripting language is used, the Web surveys can now have exactly the same logic as CATI surveys. Complex routing and randomization procedures can be built into the text, ensuring the data collected is consistent. Furthermore, the answers to previous questions can be used in the text of subsequent questions—customizing the survey for each respondent and encouraging their cooperation.

Around 10 percent of respondents who started the questionnaire failed to complete all the questions. There could be any number of reasons for this (boredom, connection problems, impatience), but since the cost of these lost interviews was close to nothing, it made little difference. In Stage Two, Continental requested that the respondent[s] sign in with their e-mail name, and were then able to offer the possibility of restarting the uncompleted survey at a later time, picking up neatly where respondents left off. The result of this is that despite the Stage Two questionnaire being substantially longer, the dropoff rate fell to around 5 to 6 percent. This was somewhat assisted by the exhortation to complete contained in a personalized e-mail and the opportunity to win one of five hand-held electronic organizers.

In line with other studies of Web usage, 80 percent of the respondents were male but, surprisingly, around 60 percent were employed and over 35 percent were between 25 and 35 years old. The study also exploded a general myth that the primary Web users remain businesses; although around half of the respondents use it for both business and personal access, of those who stated exclusively one or the other, twice as may Web users in the survey used it solely for leisure and personal reasons.

Stage Two: The In-Depth Study

While Stage One of the exercise invited anyone who clicked on the advertising banner to complete the initial survey, Stage Two was conducted among those who left a valid e-mail name in Stage One and agreed to participate further. These respondents were sent an e-mail informing them of the survey location on the Web. The second survey was much longer than the first stage, consisting of a series of in-depth lifestyle questions. Because these respondents are known to Continental, the research company could ask them to sign in and in doing so, the firm could very accurately measure the response rate. Continental could send out reminders, if necessary, and ensure that individual respondents only completed the survey once. In fact, the researchers achieved the target sample size within one week of sending the e-mail notices, and no reminders were necessary.[29]

Questions

1. What type or types of Internet samples were drawn?
2. Do you think that using the Internet was the best way to obtain the desired information? Defend your answer.
3. Are privacy issues involved in this kind of Internet research? If so, what are they?
4. What other form of survey research could have been used to gather the data? Explain.

CHAPTER eight

Primary Data Collection: Experimentation

Learning Objectives

1 *To understand the nature of experiments*

2 *To gain insight into proving causation*

3 *To learn about the experimental setting*

4 *To examine experimental validity and the threats to validity*

5 *To learn the disadvantages of experiments that limit their use in marketing research*

6 *To compare preexperimental designs, true experimental designs, and quasi-experimental designs*

7 *To gain insight into test marketing*

Tammy Green is director of advertising for Toon Warehouse, a music chain with more than 70 outlets in Texas, Louisiana, Mississippi, and Alabama. The company has been in business for 10 years, and experienced rapid growth over the first 8 years of that period. Sales for the past year exceeded $350 million, but the company has encountered a slower growth over the past two years and is considering major changes in its marketing strategy.

Sound USA is Toon Warehouse's major competitor in all markets. Sound USA has 500 outlets throughout the United States and is a subsidiary of a major media conglomerate. Toon Warehouse recently conducted a comprehensive marketing strategy evaluation that included focus groups and a large-scale telephone survey involving music cassette and CD purchasers throughout its market area. This evaluation and research pointed to a number of potential problems, but the one that Tammy is most concerned with is the finding that target customers think that Toon Warehouse's prices are too high. Toon Warehouse has positioned itself as the place to go to find what you want in music and has supported this position by offering a wider selection of music than its competitors, including Sound USA. Tammy is very concerned about the pricing issue because she knows that for Toon Warehouse to reduce its prices, the firm would have to make some reduction in the variety of music it offers. She does not want to take this action unless she is very sure that the results for Toon Warehouse will be positive. She does not think that this question can be definitively answered by surveys, focus groups, or observation-based primary data collection. Tammy is considering the possibility of testing a strategy change in the actual marketplace. However, she does not want to take the risk of testing a new "lower-price, somewhat more limited assortment" strategy throughout the entire area served by Toon Warehouse.

Experimentation may be the best way for Toon Warehouse to assess the impact of a lower pricing strategy on the variety of music it can offer its customers.

Toon Warehouse has one store in the somewhat isolated market of Amarillo, Texas, where Sound USA has two stores. Tammy is considering the possibility of testing the new strategy in Amarillo for one year. At the end of this test, she will evaluate the results of the new strategy and make a recommendation to top management regarding a possible change in the marketing strategy for Toon Warehouse.

Tammy is concerned about a number of factors. First, is Amarillo a good place to conduct the test? Second, is one year long enough or longer than necessary? Third, what factors should she consider when evaluating the results of the Amarillo test? The issues confronting Tammy Green are related to the main topic of this chapter, which pertains to experimental research. Is experimental research appropriate for this problem? How does she go about evaluating the results of the experiment? What are the inherent advantages and disadvantages of the experimental approach? Why conduct a field experiment rather than a laboratory experiment? After you read the chapter, reconsider the questions raised by Tammy's predicament to see whether you can make recommendations to her. ■

What Is an Experiment?

Research based on experimentation is fundamentally different from research based on survey or observation. In both surveys and observations, the researcher is, in essence, a passive assembler of data. The researcher asks people questions or observes what they do. In the case of experiments, the researcher becomes an active participant in the process.

In concept, an **experiment** is straightforward. The researcher changes or manipulates one thing, called an *explanatory, independent,* or *experimental variable,* to observe what effect this change has on something else, referred to as a *dependent variable.* In marketing experiments, the dependent variable is frequently some measure of sales, such as total sales or market share, and the explanatory or experimental variables typically have to do with the marketing mix, such as price, amount or type of advertising, or changes in product features.

Experiment A research approach where one variable is manipulated and the effect on another variable is observed.

Demonstrating Causation

Experimental research is often referred to as causal (not casual) research. It is called **causal research** because it is the only type of research that has the potential to demonstrate that a change in one variable caused some predictable change in another variable. To demonstrate causation—that *A* most likely caused *B*—we must be able to show three things:

1. concomitant variation
2. appropriate time order of occurrence
3. elimination of other possible causal factors.

Causal research Research designed to determine whether a change in one variable most likely caused an observed change in another.

We are using the terms causation and causality in the scientific sense. The scientific view of causation is quite different from the way the term is commonly used. The popular view of causation implies that there is a single cause of an event. For example, if we say that *X* is the cause of some observed change in *Y*, this implies that *X* is the only cause of the observed change in *Y*. The scientific view holds that *X* is only one of a number of determining conditions that caused the observed change in *Y* (concomitant variation). The everyday view of causality usually implies a completely deterministic relationship, whereas the scientific view implies a probabilistic relationship. The popular view is that if *X* causes *Y*, then *X* must always lead to *Y*. The scientific view holds that *X* can be a cause of *Y* if the presence of *X* makes the occurrence of *Y* more probable or likely (appropriate time order of occurrence). The scientific view is that we can never definitively prove that *X* is a cause of *Y*, but can only infer that a relationship exists. In other words, causal relationships are always inferred and never demonstrated conclusively beyond a shadow of a doubt (elimination of other possible causal factors). The three types of evidence just cited (concomitant variation, appropriate time order of occurrence, and elimination of other possible causal factors) are all used to infer causal relationships.

Concomitant Variation

Concomitant variation or correlation A predictable statistical relationship between two variables.

To provide evidence that a change in *A* caused a particular change in *B*, we must first show that there is **concomitant variation** or **correlation** between *A* and *B*. In other words, we must show that they vary together in some predictable fashion. This relationship might be positive or inverse. An example of two variables that are related in a positive manner might be advertising and sales. They would be positively related if sales increased by some predictable amount when advertising increased. An example of two variables that are related in an inverse manner might be price and sales. They would be inversely or negatively related if sales increased when the price decreased and decreased when the price increased. The researcher can test for the existence and direction of statistical relationships by means of a number of statistical procedures. These procedures include chi-square analysis, correlation analysis, regression analysis, and analysis of variance. These statistical procedures are discussed later in the text (chi-square in Chapter 13; correlation analysis, regression analysis, and analysis of variance in Chapter 14.

Concomitant variation by itself does not prove causation. Simply because two variables happen to vary together in some predictable fashion does not prove that one causes the other. You might, for example, find that a high degree of correlation exists between the sales of a product in the United States and the GNP of Germany. Further examination might show that there is no true link between the two variables; it is true simply because both variables happen to be increasing at a similar rate. The proof of causation requires a demonstration of correlation, but correlation alone is not proof of causation.

Appropriate Time Order of Occurrence

The second way to show that a causal relationship probably exists between two variables is to demonstrate that there is an **appropriate time order of occurrence.** To demonstrate that *A* caused *B*, the researcher must be able to show that *A* occurred before *B* occurred. For example, to demonstrate that a price change had an effect on sales, a researcher must be able to show that the price change occurred before the change in sales was observed. However, showing that *A* and *B* vary concomitantly and that *A* occurred before *B* still does not provide evidence that is strong enough to permit the researcher to conclude that *A* is the likely cause of an observed change in *B*.

Appropriate time order of occurrence To be considered a likely cause of a dependent variable, a change in an independent variable must occur before a change is observed in the dependent variable.

Elimination of Other Possible Causal Factors

To infer that a causal relationship quite likely exists between *A* and *B*, the most difficult thing to demonstrate in many marketing experiments is that the change in *B* was not caused by some factor other than *A*. For example, we might increase our advertising expenditures and observe a particular increase in the sales of our product. Correlation and appropriate time order of occurrence are present. But has a likely causal relationship been demonstrated? The answer is clearly "No." It is possible that the observed change in sales is due to some factor other than the increase in advertising. For example, at the same time advertising expenditures were increased, a major competitor might have decreased advertising expenditures, or increased price, or pulled out of the market. Even if the competitive environment did not change, one or a combination of other factors may have influenced sales. For example, the economy in the area might have received a major boost for some reason that has nothing to do with the experiment. For any of these reasons or for many other possible reasons, the observed increase in sales might have been caused by some other factor or combination of factors, rather than or in addition to the increase in advertising expenditures. Much of the discussion in this chapter is related to the question of designing experiments that enable us to eliminate or adjust for the effects of other possible causal factors.

The Experimental Setting: Laboratory or Field

Experiments can be conducted in either a laboratory or a field setting. Most experiments in the physical sciences are conducted in a laboratory setting. The major advantage of conducting experiments in a laboratory is the ability to control many other causal factors—temperature, light, humidity, and so on—and focus on the effect of a change in *A* on *B*. In the lab, the researcher can more effectively deal with the third element of proving causation (elimination of other possible causal factors) and focus on the first two (concomitant variation and appropriate time order of occurrence).

Laboratory experments Experiments conducted in a controlled setting.

Laboratory experiments provide a number of important advantages. The major advantage—the ability to control all variables other than the experimental one—means that the ability to infer that an observed change in the dependent variable was caused by a change in the experimental or treatment variable is much stronger. As a result, laboratory experiments are generally viewed as having greater internal validity (internal validity is discussed later). On the other hand, the controlled and possibly sterile environment of the laboratory may not be a good analog of the marketplace. Because of this, the findings of laboratory experiments sometimes do not hold up when they are transferred to the marketplace. Therefore, laboratory experiments are often seen as having greater problems with external validity (external validity is also discussed later). However, laboratory experiments have many advantages and are probably being used to a greater extent today than in the past. For example, one recent laboratory experiment investigated whether consumers can evaluate nutritional information in the presence of a health claim. Results showed that both health claims and nutritional information influence beliefs about a product's healthfulness. However, health claims about a product do not influence the processing of nutritional information on a food label. Rather, health claims and nutritional information have independent effects on consumer beliefs.[1]

Field experiments Tests conducted outside the laboratory in an actual market environment.

Many marketing experiments are conducted as **field experiments.** This means that they are conducted outside the laboratory in an actual market environment. Test markets, discussed later in this chapter, are a frequently used type of field experiment. Field experiments solve the problem of having a realistic environment but open up a whole new set of problems. The major problem is that in the field the researcher cannot control all spurious factors that might influence the dependent variable. The researcher cannot control the actions of competitors, the weather, the economy, societal trends, the political climate, and the like. Therefore, field experiments have more problems related to internal validity, whereas lab experiments have more problems related to external validity.

Experimental Validity

Validity is a measurement of what we are attempting to measure. The validity of a measure is the extent to which the measure is free from both systematic and random error. In addition to the general concept of validity, in experimentation we are also interested in two specific kinds of validity: internal validity and external validity.

Internal and External Validity

In an experimental design, any extraneous variable that may interfere with our ability to make causal inferences is considered a threat to validity.

Internal validity The extent to which competing explanations for experimental results can be avoided.

Internal validity refers to the extent to which competing explanations for experimental results can be avoided. If a researcher can show that the experimental or treatment variable actually produced the differences observed in the dependent variable, then the experiment can be said to be internally valid. This kind of validity requires evidence to demonstrate that variation in

The Difference Between Internal and External Validity

The problem of internal versus external validity was recently addressed in a research project on the effectiveness of racially exclusive real estate advertising. A field experiment found that African Americans in real estate advertisements produced a positive effect for African-American respondents in terms of (1) liking the models pictured in the photographs and (2) identifying with the models pictured in the photographs.

In discussing their research, the authors said that they would have liked to have conducted a laboratory experiment. However, they were more concerned here about issues of external validity because of the recent court decisions and opted to conduct a study that would more closely reflect what happens when actual housing prospects view real estate advertising. Hence, they employed a field experiment approach using a mail survey, rather than the artificial laboratory situation.[2] ■

the dependent variable was caused by exposure to the treatment conditions and not by other causal factors.

External validity refers to the extent to which the causal relationships measured in an experiment can be generalized to outside people, settings, and times. The issue here is: How representative are the subjects and the setting used in the experiment to other populations and settings on which we would like to project the results? In general, field experiments offer a higher degree of external validity and a lower degree of internal validity than laboratory experiments.

External validity The extent to which the causal relationships measured in an experiment can be generalized to outside people, settings, and times.

Experimental Notation

We believe that our further discussion of experiments will be facilitated by using the following standard system of notation:[3]

- X indicates the exposure of individuals or groups to an experimental treatment. The experimental treatment is the factor whose effects we want to measure and compare. Experimental treatments might be such factors as different prices, package designs, point-of-purchase displays, advertising approaches, or product forms. Possible experimental treatments include all the possible elements of the marketing mix.

- *O* (for Observation) refers to the process of taking measurements on the test units. Test units are individuals or groups of individuals or entities (retail stores) whose responses to the experimental treatments are being tested. Test units might include individual consumers, groups of consumers, retail stores, total markets, or any other entities that might be the targets of a firm's marketing program.
- Different time periods are represented by the horizontal arrangement of the *X*s and *O*s. For example,

$$O_1 \quad X \quad O_2$$

would describe an experiment in which a preliminary measurement was taken on one (or more) test unit O_1, that one (or more) test unit was exposed to the treatment or experimental variable *X;* and that a measurement of the test unit(s) was taken after the exposure, O_2. The *X*s and *O*s can also be arranged vertically to show simultaneous exposure and the measurement of different test units. For example, we might have the following design:

$$\begin{matrix} X_1 & O_1 \\ X_2 & O_2 \end{matrix}$$

This design shows two different groups of test units. It shows that each group of test units received a different experimental treatment at the same time (X_1 and X_2). And it shows that the two groups were measured simultaneously (O_1 and O_2).

Extraneous Variables: Threats to Experimental Validity

In interpreting experimental results, it would be convenient to conclude that the observed response is due to the effect of the experimental or treatment variable. However, many things stand in the way of our ability to reach this conclusion. In anticipation of possible problems in interpretation, an experiment must be designed so that extraneous factors can be eliminated as possible causes of the observed effect. Examples of extraneous factors or variables follow.[4]

History Things that happen or outside variables that change between the beginning and end of an experiment.

History

History refers to any variable or event other than the one manipulated by the researcher (experimental or treatment variable) that takes place between the beginning and end of an experiment and that might affect the value of the dependent variable. Early tests of Prego Spaghetti Sauce by the Campbell Soup Company provide an example of the possible problems with this type of extraneous variable. Campbell executives claim that Ragu greatly increased its advertising levels and use of cents-off deals during their test. They believe that this increased marketing activity was designed to get shoppers to buy Ragu and make it impossible for Campbell to get an accurate reading of potential sales for their Prego product.

Maturation

Maturation refers to changes in subjects during the course of an experiment that are a function of time, such things as getting older, hungrier, tireder, and the like. People's responses to a treatment variable throughout the course of an experiment may change due to these maturation factors rather than to the treatment or experimental variable. The likelihood that maturation will be a serious problem in a particular experiment depends on the length of the experiment. The longer the experiment runs, the more likely it is that maturation will present problems for interpreting the results.

Maturation Changes in subjects that take place during an experiment that are not related to the experiment but may affect their responses to the experimental factor.

Instrument Variation

Instrument variation refers to any changes in measurement instruments that might explain differences in the measurements taken. This is a serious problem in marketing experiments in which people are used as interviewers or observers to measure a dependent variable. Measurements on the same subject may be taken by different interviewers or observers at different times. Any differences between these measurements may reflect differences in the way the interviewing or observation was done. On the other hand, the same interviewer or observer may be used to take measurements on the same subject over time. In this case, differences may reflect the fact that the particular observer or interviewer has become less interested and is doing a sloppier job over time.

Instrument variation Differences or changes in measurement instruments (such as interviewers or observers) that explain differences in measurements.

Selection Bias

The threat to validity of **selection bias** occurs when the experimental or test group is systematically different from a population on which we would like to project the experimental results or from a control group with which we would like to compare results.

In projecting the results onto a population that is systematically different from the test group, we may get very different results from those we got in the test because of differences in the makeup of the two groups. In a similar manner, an observed difference between a test group and an untreated control group (not exposed to the experimental or treatment variable) may be due to differences in the two groups and not to the effect of the experimental or treatment variable. We can ensure the equality of groups by either matching or randomization. *Randomization* involves assigning subjects to test groups and control groups at random. *Matching* involves what the name suggests—we make sure that there is a one-to-one match between people or other units in the test and control groups in regard to key characteristics (such as age).

Selection bias Systematic differences between the test group and the control group due to a biased selection process.

Mortality

Mortality refers to the loss of test units during the course of an experiment. There is no easy way to know if the participants who left would have responded to the experimental or treatment variable in the same way as those who continued for the entire experiment. Like a control group, an experimental group that is representative of a certain population may become nonrepresentative because of the systematic loss of subjects with certain characteristics. For example, in a study of the music preferences of the

Mortality Loss of test units or subjects during the course of an experiment. The problem is that those who leave may be systematically different from those who stay.

U.S. population, if we lost nearly all of the subjects under the age of 25 during the course of the experiment, then we would be likely to get a biased picture of music preferences at the end of the experiment. In this case, our results would probably lack external validity.

Testing effect An effect that is a by-product of the research process and not the experimental variable.

Testing Effect

The process of experimentation itself may produce its own **testing effect** on participants' responses. For example, measuring attitudes toward a product before exposing subjects to an ad may act as a treatment and influence perceptions of the ad. Testing effects come in two forms:

- *Main testing effects* are the possible effects of earlier observations on later observations. For example, students taking the SAT for the second time tend to do better than those taking the test for the first time. This is true even though students have no information about the items they actually missed on the first test. This effect can also be reactive; for example, the answers given on an attitude test have an effect on the attitudes of the test takers, which is reflected in the answers given when taking the same test again.
- *Interactive testing effects* are the effects of a prior measurement on subjects' responses to a later measurement. For example, if we ask subjects about their awareness of advertising for various products (preexposure measurement) and then expose them to advertising for one or more of these products (treatment variable), the postmeasurements are likely to reflect the joint effect of the preexposure and the treatment condition.

Regression to the mean The tendency for people's behavior to move toward the average for that behavior during the course of an experiment.

Regression to the Mean

Regression to the mean refers to the observed tendency of subjects with extreme behavior to move toward the average for that behavior during the course of an experiment. Test participants may exhibit extreme behavior due to chance, but in some cases they may have been specifically chosen because of their extreme behavior. For example, people may have been chosen for an experimental group because they are extremely heavy users of a particular product or service. It has been observed that in these situations it is likely for these extreme cases to move toward the average during the course of an experiment. The problem is that this movement toward the average, which has nothing to do with the treatment or experimental variable, may be interpreted to have been caused by the experimental or treatment variable.

Experimentation: Summary of Basic Issues

Experimental design A test in which the researcher has control over one or more independent variables and manipulates them.

Experimental Design and Treatment

In an **experimental design,** the researcher has control over one or more independent variables and manipulates them. In the experiments we discuss, typically only one independent variable is manipulated. Nonexperimental designs involve no manipulation and are typically referred to as *ex post facto* (after the fact) *research.* In this type of research, an effect is observed and then some attempt is made to attribute this effect to some causal factor. An experimental design includes four factors:

1. the *treatment* or experimental variable (independent variable) to be manipulated
2. the *subjects* to participate in the experiment
3. a *dependent variable* to measure
4. some *plan* or *procedure* for dealing with extraneous causal factors.

The **treatment** is the independent variable that is manipulated. *Manipulation* refers to the process in which the researcher sets the levels of the independent variable to test a particular causal relationship. To test the relationship between price (independent variable) and sales of a product (dependent variable), a researcher might expose subjects to three different levels of price and record the level of purchases under each level. Price is the variable that is manipulated; it is the single treatment factor, with three treatment conditions or levels of price.

Treatment The independent variable that is manipulated in an experiment.

An experiment can include a test or treatment group as well as a control group. A *control group* is a group in which the independent variable is not changed during the course of the experiment. A *test group* is a group that is exposed to a manipulation (change) of the independent variable.

Experimental Effects

The term **experimental effect** refers to the effect of the treatment variables on the dependent variable. The goal is to determine the effect of each treatment condition (level of treatment variable) on the dependent variable. For example, suppose that three different markets are selected to test three different prices or treatment conditions of a product. Each price will be tested in each market for a three-month period. In market one, a price 2 percent lower than the existing price for the product is tested; in market two, a price 4 percent lower is tested; and in market three, a price 6 percent lower is tested. At the end of the three-month test, sales in market one are observed to have increased by less than 1 percent over sales for the preceding three-month period. In market two, sales have increased by 3 percent; and in market three, sales have increased by 5 percent. The change in sales observed in each market would be the experimental effect.

Experimental effect The effect of the treatment variable(s) on the dependent variable.

The Control of Other (Extraneous) Causal Factors

Other or extraneous causal factors are variables that can affect the dependent variable and should be controlled in some manner to establish a clear picture of the effect of the manipulated variable on the dependent variable. Extraneous causal factors are ordinarily referred to as *confounding variables* because they confound the treatment condition, making it impossible to determine whether changes in the dependent variable are due solely to the treatment conditions.

Four basic approaches are used to control extraneous factors: randomization, actual physical control, experimental design control, and statistical control.

Randomization The random assignment of group subjects to treatment conditions to ensure equal representation of characteristics in all groups.

Randomization involves randomly assigning subjects to treatment conditions, so that we can reasonably assume that those extraneous causal factors related to the subjects' characteristics will be represented equally in each treatment condition, thus canceling out any extraneous effects.

Physical control Holding the value or level of extraneous variables constant throughout the course of an experiment.

Physical control of extraneous causal factors involves somehow holding the value or level of the extraneous variable constant throughout the experiment. Another approach to physical control is matching. Under this approach, respondents are matched for important personal characteristics such as, age, income, or lifestyle, before being assigned to different treatment conditions. The goal is to make sure there are no important differences between the characteristics of respondents in both test and control groups. Specific matching procedures are discussed later in this chapter.

Design control Use of an experimental design to control extraneous causal factors.

Design control refers to the control of extraneous causal factors by means of specific types of experimental designs developed for this purpose. These designs will be discussed later in this chapter.

Statistical control Adjusting for the effects of confounding variables by statistically adjusting the value of the dependent variable for each treatment condition.

Statistical control procedures can account for extraneous causal factors if they can be identified and measured throughout the course of the experiment. These procedures (for example, analysis of covariance) can take into account the effects of a confounded variable on the dependent variable by statistically adjusting the value of the dependent variable within each treatment condition.

Why Are Experiments Not Used More Often?

The preceding discussion shows that experiments are an extremely powerful form of research—the only type of research that can truly explore the existence and nature of causal relationships between variables of interest. Given these advantages over other research designs for primary data collection, why is experimental research not used more often? There are many reasons for this, including the cost of experiments, security issues, problems associated with implementing experiments, and the dynamic nature of the marketplace.

The High Cost of Experiments

To some degree, when making comparisons of the costs of experiments with the costs of survey- or observation-based research, we are comparing apples to oranges. It is clear that experiments can be costly in both money and time. In many cases, managers anticipate that the costs of doing an experiment will exceed the value of the information gained. Consider, for example, the costs of testing three alternative advertising campaigns in three different geographic areas. Three different campaigns must be produced; airtime must be purchased in all three markets; the timing in all three markets must be carefully coordinated; some system must be put into place to measure sales before, during, and after the test campaigns have run; measurements of other extraneous variables must be made; extensive analysis of the results must be performed; and a variety of other tasks must be completed to execute the experiment. All this could cost $1 million or more.

Security Issues

A field experiment or test market involves exposing a marketing plan or some key element of a marketing plan in the actual marketplace. Undoubtedly, competitors will find out what is being considered well in advance of a full-scale market introduction. This advance notice gives competitors an opportunity to decide if and how to respond. In any event, the element of surprise is lost. In some instances, competitors have actually "stolen" concepts that were being tested in the marketplace and gone into national distribution before the company testing the product or strategy element completed the test market.

Implementation Problems

A number of problems may hamper the implementation of experiments. They include the difficulty of gaining cooperation within an organization, contamination problems, differences between test markets and the total population, and the lack of availability of a group of people or a geographic area to act as a control group.

It may be extremely difficult to obtain cooperation within an organization to execute certain types of experiments. For example, a regional marketing manager might be reluctant to permit his or her market area to be used as a test market for a reduced level of advertising or a higher price. Quite naturally, there would be concern that the experiment might lower sales for the area.

Contamination refers to the fact that buyers from outside the test area may come into the area to purchase the product because of the experiment. These purchases by outsiders will distort the results of the experiment. Outside buyers might live on the fringes of the test market area and receive TV advertisements intended only for those in the test area that offer a lower price, a special rebate, or some other incentive to buy a product. Their purchases would tend to indicate that the particular sales-stimulating factor being tested was more effective than actually was the case.

Contamination The inclusion in a test of a group of respondents who are not normally there; for example, outside buyers who see an advertisement intended only for those in the test area and enter the area to purchase the product being tested.

A third problem relates to the fact that in some cases the behavior of consumers in test markets may be so different from the population as a whole that the experimental results have a relatively small effect. This problem can be dealt with by carefully matching test markets and using other strategies designed to ensure a higher degree of equivalency of test units.

Fourth, in some situations no geographic area or group of people may be available to serve as a control group. For example, when only a small number of purchasers ever buy industrial products in a geographic area, an attempt to test a new industrial product among a subset of purchasers in this area would be doomed to failure.

Selected Experimental Designs

In the following section, examples of preexperimental, true experimental, and quasi-experimental designs are discussed.[5] In outlining these experimental designs, we use the system of notation introduced earlier.

Three Preexperimental Designs

Preexperimental design A design that offers little or no control over extraneous factors.

Studies using **preexperimental designs** are usually difficult to interpret because they offer little or no control over the influence of extraneous factors and, as a result, are often not much better than descriptive studies when it comes to making causal inferences. With these designs the researcher has little control over exposure to the treatment variable and comparative measurements. However, these designs are frequently used in commercial marketing research because they are simple and inexpensive. They are useful for suggesting new hypotheses but do not offer strong tests of hypotheses.

One-shot case study design A preexperimental design with no control group and an after-measurement only.

The One-Shot Case Study The **one-shot case study design** involves exposing test units (people or test markets) to a treatment or experimental variable for some period of time and then taking a measurement of the dependent variable. Symbolically, the design is shown as

$$X \quad O_1$$

There are two basic weaknesses in this design: No pretest observations are made of the test units that will receive the treatment, and there is no control group of test units that will not receive the treatment. As a result of these deficiencies, the design does not deal with the effects of any of the possible extraneous variables. Therefore, the design lacks internal validity and, most likely, external validity as well. While this design is useful for suggesting causal hypotheses, it does not provide a strong test of them. Many test markets for new products (not previously on the market) are based on this design. Examples of this and other preexperimental designs are shown in Figure 8.1.

One-group pretest/posttest design A preexperimental design with pre- and post-measurements but no control group.

The One-Group Pretest/Posttest Design The **one-group pretest/posttest design** is the design employed most frequently for testing changes in established products or marketing strategies. The fact that the product was on the market prior to the change provides the basis for the pretest measurement (O_1). The design is shown symbolically as

$$O_1 \quad X \quad O_2$$

Pretest observations are made on a single group of subjects or a single test unit (O_1) that later receives the treatment. Then a posttest observation is made (O_2). The treatment effect is estimated by $O_2 - O_1$.

History is a threat to the internal validity of this design because an observed change in the dependent variable might be due to an event outside the experiment that took place between the times of the pretest and posttest measurements. In laboratory experiments this threat can be controlled by insulating respondents from outside influences. Unfortunately, this type of control is impossible in field experiments.

Figure 8.1

Examples of Preexperimental Designs

Blue Cross/Blue Shield is in the process of instituting a new sales training program for its existing sales force. The program is designed to increase the productivity of individual salespeople and thus the entire sales force. Butler Moore, vice president in charge of sales, wants to do a small-scale research project to determine whether the course is producing the desired results. Jill Marion, director of marketing research, has proposed three preexperimental designs, as outlined below.

One-Shot Case Study Design

This design has the following features:

Basic design: $X\ O_1$

Sample: Volunteers from among those who have taken the course.

Treatment *(X):* Taking the course.

Measurement *(O_1):* Actual sales performance for the six-month period after the course.

Weaknesses:

- No conclusive inferences can be drawn from the results.
- The posttest measurement of sales may be the result of many uncontrolled factors. It cannot be judged better or worse in the absence of a pretreatment of observation of sales performance.
- There is no control group of salespeople who did not receive the treatment (take the course).

Static-Group Comparison

This design has the following features:

Basic design:

- Experimental group: X O_1
- Control group: O_2

Sample: Volunteers for both test and control groups.

Treatment: Take the course.

Measurements *(O_1 O_2):* O_1 is actual sales performance of experimental group for six months after the course. O_2 is actual sales performance for control group that did not take course (treatment).

Weaknesses:

- No pretest measure to help deal with such threats as history and maturation.
- Because subjects were not assigned to the two groups at random, differences in performance between the two groups may be attributed to differences in the groups (one group had more good salespeople to begin with), rather than the sales training course.

One-Group Pretest/Posttest Design

This is a somewhat better design:

Basic design: $O_1\ \ X\ \ O_2$

Sample: Volunteers for both test and control groups.

Treatment: Take the course.

Measurement *(O_1 O_2):* O_1 is actual sales performance for the six months prior to course and O_2 is actual sales performance for the six months after the course.

Comparison: Same as the static-group comparison design, except a pretest measure of sales performance (O_2) is taken.

Weaknesses:

- Better than one-shot case study design, but still has many serious problems.
- Difference between pretest and posttest measures may be attributable to a number of things other than the sales training course.
- These other things (extraneous factors) include:
  - Better or worse economic conditions may have contributed to the observed change in the dependent variable (history threat).
  - Salespeople may have matured over the period (gotten better) in ways that had nothing to do with the course (maturation).
  - The pretest measure and the fact that the sales force knew their performance was being monitored may have affected their performance (testing effect).
  - Some salespeople may have dropped out (left the company) over the period (mortality).

Maturation is another threat to this type of design. An observed effect might be due to the fact that subjects have grown older, smarter, or more experienced between the pretest and the posttest.

This design has only one pretest observation. As a result, we know nothing of the pretest trend of the dependent variable. The posttest score might be higher because of the increasing trend of the dependent variable, a situation in which the effect is not from the treatment of research interest.

Static-group comparison design A preexperimental design that utilizes an experimental and a control group. However, subjects or test units are not randomly assigned to the two groups and no premeasurements are taken.

The Static-Group Comparison The **static-group comparison design** uses two treatment groups one; (the experimental group) is exposed to the treatment and one (the control group) is not. The two groups must be considered as nonequivalent because subjects are not randomly assigned to the groups. The design can be shown symbolically as follows:

Experimental group:	X	O_1
Control group:		O_2

The treatment effect is estimated as $O_1 - O_2$. The most obvious flaws in this design are the absence of pretests and the fact that any posttest differences between the groups may be due to the treatment effect, selection differences between the nonequivalent groups, or many other reasons.

Three True Experimental Designs

True experimental design Research using an experimental group and a control group, with randomized assignment of test units to both groups.

In a **true experimental design,** the experimenter randomly assigns treatments to randomly selected test units. The random assignment of test units to treatments is denoted by *(R)* in our notation system. Randomization is an important mechanism that makes the results of true experimental designs better (more valid) than the results from preexperimental designs. True experimental designs are superior to preexperimental designs because randomization takes care of many extraneous variables. The principal reason for choosing to conduct randomized experiments over other types of research design is that they make causal inference clearer.[6] Three true experimental designs are discussed in this section.

Before and after with control group design A true experimental design that includes the random assignment of subjects or test units to experimental and control groups and the premeasurement of both groups.

Before and After with Control Group The **before and after with control group design** can be presented symbolically as

Experimental group:	*(R)*	O_1	X	O_2
Control group:	*(R)*	O_3		O_4

Because the test units in this design are randomly assigned to the experimental and control groups, the two groups can be considered equivalent. Therefore, they are likely to be subject to the same extraneous factors, except for the treatment of research interest in the experimental group. For this reason, the difference between the pre- and postmeasurements of the control group ($O_4 - O_3$) should provide a good estimate of the effect of all the extraneous influences experienced by each group. To get the true impact of the treatment variable *X*, the extraneous influences must be removed from the difference between the pre- and postmeasurements of the experimental group. Thus, the true impact of *X* is estimated by $(O_2 - O_1) - (O_4 - O_3)$. This design generally controls for all but two major threats to validity: mortality and history.

Mortality is a problem if certain units drop out during the study and if the units dropping out differ systematically from the ones that remain. This results in a selection bias, because the experimental and control groups are composed of different subjects at the posttest than they were at the pretest. History is a problem in situations in which events other than the treatment variable affect the experimental group but not the control group, or vice versa. Examples of true experimental designs are provided in Figure 8.2.

Solomon four-group design Research using two experimental groups and two control groups to control for all extraneous variable threats.

The Solomon Four-Group Design

The **Solomon four-group design** is similar to the previous design; however, a second set of experimental and con-

Figure 8.2

Examples of True Experimental Designs

After-Only with Control Group Design

This design has the following features:

Basic design:

- Experimental group: *(R)* X O_1
- Control group: *(R)* O_2

Sample: Random sample of stores that sell shampoo. Stores are randomly assigned to test and control groups. Groups can be considered equivalent.

Treatment *(X)*: Placing the point-of-purchase display in stores in the experimental group for one month.

Measurements *(O_1, O_2)*: Actual sales of company's brand during the period that the point-of-purchase displays are in the test stores.

Comments: Because of the random assignment of stores to groups, the test group and control group can be considered equivalent. Measurement of the treatment effect of *X* is $O_1 - O_2$. If $O_1 = 125{,}000$ units and $O_1 = 113{,}000$ units, then the treatment effect = 12,000 units.

Before and After with Control Group Design

This design has the following features:

Basic design:

- Experimental group: *(R)* O_1 X O_2
- Control group: *(R)* O_3 O_4

Sample: Same as previous.

Treatment *(X)*: Same as previous.

Measurements *(O_1 to O_4)*: O_1 and O_2 are pre- and postmeasurements for the experimental group; O_3 and O_4 are the same for the control group.

Results:

O_1 = 113,000 units
O_2 = 125,000 units
O_3 = 111,000 units
O_4 = 118,000 units

Comments: Random assignment to groups means that they can be considered equivalent. Because groups are equivalent, it is reasonable to assume that they will be equally affected by the same extraneous factors. The difference between the pre- and postmeasurements for the control group ($O_4 - O_3$) provides a good estimate of the effects of all extraneous factors on both groups. Based on these results, $O_4 - O_3$ = 7,000 units. The estimated treatment effect is $(O_2 - O_1) - (O_4 - O_3)$, (125,000 − 113,000) − (118,000 − 111,000) = 5,000 units.

trol groups is added to control for all extraneous variable threats to internal validity and the interactive testing effect. This design is presented symbolically as follows.

Experimental group 1:	(R)	O_1	X	O_2
Control group 1:	(R)	O_3		O_4
Experimental group 2:	(R)		X	O_5
Control group 2:	(R)			O_6

The second experimental group receives no pretest but is otherwise identical to the first experimental group. The second control group receives only a posttest measurement.

This design provides several measures of the experimental treatment effect of X. They are $(O_2 - O_1) - (O_4 - O_3)$, $(O_6 - O_5)$, and $(O_2 - O_4)$. If there is agreement among these measures, the inferences that can be made about the effect of the treatment can be much stronger. In addition, with this design it is possible to directly measure the interaction of the treatment and before-measure effects $[(O_2 - O_4) - (O_5 - O_6)]$.

After-only with control group design True experimental design that involves random assignment of subjects or test units to experimental and control groups, but no premeasurement of the dependent variable.

After-Only with Control Group

The **after-only with control group design** differs from the static-group comparison design (with nonequivalent groups) discussed earlier in its assignment of the test units. In the previously presented design, the test units are not randomly assigned to treatment groups. As a result, it is possible for the groups to differ in regard to the dependent variable prior to the treatment presentation. The after-only with control group design deals with this shortcoming and can be shown symbolically as

Experimental group:	(R)	X	O_1
Control group:	(R)		O_2

Notice that the test units are randomly *(R)* assigned to experimental and control groups. This random assignment of test units to the groups should produce experimental and control groups that are approximately equal in regard to the dependent variable prior to presenting the treatment to the experimental group. In addition, it can reasonably be assumed that test-unit mortality (one of the threats to internal validity) will affect each group in the same way.

Considering this design in the context of the shampoo example described in Figure 8.2, we can see a number of problems. Events other than the treatment may have occurred during the experimental period in one or more of the stores in the experimental group. If a particular store in the experimental group ran a sale on certain other products and, as a result, had a larger (more than average) number of customers in the store, shampoo sales might be increased due to the heavier traffic. Events such as these, which are store-specific (history), may distort the overall treatment effect. Also, there is a possibility that a few stores may drop out during the experiment (mortality threat), resulting in a selection bias because the stores in the experimental group will be different at the posttest.

If the experimenter added second experimental and control groups, and the stores in the second experimental group were subjected to the new point-of-sale advertising campaign, then posttest measures of shampoo sales for stores in the second experimental and control group would also be taken (O_5 and O_6).

If the marketer observed an agreement between the measures $[(O_2 - O_1) - (O_4 - O_2)]$, $(O_6 - O_5)$, and $(O_2 - O_4)$, then the inference about the effects of a point-of-sale advertising campaign would be much more conclusive.

Quasi-experiments

When designing a true experiment, the researcher must often create an artificial environment to control independent and extraneous variables. Because of this artificiality, questions are raised about the external validity of the experimental findings. **Quasi-experimental designs** have been developed to deal with this problem. They are usually more feasible in field settings than are true experiments.

Quasi-experimental design A study in which the researcher lacks complete control over the scheduling of the treatment or must assign respondents to treatment in a nonrandom manner.

In quasi-experiments the researcher lacks complete control over the scheduling of treatments or must assign respondents to treatments in a nonrandom fashion. These designs are frequently used in marketing research studies because cost and field constraints often do not permit the researcher to exert direct control over the scheduling of treatments and the randomization of respondents. Selected examples of these types of designs follow.

Interrupted Time-Series Designs

Interrupted time-series designs involve repeated measurement of an effect, both before and after a treatment is introduced, which "interrupts" previous data patterns. Interrupted time-series experimental designs can be shown symbolically as

Interrupted time-series design Research in which the treatment "interrupts" ongoing repeated measurements.

$$O_1 \quad O_2 \quad O_3 \quad O_4 \qquad X \qquad O_5 \quad O_6 \quad O_7 \quad O_8$$

A common example of this type of design in marketing research involves the use of consumer purchase panels. We might use a panel to make periodic measures of consumer purchase activity (the *O*s). We might introduce a new promotional campaign (the *X*) and examine the panel data for an effect. The researcher has control over the timing of the promotional campaign but cannot be sure when the panel members were exposed to the campaign, or if they were exposed at all.

This design is similar to the one-group pretest/posttest design, $O_1\ X\ O_2$. However, time-series experimental designs have greater interpretability than the one-group pretest/posttest design because the many pretest/posttest measurements that are taken provide more understanding of extraneous variables. If, for example, sales of a product were on the rise and a new promotional campaign was introduced, the true effect of this campaign could not be estimated if only a pretest and posttest design was used. However, the rising trend in sales would be obvious if a number of pretest and posttest observations had been made. The time-series design helps to determine the underlying trend of the dependent variable and provides better interpretability in regard to the treatment effect.

This design has two fundamental weaknesses. The primary weakness is the experimenter's inability to control history. Although maintaining a careful log of all possible relevant external happenings can reduce this problem, the experimenter has no way of determining the appropriate number and timing of pretest and posttest observations.

The other weakness of this design comes from the possible interactive effects of testing and evaluation apprehension resulting from the repeated measurements taken on test units. For example, panel members may become such "expert" shoppers or so much more conscious of their shopping habits that it may be inappropriate to make generalizations to other populations.

Multiple time-series design An interrupted time-series design with a control group.

Multiple Time-Series Designs

In some studies based on time-series designs, we are able to find a group of test units to serve as a control group. If a control group can be added to the straight time-series design, then we can be more certain of our interpretation of the treatment effect. This design, called the **multiple time-series design** can be shown symbolically as

Experimental Group 1:	O_1	O_2	O_3	X	O_4	O_5	O_6
Control Group 1:	O_1	O_2	O_3	X	O_4	O_5	O_6

The researcher must take care in selecting the control group. For example, an advertiser might test a new advertising campaign in a test city. That city would constitute the experimental group, and another city that was not exposed to the new campaign would be chosen as the control group. It is important that the test and control cities be roughly equivalent in regard to those characteristics related to the sale of the product (for example, the competitive brands available).

Test Markets

Test market Testing a new product or some element of the marketing mix using experimental or quasi-experimental designs.

A common form of experimentation used by marketing research practitioners is test marketing. The term **test market** is used by marketing researchers rather loosely to refer to any research that

- involves testing a new product or any change in an existing marketing strategy (product, price, place, or promotion) in a single market, a group of markets, or a region of the country.
- involves the use of experimental procedures.

Test-Market Usage and Objectives

New product introductions play a key role in shaping a firm's financial success or failure. The conventional wisdom in the corporate world is that new products should contribute more profits than was previously expected due to higher levels of competition and a faster pace of change. However, according to various published sources, 70 to 80 percent of all new packaged goods fail. In addition, data reported by Burke Marketing Research Services indicate that 65 percent of all new product dollars are spent on marginal or losing brands. To make up for the failures and to maintain corporate profitability at necessary levels, those products that succeed must produce a return on investment averaging greater than 30 percent.

Test-market studies have the goal of helping marketing managers make better decisions about new products and additions or changes to existing products or marketing strategies. Test-market studies do this by providing a real-world test for evaluating products and marketing programs. Marketing managers use test markets to evaluate proposed national programs with all of their separate elements on a smaller, less costly scale. The basic idea is to determine whether the estimated profits from rolling the product out nationally justify the potential risks. Test-market studies are designed to provide information on the following issues:

- estimates of market share and volume that can be projected to the total market.
- the effect that the new product will have on the sales of similar products (if any) already marketed by the company. The extent to which the new product takes business away from the company's existing products is referred to as the **cannibalization rate.**
- characteristics of consumers who buy the product. Demographic data will almost surely be collected, and lifestyle, psychographic, and other types of classification data may be collected. This information will be useful in helping the firm refine the marketing strategy for the product. For example, knowing the demographic characteristics of likely purchasers will help in developing a media plan that will more effectively and efficiently reach target customers. Knowing the psychographic and lifestyle characteristics of target customers will provide valuable insights into how to position the product and the types of promotional messages that will appeal to them.
- the behavior of competitors during the test may provide some indication of what they will do if the product is introduced nationally.

Cannibalization rate
The extent to which a new product takes business away from a company's existing products.

One alternative to traditional test markets is the growing area of simulated test markets (STMs). STMs use survey data and mathematical models to simulate test-market results, at a much lower cost. Details of how STMs are actually used are provided later in the chapter.

Test markets employ experimental designs. Traditional test markets, by definition, are field experiments, whereas STMs tend to rely on a laboratory approach. Traditional test markets rely almost exclusively on preexperimental and time-series designs. STMs use preexperimental, time-series, and in some cases, true experimental designs.

Costs of Test Marketing

Test marketing is expensive. One test often takes six months to a year or longer and can cost millions of dollars. In fact, it usually takes 30 to 60 days just to get a new product onto store shelves. This estimate refers only to *direct costs,* which can include

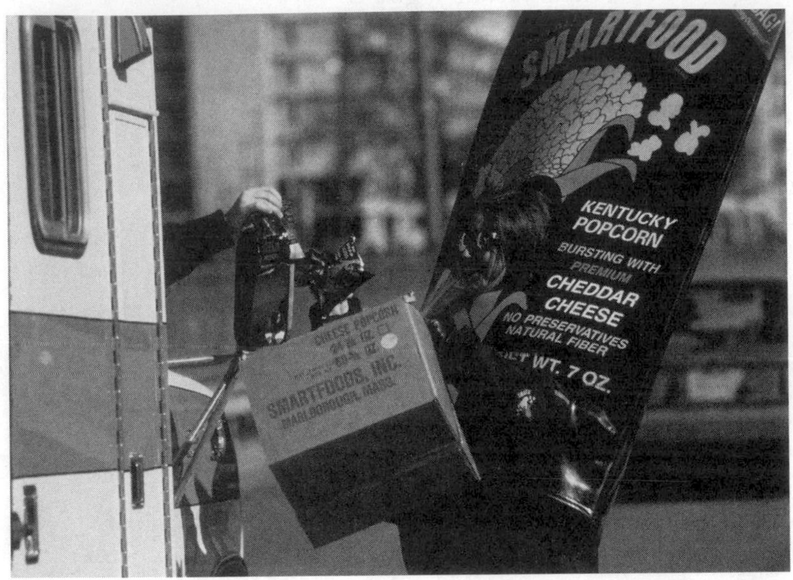

The cost of sampling involved in experimentation can be a significant expense when conducting test marketing.

- production of commercials
- payments to advertising agency for services
- media time at a higher rate because of low volume
- syndicated research information
- customized research information and associated data analysis
- point-of-purchase materials
- coupons and sampling
- high trade allowances to obtain distribution.

Many possible *indirect costs* are also associated with test marketing, including the

- cost of management time spent on the test market
- diversion of sales activity from existing products
- possible negative impact of a test-market failure on other products with the same family brand
- possible negative trade reactions to a product if it develops a reputation of not doing well
- risk of competitors finding out about the test marketing, allowing them to develop a better strategy or preempt a national campaign.

The costs of test markets are high, and as a result, they should be used only as the last step in a research process that has already shown the new product or strategy to have considerable potential. In some situations, it may be cheaper to go ahead and launch the product, even if it fails.[7]

Deciding Whether to Conduct a Test Market

Test markets offer at least two important benefits to the firm conducting the test:

- First and foremost, a test market provides a vehicle with which to obtain a good estimate of a product's sales potential under realistic market conditions. On the basis of these test results, the researcher can develop estimates of the product's national market share and use this figure to develop estimates of a product's financial performance.

Virtual Shopping

Recent advances in computer graphics and three-dimensional modeling promise to bring simulated test marketing to a much broader range of companies, products, and applications. How? By allowing the marketer to re-create—quickly and inexpensively—the atmosphere of an actual retail store on a computer screen using virtual reality. For example, a consumer can view shelves stocked with any kind of product. The shopper can "pick up" a package from the shelf by touching its image on the monitor. In response, the product moves to the center of the screen, where the shopper can use a three-axis trackball to turn the package so that it can be examined from all sides. To "purchase" the product, the consumer touches an image of a shopping cart, and the product moves to the cart. Just as in a physical store, products pile up in the cart as the customer shops. During the shopping process, the computer unobtrusively records the amount of time the consumer spends shopping in each product category, the time the consumer spends examining each side of a package, the quantity of product the consumer purchases, and the order in which items are purchased.

Computer-simulated environments like this one offer a number of advantages over older research methods. First, unlike focus groups, concept tests, and other laboratory approaches, the virtual store duplicates the distracting clutter of an actual market. Consumers can shop in an environment with a realistic level of complexity and variety. Second, researchers can set up and alter the tests very quickly. Once images of the product are scanned into the computer, the researcher can make changes in the assortment of brands, product packaging, pricing, promotions, and shelf space within minutes. Data collection is also fast and error-free because the information generated by the purchase is automatically tabulated and stored by the computer. Third, production costs are low because displays are created electronically. Once the hardware and software are in place, the cost of a test is largely a function of the number of respondents, who generally are given a small incentive to participate. Fourth, the simulation has a high degree of flexibility. It can be used to test entirely new marketing concepts or to fine-tune existing programs. The simulation also makes it possible to eliminate much of the noise that exists in field experiments.

The most important benefit of the methodology, however, is the freedom it gives marketers to exercise their imagination[s]. It transforms the simulated test market from a go-or-no-go hurdle that occurs late in the planning process to an efficient marketing laboratory for experimenting with new ideas. Product managers can test new concepts before incurring manufacturing or advertising costs, paying slotting allowances to the trade, alerting competitors, or knowing whether the new ideas are good, bad, terrible, or fantastic.[8] ■

In PRACTICE

- Second, the test should identify weaknesses of the product and the proposed marketing strategy, and give management an opportunity to correct any weaknesses. It will be much easier and less expensive to correct these problems at the test-market stage than to correct them after the product has gone into national distribution.[9]

On the other hand, these benefits must be weighed against a number of costs and other negative features associated with test markets. The financial costs of test markets were discussed previously and can be significant. Another problem with test markets is that they give competitors an early indication of what a company is planning to do. They may choose to make adjustments in their marketing strategy or, if your idea is easily copied and not legally protected, they may actually emulate the idea and move quickly into national distribution. Four major factors should be taken into account in determining whether to conduct a test market:

- First, weigh the cost and risk of failure against the probability of success and associated profits. If estimated costs are high and the likelihood of success is uncertain, then lean toward doing a test market. On the other hand, if expected costs are low and the risk of product failure is also low, then an immediate national rollout without a test market may be the appropriate strategy.
- As suggested earlier, the likelihood and speed with which competitors can copy a product and introduce it on a national basis must also be considered. If it can be easily copied, then it may be appropriate to go ahead and introduce the product without a test market.
- Consider the investment required to produce the product for the test market versus the investment required to produce the product in the quantities necessary for a national rollout. In some cases, the difference in investment required may be small and it may make sense to introduce the product nationally without a test market. However, where there is a large difference between the investment required to produce the product for test marketing and the investment required to produce the product for a national rollout, conducting a test market before making a decision to introduce the product nationally makes good sense.
- The final consideration relates to the damage that an unsuccessful new-product launch can inflict on a company's reputation. Failure may hurt the company's reputation with other members of the channel of distribution (retailers) and damage the company's ability to gain their cooperation in future product launches. In those cases where this is a particular concern, test marketing is called for.

Steps in a Test Market Study

Once you have decided to conduct a test market, certain steps must be carried out to achieve a satisfactory result.

Define the Objective

As always, the first step in the process is to define the objectives of the test. Typical test market objectives are to

- develop share and volume estimates.
- determine the characteristics of people who are purchasing the product.
- determine the frequency and purpose of purchase.
- determine where (retail outlets) purchases are made.
- measure the effect of sales of the new product on sales of the similar existing products in the product line.

Select a Basic Approach After specifying the objectives of the test-market exercise, the next step is to decide on the type of test-market method that is appropriate, given the stated objectives. Here are three basic approaches.

- *Simulated test market.* STMs do not involve actual testing in the marketplace. Under this approach, we expose a sample of individuals, representative of the target group, to various stimuli (new product concepts) and ask them to make simulated purchase choices between them. The results are used as input to mathematical models to make projections of how the new product will sell if available nationally.
- *Standard test market.* This approach involves an actual market test on a limited basis.
- *Controlled test market.* In this method the test market is handled by an outside research company such as Information Resources (see Chapter 6 for a more detailed discussion). This approach uses minimarkets operated by the testing company as well as controlled store panels. The companies handling the test typically guarantee the distribution of the new product in stores that cover some percentage of the minimarkets. They typically provide warehouse facilities and have their own field representatives to sell the product to retailers. They are also typically responsible for stocking shelves and tracking sales either manually or electronically.

Develop Detailed Procedures for the Test After we have developed the objectives and a basic approach for the test, then we must develop a detailed plan for conducting the test. Manufacturing and distribution decisions must be made to ensure that enough of the product is available in the test stores. In addition, the detailed marketing plan to be used for the test must be completed. The basic positioning approach must be selected, the execution of that approach in terms of actual commercials must be developed, a pricing strategy chosen, a media plan developed, and various promotional activities specified.

Select Markets for the Test The selection of markets for the test is an important decision. A number of factors must be taken into account:

- The market should not be overtested. Markets that have been used extensively by other companies for testing purposes may not respond in the same way as if they have not been used.
- The market should have normal development, that is, sales in the market of the particular product should be typical, not unusually high or unusually low.

- Markets with unusual demographic profiles should be avoided. For example, college towns and retirement areas are not particularly good areas for testing most new products.
- The selected cities should reflect significant regional differences. If sales of a certain product type vary significantly by region, then all the major regions should be represented by at least one city in the test.
- The markets chosen should have little media spillover into other markets and receive relatively little media contact from outside the area. For example, if the television stations in a particular market reach a large area outside it, the advertising used for the test product may pull in a large number of consumers from outside the local market. This eventuality will make the product appear to be more successful than it really is.
- Media usage patterns for the market should be similar to national norms. For example, television viewership should not differ significantly from national patterns. This might bias the estimates that you make for the national market.
- The markets chosen should be big enough to provide meaningful results but not so big that testing becomes too expensive.
- Distribution channels in the chosen markets should reflect national patterns. For example, all the types of stores that sell the particular product should be present in the market and in their approximate national proportions.
- The competitive situation in the markets chosen should be similar to the national situation for the product category. For example, it would not be pertinent to use a market in which one or more national competitors are not present.
- The demographic profiles of the cities used should be similar to each other and similar to the national demographic profile.[10]

As the list indicates, many of the selection criteria relate to using cities that are microcosms of the region or country where the product will ultimately be sold. The basic motivation for taking this approach is to make sure that the test-market results can be projected to the total area where the product will be sold. This objective is critical to meet an important objective: developing reliable estimates of sales of the new product from the test market. A list of the most typical metropolitan areas in the United States, prepared by *American Demographics* is provided in Table 8.1. The cumulative index in the table is an index of similarity to the national market that considers housing value, age, and race characteristics of each market simultaneously. A value of 0.0 indicates a perfect match to the national market on these characteristics.[11]

Execute the Plan Once a plan is in place, the next step is executing it. Before beginning the test, it is important to decide how long the test should run. The average test runs for 6 to 12 months; however, shorter and longer tests are common. The test must run long enough for an adequate number of repeat-purchase cycles to be observed. This provides a measure of the "staying power" of a new product or marketing program. The shorter the average purchase period, the shorter the test needs to be. For example, cigarettes, soft drinks, and packaged goods are purchased every few days, whereas shaving

Table 8.1

The Most Typical Metropolitan Areas

Rank	Metropolitan Area	1990 Population	Cumulative Index	Housing Value Index	Age Index	Race Index
1	Detroit, MI	4,382,000	22.8	11.8	1.5	9.5
2	St. Louis, MO–IL	2,444,000	22.8	15.1	1.6	6.2
3	Charlotte–Gastonia, Rock Hill, NC–SC	1,162,000	24.1	13.5	2.7	7.9
4	Fort Worth–Arlington, TX	1,332,000	25.1	17.0	5.9	2.2
5	Kansas City, MO–KS	1,566,000	25.4	17.9	2.7	4.8
6	Indianapolis, IN	1,250,000	25.5	16.7	2.4	6.3
7	Philadelphia, PA–NJ	4,857,000	26.7	18.0	1.7	7.1
8	Wilmington, NC	120,000	27.2	15.1	4.1	8.0
9	Cincinnati, OH–KY–IN	1,453,000	27.2	19.1	1.6	6.6
10	Nashville, TN	985,000	27.6	18.5	2.9	6.2
11	Dayton-Springfield, OH	951,000	27.6	19.5	1.9	6.2
12	Jacksonville, FL	907,000	27.6	17.2	2.5	7.9
13	Toledo, OH	614,000	27.9	20.0	2.4	5.5
14	Greensboro–Winston-Salem–High Point, NC	942,000	27.8	17.6	2.9	7.3
15	Columbus, OH	1,377,000	28.4	19.0	3.8	5.7
16	Charlottesville, VA	131,000	28.5	16.9	6.3	5.2
17	Panama City, FL	127,000	28.6	20.1	2.6	6.0
18	Pensacola, FL	344,000	38.7	21.8	2.2	4.7
19	Milwaukee, WI	1,432,000	28.8	23.4	1.4	4.1
20	Cleveland, OH	1,831,000	28.9	18.2	3.4	7.4

Source: Judith Waldrop, "All American Markets," *American Demographics* (January 1992), p. 27. Reprinted from *American Demographics* magazine, courtesy of Intertec Publishing Corp., Stamford, Connecticut.

cream and toothpaste are purchased only every few months. The latter types of products would therefore require a longer test. Regardless of the product type, the test will need to be continued until the repeat-purchase rate stabilizes. There is a tendency for the percentage of people making repeat purchases to drop for some period of time before reaching a level that remains relatively constant. The repeat-purchase rate is critical to the process of estimating the ultimate sales of the project. If the test ends too soon, sales will be overestimated.

Two other factors should be considered before beginning the test: the expected speed of competitor reactions and the costs of running the test. If there is reason to expect that competitors will react quickly by introducing their own version of the new product, then the test should be as short as possible. Minimizing the length of the test reduces the amount of time competitors have to react. Always balance the value of the additional information to be gained from the test against the cost of continuing to run the test. At some point, the value of the information will be outweighed by the cost of obtaining it.

Analyze the Test Results Although the data should continually be reviewed as an experiment proceeds, it is after an experiment is completed that a more careful and thorough evaluation of the data should be made. This analysis should focus on four areas:

- *Purchase data.* Purchase data are often the most important data produced by the experiment. The levels of initial purchase (trial) throughout the course of the experiment provide an indication of how well the advertising and promotion program worked. The repeat rate (percentage of initial triers who made second and subsequent purchases) provides an indication of how well the product met the expectations created through advertising and promotion. The trial and repeat-purchase results provide the basis for estimating sales and market share for the product if it is to be distributed nationally.
- *Awareness data.* How effective was the media weight and media plan in creating product awareness? Do consumers know how much the product costs? Do they know its key features?
- *Competitive response.* Ideally, it was possible to monitor the response of competitors during the period of the test market. For example, competitors may have tried to distort test results by offering special promotions, price deals, and quantity discounts. This may provide some indication of what they would do if you move into national distribution, as well as some basis for estimating the effect of these actions.
- *Source of sales.* Assuming this is a new entry in an existing product category, it is important to determine where sales are coming from. In other words, which brands did the people who purchased the test product previously purchase? This gives a true indication of the real competition. If the company has an existing brand on the market, identifying the source of sales indicates to what extent the new product is likely to take business away from existing brands and from the competition.

These data will help a company decide whether to go back and improve the product or marketing program, drop the product, or move into national or regional distribution.

Simulated test market (STM) or pretest market
As an alternative to traditional test market, survey data and mathematical models are used to simulate test-market results for a much lower cost.

Simulated Test Markets **Simulated test markets (STMs),** sometimes referred to as pretest markets, use survey data and mathematical models to simulate test market results, for a much lower cost. Although there has been a decline in the use of traditional test markets, like the ones described earlier in the chapter, there has been a corresponding increase in the use of STMs. STMs do not involve actual market tests; they rely on laboratory approaches and mathematical modeling. Under the STM approach, a model of consumer responses to a new product is developed. This model is used to develop volume estimates and to provide information for evaluating features of the product and the anticipated marketing mix. A typical STM process includes the following steps:

- Intercept consumers at shopping malls (the mall-intercept approach is discussed in Chapter 7).
- Screen them for category use or target-market membership. This is achieved via screening questions on a separate questionnaire or as the initial questions on the main questionnaire.
- Those who qualify are exposed to the new product concept or prototype and, in many cases, prototype advertising for the new product.
- Participants are given an opportunity to buy the new product in a real or laboratory setting.
- Interview those who purchased the new product after an appropriate time interval to determine their assessment of it and their likelihood to make further purchases.
- Trial and repeat-purchase estimates, developed previously, provide the input for a mathematical model that is used to project share or volume for the product if it is distributed nationally. In addition, management must supply information about proposed advertising, distribution, and other elements of the proposed marketing strategy for the new product.[12]

Several STM systems are currently in widespread use. The four most popular STMs and the companies offering them are Litmus® (Yankelovich Partners), BASES® (The BASES Group), MicroTest® (Research International) and ASSESSOR® (The MARC Group).

There are four major reasons for the growing popularity of STMs. First, they are relatively surreptitious. Given the fact that laboratory designs are employed, competitors are unlikely to know a test is being conducted; they are privy neither to the details of the test nor the nature of the new product being tested. Second, testing can be done more quickly than in standard test markets. STM experiments can usually be completed in three to four months; those in standard test markets almost always take longer. Third, STM tests are much less costly to conduct than tests in standard test markets. A typical STM study can be conducted for $50,000 to $100,000; in contrast, cost of a typical standard test-market study can easily approach $1 million. Finally, and perhaps most important, some evidence shows that STMs can be quite accurate. For example, one published validation study showed that ASSESSOR produced predictions of market share that were, on average, within 0.8 share points of the actual shares achieved for the products tested. In terms of the variance of the estimates produced by ASSESSOR, the study showed that 70 percent of the predictions fell within 1.1 share points of actual results.[13]

Alternatives to Test Marketing

In addition to traditional test marketing and STMs, companies can gauge a product's potential in a few other ways. One alternative is a *rolling rollout,* which usually follows a pretest. A product is launched in a certain region rather than in one or two cities. Within a matter of days, scanner data can provide information on how the product is doing. The product can then be launched in additional regions, fixing ads and promotions along the way to a national introduction. General Mills has used this approach for products such as Multi-Grain Cheerios.

In PRACTICE

Test Market Accuracy Is Elusive

Test marketing is "the most difficult and abused variety of marketing research," but it is also the most valuable, said Doss Struse, director of marketing research services for General Mills, Minneapolis.

Companies will use almost every methodology and experimental design in their tests, "including many which are pretty poor from the standpoint of science." The role of marketing has become a specialized practice in controlled experiments, Struse said, usually when large marketing expenses are incurred in a business or a high risk in capital investment or marketing expense. "Over the years as marketing research has striven to mature as a scientific discipline, we have sought to gain more control over the testing environment. Marketing researchers have adopted each wave of innovation offering more control."

But greater control does not necessarily lead to better accuracy and validity, he warned. Many other elements of a test are just as important:

- In projecting results, one has to take the outcome of the test and figure out how to properly transfer it to another context in the future.
- Virtually every test market involves the notion of time. Yet, the analytic models researchers use to decipher the results are relatively weak.
- Developing the appropriate statistical controls by selecting matched panels of consumers or shares of market is considerably trickier in practice than in theory, and it generally is done incorrectly throughout the industry.
- Almost all the tests run by marketing researchers have an incredible confounding of effects.

In addition to these technical issues, there are numerous implementation issues. Four stand out among them.

First, when researchers run a test using paid media, they must appropriately represent what they would do on a broader scale. Second, they have to cope with how to translate promotion events from a continuing national scale to a test area. Third, researchers arrange or are forced to arrange tests that never can be duplicated in the "real world." Fourth, researchers often base their selection of tools on what is popular rather than on what will give appropriate results. "We've been guilty of buying high-tech tools which turn out to be unrealistic and underpowered statistically for the problem at hand," Struse said.[14] ■

Another alternative is to try out a product in a foreign market before rolling it out globally. One or a few countries serves as a test market for a continent or even the world. This type of *lead country* strategy has been used by Colgate–Palmolive Company. The company launched Palmolive Optims shampoo and conditioner in the Philippines, Australia, Mexico, and Hong Kong. Later, the products were rolled out in Europe, Asia, Latin America, and Africa.

Some marketers think that classic test marketing may make a comeback. For totally new products more thorough testing may prove necessary, whereas for other types of introductions, such as line extensions, an alternative approach may be more appropriate.

Summary

Experimental research provides evidence about whether the change in an independent variable causes some predictable change in a dependent variable. In order to show that a change in *A* was the likely cause of an observed change in *B,* we must show three things: correlation, appropriate time order of occurrence, and the elimination of other possible causal factors. Experiments can be conducted in a laboratory or in a field setting. The major advantage of conducting experiments in a laboratory is that in this environment the researcher can control extraneous factors. However, in market research, laboratory settings often do not appropriately replicate the marketplace. Experiments conducted in the marketplace are called field experiments. The major difficulty with field experiments is that the researcher cannot control all the other factors that might influence the dependent variable.

In experimentation, we are concerned with internal and external validity. Internal validity refers to the extent to which competing explanations of the experimental results can be avoided. External validity refers to whether the causal relationships measured in an experiment can be generalized to other settings. Extraneous variables are other independent variables that may affect the dependent variable. They stand in the way of our ability to conclude that an observed change in the dependent variable was due to the affect of the experimental or treatment variable. Extraneous factors discussed include history, maturation, instrument variation, selection bias, mortality, testing effects, and statistical regression.

In an experimental design, the researcher has control over one or more independent variable and manipulates one or more independent variable. Nonexperimental designs involve no manipulation and are referred to as ex post facto research. An experimental design includes four elements: the treatment, subjects, a dependent variable that will be measured, and a plan or procedure for dealing with extraneous causal factors. An experimental or treatment effect refers to the effect of a treatment variable on a dependent variable. Four basic approaches are used to control extraneous factors: randomization, actual physical control, experimental design control, and statistical control.

Experiments have an obvious advantage: they are the only type of research that can demonstrate the existence and nature of causal relationships between variables of interest. Yet the amount of actual experimentation done in marketing research is limited because of the high cost of experiments, security issues, and implementation problems. However, evidence suggests that the use of experiments in marketing research is growing.

Preexperimental designs offer little or no control over the influence of extraneous factors and are thus generally difficult to interpret. Examples include the one-shot case study, the one-group pretest/posttest design, and the static-group comparison. In a true experimental design, the researcher is able to eliminate all extraneous variables as competitive hypotheses to the treatment. Examples of true experimental design are the before and after with control group design and after-only with control group design.

In quasi-experimental designs, the researcher has control over data collection procedures but lacks complete control over the scheduling of treatments. The treatment groups in a quasi-experiment are normally formed by assigning respondents to treatments in a nonrandom fashion. Examples of quasi-experimental designs are the interrupted time-series design and the multiple time-series design.

Test marketing involves testing a new product or some element of the marketing mix by using experimental or quasi-experimental designs. Test markets are field experiments, and they are extremely expensive to conduct. The steps in conducting a test market study include defining the objectives for the study, selecting a basic approach to be used, developing detailed procedures for the test, selecting markets for the test, and analyzing the test results.

Key Terms & Definitions

Experiment A research approach where one variable is manipulated and the effect on another variable is observed.

Causal research Research designed to determine whether a change in one variable most likely caused an observed change in another.

Concomitant variation or correlation A predictable statistical relationship between two variables.

Appropriate time order of occurrence To be considered a likely cause of a dependent variable, a change in an independent variable must occur before a change is observed in the dependent variable.

Laboratory experiments Experiments conducted in a controlled setting.

Field experiments Tests conducted outside the laboratory in an actual market environment.

Internal validity The extent to which competing explanations for experimental results can be avoided.

External validity The extent to which the causal relationships measured in an experiment can be generalized to outside people, settings, and times.

History Things that happen or outside variables that change between the beginning and end of an experiment.

Maturation Changes in subjects that take place during an experiment that are not related to the experiment but may affect their responses to the experimental factor.

Instrument variation Differences or changes in measurement instruments (such as interviewers or observers) that explain differences in measurements.

Selection bias Systematic differences between the test group and the control group due to a biased selection process.

Mortality Loss of test units or subjects during the course of an experiment. The problem is that those who leave may be systematically different from those who stay.

Testing effect An effect that is a by-product of the research process and not the experimental variable.

Regression to the mean The tendency for people's behavior to move toward the average for that behavior during the course of an experiment.

Experimental design A test in which the researcher has control over one or more independent variables and manipulates them.

Treatment The independent variable that is manipulated in an experiment.

Experimental effect The effect of the treatment variable(s) on the dependent variable.

Randomization The random assignment of group subjects to treatment conditions to ensure equal representation of characteristics in all groups.

Physical control Holding the value or level of extraneous variables constant throughout the course of an experiment.

Design control Use of an experimental design to control extraneous causal factors.

Statistical control Adjusting for the effects of confounding variables by statistically adjusting the value of the dependent variable for each treatment condition.

Contamination The inclusion in a test of a group of respondents who are not normally there; for example, outside buyers who see an advertisement intended only for those in the test area and enter the area to purchase the product being tested.

Preexperimental design A design that offers little or no control over extraneous factors.

One-shot case study design A preexperimental design with no control group and an after-measurement only.

One-group pretest/posttest design A preexperimental design with pre- and postmeasurements but no control group.

Static-group comparison design A preexperimental design that utilizes an experimental and a control group. However, subjects or test units are not randomly assigned to the two groups and no premeasurements are taken.

True experimental design Research using an experimental group and a control group, with randomized assignment of test units to both groups.

Before and after with control group design A true experimental design that includes the random assignment of subjects or test units to experimental and control groups and the premeasurement of both groups.

Solomon four-group design Research using two experimental groups and two control groups to control for all extraneous variable threats.

After-only with control group design True experimental design that involves random assignment of subjects or test units to experimental and control groups, but no premeasurement of the dependent variable.

Quasi-experimental design A study in which the researcher lacks complete control over the scheduling of the treatment or must assign respondents to treatment in a nonrandom manner.

Interrupted time-series design Research in which the treatment "interrupts" ongoing repeated measurements.

Multiple time-series design An interrupted time-series design with a control group.

Test market Testing a new product or some element of the marketing mix using experimental or quasi-experimental designs.

Cannibalization rate The extent to which a new product takes business away from a company's existing products.

Simulated test market (STM) or pretest market As an alternative to traditional test market, survey data and mathematical models are used to simulate test market results for a much lower cost.

Questions for Review & Critical Thinking

1. Pets-R-Us has developed a new frozen food for parakeets. You defrost it and serve it in its tray to your parakeet. Pets-R-Us is considering skipping test marketing and going directly into a national rollout. What are the advantages of doing it this way? What are the disadvantages of not doing any test marketing?
2. You are getting ready to test market a new snack food that is targeted at nutrition-conscious college students. How would you go about selecting test cities for this product? What are some cities that you might choose? Why would you choose those cities?
3. Why is experimentation best suited for determining causation?
4. What are some of the independent variables that should be dealt with in an experiment to test consumer reactions to new fast-food items?
5. The student center at your university or college is considering three alternative brands of frozen pizza to be offered on the menu. They want to offer only one of the three and want to find out which one students prefer. Design an experiment to determine which brand of pizza the students prefer.
6. The night students at a university are much older than the day students. Introduce an explicit control for day versus night students in the preceding experiment.
7. Why are quasi-experiments much more popular in marketing research than true experiments?
8. How does the history effect differ from the maturation effect? What specific actions might you take to deal with each in an experiment?
9. The manufacturer of microwave ovens has designed an improved model that will reduce energy costs and cook food evenly throughout. However, this new model will increase the product's price by 30 percent because of extra components and engineering design changes. The company wants to determine what effect the new model will have on sales of its microwave ovens. Propose an appropriate experimental design that can provide this information for management. Why was this design selected?
10. Discuss various methods by which extraneous causal factors can be controlled.
11. Explain how various measurements of the experimental effect in a Solomon four-group design can provide estimates of the effects of certain extraneous variables.
12. Discuss the alternatives to traditional test marketing. Explain the advantages, disadvantages of these alternatives to traditional test marketing.

Market Analysts and Promotional Specialists, Inc.

Real-Life Research

Market Analysts and Promotional Specialists, Inc. (MAPS) is a marketing consulting firm that specializes in the development of promotional campaigns. The firm was formed five years ago by two young marketing graduate students, David Roth and Lisa Ryan. The students soon overcame their initial lack of experience and since have become known for their innovativeness and creativity. Their clients include industrial wholesalers, retail product manufacturers, food brokers, and distributors, as well as retail outlets.

In 1994, Dixie Brewing company enlisted MAPS to develop a new promotional campaign for its line of beers. At the time, Dixie was the last of the microbreweries in New Orleans and distributed its products within a 200-mile radius of the city. The company had enjoyed a good reputation for a number of years but recently tarnished its image by accidentally distributing a shipment of bad beer. Dixie also was losing market share because of increased competition from national brewers. Recently Miller High Life purchased Crescent Distributors, a large liquor distributor in the New Orleans area, and was beginning to implement aggressive promotional tactics in the local market.

Dixie was concerned primarily with its retail merchandising methods. MAPS immediately began to study Dixie's product line and the present shelf space allocations in various stores throughout the market area. Because of MAPS's previous work with food brokers, it realized that proper shelf placement was extremely important in supermarket merchandising.

The company's product line consisted of two beers, Dixie and Dixie Light. Both beers were sold in 32-ounce glass bottles, 12-ounce glass bottle six-packs, and 12-ounce can six-packs.

In New Orleans, beer may be purchased in supermarkets and convenience stores. Also, in most stores, beer can be purchased either warm or cold. In studying the refrigerated closets holding beverages, MAPS noticed that most were small, 8 to 12 feet in length, and usually had glass doors on the front. Because of the relatively small size of the entire cold beer display, David and Lisa believed that the typical consumer would view the case from left to right. As such, they believed Dixie should place its products on the extreme left side of all cold beer cases.

Warm beer was displayed in a much different manner. Most stores displayed beverage products in bulk and usually devoted an entire aisle for such displays. David and Lisa reasoned that the normal consumer could not view all the brands at once and would thus have to "shop" or walk into the aisle. For this reason, they recommended that Dixie place its beer in the middle of the other brands.

Because Dixie Light was produced in response to Miller Lite, David and Lisa recommended that it be placed to the left of Miller Lite in both warm and cold beer displays. Traditionally, Dixie Light had been placed next to its standard beer brand. Dixie had noticed a significant decrease in its regular brand's market share on the introduction of Dixie Light.

To test its theories, MAPS selected a convenience store located in a suburb of New Orleans. The store contained both warm and cold beer displays. This store was then used in an experiment to measure the effect of shelf placement on beer sales. One treatment consisted of setting up the displays as they were currently being used in stores across town. The second treatment arranged the displays according to the new MAPS plan. All other factors, such as price and number of bottles, were held constant throughout the experiment. The first version of the setup was used for the first two weeks in April, and the second treatment was run for the last two weeks in April.

The following statistics show the percentage of beer purchased by brand for each treatment:

Brand	Treatment #1	Treatment #2
Dixie	18%	23%
Miller	18%	15%
Bud	19%	18%
Coors	13%	13%
Dixie Light	10%	8%
Miller Lite	13%	14%
Coors Light	9%	9%

Questions

1. Critique the research design with respect to internal and external validity considerations.
2. Discuss the advantages and disadvantages of using the convenience store in this experiment.
3. Based on the information given, what conclusions can be made about the MAPS plan?
4. Recommend a research design that would produce more interpretable results.

CD Opportunity

1. The Ethical Dilemmas for this part will help you understand ethical issues surrounding research design. The Marketing Research Across the Organization exercises on your CD will show you how the research design is affected by different functional areas in the firm.
2. The PowerPoint presentation found on your CD will help you organize your thoughts about the chapter content. Instructions for creating PowerNotes are included.

PART three

Data Acquisition

Check it out!

Remember to visit http://mcdaniel.swcollege.com for information to help you with the material in Part Three. MR Online in the Resource Center of http://marketing.swcollege.com can also help you review for your final exam!

The Concepts of Measurement and Attitude Scales

Learning Objectives

1 *To understand the concept of measurement*

2 *To understand the four levels of scales and their typical usage*

3 *To become aware of the concepts of reliability and validity*

4 *To become familiar with the concept of scaling*

5 *To learn about the various types of attitude scales*

6 *To realize the importance of purchase intent scales in marketing research*

7 *To examine some basic considerations when selecting a type of scale*

CHAPTER *nine*

Golfers know that they are playing a game where so many things can go wrong and frequently do. They are forever searching for the ball or looking for the latest high-tech club or gizmo that will inspire confidence and lower their golf score. Therein lies the foundation for the multimillion dollar golf industry.

Maxfli Golf, a Greenville, South Carolina, manufacturer of golf balls and other golf accessories, decided that a new promotion program might quickly boost its market share. The company brought in Wallace Church Associates, New York, to handle the design duties and BBDO South, Atlanta, to develop new TV and print ads.

The research findings and insights of Wallace Church and BBDO resulted in a new positioning for Maxfli that projects a youthful, yet still respectful, attitude toward the game of golf.

Guiding these efforts were a number of research studies, including segmentation work and a variety of qualitative and quantitative approaches. "We needed to develop a market-driven identity for Maxfli based on consumer wants and needs," says Cheryl Swanson, senior vice president, strategic planning at Wallace Church Associates.

The research process started with focus groups to uncover what motivates golf ball purchases. "We wanted to find out how people talk about golf balls," says Terry Rooke, executive vice president, director of research, BBDO South. "Do they identify a ball by its company, by the brand that's on the ball, or by some numeric designation?"

After the focus groups, BBDO used a Market Facts national panel as a cost-effective way to generate a representative sample of golfers to contact by telephone. "The golf category is a low-incidence one," Rooke says. "Total golfers only represent about 10 percent of the population and heavy golfers are a small subset of that, so it's not something that you typically would survey for randomly because the costs would be prohibitive."

The research showed that while many golfers are quality oriented, there is an even bigger segment that could be called the fashion crowd of golf. "They want to play the right brand and the right ball because it's stylish to do so, not because they're committed to the game of golf. These are often the country club or corporate golfers, the wannabes who want to play with excellent golfers, none of whom might be committed to becoming a par golfer but who want to use the products that par golfers use."

Find out more about how Maxfli applied this new, youthful orientation to its Web page at

http://www.maxfli.com

BBDO also conducted a Brand Fitness Study on Maxfli, a proprietary approach that seeks to identify the type of person associated with a brand (user imagery), the product-based imagery (what does the product do for you?), and the personal drives imagery (the underlying motivating factors). "We map the three dimensions of imagery for our brands as well as all competing brands and by using correspondence mapping we're able to find both important and unique space as well as where brands overlap with competitors," Rooke says.

Based on the research findings and the insights of Wallace Church and BBDO, the new positioning for Maxfli projected a youthful attitude, but one that treated the game of golf with respect. "We went with the design that best signaled the positioning we had chosen, that Maxfli stood for winning and a youthful approach, not in terms of years but in a way of living life," Rooke says.

"We were trying to appeal to a more contemporary, aggressive golfer, one who would take more risks, who knew what they wanted and would be more assertive in their approach. A lot of golfers buy on image. Whatever they feel good about they pick. It's almost like apparel or cosmetics. The ball you choose says a lot about you."[1]

Data regarding the concepts of "quality oriented" and the "fashion-crowd segment" were based on measurement, as was user imagery, product-based imagery, and personal drives imagery. How does a researcher go about measuring a construct? How does one determine the reliability and validity of the information? What factors should be considered when selecting an attitude scale? These are some of the issues we will explore in Chapter 9. ■

The Concept of Measurement and Measurement Scales

Measurement

Measurement The process of assigning numbers or labels to people or things in accordance with specific rules to represent quantities or qualities of attributes.

Rule A guide, a method, or a command that tells a researcher what to do.

Measurement is the process of assigning numbers or labels to objects, persons, states, or events in accordance with specific rules to represent quantities or qualities of attributes. Measurement, then, is a procedure used to assign numbers that reflect the amount of an attribute possessed by an event, person, or object. Note that the event, person, or object is not what is measured, but rather its attributes. A researcher, for example, does not measure a consumer, but measures the attitudes, income, brand loyalty, age, and other relevant factors about the consumer.

Another key aspect of measurement is the concept of rules. A **rule** is a guide, a method, or a command that tells a researcher what to do. For example, a rule might say, "Assign the numbers 1 through 5 to people according to their disposition to do household chores. If they are extremely willing to do any and all household chores, assign them a 1. If they are not willing to do any household chores, assign them a 5." In the same manner, specific rules would also be assigned for numbers 2, 3, and 4.

A problem that is often encountered with rules is a lack of clarity or specificity. Some things are easy to measure because the rules are easy to create and follow. The measurement of gender, for example, is quite simple, and concrete criteria can be offered to determine sex. The researcher is then told to assign a 1 for male and a 2 for female. Unfortunately, many characteristics of interest to a market researcher, such as brand loyalty, purchase intent, or total family income, are much more difficult to measure because it is difficult to devise rules to measure the true value of these consumer attributes. Let us examine how a researcher should measure a phenomenon.

Measurement Scales

A **scale** is a set of symbols or numbers constructed to be assigned by a rule to individuals or their behaviors or attitudes. The assignment on the scale is indicated by the individual's possession of whatever the scale is supposed to measure.

Scale A set of symbols or numbers so constructed that they can be assigned by a rule to individuals or their behaviors or attitudes.

Creating a measurement scale begins with determining the level of measurement that is either desirable or possible. Table 9.1 on page 250 describes the four basic levels of measurement: nominal, ordinal, interval, and ratio. These four levels lead to the four kinds of scales discussed below.

Nominal Scales

Nominal scales are commonly used in marketing research. A **nominal scale** partitions data into categories that are mutually exclusive and collectively exhaustive. This implies that every bit of data will fit into single categories and that all the data will fit somewhere in the scale. The term nominal means namelike, implying that the numbers assigned to objects or phenomena name or classify but have no true numeric meaning. The numbers cannot be ordered, added, or divided. They are simply labels or identification numbers and nothing else—examples of nominal scales are

Nominal scale A scale that partitions data into mutually exclusive and collectively exhaustive categories.

Sex	(1) Male	(2) Female	
Geographic area	(1) Urban	(2) Rural	(3) Suburban

The only quantification in numerical scales is the number and percentages of objects in each category; for example, 50 males (48.5 percent) and 53 females (51.5 percent). Computing a *mean* or average, for example, of 2.4 for a geographic area would be meaningless; only the *mode*, the value that appears most often, would be appropriate. For example, cities with a population of 500,000.

Ordinal Scales

Ordinal scales maintain the labeling characteristics of nominal scales, but also have the ability to order data. Ordinal measurement is possible when a transitivity postulate can be applied. A *postulate* is an assumption that is an essential prerequisite to carrying out an operation or line of thinking. The *transitivity postulate* can be described by the notion that

Ordinal scale A nominal scale that can order data.

"if *a* is greater than *b,* and *b* is greater than *c,* then *a* is greater than *c.*" Other terms that can be substituted are "is preferred to," "is stronger than," or "precedes." Here is an example of an ordinal scale:

Please rank the following fax machines from 1 to 5, with 1 being the most preferred and 5 the least preferred:

Panasonic ________

Toshiba ________

Sharp ________

Savin ________

Ricoh ________

Ordinal numbers are used strictly to indicate rank order. The numbers do not indicate absolute quantities, nor do they imply that the intervals between

Table 9.1

The Four Major Levels of Measurement

Level	Description	Basic Empirical Operations	Typical Usage	Typical Descriptive Statistics
Nominal	Uses numerals to identify objects, individuals, events, or groups	Determination of equality or inequality	Classification (male/female; buyer/ nonbuyer)	Frequency counts, percentages/modes
Ordinal	In addition to identification, the numerals provide information about the relative amount of some characteristic posed by an event, object, etc.	Determination of greater or lesser	Rankings/ratings (preferences for hotels, banks, social class; ratings of foods based on fat content, cholesterol)	Median (mean and variance metric)
Interval	Possesses all the properties of nominal and ordinal scales, plus the intervals between consecutive points are equal	Determination of equality of intervals	Preferred measure of complex concepts/constructs (temperature scale, air pressure scale, level of knowledge about brands)	Mean/variance
Ratio	Incorporates all the properties of nominal, ordinal, and interval scales, plus it includes an absolute zero point	Determination of equality of ratios	When precision instruments are available (sales, number of on-time arrivals, age)	Geometric mean/ harmonic mean

*Because higher levels of measurement contain all the properties of lower levels, we can convert higher-level scales into lower-level ones (i.e., ratio to interval or ordinal or nominal; or interval to ordinal or nominal; or ordinal to nominal).

Source: Adapted from S. S. Stevens, "On the Theory of Scales of Measurement," *Science* 103 (June 7, 1946), pp. 677–680. With permission from the American Association for the Advancement of Science.

the numbers are equal. For example, the person ranking the fax machines might like Toshiba only slightly more than Savin and view Ricoh as totally unacceptable. Such information would not be obtained from an ordinal scale.

Because ranking is the objective of an ordinal scale, any rule prescribing a series of numbers that preserves an ordered relationship is satisfactory. In other words, Panasonic could have been assigned a value of 30; Sharp, 40; Toshiba, 27; Ricoh, 32; and Savin, 42; or any other series of numbers, as long as the basic ordering was preserved. In this example, Savin was 1; Sharp, 2; Ricoh, 3; Panasonic, 4; and Toshiba, 5. Common arithmetical operations such as addition or multiplication cannot be used with ordinal scales. The appropriate measure of *central tendency* is the mode or the median.

A controversial (yet rather common) use of ordinal scales is to rate various characteristics. In this case, the researcher assigns numbers to reflect the relative ratings of a series of statements, then uses these numbers to interpret relative distance. Recall that our market researchers examining role ambiguity used a scale ranging from very certain to very uncertain. Note that the following values had been assigned:

(1)	(2)	(3)	(4)	(5)
Very certain	Certain	Neutral	Uncertain	Very uncertain

If a researcher can justify the assumption that the intervals are equal within the scale, then the more powerful parametric statistical tests can be applied. Parametric statistical tests will be discussed in Chapter 14. Indeed, some measurement scholars argue that we should normally assume equal intervals.

> The best procedure would seem to be to treat ordinal measurements as though they were interval measurements but to be constantly alert to the possibility of gross inequality of intervals. As much as possible about the characteristics of the measuring tools should be learned. Much useful information has been obtained by this approach, with resulting scientific advances in psychology, sociology, and education. In short, it is unlikely that researchers will be led seriously astray by heeding this advice, if they are careful in applying it.[2]

Interval scale An ordinal scale with equal intervals between points to show relative amounts, which may include an arbitrary zero point.

Interval Scales

Interval scales contain all the features of ordinal scales with the added dimension that the intervals between the points on the scale are equal. The concept of temperature is based on equal intervals. Market researchers often prefer to use interval scales over ordinal scales because they can measure how much of a trait one consumer has (or does not have) over another. Interval scales enable a researcher to discuss the differences separating two objects. The scale possesses properties of order and difference but with an arbitrary zero point, for example, Fahrenheit and centigrade scales. Thus, the freezing point of water is 0° on one scale and 32° on the other.

The arbitrary zero point of interval scales restricts the statements that a researcher can make about the scale points. One can say that 80°F is hotter than 32°F or that 64°F is 16° cooler than 80°F. However, one cannot say that 64°F is twice as warm as 32°F. Why? Because the zero point on the Fahrenheit scale is arbitrary. To prove our point, consider the transformation of the two temperatures to Celsius using the following formula:

$$C = (F - 32) \times 5/9.$$

Thus, 32°F equals 0°C and 64°F equals 17.8°C. Our previous statement for Fahrenheit (64° is twice as warm as 32°) does not hold for Celsius. The same would be true if we were evaluating fax machines for which factors were liked the most using an interval scale. If Toshiba is given score of 20 and Sharp a 10, we cannot say that Toshiba is liked twice as much as Sharp. This is because a zero point defining the absence of liking has not been identified and assigned a value of zero on the scale.

Interval scales are amenable to such computations as an arithmetic mean, standard deviation, and correlation coefficients, and the powerful parametric statistical tests, such as *t*-tests and *F*-tests, can be applied. In addition, researchers can take a conservative approach and use nonparametric tests if there is concern about the assumption that intervals are equal.

Ratio scale An interval scale with a meaningful zero point so that magnitudes can be compared arithmetically.

Ratio Scales

Ratio scales have all the powers of the scales previously discussed, as well as providing a meaningful absolute zero or origin. Because there is universal agreement about the location of the zero point, comparisons among the magnitudes of ratio-scaled values are acceptable. Thus, a ratio scale reflects the actual amount of a variable. Physical characteristics of a respondent, such as age, weight, or height, are examples of ratio-scaled variables. Other ratio scales are based on area, distance, money amounts, return rates, population counts, and lapsed periods of time.

Because some objects have none of the properties being measured, a ratio scale originates at zero, thus having an absolute empirical meaning. For example, an investment (albeit a poor one) could have no rate of return, or a census tract in New Mexico could be devoid of any persons. An absolute zero implies that all arithmetic operations are possible, including multiplication and division. Numbers on the scale indicate the actual amounts of the property being measured. If a large bag of McDonald's french fries weighs 8 ounces and a regular bag at Burger King weighs 4 ounces, then the large McDonald's bag of fries weighs twice as much as a regular Burger King bag.

Sources of Measurement Differences

An ideal market research study would provide information that is accurate, precise, lucid, and timely. Accurate data implies accurate measurement, or M = A, where M refers to measurement and A stands for complete accuracy. In market research, this ideal is rarely, if ever, obtained. Instead we have

$$M = A + E, \text{ where } E = \text{error}$$

Errors can be either random or systematic, as noted in Chapter 7. **Systematic error** is error that results in a constant bias in the measurements. The bias results from faults in the measurement instrument or process. For example, if we are using a faulty ruler (1 inch is actually 1½ inches) in Pillsbury's test kitchens to measure the height of chocolate cakes using alternative recipes, all cakes will be recorded below their actual height. **Random error** also influences the measurements, but not systematically. Random error is transient in nature and does not occur consistently. For example, a person may not answer a question truthfully simply because he or she is in a bad mood that day.

Systematic error Error that results in a constant bias in the measurements.

Random error Error that affects measurement in a transient, inconsistent manner.

Two scores on a measurement scale can differ, for a number of reasons. Only the first reason listed below does not involve error. The remaining seven sources of measurement differences are either random error or systematic.

1. *A true difference in the characteristic being measured*. A perfect measurement difference would be solely the result of actual differences. If John rates McDonald's service as 1 (excellent) and Sandy rates service as 4 (average), then the difference is due only to actual attitude differences.
2. *Differences due to stable characteristics of individual respondents,* such as personality, values, and intelligence. Sandy has an aggressive, rather critical personality and he gives no one and nothing the benefit of a doubt. He was actually quite pleased with the service he received at McDonald's, but he expects such service and so gave it an average rating.
3. *Differences due to short-term personal factors,* such as temporary mood swings, health problems, time constraints, fatigue, or other transitory factors. Earlier today, John won $400 in a "Name that Tune" contest on a local radio station. He stopped by McDonald's for a burger after he had picked up his winning check. His reply on the service-quality questionnaire might have been quite different if he had been interviewed yesterday.
4. *Differences caused by situational factors,* such as distractions or others present in the interview situation. Sandy is giving his replies while trying to watch his four-year-old nephew, who is running amok on the McDonald's playground; John had his new fiancée along when he was interviewed. Replies of both men might have been different if they had been interviewed at home while no other friend or relative was present.
5. *Differences resulting from variations in administering the survey.* Interviewers can ask questions with different voice inflections, causing response variation. Different interviewers can cause responses to vary. This may be due to rapport, manner of dress, sex, race, or a host of other factors. Interviewer bias can be as subtle as a nodding of the head. One interviewer who tended to nod unconsciously was found to have biased some respondents. They thought that the interviewer was agreeing with them when it was in fact a way of saying, "Okay, I'm recording what you say—tell me more."

6. *Differences due to the sampling of items included in the questionnaire.* When researchers attempt to measure the quality of service at McDonald's, the scales and other questions used represent only a portion of items that could have been used. The scales created by the researchers reflect their interpretation of the construct (service quality) and the way it is measured. If the researchers had used different words or items had been added or removed, then the outcome with respect to scale values reported by John and Sandy might have been different.
7. *Differences due to a lack of clarity in the measurement instrument.* A question may be ambiguous, complex, or incorrectly interpreted. A question asking, "How far do you live from McDonald's?" with answers such as (1) less than 5 minutes, (2) 5 to 10 minutes, and so forth, is ambiguous. If someone is walking, it is undoubtedly longer than a person driving a car or riding a bike.
8. *Differences due to mechanical or instrument factors.* Blurred questionnaires, lack of space to fully record an answer, missing pages in a questionnaire, or a balky pen can result in differences in responses.[3]

Reliability

A measurement scale that provides consistent results over time is reliable. If a ruler consistently measures a chocolate cake as 9 inches high, then the rule is said to be reliable. Reliable scales, gauges, and other measurement devices can be used with confidence, with the knowledge that transient and situational factors are not interfering with the measurement process. Reliable instruments provide stable measures at different times under different conditions. A key question regarding reliability is, "If we measure some phenomenon over and over again with the same measurement device, will we get the same or highly similar results?" If the answer is affirmative, the device is reliable.

Reliability Measures that are consistent from one administration to the next.

Therefore, **reliability** is the degree to which measures are free from random error and therefore provide consistent data. The less error there is, the more reliable an observation should be, so that a measurement that is free of error should be a correct measure. Therefore, a measurement is reliable if the measurement does not change when the concept being measured remains constant in value. Conversely, if the concept being measured does change in value, the reliable measure will indicate that change. How can a measuring instrument be unreliable? If your weight stays constant at 150 pounds, but repeated measurements on your bathroom scale show your weight to fluctuate, the lack of reliability may be due to a weak spring inside the scale.

There are three ways to assess reliability: test-retest, equivalent forms, and internal consistency (see Table 9.2).

Test-retest reliability The ability of the same instrument to produce consistent results when used a second time under conditions as nearly the same as possible.

Stability Lack of change in results from test to retest.

Test-Retest Reliability

Test-retest reliability is obtained by repeating the measurement using the same instrument under as nearly the same conditions as possible. The theory behind test-retest is that if random variations are present, they will be revealed by variations in the scores between the two tests. **Stability** means that very few differences in scores are found between the first

Table 9.2

Assessing the Reliability of a Measurement Instrument

Test-retest reliability	Use the same instrument a second time under as nearly the same conditions as possible.
Equivalent form reliability	Use two instruments that are as similar as possible to measure the same object during the same time period.
Internal consistency reliability	Compare different samples of items being used to measure a phenomenon during the same time period.

and second administration of the tests; the measuring instrument is said to be stable. For example, assume that a 30-item department store image measurement scale was administered to the same group of shoppers at two points in time. If the correlation between the two measurements was high, the reliability would be assumed to be high.

There are several problems with test-retest reliability. First, it is often difficult to locate and gain the cooperation of respondents for a second testing. Second, the first measurement may alter the person's response on the second measurement. Third, environmental or personal factors may change, causing the second measurement to change.

Equivalent Form Reliability The problems of the test-retest approach can be avoided by creating equivalent forms of a measurement instrument. For example, assume that the researcher is interested in identifying inner-directed versus outer-directed lifestyles. Two questionnaires would be created containing measures of both inner-directed and outer-directed behavior. These measures would receive about the same emphasis on each questionnaire. Although the questions used to ascertain the lifestyles would be different on each questionnaire, the same number of questions used to measure each lifestyle would be approximately equal. The recommended interval for administering the second equivalent form is two weeks, although in some cases they are given one after the other or even simultaneously. **Equivalent form reliability** is determined by measuring the correlation of the scores on the two instruments.

Equivalent form reliability
The ability to produce similar results using two instruments as similar as possible to measure the same thing.

Two problems with equivalent forms should be noted. First, it is difficult, perhaps impossible, to create two totally equivalent forms. Second, if equivalence can be achieved, it may not be worth the time, trouble, and expense involved. The theory behind the equivalent forms approach to reliability assessment is the same as for the test-retest approach. The primary difference between the test-retest and the equivalent forms methods is the testing instrument itself. Test-retest uses the same instrument, whereas equivalent forms use different but highly similar measuring instruments.

Internal consistency reliability Ability to produce similar results using different samples to measure a phenomenon during the same time period.

Split-half technique A method of assessing the reliability of a scale by dividing into two the total set of measurement items and correlating the results.

Internal Consistency Reliability **Internal consistency reliability** assesses the ability to produce similar results using different samples to measure a phenomenon during the same time period. The theory of internal consistency rests on the notion of equivalence. Equivalence is concerned with how much error may be introduced by using different samples of items to measure a phenomenon. It is concerned with variations at one point in time among samples of items. A researcher can test for item equivalence by assessing the homogeneity of a set of items. The total set of items used to measure a phenomenon, such as inner-directed lifestyles, is divided into two halves; the total score of the two halves is then correlated (see Table 9.3). Use of the **split-half technique** typically calls for scale items to be randomly assigned to one half or the other. The problem with this method, however, is that the estimate of the coefficient of reliability is totally dependent on how the items were split. Different splits result in different correlations but should not.

To overcome the split-halves problems, many researchers now use the *Cronbach Alpha.* This technique computes the mean reliability coefficient estimates for all possible ways of splitting a set of items in half. A lack of

Table 9.3

Statements Used to Measure Inner-Directed Lifestyles

I often don't get the credit I deserve for things I do well.
I try to get my own way regardless of others.
My greatest achievements are ahead of me.
I have a number of ideas that someday I would like to put into a book.
I am quick to accept new ideas.
I often think about how I look and what impressions I am making on others.
I am a competitive person.
I feel upset when I hear that people are criticizing or blaming me.
I'd like to be a celebrity.
I get a real thrill out of doing dangerous things.
I feel that almost nothing in life can substitute for great achievement.
It's important for me to be noticed.
I keep in close touch with my friends.
I spend a good deal of time trying to decide how I feel about things.
I often think I can feel my way into the innermost being of another person.
I feel that ideals are powerful motivating forces in people.
I think someone can be a good person without believing in God.
The eastern religions are more appealing to me than Christianity.
I feel satisfied with my life.
I enjoy getting involved in new and unusual situations.
Overall, I'd say I'm happy.
I feel I understand where my life is going.
I like to think I'm different from other people.
I adopt a commonsense attitude toward life.

In PRACTICE

The Truth About What Respondents Say

Martin Weinberger is executive vice president of Oxtoby–Smith, Inc., New York, one of America's largest and oldest marketing research companies. His 25 years of experience in the research industry have led him to develop several perspectives regarding measurement in consumer research.

1. *Sometimes consumers don't tell the truth; sometimes they are willing to reveal it.* Several years ago, a major catalog company was having trouble with its boys' slacks—it was getting an unusually large number of returns. Consumers were writing that the reason for the return was that the slacks did not fit properly. On the basis of that information, the catalog sales company believed something must be wrong with the diagrams and instructions it provided to consumers for ordering the right size slacks. Oxtoby–Smith was asked to find out what was wrong with the diagrams or the instructions so the client could fix them. We were given the names of consumers who had returned the boys' slacks.

   We sent our interviewers into the field, carrying the heavy catalog, with the diagrams and the instructions. What we found was not what we had expected to find. The consumers told us the slacks had fit perfectly well. The mothers had ordered three or four pairs of slacks for their teenage sons in the hope that the son would find one pair he would be willing to wear. Then the mother had to face returning the other two or three pairs. The mothers felt uncomfortable giving any explanation for the return of the slacks other than "poor fit." This finding indicated that the diagrams were not the problem. The instructions were not the problem. The catalog company had to learn to live with the returns in the same way the mothers had to live with the habits of their teenage sons.

2. *Sometimes consumers claim more than they know; sometimes they are just confused.* It has been well established that consumers sometimes claim awareness of brands that do not exist. That is why it is important to include fictitious brand names in studies of brand awareness to see how much claiming is going on. In fact, I have done a study in which a fictitious brand name had *more* brand awareness than the client's brand and the client considered changing the name of its brand to the fictitious brand name!

3. *Sometimes consumers don't know why they buy the brands they buy.* This section could be subtitled "Why you should not ask why." I have conducted a large number of studies asking consumers, at the client's request, *why* they buy the products they buy, and I have looked at their answers to that question. At the same time, I have looked at their answers to other questions. I have found that consumers often do not really *know* why they buy the brands they buy.

continued

A simple case in point is a food or beverage product. Ask consumers why they buy a brand, and they usually will tell you "because it tastes good." If you give a consumer a blind product test, you may find out that this individual cannot differentiate between his or her preferred brand X and brand Y. If you use a double-blind paired comparison, in one paired blind test a consumer will prefer X and in another paired blind test the same individual will prefer Y.

4. *Consumers not only have opinions, they have passions.* Generally, consumers are very cooperative. They will answer almost any questions you ask them. But, my experience teaches me that you need to know more than just their opinions; you need to know their passions.

For example, a manufacturer of toilet paper that is thinking of introducing a scented version might ask us to find out which of a series of scents is preferred by consumers. We could test the scents and tell them scent A is more widely preferred than scent B. However, we would be remiss in our job if we failed to find out whether consumers would be disposed toward toilet paper *with any scent at all* and what the scent preferences are of those who *like* the idea of scented toilet paper. Possibly those who are interested in toilet paper with scents prefer scent B over scent A, whereas scent A appeals to those who, in the marketplace, would be buying *unscented paper.*[4] ■

correlation of an item with other items in the scale is evidence that the item does not belong in the scale and should be omitted. One limitation of the Cronbach Alpha is that the scale items require equal intervals. If this criterion cannot be met, another test called the *KR-20* can be used. The KR-20 technique is applicable for all dichotomous or nominally scaled items.

Validity

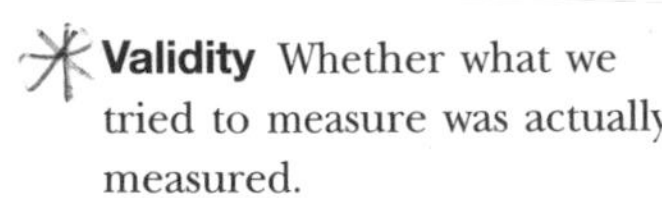

Validity Whether what we tried to measure was actually measured.

Recall that the second characteristic of a good measurement device is validity. **Validity** addresses the issue of whether what we tried to measure was actually measured. When Coke first brought out "New Coke," it had conducted more than 5,000 interviews purporting to show that New Coke was favored over original Coke. Unfortunately, its measurement instrument was not valid. This led to one of the greatest marketing debacles of all time! The validity of a measure refers to the extent to which the measurement instrument and procedure are free from both systematic and random error. Thus, a measuring device is valid if differences in scores solely reflect true differences in the characteristic we are seeking to measure rather than systematic or random error. A necessary precondition for validity is that the measuring instrument is reliable. An instrument that is not reliable will not yield consistent results when measuring the same phenomenon over time.

A scale or other measuring device is worthless to a researcher if it lacks validity, because it is not measuring what it is supposed to. On the surface, this seems like a rather simple notion, yet validity often is based on subtle distinctions. Assume that a teacher gives an exam that has been constructed to measure marketing research knowledge, and the test consists strictly of applying a number of formulas to simple case problems. Gloria receives a low score on the test and protests to the teacher that she "really understands marketing research." Her position, in essence, is that the test was not valid. Rather than measuring knowledge of marketing research, the test measured memorization of formulas and the ability to use simple math to find solutions. The teacher could repeat the exam only to find that Gloria's scores still fall in the same order. Does this mean that Gloria's protestations were incorrect? Not necessarily; the teacher may be systematically measuring the ability to memorize rather than a true understanding of marketing research.

Unlike the teacher, who was attempting to measure market research knowledge, a brand manager is more interested in successful prediction. The manager, for example, wants to know if a purchase intent scale successfully predicts the trial purchase of a new product. Thus, validity can be examined from a number of different perspectives, including face, content, criterion-related, and construct (see Table 9.4).

Table 9.4

Assessing the Validity of a Measurement Instrument

Face validity	Researchers judge the degree to which a measurement instrument seems to measure what it is supposed to.
Content validity	The degree to which the instrument items represent the universe of the concept under study.
Criterion-related validity	The degree to which a measurement instrument can predict a variable that is designated as a criterion. a. *Predictive validity:* The extent to which a future level of a criterion variable can be predicted by a current measurement on a scale. b. *Concurrent validity:* The extent to which a criterion variable measured at the same point in time as the variable of interest can be predicted by the measurement instrument.
Construct validity	The degree to which a measure confirms a hypothesis created from a theory based upon the concepts under study. a. *Convergent validity:* The degree of association among different measurement instruments that purport to measure the same concept. b. *Discriminant validity:* The lack of association among constructs that are supposed to be different.

Face validity A measurement that seems to measure what it is supposed to measure.

Face Validity **Face validity** is the weakest form of validity. It is concerned with the degree to which a measurement "looks like" it measures what it is supposed to. It is a judgment call by the researcher, made as the questions are designed. As each question is scrutinized, there is an implicit assessment of its face validity. Revisions enhance the face validity of the question until it passes the researcher's subjective evaluation. Alternatively, face validity can refer to the subjective agreement of researchers, experts, or people familiar with the market, product, or industry that a scale logically appears to be accurately reflecting what it is supposed to measure. A straightforward question such as "What is your age?" followed by a series of age categories generally is agreed to have face validity. Most scales used in market research attempt to measure attitudes or behavioral intentions, which are much more elusive.

Content validity The degree to which the instrument items represent the universe of the concept under study.

Content Validity **Content validity** is the representativeness or sampling adequacy of the content of the measurement instrument. In other words, does the scale provide adequate coverage of the topic under study? Say that McDonald's has hired Raymond to measure the image of the company among adults 18 to 30 years of age who eat fast-food hamburgers at least once a month. Raymond devises a scale that asks consumers to rate the following:

Modern building	1	2	3	4	5	Old-fashioned building
Beautiful landscaping	1	2	3	4	5	Poor landscaping
Clean parking lots	1	2	3	4	5	Dirty parking lots
Attractive signs	1	2	3	4	5	Unattractive signs

A McDonald's executive would quickly take issue with this scale, claiming that a person could evaluate McDonald's on this scale as either good or bad and never have eaten a McDonald's burger. In faxct, the evaluation could be made simply by driving past a McDonald's location. The executive could further argue that the scale lacks content validity because many important components of image, such as the quality of the food, cleanliness of the eating area and restrooms, and promptness and courtesy of service, had been omitted.

The determination of content validity is not always a simple matter. It is probably not possible to identify all the facets of McDonald's image. Content validity ultimately becomes a judgmental matter. Content validity should be approached by first carefully defining precisely what is to be measured. Second, doing an exhaustive literature search and conducting focus groups will help to identify all possible items for inclusion on the scale. Third, a panel of experts can be asked their opinions on whether an item should be included. Finally, the scale can be pretested and an open-ended question asked that might identify other items to be included. For example, after a more

A survey asking only about the exterior building and grounds may not be the most suitable method of determining McDonald's image among 18 to 30 year olds. The content validity of the survey could be called into question.

refined image scale for McDonald's has been administered, a follow-up question could be, "Do you have any other thoughts about McDonald's that you would like to express?" Answers to this pretest question may provide clues for other image dimensions not previously covered.

Criterion-Related Validity

Criterion-related validity examines the ability of a measuring instrument to predict a variable that is designated as a criterion. To illustrate, assume that we wish to devise a test to identify marketing researchers who are exceptional at moderating focus groups. We begin by having impartial marketing research experts determine from a directory of marketing researchers who they judge to be best at moderating focus groups. We then construct 300 items to which group moderators are asked to reply "Yes" or "No," such as "I believe it is important to compel shy group participants to speak out" and "I like to interact with small groups of people." We then go through the responses and select the items that the good focus group moderators answered one way and the remainder the other way. Assume that this process produces 84 items, which we put together to form what we call the Test of Effectiveness in Focus Group Moderating (TEFGM). We feel that this test will identify good focus group moderators. The criterion of interest here is the ability to conduct a good focus group. We might explore the criterion-related validity of TEFGM further by administering the test to a new group of moderators that has previously been divided into those who are good moderators and those who are not. We can determine in this way how well the test identifies the group to which each marketing researcher is assigned. Thus, criterion-related validity is concerned with detecting the presence or absence of one or more criterion considered to represent constructs of interest.

Criterion-related validity The degree to which a measurement instrument can predict a variable that is designated as a criterion.

Two subcategories of criterion-related validity are predictive validity and concurrent validity. **Predictive validity** is the extent to which a future level of a criterion variable can be predicted by a current measurement on a scale. A voter motivation scale, for example, is used to predict the likelihood of a person voting in the next election. A savvy politician is not interested in what the community as a whole perceives as important problems, but only in what persons who are likely to vote perceive as important problems. These are the issues that the politician will address in speeches and advertising. Another example of predictive validity is the extent to which a purchase intent scale for a new Pepperidge Farm pastry predicts actual trial of the product.

Predictive validity The degree to which the future level of a criterion can be forecast by a current measurement scale.

Concurrent validity is concerned with the relationship between the predictor variable and the criterion variable, both of which are assessed at the same point in time, for example, the ability of a home pregnancy test to accurately determine whether a woman is pregnant right now. Such a test with low concurrent validity could cause a lot of undue stress.

Concurrent validity The degree to which a variable, measured at the same point in time as the variable of interest, can be predicted by the measurement instrument.

Construct Validity

Construct validity, although often not consciously addressed by many market researchers on a day-to-day basis, is extremely important to marketing scientists. It involves understanding the theoretical foundations underlying the obtained measurements. A measure has **construct validity** if it behaves according to the underlying theory. Instead of addressing the major issue of interest to the brand manager (whether the scale adequately

Construct validity The degree to which a measurement instrument represents and logically connects observed phenomena to a construct via an underlying theory.

predicts whether a consumer will try a new brand), construct validity is concerned with the theory behind the prediction. Purchase behavior is something we can observe directly; someone either buys product A or does not. Yet scientists have developed constructs on lifestyles, involvement, attitude, and personality that help understand why someone purchases something or does not. These constructs are largely unobservable. We can observe behavior related to the constructs—that is, buying a product. We cannot observe the constructs themselves—such as an attitude. Constructs help scientists communicate and build theories to explain phenomena.

Convergent validity A high degree of correlation among different measurement instruments that purport to measure the same concept.

Discriminant validity A low degree of correlation among constructs that are supposed to be different.

Two statistical approaches for assessing construct validity are convergent and discriminant validity. **Convergent validity** is a high degree of correlation among different measures that purport to measure the same construct. **Discriminant validity** is the degree of correlation among constructs that are supposed to be different. Assume that we develop a multiitem scale that measures the propensity to shop at discount stores. Our theory suggests that this propensity is caused by four personality variables: high level of self-confidence, low need for status, low need for distinctiveness, and high level of adaptability. Further, our theory suggests that the propensity to shop at discount stores is not related to brand loyalty or high-level aggressiveness.

Evidence of construct validity would exist if our scale

- correlates highly with other measures of propensity to shop at discount stores, such as reported stores patronized and social class (convergent validity)
- has a low correlation with the unrelated constructs of brand loyalty and a high level of aggressiveness (discriminant validity)

Relating the Measures to Assess Validity All the types of validity discussed here interrelate somewhat in theory and practice. For example, predictive validity would be important on a scale devised to predict whether people will shop at a discount store. A researcher developing a discount store patronage scale would probably first attempt to understand the construct that provided the basis for prediction. The researcher would put forth a theory about discount store patronage, which would provide the foundation of construct validity. Next, the researcher would be concerned with which specific items to include on the discount store patronage scale and whether they related to the full range of the construct. Thus, the researcher would ascertain the degree of content validity. The issue of criterion-related validity could be addressed in a pretest by measuring the scores on the discount store patronage scale against actual store patronage.

Reliability and Validity Illustrated

The concepts of reliability and validity are illustrated conceptually in Figure 9.1. Situation 1 shows holes all over the target. It could be due to the use of an old rifle, being a poor shot, or many other factors. This complete lack of consistency means that there is no reliability. Because the instrument lacks reliability, thus creating huge errors, it cannot be valid. Measurement reliability is a necessary condition for validity.

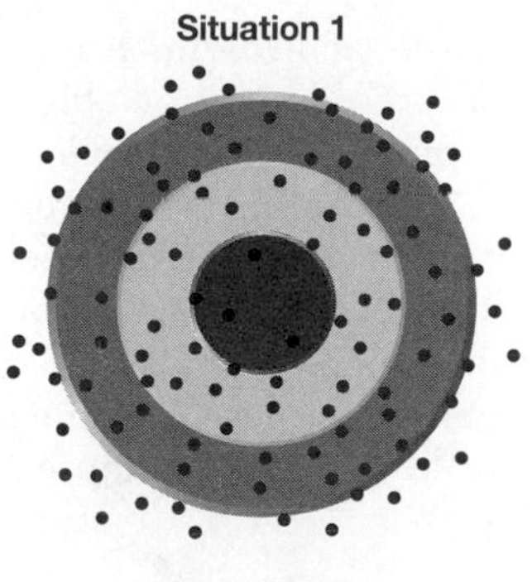

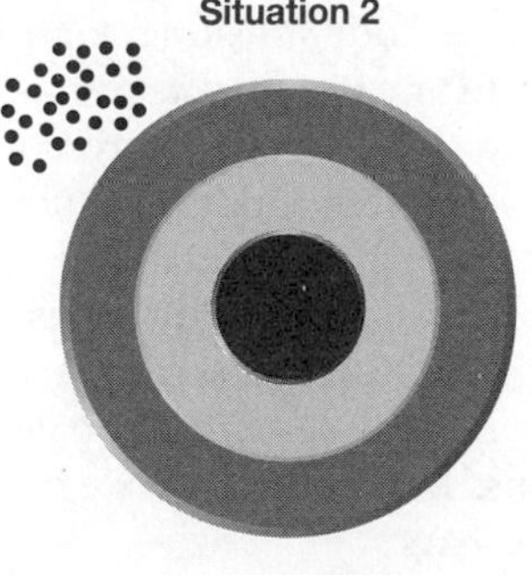

Situation 3

Highly Reliable
and Valid

Figure 9.1

Illustrations of Possible Reliability and Validity Situations in Measurement

The second target denotes a very tight pattern (consistency), but is far removed from the bull's eye. This illustrates that we can have a high level of reliability in an instrument (little variance) that lacks validity. The instrument is consistent, but it does not measure what it is supposed to measure. The shooter has a steady eye, but the sights are not adjusted properly. Situation 3 shows the criteria that researchers strive to achieve in a measurement instrument that is reliable, consistent, and valid (on target with what we are attempting to measure).

Attitude Scales

The measurement of attitudes is difficult and uses less precise scales than those found in the physical sciences. An attitude is a construct that exists in the minds of the consumers and is not directly observable, unlike, for example, weight in the physical sciences. Attitude scaling is based on various operational definitions created to measure attitude constructs. In many cases, attitudes are measured at a nominal or ordinal level. Some more sophisticated scales enable the market researcher to measure at the interval level. It is important not to attribute the more powerful properties of an interval scale to the lower-level nominal or ordinal scales.

Scaling Defined

The term **scaling** refers to procedures for attempting to determine quantitative measures of subjective and sometimes abstract concepts. It is defined as a procedure for the assignment of numbers (or other symbols) to a property of objects to impart some of the characteristics of numbers to the properties in question. A scale is a measurement tool. Thus, we assign a number scale to the various levels of heat and cold and call it a thermometer, as you recall from earlier in this chapter. Actually, we assign numbers to indicants of the properties of objects. The rise and fall of mercury in a glass tube is an indicant of temperature variations.

Scaling Procedures for attempting to determine quantitative measures for subjective or abstract concepts.

Unidimensional scale A scale that measures only one attribute.

Multidimensional scale A scale that measures more than one attribute.

Scales are either unidimensional or multidimensional. **Unidimensional scaling** is designed to measure only one attribute of a respondent or object. Thus, we may create a scale to measure consumers' price sensitivity. We may use several items to measure price sensitivity, but we will combine them into a single measure, placing all interviewees along a linear continuum, called the degree of price sensitivity. **Multidimensional scaling** recognizes that a concept or object might be better described using several dimensions rather than one. For example, target customers for Jaguar automobiles may be defined in three dimensions: level of wealth, degree of price sensitivity, and appreciation of fine motor cars.

Graphic Rating Scales

Graphic rating scale A scale showing a graphic continuum that is typically anchored by two extremes.

Graphic rating scales present respondents with a graphic continuum typically anchored by two extremes. Figure 9.2 depicts three types of graphic rating scales that might be used to evaluate La-Z-Boy recliners. Scale A represents the simplest form of a graphic scale. Respondents are instructed to check their response along the continuum. After a check mark is made, a score is assigned by dividing the line into as many categories as desired and assigning the score based on the category into which the mark has been placed. For example, if the line is 6 inches long, every inch could represent a category. Scale B offers respondents slightly more structure by assigning numbers along the scale.

Graphic rating scales are not limited to simply placing a check mark along a continuum, as illustrated by scale C. Scale C has been used successfully by many researchers to speed up the interviewing process. The interviewer has the scale mounted on a card that is held in front of respondents, who are asked to touch the thermometer that best depicts their feelings.

Figure 9.2

Three Types of Graphic Rating Scales

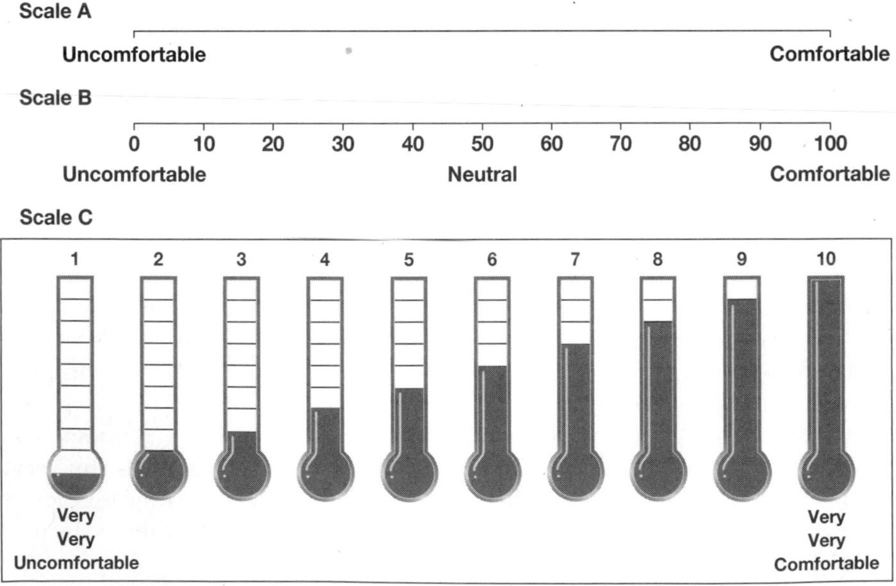

Graphic rating scales can be constructed easily and are simple to use. They also enable a researcher to discern fine distinctions, assuming that the rater has adequate discriminatory abilities. Numerical data obtained from such scales are typically treated as interval data.

One disadvantage of this type of measurement is that if the anchors are too extreme, respondents tend to be forced toward the middle of the scale. Also, graphic rating scales may not be reliable as itemized rating scales.

Itemized Rating Scales

Itemized rating scale A scale showing a limited number of ordered categories.

Itemized rating scales are similar to graphic rating scales, except that respondents must select from a limited number of ordered categories rather than placing a check mark on a continuous scale (purists would argue that scale C in Figure 9.2 is an itemized ratings scale). Figure 9.3 on page 266 illustrates itemized rating scales taken from nationwide market research surveys. As the figure shows, researchers often hand a copy of the basic scale to a respondent and ask for a rating after the interviewer reads off a characteristic. Starting points are rotated on each questionnaire to eliminate order bias, since starting with the same characteristic each time may act as a source of bias.

Scale A was part of a questionnaire used to evaluate watches with a Sears logo. Scale B was on a screening questionnaire used for in-home placement of a new shampoo concept. The manufacturer wanted an equal number of users in each hair condition category. Scale C was also part of an in-home product test. It was administered after teenagers had used the sample product for two weeks. Scale D was used in a study of children's TV ads. Examples of other itemized rating categories are shown in Table 9.5.

Table 9.5 Selected Itemized Rating Scales

Purchase Intent	**Quality**	**Style**	**Cost**	**Color Brightness**
Definitely will buy	Very good	Very stylish	Extremely expensive	Extremely bright
Probably will buy	Good	Somewhat stylish	Expensive	Very bright
Probably will not buy	Neither good nor bad	Not very stylish	Neither expensive nor inexpensive	Somewhat bright
Definitely will not buy	Fair	Completely unstylish	Slightly inexpensive	Slightly bright
	Poor		Very inexpensive	Not bright at all
Level of Agreement	**Dependability**	**Satisfaction**	**Ease of Use**	**Modernity**
Strongly agree	Completely dependable	Completely satisfied	Very easy to use	Very modern
Somewhat agree	Somewhat dependable	Somewhat satisfied	Somewhat easy to use	Somewhat modern
Neither agree nor disagree	Not very dependable	Neither satisfied nor dissatisfied	Not very easy to use	Neither modern nor old-fashioned
Somewhat disagree	Not dependable at all	Somewhat dissatisfied	Difficult to use	Somewhat old-fashioned
Strongly disagree		Completely dissatisfied		Very old-fashioned

Figure 9.3

Itemized Rating Scales Used in National Surveys

Source: Scale D is adapted from Fred Cutler, "To Meet Criticisms of TV Ads, Researchers Find New Ways to Measure Children's Attitudes," *Marketing News* (January 27, 1978), p. 16. Reprinted with permission from *Marketing News,* published by the American Marketing Association.

Scale A

Now, I'd like to ask you about just two watches specifically. The first one is the SEARS watch. I'm going to mention some characteristics of watches, and, as I mention each one, please tell me whether you think the SEARS watch is (HAND RESPONDENT RATING CARD) excellent, very good, good, fair, or poor for the particular characteristic.

The first characteristic is (READ CHARACTERISTIC CIRCLED BELOW). Do you feel that the SEARS watch is excellent, very good, good, fair, or poor for (CHARACTERISTIC)? (CONTINUE FOR *ALL* CHARACTERISTICS BELOW)

Starting Point	Excellent		Good	Very Good	Fair	Poor
X	Value for the money	☐ 5	☐ 4	☐ 3	☐ 2	☐ 1
X	Brand name	☐ 5	☐ 4	☐ 3	☐ 2	☐ 1
ⓧ	Accuracy	☐ 5	☐ 4	☐ 3	☐ 2	☐ 1
X	Durability	☐ 5	☐ 4	☐ 3	☐ 2	☐ 1
X	Manufacturer's reputation	☐ 5	☐ 4	☐ 3	☐ 2	☐ 1
X	After-sales service	☐ 5	☐ 4	☐ 3	☐ 2	☐ 1
X	Styling ☐ 5	☐ 4	☐ 3	☐ 2	☐ 1	

Scale B

9. Which statement on this card (HAND RESPONDENT CARD B) best describes the present condition of your hair?

1 ( ) Very damaged 2 ( ) Somewhat damaged 3 ( ) Slightly damaged 4 ( ) Not at all damaged

Scale C

Now, I would like to get your opinion on some characteristics of Stridex Cleansing Pads. (HAND RATING CARD) Using the phrases on this card, please tell me which one best indicates how much you agree or disagree that Stridex Cleansing Pads . . . (START WITH CHECKED CHARACTERISTICS AND CONTINUE UNTIL ALL ARE ASKED)

Start	Agree Strongly	Agree Somewhat	Disagree Somewhat	Disagree Strongly
( ) Help prevent blemishes	____ 9–4	____ –3	____ –2	____ –1
( ) Help to clear up blemishes	____ 10–4	____ –3	____ –2	____ –1
( ) Are convenient to use	____ 11–4	____ –3	____ –2	____ –1
(✓) Are not irritating	____ 12–4	____ –3	____ –2	____ –1
( ) Leave face feeling fresh	____ 13–4	____ –3	____ –2	____ –1
( ) Make you feel confident you are doing everything you can to help your skin look good	____ 14–4	____ –3	____ –2	____ –1

Scale D

Very Very Good

Very Very Poor

Itemized rating scales are easy to construct and administer, but do not allow for the fine distinctions that can be achieved in a graphics rating scale. However, the definitive categories found in itemized rating scales usually produce more reliable ratings than graphics rating scales do.

Rank-Order Scale

Itemized and graphic scales are **noncomparative** because respondents make a judgment without reference to another object, concept, or person. **Rank-order scales,** on the other hand, are **comparative** because respondents are asked to judge one item against another. Rank-order scales are widely used in market research for several reasons. They are easy to use and they form an ordinal scale of the items evaluated. Instructions are easy to understand and the process typically moves at a steady pace. Some researchers claim that it forces respondents to evaluate concepts in a realistic manner. For example, Table 9.6 illustrates a series of rank-order scales taken from a study on eye shadows.

Noncomparative scale A scale that does not compare objects, concepts, or person, such as graphic rating and itemized rating scales.

Rank-order scale A scale that ranks an object, concept, or person in a certain order.

Comparative scale A scale that compares another object, concept, or person; rank-order scales are comparative.

Table 9.6

A Series of Rank-Order Scales Used to Evaluate Eye Shadows

Please rank the following eye shadows with 1 being the brand that best meets the characteristic being evaluated and 6 being the brand that least meets the characteristic being evaluated. The six brands are listed on card C. (HAND RESPONDENT CARD C.) Let's begin with the idea of having high-quality compacts or containers. Which brand would rank as having the highest-quality compacts or containers? Which is second? (RECORD BELOW)

	Having a High-Quality Container Q.48	Having a High-Quality Applicator Q.49	Having a High-Quality Eye Shadow Q.50
Avon	________	________	________
Cover Girl	________	________	________
Estee Lauder	________	________	________
Maybelline	________	________	________
Natural Wonder	________	________	________
Revlon	________	________	________

Card C

Avon	Cover Girl	Estee Lauder
Maybelline	Natural Wonder	Revlon

Rank-order scales possess several disadvantages. If all the alternatives in a respondent's set of choices are not included, the results could be misleading. For example, a respondent's first choice for all the dimensions of eye shadow quality might have been Max Factor, which was not included on card C. A second problem is that the concept being ranked may be completely outside a person's set of choices, thus producing meaningless data. For example, perhaps a respondent doesn't use eye shadow and feels that the product isn't appropriate for any woman. Another limitation is that a rank-order scale gives the researcher only ordinal data. Nothing is learned about how far apart the items stand or how intense a person feels about the ranking of an item. Finally, we don't know why the items were ranked as they were.

Q-Sorting

Q-sorting Distributing a set of objects into piles according to specified rating categories.

Q-sorting is basically a sophisticated form of rank ordering. A set of *objects*—verbal statements, slogans, product features, potential customer services, and so forth—is given to individuals to sort into piles according to specified rating categories (see Table 9.5). For example, some cards may each show a feature that can be designed into a new automobile. Respondents could be asked to sort the cards according to how well they like each potential feature. With a large number of cards—Q-sorts usually contain from 60 to 120 cards—it would be very difficult to rank-order them. For statistical convenience, the sorter is instructed to put varying numbers of cards into several piles, with the whole making up a normal statistical distribution.

Here is a Q-sort distribution of 90 items:

Excellent Feature										Poor Feature
3	4	7	10	13	16	13	10	7	4	3
10	9	8	7	6	5	4	3	2	1	0

This is a rank-order continuum from Excellent Feature to Poor Feature, with varying degrees of approval and disapproval between the extremes.

The numbers 3, 4, 7, . . . , 7, 4, 3 represent the number of cards that are to be placed in each pile. The numbers below the line are the values assigned to the cards in each pile. That is, the three cards at the extreme left, Excellent Feature, are each assigned a value of 10, the four cards in the next pile are assigned a value of 9, and so on through the distribution to the three cards at the extreme right, which are assigned a value of zero. The center pile is a neutral pile. The respondent is told to put cards into the neutral pile that are left over after the other choices have been made; these are cards about which the respondent is ambiguous or cannot make a decision. This Q distribution has 11 piles with varying numbers of cards in each pile, the cards in the piles being assigned values from 0 through 10. A Q-sort scale can be used to determine the relative ranking of items by individuals and to derive clusters of individuals who exhibit the same preferences. These clusters of people may then be analyzed as a potential basis for market segmentation.

Paired Comparisons

Paired comparison scales ask respondents to pick one of two objects from a set based on some stated criteria. Respondent therefore make a series of paired judgments between objects. Table 9.7 shows a paired comparison scale used in a national study for suntan products. Only part of the scale is shown, as the data collection procedure typically requires respondents to compare all possible pairs of objects.

Paired comparison scale A scale showing a series of only two objects as choices.

Paired comparisons overcome several problems of traditional rank-order scales. First, it is easier for people to select one item from a set of two than to rank a large set of data. Second, the problem of order bias is overcome. On the negative side, because all possible pairs are evaluated, as the number of objects to be evaluated increases arithmetically, the number of paired comparisons also increases geometrically. Therefore, the number of objects to be evaluated should remain fairly small to prevent interviewee fatigue and confusion.

Constant Sum Scales

Constant sum scales are used more often by market researchers than paired comparisons because they avoid the long list of paired items. This technique requires respondents to divide a given number of points, typically 100, among two or more attributes based on their importance. Respondents must value each individual item relative to all other items. The number of points allocated to each alternative indicates the rank assigned to it. The value assigned to each alternative is indicative of its relative magnitude. A constant sum scale used in a national study of tennis sportswear is shown in Table 9.8 on page 270. An advantage of the constant sum scale over the rank-order or paired comparison scale is that if respondents perceive two characteristics to have equal value, they can give them the same ranking.

Constant sum scale A scale on which a set number of points is distributed among two or more attributes.

Table 9.7 A Paired Comparison Scale for Suntan Products

14. Thinking about sun products in general, here are some characteristics used to describe them. Please tell me which characteristic in each pair is more important to you when selecting a sun care product.

a. Tans evenly	b. Tans without burning
a. Prevents burning	b. Protects against burning and tanning
a. Good value for the money	b. Goes on evenly
a. Not greasy	b. Does not stain clothing
a. Tans without burning	b. Prevents burning
a. Protects against burning and tanning	b. Good value for the money
a. Goes on evenly	b. Tans evenly
a. Prevents burning	b. Not greasy

Table 9.8

A Constant Sum Scale Used in a Tennis Sportswear Study

Below are seven characteristics of women's tennis sportswear. Please allocate 100 points among the characteristics such that the allocation represents the importance of each characteristic to you. The more points that you assign to a characteristic, the more important it is. If the characteristic is totally unimportant, you should not allocate any points to it. When you've finished, please double-check to make sure that your total adds to 100.

Characteristic of Tennis Sportswear	Number of Points
Is comfortable to wear	________
Is durable	________
Is made by well-known brand or sports manufacturers	________
Is made in the U.S.A.	________
Has up-to-date styling	________
Gives freedom of movement	________
Is a good value for the money	________
	100 Points

A major disadvantage of this scale is that as the number of characteristics or items increases, so respondents may become confused. That is, respondents may have difficulty allocating the points to total 100. Most researchers feel that 10 items should be the outer limit on a constant sum scale.

The Semantic Differential

The semantic differential was developed by Charles Osgood, George Suci, and Percy Tannenbaum.[5] The focus of the original research was the measurement of the meaning of an object to a person. For example, the object might be a savings and loan association, whereas the meaning might be the image of that association to a certain group.

Semantic differential scale A scale that rates opposite pairs of words or phrases on a continuum, which are then plotted as a profile or image.

The construction of a **semantic differential scale** begins with the determination of a concept to be rated, such as a company, brand, or store image. The researcher selects dichotomous (opposite) pairs of words or phrases that could be used to describe the concept. Respondents then rate the concept on a scale (usually from 1 to 7). The mean of these responses for each pair of adjectives is computed and plotted as a profile or image.

Figure 9.4 is an actual image profile of an Arizona savings and loan association, as perceived by noncustomers with family incomes of $45,000 and above. A quick glance shows that the S&L is thought of as somewhat old-fashioned with rather plain facilities. It is considered to be well-established, reliable, successful, and probably very nice to deal with. The institution has parking problems and perhaps entry and egress difficulties. Its advertising is viewed as dismal.

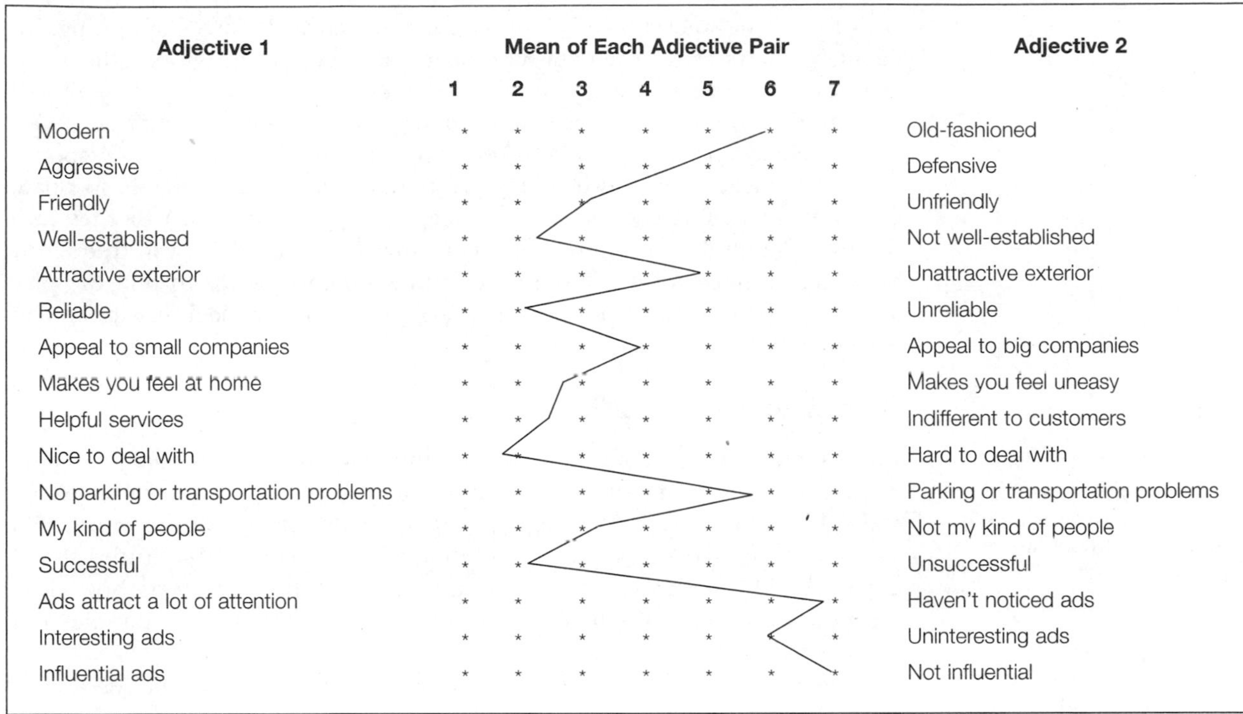

Figure 9.4

A Semantic Differential Profile of an Arizona Savings and Loan Association

The semantic differential is a quick and efficient means of examining the strengths and weaknesses of a product or company image versus the competition's. More importantly, however, the semantic differential has been shown to be sufficiently reliable and valid for decision making and prediction in marketing and the behavioral sciences.[6] Also, the semantic differential has proved to be statistically robust (applicable) from one group of subjects to another when applied to corporate image research.[7] This makes it possible to measure and compare images held by interviewees with diverse backgrounds.

Although these advantages have led many researchers to use the semantic differential as an image measurement tool, it is not without its disadvantages. First, there is a lack of standardization. The semantic differential is a highly generalized technique that must be adapted for each research problem. There is no single set of standard scales, and hence their development becomes an integral part of the research.

The number of divisions on the semantic differential scale also presents a problem. If too few divisions are used, the scale is crude and lacks meaning; if too many are used, the scale goes beyond the ability of most people to discriminate. Researchers have found the seven-point scale to be the most satisfactory.

Another disadvantage of the semantic differential is the "halo effect." The rating of a specific image component may be dominated by an interviewee's overall impression of the concept being rated. There may be significant bias if the image is hazy in the respondent's mind. To partially counteract the halo effect, the scale adjectives should be randomly reversed so that all the "good" phrases are not placed on one side of the scale and the "bad" on the other.

This forces the interviewee to evaluate the adjectives before responding. To facilitate analysis after the data have been gathered, all the "good adjectives" are placed on one side and the negative ones on the other.

Another problem occurs when analyzing a seven-point semantic differential scale in that care must be taken in interpreting a score of 4. A response of 4 will indicate one of two things—respondents are either unable to relate the given pair of adjectives to the concept (they do not know) or they may simply be neutral or indifferent. In many image studies, there will frequently be a large number of 4 responses. This phenomenon tends to pull the profiles toward the neutral position, causing the profiles to lack clarity and to provide few distinctions.

Stapel Scale

Stapel scale A scale that provides a single description in the center, which is usually measured by plus or minus 5 points.

The **Stapel scale** is a modification of the semantic differential. A single description containing an adjective and a noun is placed in the center of the scale. The scale is typically designed with 10 points ranging from +5 to −5. The technique measures both the direction and intensity of attitudes simultaneously. The semantic differential, on the other hand, reflects how close the descriptor adjectives fit the concept being evaluated. An example of a Stapel scale is shown in Figure 9.5.

The primary advantage of the Stapel scale is that it enables the researcher to avoid the arduous task of creating bipolar adjective pairs. Some researchers also claim that the scale permits finer discrimination in measuring attitudes. On the negative side is the problem that descriptor adjectives can be phrased in a positive, neutral, or a negative vein. The choice of phrasing has been shown to affect the scale results and a person's ability to respond correctly.[8] The popularity of the semantic differential has declined extensively in the 1990s, primarily because of the increase in telephone interviewing. The

Figure 9.5

Example of a Stapel Scale

+5	+5
+4	+4
+3	+3
+2	+2
+1	+1
Friendly Personnel	Competitive Loan Rates
−1	−1
−2	−2
−3	−3
−4	−4
−5	−5

Select a *plus* number for words that you think describe the savings and loan accurately. The more accurately you think the words describe the company, the larger the plus number you should choose. Select a *minus* number for words you think do not describe the savings and loan accurately. The less accurately you think the words describe the institution, the larger the minus number you should choose. Therefore, you can select any number from +5 for words that you think are very accurate all the way to −5 for words that you think are very inaccurate.

Global ISSUES

Caution Should be Used in Interpreting Scales Used in Global Research

SABRA BROCK, VICE PRESIDENT OF CITICORP, NOTES THAT DEVISING SCALES AND OTHER types of questions requires careful planning when conducting marketing research in Asia. In Asia, many countries have the capability of conducting some kinds of Western-style marketing research. Japan, Hong Kong, Singapore, and the Philippines have fairly advanced research industries. Other countries in Asia such as China, South Korea, Indonesia, and India have research capabilities, but they are so underdeveloped as to require special supervision. Asia also has fewer research and marketing firms that can act as data "translators," people who can transform computer tables and research results into specific marketing directions.

Attitudes toward research vary from country to country in Asia, as do reactions to pricing, distribution, and promotion strategies. Most Asians respond differently to being interviewed than Americans. They frequently have less patience with the abstract and rational phrasing commonly used in questionnaires, particularly where literacy rates are low.

The interpretation of research tools like scales is different among educated Asians. The Japanese desire not to contradict, for example, makes for more yea-saying and upward scale bias than in a Western culture.

Apart from the varying reactions to research, there also are design implications to the distinct pricing and distribution strategies employed in Asia. For example, when querying Asians about pricing, the researcher must realize that they are especially prone to equating high price with high quality. In countries where imports are restricted or highly taxed, like South Korea and the Philippines, "imported" and especially "made in USA" are strong product claims.

Among the Chinese countries in Asia, many distinct dialects are spoken. A Hong Kong native speaks the Cantonese dialect and must study Mandarin to communicate easily in Taiwan. These language dissimilarities are critical in questionnaire development. In Hong Kong, written and oral Cantonese are different enough to necessitate rewriting a questionnaire when the methodology changes from self-administered to interviewer-read.[9] ■

Stapel scale has never had much popularity in commercial research and is used even less than the semantic differential.

Likert Scales

Likert scale A scale that shows a series of attitudes toward an object, which are given numerical values ranging from favorable to unfavorable.

The **Likert scale** is another scale that avoids the problem of developing pairs of dichotomous adjectives. The scale consists of a series of statements that express either a favorable or an unfavorable attitude toward the concept under study. Respondents are asked for their level of agreement or disagreement with each statement. Each respondent is then given a numerical score to reflect how favorable or unfavorable their attitude is toward each statement. The scores are then totaled to measure each respondent's attitude.

Table 9.9 shows a Likert scale for people who have admitted on a screening questionnaire that they have a foot odor problem but have not tried Johnson's Odor-Eaters Insoles. The scale was taken from a national study on the product.

The Likert scale only requires the respondent to consider one statement at a time with the scale running from one extreme to another. A series of statements (attitudes) can be examined, yet there is only a single set of uniform replies for the respondent to give.

Rensis Likert created his scale to measure a person's various attitudes toward concepts (e.g., unions) and activities (e.g., swimming). He recommended the following steps in building the scale:

1. The researcher identifies the concept to be scaled. Let us assume that it is snow skiing.
2. The researcher assembles a large number (e.g., 75 to 100) of statements concerning the public's sentiments toward snow skiing.
3. Each test item is classified by the researcher as generally "favorable" or "unfavorable" with regard to the attitude under study. No attempt is made to scale the items; however, a pretest is conducted that involves the full set of statements and a limited sample of respondents.
4. In the pretest the respondent indicates agreement (or not) with every item, checking one of the following direction-intensity descriptors:
   a. Strongly Agree
   b. Agree
   c. Undecided
   d. Disagree
   e. Strongly disagree
5. Each response is given a numerical weight (e.g., 5, 4, 3, 2, 1).
6. The individual's total attitude score is represented by the algebraic summation of weights associated with the items checked. In the scoring process, weights are assigned so that the directionality of attitude—favorable to unfavorable—is consistent over items. For example, if 5 was assigned to "strongly approve" for favorable items, then 5 should be assigned to "strongly disapprove" for unfavorable items.
7. After seeing the results of the pretest, the analyst selects only those items that appear to discriminate well between high and low total scorers. This may be done by first finding the highest and lowest quartiles of subjects

Table 9.9

A Likert Scale for People with Foot Odor Problems Who Have Not Tried Johnson's Odor-Eaters

(SHOW CARD J) Now I would like to find out your impressions about Johnson's Odor-Eaters, which you said you were familiar with but had not tried. As I read each characteristic, please tell me, using the statements on this card, if you strongly agree, agree, neither agree nor disagree, disagree, or strongly disagree.

	Strongly Agree	Agree	Neither Agree nor Disagree	Disagree	Disagree Strongly
They might make my feet feel hot	5	4	3	2	1
I am satisfied with what I am using	5	4	3	2	1
My problem is not serious enough	5	4	3	2	1
Too much trouble to cut them to fit to size	5	4	3	2	1
Price is too expensive	5	4	3	2	1
Might make my shoes too tight	5	4	3	2	1
I'm embarrassed to buy them	5	4	3	2	1
The advertising has not convinced me that the product is effective	5	4	3	2	1
Other insoles I've tried didn't work	5	4	3	2	1
Foot sprays work better	5	4	3	2	1
Foot powders work better	5	4	3	2	1
I've never used an insole	5	4	3	2	1
Wouldn't last more than a couple of weeks	5	4	3	2	1
Would look unattractive in my shoes	5	4	3	2	1
Would have to buy more than one pair	5	4	3	2	1
Would have to move them from one pair of shoes to another	5	4	3	2	1
No product for foot odor works completely	5	4	3	2	1
They might get too wet from perspiration	5	4	3	2	1
Don't know what an insole would feel like in my shoe	5	4	3	2	1

CARD J

Strongly Agree	Agree	Neither Agree nor Disagree	Disagree	Strongly Disagree

on the basis of total score. Then, the mean differences on each specific item are compared between these high and low groups (excluding the middle 50 percent of subjects).

8. The 20 to 25 items finally selected are those that have discriminated "best" (exhibited the greatest difference in mean values) between high versus low total scorers in the pretest.

9. Steps 3 through 5 are then repeated in the main study.

Likert created his scale so that a researcher could look at a summed score and tell whether a person's attitude toward a concept was positive or negative. For example, the maximum favorable score on a 20-item scale would be 100; therefore, a person scoring 92 would be presumed to have a favorable attitude. Two people could both score 92 and yet have rated various statements differently, so specific attitudes toward components could differ markedly. For example, respondent A might strongly agree (5) that a bank has good parking and strongly disagree (1) that its loan programs are the best in town. Respondent B could have the exact opposite attitude, yet both summed scores would be 6.

In the world of commercial market research, Likert scales are very popular. They are quick and easy to construct and can be administered over the phone, or a respondent can be given a "reply category" card and be asked to call out an answer. Commercial researchers rarely follow the textbook process just outlined. Instead, the scales are usually developed jointly by a client project manager and a researcher. Many times the scales are created after holding a focus group.

Most important, the commercial researcher usually has a totally different motivation for using the scale. Instead of trying to discern positive and negative attitudes of individual respondents, he or she is more interested in attitudes toward the various components of the scale. Thus, referring back to the Odor-Eaters scale, the company was interested in determining what factors were causing target customers not to purchase Odor-Eaters. It was not really concerned whether respondent A had a positive or negative attitude toward Odor-Eaters. This notion is also often true for the semantic differential.[10]

Purchase Intent Scales

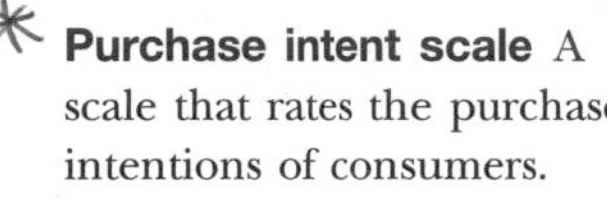
Purchase intent scale A scale that rates the purchase intentions of consumers.

Perhaps the single scale used most often in commercial market research is the **purchase intent scale.** The ultimate issue for marketing managers is: Will consumers buy the product or not? And if so: What percentage of the market can the company expect to obtain? The purchase intent question is normally an important one for all new products and services, product modifications, and new retail services or service modifications by a retailer, and even by nonprofit organizations.

During new product development, the purchase intent question is asked during concept testing to get a rough idea of demand. The manager wants to quickly eliminate potential "turkeys," take a careful look at those products for which purchase intent was moderate, and push forward those projects that seem to have star potential. At this stage, the investment is minimal and modifying the product or repositioning the concept is an easy task. As the product moves through development, the product itself, promotional strategy, price levels, and distribution channels become more concrete and focused. Purchase intent is evaluated at each stage of development and demand estimates are refined. The crucial go-no go decision for a national or regional rollout typically comes after test marketing. Immediately before test marketing, commercial researchers have another critical stage of evaluation. Here the final, or nearly final, version of the product is placed in consumers' homes in test cities around the country. After a period of in-home use (usually two to six weeks), a follow-up survey is conducted among participants to find out their likes and dislikes, how the product compares with what they use now, and what they would pay for it. The critical question near the end of the questionnaire is purchase intent.

Table 9.10, question 21, is a purchase intent question taken from a follow-up study on in-home placement of a fly trap. The trap consisted of two 3-inch discs held about ¼ inch apart by three plastic pillars looking somewhat like a large, thin yo-yo. The trap worked on the same principle as the Roach Motel. It contained a pheromone to attract the flies and a glue that would remain sticky for six months. Supposedly, the flies flew in, but never flew out! Centered on the back side of one of the discs was an adhesive tab so that the disc could be attached to a kitchen window. The concept was to eliminate flies in the kitchen area without resorting to a pesticide. Question 22 in Table 9.10 was designed to aid in positioning the product, and question 23 was traditionally used by the manufacturer as a double-check on purchase intent. That is, if 60 percent of the respondents claimed that they definitely would buy the product and 90 percent said they definitely would not recommend the product to their friends, the researcher would question the validity of the purchase intent.

The purchase intent scale has been found to be a good predictor of consumer choice for frequently purchased and durable consumer products.[11] The scale is very easy to construct and consumers are simply asked to make a subjective judgment on their likelihood of buying a new product. From past

Table 9.10

Purchase Intent Scale and Related Questions for an In-home Product Placement of Fly Traps

21. If a set of three traps sold for approximately $1.00 and was available in the stores where you normally shop, would you:

	(51)
definitely buy the set of traps	1
probably buy	2
probably not buy—SKIP TO Q23	3
definitely not buy—SKIP TO Q23	4

22. Would you use the traps (a) instead of or (b) in addition to existing products?

	(52)
instead of	1
in addition to	2

23. Would you recommend this product to your friends?

	(53)
definitely	1
probably	2
probably not	3
definitely not	4

experience in analyzing product categories, a marketing manager can translate consumer responses on the scale to estimates of purchase probability. Obviously, all those who claim that they "definitely will buy" the product will not do so; in fact, a few who state that they "definitely will not buy" will buy it. Assume that the manufacturer of the fly trap is a major producer of both pesticide and nonpesticide pest control products. Based on historical follow-up studies, the manufacturer has learned the following about the purchase intent of nonpesticide pest control product for home use:

- 63 percent of consumers who "definitely will buy" actually purchase within 12 months
- 28 percent of consumers who "probably will buy" actually purchase within 12 months
- 12 percent of consumers who "probably will not buy" actually purchase within 12 months
- 3 percent of consumers who "definitely will not buy" actually purchase within 12 months.

Suppose that the fly trap study resulted in the following data:

- 40 percent of consumers say they "definitely will buy"
- 20 percent of consumers say they "probably will buy"
- 30 percent of consumers say they "probably will not buy"
- 10 percent of consumers say they "definitely will not buy."

Assuming that the sample is representative of the target market, then:

$$(.4)(63\%) + (.2)(28\%) + (.3)(12\%) + (.1)(3\%)$$
$$= 34.7\% \text{ market share}$$

Most marketing managers would be deliriously happy at a market share prediction this high for a new product. Unfortunately, while the purchase intent prediction was high for the fly traps, because of consumer confusion the product was killed after the in-home placement.

While market research firms routinely conduct studies containing a purchase intent scale, clients do not always have historical data to use as a basis for weighing the results. A reasonable but conservative estimate would be that 70 percent of the "definitely will buy" do buy, 35 percent of the "probably will buy" do buy, 10 percent of the "probably will not buy" do buy, and 0 percent of the "definitely will not buy" do buy.[12] Higher weights are common in the industrial market.

Some companies use the purchase intent scale to make go–no go decisions in product development without reference to market share. Typically, the managers simply add the "definitely will buy" and "probably will buy" and use that against a predetermined go–no go threshold. One consumer goods manufacturer, for example, requires a combined buying score of 80 percent or higher at the concept testing stage and 65 percent for liking a product to move from in-home placement tests to test marketing.

Some Basic Considerations When Selecting a Scale

With the exception of purchase intent, for most nonimage studies the question arises as to which scale is the most appropriate to use. We have presented the most commonly used scales and their advantages and disadvantages. Now let's review them in terms of specific applications.

Selecting a Rating, Ranking, Sorting, or Purchase Intent Scale

Most commercial researchers lean toward scales that can be administered over the telephone to save interviewing expense. The costs of administration and development are also important considerations. For example, a rank-order scale can be quickly created, whereas a semantic differential (rating scale) is often a long and tedious process. The decision-making needs of the client are always of paramount importance. Can a decision be made using ordinal data or must we have interval information? Researchers must also consider that respondents usually prefer nominal and ordinal scales because of their simplicity. Ultimately, the choice of which type of scale to use will depend on the problem at hand and the questions that must be answered. It is common to find several types of scales in one research study. For example, an image study for a grocery chain might have a ranking scale of competing chains and a semantic differential to examine components of the chain's image.

Balanced Versus Nonbalanced Alternatives A **balanced scale** has the same number of positive and negative categories; a **nonbalanced scale** is weighted toward one end or the other. If the researcher expects a wide range of opinions, then a balanced scale is probably in order. If past research or a preliminary study has determined that most opinions are positive, then the scale should contain more positive gradients than negative to enable the researcher to ascertain the degree of positiveness toward the concept being researched. We have conducted a series of studies for the YMCA and know that the overall image of the institution is positive. In tracking the YMCA's image, we have used the following simple categories: (1) outstanding, (2) very good, (3) good, (4) fair, (5) poor.

Balanced scale A scale with the same number of positive and negative categories.

Nonbalanced scale A scale with an uneven number of positive and negative categories.

Number of Categories The number of categories to be included in a scale is another question that must be resolved by the market researcher. If the number of categories is too small—for example, good, fair, poor—the scale is crude and lacks richness. A three-category scale does not reveal the intensity of feeling that, say, a 10-category scale offers. Yet, a 10-category scale may go beyond a person's ability to accurately discriminate from one category to another. Research has shown that rating scales should typically have from five to nine categories.[13] When a scale is being administered over the telephone, five categories seem to be the most that respondents can adequately handle.

Odd or Even Number of Categories An even number of categories in a scale means that there is no neutral point. Without a neutral point, respondents are forced to indicate some degree of positive or negative feeling on an issue. Persons who are truly neutral are not allowed to express this feeling. On the other hand, some commercial market researchers say that putting a neutral point on a scale gives respondents an easy way out. Assuming that they have no really strong opinion, people do not have to concentrate on their actual feelings and can easily say that they are neutral. However, researchers also point out that it is rather unusual to be highly emotional about a new flavor of salad dressing, a package design, or a test commercial for a pickup truck.

Forced Versus Nonforced Choice If a neutral category is included, those who pick it typically will do so because they are neutral and because they lack enough knowledge to answer the question. Some researchers have resolved this issue by adding a "don't know" response as an additional category. For example, a semantic differential might be set up as follows:

Friendly	1 2 3 4 5 6 7	Unfriendly	Don't know
Unexciting	1 2 3 4 5 6 7	Exciting	Don't know

Adding a "don't know" option, however, can also be an easy out for lazy respondents.

A neutral point on a scale without a "don't know" option still does not force respondents to give a positive or negative opinion. A scale without either a neutral point or a "don't know" option forces even those with no information about an object to state an opinion. The argument for forced choice is the same as for a scale with an even number of categories. The arguments against forced choice are that inaccurate data are recorded or that respondents refuse to answer that type of question. A questionnaire that continues to require respondents to provide opinions when, in fact, they lack information to make such decisions can create ill will and result in termination of the interview.

Summary

Measurement consists of using rules to assign numbers to objects in such a way as to represent quantities of attributes. Thus, it is a procedure used to assign numbers that reflect the number of attributes possessed by an event, person, or object. A measurement rule is a guide, a method, or command that tells the researcher what to do. Accurate measurement requires rules that are both clear and specific. Measurement includes order, distance, and origin.

There are four basic levels of measurement: nominal, ordinal, interval, and ratio. A nominal scale partitions data into categories that are mutually exclusive and collectively exhaustive. The numbers assigned to objects or phenomena are numerical but have no number meaning; they are simply labels. Ordinal scales maintain the identification characteristics of nominal scales, plus have the ability to order data. Interval scales contain all the features of ordinal scales, with the added dimension that the intervals between the points on the scale are equal. Interval scales enable the researcher to discuss differences separating two objects and allow computations of the arithmetic mean, the standard deviation, and correlation coefficients. Ratio scales have all the powers of the scales previously discussed and have the added concept of an absolute zero or origin, which enables comparison of the absolute magnitude of the numbers and reflects the actual amount of the variable.

Measurement data consist of both accurate information and errors. Systematic errors result in a constant bias in the measurements. Random errors also influence the measurements but are not systematic; they are transient in nature and do not occur in a consistent manner. Reliability is the degree to which measures are free from random error and therefore provide consistent data. There are three ways to assess reliability: test-retest, internal consistency, and use of equivalent forms. Validity refers to the notion of actually measuring what one is attempting to measure. The validity of a measure refers to the extent to which the measurement device or process is free from both systematic and random error. Concepts of validity include face, content, criterion, and construct validity.

Scaling refers to procedures for attempting to determine quantitative measures of subjective and sometimes abstract concepts. It is a procedure for the assignment of numbers or other symbols to a property of objects to impart some of the characteristics of the numbers to the properties in question. Scales are either unidimensional or multidimensional. A unidimensional scale is designed to measure only one attribute of a respondent or object. Multidimensional scaling recognizes that a concept or object might be better described using several dimensions rather than one.

One type of scale is called a graphic rating scale. Respondents are presented with a graphic continuum typically anchored by two extremes. Itemized rating scales are similar to graphic rating scales, except that respondents must select from a limited number of categories rather than placing a check mark in a continuous scale. A rank-order scale is comparative because respondents are asked to judge one item against another. A Q-sort is a sophisticated form of rank ordering. Respondents are asked to sort a large number of cards into piles of predetermined sizes. Paired comparison scales present two objects from a set and ask respondents to pick one based on some stated criterion. Constant sum scales ask respondents to divide a given number of points, typically 100, among two or more attributes based on their importance. This scale requires respondents to value each individual item relative to all other items. The number of points allocated to each alternative indicates the ranks assigned to them by respondents.

The semantic differential was developed to measure the meaning of an object to a person. The construction of a semantic differential scale begins with a determination of the concept to be rated, such as a brand, and then the researcher selects dichotomous pairs of words or phrases that can be used to describe the concept. Respondents then rate the concept usually on a scale of 1 to 7. The mean of these responses for each pair of adjectives is computed and plotted as a profile or image. The Stapel scale is one in which a single descriptive phrase is placed in the center of the scale. Typically, it is designed to simultaneously measure both the direction and intensity of attitudes. The Likert scale also avoids the problem of developing pairs of dichotomous adjectives. The scale consists of a series of statements that express either a favorable or unfavorable attitude toward the concept under study. Respondents are asked the level of agreement or disagreement with each statement. They are then given a numerical score to reflect how favorable or unfavorable their attitude is toward each statement. Scores are then totaled to measure each respondent's attitude.

The scale used most often and the one that is probably the most important to marketing researchers is the purchase intent scale. The purchase intent scale is used to measure respondents' intention to buy or not buy a product. The purchase intent question usually asks people to state whether they would "definitely buy," "probably buy," "probably not buy,"or "definitely not buy" the product under study. The purchase intent scale has been found to be a good predictor of consumer choice of frequently purchased consumer durable goods.

When attempting to select a particular scale for a study, researchers consider several factors. The first is whether to use a rating, ranking, or choice scale. Next, consideration must be given to the use of a balanced scale versus a nonbalanced scale. The number of categories must also be determined. Another factor is whether to use an odd or even number of scale categories. Finally, the researcher must consider whether to use forced versus nonforced choice sets.

Key Terms & Definitions

Measurement The process of assigning numbers or labels to people or things in accordance with specific rules to represent quantities or qualities of attributes.

Rule A guide, a method, or a command that tells a researcher what to do.

Scale A set of symbols or numbers so constructed that they can be assigned by a rule to individuals or their behaviors or attitudes.

Nominal scale A scale that partitions data into mutually exclusive and collectively exhaustive categories.

Ordinal scale A nominal scale that can order data.

Interval scale An ordinal scale with equal intervals between points to show relative amounts, which may include an arbitrary zero point.

Ratio scale An interval scale with a meaningful zero point so that magnitudes can be compared arithmetically.

Systematic error Error that results in a constant bias in the measurements.

Random error Error that affects measurement in a transient, inconsistent manner.

Reliability Measures that are consistent from one administration to the next.

Test-retest reliability The ability of the same instrument to produce consistent results when used a second time under conditions as nearly the same as possible.

Stability Lack of change in results from test to retest.

Equivalent form reliability The ability to produce similar results using two instruments as similar as possible to measure the same thing.

Internal consistency reliability Ability to produce similar results using different samples to measure a phenomenon during the same time period.

Split-half technique A method of assessing the reliability of a scale by dividing into two the total set of measurement items and correlating the results.

Validity Whether what we tried to measure was actually measured.

Face validity A measurement that seems to measure what it is supposed to measure.

Content validity The degree to which the instrument items represent the universe of the concept under study.

Criterion-related validity The degree to which a measurement instrument can predict a variable that is designated as a criterion.

Predictive validity The degree to which the future level of a criterion can be forecast by a current measurement scale.

Concurrent validity The degree to which a variable, measured at the same point in time as the variable of interest, can be predicted by the measurement instrument.

Construct validity The degree to which a measurement instrument represents and logically connects observed phenomena to a construct via an underlying theory.

Convergent validity A high degree of correlation among different measurement instruments that purport to measure the same concept.

Discriminant validity A low degree of correlation among constructs that are supposed to be different.

Scaling Procedures for attempting to determine quantitative measures for subjective or abstract concepts.

Unidimensional scale A scale that measures only one attribute.

Multidimensional scale A scale that measures more than one attribute.

Graphic rating scale A scale showing a graphic continuum that is typically anchored by two extremes.

Itemized rating scale A scale showing a limited number of ordered categories.

Noncomparative scale A scale that does not compare objects, concepts, or person, such as graphic rating and itemized rating scales.

Rank-order scale A scale that ranks an object, concept, or person in a certain order.

Comparative scale A scale that compares another object, concept, or person; rank-order scales are comparative.

Q-sorting Distributing a set of objects into piles according to specified rating categories.

Paired comparison scale A scale showing a series of only two objects as choices.

Constant sum scale A scale on which a set number of points is distributed among two or more attributes.

Semantic differential scale A scale that rates opposite pairs of words or phrases on a continuum, which are then plotted as a profile or image.

Stapel scale A scale that provides a single description in the center, which is usually measured by plus or minus 5 points.

Likert scale A scale that shows a series of attitudes toward an object, which are given numerical values ranging from favorable to unfavorable.

Purchase intent scale A scale that rates the purchase intentions of consumers.

Balanced scale A scale with the same number of positive and negative categories.

Nonbalanced scale A scale with an uneven number of positive and negative categories.

Questions for Review & Critical Thinking

1. What is measurement?
2. Differentiate among the four types of measurement scales and discuss the types of information contained in each.
3. How does reliability differ from validity? Give examples of each.
4. Give an example of a scale that would be reliable but not valid. Also give an example of a scale that would be valid but not reliable.
5. What are three methods of assessing reliability?
6. What are three methods of assessing validity?
7. Discuss some of the considerations in selecting a rating, ranking, or purchase intent scale.
8. What are some of the arguments for and against having a neutral point on a scale?
9. Compare and contrast the semantic differential, Stapel scale, and Likert scale. Under what conditions would a researcher use each one?
10. Develop a Likert scale to evaluate the parks and recreation department in your city.
11. Develop a purchase intent scale for students eating at a university's cafeteria. How might the reliability and validity of this scale be measured? Why do you think purchase intent scales are so popular in commercial marketing research?
12. What are the disadvantages of a graphic rating scale?
13. Develop a rank-order scale for the beer preferences of college students. What are the advantages and disadvantages of this type of scale?
14. What are some adjective pairs or phrases that could be used in a semantic differential to measure the image of your university?

Comment Cards—Who Is Fooling Whom?

Real-Life Research

Joseph Duket is president of Q&A, Inc., a Smyrna, Georgia, research firm. His hobby is collecting comment cards wherever he can find them. Below Mr. Duket discusses his thoughts on comment cards.

These innocuous little cards come in every size and shape imaginable, from official-looking trifolds addressed to "Chief Executive Officer" to simple index cards with a few lines for open-ended feedback. Studies have shown that 26 out of 27 dissatisfied customers—96 percent—never voluntarily complain. Yet companies large and small use comment cards to measure customer satisfaction. Compounding the dubious reliability of comment cards, companies create further bias in the design of their rating scales. As shown in the chart on the following page, one must wonder how confused customers are with this semantic hodgepodge. With the exception of one company that didn't think highly enough of itself to warrant an "excellent" score ("very good" was its top rating) and another that chose to deceive itself by assigning "below average" as its lowest score, the only terms which were universally acceptable were "excellent" and "poor." All other terms and ratings points in between are nebulous, to say the least. According to Funk & Wagnalls, the term excellent means "being of the very best quality." As a superlative term, it requires no qualifier or adjective to increase its impact. One person or company cannot be more excellent than another. If you're doing the best job or providing the best quality, no one can do better.

For the word poor, however, Funk & Wagnalls uses the synonyms inferior and unsatisfactory in its definition. Confusion arises when the word inferior is described as "lower in quality, worth, or adequacy; mediocre; ordinary." Mediocre is then defined as "of only average quality." So, taking this exercise in interpretation to the extreme, poor performance could actually mean an average rating.

Good is perhaps the most misunderstood term used in rating scales. What exactly is good performance when it comes to customer satisfaction? As clearly shown in the examples, some companies consider good to be synonymous with above average, while others consider good to be the same as average.

Average, the term many firms use as their midpoint in the scale, can be misconstrued, as well. Average can be defined as the arithmetic mean (as in batting average) or a synonym for ordinary or mediocre. If used as the mean, who determines what average performance is? According to many people, the average customer service for Ritz Carlton hotels or Nordstrom department stores is excellent. And, on the other hand, the average (mean) service level for many fast food restaurants is poor.

Depending on which scale you're using, words can have far different meanings. On a three-point scale, fair can be synonymous with acceptable or satisfactory while on a four- or five-point scale it's comparable to below average or needs improvement. There is danger in using the term needs improvement for a "D" rating, since employees and managers can look upon a "C" as good enough not to warrant improvement. Does the company only need to improve when it has reached the point where customers are defecting in droves? In the real world of customer service, any score other than excellent needs improvement.

Many companies, either consciously or unconsciously, stack the deck in their favor by employing rating scales skewed to the positive side. Such scales as:

Excellent	Very good	Good	Fair	Poor
Excellent	Good	Average	Below Average	
Very good	Satisfactory	Unsatisfactory		
Excellent	Okay	Poor		
Excellent	Good	Poor		

will obviously produce much higher positive scores than if more equitable scales were given or more relevant terms used. Companies can also lull themselves into a false sense of security, as in the example of the company above that used "below average" as its lowest rating. I can hear the customer service manager explaining to the CEO now, "Well, our customer satisfaction scores are below average, but at least we're not failing."

The most disturbing aspect of this name selection process—and the one which has the most detrimental effect on business—involves the middle-of-the-road satisfaction score. Whether it's called average, good, fair, okay, acceptable, or satisfactory, the fact remains that no business should accept such a rating as positive. At best, a "C" means the company is providing the bare basics of quality or service. Just as it means in the scholastic arena, a "C" student is doing just enough to get by—nothing more and nothing less. It's a marginal passing score that should not be considered acceptable if the business expects to retain customers and prevent defections. And, most certainly, it should never be misconstrued to be a good score.

I don't know too many parents with high aspirations of their child attending a good college who would look at a report card of all Cs and say, "You're doing okay!" or "Good job!" And I can't imaging any proud parent telling a child with a D that he or she did "fair." Yet companies continue to pat themselves on the back for mediocre performance by attaching such words to their rating scales.[14]

Questions

1. Is Mr. Duket primarily speaking about reliability or validity problems with comment cards? Explain your answer.
2. Given the problems with comment cards, should management simply do away with them? Why?
3. What could be done to improve the data quality of comment cards?
4. If the objective of comment cards is as an aid to building long-term relationships with customers (satisfied customers will be repeat customers), what other marketing research techniques could be applied to reach this objective?

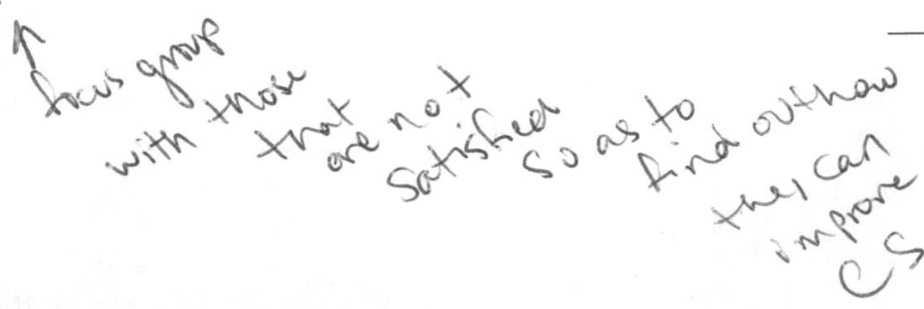

CHAPTER *ten*

Questionnaire Design

Learning Objectives

1 *To learn the objectives of questionnaire design*

2 *To understand the role of the questionnaire in the data collection process*

3 *To become familiar with the criteria for a good questionnaire*

4 *To learn the process for questionnaire design*

5 *To become knowledgeable about the three basic forms of questions*

6 *To understand the key role of the questionnaire in data collection costs*

7 *To learn the necessary procedures for the successful implementation of a survey*

8 *To understand how software and the Internet are impacting questionnaire design*

Kraft Foods already knew that consumers think frozen pizza tastes like cardboard. Carryout from the local pizzeria, they believe, will always beat a pie that heats in the oven. How could Kraft change that mind-set with its new product, DiGiorno Rising Crust Pizza? Kraft had to pinpoint why people eat pizza, regardless of whether it's frozen or carryout. SMI–Alcott mailed a survey to 1,000 pizza lovers and asked them about their habits. When did they eat pizza? Could they describe the last two times they had it? Results showed that people ate pizza during fun social occasions or at home, when no one—especially mom—wanted to be stuck in the kitchen. Other activities, maybe a party, a big sports game on TV, or just a quiet night with their mate, were more important than making a five-course meal. People said they mostly ate frozen pizza for convenience, when time was short, but called for delivery for a variety of reasons. They also questioned the quality of frozen pizza, saying it couldn't offer the same taste as carryout.

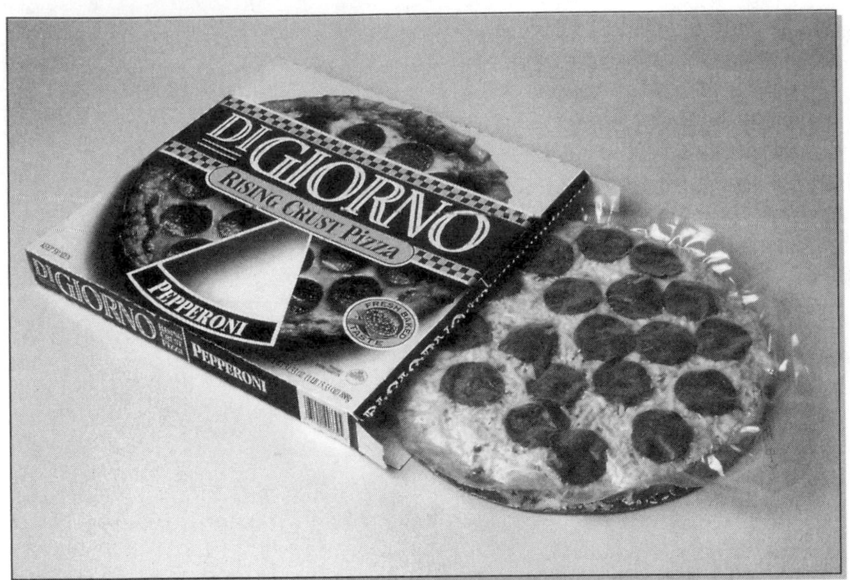

Focus groups with women ages 25 to 54, conducted by Loran Marketing Group, supported the findings. Participants said they wanted a frozen pizza with a fresh-baked taste, but so far hadn't found one in the grocery store. Then the groups watched a demonstration of DiGiorno, its crust rising as it baked in the oven. The image clicked—and convinced skeptical consumers that even a frozen pizza could really deliver.

Of course, it had to taste good, too. Product Dynamics ran a series of blind taste tests with consumers to rate DiGiorno against both frozen and carryout pies. No problem there: It scored the highest among frozen brands and placed second to only one carryout product. Ideas for the ad campaign were presented to a group of consumers in a series of interviews. Again, Kraft heard that people wanted a frozen pizza with the taste and crust of carryout. And, these folks added, they'd need proof that DiGiorno was for real before picking it up in the frozen-foods aisle. This insight underscored the need to actually show DiGiorno rising in the oven during the commercials.

Kraft also learned that people had trouble pronouncing "DiGiorno," the Italian name chosen to lend authenticity to the product. If they couldn't say it, how would they remember it? A simple solution: Final copy for the TV spots made sure that the brand name was repeated several times.

Find out more about DiGiorno by visiting

http://www.Kraftfoods.com

and opening the Fridge in the KRAFT Family of Brands

Nielsen data show a steady rise in sales for DiGiorno since its launch in 1996. It now boasts $300 million in revenues, placing it second in its category (Tombstone, another Kraft brand, ranks number one). Brand awareness, according to Millward Brown, has jumped significantly, too—from 23 percent in 1996 to 77 percent. And watch out, pizza man: 49 percent of Millward Brown participants say that DiGiorno is a worthy substitute for carryout.[1]

Survey research and focus groups enabled Kraft Foods to build demand for DiGiorno. The cornerstone of survey research is the questionnaire. What are the objectives of questionnaire design? A poor questionnaire can lead to interviewer frustration and confused respondents. This in turn leads to interviews being terminated by respondents. What steps are involved in questionnaire development? What impact is the Internet having on questionnaires? We explore these and other issues in Chapter 10.

A questionnaire can play a vital role in research, so some primary considerations must be kept in mind when developing it. In this chapter we present a step-by-step procedure for designing a questionnaire, including guidelines for evaluating questions for appropriateness and an overview of alternative question forms. We then describe the instructions for supervisors and interviewers that must accompany a questionnaire. Next, we discuss how the Internet and new software are affecting questionnaire development. Finally, we explain the differences between observation forms and questionnaires. ■

The Role of a Questionnaire

Questionnaire Defined

Every form of survey research relies on the use of a questionnaire. The questionnaire is the common thread for almost all data collection methods. A **questionnaire** is a set of questions designed to generate the data necessary for accomplishing the objectives of the research project. It is a formalized schedule for collecting information from respondents. You have no doubt seen many and even filled one out recently. Creating a good questionnaire requires both hard work and creativity.

Questionnaire A set of questions designed to generate the data necessary for accomplishing the objectives of the research project.

A questionnaire provides standardization and uniformity in the data-gathering process. It standardizes the wording and sequencing of the questions. Every respondent sees or hears the same words and questions; every interviewer asks identical questions. Without such a procedure, every interviewer could ask whatever he or she felt at the moment, and the researcher would be left wondering whether respondents' answers were a consequence of interviewer influence, prompting, or interpretation. A valid basis for comparing respondents' answers would not exist, and the jumbled mass of data would be impossible to tabulate. The questionnaire, then, is a control device, but it is also a unique device.

The questionnaire (sometimes referred to as an interview schedule or survey instrument) plays a critical role in the data collection process. An elaborate sampling plan, well-trained interviewers, proper statistical analysis techniques, and good editing and coding are all for naught if the questionnaire is poorly designed. Improper design can lead to incomplete information, inaccurate data, and higher costs. The questionnaire and the interviewer are the production line of marketing research. It is here that the product, be it good or bad, is created. The questionnaire is the workers' (interviewers') tool that creates the basic product (respondent information).

The Critical Link

Figure 10.1 illustrates the pivotal role a questionnaire has in research. It is positioned between the survey objectives (drawn from the manager's problem) and the respondents' information. The objectives are translated into specific questions to solicit information from respondents. Assume that

Figure 10.1

The Questionnaire's Role in the Research Process

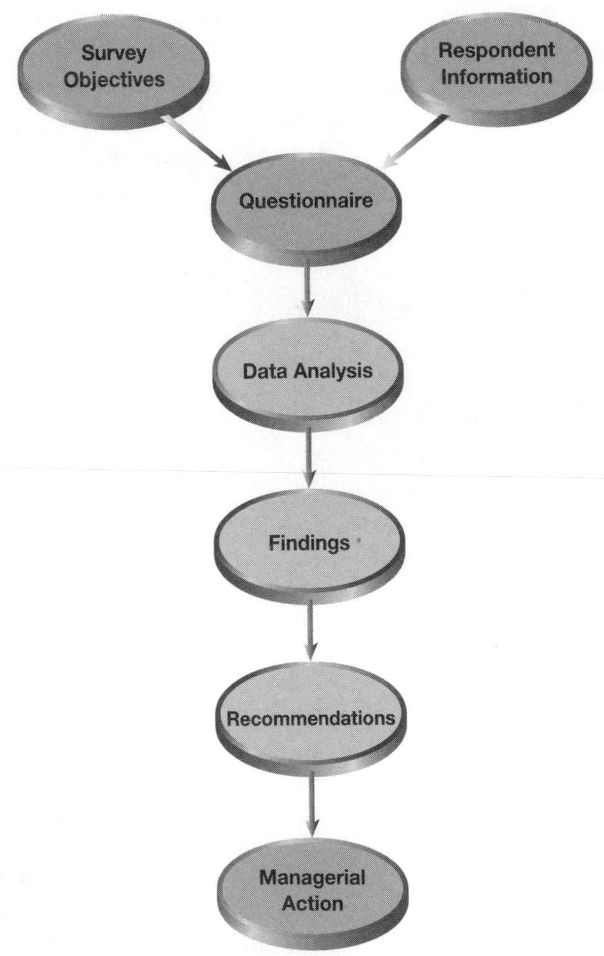

Timex is considering the development of a child's wristwatch. The timepiece would be made of a plastic casing with printed circuits inside. The engineering staff believes that it can come up with a watch that will withstand the potential abuse of the normal activities of a child between 8 and 13 years old. Preliminary market research is called for to determine the acceptability of the watch to the market. One objective is to determine children's reactions to the watch. But a child of eight cannot respond to questions that use words such as acceptability, efficiency, and likelihood of purchase.

The marketing researcher must translate the objectives into language that is understandable to the children as respondents. The process illustrates the pivotal role of the questionnaire: The researcher must translate the survey objectives into a form that is understandable to respondents and that draws the requisite information out of them. The questionnaire must also be designed so that responses can be easily tabulated and translated into findings and recommendations that satisfy the manager's information requirements. The way questionnaires are designed and implemented plays a key role in total survey costs, a subject we discuss in detail later in the chapter.

Criteria for a Good Questionnaire

In designing a good questionnaire, a number of considerations must be kept in mind: Does it provide the necessary decision-making information for management? Does it consider the type of respondents? Does it meet editing, coding, and data-processing requirements?

Does It Provide the Necessary Decision-Making Information?

The primary role of any questionnaire is to provide the required information necessary for management decision making. Any questionnaire that fails to provide important insights for management or decision-making information should be discarded or revised. This means that managers who will be using the data should always approve the questionnaire. By signing off on the questionnaire, the manager is implying, "Yes, this instrument will supply the data I need to reach a decision." If the manager does not sign off, then the marketing researcher will continue to make revisions to the questionnaire.

Does It Fit Respondent Requirements?

As companies have recognized the importance of marketing research, the number of surveys taken annually has mushroomed. Poorly designed, confusing, and lengthy surveys have turned off thousands of potential respondents. It is estimated that more than 40 percent of all persons now contacted refuse to participate in surveys.

The researcher who is designing a questionnaire must not only consider the topic and the type of respondents, but also the interviewing environment and questionnaire length. One recent study found that when respondents attach little interest or importance to the survey topic, questionnaire length is relatively unimportant. They decide not to participate in the survey no matter how long or short the questionnaire is. The study also found that consumers do answer somewhat longer questionnaires when they are interested in the topic and when they perceive little difficulty in answering the questions.[2]

A questionnaire should be designed explicitly for the intended respondents. Although parents typically purchase cold cereals, it is the children, either directly or indirectly, who often decide which brand. Thus, a taste-test questionnaire for children should be formulated in language children understand. On the other hand, an interview schedule for adult purchasers should be worded in language that is suitable for adult interviewees. One of the most important tasks of questionnaire design is to "fit" the questions to the prospective respondents. The questionnaire designer must strip away any marketing jargon and business terminology that may be misunderstood by respondents. In fact, it is always best to use simple, everyday language, as long as it is not insulting or demeaning.

What About Editing and Data-Processing Requirements?

Editing Checking the questionnaire to ensure that skip patterns were followed and the required questions filled out.

Once information is gathered, it must be edited. **Editing** refers to going through the questionnaire to make certain that the "skip patterns" were followed and the required questions filled out. A *skip pattern* is the sequence in which questions are asked. Table 10.1 denotes a skip pattern from 4a to 5a for persons who answered "no" to question 4a.

Table 10.1

A Questionnaire Skip Pattern

4a. Do you usually use a cream rinse or a hair conditioner on your child's hair?
(1) No (SKIP TO 5a)
(2) (ASK Q 4b)

4b. Is that a cream rinse that you pour on or a cream rinse that you spray on?
(1) ( ) Cream rinse that you pour on
(2) ( ) Cream rinse that you spray on

4c. About how often do you use a cream rinse or a hair conditioner on your child's hair? Would you say less than once a week, once a week, or more than once a week?
(1) ❑ Less than once a week
(2) ❑ Once a week
(3) ❑ More than once a week

5a. Thinking of the texture of your child's hair, is it . . . ? (READ LIST)
1 ❑ Fine
2 ❑ Coarse
3 ❑ Regular

5b. What is the length of your child's hair? (READ LIST)
1 ❑ Long
2 ❑ Medium
3 ❑ Short

All "open-ended" questions should be recorded verbatim by the interviewer. An open-ended question is one that does not contain precoded possible responses. Open-ended questions are sometimes coded by listing the answers from a number of randomly selected completed questionnaires. If at all possible, the open-ended questions should be precoded. Those responses with the greatest frequency are then listed on a coding sheet like the one shown in Table 10.2. The editor uses the coding sheet to list the responses to the open-ended question. Today sophisticated neural network systems software is decreasing the necessity of having to manually code open-ended questions.

A Questionnaire Serves Many Masters

In summary, a questionnaire must accomplish a number of things. First, it must accommodate all the research objectives in sufficient depth and breadth to satisfy the information requirements of the manager. Next, it must "speak" to respondents in understandable language and at the appropriate intellectual level. Furthermore, it must be convenient for an interviewer to administer, and it must allow the interviewer to quickly record respondents' answers. At the same time, it must be easy and fast to edit and check for completeness. It should also facilitate coding and data entry. Finally, the questionnaire must be translatable back into findings that respond to the manager's original questions.

The Questionnaire Development Process

Designing a questionnaire involves a logical series of steps, as shown in Figure 10.2. on page 294. The steps may vary slightly from researcher to

Table 10.2

Coding Sheet for the Question "What Is Your Occupation?"

Category	Code
Professional/technical	1
Manager, official, self-employed	2
Clerical, sales	3
Skilled worker	4
Service worker	5
Unskilled laborer	6
Farm operator or rancher	7
Unemployed or student	8
Retired	9

researcher, but still tend to follow the same general sequence. Committees and lines of authority can complicate the questionnaire design process. It is often wise to clear each step of the design process with the individual who has the ultimate project authority. This is particularly true for step one, determining the decision-making information needed. Many work hours have been wasted on questionnaire design when a researcher developed a questionnaire to answer one type of question and the "real" decision maker wanted something entirely different. The design process itself, such as question wording and format, can raise additional issues or unanswered questions. This, in turn, can send the researcher back to step one for a clearer delineation of the information sought.

Step One: Determine Survey Objectives, Resources, and Constraints

The research process often begins when a marketing manager, brand manager, or new product development specialist has a need for decision-making

Figure 10.2

The Questionnaire Development Process

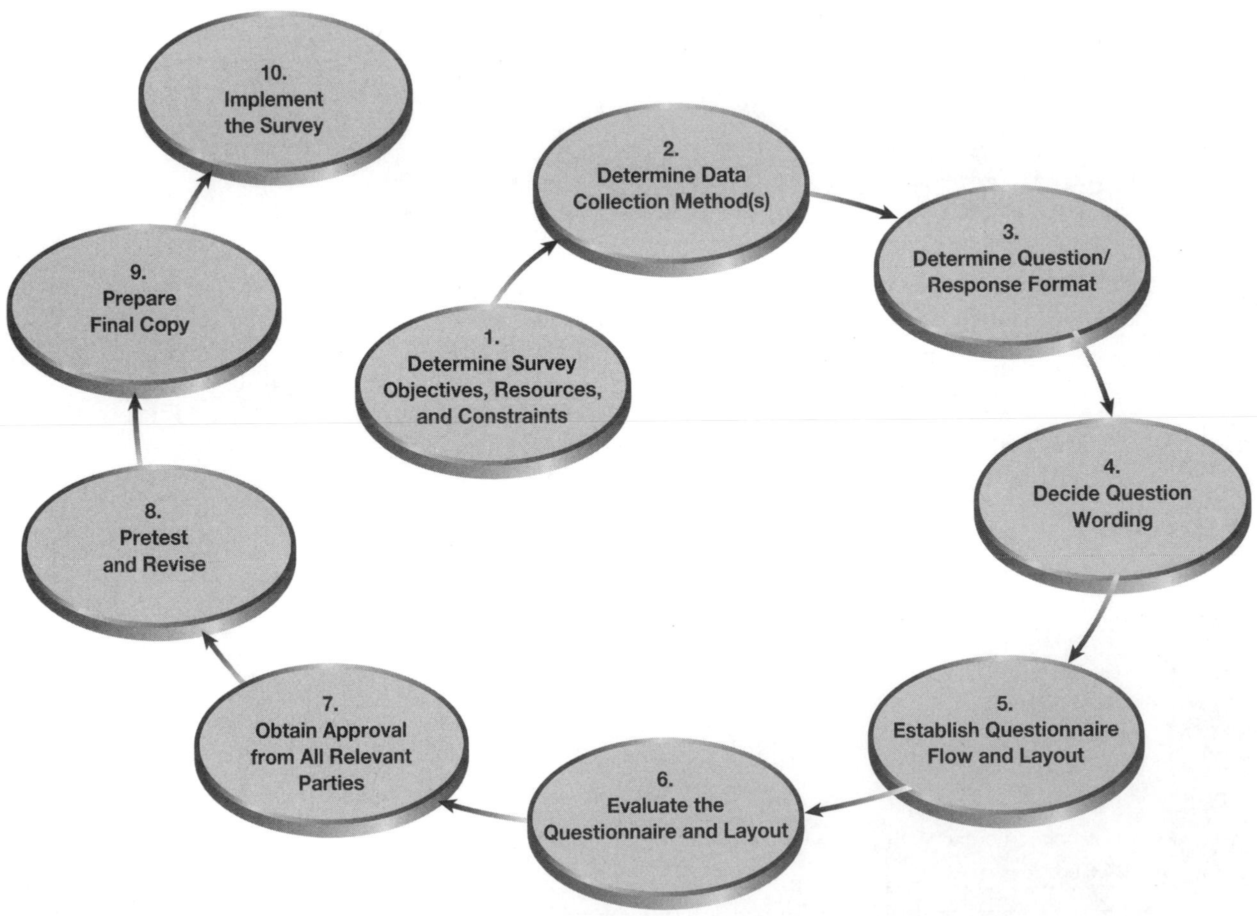

information that is not available. In some firms it is the responsibility of the manager to evaluate all secondary sources to make certain that the needed information has not already been gathered. In other companies, the manager leaves all research activities, primary and secondary, to the research department. The discussion of the research process in Chapter 2 covers this issue in more detail.

Although a brand manager may initiate the research request, everyone affected by the project, such as the assistant brand manager, group product manager, and even the marketing manager, should provide input into exactly what data are needed. **Survey objectives,** sometimes called **information objectives,** should be spelled out as clearly and precisely as possible. If this step is completed in a thorough fashion, the rest of the process will follow more smoothly and efficiently.

Survey or information objectives The decision-making information sought through the questionnaire.

Step Two: Determine the Data Collection Method

Chapter 7 discussed the variety of ways that survey data can be gathered, such as interviews in person or on the telephone and self-administered surveys filled out by mail or on the Internet. Each method has an impact on the questionnaire design. For example, an in-person questionnaire designed for mall interviews will have certain constraints, such as a time limitation, not found in an in-home interview. A mailed questionnaire that is to be self-administered must have explicit instructions and should usually be rather short. Because no interviewer is present, opportunities to clarify questions are lacking. A telephone interview often requires a rich verbal description of concepts to make certain respondents understand the ideas being discussed. In contrast, in a face-to-face interview or an Internet survey the respondents can be shown a picture or a concept can be demonstrated.

Step Three: Determine the Question-Response Format

Once the data collection method has been determined, the actual questionnaire design process begins. The first phase in the process concerns itself with the types of questions to be used in the survey. Three major types of question-response formats are used in marketing research: open-ended, closed-ended, and scale-response questions.

Open-ended Questions

Open-ended questions are those in which respondents can reply in their own words. The researcher does not limit the response choices. Often open-ended questions require probes from the interviewer. A *probe* is encouragement from an interviewer for a respondent to elaborate or continue the discussion. The interviewer may say, "Is there anything else?" or "Would you elaborate on that?" Probes aid in clarifying a respondent's interests, attitudes, and feelings. Computer software is playing an increasingly important role in analyzing and recording probes to open-ended questions.

Open-ended questions Questions that ask respondents to reply in their own words.

Open-ended questions offer several advantages to the researcher. They enable respondents to give their general reactions to questions such as the following:

1. *What advantages, if any, do you think ordering from a mail-order catalog company offers compared with local retail outlets? (PROBE: What else?)*
2. *Why do you have one or more of your rugs or carpets professionally cleaned, rather than you or someone else in the household cleaning them?*
3. *What is there about the color of ___ (the product of interest) that makes you like it the best? (PROBE: What color is that?)*
4. *Why do you say that ___ (the brand you use most often) is better?*

Each of these questions was taken from a different nationwide survey covering four products and services. Note that in questions 2 and 4, the open-ended question is part of a skip pattern. In question 2, for example, respondents have already indicated that they use a professional carpet cleaning service and do not depend on members of the household for rug cleaning.

Another advantage of open-ended responses is that they can provide the researcher with a rich array of information. Respondents answer from their own frame of reference. Answers are given in down-to-earth language rather than in laboratory or marketing jargon. This is often helpful in designing promotional themes and campaigns. It enables copywriters to use the consumers' lingo. This rich array of information can now be captured even in computer-assisted interviews.

An analysis of open-ended data often sheds additional light on the motivations or attitudes behind closed-ended response patterns. It is one thing to know that color ranks second in importance out of five product attributes. But it might be much more valuable to know why color is so important. For example, a recent study on mobile home park residents uncovered a great deal of dissatisfaction with the trash pick-up service, but further inspection of the open-ended responses uncovered the reason: Neighbors' dogs were allowed to run free and were overturning the receptacles. Similarly, open-ended questions may suggest additional alternatives that were not listed in closed-ended questions. For example, a previously unrecognized advantage of using a mail-order catalog might be uncovered from question 1. This advantage would have been omitted from a closed-ended question on the same subject.

One manufacturer with whom the authors consult always ends a product placement questionnaire with the following: "Is there anything else that you would like to tell us about the product that you have tried during the past three weeks?" This question seeks to discover any final tidbit of information that might provide additional insight for the researcher.

Open-ended questions have their problems, too. One factor is the time-and-money-consuming process of editing and coding. Editing open-ended responses requires collapsing the many response alternatives into some reasonable number. If too many categories are used, data patterns and response frequencies are difficult for the researcher to interpret. If the categories are too broad, the data are too general and important meaning may be lost. Even if a proper number of categories is used, editors may have to interpret what the interviewer has recorded and force the data into a category.

A related problem is that not all interviewers handle open-ended questions well. Although training sessions continually stress the importance of recording open-ended questions verbatim, it is often not practiced in the field. Slow writers may unintentionally miss important comments or may not probe adequately. Good probes that ask "Can you tell me a little more?" or "Is there anything else?" generally have better-quality answers than poor probes.

Assume that this question was asked in a food study: "What, if anything, do you normally add to a taco that you prepare at home besides meat?" The question is open ended and the coding categories might be:

Response	Code
Avocado	1
Cheese (Monterey Jack, Cheddar)	2
Guacamole	3
Lettuce	4
Mexican hot sauce	5
Olives (black or green)	6
Onions (red or white)	7
Peppers (red or green)	8
Pimento	9
Sour cream	0
Other	X

The open-endedness of the question is partially overcome by precoding the possible responses. However, it might have been better simply to list the possible answers on the questionnaire. A space could have been provided to write in any nonconforming reply in the "other" category. In a telephone interview, the question would still qualify as open ended because the respondent would not see the categories and the interviewer would be instructed not to divulge them. Precoding necessitates sufficient familiarity with previous studies of a similar nature to anticipate respondents' answers. Otherwise, a pretest with a fairly large sample is needed.

Open-ended questions may be biased toward articulate interviewees. Those with elaborate opinions and the ability to express them are likely to have greater input than those who are shy, inarticulate, or withdrawn. Yet they are equally likely prospects for buying a product. How would an editor code the response "I usually add a green, avocado-tasting hot sauce"? Or "I cut up a mixture of lettuce and spinach"? Or "I'm a vegetarian. I don't use meat at

In PRACTICE

Using Technology to Record Open-ended Responses

Adults and Surveys has developed a system called A&S Voice/CATI.When an open-ended question comes up on the screen, the interviewer has the capability to record the entire response in the respondent's own voice onto PC disk rather than a tape recorder. The assumption is that the interview is taking place via PC rather than a dumb terminal. The system affords some important new benefits for analysts of open-ended responses:

- By recording the entire open-ended response, the interviewer does not break spontaneity by interrupting to clarify and write or type the response.
- How a thing is said is captured along with what is said.
- It's even possible to record how the interviewers ask the questions and the give-and-take between the interviewer and the respondent.

The system stores the response on a computer as a digital file on hard disk or floppies. Hence, the verbatim response can be sorted like any other computer file. The data can be transmitted via telephone lines like any other data.

In analyzing a customer satisfaction study, for example, the analyst can sort respondents who are satisfied and those who are dissatisfied and listen to each group's actual comments as to why. During analysis and report presentation or preparation, actual-voice, open-ended responses can be sorted by answers to any other question in the questionnaire and by traditional classification questions (sex, age, income, etc.).[3] ■

all. My taco is filled only with guacamole"? A basic problem with open-ended questions lies in their interpretation. In fact, a two-phased judgment must be made. First, the researcher must decide on the proper set of categories and then each response must be evaluated according to which category it falls into.

A final difficulty with open-ended questions is their inappropriateness on some self-administered questionnaires. If no interviewer is there to probe, a shallow, incomplete, or unclear answer may be recorded. If the taco question had appeared on a self-administered interview schedule without precoded choices, the answers might read, "I use a little bit of everything" or "I use the same things that restaurants do." These answers would have virtually no value to a researcher.

Closed-ended questions Questions that ask respondents to choose between two or more answers.

Closed-ended Questions

A **closed-ended question** is one that requires the respondent to make a selection from a list of responses. The primary advantage of closed-ended questions is simply the avoidance of many of the problems of open-ended questions. Reading the response alternatives may jog a person's memory and provide a realistic response. And because the option of expounding on a topic is not given, there is no bias toward articulate respondents. Interviewer and coder bias are removed because they are simply checking a box, circling a category, recording a number, or punching a key. Finally, the coding and data-entry process is greatly simplified.

There are important differences between precoded open-ended questions and multiple-choice questions. An open-ended question allows respondents to answer in a freewheeling format. The interviewer simply checks the points on the precoded answers as they are given. Probing is used, but a list is never read. If an answer is given that is not precoded, it is written verbatim in the "other" column. In contrast, a closed-ended question requires that the alternatives be read or shown to respondents.

Traditionally, marketing researchers have separated the two-item response option from the many-item type. A two-choice question is called **dichotomous** and the many-item type is often called **multiple choice** or multichotomous. With the dichotomous closed-ended question, the response categories are sometimes implicit. For instance, how would you respond to the following question: "Did you buy gasoline for your automobile in the last week?" Obviously, the implicit options are "Yes" or "No." Regardless of the fact that a respondent may say, "I rented a car last week, and they filled it up for me. Does that count?" the questions would still be classified as dichotomous closed ended.

Dichotomous questions
Questions that ask respondents to choose between two answers.

Multiple-choice questions
Questions that ask respondents to choose among a list of more than two answers.

Dichotomous Questions

The simplest form of a closed-ended question is the dichotomous choice. A few examples are:

1. *Did you heat the Danish roll before serving it?*

Yes	*1*
No	*2*

2. *The federal government doesn't care what people like me think.*

Agree	*1*
Disagree	*2*

3. *Do you think that inflation will be greater or less than last year?*

Greater than	*1*
Less than	*2*

Note that respondents are limited to two fixed alternatives. Such questions are easy to administer and usually evoke rapid responses. Many times a neutral or no opinion/don't know option is added to the dichotomous alternatives. Sometimes interviewers will jot down DK for "don't know" or NR for "no response" if the neutral option is omitted from the questionnaire.

Dichotomous questions are prone to a large amount of measurement error. Because alternatives are polarized, the wide range of possible choices between the poles is omitted. Thus, question wording is critical to obtaining accurate responses. The same question phrased positively and negatively may well result in opposing answers. In the third question, response may vary depending upon whether greater than or less than is listed first. These problems can be overcome using a split ballot technique. One-half of the questionnaires are worded with greater than listed first and the other half with less than first. This procedure aids in reducing potential bias.

Multiple-Choice Questions Multiple-choice questions have about the same advantages and disadvantages as closed-ended questions. Replies do not have to be coded like open-ended questions but limited information is provided. Interviewees are asked to give one alternative that correctly expresses their opinion or, in some instances, to indicate all alternatives that apply. Some examples of multiple-choice questions follow:

1. *I'd like you to think back to the last footwear of any kind that you bought. I'll read you a list of descriptions and would like for you to tell me which category this footwear falls into. (READ LIST AND CHECK THE PROPER CATEGORY)*

Dress or formal	*1*
Casual	*2*
Canvas-trainer-gym shoes	*3*
Specialized athletic shoes	*4*
Boots	*5*

2. *(HAND RESPONDENT CARD) Please look at this card and tell me the letter that indicates the age group you belong to:*

A. Under 17	*1*
B. 17–24 Years	*2*
C. 25–34 Years	*3*
D. 35–49 Years	*4*
E. 50–64 Years	*5*
F. 65 and Over	*6*

3. *In the last three months, have you used Noxzema Skin Cream . . . ? (CHECK ALL THAT APPLY)*

as a facial wash	*1*
for moisturizing the skin	*2*
for treating blemishes	*3*
for cleansing the skin	*4*
for treating dry skin	*5*
for softening skin	*6*
for sunburn	*7*
for making the facial skin smooth	*8*

Question 1 may not cover all possible alternatives and thus would not capture a true response. Where, for example, would an interviewer record work shoes? The same thing can be said for question 3. Not only are all possible alternatives not included, but also there is no possibility for respondents to elaborate on or qualify their answers. Part of the problem could be easily overcome by adding an "Any other use? (RECORD VERBATIM)" alternative to both questions.

Disadvantages of Closed-ended Questions

Each type of closed-ended question represents unique disadvantages. For dichotomous questions, researchers find that frequently responses fail to communicate any intensity of feeling from respondents. In some cases, the matter of intensity does not apply, as in the example about purchasing gasoline. But instances do arise in which respondents feel strongly about an issue but the intensity is lost because of the dichotomous response format. Suppose that interview had continued with this question: "Would you purchase gasoline priced $1 above current prices but that would guarantee twice the miles per gallon?" The likelihood is that the responses might range in intensity, like these quotes: "No, absolutely not"; "Gee, I doubt it"; "Well, I might try it"; or "You bet!"

The multiple-response close-ended question has two additional disadvantages. First, the researcher must spend time generating the list of possible responses. This phase may require intensive analysis of focus group tapes, brainstorming, or secondary data investigation. In any case, it requires more time and effort than the open-ended alternative or the dichotomous format. Another problem with closed-ended multiple-response questions is the range of possible answers. If the list is too long, respondents may become confused or uninterested. One way to help overcome this problem is to show interviewees a card and read down the list with them. A related problem with any list is position bias. Respondents typically choose from among the first and last alternatives, all other things being equal. Position bias can be overcome by marking an alternative with an X and instructing the interviewer to begin reading the list at the marked alternative instead of at the beginning of the list. The first question is marked with an X at alternative one, the second question at alternative two, and so forth.

Scaled-Response Questions

Consider the differences between the following two questions:

1. *Now that you have used the product, would you say that you would buy it or not? (CHECK ONE)*
   - ❑ *Yes, would buy it.*
   - ❑ *No, would not buy it.*
2. *Now that you have used the product, would you say that you would . . . ? (CHECK ONE)*
   - ❑ *definitely buy it.*
   - ❑ *probably buy it.*
   - ❑ *might or might not buy it.*
   - ❑ *probably would not buy it.*
   - ❑ *definitely would not buy it.*

The first question fails to capture any intensity. It determines the direction (yes versus no), but it does not compare with the second one for completeness or sensitivity of response. The latter question is also ordinal in nature.

A primary advantage of **scaled-response questions** is that scaling permits the measurement of the intensity of respondents' answers to multiple-choice

Scaled-response questions Multiple-choice questions in which the choices are designed to capture the intensity of respondents' answers.

questions. Another advantage is that many scaled-response questions incorporate numbers, which may be used directly as codes. The marketing researcher is able to employ much more powerful statistical tools by using some scaled-response questions, as discussed in Chapter 14.

The most significant problems of scaled-response questions evolve from respondent misunderstanding. Scaled questions sometimes tax respondents' ability to remember and answer. First, the questionnaire must explain the response category options, then respondents must translate them into their own frames of reference. To overcome the first problem, interviewers are usually provided with a detailed description of the allowed response categories and even instructed to elicit an affirmation that respondents understand the scale before asking the questions. Take a look at Table 10.3 for examples of a telephone interviewer's instructions for scaled-response questions. In the case of self-administered questionnaires, the researcher often presents an example of how to respond to a scale as part of the instructions.

Step Four: Decide on the Question Wording

Once the marketing researcher has decided on the specific types of questions and response formats, the next task is the actual writing of the questions. The wording of specific questions always poses a significant investment of time for a marketing researcher. It is a skill developed over time and subject to constant improvement. Four guidelines are useful to bear in mind in composing the wording and sequencing of each question.

1. *The wording must be clear.* If the researcher decides that a question is absolutely necessary, that question must be stated so that it means the same thing to all respondents. Ambiguous terminology should be avoided, such as "Do you live within five minutes of here?" or "Where do you usually shop for clothes?" The first example depends on the mode of transportation (perhaps the respondent walks), driving speed, perceived elapsed time, and other factors. It would normally be prudent to show respondents a map with certain areas delineated and ask whether they live within the area. The second question depends on the type of clothing, the occasion, the member of the family who is shopping, and the meaning of the word where.

   Clarity also implies the use of reasonable terminology. A questionnaire is not a vocabulary test. Jargon should be avoided and verbiage should be geared to the target audience. A question such as "State the level of efficacy of your preponderant dishwasher liquid" probably would be greeted by lots of blank stares. It would be simpler and better to ask, "Are you (1) very satisfied, (2) somewhat satisfied, or (3) not satisfied with your current brand of dishwasher liquid?" It is best to use words that have precise meanings, universal usage, and minimal connotative confusion. When respondents are uncertain of what a question means, the incidence of "no response" increases.

   Clear writing means custom-tailoring the wording to each target respondent group. If, for example, lawyers are to be interviewed, the wording should be appropriate to lawyers. If construction laborers are to

Table 10.3

Sample Telephone Interviewer Instructions for a Scaled-Response Question Form

Example 1

I have some statements that I will read to you. For each one, please indicate whether you "strongly agree," "agree," "disagree," "strongly disagree," or "have no opinion." I will read the statement, and you indicate *your* opinion as accurately as possible. Are the instructions clear?

(IF THE RESPONDENT DOES NOT UNDERSTAND, REPEAT RESPONSE CATEGORIES. GO ON TO READ STATEMENTS AND RECORD RESPONSES. CIRCLE RESPONDENT'S OPINION IN EACH CASE.)

Example 2

4. Now I'm going to read you a list of statements that may or may not be important to you in deciding where to shop for stereo equipment. Let's use your telephone dial as a scale. #1 would mean "definitely disagree" and #6 would mean "definitely agree." Or you can pick any number in between that best expresses your feelings.

Let's begin. To what extent do you agree or disagree that (INSERT STATEMENT) is an important aspect when deciding where to shop for stereo equipment?

Example 3

Now I will read a list of statements about automotive servicing that may or may not be *important* to you when servicing your car.

Let's use your telephone dial as a scale.

Number 1 would mean you *disagree completely* with the statement.

Number 2 would mean you *disagree* with the statement.

Number 3 would mean you *somewhat disagree* with the statement.

Number 4 would mean you *somewhat agree* with the statement.

Number 5 would mean you *agree* with the statement.

Number 6 would mean you *agree* completely with the statement.

Do you have any questions about the scale?

1. To what extent do you agree or disagree that (FILL IN THE STATEMENT) is a feature you consider when selecting a place to have your car serviced?

be questioned, the terminology must be modified appropriately. This advice is painfully obvious, but there are instances in which the failure to relate to respondents' frames of reference has been disastrous. A case in point is the use of the word bottles in this question: "How many bottles of beer do you drink in a normal week?" In some southern states, beer is sold in bottled amounts of 32, 12, 8, 7, 6, and even 4 ounces. So a "heavy" drinker of eight bottles may consume only 32 ounces per week (8 × 4 oz.); in contrast, a "light" drinker might only consume three bottles but 96 ounces (3 × 32 oz.).

Understanding can also be improved by stating the purpose of the survey at the beginning of an interview. Usually, respondents should understand the nature of a study and what is expected of them, but not necessarily know who is sponsoring the project. This aids interviewees in placing questions in the proper perspective.

It is always best to avoid placing two questions in one, sometimes called a double-barreled question. For example, the question "How did you like the taste and texture of the coffee cake?" should be broken into two questions: one concerning taste and the other texture. Each question should address only one aspect requiring evaluation.

2. *Select words that avoid biasing respondents.* A question such as "Do you often shop at lower-class stores like KMart?" evokes an obvious response. Similarly, "Have you purchased any high-quality Black & Decker tools in the past six months?" also biases respondents. Questions can be leading, such as, "Weren't you pleased with the good service you received last night at the Holiday Inn?" Unfortunately, bias may be much more subtle than these examples illustrate.

   Sponsor identification too early in the interviewing process can distort answers. It does not take long, for example, for a person to recognize that a survey is being conducted for a beer company if almost every question relates to its product line. Or consider an opening statement such as "We are conducting a study on the quality of banking for Northeast National Bank, and would like to ask you a few questions."

3. *Consider the ability of respondents to answer the questions.* In some cases respondents may have never acquired the information necessary to answer some questions. Asking a husband which brand of sewing thread his wife most prefers might fall into this category. Asking respondents about a brand or store that they have never encountered creates the same problem. When a question is worded to imply that respondents should be able to answer it, then often replies will be forthcoming, but they will be nothing more than wild guesses. This creates measurement error, since uninformed opinions are being recorded.

   A second problem is forgetfulness. For example, "What was the name of the last movie you saw in a theater?" "Who were the stars?" "Did you have popcorn?" "How many ounces were in the container?" "What price did you pay for the popcorn?" "Did you purchase any other snack items?" "Why or why not?" You probably cannot remember the answers to all these questions. The same is true for typical respondents. Yet a brand manager for Mars, Inc., wants to know what brand of candy respondents purchased last, what alternative brands were considered, and what factors led to the brand selected. Because brand managers want answers to these questions, market researchers ask them. This, in turn, also creates measurement error. Often respondents will give the name of a well-known brand, like Milky Way or Hershey. In other cases, respondents will mention a brand that they often purchase, but it may not be the last brand purchased.

   To avoid the problem of respondents being unable to recall facts, time periods should be kept relatively short. For example, "Did you purchase a candy bar within the past seven days?" If the reply is "Yes," then brand and purchase motivation questions can be asked. Alternatively, a poor question would be, "How many movies have you rented in the past year to view at home on your VCR?" Instead, the researcher might ask:

   a. How many movies have you rented in the past month to view on your VCR?

b. Would you say that in the last month, you rented more movies, fewer movies, or about the average number of movies you rent per month? (IF "MORE" OR "LESS" ASK:)

c. What would you say is the typical number of movies you rent per month?

4. *Consider the willingness of respondents to answer a question.* A respondent's memory may be totally clear, yet he or she may not be willing to give a truthful reply. Reporting an event is likely to be distorted in a socially desirable direction. If an event is perceived as embarrassing, sensitive in nature, threatening, or divergent from someone's self-image, it is likely either not to be mentioned at all or to be distorted in a desirable direction.

Embarrassing topics that deal with such things as borrowing money, personal hygiene, sexual activities, and criminal records must be phrased in a careful manner to minimize measurement error. One technique is to ask the question in the third person. For example, "Do you think that most people charge more on their credit cards than they should? Why?" By asking about "most people" rather than about the respondents themselves, researchers may be able to learn about respondents' attitudes about credit and debt.

A third method for soliciting embarrassing information is to state that the behavior or attitude is common prior to asking the question. For example, "Millions of Americans suffer from hemorrhoids; do you or any member of your family suffer from this problem?" This technique is called "using counterbiasing statements," and makes embarrassing topics less intimidating for respondents to discuss.

Step Five: Establish Questionnaire Flow and Layout

After the questions have been properly formulated, the next step is to sequence them and develop a layout for the questionnaire. Questionnaires are not constructed haphazardly. There is a logic to the positioning of each section of the questionnaire; this logic is depicted in Table 10.4 on page 306. Experienced marketing researchers are well aware that questionnaire development is the key to obtaining interviewer-interviewee rapport. The greater the rapport, the more likely the interviewer will obtain a completed interview with more carefully thought-out and detailed answers. Researcher wisdom has developed the following guidelines concerning questionnaire flow.

1. *Use the screener questions to identify qualified respondents.* Most market research employs some variation of quota sampling. Only qualified respondents are interviewed, and specific minimum numbers (quotas) of various types of qualified respondents may be desired. A study on food products generally has quotas for users of specific brands, a magazine study screens for readers, a cosmetic study screens for brand awareness, and so forth.

Screeners Questions used to screen for appropriate respondents.

The **screeners** (screen questions) may appear on the questionnaire. In many cases, a separate screening questionnaire is provided and filled

Table 10.4

How a Questionnaire Should Be Organized

Location	Type	Examples	Rationale
Screeners	Qualifying questions	"Have you been snow skiing in the past 12 months?" "Do you own a pair of skis?"	To identify target respondents. Survey of ski owners who have skied in the past year.
First few questions	Warm-ups	"What brand of skis do you own?" "How many years have you owned them?"	Easy-to-answer questions show respondent that survey is simple.
First third of questions	Transitions	"What features do you like best about the skis?"	Relate to research objectives, slightly more effort needed to answer.
Middle half of second third	Difficult and complicated	Following are 10 characteristics of snow skis. Please rate your skis on each characteristic using the scale below.	Respondent has committed to completing questionnaire and can see that just a few questions are left.
Last section	Classification and demographics	"What is the highest level of education you have attained?"	Some questions may be considered personal and respondent may leave them blank, but they are at the end of the survey.

out for everyone interviewed. The demographic information obtained in this way provides a basis for comparison against persons who qualify for the full study. A long screener can significantly increase the cost of a study, however, because it means that more information is obtained from every respondent contact. Short screeners, such as the one shown in Table 10.5, quickly eliminate unqualified persons and enable the interviewer to move immediately to the next potential respondent. Longer screeners, on the other hand, provide important information on the nature of nonusers, nontriers, or persons unaware of the product or service being researched.[4]

Most importantly, screeners provide a basis for estimating the costs of a survey. A survey for which everyone qualifies to be interviewed is going to cost much less than one with a 5 percent incidence rate, all else being equal. Many surveys are placed with field services at a flat rate per completed questionnaire. The rate is based on a stated "average interview time" and incidence rate. The screener is used to determine whether, in fact, the incidence rate holds true in a particular city. If it does not, the flat rate is adjusted accordingly.

2. *After obtaining a qualified respondent, begin with a question that catches the respondent's interest.* After introductory comments and screens to find a qualified respondent, the initial questions should be simple, interesting,

Table 10.5

A Screening Questionnaire that Seeks Men 15 Years of Age and Older Who Shave at Least Three Times a Week with a Blade Razor

Hello. I'm from Data Facts Research. We are conducting a survey among men, and I'd like to ask you a few questions.

1. Do you or does any member of your family work for an advertising agency, market research firm, or a company that manufactures or sells shaving products?

(TERMINATE AND RECORD ON CONTACT RECORD SHEET)	Yes ❑
(CONTINUE WITH Q.2)	No ❑

2. How old are you? Are you . . . ? (READ LIST)

(TERMINATE AND RECORD ON CONTACT RECORD SHEET)	Under 15 yrs. old ❑
(CHECK QUOTA CONTROL FORM—IF QUOTA GROUP FOR WHICH THE RESPONDENT QUALIFIES *IS NOT* FILLED, THEN CONTINUE. IF QUOTA GROUP *IS* FILLED, THEN TERMINATE AND RECORD)	15 to 34 yrs. old ❑ Over 34 yrs. old ❑

3. The last time you shaved, did you use an electric razor or a razor that uses blades?

(TERMINATE AND RECORD ON CONTACT RECORD SHEET)	Electric razor ❑
(CONTINUE WITH Q.4)	Blade razor ❑

4. How many times have you shaved in the past seven days?

(TERMINATE AND RECORD ON CONTACT RECORD SHEET)	One or two times ❑
(CONTINUE WITH Q.5)	Three or more times ❑

and nonthreatening. To open a questionnaire with an income or age question might be disastrous. These are often considered threatening and immediately put the respondent on the defensive. The initial question should be easy to answer without much forethought.

3. *Ask general questions first.* Once the interview proceeds beyond the opening warm-up questions, the questionnaire should proceed in a logical fashion. General questions should be covered first to get the person thinking about a concept, company, or type of product, and then the questionnaire should move to the specifics. For example, a questionnaire on shampoo might begin, "Have you purchased a hair spray, hair conditioner, or hair shampoo within the past six weeks?" Then it would continue with questions about the frequency of shampooing, brands purchased in the past three months, satisfaction and dissatisfaction with brands purchased, repurchase intent, the characteristics of an ideal shampoo, respondent's hair characteristics, and finally demographics.
4. *Ask those questions that require work in the middle of the questionnaire.* Initially, the respondent is only vaguely interested and has a minimal comprehension about the nature of the survey. As the interest-building questions transpire, the interview process builds momentum and the respondent's

commitment to the interview. When the interviewer shifts to questions with scaled-response formats, the respondent must be motivated to understand the response categories and options. Alternatively, some questions might ask for some recall or an opinion. The built-up interest in and commitment to the survey and rapport with the interviewer sustain the respondent in this part of the interview. Even if the self-administered method is used, the approach is the same: Build interest and commitment early to motivate the respondent to finish the rest of the questionnaire.

5. *Insert prompters at strategic points.* Good interviewers can sense when a respondent's interest and motivation are sagging and will attempt to build them back up. However, it is always worthwhile for the questionnaire designer to insert short encouragements at strategic locations in the questionnaire. These may be simple statements such as, "I only have a few more questions to go" or "This next section will be easier." On the other hand, they may be inserted as part of the introduction to a new section: "Now that you have helped us with those comments, we would like to ask you a few more questions."
6. *Position sensitive, possibly threatening, and demographic questions at the end.* Sometimes the objectives of a study necessitate questions on topics about which respondents may feel uneasy. Embarrassing topics should be covered near the end of the questionnaire. Placing these questions at the end ensures that most of the questions will be answered before the respondent becomes defensive or breaks off the interview. Moreover, rapport has been established between the respondent and the interviewer by this time, increasing the likelihood of obtaining an answer. Another argument for placing sensitive questions toward the end is that by the time sensitive questions are asked, interviewees have been conditioned to respond. In other words, the pattern of response has been repeated many times. The interviewer asks a question and the respondent gives an answer. By the time potentially embarrassing questions are asked, the respondent has become conditioned to reply.

Step Six: Evaluate the Questionnaire and Layout

Once a rough draft of the questionnaire has been designed, the marketing researcher is obligated to take a step back and critically evaluate it. This phase may seem redundant, given all the careful thought that went into each question. But recall the crucial role played by the questionnaire. At this point in the questionnaire development, the following items should be considered: (1) Are the questions necessary? (2) Is the survey too long? and (3) Will the questions provide the answers to the survey objectives?

Are the Questions Necessary?

Perhaps the most important criterion for this phase of questionnaire development is ascertaining the necessity for a given question. Sometimes researchers and brand managers want to ask questions because "they were on the last survey we did like this," or because "it would be nice to know." Excessive demographic questions are common. Educational data, the number of children in multiple age categories, and extensive spousal information are simply not warranted by the nature of many studies.

Each question must serve a purpose. It must be a screener, an interest generator, a required transition, or directly and explicitly related to the stated objectives of a particular survey. Any question that fails to satisfy at least one of these criteria should be omitted.

Is the Questionnaire Too Long? At this point the researcher should role-play the questionnaire with volunteers acting as respondents. Although there is no magic number of interactions, the length of time it takes to complete the questionnaire should be averaged over a minimum of five trials. Any questionnaire to be administered in a mall or over the telephone that averages longer than 20 minutes should be a candidate for cutting. Sometimes mall interviews can run slightly longer if an incentive is provided to respondents. In-home interviews that last more than 45 minutes should also offer respondents some incentive. Common incentives are movie tickets, pen and pencil sets, and cash or checks. The use of incentives often actually lowers the survey costs because response rates increase and terminations during the interview decrease. If checks are used instead of cash, the canceled checks can be used to create a list of survey participants for follow-up purposes.

Will the Questions Provide the Desired Information to Accomplish Research Objectives? The researcher must make certain that a sufficient number and type of questions are contained within the questionnaire to meet management's decision-making needs. A suggested procedure is to carefully review the written objectives for the research project, then go down the questionnaire and write each question number next to the objective that the particular question will help to accomplish. For example, question 1 applies to objective 3, question 2 to objective 2, and so forth. If a question cannot be tied to an objective, the researcher should determine whether the list of objectives is complete. If the list is sufficient, the question should be omitted. If, after going through the entire questionnaire, an objective has no matching question listed beside it, then an appropriate question should be added.

Allow Plenty of Space for Open-ended Responses An open-ended question that allows half a line for a reply usually will receive a reply of that length and nothing more. Generally speaking, three to five lines (using paper 8½ inches wide) are sufficient for open-ended replies. The researcher must use his or her judgment on how much detail is desirable for an open-ended reply. An answer for "Which department store did you visit most recently?" requires little space. However, a follow-up question that asks, "What factors were most important in your decision to go to (name of department store)?" requires substantially more lines for the response.

Print Instructions in Capital Letters To avoid confusion and to clarify what is a question and what is an instruction, all instructions should be in capital letters. Capitalizing helps bring the instructions to the interviewers' or respondents' attention. For example, "IF THE ANSWER IS 'YES' TO QUESTION 13, SKIP TO QUESTION 17."

Step Seven: Obtain Approval from All Relevant Parties

When the first draft of the questionnaire has been completed, copies of it should be distributed to all parties that have direct authority over the project. Practically speaking, managers may step in at any time in the design process with new information, requests, or concerns, which often necessitates revisions. But it is still important to get final approval of the first draft, even if managers have already interceded in the development process.

Managerial approval commits management to obtaining a body of information via a specific instrument (the questionnaire). If certain questions are not asked, the data will not be gathered. Thus, questionnaire approval tacitly reaffirms what decision-making information is needed and how it will be obtained. For example, assume that a new product questionnaire asks about shape, material, end use, and packaging, but not about color preferences. By approving the questions, the product development manager is implying that he or she knows what color the product will be or that color is not important to determine at this time.

Step Eight: Pretest and Revise

Pretest A trial run of a questionnaire.

When final managerial approval has been obtained, the questionnaire must be pretested. No survey should be taken without a **pretest.** Moreover, a pretest does not mean that one researcher should administer the questionnaire to another researcher. Ideally, a pretest is conducted by excellent interviewers who will ultimately be working on the job on target respondents for the study. They are instructed to look for misinterpretations and general reactions of respondents, as well as lack of continuity, poor skip patterns, and additional alternatives for precoded and closed-ended questions. The pretest should also be conducted in the same mode as the final interview. If the study is to be door to door, then the pretest should be the same.

After the pretest is completed and any necessary changes made, management's approval should be reobtained before taking the questionnaire into the field. If the pretest resulted in extensive design and question alterations, a second pretest would be in order.

Today's global marketers offer a variety of products to their customers throughout the world. Many times a new product concept is tested simultaneously in a number of different countries, requiring questionnaires in a variety of languages. Fortunately, new software programs help ease the language problem, as the Global Issues box explains.

Step Nine: Prepare Final Questionnaire Copy

Even the final-copy phase does not allow the researcher to relax. Precise typing instructions, spacing, numbering, and precoding must be set up, monitored, and proofread. In some instances the questionnaire must be photoreduced to save space or be specifically folded and stapled. In general, the quality of the printing or copying and the paper used relates to who will see the questionnaire. In a mail survey, compliance and subsequent response rates may be affected positively by a professional appearance. In telephone interviews, in contrast, the quality is of much less importance, since the copy is typically read from a computer screen.

Step Ten: Implement the Survey

The completion of the questionnaire establishes the basis for obtaining the desired decision-making information from the marketplace. A series of forms and procedures must be issued with the questionnaire to make certain that the data are gathered correctly, efficiently, and at a reasonable cost. Depending on the data collection method, these include the supervisor's instructions, the interviewer's instructions, screeners, call record sheets, and visual aids.

Supervisor's Instructions

As discussed in Chapter 3, most research interviewing is conducted by field services. It is the service's job to complete the interviews and send them back to the researcher. In essence, field services are the production line of the marketing research industry.

Supervisor's instructions Written directions to the field service on how to conduct a survey.

Supervisor's instructions inform field service supervisors of the nature of the study, start and completion dates, quotas, reporting times, equipment and facility requirements, sampling instructions, the number of interviewers required, and validation procedures. In addition, detailed instructions are required for any taste test that involves food preparation. Quantities are typically measured and cooked using rigorous measurement techniques and devices. The supervisor's instructions are a vitally important part of any

Global ISSUES

Consistency Is the Key in Global Research

WHEN COLLECTING AND PROCESSING DATA FOR INTERNATIONAL RESEARCH, CONSISTENCY is paramount.If the data are not collected and processed consistently, then the results cannot be compared regionally, and eventually project cost and turnaround time will increase. Attention to details and their standardization are imperative.

Specialized software packages for survey design can be tremendously helpful, allowing a library of standard questions, responses, and even routing logic to be compiled. They can be easily retrieved and used to create the different versions of the survey, to achieve consistency in the wording of questions and responses.

Some of these software packages also interface to, or contain, translation utilities. Using these utilities, a researcher can create a database of commonly used phrases, translated into different languages and easily retrieved and used.[5] ■

study. They establish the parameters under which the research is conducted. Without clear instructions, an interview could be conducted 10 different ways in 10 cities. Table 10.6 shows a sample page from a set of supervisor's instructions.

Interviewer's instructions Written directions to the interviewer on how to conduct an interview.

Interviewer's Instructions **Interviewer's instructions** cover many of the same points as supervisor's instructions but are geared to the actual interview. The nature of the study is explained, sampling methodology is given, and reporting forms and times are given. Often a sample interview is

Table 10.6

A Sample Page of Supervisor's Instructions for a Diet Soft Drink Taste Test

Purpose	To determine the ability of diet soft drink users to discriminate among three samples of Diet Dr. Pepper and give opinions and preferences between two of the samples.
Staff	3 to 4 experienced interviewers per shift.
Location	One busy shopping center in a middle to upper-middle socioeconomic area. The center's busiest hours are to be worked by a double shift of interviewers. In the center, 3 to 4 private interviewing stations are to be set up and a refrigerator and good counter space made available for product storage and preparation.
Quota	192 completed interviews broken down as follows: ■ A minimum of 70 Diet Dr. Pepper users ■ A maximum of 122 other diet brand users
Project materials	For this study, you are supplied the following: ■ 250 Screening Questionnaires ■ 192 Study Questionnaires ■ 4 Card A's
Product/preparation	For this study, our client shipped to your refrigerated facility 26 cases of soft drink product. Each case contains 24 10-oz. bottles—312 coded with an *F* on the cap, 312 with an *S*. Each day, you are to obtain from the refrigerated facility approximately 2 to 4 cases of product—1 to 2 of each code. Product must be transported in coolers and kept refrigerated at the location. It should remain at approximately 42°F. In the center, you are to take one-half of the product coded *F* and place the #23 stickers on the bottles. The other half of the F product should receive #46 stickers. The same should be done for product *S*—one-half should be coded #34, the other half #68. A supervisor should do this task before interviewing begins. Interviewers will select product by *code number.* Code number stickers are enclosed for this effort. Each respondent will be initially testing three product samples as designated on the questionnaire. Interviewers will come to the kitchen, select the three designated bottles, open and pour 4 oz. of each product into its corresponding coded cup. The interviewer should cap and *refrigerate* leftover product when finished pouring and take only the three *cups* of product on a tray to respondent.

included with detailed instructions on skip patterns, probing, and quotas. A sample page of interviewer's instructions is shown in Table 10.7.

Call record sheets
Interviewers' logs listing the number and results of a contact.

Call Record Sheets **Call record sheets** are used to measure the efficiency of the interviewers. The form normally indicates the number of contacts and their results (see Table 10.8 on page 314). From these sheets a supervisor can examine the calls per hour, contacts per completed interview, average time per interview, and similar measures to analyze an interviewer's efficiency. If, for example, contacts per completed interview are high, the field supervisor

Table 10.7

A Sample Page of Interviewer's Instructions for a Magazine Readership Study

Purpose	The purpose of this study is to determine a relationship between people's attitudes and the magazines they read regularly.
Method	All interviewing is to be conducted by telephone within your local dialing area. We will neither use nor pay for any work not conducted in exact accordance with our job instructions.
When to interview	Begin interviewing immediately. All interviewing is to be conducted from 5:30 P.M. to 9:30 P.M. weekdays and all day Saturday. You may also interview on Sunday. All work is to be completed by Sunday, November 5.
Sample lists	You have been provided with sample lists. You are to interview the person in the household who reads the magazine and is a qualified respondent. Use the sample lists and try to complete interviews with subscribers or readers of affluent publications.
Eligible respondents	A respondent is eligible if ■ The total annual family income is above $25,000 ■ He or she is employed in one of the prelisted categories in Q.B.
Quota	You are to complete a total of 13 interviews.
Call record sheets	You are to use the call record sheet to list the name and telephone number of each call you make. All telephone numbers and listings are to be done during the interviewing hours. We *will not* pay for additional time for looking up numbers and listings. Record the outcome of each call you make.
Validation forms	We have included validation forms on which you must list information about completed interviews. A properly filled out validation form must accompany each delivery of work you make to your supervisor. Fill in all the information required at the top of the form. Then fill in the following: ■ Under "Quota Group" name of magazine. ■ Under "Sex," sex of respondent. ■ Under "Respondent Name," write in the full name. ■ Under "Telephone Number," write in the phone number.

should examine the reasons behind it. Perhaps the interviewer is not using a proper approach or the area may be difficult to cover.

A researcher can use aggregated data for all the field service interviewers to measure field service efficiency. A high cost per interview for a field service might be traced to a large number of contacts per completed interview. This, in turn, may be due to poor interviewer selection and training by the field service.

Field management companies Firms that provide support services such as formatting questionnaires, writing screeners, and collecting data to full-service research companies.

Field Management Companies

Conducting fieldwork is much easier today than in years past. The stereotypical "kitchen table" field service is passing into history. In its place are companies that specialize in field management. **Field management companies** such as QFact, On-Line Communications, and Direct Resource generally provide questionnaire formatting, screener writing, development of instructional and peripheral materials, shipping departments, field auditing, and all coordination of the data collection, coding, and tabulation services required for the project. Upon study completion, they typically provide a single consolidated invoice for the project. Usually lean on staff, these companies are designed to provide the services clients need without attempting to compete with the design and analytical capabilities of full-service companies and ad agency research staffs.

Table 10.8 A Sample Call Record Sheet

	Date	Date	Date	Date
Total completions	____	____	____	____
Quota A	____	____	____	____
Quota B	____	____	____	____
Terminated at	____	____	____	____
Q. A	____	____	____	____
Q. B	____	____	____	____
Q. C—No deodorant/antiperspirant	____	____	____	____
Q. D—No roll-on	____	____	____	____
Q. E—Ban full	____	____	____	____
Q. E—"Other" full	____	____	____	____
Q. F—Refusal	____	____	____	____
Q. G—No telephone	____	____	____	____
Total incomplete contacts	____	____	____	____
No one home	____	____	____	____
No woman available	____	____	____	____
Refused	____	____	____	____
Language/hearing	____	____	____	____
Respondent break-off	____	____	____	____
Other	____	____	____	____
Briefing hours	____	____	____	____
Interviewing hours	____	____	____	____
Travel hours	____	____	____	____
Mileage	____	____	____	____

In fact, a number of full-service companies and qualitative professionals also have discovered that field management can cost-effectively increase their productivity by allowing them to take on more projects using fewer of their internal resources. One example of this is the newly formed business relationship between Heakin Research and The MARC Group, which hired Heakin to handle field management on particular types of studies. Likewise, several qualitative researchers have developed ongoing relationships with field management companies who function as extensions of the consultant's staff, setting up projects and freeing up the researcher to conduct groups, write reports, and consult with clients.

Like any other segment of the research industry, field management has its limitations. By definition, field management companies are not in the habit of providing design and analytical capabilities. This means that their clients may, on occasion, need to seek other providers to meet their full-service needs. Additionally, as this is a relatively new segment of the industry, experience, services, and standards vary tremendously from firm to firm. It is advisable to carefully screen prospective companies and check references. These limitations notwithstanding, field management provides a way for researchers to increase their productivity while cost-effectively maintaining the quality of the information on which their company's decisions and commitments are made.[6]

The Impact of Software Technology and the Internet on Questionnaire Development

Like most other aspects of business, the Internet has affected questionnaire development and use in several ways. For example, a market research company can now create a questionnaire, send it as an e-mail attachment for comments and approval, and once it is approved, can place it on the client's server to be used as an Internet survey.

Software for Questionnaire Development

Software for questionnaire development has advanced at a rapid rate in the past several years. Sensus Multimedia by Sawtooth Technologies is a multimedia PC-based package. This means that, along with a traditional questionnaire, researchers can use sounds, images, and animations or movie clips. Sensus can also incorporate earlier responses into later questions. It even can do calculations that follow through to later answers. For instance, suppose you fill out a survey on tractors, and say that you have two Fords, three John Deeres, and four International Harvesters. In a later question, the package could then ask you, "Thinking about your nine tractors. . . . " It could then go on and ask you questions about your two Ford tractors, your three John Deeres, and four International Harvesters. Sensus Multimedia costs about $2,000.

A second software program is called Survey Said. With this software, researchers can create PC-based and Internet-based surveys. The Internet surveys require HTML (hyper-text markup language) or Java "applets." HTML allows the researcher to create links (which move you to other pages when you click on them). HTML also allows you to embed pictures, sounds, and movies right into a page created for the Web.

Survey Said allows the marketing research to create and modify survey content in a program it calls the Survey Librarian. Once the researcher calls up the survey, an editing window appears which provides the researcher with all the question alternatives available. Survey Said cannot do calculations and feed sums from earlier answers back to the respondent. However, a detailed skip pattern is available to guide respondents to different questions depending on their answers.

In summary, Survey Said is a versatile program that is easy to use. Its data collection facilities allow several surveys to be up and running on one website. At a price of $1,000, it is a real value.

Decisive Survey, Inc. offers very powerful software packages. Their larger version, Decision Source, can process unlimited numbers of surveys, requires a dedicated Web server, and commands a high price. This is software used by enormous organizations, like America Online, that sometimes need to gather millions of responses from their customers.

Decisive's smaller, 10,000 respondent product—Decisive Survey—is a "real-time information" system, which can provide ongoing "feedback" from customers to manufacturers to service providers, or from employees of large organizations to their managers. It offers four basic styles of questions:

- choose one
- choose all, that apply
- rating
- enter text.

Decisive Survey does not allow for scaled responses, except as simple text. It does not do rankings, point allocation, or sliding-scale questions. Decisive Survey, unlike Survey Said, gets its responses back in the form of e-mail. Each survey comes into a designated e-mail address on a website, rather than into a dedicated file. Decisive, like the others, does some summary statistics, but not early as much as a dedicated data analysis package, such as SPSS or SAS. Also like the others, it will export data to these packages, but only as a plain text (or ASCII) file.[7]

Internet Self-Service Questionnaire Builders

WebSurveyor is a leading Internet self-service questionnaire-building site. WebSurveyor's http://www.WebSurveyor.com enables a marketing researcher to create an online survey quickly and then view real-time results anytime and anywhere using remote access to reach the marketing researcher's Web browser. The advantage of WebSurveyor is that the marketing research client has no questionnaire software to install, and no programming or administration is involved. All operations are automated and performed through the WebSurveyor website. This includes survey design, respondent invitation, data collection, analysis, and results reporting. If, however, a client wishes, it can use it's own web server using WebSurveyor's self-hosted solutions. The WebSurveyor hosted process works as follows:

1. The researcher creates a customized survey on the WebSurveyor website.
2. Instructions are automatically e-mailed to the researcher to enable the research supplier to link the survey to its website.
3. WebSurveyor's "invitations" randomly pop up on the research supplier's website to recruit visitors for participation in a survey. The research firm can also invite respondents by e-mail, banners, and hotlinks on its or another website.
4. Respondents complete the survey and data are automatically collected and tabulated in WebSurveyor's centralized data center.
5. The research company and any authorized users can remotely access the research supplier's password-protected account on the WebSurveyor website to instantly view and print real-time reports and download datasets, anytime from anywhere worldwide.

A marketing research supplier can quickly design a survey using its own questions or WebSurveyor's online library of fully customizable questions, response types, and preconfigured surveys. WebSurveyor uses "cookies" to prevent respondents from taking a survey more than once. The site also offers a technical translation service to create a survey in numerous foreign languages. WebSurveyor, and firms like it, are the leading edge of survey research support on the Internet.[8]

The Questionnaire's Role in Costs and Profitability

A discussion of questionnaires would not be complete without mentioning their impact on costs and profitability. Marketing research suppliers typically bid against other suppliers to implement a client's project. If costs are overestimated, then a supplier will usually lose a job to a lower-cost competitor. In all survey research, the questionnaire and incidence rate (see Chapter 7) are the core determinants of a project's estimated costs. One of the United States' largest research suppliers examined its costs and bids for all of its projects conducted by central-location telephone (CLT) interviewing. It found that during a recent year-and-a-half period, it had overestimated project costs 44 percent of the time. This translated into millions of dollars of lost sales opportunities due to overbidding.

To avoid overbidding, managers must better understand questionnaire costs. The MARC Group, a large international marketing research firm, found that in a CLT study with a 50 percent incidence rate (50 percent of the respondents called would qualify to be interviewed) and lasting an average of 15 minutes, only 30 percent of the data collection costs were related to asking the questions. Seventy percent of the costs concerned reaching qualified respondents.[9] Table 10.9 depicts the numerous roadblocks an interviewer can encounter in obtaining a completed interview. Each roadblock to getting a completed interview adds to the costs. MARC, for example, has found that simply adding a security screener to a questionnaire can add as much as 7 percent to the cost of interviewing.

Another major cost in survey research is when respondents terminate an interview. People end interviews for four major reasons: the subject matter, redundant or difficult to understand questions, questionnaire length, and changing the subject during an interview. People like to talk about some subjects and not others. Gum is no problem, but mouthwash results in many terminations. Figure 10.3 reveals that a 20-plus minute interview on gum results in few terminations (actual data). However, many people terminate a mouthwash interview either within two minutes or in the 19- to 20-minute range. Terminations on a leisure travel interview don't become a serious problem until the interview reaches 17 minutes in length. Terminations mean that the interview must be redone and all of the time spent interviewing the

Table 10.9 The Difficulty of Finding Qualified Respondents in a Central-Location Telephone Interview

1. Failed attempts
   - Busy
   - No answer
   - Answering machine
   - Business number
   - Phone/language problem
   - Discontinued line

2. Cooperation problems
   - Respondent not at home
   - Refused to be interviewed

3. Screener determines respondent not eligible
   - Failed security test (works for marketing research firm, advertising agency, or the client)
   - Doesn't use the product
   - Demographic disqualification (wrong gender, age, etc.)
   - Quota filled (survey has quota of 500 users of Tide and 500 users of other clothes washing powder. Interviewer already has 500 Tide users; the current respondent uses Tide.)

4. Respondent terminated during interview

5. Completed interview

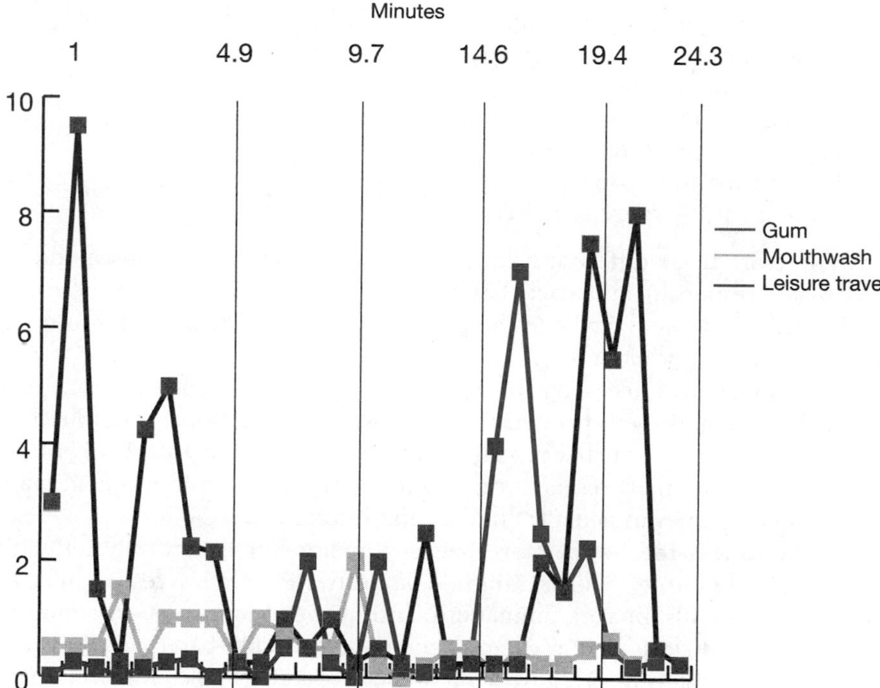

Figure 10.3

Actual Respondent Termination Patterns for Interviews in Three Different Product Categories

respondent was wasted. Preliminary research has found that callbacks on terminated interviews can sometimes result in a completed interview. The same research on callbacks to persons who originally refused to be surveyed was, however, not productive.[10]

Once managers better understand their actual costs of data collection, they should be able to bid on jobs with a higher degree of cost accuracy. This should result in less overpricing and therefore more winning contracts.

Summary

This chapter examines the objectives of the questionnaire, as well as its construction, evaluation, and impact on project costs and profitability. After defining a questionnaire and explaining its role in the data collection process, the criteria for a good questionnaire are established. These criteria are categorized into the following topic areas:

1. achieving the goals of the study
2. fitting the questionnaire to respondents
3. editing, coding, and data processing.

The bulk of this chapter is devoted to the process of developing a questionnaire. This process is addressed sequentially, beginning with survey objectives, resources, and constraints. The process continues with these steps:

1. Determine the data collection method.
2. Determine the question-response format.

3. Decide on question wording.
4. Establish questionnaire flow and layout.
5. Evaluate the questionnaire.
6. Obtain approval from all relevant parties.
7. Pretest and revise the questionnaire.
8. Prepare the final copy.
9. Implement the questionnaire.

There are three different types of questions (open-ended, closed-ended, and scaled-response) and each has advantages and disadvantages. Certain guidelines, if followed, facilitate the proper working and positioning of questions within the questionnaire.

The procedures necessary for implementing survey research ensure that the data are gathered properly. Supervisor's instructions, interviewer's instructions, call record sheets, and visual aids are discussed in this context. We also note that many research organizations are now turning to field management companies to actually conduct the interviews.

Software and the Internet are having a major impact on questionnaire design. For example, Sensus Multimedia software enables researchers to incorporate sounds, images, animations, and movie clips into questionnaires. Survey Said and Decisive Survey make the creation of PC-based and Internet surveys much easier. Informative's SurveyBuilder.com enables researchers to go to the SurveyBuilder site and create on-line surveys. The survey appears on the researcher's own website but is tabbed to and recommendations made by SurveyBuilder. Anyone with the correct password can review the survey findings.

The chapter concludes with the role of the questionnaire in survey research costs. If a researcher overestimates data collection costs, chances are he or she will lose the project to another supplier. Most data collection costs are not those of conducting an actual interview but of finding qualified respondents. The nature of the topic discussed can influence respondents' propensity to terminate an interview.

Key Terms & Definitions

Questionnaire A set of questions designed to generate the data necessary for accomplishing the objectives of the research project.

Editing Checking the questionnaire to ensure that skip patterns were followed and the required questions filled out.

Survey or information objectives The decision-making information sought through the questionnaire.

Open-ended questions Questions that ask respondents to reply in their own words.

Closed-ended questions Questions that ask respondents to choose between two or more answers.

Dichotomous questions Questions that ask respondents to choose between two answers.

Multiple-choice questions Questions that ask respondents to choose among a list of more than two answers.

Scaled-response questions Multiple-choice questions in which the choices are designed to capture the intensity of respondents' answers.

Screeners Questions used to screen for appropriate respondents.

Pretest A trial run of a questionnaire.

Supervisor's instructions Written directions to the field service on how to conduct a survey.

Interviewer's instructions Written directions to the interviewer on how to conduct an interview.

Call record sheets Interviewers' logs listing the number and results of a contact.

Field management companies Firms that provide support services such as formatting questionnaires, writing screeners, and collecting data to full-service research companies.

Questions for Review & Critical Thinking

1. Explain the role of the questionnaire in the research process.
2. How do respondents influence the design of a questionnaire? Suggest some examples, such as questionnaires designed for engineers, welfare recipients, baseball players, generals in the army, and migrant farmworkers.
3. Discuss the advantages and disadvantages of open-ended questions and closed-ended questions.
4. Outline the procedure for developing a questionnaire. Discuss the questionnaire development for a new sandwich for McDonald's.
5. Give examples of poor questionnaire wording. What is wrong with each of these questions?
6. Once a questionnaire is developed, what other factors need to be considered before putting it into the hands of interviewers?
7. Why is pretesting a questionnaire important? Are there some situations in which pretesting can be forgone?
8. Design three open-ended and three closed-ended questions to measure consumers' attitudes toward BMW automobiles.
9. What is wrong with the following questions?
   a. How do you like the flavor of this high-quality Maxwell House coffee?
   b. What do you think of the taste and texture of this Sara Lee coffee cake?
   c. We are conducting a study for Bulova watches. What do you think of the quality of Bulova watches?
   d. How far do you live from the closest mall?
   e. Who in your family shops for clothes?
   f. Where do you buy most of your clothes?
10. What do you see as the major advantages of using a field management company to administer surveys? What about drawbacks?

Working the Net

1. How might the Internet impact questionnaire design in the future?
2. Use Infoseek, or another search engine, and type "questionnaire design." Report to the class on two questionnaire design software programs you find on the Net.
3. Go to http://www.WebSurvey.com. What does WebSurvey claim are the benefits of WebSurvey.com?

Real-Life Research

S. T. Arrow owned a chain of dry cleaners in Portland, Oregon. Competition from One-Hour Martinizing and a regional chain had lowered Arrow's market share from 14 percent to 12 percent. Moreover, his overall profits had fallen 11 percent from the previous year. Arrow decided that an aggressive marketing strategy was in order. Before establishing such a strategy, he felt that a thorough study of the dry cleaning market was needed. The following questionnaire was created by Arrow and was given to customers as they left one of his stores.

Dry Cleaning Questionnaire

Name ______________________

Address ______________________

Phone number ______________________

Where do you take your dry cleaning and laundry?

____

How much do you spend on dry cleaning/laundry? ______________________

Sex: Male _____ Female _____

Age Group: Under 30 _____ 30–40 _____ 40–50 _____ 50–60 _____ Over 60 _____

Marital Status: Single _____ Married _____

Income: Under \$5,000 _____ \$5,000–\$25,000 _____ \$25,000–\$60,000 _____
Over \$60,000 _____

Number living in home: Alone _____ 2 people _____ 3 people _____
4 people _____ 5 people or more _____

Home: _____Rent _____Own What type of housing? ______________________

Education: High school graduate _____ Associate degree _____
Bachelor's degree _____ Master's degree _____ More _____

1. How long have you been using your dry cleaner?
2. How would you rate it? Great _____ Good _____ OK _____
Not too good _____ Bad _____
3. The dry cleaning establishment

Convenience	I now use offers	I would like to use would offer
–All work done on premises	_____	_____
–Wash'n'wear cleaning services	_____	_____
–Pressing while you wait	_____	_____
–Washing while you wait	_____	_____
–A drive-through window	_____	_____
–Computerized receipts and organization	_____	_____
–Shirt laundry service	_____	_____
–An outlet for drop off/pick up	_____	_____

–Machines to pick up/drop off after hours	________	________
–A special for people moving into a new location where the cleaners pick up, clean, and deliver rugs and drapes for new home	________	________
4. Services		
–Shoe repair	________	________
–Shoe shining	________	________
–Mending	________	________
–Altering and tailoring	________	________
–Hand pressing	________	________
–Dyeing	________	________
–Summer/winter clothing storage	________	________
–Hand laundering	________	________
–Sponging and pressing	________	________
–Fur storage	________	________
5. For sale		
–Ties and other accessories	________	________
–Spot removers, lint brushes, etc.	________	________
–Buttons, thread, zippers, etc.	________	________
–Woolite	________	________
6. Who in your home drops off/picks up the dry cleaning/laundry?		
–Wife/mother/self	________	________
–Husband/father/self	________	________
–Each decides when own clothing is ready	________	________
–We take turns	________	________
7. Who within the household decides that the clothing is in need of dry cleaning?		
–Wife/mother/self	________	________
–Husband/father/self	________	________
–Each decides their own clothing is ready	________	________
–Other family member/self	________	________
8. Please check one for each topic.	A. I am this type	B. I would like to remain as this type
–I hate housework. I just hate having to do it.	________	________
–I'd rather pay more to enjoy more. It's easier to pay someone to clean my home and clothes, so I'm free to do what I want to do.	________	________
–I enjoy being at home. Home is where I'm happiest.	________	________
–I like cleaning my home. It gives me a good feeling.	________	________
–Since I have small children, I'm at home, so I clean. But if I were working, it would be easier to have someone come in.	________	________
–I don't feel right having someone else cleaning up after me. I find myself cleaning before they come and after they leave. They don't clean the way I do.	________	________

9. Check the phrase in each group that best describes you (Check one for each column.)	Your present dry cleaner	The way you would like your dry cleaner to be or remain as
A. Makes me feel like an intruder	______	______
Keeps me waiting	______	______
Businesslike	______	______
Always has a friendly word	______	______
B. Gives the feeling he's/she's too busy for me	______	______
Forgets my name when crowded	______	______
Always says hello even when busy	______	______
Takes the time to treat me individually, no matter what	______	______
C. There's a chemical odor and the posters are outdated and curled at the ends	______	______
There's nothing noticeable about the shop, good or bad	______	______
The shop smells clean, the clothes are scientifically racked, and the posters are helpful	______	______
D. Standardized service	______	______
Efficient, but distant	______	______
Interested in personal requirements	______	______
Goes out of the way to please	______	______
E. The shop leaves an unkempt impression	______	______
Neat but cluttered store	______	______
There is space to move around	______	______
The shop has a warm, cared-for look	______	______
F. The store could use a thorough cleaning	______	______
The shop is acceptably clean	______	______
Assuringly sanitary store	______	______
G. There's never an answer to questions	______	______
I must point out spots, belts, loose buttons	______	______
We discuss whether it can be cleaned	______	______
The dry cleaner explains particular processes and new chemicals	______	______

Questions

1. Critique S. T. Arrow's questionnaire.
2. What additional topics should have been covered?
3. Discuss the sampling procedure.
4. Did S. T. Arrow develop his questionnaire?

CHAPTER *eleven*

Basic Sampling Issues

Learning Objectives

1 *To understand the concept of sampling*

2 *To learn the steps in developing a sampling plan*

3 *To distinguish between probability samples and nonprobability samples*

4 *To understand the concepts of sampling error and nonsampling error*

5 *To review the types of probability sampling methods*

6 *To gain insight into nonprobability sampling methods*

Jenny Johnson is vice president of marketing for Tropicana Mart. Tropicana Mart has 12 supermarkets in the Miami area that cater to ethnic shoppers, particularly Cuban-Americans. The company has grown from a single small store 10 years ago to over 15 stores today. Stores built in recent years all exceed 100,000 square feet and offer a full range of standard and ethnic food items.

Tropicana Mart has always stressed customer service. Their research has shown that customer service is very important to their customers and that customers believe Tropicana Mart does a good job in this area. However, rapid growth has strained Tropicana Mart's ability to provide the outstanding customer service on which their success has been substantially built. The CEO has charged Jenny with developing a program to manage customer service in a more objective way. The first phase of this program is to develop a system to continuously track customer satisfaction with the service provided by Tropicana Mart. Jenny invited two research suppliers in whom she has a great deal of confidence and positive past experiences to submit proposals to design and implement a customer satisfaction monitoring system.

The rapid growth experienced by Tropicana Mart has compromised its ability to provide top-notch customer service. In order to reconnect with its customers, Tropicana Mart must decide the survey method that will give them the most representative sample of people.

The two firms proposed different approaches to data collection. The first firm proposed a measurement system built around telephone interviewing. Under this proposal, the firm would generate telephone numbers at random, conduct all interviews from its central-location telephone facility, and survey 400 customers each month. The firm calculated that a sample of this size will provide estimates of customer satisfaction that are within ± 5 percent of true population values with 95 percent confidence.

The second firm proposed a customer satisfaction measurement program that uses mail surveys to collect the necessary data. This firm argued that the necessary data could be collected by mail at a lower cost without sacrificing quality. Also, they contended that customers will be more honest in a mail survey than in a telephone survey. The monthly cost of the program under a telephone approach would be $8,400 compared to $6,900 under the mail approach.

Jenny asked Juan Perez, marketing research manager for Tropicana Mart, to evaluate the proposals and make a recommendation. Juan provided some preliminary thoughts on the pros and cons associated with the two methodologies from a sampling perspective:

- The estimated response rate for the mail survey is 25 percent. Obviously, this means that 75 percent of the people who receive the survey will not respond to it. If the people who do respond are systematically different from those who do not, then the results will be biased and not truly representative of Tropicana Mart's customers.
- The telephone survey has an estimated response rate of 70 percent. This means that less than one-third (30%) of those that the firm attempts to survey will be unreachable or will refuse to participate. Although the telephone approach still has a substantial nonresponse rate, the potential for nonresponse bias will be much smaller and the results are more likely to be representative of the true sentiments of Tropicana Mart customers.
- The telephone survey approach offers the advantage of faster turnaround because the surveys can be completed, tabulated, and a report produced in approximately two weeks. The same process requires almost six weeks under a mail approach because of the time required for people to receive the survey, complete it, and send it back. In addition, the mail approach requires a second mailing of questionnaires if a 25 percent response rate is to be achieved.

Jenny and Juan are weighing the pros and cons of the two approaches in relation to their relative cost in order to arrive at a final decision. The mail survey will be cheaper, but it suffers from problems of bias, lack of representativeness, and slow turnaround. The telephone survey is more expensive, but promises to provide data that are more representative of Tropicana Mart customers. They are weighing the alternatives and trying to arrive at the best decision.

The issues confronting Jenny Johnson are related to the central topic of this chapter. The question is one of choosing the "best" approach, in a given situation, for selecting a sample of people from whom to collect data. As this example suggests, different alternatives have different costs, data-quality levels, and levels of sampling accuracy associated with them. The challenge, as always, is to obtain the required information at the appropriate level of quality at the lowest possible cost. These issues are covered in this chapter. After you have had an opportunity to read this chapter, return to Jenny Johnson's dilemma, and see what choice you would make between the two alternatives. ■

Definition of Important Terms

Population or Universe

Population or universe The total group of people from whom information is needed.

In the area of sampling, the terms **population** and **universe** are used interchangeably.[1] In this discussion, we will use the term *population.* The population or population of interest is the total group of people from whom we need to obtain information. One of the first things the analyst must do is to define the population of interest. This often involves defining the target market for the product or service in question.

For example, a researcher conducting a product concept test for a new nonprescription product to relieve cold symptoms, such as Contac, might take the position that the population of interest includes everyone, because everyone suffers from colds from time to time. However, although everyone suffers from colds from time to time, not everyone buys a nonprescription product to relieve cold symptoms, In this case, the first task would probably be to ask people whether they had purchased or used one or more of a number of competing brands during some time period. Only those who had purchased or used one of these brands would be included in the population of interest.

Defining the population of interest is a key step in the sampling process. The issue is: Whose opinions are needed to fulfill the objectives of the research? There are no specific rules to follow in defining the population of interest. The researcher must apply good logic and judgment. Often the definition of a population is based on the characteristics of current or target customers.

Sample Versus Census

Census Data obtained from or about every member of the population of interest.

The term **census** refers to those situations where data are obtained from or about every member of the population of interest. Censuses are not often employed in marketing research. In most marketing research situations, the population includes many thousands, hundreds of thousands, or millions of individuals. The cost and time required to take a census of population of this magnitude are so great as to preclude the possibility of its use.

Sample A subset of the population of interest.

It has been demonstrated time and time again that a relatively small but carefully chosen sample can quite accurately reflect the characteristics of the population from which it is drawn. A **sample** is a subset of the population. Information is obtained from or about a subset of the population to make estimates about various characteristics of the total population. Ideally, the subset of the population from or about which information is obtained should be a representative cross section of the total population.

Although censuses are not often used in marketing research, in some instances they are appropriate and feasible. For example, censuses may be the best approach when a particular industrial products firm has only a small number of customers for the highly specialized products it sells. In these situations it may be possible to obtain information from the entire population of customers.

The idea of taking a census may be appealing since it is perceived to be more accurate than a sample, but this is not necessarily true. Particularly when we are trying to do a census of a human population, there are many impediments to actually obtaining information from every member of a population. We may not be able to obtain a complete and accurate list of all population members, or certain members may refuse to provide information to us. A census is seldom attainable even in relatively small populations, and the problems of achieving one of a large population are formidable. You may have read or heard about these types of problems in connection with the U.S. Census of Population that occurs every decade.[2]

Steps in Developing a Sampling Plan

The process of developing a sampling plan can be separated into seven steps, which are summarized in Figure 11.1. Each step in the process is discussed here.

Step One: Define the Population of Interest

The basic problem is to specify the characteristics of those individuals or things (companies, stores, etc.) from whom information is needed to meet the objectives of the research. The population of interest is often specified in terms of some combination of the following characteristics: geography,

Figure 11.1

Steps in Developing a Sample Plan

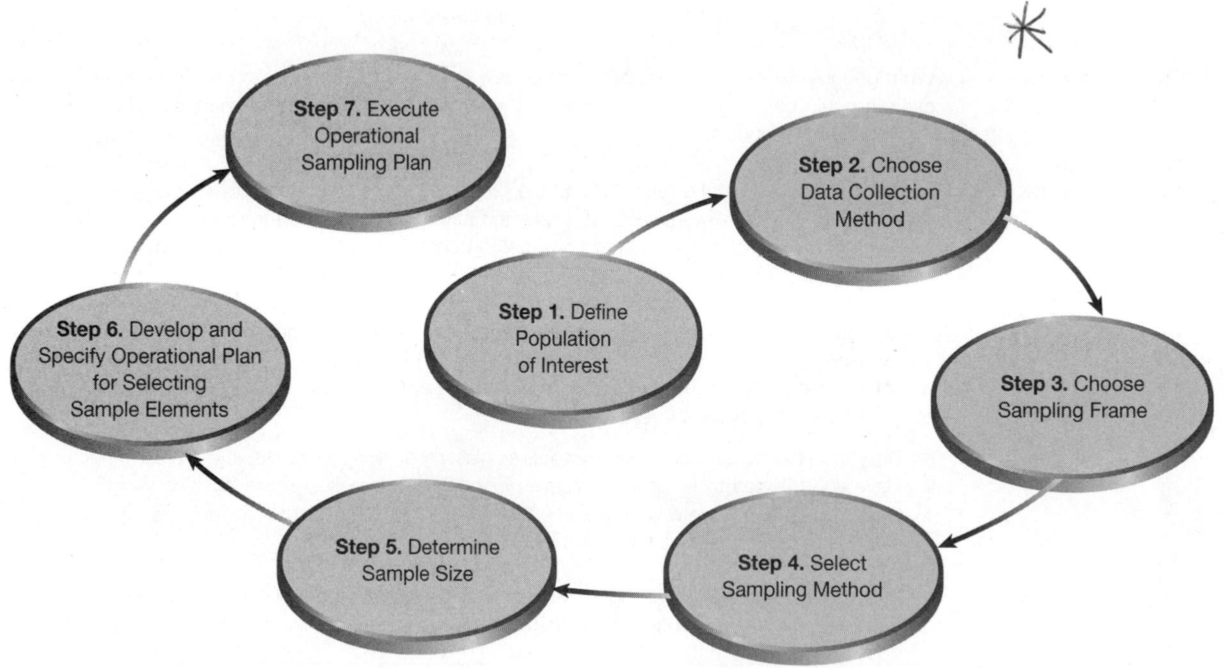

demographic characteristics, product or service use characteristics, or awareness measures. These bases for population definition are discussed in Table 11.1. In surveys, the question of whether particular individuals do or do not belong to a population of interest is often dealt with by means of screening questions at the beginning of the questionnaire (see Chapter 10). Even if we have a list of population members and a sample from that list, screening questions are still used to qualify potential respondents. Figure 11.2 provides a sample sequence of screening questions.

In addition to defining who will be included in the population of interest, it is sometimes important to define who will be excluded. Most commercial marketing research surveys exclude certain individuals for so-called security reasons. Frequently the first question on a questionnaire will ask whether the individual or anyone in the household works in marketing research, in advertising, or in the product or service area dealt with in the survey (see question 5 in Figure 11.2). If the answer is "Yes," the interview is terminated. This is referred to as a *security question,* because individuals in the industries in question may be competitors or work for competitors, and researchers do not want to give them any indication of what they may be planning to do.

There may be other reasons to exclude individuals. For example, Coca-Cola might wish to survey individuals who drink five or more cans, bottles,

Table 11.1

Some Bases for Defining the Population of Interest

Basis	Discussion
Geography	What geographic area is to be sampled? Usually this question depends on a client's scope of operation. It could be a city, county, metropolitan area, state, group of states, the entire United States, or a number of countries.
Demographics	Given the objectives of the research and the target market for the product, whose opinions, reactions, and so on are relevant? Are we interested in getting information from women over 18? Women 18–34? Women 18–34 with household incomes over $35,000 per year, who work and have preschool children?
Use	In addition to the preceding, the population of interest is frequently defined in terms of some product or service use requirement. This is usually stated in terms of some use versus nonuse or the use of some quantity of the product or service over some period of time. The following examples of use-screening questions illustrate the point: ■ Do you drink five or more cans, bottles, or glasses of diet soft drinks in a typical week? ■ Have you traveled to Europe for vacation or business purposes in the last two years? ■ Have you or has anyone in your immediate family been in a hospital for an overnight or extended stay in the past two years?
Awareness	We may be interested in surveying individuals who are aware of the company's advertising to explore what the ad communicated to them about the characteristics of the product or service.

Figure 11.2

Example of Screening Question Sequence to Determine Population Membership

Hello. I'm _________ with _________ Research. We're conducting a survey about products used in the home. May I ask you a few questions?

1. Have you been interviewed about any products or advertising in the past 3 months?
   Yes — TERMINATE AND TALLY
   No — *CONTINUE*

2. Which of the following hair care products, if any, have you used in the past month? (HAND PRODUCT CARD TO RESPONDENT. CIRCLE ALL MENTIONS.)
   1 Regular Shampoo
   2 Dandruff Shampoo
   3 Cream Rinse/Instant Conditioner
   4 "Intensive" Conditioner
   IF NONE OF PRODUCTS IN BOX IS CIRCLED, TERMINATE AND TALLY

INSTRUCTIONS:
IF "4" IS CIRCLED–SKIP TO Q. 4 AND CONTINUE FOR "INTENSIVE" QUOTA
IF "3" IS CIRCLED *BUT NOT* 4–ASK Q. 3 AND CONTINUE FOR "INSTANT" QUOTA

3. You said that you have used a cream rinse/instant conditioner in the past month. Have you used either a cream rinse or an instant conditioner in the past week, or not?
   Yes (used in the past week) — *CONTINUE FOR "INSTANT" QUOTA*
   No (not used in past week) — TERMINATE AND TALLY

4. Into which of the following groups does your age fall? (READ LIST, CIRCLE AGE.)
   X Under 18 — CHECK AGE QUOTAS
   1 18–24
   2 25–34
   3 35–44
   X 45 or over

5. Previous surveys have shown that people who work in certain jobs may have different reactions to certain products. Now, do you or does any member of your immediate family work for an advertising agency, a market research firm, a public relations firm, or a company that manufactures or sells personal care products?
   Yes — TERMINATE AND TALLY
   No — *CONTINUE*

IF RESPONDENT QUALIFIES, INVITE HER TO PARTICIPATE AND COMPLETE NAME GRID BELOW.

or glasses of soft drink in a typical week but who do not drink Coke, because the company wants a better understanding of heavy soft drink users who do not drink their product. Therefore, they might wish to exclude individuals who indicate they have drunk Coke in the last week.

Step Two: Choose a Data Collection Method

The selection of a data collection method, as indicated in the opening vignette, has considerable impact on the subsequent steps in the sampling

In PRACTICE

Gallup Pioneers Modern Sampling Methods

"A New Technique for Objective Methods for Measuring Reader Interest in Newspapers" was the title of George Gallup's Ph.D. thesis at the University of Iowa. Working with the *Des Moines Register and Tribune* and the 200-year-old statistical theory of probabilities of Swiss mathematician Jakob Bernoulli, Gallup developed sampling techniques. He showed that you did not have to talk to everybody as long as you randomly selected respondents according to a sampling plan that takes into account whatever diversity was relevant in the universe of potential respondents-geographic, ethnic, economic. Although not everybody understood or believed his ideas then—or now—this intellectual invention was a big deal.

On many occasions Gallup used a particular example to explain what he was doing: "Suppose there are 7,000 white beans and 3,000 black beans well churned in a barrel. If you scoop out 100 of them, you'll get approximately 70 white beans and 30 black beans in your hand, and the range of your possible error can be computed mathematically. As long as the barrel contains many more beans than your handful, the proportion will remain within that margin of error 997 times out of 1,000."

In the early 1930s George Gallup was in great demand around the country. He became head of the Journalism Department at Drake University and then switched to Northwestern. During this period he was doing readership surveys for newspapers throughout the northeastern United States. In the summer of 1932 a new advertising agency, Young and Rubicam, invited him to New York to create a research department and procedures for evaluating the effectiveness of advertising. In that same year, he used his polling techniques to help his mother-in-law get elected secretary of state of Iowa. Based on this experience, he was confident that his sampling methodology was valid not only for beans and newspaper readers but for voters also. As long as you understood the sampling universe—white/black, male/female, rich/poor, urban/rural, Republican/Democratic—you could predict elections or calculate attitudes on public opinion questions by interviewing a relatively small number of people, provided that small number was representative of the total population from which it was drawn. Gallup proved that population values could be accurately estimated by means of scientific samples and made a fortune in the process.[3] ■

process. For example, telephone interviewing has certain inherent advantages and mall-intercept interviewing has certain inherent disadvantages in regard to sampling (refer to Chapter 7 for the pros and cons of each survey method).

Step Three: Choose a Sampling Frame

The third step in developing a sample plan is to identify the sampling frame. The **sampling frame** is a list of the population elements or members from which we select units to be sampled. In an ideal situation, we have obtained such a list, which is complete and accurate. All too often we have no such list. For example, the population for a particular study may be defined to include those individuals who have played three or more 18-hole rounds of golf in the last 30 days. There is obviously no list that provides a complete enumeration of these individuals. In these instances, instead of a sample frame in the traditional sense, we will have to reflect the sample frame through some procedure that will produce a representative sample of individuals with the desired characteristics. For example, a telephone book might be the sample frame for a telephone survey sample. This simple example illustrates that there is seldom a perfect correspondence between the sampling frame and the population of interest. The population of interest might be all households in the city in question. However, the telephone book would not include households that do not have telephones and those with unlisted numbers.

Sampling frame List of population elements from which to select units to be sampled.

There is substantial evidence that those with listed numbers and those with no listing are significantly different in a number of important characteristics. Data have shown that voluntarily unlisted subscribers are more likely to be renters, live in the central city, have recently moved, have larger families, have younger children, and have lower incomes than their counterparts with listed numbers.[4] There are also significant differences between the two groups in terms of the purchase, ownership, and usage patterns of certain products.

Unlisted numbers are more prevalent in the West, in metropolitan areas, and among nonwhites and people in the 18 to 34 age group.[5] These findings have been confirmed in a number of studies.[6] The implications are clear: if representative samples are to be obtained in telephone surveys, sampling procedures must include an appropriate proportion of households with unlisted numbers.

The extent of the problem is suggested by the data in Table 11.2 on page 334. In such cases, a procedure may be used to generate a list of the elements of the population to be sampled. **Random-digit dialing** involves generating lists of telephone numbers at random. Developing an appropriate sampling frame is often one of the most challenging problems facing the researcher in the area of sampling.[7]

Random-digit dialing Method of generating lists of telephone numbers at random.

Step Four: Select a Sampling Method

The fourth step in the process involves selecting a sampling method. This selection depends on the objectives of the study, the financial resources available, time limitations, and the nature of the problem under investigation. The major sampling methods can be grouped under two headings: probability sampling methods and nonprobability sampling methods. Each type provides a number of alternatives.

Probability samples must be selected so that every element of the population has a known, nonzero probability of selection.[8] The **simple random sample** is the best known and most widely used probability sampling method.

Probability sample A sample in which every element of the population has a known, nonzero probability of selection.

Simple random sample A probability sampling in which the sample is selected in such a way that every element of the population has a known and equal probability of inclusion in the sample.

Table 11.2

The 25 Metropolitan Statistical Areas with the Highest Incidence of Unlisted Phones (1997)

The proportion of U.S. telephone households not included in white-page telephone directories in the top 100 Metropolitan Statistical Areas (MSAs) ranges between 7.0 percent and 71.6 percent. As the national average unlisted rate for the top 100 MSA markets reaches 29.6 percent (compared to 24.1% for all U.S. telephone households), the need for representative random-digit sampling techniques is more critical than ever. The table below presents the unlisted rates for the top 100 MSAs.

MSA	Total MSA Households	Percent Households with Phones	Percent Households with Unlisted Phones	MSA Rank Based on Percent Unlisted Household
Sacramento, CA PMSA	563,000	97.6	71.6	1
Oakland, CA PMSA	822,700	98.0	71.4	2
Fresno, CA	284,300	95.8	71.1	3
Los Angeles–Long Beach, CA PMSA	3,023,300	96.7	69.8	4
San Diego, CA	940,100	97.8	68.9	5
San Jose, CA PMSA	540,500	98.8	68.9	6
Orange County, CA PMSA	875,300	98.5	67.0	7
Riverside–San Bernardino, CA PMSA	987,200	96.0	65.5	8
Bakersfield, CA	203,400	94.7	64.8	9
San Francisco, CA PMSA	665,100	98.3	64.4	10
Ventura, CA PMSA	228,000	98.4	63.5	11
Las Vegas, NV–AZ	465,100	96.2	59.8	12
Portland–Vancouver, OR–WA PMSA	668,100	97.2	44.9	13
Tacoma, WA PMSA	239,700	97.1	44.4	14
Honolulu, HI	283,800	98.0	42.6	15
Jersey City, NJ PMSA	205,100	93.3	42.0	16
Tucson, AZ	301,700	94.5	40.1	17
El Paso, TX	205,200	91.9	39.5	18
Seattle–Bellevue–Everett, WA PMSA	880,100	98.2	38.8	19
San Antonio, TX	510,900	93.4	38.4	20
Detroit, MI PMSA	1,607,000	96.6	38.1	21
Phoenix–Mesa, AZ	986,000	94.7	36.8	22
Chicago, IL PMSA	2,774,200	96.1	35.9	23
Miami, FL PMSA	718,600	95.2	33.6	24
Houston, TX PMSA	1,328,900	93.7	33.0	25

Note: The unlisted rate is determined by comparing the estimated number of telephone households with the actual number of households found in telephone directories. Estimated telephone households are computed by taking projected household estimates at the county level calculated by Strategic Mapping, Inc. and applying a figure from the U.S. Census that indicates the percent of households with a telephone.

Source: Courtesy of Survey Sampling, Inc.

The simple random sample must be selected so that every member or element of the population has a known and equal probability of being selected. Under probability sampling, the researcher must closely adhere to precise selection procedures that avoid arbitrary or biased selection of elements. When these procedures are followed strictly, the laws of probability are in effect. This allows calculation of the extent to which a sample value can be expected to differ from a population value. This difference is referred to as **sampling error.**

Sampling error The difference between the sample value and the true value of the population mean.

Nonprobability samples include elements from a population that are selected in a nonrandom manner. Nonrandomness occurs due to accident when population elements are selected on the basis of convenience—because they are easy or inexpensive to reach. Purposeful nonrandomness would involve a sampling plan that systematically excluded or overrepresented certain subsets of the population. For example, a sample designed to represent the opinions of all women over the age of 18 that was based on a telephone survey conducted during the day on weekdays would systematically exclude working women.

Nonprobability sample A sample that includes elements from the population that are selected in a nonrandom manner.

Probability samples offer several advantages, including the following:

- The researcher can be sure of obtaining information from a representative cross section of the population of interest.
- Sampling error can be computed.
- The survey results are projectable to the total population. For example, if 5 percent of the individuals sampled in a research project based on a probability sample gave a particular response, the researcher can project this percentage, plus or minus the sampling error, to the total population.

On the other hand, certain disadvantages are associated with probability samples:

- They are more expensive than nonprobability samples of the same size in most cases. A certain amount of professional time must be spent in developing the sample design.
- Probability samples take more time to design and execute than nonprobability samples. The procedures that must be followed in the execution of the sampling plan increase the amount of time required to collect data.

The disadvantages of nonprobability samples are essentially the reverse of the advantages of probability samples:

- Sampling error cannot be computed.
- The researcher does not know the degree to which the sample is representative of the population from which it was drawn.
- The results of nonprobability samples cannot be projected to the total population.

Seeing the potential for frame error is critical to generating valid results, as sampling errors can cause marketing and public relations disasters. Can you think of any other high-profile flops that could be attributed to sampling errors?

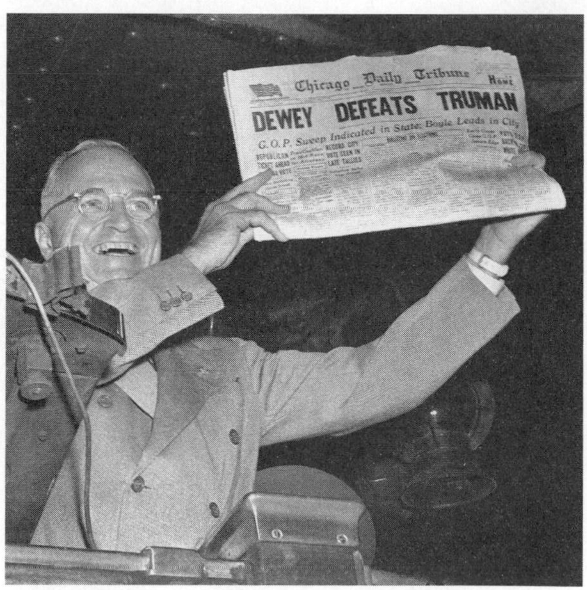

Given the disadvantages of nonprobability samples, one may wonder why they are used. In fact they are used frequently by marketing researchers. The reasons for their use relate to their inherent advantages:

- Nonprobability samples cost less than probability samples. This characteristic of nonprobability samples may have considerable appeal when accuracy is not of utmost importance. Exploratory research is an example of this type of situation.
- Nonprobability samples ordinarily can be gathered more quickly than probability samples. The reasons for this were discussed earlier.
- Nonprobability samples can produce samples of the population that are reasonably representative if executed properly.[9]

Issues related to public beliefs in regard to sampling issues are summarized in the In Practice feature on 900 number polls.

In addition to choosing between probability and nonprobability samples, the researcher must choose among types of samples under each of these major categories. These options are summarized in Figure 11.3. and are discussed in greater detail later in the chapter.

Step Five: Determine the Sample Size

Once the sampling method has been chosen, the next step is to determine the appropriate sample size. The issue of sample-size determination is covered in detail in Chapter 12, where we discuss the role that the available budget, various rules of thumb, the number of subgroups to be analyzed, and traditional statistical methods play in this process. In the case of nonprobability samples, we can rely only on the budget figures, the rules of thumb, and the number of subgroups to be analyzed in determining sample size. However, with probability samples, formulas are used to calculate the sample

Figure 11.3

Classification of Sampling Methods

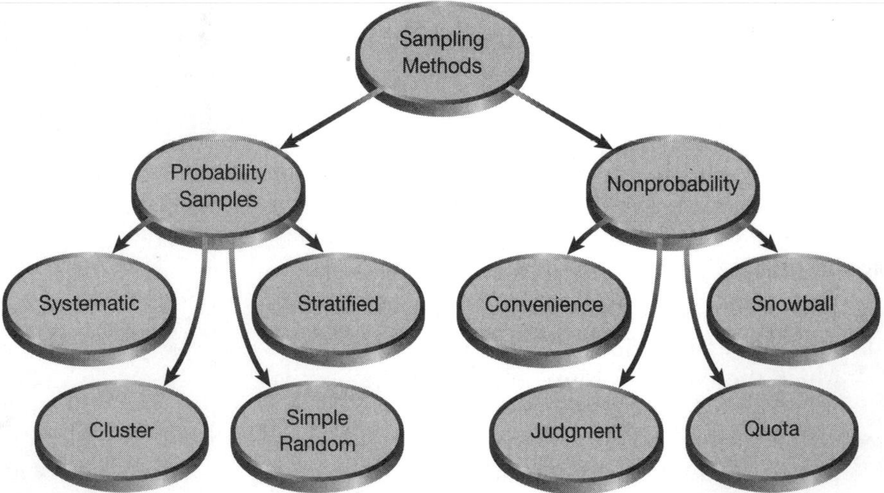

In PRACTICE

900 Polls Produce Biased Results

We have all seen the 900 number telephone polls on CNN and other news programs. These polls violate all the statistical principles on which legitimate research surveys are based. The responses from self-selection 900 number polls are not projectable to any definable population group because they are biased. They are based on responses only from people aware of the poll, interested enough to respond, willing and able to pay to respond, and able to reach the given number. There is also the possibility that a given individual may make multiple calls to a 900 number poll.

Though these polls are clearly not representative, a recent poll conducted by the R. H. Bruskin Company based on a national telephone probability survey of 1,000 adults indicates that substantial proportions of the general population believe these polls are legitimate and representative in certain respects:

- 45 percent believe that the results of these call-in polls are believable.
- 40 percent believe that the results of these polls should be believed because thousands of people participated in the poll.
- 40 percent believe that those who call in on these kinds of polls have the same opinions as those who do not call in.
- 38 percent believe that those who respond to these kinds of polls are typical of the entire U.S. population.
- 36 percent believe that the results of these polls would not be reported if they were not accurate.
- 34 percent believe that the results of these polls should be believed because they are sponsored by major television, newspaper, or magazine organizations.
- 24 percent believe that these polls are scientific.
- 24 percent believe that the results of these polls accurately represent what the country as a whole thinks.[10] ■

size required, given target levels of acceptable error (the difference between the sample result and the population value) and *levels of confidence* (the likelihood that the confidence interval, which is the sample result plus or minus the acceptable error, will take in the true population value). As noted earlier, the ability to make statistical inferences about population values based on sample results is a major advantage of probability samples.

Step Six: Develop the Operational Procedures for Selecting Sample Elements

The sample selection procedures for the data collection phase of a project should specify whether a probability or nonprobability sample is being used.[11]

The procedures are much more critical to the successful execution of a probability than to a nonprobability sample. Probability sample procedures should be detailed, clear, and unambiguous and should take all discretion about the selection of specific sample elements away from interviewers. Failure to develop a proper operational plan for selecting sample elements can jeopardize the entire sampling process. An example of an operational sampling plan is provided in Figure 11.4.

Step Seven: Execute the Sampling Plan

The final step in the sampling process involves the execution of the operational sampling plan discussed in the previous step. It is important that this step include adequate checking to make sure that data collectors are following specified procedures. Refer to Chapter 10 for a discussion of data collection procedures.

Figure 11.4

An Example of an Operational Sampling Plan

Source: Reprinted from interviewer guide by permission of Belden Associates, Dallas, Texas. The complete guide was over 30 pages long and contained maps and other aids for the interviewer.

In the instructions that follow, reference is made to follow your route around a "block." In cities this will be a city block. In rural areas, a "block" is a segment of land surrounded by roads.

1. If you come to a dead end along your route, proceed down the opposite side of the street, road, or alley, traveling in the other direction. Continue making right turns, where possible, calling at every third occupied dwelling.
2. If you go all the way around a block and return to the starting address without completing four interviews in listed telephone homes, attempt an interview at the starting address. (This should seldom be necessary.)
3. If you work an entire block and do not complete the required interviews, proceed to the dwelling on the opposite side of the street (or rural route) that is nearest the starting address. Treat it as the next address on your Area Location Sheet and interview that house only if the address appears next to an "X" on your sheet. If it does not, continue your interviewing to the left of that address. Always follow the right turn rule.
4. If there are no dwellings on the street or road opposite the starting address for an area, circle the block opposite the starting address, following the right turn rule. (This means that you will circle the block following a clockwise direction.) Attempt interviews at every third dwelling along this route.
5. If, after circling the adjacent block opposite the starting address, you do not complete the necessary interviews, take the next block found, following a clockwise direction.
6. If the third block does not yield the dwellings necessary to complete your assignment, proceed to as many blocks as necessary to find the required dwellings; these blocks follow a clockwise path around the primary block.

Sampling and Nonsampling Errors

Consider a situation in which the goal is to determine the average age of the members of a particular population.[12] If we can obtain accurate information about all members of the population, we can compute the population parameter "average age." A **population parameter** is a value that defines a true characteristic of a total population. Assume that μ (population parameter, in this case, average age) is 36.3 years. Since it is almost always impossible to measure an entire population. The researcher instead takes a sample and makes inferences about population parameters from sample results. To compute average age, the analyst might take a sample of 400 from a population of 250,000. An estimate of the average age of the members of the population ($\overline{X}$) would be calculated from the sample values. Assume that the average age of the sample members is 35.8 years. A second random sample of 400 might be drawn from the same population and the average again computed. In the second case, the average might be 36.8 years. Additional samples might be chosen and means computed for the various samples. The researcher would find that the means computed for the various samples would in most cases be fairly close but not identical to the true population value.

Population parameter
A value that defines a true characteristic of a total population.

The accuracy of sample results is affected by two general types of error: *sampling error* and *nonsampling (measurement) error.* The following formula portrays the effect of these two types of error on the problem of estimating a population mean:

$$\overline{X} = \mu \pm \epsilon_s \pm \epsilon_{ns}$$

$\overline{X}$ = sample mean
μ = true population mean
ϵ_s = sampling error
ϵ_{ns} = nonsampling or measurement error

Sampling error results when the sample selected is not perfectly representative of the population. There are two types of sampling error: random and administrative error. *Administrative error* relates to problems in the administration or execution of the sample. That is, flaws in the design or execution of the sample cause it to be unrepresentative of the population. This type of error can be avoided or minimized by careful attention to the design and execution of the sample. *Random sampling error* is due to chance and cannot be avoided. This type of error can only be reduced by increasing sample size. *Measurement* or *nonsampling error* includes everything other than sampling error that can cause inaccuracy and bias in the study results.

Probability Sampling Methods

Simple Random Sampling

Simple random sampling is considered to be the purest form of probability sample. As mentioned earlier, a probability sample is a sample in which every element of the population has a known and equal probability of being selected into the sample. For a simple random sample, that *known* and equal probability is computed as follows:

$$\text{Probability of selection} = \frac{\text{Sample size}}{\text{Population size}}$$

For example, if the population size is 10,000 and the sample size is 400, then the probability of selection is 4 percent. It is computed as follows:

$$.04 = \frac{400}{10{,}000}$$

If a sampling frame (a listing of all the elements of the population) is available, the researcher can select a simple random sample as follows:

1. Assign a number to each element of the population. A population of 10,000 elements would be numbered from 1 to 10,000.
2. Using a table of random numbers (see Table 1 in the Appendix at the end of the text), you would begin at some arbitrary point and move up, down, or across until 400 (sample size) five-digit numbers between 00001 and 10,000 are chosen.
3. The numbers selected from the table identify specific population elements to be included in the sample.

Simple random sampling is appealing because it seems simple and meets all necessary requirements of a probability sample. It allows researchers to project sample results to the target population. The procedure guarantees that every member of the population has a known and equal chance of being selected for the sample. It can be employed quite successfully in telephone surveys through the use of random digit dialing. Also, simple random sampling can be used to select respondents from computer files. Computer programs are available or can be readily written to select random samples from computer files such as customer lists.

Simple random samples also have some disadvantages. The process can result in expensive interviewing costs. Large samples or samples spread over a large geographic area can make data collection time-consuming and costly. Also, in the real world of marketing research simple random sampling may not be feasible. All the elements in a population have to be identified and then labeled or numbered before drawing the sample, and many populations defy such identification or labeling. Where would one get a complete list of every person over 16 years of age in Chicago? What about a complete list of all early triers of microbrewed beers in California?

A simple random sample does not guarantee that the sample drawn will represent the target population—it may not include specific subgroups of the population. As a result, a sample may have too many or too few people from certain subgroups. A simple random sample of people who have ordered pizza at home by telephone may result in Domino's Pizza being overrepresented and Pizza Hut being underrepresented relative to their true market share. Random samples may represent a population well, on average, but a specific random sample (and particularly a small one) may not represent subpopulations well at all.

Systematic Sampling

Systematic sampling is a sampling method that uses a fixed *skip interval* to draw elements from a numbered population. This method is often used as a substitute for simple random sampling. Its popularity is based on its simplicity. Systematic sampling produces samples that are almost identical to those generated via simple random sampling.

Systematic sample
A probability sampling in which the entire population is numbered and elements are drawn using a skip interval.

To use this approach, it is necessary to obtain a listing of the population, just as in the case of simple random sampling. The researcher must determine a skip interval and select names based on this skip interval. This interval can be computed by using the following formula:

$$\text{Skip interval} = \frac{\text{Population size}}{\text{Sample size}}$$

An example is to use the local telephone directory and compute a skip interval of 100, so that every hundredth name will be selected for the sample. The use of this formula ensures that the entire list will be covered.

A random starting point should be used in systematic sampling. For example, using a telephone directory, draw a random number to determine the page on which to start. Suppose it is page 53. Determine another random number to decide the column on that page. Assume it is the third column. Draw a final random number to determine the actual starting position in that column, say, the seventeenth name. From that beginning point employ the skip interval.

The main advantage of systematic sampling over simple random sampling is economy. It is often simpler, less time-consuming, and less expensive to use systematic sampling than simple random sampling. The greatest danger in the use of systematic sampling lies in the listing of the population. Some populations may contain hidden patterns that the researcher may inadvertently pull into the sample. However, this danger is remote when alphabetical listings are used.

Stratified Samples

Stratified sample A probability sample that selects elements from relevant population subsets to be more representative of an entire population.

Stratified samples are probability samples that are distinguished by the following procedural steps:

1. The original or parent population is divided into two or more mutually exclusive and exhaustive subsets (for example, male and female).
2. Simple random samples of elements from the two or more subsets are chosen independently from each other.

Requirements for a stratified sample do not specify the bases that should be used to separate the original or parent population into subsets. However, common sense dictates that the population be divided on the basis of factors that relate to the characteristic of the population we are really interested in measuring. For example, if someone is conducting a political poll to predict the outcome of an election and can show that there is a significant difference between the way men are likely to vote and the way women are likely to vote, then gender would be an appropriate basis for stratification. Without doing a stratified sampling based on gender, the researcher would have expended time, effort, and resources for no benefit. In gender stratification, one stratum is made up of men and another stratum is made up of women. These strata are mutually exclusive and exhaustive in that every population element can be assigned to one and only one stratum (male or female) and no population elements are unassignable. The second stage in the process involves drawing simple random samples independently from each stratum.

Stratified samples are used rather than simple random samples because of their potential for greater statistical efficiency.[13] This means that if we have two samples from the same population, one a properly stratified sample and the other a simple random sample, the stratified sample will have a smaller sampling error. If, on the other hand, the goal is to attain a certain target level of sampling error, it can be achieved with a smaller stratified sample. Stratified samples are statistically more efficient because one source of variation has been eliminated.

You might ask the question "If stratified samples are statistically more efficient, why are they not used all the time?" There are two reasons:

1. Frequently the information necessary to properly stratify the sample is not available. For example, little may be known about the demographic characteristics of the consumers of a particular product. Note that we said *properly* stratify the sample. To properly stratify the sample and get the benefits of stratification, there must be are significant differences between the members of two or more strata in regard to the measurement of interest.
2. Even if the necessary information is available, the value of the information gained may not justify the time or costs of stratification.

In the case of a simple random sample, the researcher depends entirely on the laws of probability to generate a representative sample of the population. In the case of a stratified sample, the researcher, to some degree, forces the sample to be representative by making sure that important or salient dimensions of the population are represented in the sample in their true population proportions. For example, the researcher may know that, although men and women are equally likely to be users of a particular product, women are much more likely to be heavy users of that product. In a study designed to analyze consumption patterns of the product, failure to properly represent women in the sample will result in a biased view of consumption patterns. Assume that women make up 60 percent of the population of interest and men account for 40 percent of the population. A simple random sample of the population, even if everything were done absolutely correctly, might result in a sample that is made up of 55 percent women and 45 percent men. This would be due to sampling fluctuations. This is the kind of error we get when we flip a coin 10 times. The correct result would be five heads and five tails, but more than half of the time we would get a result other than five heads and five tails. In similar fashion, even a properly drawn and executed simple random sample will seldom generate a sample made up of 60 percent women and 40 percent men from a population made up of 60 percent women and 40 percent men. However, in the case of a stratified sample, the researcher will force the sample to have 60 percent women and 40 percent men.

As noted, the added precision of a stratified sample comes at some cost. Three steps are involved in implementing a properly stratified sample:

1. Identify salient (important) demographic or classification factors—factors that are correlated with the behavior of interest. For example, in a study of consumption rates for a particular product, there may be reason to believe that men and women have different average consumption rates. To use gender as a basis for meaningful stratification, the researcher must be able to show with actual data that there are significant differences in the consumption levels of men and women. In this manner, various salient factors are identified. Research indicates that after the six most important salient factors have been identified, the identification of additional salient factors adds little in the way of additional sampling efficiency.[14]
2. Next, determine what proportions of the population fall into the various subgroups under each stratum (so if gender has been determined to be a salient factor, what proportion of the population is male and what proportion is female?). Using these proportions, determine how many respondents are required from each subgroup. However, before making a final determination, a decision must be made about whether to use proportional allocation or disproportional or optimal allocation.[15]
   - Under **proportional allocation,** the number of elements selected from a stratum is directly proportional to the size of the stratum in relation to the size of the population. With proportional allocation, the proportion of elements to be taken from each stratum is given by the formula n/N, where $n =$ the size of the stratum and $N =$ the size of the population.
   - **Disproportional** or **optimal allocation** produces the most efficient samples and the most precise or reliable estimates for a given sample size. This approach requires a *double weighting scheme.* Under this double weighting scheme, the number of sample elements to be taken from a given stratum is proportional to the relative size of the stratum and

Proportional allocation A sampling in which the number of elements selected from a stratum is directly proportional to the size of the stratum relative to the population.

Disproportional or optimal allocation A sampling in which the number of elements taken from a given stratum is proportional to the relative size of the stratum and the standard deviation of the characteristic under consideration.

the standard deviation of the distribution of the characteristic under consideration for all elements in the stratum. This is done for two reasons. First, the size of a stratum is important because those strata with a larger number of elements are more important in determining the population mean. Therefore, these strata are more important in deriving estimates of population parameters. Second, it also makes sense that relatively more elements should be drawn from those strata having larger standard deviations (more variation) and that relatively fewer elements should be drawn from those strata having smaller standard deviations. By allocating relatively more of a sample to those strata in which the potential for sampling error is greatest (largest standard deviation), we get more bang for our buck and improve the overall accuracy of our estimates. There is no difference between proportional allocation and disproportional allocation if the distributions of the characteristic under consideration have the same standard deviations from stratum to stratum.

3. Finally, select separate simple random samples from each stratum. Actually, this process is implemented somewhat differently in reality. Assume that a stratified sampling plan requires that 240 women and 160 men be interviewed. We would sample from the total population, including both men and women, and keep track of the number of men and women interviewed during the process. Let us say, for example, that at some point in the process we had interviewed 240 women and 127 men. From that point on, we would interview only men until we had reached the target of 160 men. In this manner, the process would generate a sample in which the proportion of men and women would meet the sample required by the allocation scheme in step 2.

Stratified samples are not used as often as might be expected in marketing research. The problem is that the researcher frequently does not have, in advance, the information necessary to properly stratify the sample. Stratification cannot be based on guesses or hunches, but must be based on hard data regarding the characteristics of a population and the relationship between these characteristics and the behavior under investigation. Stratified samples are frequently used in political polling and media audience research. In those areas, the researcher is much more likely to have the information necessary to implement the stratification process just described.

Cluster Samples

Cluster sample A probability sample drawn from a sample of geographic areas.

The types of samples discussed up until now have all been single-unit samples, where each sampling unit is selected separately. In the case of **cluster samples,** the sampling units are selected in groups.[16] There are two basic steps in cluster sampling:

1. The population of interest is divided into mutually exclusive and exhaustive subsets.
2. A random sample of the subsets is selected.

If the researcher samples all elements in the subsets selected, the procedure is a one-stage cluster sample. However, if a sample of elements is selected in some probabilistic manner from the selected subsets, then the procedure is a two-stage cluster sample. Both stratified and cluster sampling involve dividing the population into mutually exclusive and exhaustive subgroups. However, for stratified samples, a sample of elements is selected from each subgroup. In the case of cluster sampling, the researcher selects a sample of subgroups and then either collects data from all the elements in the subgroup (one-stage cluster sample) or from a sample of the elements (two-stage cluster sample).

All of the probability sampling methods discussed up to this point require sample frames that list or provide some organized breakdown of all the elements in the target population. Under cluster sampling, the researcher develops sample frames that include groups or clusters of elements of the population without actually listing individual elements. Sampling is executed with such frames by taking a sample of the clusters in the frame and generating lists or other breakdowns for only those clusters that have been selected for the sample. Finally, a sample is selected from the elements of the clusters selected.

Cluster sampling involves randomly selecting geographic units in which to conduct a survey. Because the number of sample clusters is limited, this can be a time-saving and cost-effective method of research.

The *area sample,* where the clusters are units of geography (say, city blocks), is the most popular type of cluster sample. A researcher conducting a door-to-door survey in a particular metropolitan area might randomly choose a sample of city blocks from that metropolitan area. After selecting a sample of clusters, a sample of consumers would be interviewed from each cluster. All interviews would be conducted in the clusters selected and none in other clusters. By interviewing only within the cluster selected, the researcher would dramatically reduce interviewer travel time and expenses. Cluster sampling is considered to be a probability sampling technique because of the random selection of clusters and the random selection of elements within each cluster selected.

Under cluster sampling it is assumed that the elements in a cluster are just as heterogeneous as the total population. If the characteristics of the cluster elements are very similar, then that assumption is violated and the researcher has a problem. In the example just described, there may be little heterogeneity within clusters because the residents of clusters are similar to each other and different from those in other clusters. Typically, this potential problem is dealt with in the sample design by selecting a large number of clusters for the sample and sampling a relatively small number of elements from each cluster.

This type of cluster sample incorporates two stages. Stage 1 involves the selection of clusters and stage 2 involves the selection of elements from within clusters. Multistage area sampling or multistage area probability samples involve three or more steps.[17] These types of samples are used for national or large regional surveys. Under samples of this type the researcher randomly selects geographic areas in progressively smaller units. For example, a statewide door-to-door survey might include the following steps:

1. Choose counties within the state to make sure that different areas are represented in the sample. Counties within the state should be selected with a probability proportional to the number of sampling units (households) within the county. Counties with a larger number of households would have a higher probability of selection than counties with a smaller number of households.
2. Select residential blocks within the selected counties.
3. Select households within the residential blocks selected.

Cluster samples are generally less statistically efficient than other types of probability samples. In other words, a cluster sample of a certain size will have a larger sampling error than a simple random sample or a stratified sample of that same size. To illustrate the greater cost efficiency and lower statistical efficiency of a cluster sample, consider the following situation. We need to select a sample of 200 households in a particular city for in-home interviews. If these 200 households were selected via a simple random sample, they would be scattered across the city. A cluster sample might be implemented by selecting 20 residential blocks in the city and randomly selecting 10 households within each block to be interviewed. It is easy to see that interviewing costs will be dramatically reduced under the cluster sampling approach. Interviewers would dramatically reduce their mileage and travel time. In regard to sampling error, the advantage would go to the simple random sample. Interviewing 200 households scattered across the city would increase the chance of getting a representative cross section of respondents. If all the interviewing was conducted in 20 randomly selected city blocks within the city, it is possible that certain ethnic, social, or economic groups could be missed or over- or underrepresented.

Because cluster samples are, in nearly all cases, statistically less efficient than simple random samples, it is possible to view a simple random sample as a special type of cluster sample, where the number of clusters is equal to the total sample size, and one sample element is selected per cluster. At this point, the statistical efficiency of the cluster sample and the simple random sample are equal. From this point on, by decreasing the number of clusters and increasing the number of sample elements per cluster, the statistical efficiency of the cluster sample would decline. At the other extreme, we might select a single cluster and select all the sample elements from that cluster. For example, we might select one relatively small geographic area in a city and interview 200 people from that area. But would a sample selected in this manner be representative of the entire metropolitan area?

Nonprobability Sampling Methods

In a general sense, any sample that does not meet the requirements of a probability sample is, by definition, a nonprobability sample. We have already noted that a major disadvantage of nonprobability samples is the inability to calculate sampling error. This suggests the even greater difficulty of evaluating the overall quality of nonprobability samples. We know that they do not meet the standard required of probability samples, but the question is: How far do they deviate from that standard? The user of the data from a nonprobability sample must make this assessment. The assessment must be based on a careful evaluation of the methodology used to generate the nonprobability sample. Is it likely that the methodology employed would generate a reasonable cross section of the target population? Or is the sample hopelessly biased in some particular direction? Four types of nonprobability samples are frequently used: convenience, judgment, quota, and snowball samples.

Convenience Samples

Convenience sample A nonprobability sample used primarily because data are easy to collect.

Convenience samples are used, as their name implies, for reasons of convenience, which is because they are easy to collect. Companies like Frito Lay often do preliminary tests of new product formulations developed by their R&D departments using employees. At first, this may seem to be a highly biased approach to the problem. However, they are not asking employees to evaluate their existing products or to compare their products with competitive products. They are asking employees only to provide gross sensory evaluations of new product formulations (such as saltiness, crispiness, greasiness). In situations like this, convenience samples may represent an efficient and effective means of obtaining the required information. This is particularly true in dealing with an exploratory situation, in which there is a pressing need to get an approximation of the true value inexpensively.

Reports from the industry indicate that the use of convenience sampling is growing at a faster rate than the growth of probability sampling. The reason for this, as suggested in the following In Practice feature on SSI-LITe, is the growing availability of databases of consumers in low-incidence and hard-to-find categories. For example, if a company has developed a new athlete's foot remedy and needs to conduct a survey among people who suffer from the malady, it would find that these individuals make up only 4 percent of the population. This means that in a telephone survey, researchers would have to actually talk with 25 people before finding one individual who suffers from the problem. An attractive alternative is to purchase a list of individuals known to suffer from the problem. The cost of the survey and the time necessary to complete it can be dramatically reduced. Although the list was developed from individuals who had used coupons when purchasing the product or who had sent in for manufacturers' rebates and was, therefore, not a perfectly representative sample frame, companies are increasingly willing to make the trade-off of lower cost and faster turnaround for a lower-quality sample. Examples of some of the more than 1,500 lists available from Survey Sampling, Inc. are provided in Table 11.3 on page 349.

In PRACTICE

SSI Provides Useful Convenience Samples

SSI-LITe (SSI's Low Incidence Targeted samples) is a form of convenience sampling, which the research industry can use to assist in screening for low-incidence segments of the population. To the degree that SSI's sampling service acts as a barometer of research activity, SSI-LITe sales suggest that the use of convenience samples is growing at a faster rate than the use of probability samples.

Probability sampling in the strictest sense allows each potential respondent an opportunity to be selected for a study. The probabilities of selection can be controlled and calculated as a result of sample selection. Research results can serve both enumerative as well as analytical purposes. This is not the case when a subjective selection of respondents is used, as with SSI-LITe and other nonprobability samples. Yet the practical constraints of time and budgets clearly make a case for the use of nonprobability samples.

When less than 1 percent of U.S. households purchase a certain brand, research options may become quite limited, and targeted samples, such as SSI-LITe, provide researchers with the opportunity to gain an understanding of attitudes and behaviors that they could not otherwise gain. The problem occurs when the researcher or research user attempts to project the findings to the total population, which can lead to costly wrong decisions. The researcher must understand the limitations when the research design employs anything other than a probability sample.[18] ■

Judgment Samples

Judgment sample A nonprobability sample in which the selection criteria are based on personal judgment that the element is representative of the population under study.

The term **judgment sample** is applied to any situation in which the researcher is attempting to draw a representative sample based on judgmental selection criteria. Most test markets and many product tests conducted in shopping malls are essentially judgmental samples. In the case of test markets, one or a few markets are selected based on the judgment that they are representative of the population as a whole. Malls are selected for product taste tests based on the researcher's judgment that the particular mall attracts a reasonable cross section of consumers who fall into the target group for the product being tested.

Quota Samples

Quota sample A nonprobability sample in which a population subgroup is classified on the basis of researcher judgment.

Because **quota samples** are typically selected in such a way that the demographic characteristics of interest to the researcher are represented in the sample in the same proportions as they are in the population, it is easy to understand how quota samples and stratified samples might be confused. There are, however, two key differences between a quota sample and a

Table 11.3

Survey Sampling of LITe Categories Under the Letter A

Category	Description	Count
Acne Remedies	use, by frequency	1,253,560
Aerobics	run, job, walk, fitness, exercise, interest in	1,495,990
Aerobics/Fitness Classes	take part in and by location	209,437
Affluence	prime timers (over 50)	1,076,238
Affluence	subscribe to or buy magazines about	*call for count*
Affluence	young (under 40)	364,882
Affluent, Ultra		*call for count*
Ailments	see Suffers From	*call for count*
Air Force	active military member	*call for count*
Air Force	member in household	133,721
Airline Inflight/Train Enroute	subscribe to or buy magazines about	*call for count*
Airline Visa/MC	use	490
Alcoholic Beverages	various, use, by type	804,435
Alcoholic Beverages		*call for count*
Allergies	see Suffers from	
Allergy Medicines	see Cold/Allergy Medicines	
Almanacs and Directories	subscribe to or buy magazines about	*call for count*
American Express Card	have	1.103,585
American Express Card	have	1,994,490
American Express Gold Card	have	151,260
Annuities	have	340,915
Annuities	have or want	438,400
Annuities	want	226,909
Answering Machines	own	4,520,350
Antacids	frequency of use, by brand	1,054,470
Antacids	various, by brands	1,262,248
Apartments	own or rent	3,327,960
Apparel	order by mail	5,763,138
Army	active military member in household	*call for count*
Army	member in household	318,167
Art & Antiques	interest in collecting	3,231,000
Art & Antiques	subscribe to or buy magazines about	*call for count*
Asian		304,000
Astrology/Occult		1,268,900
AT&T Calling Card	see Calling Card	
AT&T Universal Credit Card		389,030
Athlete's Foot Remedies	use, by frequency	*call for count*
Athletic Equipment	buy by mail	295,530
Automatic Dishwash Detergents	use, by frequency	939,626
Automobile Insurance	current carrier, month renew	1,282,816
Automobile Owners	by make, model	328,439
Automobile-Frequent Renters		216,457
Automobiles	plan to buy	1,165,854
Automotive	read about/hobby	*call for count*
Automotive	subscribe to or buy magazines about	*call for count*
Automotive Products	buy by mail	570
Automotive Work	as hobby	5,360,000
Automotive Work		4,603,000

Source: Courtesy of Survey Sampling, Inc. Copyright © 1999 Survey Sampling, Inc.

stratified sample. First, respondents for a quota sample are not selected on a random basis, as they must be for a stratified sample. Second, in a stratified sample, the classification factors used for stratification must be selected on the basis of the existence of a correlation between the classification factor and the behavior of interest. There is no such requirement in the case of a quota sample. The demographic or classification factors of interest in a quota sample are selected on the basis of researcher judgment.

Snowball Samples

Snowball sample A non-probability sample in which the selection of additional respondents is based on referrals from the initial respondents.

Snowball samples use sampling procedures that select additional respondents on the basis of referrals from the initial respondents. This procedure is used to sample from low-incidence or rare populations. By *low-incidence* or *rare populations* we are referring to populations that make up a very small percentage of the total population. The costs of finding members of these rare populations may be so great as to force the researcher to use a technique like snowball sampling for cost-efficiency. For example, an insurance company might be interested in obtaining a national sample of individuals who have switched from the indemnity form of health care coverage to a health maintenance organization in the last six months. It would be necessary to sample an extremely large number of consumers nationally to locate 1,000 consumers who fall into this population. It would be far more economical to conduct an initial sample to identify 200 people who fall into the population of interest and obtain the names of an average of four other people from each of the respondents to the initial survey to complete the sample of 1,000.

The main advantages of snowball sampling relate to the dramatic reduction in search costs. However, this savings comes with disadvantages. The total sample is likely to be biased because the individuals whose names were obtained from those sampled in the initial phase are likely to be similar to those initially sampled. As a result, the sample may not be a good cross section of the total population. There should be some limits on the number of respondents obtained through referral, though there are no specific rules regarding what these limits should be. Also, this approach may be hampered by the fact that respondents may be reluctant to give referrals.[19]

Internet Samples

The growth of surveying over the Internet has, to some extent, been hindered by problems associated with the ability to generate representative samples via that medium. There are two fundamental problems. First, the on-line population is still not representative of the total population. Though the on-line population looks more like the general population every day, the cyber world is still younger, better educated, and more likely to be male.[20] Second, there is no central database of all e-mail addresses that can be used as a basic sample frame from which to draw a sample. As a result, it is still difficult to established the fact that any sample of on-line users is a representative probability sample.

In some special situations, samples of specialized groups of Internet users can be defended as representative probability samples. We have conducted surveys of customers for business-to-business studies (for example, semiconductor

Online Survey Sampling Pitfalls

Going ON-LINE

POSTING SURVEYS IN PUBLIC AREAS WITH NO CONTROL OVER access is an invitation for disaster in the form of highly biased samples. There are often individuals who have a vested interest in a survey or certain questions on a survey showing a certain result, as *Byte* Magazine found. A single advocate for a particular outcome may stumble across the survey and post the existence of the survey to a particular news or advocacy group, thereby rallying a large population segment to vote a particular way on the survey. The results of three questions from the *Byte* survey are shown in Figure 11.5. Based on these results, one might conclude that UNIX and OS/2 are surprisingly popular. Analysis of the locations from which respondents came indicated that they were 12 times more likely to come from http://www.IBM.com (OS/2 is an IBM product) than are typical *Byte* site visitors. These individuals are OS/2 and UNIX supporters who wanted to make sure that their favorites did well in the survey. One way to avoid this possibility is to invite individuals to participate via e-mail or other means and to provide each invited person with a unique password or ID number. ■

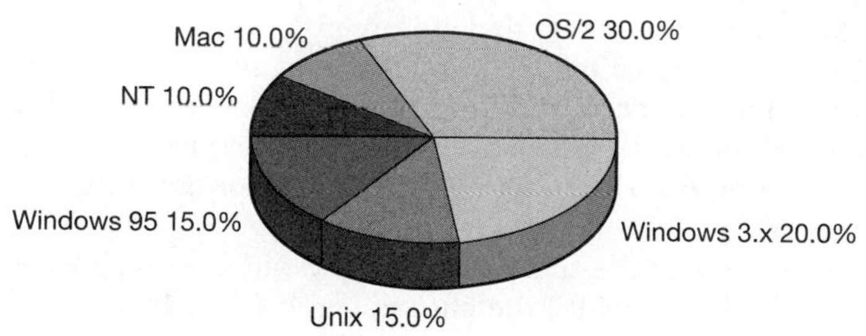

Figure 11.5

Internet Survey Results

Source: "*Byte* Learns a Lesson in Web Surveys," *Byte* Magazine (September 1996), p. 32. Reprinted with permission, CMP Media, Inc., BYTE/BYTE.com. 600 Community Drive, Manhasset NY. All Rights Reserved.

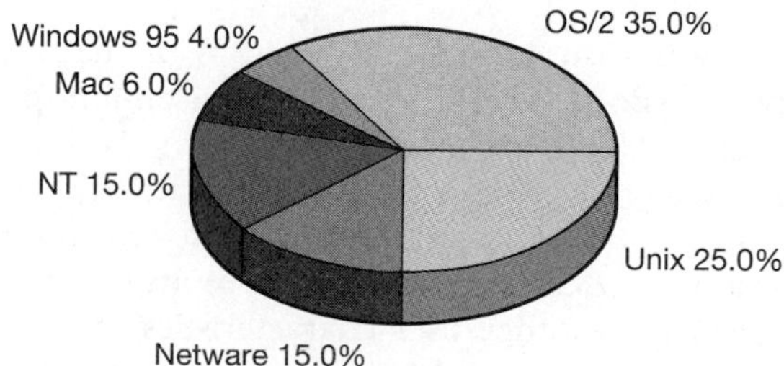

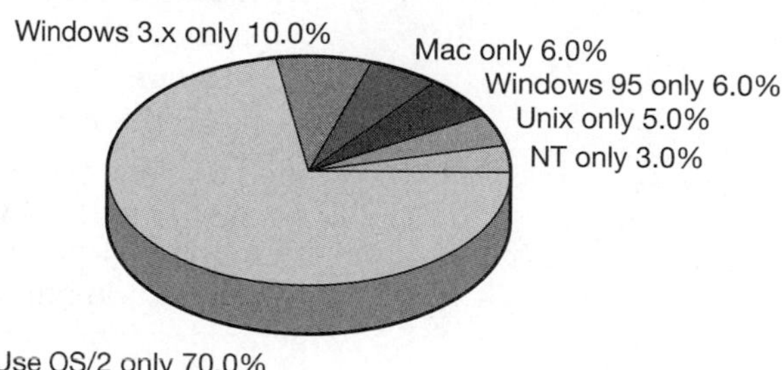

device buyers) with our client having e-mail addresses for all their customers. Random samples were drawn, recruiting with significant incentives ($50 to $100 cash) via e-mail was used, and very high response rates (70 to 80%) were achieved. These Internet samples can be defended as representative probability samples. In fact, in most of these cases, response rate exceeded those previously achieved with the same populations by means of central-location telephone interviewing. However, if there is a need to survey new car buyers, then there would be no list of all buyers with e-mail addresses, and any sample produced for a small subset of these buyers for whom e-mail addresses were available from some source would produce estimates that were highly suspect.

Highly reputable research firms, such as Harris Black International Ltd., are now saying that they can generate results from Internet samples that are representative of large general populations. For example, Harris Black claims to have tested Internet samples to predict the outcome of 22 political races in the fall of 1998, and have correctly predicted the outcomes of 21 of these races.[21] Though they and others making similar claims have not been totally clear on methodologies, two elements have emerged. Those organizations that are heavily promoting on-line interviewing have, in most cases, recruited very large panels of Internet users. To see the techniques they use, go to http://vr.harrispollonline.com/register. Harris Black claims to have over 3 million individuals on its panel, with a goal of reaching 5 million. They have basic demographic data on panel members; to see what they have, sign up for the Harris poll.

Large panel sizes permit these organizations to pull samples from their databases that are "sort of representative," in that they accurately mirror a particular population for a number of known demographic characteristics. For example, if we know from other data that 40 percent of a particular population is under 35 years of age and that 60 percent is 35 years or older, then we can make sure that the sample we pull has this same distribution. This assumes that age is significantly related to usage of the particular type of product, under scrutiny. We would do this same balancing act for a number of demographic characteristics.

We determine the sample at the start of a study, but after the data have been collected and we have the results, the analysis can be "weighted back" to the known characteristics of the population. So, for example, when the age distribution of a population is known, we can weight or adjust the results to the known 40/60 split. Most of the popular statistical software packages, such as STATISTICA, SPSS and Minitab, have the capability to make these adjustments.

Certainly on-line interviewing will continue to grow. With that growth, many of the current problems associated with sampling the on-line population will take care of themselves. Until that time, research firms will use procedures such as those discussed here to try to compensate for the current shortcomings of on-line sampling. It is difficult to estimate the effects on data quality of using these techniques.[22] Biases present in the results may be exaggerated by their use. There may be other user characteristics that are not being used in selection or weighting procedures that are more important than the ones available to us.

Summary

The population, or universe, is the total group of people in whose opinions one is interested. A census involves collecting desired information from all the members of the population of interest. A sample is simply a subset of a population. The steps in developing a sampling plan are to: define the population of interest, choose the data collection method, choose the sampling frame, select the sampling method, determine the sample size, develop and specify an operational plan for selecting sampling elements, and execute the operational sampling plan. The sampling frame is the means of listing the elements of the population from which the sample will be drawn or specifying a procedure for generating the elements of the population to be sampled.

Probability sampling methods are selected in such a way that every element of the population has a known, nonzero probability of selection. Nonprobability sampling methods include all methods that select specific elements from the population in a nonrandom manner. Probability samples have several advantages over nonprobability samples, including a reasonable certainty that the information will be obtained from a representative cross section of the population, a sampling error that can be computed, and survey results that can be projected to the total population. However, probability samples are more expensive than nonprobability samples and usually take much more time to design and execute. Recent evidence indicates that convenience samples are growing in popularity.

The accuracy of sample results is affected by sampling error and nonsampling error. Sampling error is the error that results because the sample selected is not perfectly representative of the population. There are two types of sampling error: random and administrative. Random sampling error is due to chance and cannot be avoided.

Probability sampling methods include simple random samples, systematic samples, stratified samples, and cluster samples. Nonprobability sampling techniques include convenience samples, judgment samples, quota samples, snowball samples, and Internet samples.

Key Terms & Definitions

Population or universe The total group of people from whom information is needed.

Census Data obtained from or about every member of the population of interest.

Sample A subset of the population of interest.

Sampling frame List of population elements from which to select units to be sampled.

Random-digit dialing Method of generating lists of telephone numbers at random.

Probability sample A sample in which every element of the population has a known, nonzero probability of selection.

Simple random sample A probability sampling in which the sample is selected in such a way that every element of the population has a known and equal probability of inclusion in the sample.

Sampling error The difference between the sample value and the true value of the population mean.

Nonprobability sample A sample that includes elements from the population that are selected in a nonrandom manner.

Population parameter A value that defines a true characteristic of a total population.

Systematic sample A probability sampling in which the entire population is numbered, and elements are drawn using a skip interval.

Stratified sample A probability sample that selects elements from relevant population subsets to be more representative of an entire population.

Proportional allocation A sampling in which the number of elements selected from a stratum is directly proportional to the size of the stratum relative to the population.

Disproportional or optimal allocation A sampling in which the number of elements taken from a given stratum is proportional to the relative size of the stratum and the standard deviation of the characteristic under consideration.

Cluster sample A probability sample drawn from a sample of geographic areas.

Convenience sample A nonprobability sample used primarily because data are easy to collect.

Judgment sample A nonprobability sample in which the selection criteria are based on personal judgment that the element is representative of the population under study.

Quota sample A nonprobability sample in which a population subgroup is classified on the basis of researcher judgment.

Snowball sample A nonprobability sample in which the selection of additional respondents is based on referrals from the initial respondents.

Questions for Review & Critical Thinking

1. Describe five distinct populations at your college or university.
2. What are some situations in which a census would be better than a sample? Why are samples usually taken rather than censuses?
3. Develop a sampling plan for examining undergraduate business students' attitudes toward children's advertising.
4. Give an example of a perfect sample frame. Why is a telephone directory often not an acceptable sample frame of a particular city?
5. Distinguish between probability and nonprobability samples. What are the advantages and disadvantages of each? Why are nonprobability samples so popular in marketing research?
6. Distinguish among a systematic sample, a cluster sample, and a stratified sample. Cite examples of each.
7. What is the difference between a stratified sample and a quota sample?
8. American National Bank has 1,000 customers. The manager wishes to draw a sample of 100 customers. How would this be done using systematic sampling? What impact would it have on the technique, if any, if the list were ordered by average size of deposit?
9. Simple random samples are rarely used for door-to-door interviewing. Why do you think this is true?

Working the Net

1. Go to the Survey Sampling site at http://www.ssisamples.com and click on Products. What lists are offered under the category "Smokers"? What lists are under the category "Music choices"?
2. Go to Survey Sampling at http://www.ssisamples.com and click on Products. What is offered in the way of random-digit telephone samples? When would you use samples of this type? What is offered in regard to business samples? Provide two examples of situations in which you might use such business samples.

Real-Life Research

Florida National Bank

Florida National Bank (FNB) operates branches in 65 cities and towns throughout Florida. The bank offers a complete range of financial services, including Visa and Mastercard credit cards. FNB has 62,500 people in the state using its credit cards. From the original application, it has certain information about these individuals, including name, address, ZIP, telephone number, income, education, and assets. FNB is interested in determining whether there is a relationship between the volume of purchases charged on credit cards and the demographic characteristics of the individual cardholders. For example, are individuals in certain parts of the state more or less likely to be heavy users of the card? Is there a relationship between the people's income and their level of card usage? Is there a relationship between people's level of education and card usage? These data can be used to more effectively target offerings sent through the mail if significant relationships are found. Paul Bruney is research director for FNB, and he is currently in the process of developing a design for the research. If you were Bruney, how would you answer the following questions?

Questions

1. How would you define the population of interest for the study?
2. What sample frame or frames might you use for the project?
3. What procedure would you use to select a simple random sample from the sampling frame you chose above?
4. Would a stratified sample make sense in this situation? Why or why not? How would you approach the process of developing a stratified sample from the sampling frame you chose?
5. Could you use your sample frame to draw a cluster sample? How would you go about it? Would it make any sense to do this?
6. Which of the three probability sampling methods covered in this chapter would you choose for this study? Why would you choose that option?
7. Give an example of a situation in which it would be appropriate to use a list available from SSI-LITe. Justify your choice.

CHAPTER *twelve*

Sample Size Determination

Learning Objectives

1. *To learn the financial and statistical issues in determining the sample size*

2. *To discover the methods for determining the sample size*

3. *To gain an appreciation of a normal distribution*

4. *To understand population, sample, and sampling distribution*

5. *To distinguish between point and interval estimates*

6. *To recognize problems involving sampling means and proportions*

Computer World is a chain of computer super stores operating in several southwestern states. Computer World wants to develop information about the characteristics of its current customers. However, the company does not have a budget for a commercial marketing research firm to do the research at the current time. Joe Langan, marketing director for Computer World, is currently completing the Executive MBA Program at Texas State University. Through the program, he has met Dr. Lara Gates, who teaches the marketing research course in the MBA program. He knows that her class conducts projects for firms in the area every semester, and has heard positive feedback from students and businesspeople who have participated in the program. He has contacted her and reached an agreement whereby her class will do the research project for Computer World.

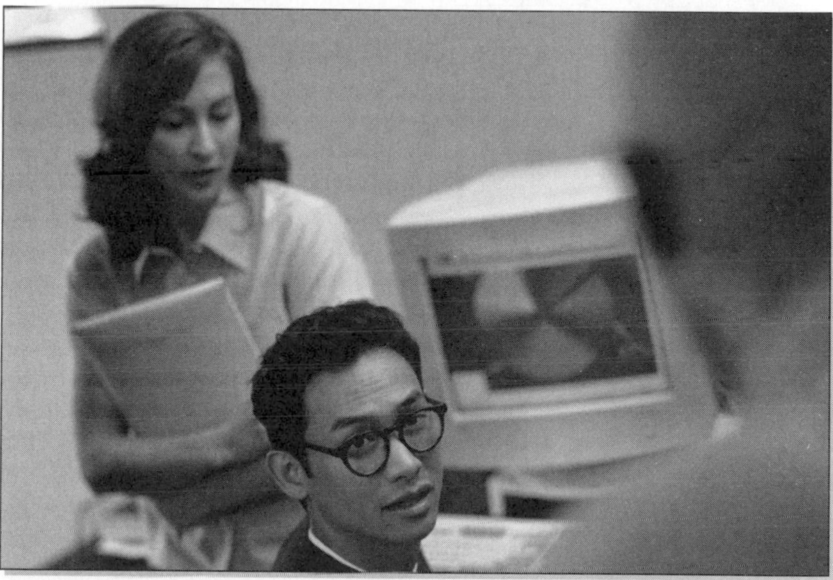

Developing an appropriate sample plan for Computer World is key to the estimation of demographic and psychographic group size. Sample size calculations are the cornerstone of the plan and the determinant of its success.

Lara has created teams responsible for executing different aspects of the research. Bryan Buckler is a member of the team responsible for developing the sample plan. The team has decided, after an initial meeting with Joe, that a simple random sample is the appropriate type of sample for the project. Bryan is responsible for determining how large the sample should be. He recognizes that a major goal of the research is to estimate the proportions or percentages of Computer World customers that fall into various demographic and psychographic groups. In addition, he has determined that Computer World wants estimates of population values that are within plus or minus (±) 5 percent of the true values. He remembers, from an earlier statistics course, that you can make such inferences about sample results, but you can make them only with some level of confidence, never with certainty. Referring to the statistics book from his earlier course, he has determined that the team can make inferences such as "We are 95 percent confident that the true population value is within ± 5 percent of the estimates based on our sample."

He has discussed this with other members of his team and with Joe. Both his team and Joe agree that an error of ± 5 percent with 95 percent confidence is acceptable. He is now trying to figure out how to calculate the sample size necessary to meet these requirements.[1]

The issues covered in this chapter are the same ones that Bryan and his team are facing. After completing the reading, it should be possible to answer the various questions the team is attempting to answer and know how to approach the sample size calculation that Bryan is considering. ■

Determining the Sample Size for Probability Samples

Financial, Statistical, and Managerial Issues

The process of determining a sample size for probability samples involves financial, statistical, and managerial issues. Other things being equal, the larger the sample, the less the sampling error. However, larger samples cost more money, and the funds available for a particular project are always limited. In addition, though the costs of larger samples tend to increase on a linear basis, the level of sampling error decreases at a rate only equal to the square root of the relative increase in sample size. In other words, if the sample size is quadrupled, data collection costs will also quadruple, but the level of sampling error will decrease by only one-half. Finally, managerial issues must be reflected in sample size calculations. How accurate do our estimates need to be, and how confident do we need to be that the chosen confidence interval includes the true population values? There are a number of possibilities. In some cases, there is a need to be very precise (small sampling error) and very confident that population values fall in the small range of sampling error (confidence interval). In other cases, there is no such need to be as precise or confident.

Budget Available

Frequently, the sample size for a project is determined by the budget available. Sample size, in essence, is frequently determined backwards. A brand manager may have $20,000 available in the budget for a particular marketing research project. After deducting other project costs (such as research design, questionnaire development, data processing, and analysis), the remainder determines the size of the sample that can be surveyed. There are limits, of course. If the dollars available are enough for only a clearly inadequate sample, a decision must be made: Either additional funds must be found or the project should be canceled.

Although this approach may seem highly unscientific and arbitrary, it is a fact of life in a corporate environment that the amount of research possible is based on the budgeting of financial resources. Financial constraints challenge the researcher to develop research designs that will generate data of adequate quality for decision-making purposes with limited resources. This "budget available" approach forces the researcher to carefully consider the value of information in relation to its cost.

Rules of Thumb

Potential clients may specify in their requests for proposal that they want a sample of 200, 400, 500, or some other specific size. Sometimes this number is based on the target sampling error, and in other cases it is based on nothing more than past experience and sample sizes used for similar studies. The justification for the specified sample size may boil down to a "gut feel" that it is an appropriate level.

It may be that the sample size requested is judged to be adequate to support the objectives of the proposed research. If the researcher determines that the sample size requested is not adequate, he or she should present arguments for a larger sample size to the client and let the client make the final decision. If the client rejects the arguments for a larger sample size, the researcher may decline to submit a proposal in the belief that the sample size is so inadequate that it will fatally cripple the research effort.

Number of Subgroups to Be Analyzed

In any sample-size determination problem, the number and anticipated size of subgroups to be analyzed must be considered. For example, we might decide that a sample of 400 is quite adequate overall. However, if male and female respondents must be analyzed separately and the sample is expected to be 50 percent male and 50 percent female, then the expected sample size for each subgroup is only 200. Is this number adequate to make the desired statistical inferences about the characteristics of the two groups? If, in addition, the results are to be analyzed by both sex and age, the problem gets even more complicated. Assume that it is important to analyze four subgroups of the total sample as follows:

- men under 35
- men 35 and over
- women under 35
- women 35 and over.

If each group is expected to make up about 25 percent of the total sample, then there will be only 100 respondents in each subgroup. Is this an adequate number to permit us to make the kinds of statistical inferences about these groups that the objectives of the research require?

Other things being equal, the larger the number of subgroups that need to be analyzed, the larger the required total sample size. It has been suggested that the sample should be large enough so that there will be 100 or more respondents in each major subgroup and a minimum of 20 to 50 respondents in each of the less important subgroups.

Traditional Statistical Methods

In Chapter 11 we discussed some of the advantages and disadvantages of using a simple random sample. In this chapter we cover the traditional approaches for determining the sample size for a simple random sample. Three pieces of information are required to make the necessary calculations when using a sample result:

- an estimate of the population standard deviation.
- the acceptable level of sampling error.
- the desired level of confidence that the sample result will fall within a certain range (result ± sampling error) of true population values.

With these three pieces of information, we can calculate the size of the simple random sample required.

In PRACTICE

Sample Costs Versus Costs of Being Wrong

Marketers, all too often, try to save a few bucks on sample size and risk millions in opportunity loss. This observation comes from Thomas Semon, expert columnist for *Marketing News*. He noted that an ad agency he once worked for bragged about using samples of 120 for copy research. Samples of this size can be fine in some cases but not in others. There is not a one-size-fits-all sample size for any type of research. The really critical factor is the size of the expected difference or change to be measured—the smaller the expected difference or change, the larger the sample must be, squared.

In testing two versions of an ad, a current or control version and a new version, we might adopt the rule that the new version will be adopted if it scores significantly higher than the current or control version. "Significance" might be set at either the 90 percent or 95 percent confidence level.

This type of decision criterion protects against the risk that random sampling error results in an overestimate of the favorable response and leads to the false conclusion that the new version should be adopted. However, the opposite problem (underestimate of the favorable response, leading to the false conclusion that the new version should be rejected) is just as likely, and the decision criterion specified does not protect against this possibility. In this example, a sample size of 120 does not have the statistical power to protect against the opportunity loss that may result from a failure to recognize superiority of the new version.

When the effect size, the needed or expected difference, is large (e.g., more than 10 percentage points), then statistical power is typically not a problem. However, very small effect sizes (e.g., 2 percentage points) may require such large sample sizes as to be impractical from a cost perspective.[2] ■

The Normal Distribution

General Properties

A **normal distribution** is a continuous distribution that is bell-shaped and symmetrical about the mean—mean, median, and mode being equal. Sixty-eight percent of the observations fall within plus or minus one standard deviation of the mean, approximately 95 percent fall within plus or minus two standard deviations, and approximately 99.5 percent fall within plus or minus three standard deviations.

Normal distribution A continuous distribution that is bell-shaped and symmetrical about the mean—mean, median, and mode being equal. Sixty-eight percent of the observations fall within plus or minus one standard deviation of the mean, approximately 95 percent fall within plus or minus two standard deviations, and approximately 99.5 percent fall within plus or minus three standard deviations.

The concept of a normal distribution is crucial to classical statistical inference. There are several reasons for its importance. First, many variables encountered by marketers have probability distributions that are close to the normal distribution. Examples include the number of cans, bottles, or glasses of soft drink consumed by soft-drink users; the number of times that people who eat at fast-food restaurants go to restaurants of this type in an average month; and the average hours per week spent viewing television. Second, the normal distribution is useful for a number of theoretical reasons. One of the most important of these relates to the **central limit theorem.** According to this theorem, for any population (regardless of its distribution), a distribution of sample means ($\overline{X}$) approaches a normal distribution as the sample size increases. We demonstrate the importance of this factor later in the chapter. Third, the normal distribution is a useful approximation of many discrete probability distributions.

Central limit theorem A distribution of a large number of sample means or sample proportions that approximate a normal distribution, regardless of the actual distribution of the population from which they were drawn.

If, for example, we measured the heights of a large sample of men in the United States and plotted those values on a graph, a distribution similar to the one shown in Figure 12.1 would result. This distribution is a normal distribution that has a number of important characteristics, including the following:

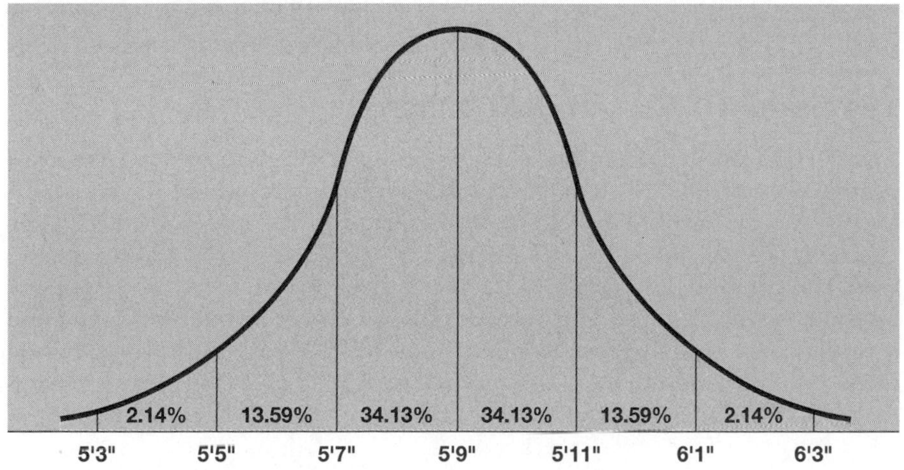

Figure 12.1

Distribution of the Heights of Men in the United States Based on a Large Sample

This group of cadets provides a visual example of a normal distribution curve. Clearly there is a much higher frequency of men whose height falls close to the mean than of men who are significantly taller or shorter than the mean.

1. The normal distribution is bell-shaped and has only one mode. The mode is a measure of central tendency and is the particular value that occurs most frequently. A bimodal (two modes) distribution would have two peaks or humps.
2. A normal distribution is symmetric about its mean. This is another way of saying that it is not skewed and that the three measures of central tendency (mean, median, and mode) are all equal to the same value.
3. A particular normal distribution is uniquely defined by its mean and standard deviation.
4. The total area under a normal curve is equal to one, meaning that it takes in all observations.
5. The area of a region under the normal distribution curve between any two values of a variable equals the probability of observing a value in that range when randomly selecting an observation from the distribution. For example, on a single draw there is a 34.13 percent chance of selecting a man between 5 feet, 7 inches and 5 feet, 9 inches in height from the distribution shown in Figure 12.1.
6. The normal distribution has the feature that the area between the mean and a given number of standard deviations from the mean is the same for all normal distributions. In other words, the area between the mean and plus or minus one standard deviation takes in 68.26 percent of the area under the curve or 68.26 percent of the observations. This is called the *proportional property* of the normal distribution. This feature provides the basis for much of the statistical inference that we discuss in this chapter.

The Standard Normal Distribution

Standard normal distribution A normal distribution with a mean of zero and a standard deviation of one.

Any normal distribution can be transformed into what is known as a **standard normal distribution.** The standard normal distribution has the same features as any normal distribution. However, the mean of the standard normal distribution is always equal to zero and the standard deviation is always equal to one. The probabilities provided in Table 2 in the Appendix at the end of the text are based on a standard normal distribution. A simple transformation formula can be used to transform any value X from any normal distribution to its equivalent value Z for a standard normal distribution. This transformation is based on the proportional property of the normal distribution:

$$Z = \frac{\text{value of the variable} - \text{mean of the variable}}{\text{standard deviation of the variable}}$$

Symbolically, the formula can be stated as

$$Z = \frac{X - \mu}{\sigma}$$

where

X = value of the variable
μ = mean of the variable
σ = standard deviation of the variable

The areas under (percent of all observations) a standard normal distribution for various Z values **(standard deviations)** are shown in Table 12.1. The standardized normal distribution is shown in Figure 12.2 on page 364.

Standard deviation A measure of dispersion calculated by subtracting the mean of a series from each value in a series, squaring each result, summing them, dividing the sum by the number of items minus 1, and taking the square root of this value.

Population, Sample, and Sampling Distributions

The purpose of conducting a survey based on a sample is to make inferences about the population, not to describe the sample. A population includes all possible individuals or objects from whom or about which we might collect information to meet the objectives of the research. A sample is a subset of the total population.

A **population distribution** is a frequency distribution of all the elements of a population. This frequency distribution has a mean, usually represented by the Greek letter μ, and a standard deviation, usually represented by the Greek letter σ. A **sample distribution** is a frequency distribution of the elements of an individual (single) sample. In a sample distribution, the mean is usually represented by $\overline{X}$ and the standard deviation is usually represented by S.

Population distribution A frequency distribution of all the elements of a population.

Sample distribution A frequency distribution of all the elements of an individual sample.

Table 12.1

Area Under Standard Normal Curve for *Z* Values (Standard Deviations) of 1, 2, and 3

Z Values (Standard Deviation)	Area Under Standard Normal Curve (%)
1	68.26
2	95.44
3	99.74

Figure 12.2

Standardized Normal Distribution

The term Pr (*Z*) is read "the probability of *Z*."

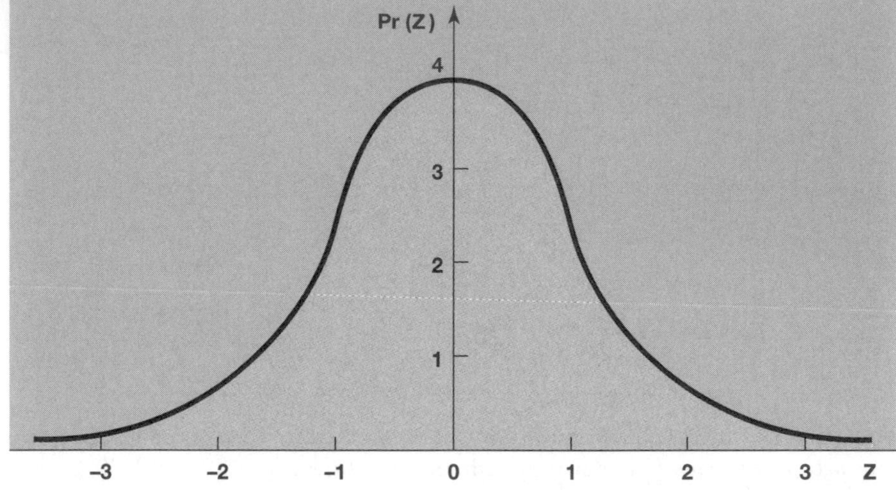

Sampling distribution of the sample mean A frequency distribution of the means of many samples drawn from a particular population, which has a normal distribution.

At this point, it is necessary to introduce a third distribution, the sampling distribution of the sample mean. Understanding this distribution is crucial to understanding the basis for computing sampling error in simple random samples. The **sampling distribution of the sample mean** is a conceptual and theoretical probability distribution of the means of all possible samples of a given size drawn from a particular population. Though this distribution is seldom calculated, its known properties have tremendous practical significance. To actually derive a distribution of sample means, a large number of simple random samples (say, 25,000) of a certain size are drawn from a particular population. Then, the means for each sample are computed and arranged in a frequency distribution. Because each sample is composed of a different subset of sample elements, the sample means will not all be exactly the same.

If the samples are sufficiently large and random, then the resulting distribution of sample means will approximate a normal distribution. This assertion is based on the central limit theorem. Once again, this theorem states that as the sample size increases, the distribution of the means of a large number of random samples taken from virtually any population approaches a normal distribution with a mean equal to μ and a standard deviation (referred to as *standard error*) equal to

$$S_{\bar{x}} = \frac{\sigma}{\sqrt{n}} \quad \text{where } n = \text{sample size}$$

It is important to note that the central limit theorem holds, regardless of the shape of the population distribution from which the samples are selected. This means that, regardless of the distribution of the population, a distribution of means of samples selected from that distribution will tend to be normally distributed. The notations ordinarily used to refer to the means and standard deviations of population, sample, and sampling distributions are summarized in Table 12.2.

Table 12.2

Symbols Used for Means and Standard Deviations of Various Distributions

Distribution	Mean	Standard Deviation
Population	μ	σ
Sample	$\overline{X}$	S
Sampling	$\mu_{\overline{X}} = \mu$	$S_{\overline{X}}$

The **standard error of the mean** ($S_{\overline{X}}$) is computed because the variance or dispersion within a particular distribution of sample means will be smaller if it is based on larger samples. Common sense tells us that individual sample means will, on the average, be closer to the population mean where larger samples are taken. The relationships among the population distribution, sample distributions, and sampling distributions of the mean are shown graphically in Figure 12.3 on page 366. The sampling distribution of the mean is discussed next, and another concept, the sampling distribution of the proportion, is introduced in sections that follow.

Standard error of the mean The standard deviation of a distribution of sample means.

Sampling Distribution of the Mean

Basic Concepts

Consider a sampling exercise in which a researcher takes 1,000 simple random samples of size 200 from the population of all consumers who have eaten at a fast-food restaurant at least once in the past 30 days to estimate the average number of times these individuals eat at a fast-food restaurant in an average month.

If the researcher computes the mean number of visits for each of the 1,000 samples and sorts them into intervals based on their relative values, the frequency distribution shown in Table 12.3 on page 367 might result. These frequencies are shown in a histogram in Figure 12.4. on page 367 In addition, a normal curve has been superimposed on this histogram, which closely approximates the shape of a normal curve. If we drew a large enough number of samples of size 200, computed the mean of each sample, and plotted those means, then the resulting distribution would be a normal distribution. The normal curve shown in Figure 12.4 is the sampling distribution of the mean for this particular problem. The sampling distribution of the mean for simple random samples that are large (30 or more observations) has the following characteristics:

1. The distribution is a normal distribution.
2. The distribution has a mean equal to the population mean.

Figure 12.3

Relationships of the Three Basic Types of Distribution

Source: Adapted from D. H. Sanders, A. F. Murphy, and R. J. Eng, *Statistics: A Fresh Approach*, p. 123. © 1980 McGraw-Hill reprinted with permission of The McGraw-Hill Companies.

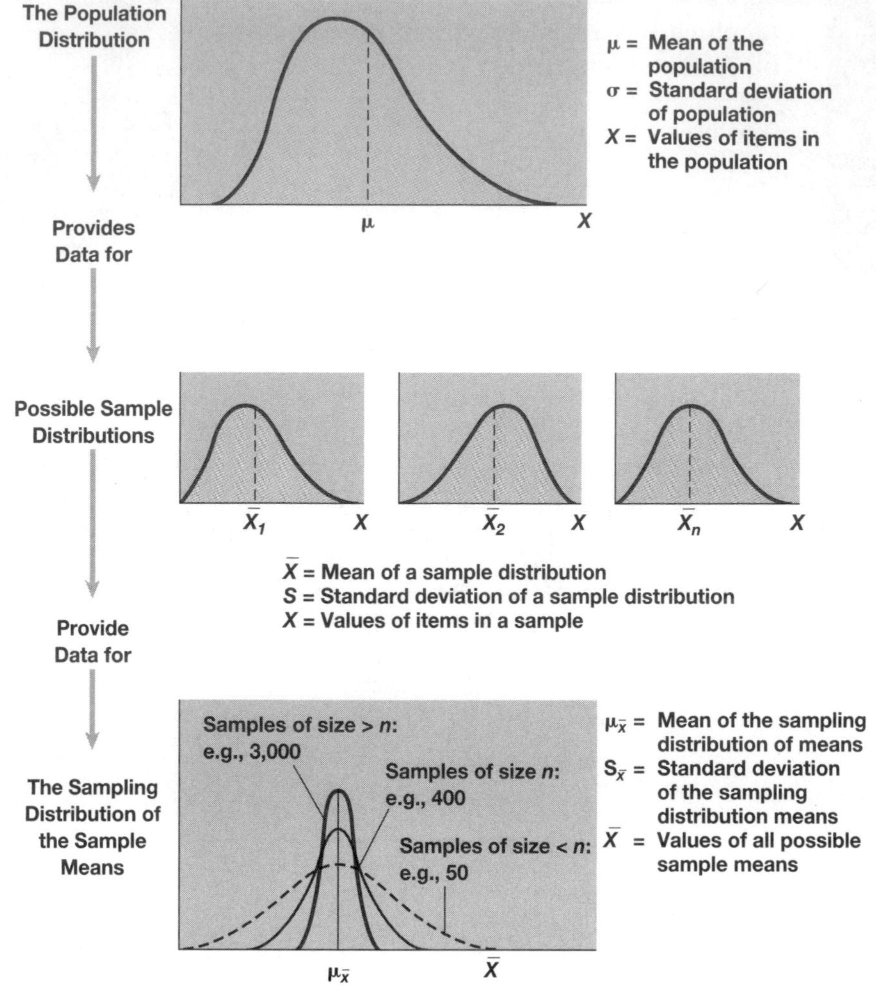

3. The distribution has a standard deviation, referred to as the *standard error of the mean,* equal to the population standard deviation divided by the square root of the sample size:

$$\sigma_{\bar{x}} = \frac{\sigma}{\sqrt{n}}$$

This statistic is referred to as the *standard error of the mean* instead of the standard deviation to indicate that it applies to a distribution of sample means rather than to the standard deviation of a sample or a population. Keep in mind that this calculation applies only to a simple random sample and not to other types of samples. Other types of probability samples (stratified samples and cluster samples) use more complex formulas for computing standard error.

Table 12.3

Frequency Distribution of 1,000 Sample Means: Average Number of Times Consumers Ate at a Fast-Food Restaurant in the Past 30 Days

Category–Number of Times	Frequency of Occurrence
2.6–3.5	8
3.6–4.5	15
4.6–5.5	29
5.6–6.5	44
6.6–7.5	64
7.6–8.5	79
8.6–9.5	89
9.6–10.5	108
10.6 –11.5	115
11.6–12.5	110
12.6–13.5	90
13.6–14.5	81
14.6–15.5	66
15.6–16.5	45
16.6–17.5	32
17.6–18.5	16
18.6–19.5	9
Total	1,000

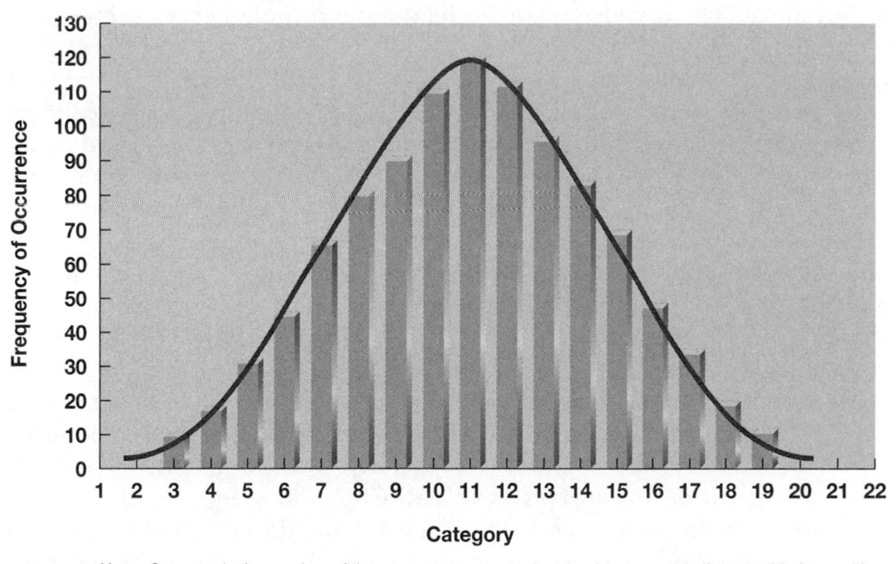

Note: Category is the number of times a person ate at a fast-food restaurant in the past 30 days, with a normal distribution superimposed.

Figure 12.4

Actual Sampling Distribution of Means

Note: Category is the number of times a person ate at a fast-food restaurant in the past 30 days, with a normal distribution superimposed.

Making Inferences on the Basis of a Single Sample

In practice we are not interested in taking all possible random samples from a particular population and generating a frequency distribution like the one shown in Table 12.3 and a histogram like the one shown in Figure 12.4. Normally, we want to take one simple random sample and make some statistical inference about the population from which the sample was drawn. The question is: What is the probability that any one simple random sample of a particular size will produce an estimate of the population mean that is within one standard error (plus or minus) of the true population mean? The answer, based on the information provided in Table 12.1, is that there is a 68 percent probability that any one sample from a particular population will produce an estimate of the population mean that is within plus or minus one standard error of the true value, because 68 percent of all sample means will fall in this range. There is a 95 percent probability that any one simple random sample of a particular size from a given population will produce a value that is within plus or minus two standard errors of the true population mean and a 99.7 percent probability that such a sample will produce an estimate of the mean that is within plus or minus three standard errors of the population mean.

Point and Interval Estimates

Point estimate Inference regarding the sampling error associated with a particular estimate of a population value.

Interval estimate Inference regarding the likelihood that a population value will fall within a certain range.

Confidence level The probability that a particular confidence interval will include the true population value.

When using the results of a sample to make estimates of a population mean, two kinds of estimates can be generated: point and interval estimates. In **point estimates,** the sample mean is the best estimate of the population mean. It is likely that a particular sample result will produce a mean that is relatively close to the population mean. However, the mean of a particular sample could be any one of the sample means shown in the distribution. A small percentage of these sample means is a considerable distance from the true population mean. The distance between the sample mean and the true population mean is called the *sampling error.*

Given that point estimates based on sample results are exactly correct in only a small percentage of all possible cases, interval estimates are generally preferred to point estimates. An **interval estimate** is an estimate regarding an interval or range of values of the variable, such as a population mean, that the researcher is attempting to estimate. In addition to stating the size of the interval, it is customary to state the probability that the interval will take in the true value of the population mean. This probability is normally referred to as the *confidence coefficient* or **confidence level,** while we refer to the interval as the *confidence interval.*

Interval estimates of the mean are derived as follows. A random sample of a given size is drawn from the population of interest and the mean of that sample is calculated. This particular sample mean is known to lie somewhere within the sampling distribution of all possible sample means, but exactly where this particular mean falls in that distribution is not known. In addition, there is a 68 percent probability that this particular sample mean lies within one standard error (plus or minus) of the true population mean. Based on this information, the statement can be made that the researcher is

68 percent confident that the true population value is equal to the sample value plus or minus one standard error. Symbolically, this statement would be shown as follows:

$$\overline{X} - 1\sigma_{\overline{x}} \leq \mu \leq \overline{X} + 1\sigma_{\overline{x}}$$

Using this same logic, the statement can be made that the researcher is 95 percent confident that the true population value is equal to the sample estimate plus or minus two standard errors (technically 1.96, but 2 is often used for convenience in calculation) and 99.7 percent confident that the true population value falls within the interval defined by the sample value plus or minus three standard errors.

All of this assumes that the standard deviation of the population is known. In most situations, this is not the case. If the standard deviation of the population were known, by definition the mean of the population would also be known, and there would be no need to take a sample in the first place. Lacking information on the standard deviation of the population, the true population value is estimated based on the standard deviation of the sample.

Sampling Distribution of the Proportion

Marketing researchers are frequently interested in estimating proportions or percentages rather than or in addition to estimating means. Common examples include the following:

- the percentage of the population who is aware of a particular ad.
- the percentage of the population who will buy a new product.
- the percentage of the population of all individuals who have visited a fast-food restaurant in the last 30 days, and have visited one four or more times during that period.
- the percentage of the population who subscribes to a specific newspaper.

In situations like these, where a population proportion or percentage is of interest, we shift to the sampling distribution of the proportion.

The **sampling distribution of the proportion** is a relative frequency distribution of the sample proportions of a large number of random samples of a given size drawn from a particular population. The sampling distribution of a proportion has the following characteristics:

Sampling distribution of the proportion A frequency distribution of the proportions of many samples drawn from a particular population which has a normal distribution.

1. It approximates a normal distribution.
2. The mean proportion for all possible samples is equal to the population proportion.
3. The standard error of a sampling distribution of proportions can be computed with the following formula:

$$S_p = \sqrt{\frac{P(1-P)}{n}}$$

where

S_p = *standard error of sampling distribution of proportion*
P = estimate of population proportion
n = sample size

Consider the need to estimate the percentage of all fast-food users who have visited a fast-food restaurant four or more times in the last 30 days. As when generating a sampling distribution of the mean, 1,000 random samples of size 200 might be selected from the population of all fast-food users and from the proportion of users who have visited a fast-food restaurant four or more times in the last month for all 1,000 samples computed. These values can then be plotted in a frequency distribution, and this frequency distribution will approximate a normal distribution. The estimated standard error of the proportion for this distribution is computed using the formula for the standard error of a proportion provided earlier.

For reasons that we hope will be clear after you read the next section, marketing researchers have a tendency to cast sample size problems as problems of estimating proportions rather than means.

Sample Size Determination

Problems Involving Means

Consider the previous example that involved estimating how many times the average fast-food restaurant user visits a fast-food restaurant in an average month. Management needs an estimate of the average number of visits to make a decision about a new promotional campaign currently under consideration. To make this estimate, the marketing research manager for the firm intends to survey a simple random sample of all fast-food users. The question is: What information is necessary to determine the appropriate sample size for the project? First, the formula for calculating the required sample size for problems that involve the estimation of a mean is as follows:

$$n = \frac{Z^2 \sigma^2}{E^2}$$

where

Z = level of confidence expressed in standard errors
σ = population standard deviation
E = acceptable amount of sampling error

Three questions must be answered to compute the sample size required:

1. What is the acceptable or **allowable** level of **sampling error** *(E)*?
2. What is the acceptable level of confidence in standard errors or Z values. (how confident that the specified confidence interval takes in the population mean)?
3. What estimate of the **population standard deviation** (σ) is required?

Allowable sampling error The amount of sampling error a researcher is willing to accept.

Population standard deviation The standard deviation of a variable for an entire population.

The level of confidence (Z) and the amount of error (E) to be used must be set by the researcher. Remember, the level of confidence and amount of error are set based not only on statistical criteria, but also on financial and managerial criteria. In an ideal world, we would like to always set the level of confidence at a very high level and the amount of error at a very small level. However, because this is a business decision, cost must be considered. An acceptable trade-off between accuracy, level of confidence, and cost must be determined. In some situations, the need for precision and a high level of confidence may be less than in others. For example, in an exploratory study a client may only be interested in discovering a basic sense of whether attitudes toward a product are generally positive or negative. Precision may not be critical. However, in a product concept test a researcher may need to make a much more precise estimate of sales for a new product, so that management can make the potentially costly and risky decision to introduce a new product.

The third item on the list of required information, an estimate of the population standard deviation, presents a more serious problem. As noted earlier, if the population standard deviation was known, then the population mean would also be known (the population mean is needed to compute the population standard deviation). There would be no need to draw a sample. The question is: How can the researcher estimate the population standard deviation before selecting the sample? One or some combination of four approaches can be used to deal with this problem:

1. *Use results from a prior survey.* In many cases, a firm may have conducted a prior survey dealing with the same or a similar issue. In this situation, the most obvious solution to the problem would be to use the results of the prior survey as an estimate of the population standard deviation in this situation.
2. *Conduct a pilot survey.* If this is to be a large-scale project, it may be possible to devote some time and resources to a small-scale pilot survey of the population. The results of this pilot survey can be used to develop an estimate of the population standard deviation, which can then be used in the sample-size determination formula.
3. *Use secondary data.* In some cases, secondary data may be available that can be used to develop an estimate of the population standard deviation.

In order to accurately estimate the average number of times a customer visits the restaurant per month, the appropriate sample size for the survey must be calculated.

4. *Use judgment.* If all else fails, an estimate of the population standard deviation can be developed based solely on judgment. This process may be implemented by seeking judgments from a variety of managers who would be in a position to make educated guesses regarding the required population parameters.

After the survey has been conducted and the sample mean and sample standard deviation have been calculated, the researcher can assess the accuracy of the estimated population standard deviation used to calculate the required sample size. At this time, if it is considered appropriate, adjustments can be made in the initial estimates of sampling error.

Consider the problem involving estimating the average number of fast-food visits made in an average month by users of fast-food restaurants. The values to be substituted into the formula follow:

- After consulting with managers in the company, the marketing researcher determines that it is necessary to produce an estimate of the average number of times that fast-food users visit fast-food restaurants. Company managers believe that a high degree of accuracy is needed, and the researcher translates this to mean that the estimate should be within 0.10 (one-tenth) of a visit of the true population value. This value (0.10) should be substituted into the formula for the value of E.
- In addition, the marketing researcher decides that, all things considered, the confidence level needs to be 95 percent that the true population mean falls into the interval defined by the sample mean plus or minus E (as just defined). Two standard errors (technically 1.96) are required to take in 95 percent of the area under a normal curve; therefore, a value of 2 is substituted into the equation for Z.
- Finally, there is the question of what value to insert into the formula for σ. Fortunately, the company had previously conducted a similar study in which the standard deviation for the variable—the average number of times consumers visited a fast-food restaurant in the last 30 days—was 1.39 times. This is the best estimate of σ available. Therefore, a value of 1.39 is substituted into the formula for the value of σ. The calculation follows.

$$n = \frac{Z^2\,\sigma^2}{E^2}$$

$$n = \frac{2^2\,(1.39)^2}{(0.10)^2}$$

$$n = \frac{4\,(1.93)}{0.01}$$

$$n = \frac{7.72}{0.01}$$

$$n = 772$$

Based on this calculation, a simple random sample of 772 is necessary to meet the requirements outlined.

Problems Involving Proportions

Consider the problem of estimating the proportion of all fast-food users who visit a fast-food restaurant four or more times in an average month. The goal is to take a simple random sample from the population of all fast-food users to estimate this proportion. A discussion of determining the appropriate values to substitute into the formula follows.

- As in the previous problem involving the estimation of a population mean on the basis of sample results, the first task is to decide on an acceptable value for E. If, for example, it is decided that an error level of $\pm$ 4 percent is acceptable, a value of .04 will be substituted into the formula for E.
- Next, assume that the researcher has determined a need to be 95 percent confident that the sample estimate is within $\pm$ 4 percent of the true population proportion. As in the previous example, we will substitute a value of 2 into the equation for Z.
- Finally, in a study of the same issue conducted one year ago, the researcher found that 30 percent of all respondents indicated they had visited a fast-food restaurant four or more times in the previous month. We will therefore substitute a value of .30 into the equation for P.

The resulting calculations are as follows:

$$n = \frac{Z^2\,[P(1 - P)]}{E^2}$$

$$n = \frac{2^2\,[.30(1 - .30)]}{.04^2}$$

$$n = \frac{4\,(.21)}{.0016}$$

$$n = \frac{.84}{.0016}$$

$$n = 525$$

Given the requirements, a random sample of 525 respondents is needed. In comparison to the process of determining the sample size necessary to estimate a mean, the researcher has one major advantage when determining the sample size necessary to estimate a proportion: If there is no basis for estimating P, it is possible to make what is sometimes referred to as the *most pessimistic* or worst-case assumption regarding the value of P. What value of P, given values of Z and E, will require the largest possible sample? A value of 0.50 will make the value of the expressions $P\,(1 - P)$ larger than any other possible value of P. There is no corresponding most pessimistic assumption that the researcher can make regarding the value of σ in problems that involve determining the sample size necessary to estimate a mean with given levels of Z and E.

Population Size and Sample Size

You may have noticed that none of the formulas for determining sample size takes into account in any way the size of the population. Students (and managers) frequently find this troubling. It seems to make sense that we should take a larger sample from a larger population. However, this is not true. Generally, there is no direct relationship between the size of the population and the size of the sample required to estimate a particular population parameter with a particular level of error and a particular level of confidence. In fact, the size of the population is of interest only in those situations where the size of the sample is large in relation to the size of the population. One rule of thumb suggests that we need to make an adjustment in the sample size if the sample size is more than 5 percent of the size of the total population. The normal presumption is that sample elements are drawn independent of one another *(independence assumption)*. This assumption is justified when the sample is small relative to the population. However, it is not appropriate when the sample is a relatively large proportion (5 percent or more) of the population. As a result, we must adjust the results obtained with the standard formulas. For example, the formula for the standard error of the mean, presented earlier, is

$$\sigma_{\bar{x}} = \frac{\sigma}{\sqrt{n}}$$

Adjusting for a sample that is 5 percent or more of the population and dropping the independence assumption, the correct formula is

$$\sigma_{\bar{x}} = \frac{\sigma}{\sqrt{n}} \sqrt{\frac{N - n}{N - 1}}$$

Finite population correction factor (FPC) An adjustment to the required sample size that is made in those cases in which the sample is expected to be equal to 5 percent or more of the total population.

The factor $(N - n) / (N - 1)$ is referred to as the **finite population correction factor (FPC).**

In those situations in which the sample is large (5 percent or more) in relation to the population, the researcher can appropriately reduce the required sample size using the FPC. This calculation is made using the following formula:

$$n' = \frac{nN}{N + n - 1}$$

where

n' = revised sample size
n = original sample size
N = population size

If the population has 2,000 elements and the original sample size is 400, then

$$n' = \frac{400(2{,}000)}{2{,}000 + 400 - 1} = \frac{800{,}000}{2{,}399}$$

$$n' = 333$$

Based on the FPC adjustment, we need a sample of only 333 rather than the original 400.

The key is not the size of the sample in relation to the size of the population, but whether the sample selected is truly representative of the population. Empirical evidence shows that relatively small but carefully chosen samples can quite accurately reflect characteristics of the population. Many well-known national surveys and opinion polls are based on samples of fewer than 2,000. The Gallup Poll, the Harris Poll, and the Nielsen Television Ratings are examples. These polls have shown that the behavior of tens of millions of people can be predicted quite accurately using samples that are minuscule in relation to the size of the population.

Determining Sample Size for Stratified and Cluster Samples

The formulas for sample size determination presented in this chapter apply only to simple random samples. There also are formulas for determining required sample size and sampling error for other types of probability samples such as stratified and cluster samples. Although many of the general concepts presented in this chapter apply to these other types of probability samples, the specific formulas are much more complicated. In addition, these formulas require information that frequently is not available or is difficult to obtain. For these reasons, determining the sample size for other types of probability samples is beyond the scope of this introductory text. Those interested in pursuing the question of sample-size determination for stratified and cluster samples should refer to advanced texts on the topic of sampling.[3]

Statistical Power

Statistical power The probability of not making a Type II error.

Although it is standard practice in marketing research to use the formulas presented in this chapter to calculate sample size, these formulas all focus on *Type I error* or alpha error—the error of concluding that there is a difference when there is not a difference. They do not explicitly deal with *Type II error*—the error of saying that there is no difference when there actually is a difference. The probability of not making a Type II error is called **statistical power.**[4] The standard formulas for calculating sample size implicitly assume a power of 50 percent. For example, if we are trying to determine which of two product concepts has stronger appeal to target customers and we would like to be able to detect a 5 percent difference in the percentages of target customers who say they are very likely to buy the products, the standard sample-size formulas would tell us we needed sample sizes of approximately 400 for each product test. Using this calculation, we are implicitly accepting the fact that there is a 50 percent chance of incorrectly concluding that the two products have equal appeal.

Table 12.4 shows the sample sizes required for specific levels of power and an alpha error of 5 percent, and specific levels of differences between the two independent proportions. Formulas are available to permit power calculations for any level of confidence. However, they are somewhat complex and not necessary to the explanation of the basic concept of power. Programs are available on the Internet to make these calculations. One of these programs is available at www.dssresearch.com/SampleSize/default.asp. To reproduce the numbers in the table:

- Click on the Two-Sample, Percentages option near the upper-left portion of the screen.
- Enter the "Sample 1 Percentage" and the "Sample 2 Percentage" in the boxes on the right side so that the figures entered reflect the differences to detect and the values are in the expected range. These figures are set at the 50 percent level.

Table 12.4

Sample Size Required to Detect Differences Between Proportions from Independent Samples at Different Levels of Power and an Alpha Error of 5 percent (σ = .05)

Difference to Detect	Power 50%	60%	70%	75%	80%	90%
0.01	19,205	24.491	30,857	34,697	39,239	52,530
0.05	766	977	1,231	1,384	1,568	2,094
0.10	190	242	305	343	389	518
0.15	83	106	133	150	169	226

Summary

Determining sample size involves financial, statistical, and managerial considerations. Other things being equal, the larger the sample, the less the sampling error. In turn, the cost of the research grows with the size of the sample.

There are several ways to determine sample size. One is the funds that are available. In essence, sample size is determined by the budget. Although seemingly unscientific, this is often a very real factor in the world of corporate marketing research. The second is the so-called rule-of-thumb approach—determining sample size by "gut feel" or common practice. Often samples of 300, 400, or 500 are specified in requests for proposals. Yet another technique for determining sample size is based on the number of subgroups to be analyzed. Generally, the more subgroups that need to be analyzed, the larger the required total sample size.

In addition to these factors, there are a number of traditional statistical techniques for determining sample size. Three pieces of data are required to make sample size calculations: an estimate of a population standard deviation, the level of sampling error that the researcher or client is willing to accept, and the desired level of confidence for a population value to fall within acceptable limits.

Crucial to statistical sampling theory is the concept of the normal distribution. The normal distribution is bell-shaped and has only one mode. It is also symmetric about the mean. The standard normal distribution has the features of a normal distribution; however, the mean of the standard normal distribution is always equal to zero and the standard deviation is always equal to one. The transformation formula is used to transform any value X from any normal distribution to its equivalent value Z from a standard normal distribution. The central limit theorem states that the distribution of the means of a large number of random samples taken from virtually any population approaches a normal distribution with a mean equal to μ and a standard deviation equal to

$$S_{\bar{x}} = \frac{\sigma}{\sqrt{n}}$$

The standard deviation of a distribution of sample means is called the standard error of the mean.

When using the results of a sample to estimate a population mean, two kinds of estimates can be generated: point and interval estimates. For point estimates, the sample mean is the best estimate of the population mean. An interval estimate is an estimate regarding an interval or range of values of a variable that the researcher is attempting to estimate. Along with the magnitude of the interval, we also state the probability that the interval will take in the true value of the population mean, that is, the confidence level. The interval is the confidence interval.

The researcher who is interested in estimating proportions rather than means uses the sampling distribution of the proportion. The sampling distribution of the proportion is a relative frequency distribution of the sample proportions of a large number of samples of a given size drawn from a particular population. The standard error of a sampling distribution of proportions is computed as follows:

$$S_p = \sqrt{\frac{P(1-P)}{n}}$$

The formula for calculating the required sample size for situations that involve the estimation of a mean is as follows:

$$n = \frac{Z^2 \sigma^2}{E^2}$$

To calculate sample size, the following are required: specification of the acceptable level of sampling error *(E)*, specification of the acceptable level of confidence in standard errors or *Z* values, and an estimate of the population standard deviation. To calculate the required sample size for problems involving proportions, we use the following formula:

$$n = \frac{Z^2 [P(1 - P)]}{E^2}$$

Sample size calculation can be enhanced by taking into account the probability of not making a Type II error. This is the error of saying there is no difference between two numbers in a statistical sense when there is, in fact, a difference. The probability of not making a Type II error is called statistical power. The standard calculation assumes a power of 50 percent. That value can be varied if higher or lower levels of power are appropriate for a given problem.

Key Terms & Definitions

Normal distribution A continuous distribution that is bell-shaped and symmetrical about the mean—mean, median, and mode being equal. Sixty-eight percent of the observations fall within plus or minus one standard deviation of the mean, approximately 95 percent fall within plus or minus two standard deviations, and approximately 99.5 percent fall within plus or minus three standard deviations.

Central limit theorem A distribution of a large number of sample means or sample proportions that approximate a normal distribution, regardless of the actual distribution of the population from which they were drawn.

Standard normal distribution A normal distribution with a mean of zero and a standard deviation of one.

Standard deviation A measure of dispersion calculated by subtracting the mean of a series from each value in a series, squaring each result, summing them, dividing the sum by the number of items minus 1, and taking the square root of this value.

Population distribution A frequency distribution of all the elements of a population.

Sample distribution A frequency distribution of all the elements of an individual sample.

Sampling distribution of the sample mean A frequency distribution of the means of many samples drawn from a particular population, which has a normal distribution.

Standard error of the mean The standard deviation of a distribution of sample means.

Point estimate Inference regarding the sampling error associated with a particular estimate of a population value.

Interval estimate Inference regarding the likelihood that a population value will fall within a certain range.

Confidence level The probability that a particular confidence interval will include the true population value.

Sampling distribution of the proportion A frequency distribution of the proportions of many samples drawn from a particular population which has a normal distribution.

Allowable sampling error The amount of sampling error a researcher is willing to accept.

Population standard deviation The standard deviation of a variable for an entire population.

Finite population correction factor (FPC) An adjustment to the required sample size that is made in those cases in which the sample is expected to be equal to 5 percent or more of the total population.

Statistical power The probability of not making a Type II error.

Questions for Review & Critical Thinking

1. Explain why the determination of sample size is a financial, statistical, and managerial issue.
2. Discuss and give examples of three methods for determining sample size.
3. A marketing researcher analyzing the fast-food industry noticed that the average amount spent at a fast-food restaurant in California was \$3.30, and the standard deviation was \$.40. Yet in Georgia, the average amount spent was \$3.25 with a standard deviation of \$.10. What do these statistics tell us about fast-food consumption expenditures in these two states?
4. Distinguish between population, sample, and sampling distributions.
5. What is the finite population correction factor? Why is it used? When should it be used?

6. Assume that previous fast-food research has shown that 80 percent of the consumers like curlicue french fries. The researcher wishes to have an error of 6 percent or less and be 95 percent confident of an estimate to be made about curlicue french-fry consumption from a survey. What sample size is necessary?
7. A researcher at Disney World knows that 60 percent of the patrons like roller-coaster rides. The researcher wishes to have an error of no more than 2 percent and to be 90 percent confident about attitudes toward a new roller-coaster ride. What sample size is required?
8. You are in charge of planning a chili cook-off. You must make sure that there are plenty of samples for the patrons of the cook-off. The following standards have been set: a confidence level of 99 percent and an error of less than 4 ounces per cooking team. Last year's cook-off had a standard deviation in the amount of chili cooked of 3 ounces. What would be the necessary sample size?
9. You are doing a survey of beer prices during spring break at Daytona Beach. Last year the average price per six-pack for premium beer was $3.00 with a standard deviation of $.20. Your survey requires a 95 percent confidence level with an acceptable level of error of $.10 per six-pack. Calculate the required sample size.
10. Based on a client's requirements of a confidence interval of 99 percent and an acceptable sampling error of 2 percent, a sample size of 500 was calculated. The cost to the client would be $20,000. The client replies that the budget for this project is $17,000. What are the alternatives?

Working the Net

What size samples would you need to have a statistical power of 70 percent for being able to detect a difference of 5 percent between the estimated percentages of recent CD buyers in two independent samples? Assume an expected percentage in the range of 50 percent and an alpha error of 5 percent. Use the sample-size calculator at www.dssresearch.com/SampleSize/default.asp to get your answer. Instructions for using this calculator are provided in the Statistical Power section.

Real-Life Research

Sky Kitchens

Sky Kitchens is the second largest airline caterer in the United States, providing nearly all the meals for passengers on three major airlines and several small commuter airlines. As part of a total quality management (TQM) program, its largest airline client, Continental Air, has recently met with representatives of Sky Kitchens to discuss a customer satisfaction program that it is planning to implement.

As part of its overall customer satisfaction program, Continental Air plans to interview a sample of its customers four times a year. As part of the survey, it intends to ask customers to rate the quality of meals provided. It intends to ask customers to rate meals on a 1 to 10 scale, where 1 means poor and 10 means excellent. It has just completed a benchmark study of 1,000 customers. In that study, meals received an average rating of 8.7 on the 10-point scale with a standard deviation of 1.65. Continental has indicated that it wants Sky Kitchens to guarantee a level of satisfaction of 8.5 in the first quarterly survey to be conducted in three months. For its quarterly surveys, it plans to use a sample size of 500. In the new contract with Sky Kitchens, Continental wants to write in a clause that will penalize Sky Kitchens $50,000 for each one-tenth of a point below an average 8.5 on the satisfaction scale on the next survey.

Questions

1. What is the 95 percent confidence interval for the estimated satisfaction level in the benchmark survey? What is the 99.5 percent confidence interval?
2. Assume that the upcoming first quarterly satisfaction survey shows an average rating on satisfaction with meals of 8.4. Compute the 95 percent confidence interval and the 99.5 confidence interval.
3. If you were negotiating for Sky Kitchens, how would you respond to Continental regarding the penalty clause?

CD Opportunity

1. Don't forget to use the PowerPoint presentation on your CD to help you review chapter concepts.
2. The Ethical Dilemmas exercises for this part will help you understand how ethical issues are involved in questionnaire design and determining sample size. The Marketing Research Across the Organization exercises on your CD will help you deepen your understanding of how data acquisition is affected by different areas of the firm.

PART *four*

Data Analysis

13

Data Processing, Basic Data Analysis, and the Statistical Testing of Differences

14

Correlation and Regression Analysis

Check it out!

Remember to visit http://mcdaniel.swcollege.com for information to help you with the material in Part Four. MR Online in the Resource Center of http://marketing.swcollege.com can also help you review for your final exam!

CHAPTER *thirteen*

Data Processing, Basic Data Analysis, and the Statistical Testing of Differences

Learning Objectives

1. *To develop an understanding of the importance and nature of quality control checks*

2. *To understand the data-entry process and data-entry alternatives*

3. *To learn how surveys are tabulated and cross-tabulated*

4. *To understand how to state and test hypotheses*

5. *To describe several common statistical tests of differences*

Adam Deem is spending this semester working as an intern for City National Bank. He has been assigned the job of conducting an image survey among current small business customers of the bank. This is a customer segment that the bank suspects is being underserved by both City National and its competitors. First, he conducted focus groups to identify the issues of greatest importance to small business firms. He then used the results of the focus groups to design a quantitative survey to find out how City National measured up on these key issues in comparison to other selected banks. The survey contained both closed-ended and open-ended questions.

Adam used the survey on a random sample of current customers drawn from the bank's database. The survey did not identify City National as the sponsor. Adam mailed 1,000 surveys, along with a cover letter explaining the purpose of the survey, that all individual responses would be confidential, and that a $25 gratuity would be paid to those who responded. He sent a reminder card one week after the initial mailing, and a second letter and copy of the questionnaire two weeks after the initial mailing. It is now four weeks after the initial mailing and 487 surveys have been returned. Returns have slowed to a trickle and the bank manager has decided to cut off data collection and have Adam move on to processing the returned surveys, tabulating the responses, analyzing the results, and preparing the written report.

Adam has not given much thought to this phase of the work, since he has been involved with completing the questionnaire and getting the various mailings out the door. His problems are how to transfer all the information from the paper survey into a computer and what to do with it after that. In particular, he is concerned with the problems associated with summarizing the responses to the open-ended questions. How can he get the information into a computer, code the open-ended questions, tabulate the responses, and all the rest? What software should he use? What should the tables look like? What statistical tests, if any, should he use? What about comparing City National's image across subgroups? ■

Look at the variety of statistical tests offered by SPSS to analyze data at

http://www.spss.com

The material in this chapter answers these and other questions. Consider the problems Adam faces after you have finished reading the chapter. At this point, all data collection has been completed. The researcher is now confronted with large stacks of anywhere from a few hundred to several thousand surveys, each ranging from a few pages to 20 or more. A recent study completed by the authors involved 1,300 ten-page questionnaires. This amounted to a stack of paper nearly 3 feet high and 13,000 pages. How does a researcher transform all the information contained in 13,000 pages of completed questionnaires into a form that permits the summarization necessary for detailed analysis? At one extreme, the researcher could read all of the interviews, make notes while reading them, and draw various conclusions from this review of the questionnaires. The folly of this approach is fairly obvious. Instead of this haphazard and inefficient approach, professional researchers follow a five-step procedure for data analysis:

1. validation and editing (quality control)
2. coding
3. data entry
4. machine cleaning data
5. tabulation and statistical analysis.

Each of these five steps is discussed in detail in this chapter.

Step One: Validation and Editing

The purpose of this step is to make sure that all of the telephone, door-to-door, mall intercept, or other personal interviews were actually conducted as specified (validation) and that the questionnaires were filled out properly and completely (editing). Researchers must be sure that the research results on which they are basing their recommendations reflect the true responses of target consumers.

Validation

validation The process of ascertaining that interviews actually were conducted as specified.

The first step is to determine, to the extent possible, that each questionnaire represents a valid interview. Here we are using the term *valid* in a different sense than in Chapter 9, where *validity* was defined as the extent to which a measurement measures what it is supposed to measure. Here, **validation** means determining that all interviews were conducted properly. The goal is to detect interviewer fraud or failure to follow key instructions. In the various questionnaire examples presented throughout the text, there is almost always a place to record the respondent's name, address, and telephone number. This information is ordinarily not used in the data analysis. It is collected only to provide a basis for validation.

Professional researchers know that interviewer cheating is common. Studies have documented the existence of various types of interviewer falsification.

For this reason, validation is an integral and necessary step in the data-processing stage of a marketing research project.

After all of the interviews are completed, a research firm representative recontacts by telephone a certain percentage of the respondents surveyed by each interviewer. This applies to door-to-door, mall intercept, and telephone surveys. Normally this percentage ranges from 10 to 20 percent. Telephone validation typically covers five areas:

1. Was the person actually interviewed?
2. Did the person who was interviewed actually qualify to be interviewed, according to the screening questions on the survey? For example, the interview may have required that the interviewee be from a family with an annual household income of $25,000 or more. During validation, the respondent would again be asked whether the family's annual household income was $25,000 or more.
3. Was the interview conducted in the required manner? For example, a mall survey should have been conducted in the designated mall. Was this particular respondent actually interviewed in the mall or someplace else, such as a restaurant or a social gathering? The researcher needs to be sure that all data were collected in the prescribed manner.
4. Did the interviewer cover the entire survey? Sometimes interviewers recognize that the respondent is in a hurry and does not have time to complete the entire survey. Respondents for the particular survey may be difficult to find, so the interviewer may be motivated to ask this respondent a few questions at the beginning and a few at the end, and then fake the rest of the interview. Validation for this particular problem involves asking respondents whether they were asked various questions from different points in the interview.
5. Finally, validation normally involves checking for other kinds of problems. Was the interviewer courteous? Did the interviewer speculate about the client's identity or the purpose of the survey? Was the interviewer neat in appearance? Does the respondent have any other comments about the interviewer or the interview experience?

Tabulating customer surveys accurately is critical to obtaining a true assessment of customer satisfaction.

Editing

Whereas validation involves checking for interviewer cheating and failure to follow instructions, **editing** involves checking for interviewer and respondent mistakes. Questionnaires are normally edited at least twice before data entry. First, they are edited by the field service firm that conducted the interviews, and then they are edited by the marketing research firm that hired the field

Editing The process of checking for interviewer mistakes.

service firm. The editing process involves manually checking for a number of problems, including the following:

1. *Determining whether the interviewer failed to ask certain questions or record answers to them.* For example, in the questionnaire shown in Figure 13.1, no answer was recorded for question 19. According to the structure of the questionnaire, all respondents should have been asked this question. However, no response was recorded. Also note that in this case the respondent's name does not give a clear indication of gender. The purpose of the first edit—the field edit—is to identify these types of problems while there is still time to recontact the respondent and determine the appropriate answer for the question that was not asked. This may also be done at the second edit—the edit by the marketing research firm—but in many instances there may not be time to recontact the respondent, and the interview may have to be discarded.

Skip pattern Requirement to pass over certain questions if a respondent gives a particular answer to a previous question.

2. *Checking questionnaires to make sure that skip patterns were followed.* A **skip pattern** is a requirement to pass over certain questions if the respondent gives a particular answer to a previous question. For example, look at question 2 on the questionnaire shown in Figure 13.1. According to the skip pattern, if the answer to this question is "Very unlikely" or "Don't know," then the interviewer should skip to question 16. Researchers need to make sure that the interviewer followed instructions. Sometimes, particularly during the first few interviews that they conduct on a particular study, interviewers may get mixed up and skip when they actually should not, or fail to skip when they should.
3. *Checking responses to open-ended questions.* Marketing researchers and their clients are usually very interested in the responses to open-ended questions. The quality of the response, or at least what was recorded, is an excellent indicator of the competence of the interviewer who recorded the response. Interviewers are normally trained to record responses verbatim and not to paraphrase or insert their own language. They are also normally instructed to "probe" the initial response.

   Figure 13.2 on page 393 shows examples of the various deficiencies just outlined. Part A of Figure 13.2 shows an example of how an interviewer has paraphrased and interpreted a response to an open-ended question. Typically, interviewers do not know the purposes of the study, know the sponsor of the study, or have the experience or training necessary to interpret respondent reactions.

   Part B of Figure 13.2 shows the result of an interviewer's failure to probe a response. The response is useless from a decision-making perspective. It comes as no surprise that the respondent goes to Burger King most often because he or she likes it.

   Part C of Figure 13.2 shows how an initial meaningless response can be expanded to something useful by means of proper probing. A proper probe to the answer "Because I like it" would be something like "Why do you like it?" or "What do you like about it?" Now the respondent indicates that he or she goes there most often because it is the most convenient fast-food restaurant to his or her place of work.

Figure 13.1

Sample Questionnaire

CONSUMER SURVEY
Cellular Telephone Survey Questionnaire

Long Branch—Asbury, N.J.

Date 7-05-00 (1–3) 001

Respondent Telephone Number 201-555-2322

Hello. My name is Sally with POST Research. May I please speak with the male or female head of the household?

IF INDIVIDUAL NOT AVAILABLE, RECORD NAME AND CALLBACK INFORMATION ON SAMPLING FORM.

(WHEN MALE/FEMALE HEAD OF HOUSEHOLD COMES TO PHONE): Hello, my name is ____________, with POST Research. Your number was randomly selected and I am not trying to sell you anything. I simply want to ask you a few questions about a new type of telephone service.

1. First, how many telephone calls do you make during a typical day? (04)

   0–2 1
   3–5 2
   6–10 . . . . (3)
   11–15 4
   16–20 5
   More than 20 6
   Don't know 7

Now, let me tell you about a new service called cellular mobile telephone service, which is completely wireless. You can get either a portable model that may be carried in your coat pocket or a model mounted in any vehicle. You will be able to receive calls and make calls, no matter where you are. Although cellular phones are wireless, the voice quality is similar to your present phone service. This is expected to be a time-saving convenience for household use.

This new cellular mobile phone service may soon be widely available in your area.

2. Now, let me explain to you the cost of this wireless service. Calls will cost 26 cents a minute plus normal toll charges. In addition, the monthly minimum charge for using the service will be $7.50 and rental of a cellular phone will be about $40. Of course, you can buy the equipment instead of leasing it. At this price, do you think you would be very likely, somewhat likely, somewhat unlikely, or very unlikely to subscribe to the new phone service? (05)

   Very likely 1
   Somewhat likely . . . . (2)
   Somewhat unlikely 3
   Very unlikely . . . . . .(GO TO QUESTION 16) 4
   Don't know . . . . . .(GO TO QUESTION 16) 5

INTERVIEWER—IF "VERY UNLIKELY" OR "DON'T KNOW," GO TO QUESTION 16.

continued

Figure 13.1

Sample Questionnaire, *continued*

3. Do you think it is likely that your employer will furnish you with one of these phones for your job?

(06)

No . . . .(GO TO QUESTION 5) 1
Don't know . . . .(GO TO QUESTION 5) 2
Yes . . . .(CONTINUE) . . . . .③

INTERVIEWER—IF NO OR DON'T KNOW, GO TO QUESTION 5; OTHERWISE CONTINUE.

4. If your employer did furnish you with a wireless phone, would you also purchase one for household use?

(07)

Yes . . . .(CONTINUE) . . . . .①
No . . . .(GO TO QUESTION 16) 2
Don't Know . . . .(GO TO QUESTION 16) 3

5. Please give me your best estimate of the number of mobile phones your household would use (write in "DK" for Don't Know).

Number of Units ______01______ (08–09)

6. Given that cellular calls made or received will cost 26 cents a minute plus normal toll charges during weekdays, how many calls on the average would you expect to make in a typical weekday?

RECORD NUMBER ______06______ (10–11)

7. About how many minutes would the average cellular call last during the week?

RECORD NUMBER ______05______ (12–13)

8. Weekend cellular calls made or received will cost 08 cents per minute plus normal toll charges. Given this, about how many cellular calls on the average would you expect to make in a typical Saturday or Sunday?

RECORD NUMBER ______00______ (14–15)

9. About how many minutes would the average cellular call last on Saturday or Sunday?

RECORD NUMBER ____________ (16–17)

10. You may recall from my previous description that two types of cellular phone units will be available. The vehicle phone may be installed in any vehicle. The portable phone will be totally portable-it can be carried in a briefcase, purse, or coat pocket. The totally portable phones may cost about 25 percent more and may have a more limited transmitting range in some areas than the vehicle phone. Do you think you would prefer portable or vehicle phones if you were able to subscribe to this service?

Portable 1
Vehicle . . . . .②
Both 3
Don't Know 4

Figure 13.1

Sample Questionnaire, *continued*

11. Would you please tell me whether you, on the average, would use a mobile phone about once a week, less than once a week, or more than once a week from the following geographic locations.

	Less than Once a Week	Once a Week	More than Once a Week	Never	
Monmouth County, NJ (IF NEVER, SKIP TO QUESTION 12)	1	2	③	4	(19)
Sandy Hook	1	2	3	④	(20)
Keansburg	①	2	3	④	(21)
Atlantic Highlands	①	2	③	4	(22)
Matawan–Middletown	1	2	3	4	(23)
Redbank	1	②	3	4	(24)
Holmdel	1	2	③	④	(25)
Eatontown	1	2	3	④	(26)
Longbranch	1	2	3	④	(27)
Freehold	1	2	3	④	(28)
Manalapan	1	2	3	④	(29)
Cream Ridge	1	2	3	4	(30)
Belmar	1	2	3	4	(31)
Point Pleasant	1	2	③	4	(32)

I'm going to describe to you a list of possible extra features of the proposed cellular service. Each option I'm going to describe will cost not more than $3.00 a month per phone. Would you please tell me if you would be very interested, interested, or uninterested in each feature:

	Very Interested	Interested	Uninterested	
12. Call forwarding (ability to transfer any call coming in to your mobile phone to any other phone).	①	2	3	(33)
13. No answer transfer (if your phone is unanswered, this service redirects calls to another number).	1	2	③	(34)
14. Call waiting-signals you that another person is trying to call you while you are using your phone.	1	②	3	(35)
15. Voice mail box—permits calls to be transferred to a recording machine that will take the caller's message and relay it to you at a later time. This service will be provided at $5.00 per month.	1	2	③	(36)

continued

Figure 13.1

Sample Questionnaire,
continued

16. What is your age group: (READ BELOW) (37)

    Under 25 1
    25–44 . . . . ②
    45–64 3
    65 and over 4
    Refused, no answer, or don't know 5

17. What is your occupation? (38)

    Manager, Official, or Proprietor . . . . ①
    Professional (Doctors, Lawyers, Architects, etc.) 2
    Technical (Engineers, Computer Programmers, Draftsmen, etc.) . . 3
    Office Worker/Clerical 4
    Sales 5
    Skilled Worker or Foreman 6
    Unskilled Worker 7
    Teacher 8
    Homemaker, Student, Retired 9
    Not now employed X
    Refused . . . . Y

18. Into which category did your total family income fall in 1992? Is it: (39)

    Under $15,000 1
    $15,000–$24,999 2
    $25,000–$49,999 3
    $50,000–$74,999 4
    $75,000 and over . . . . ⑤
    Refused, no answer, don't know 6

19. (INTERVIEWER—RECORD SEX OF RESPONDENT): (40)

    Male 1
    Female 2

20. May I have your name? My office calls about 10 percent of the people I talk with to verify that I have conducted the interview.

    Gave name 1
    Refused 2

Jordan Beasley
Name

Thank you for your time. Have a good day.

A. Example of interviewer's improper recording of a response to an open-ended question.

Question:	Why do you go to Burger King most often among fast-food/ quick-service restaurants? PROBE
Response recorded:	*The consumer seemed to think Burger King had better-tasting food and better-quality ingredients.*

B. Example of interviewer's failure to probe a response.

Question:	Same as Part A.
Response recorded:	*Because I like it.*

C. Example of interviewer's proper recording and probing.

Question:	Same as Part A.
Response recorded:	*Because I like it. (P)* I like it and I go there most often because it is the closest place to where I work. (AE)** No.*

*(P) is interviewer mark indicating he or she has probed response.

**(AE) is interviewer shorthand for "anything else." This gives the respondent an opportunity to expand the original answer.

Figure 13.2

Recording Open-Ended Questions

The person doing the editing must make judgment calls about substandard responses to open-ended questions. This individual will have to decide at what point particular answers are so limited as to be useless. Again, it may be possible to recontact respondents and re-ask questions with useless responses.

Editing is extremely tedious and time-consuming—imagine reading through the 13,000 pages of interviews in the example cited earlier. However, editing is an important step in the data-processing stage.

Step Two: Coding

Coding Defined

Coding refers to the process of grouping and assigning numeric codes to the various responses to a particular question. Most questions on surveys are closed ended and precoded. This means that numeric codes have been assigned to the various responses on the questionnaire itself. All closed-ended questions should be precoded.

Coding The process of grouping and assigning numeric codes to the various responses to a question.

Open-ended questions are another matter. They were stated as open-ended questions because the researcher either had no idea what answers to expect or wanted a richer response than is possible with a closed-ended question. As with editing, the process of coding responses to open-ended questions is tedious and time-consuming. In addition, the procedure is, to some degree, subjective. For these reasons there is some tendency to avoid open-ended questions, if possible.

The Coding Process

There are four steps in the process of coding responses to open-ended questions:[1]

1. *Listing responses.* Coders at the research firm prepare lists of the actual responses to each open-ended question on the survey. In studies of a few hundred respondents, all responses may be listed. With large samples, responses given by a sample of all respondents will be listed. The listing may be done as part of editing or as a separate step. It is often done by the same individuals who edited the questionnaires.
2. *Consolidating responses.* A sample list of responses to an open-ended question is provided in Figure 13.3. An examination of this list indicates that a number of the responses can be interpreted to mean essentially the same thing; for example, the first three responses and probably the fourth. Therefore, they can be appropriately consolidated into a single category. After going through this process of consolidation, we end up with the list shown in Figure 13.4. This is the final consolidated list of responses. A number of subjective decisions had to be made to derive this final list. For example, does response number 4 belong in category 1 or should it have its own category? These decisions normally are made by a qualified research analyst and frequently involve client input.

Figure 13.3

Sample of Responses to Open-ended Question

Question: Why do you drink that brand of beer?
(BRAND MENTIONED IN PREVIOUS QUESTION)

Sample Responses:

1. Because it tastes better.
2. It has the best taste.
3. I like the way it tastes.
4. I don't like the heavy taste of other beers.
5. It is the cheapest.
6. I buy whatever beer is on sale. It is on sale most of the time.
7. It doesn't upset my stomach the way other brands do.
8. Other brands give me headaches. This one doesn't.
9. It has always been my brand.
10. I have been drinking it for over 20 years.
11. It is the brand that most of the guys at work drink.
12. All my friends drink it.
13. It is the brand my wife buys at the grocery store.
14. It is my wife's/husband's favorite brand.
15. I have no idea.
16. Don't know.
17. No particular reason.

Response Category Descriptor	Response Items From Figure 13.3 Included	Assigned Numeric Code
Tastes better/like taste/tastes better than others	1, 2, 3, 4	1
Low/lower price	5, 6	2
Does not cause headache, stomach problems	7, 8	3
Long-term use, habit	9, 10	4
Friends drink it/influence of friends	11, 12	5
Wife/husband drinks/buys it	13, 14	6
Don't know	15, 16, 17	7

Figure 13.4

Consolidated Response Categories and Codes for Open-Ended Responses from Beer Study Introduced in Figure 13.3

3. *Setting codes.* After the final consolidated list of responses has been derived, numeric codes are assigned to each category on the list. Code assignment for the sample beer study question is shown in Figure 13.4.
4. *Entering codes.* After listing responses, consolidating responses, and setting codes, the final step is the actual entry of codes. Entering codes involves several substeps:
   a. Read responses to individual open-ended questions on questionnaires.
   b. Match individual responses with consolidated list of response categories developed in step 2.
   c. Get the numeric code for the category into which the particular response is classified.

Step Three: Data Entry

Intelligent Versus Dumb Entry

Most data entry is done by means of intelligent entry systems. **Intelligent data entry** refers to the ability of the data-entry devices or their connected computers to check certain information being entered. The data entry system can be programmed to avoid certain types of errors at the point of data entry: entry of invalid or wild codes and violation of skip patterns.

Intelligent data entry The logical checking of information being entered into a data-entry device by that machine or one connected to it.

Consider question 2 on the questionnaire in Figure 13.1. The five valid answers have the associated numeric codes 1 to 5. An intelligent data-entry system programmed for valid codes would permit the data-entry operator to enter only codes 1 to 5 in the field reserved for the response to this question. If an attempt is made to enter a code other than the ones that have been defined as valid, the device will inform the data-entry operator in some manner that there is a problem. The data-entry device, for example, might beep and display a message on the screen stating that the code is invalid. Also it will not advance to the next field. Under this type of entry, of course, it is possible to incorrectly enter a "3" rather than the correct answer "2." Referring again to Figure 13.1, we see that if the answer to question 2 is "Very unlikely" or "Don't know," then the data-entry operator should skip to question 16. An intelligent data-entry device will make this skip automatically.

The Data-Entry Process

The validated, edited, and coded questionnaires have now been given to a data-entry operator seated in front of a personal computer or computer terminal. The data-entry software system has been programmed for intelligent entry. The actual data-entry process is ready to begin. Normally, the data will be entered directly from the questionnaires. Data normally are not transferred from questionnaires to computer coding sheets by professional marketing researchers, because experience has shown that a large number of errors are made in the process of transposing data from the questionnaires to coding sheets. The process of going directly from the questionnaire to the data-entry device and the associated storage medium has proven to be more accurate and efficient. To better understand the mechanics of the process, refer again to the questionnaire in Figure 13.1. Consider the following points:

- In the upper right-hand corner of the questionnaire, the number 001 is written. This number uniquely identifies the particular questionnaire, and this should be the first questionnaire in the stack that the data-entry operator is preparing to enter. This code is an important point of reference, because it will permit the data-entry staff to refer back to the original input document if errors are identified in the data input for questionnaire number 001.
- Next to the handwritten number 001 is 1–3 in parentheses. This tells the data-entry operator that 001 should be entered into fields 1–3 of the data record. Also note that throughout the questionnaire, the numbers in parentheses indicate the proper location on the data record for the circled code or answer to each question.
- Question 1 has the number 04 in parentheses associated with the codes for the answers to the question. The answer to this question would be entered in field 04 of the data record.
- In regard to open-ended questions, refer to Figure 13.5. Note the number 2 written next to the number 48 in parentheses. As with closed-ended questions, the number in parentheses refers to the field on the data record where the response code for this question should be entered. For example, a 2 should be entered in field 48 of the data record associated with this questionnaire.

Figure 13.5

Example Questionnaire Setup for Open-Ended Questions

37. Why do you drink that brand of beer (BRAND MENTIONED IN PREVIOUS QUESTION)? (48) 2

Because it's cheaper (P) Nothing. (AE) Nothing.

As you can see from this discussion, the questionnaire codes (numbers associated with different answers to questions) and fields (places on the data record where codes for answers go) correlate with those on the data record.

Optical Scanning

An **optical scanner** is a data-processing device that can "read" responses on questionnaires. It has been widely used in schools and universities as an efficient way to capture and score responses to multiple-choice questions. However, until recently, its use in marketing research has been limited. This limited use can be attributed to two factors: set-up costs and the need to record all responses with a soft-leaded pencil. Set-up costs included the need for special paper, special ink in the printing process, and very precise placement of the bubbles for recording responses. The break-even point—the point at which the savings in data-entry costs just equal the set-up costs—was in the 10,000 to 12,000 survey range. Therefore, for most surveys, scanning was not feasible until recently.

Optical scanner A data-processing device that can "read" responses on questionnaires.

However, changes in scanning technology and the advent of personal computers have changed this equation. Now, questionnaires prepared with any one of a number of Windows word-processing software packages and printed on a laser printer or through a standard printing process, using almost any type of paper, can be readily scanned using the appropriate software and a small scanner, costing about $2,000, attached to a personal computer. In addition, the latest technology permits respondents to fill out a survey using almost any type of writing implement (any pencil, ballpoint pen, roller ball, ink pen, and so on). This eliminates the need to provide respondents with a soft-leaded pencil and greatly simplifies the process for mail surveys. Finally, using the latest technology, it is not necessary for respondents to carefully shade in the entire circle or square next to their response choice. They can shade it in, put a check, put an X, or put any type of mark in the circle or square provided for their response choice.[2]

As a result of these developments, the use of scannable surveys is growing dramatically. When you expect more than 400 to 500 surveys to be completed, scannable surveys can be cost-effective.

Step Four: Machine Cleaning Data

At this point, the data from all questionnaires have been entered and stored in the computer. It is time to do final error checking before proceeding to the tabulation and statistical analysis of the survey results. Most colleges have one or more statistical packages available for the tabulation and statistical analysis of data. STATISTICA®, SAS (Statistical Analysis System), or SPSS (Statistical Package for the Social Sciences) have proven to be the most popular computer statistical packages.

Regardless of which computer package is used to tabulate the data, the first step is to do final error checking, or what is sometimes referred to as **machine cleaning of data.** This may be done in one or both of two ways: error-checking routines and marginal reports.

Machine cleaning of data
A final computerized error check of data.

Error-checking routines
Computer programs that accept instructions from the user to check for logical errors in the data.

Marginal report
A computer-generated table of the frequencies of the responses to each question to monitor entry of valid codes and correct use of skip patterns.

Some computer programs permit users to write **error-checking routines.** These routines include statements to check for various logistical errors. For example, if a particular field on the data records should only have a 1 or a 2 code, a logical statement can be written to check for the presence of any other code in that field. Some of the more sophisticated packages generate reports indicating how many times a particular condition was violated and list the data records on which it was violated. With this list the user can refer to the original questionnaires and determine the appropriate values.

Another approach to machine cleaning often used for error checking is the **marginal report,** which is used to monitor the entry of valid codes and correct the use of skip patterns. A sample marginal report is shown in Table 13.1. The rows of this report are the fields of the data record. The columns show the frequencies with which each possible value was encoun-

Table 13.1

Sample Marginal Report (Marginal Counts of 300 Records)

Col	1	2	3	4	5	6	7	8	9	10	11	12	Bal	Tot
111	100	100	1	0	0	0	0	0	0	99	0	0	0	300
112	30	30	30	30	30	30	30	30	30	0	0	0	0	300
113	30	30	30	30	30	30	30	30	30	30	0	0	0	300
114	67	233	0	0	0	0	0	0	0	0	0	0	0	300
115	192	108	0	0	0	0	0	0	0	0	0	0	0	300
116	108	190	0	0	0	0	0	0	0	0	0	2	0	300
117	13	35	8	0	2	136	95	7	2	0	0	0	2	298
118	0	0	0	0	0	0	0	0	0	0	0	2	298	2
119	29	43	12	1	2	48	50	6	4	1	0	0	104	196
1111	6	16	6	1	1	10	18	4	2	0	0	0	236	64
1113	3	4	1	1	0	1	2	0	1	0	0	0	288	12
1115	0	0	0	1	1	0	0	2	0	0	0	0	296	4
1117	24	2	22	0	1	239	9	2	0	0	0	0	1	299
1118	0	0	0	0	0	0	0	0	0	0	0	0	299	1
1119	4	49	6	0	0	81	117	5	2	0	0	0	36	264
1120	0	0	0	0	0	0	0	0	0	0	0	36	264	36
1121	5	60	6	0	0	84	116	4	3	1	0	0	21	279
1122	0	0	0	0	0	0	0	0	0	0	0	21	279	21
1123	118	182	0	0	0	0	0	0	0	0	0	0	0	300
1124	112	187	0	0	0	0	0	0	0	0	0	0	1	299
1125	47	252	0	0	0	0	0	0	0	0	0	1	0	300
1126	102	198	0	0	0	0	0	0	0	0	0	0	0	300
1127	5	31	5	1	0	33	31	9	1	0	0	0	184	116
1128	0	0	0	0	0	0	0	0	0	0	0	2	298	2
1129	0	3	1	0	0	4	8	2	1	0	0	0	281	19
1131	7	16	3	0	2	60	21	3	0	0	0	0	188	112
1133	1	3	1	0	0	2	3	1	0	0	0	0	289	11

tered in each field. For example, the first row in Table 13.1 shows that in field 1 (column 1) of the data records for this study, there are 100 "1s" recorded, 100 "2s" recorded, 1 "3" recorded, and 99 "10s" recorded. This report permits the user to determine whether invalid codes were entered and whether skip patterns were followed properly. If all the numbers are consistent, there is no need for further cleaning. However, if logical errors are detected, then the appropriate original questionnaires must be located and the corrections must be made in the computer data file.

This is the final error check in the process. When this step is completed, the computer data file should be "clean" and ready for tabulation and statistical analysis. Figure 13.6 on page 400 shows the data for the first 50 respondents out of a total of 400 for the study associated with the questionnaire shown in Figure 13.1. You might note that the apparent gaps in the data are a result of the skip called for in question 4. Also note that the gender data for respondent 001 has been filled in with a 2 for "female."

Step Five: Tabulation and Analysis of Survey Results

At this point the survey results are stored in a computer file and should be free of all logical data entry and interviewer recording error. By *logical errors* we mean violated skip patterns and impossible codes (a 3 was entered when 1 and 2 are the only possible codes). The procedures described previously cannot identify situations in which an interviewer or data-entry operator entered a 2 for a "no" response instead of the correct 1 for a "yes" response. The next step is to tabulate the survey results.

One-Way Frequency Tables

The most basic tabulation is the **one-way frequency table.** An example of this type of table is shown in Table 13.2 on page 401. A one-way frequency table shows the number of respondents who gave each possible answer to each question. Table 13.2 shows that 144 consumers (48 percent) said they would choose a hospital in Fort Worth, 146 (48.7 percent) said they would choose a hospital in Dallas, and 10 people (3.3 percent) said they didn't know which one they would choose. A computer printout will be generated showing one-way frequency tables for every question on the survey. In most instances, this will be the first summary of survey results seen by the research analyst.

One-way frequency table A table showing the number of responses to each answer of a survey question.

In addition to frequencies, one-way frequency tables typically indicate the percentage of those responding to a question that gave each possible response.

Figure 13.6

Printout of Data for the First 50 Respondents for Cellular Telephone Survey (See Figure 13.1)

```
001323101060500  234431132444443132321521
00224                               23412
00334                               49622
00414                               36221
00524                               33312
00634                               22612
00714                               21321
008221  020405031033423244443444422229321
00925                               36311
01044                               23311
01161310240050330134234444434443322330321
012622  014007200733444444444444132330511
013221  0106030603231312333323322123216211
01424                               29321
01514                               40121
01624                               22612
01774                               20622
01854                               34621
01924                               25212
02024                               23622
02114                               16611
02214                               36211
02314                               36221
024131     00101004102213344444444442229611
02524                               26621
026131  010103020312422142224441422322611
02724                               10122
02814                               59622
02924                               39622
03024                               49611
03134                               53621
03234                               32622
03321  01           124444444444442112220211
03424                               32622
035311  0410300430133131131113131211220121
03623230301050201334414433344244232320622
03724                               37622
03814                               40121
03934                               30121
04024                               16121
04124                               26311
04264                               26411
04324                               20321
04414                               26311
04524                               19321
04634                               19222
04724                               29621
04824                               31422
04924                               33121
05014                               21311
```

Table 13.2

One-Way Frequency Table

Q.30 If you or a member of your family were to require hospitalization in the future, and the procedure could be performed in Fort Worth or Dallas, where would you choose to go?

	Total
Total	300 100%
To a hospital in Fort Worth	144 48.0%
To a hospital in Dallas	146 48.7%
Don't know/No response	10 3.3%

Bases for Percentages

When running one-way frequency tables, the researcher must determine the bases to be used for the percentages. There are three choices:

1. *Total respondents.* If 300 people are interviewed, and the decision is to use total respondents as the base for calculating percentages, then the percentages in each one-way frequency table will be based on 300 respondents.
2. *Number of people asked the particular question.* Because most questionnaires have skip patterns, not all respondents will be asked all questions. For example, question 4 on a survey might ask whether the person owns a dog or cat. Assume that 200 respondents indicated they own a dog or a cat. If questions 5 and 6 on that survey should have been asked only of individuals who own a dog or a cat, then question 5 and question 6 should have been asked of only 200 respondents. In most instances, it is appropriate to use 200 as the base for percentages associated with the one-way frequency tables for questions 5 and 6.
3. *Number answering.* An alternative base for computing percentages in one-way frequency tables is the number of people who actually answered a particular question. Under this approach, if 300 people were asked a particular question, but 28 indicated "Don't know" or gave no response to the question, then the base for the percentages would be 272.

Ordinarily, the number of people who were asked a particular question is used as the base for all percentages throughout the tabulations, but there may be special cases where other bases are more appropriate. One-way frequency tables using the three different bases for calculating percentages are shown in Table 13.3 on page 402.

Table 13.3

One-Way Frequency Table with Percentages Shown for Total Respondents, Total Respondents Who Were Asked the Question, and Total Respondents Answering (Gave Response Other Than "Don't Know")

Q.35 Why would you not consider going to St. Paul for hospitalization?

	Total* Respondents	Total Asked	Total Answering
Total	300 100%	60 100%	52 100%
They aren't good/poor service	18 6.0%	18 30.0%	18 34.6%
Fort Worth doesn't have the services/equipment that Dallas does.	17 5.7%	17 28.3%	17 32.7
Fort Worth is too small	6 2.0%	6 10.0%	6 11.6%
Bad publicity	4 1.3%	4 6.7%	4 7.7%
Other	11 3.7%	11 18.3%	11 21.2%
Don't know/no response	8 2.7%	8 13.3%	

*A total of 300 respondents were surveyed. Only 60 answered the question, because in the previous question they said they would not consider going to Fort Worth for hospitalization. The total adds to more than 60 (64) because of multiple answers given by some respondents.

Selecting the Base for One-Way Frequency Tables Showing Results from Multiple-Response Questions

Some questions, by their nature, solicit more than one response from respondents. For example, consumers might be asked to name all the hospitals that come to mind. Most people will be able to name more than one hospital. Therefore, when these answers are tabulated, there will be more responses than people. If 200 consumers are surveyed and the average consumer names three hospitals, then the 200 respondents will have given 600 answers. The question is: Should percentages in one-way frequency tables showing the results to these questions be based on the number of respondents or the number of responses? Common practice among marketing researchers is to compute percentages for multiple-response questions on the basis of the number of respondents. This is based on the logic that we are primarily interested in the proportion of people that gave a particular answer.

Cross-tabulations

Cross-tabulations are likely to be the next step in analysis. They represent a simple-to-understand, yet powerful analytical tool. Many marketing research studies, possibly most, go no further than cross-tabulations in terms of analysis. The idea is to look at the responses to one question in relation to the responses to one or more other questions. Table 13.4 shows a simple cross-tabulation. Here we are examining the relationship between cities consumers are willing to consider for hospitalization and their age. This cross-tabulation shows frequencies and percentages, and the percentages are based on column totals. This table shows an interesting relationship between age and likelihood of choosing Fort Worth or Dallas for hospitalization. Consumers in successively older age groups are increasingly likely to choose Fort Worth and increasingly less likely to choose Dallas.

Cross-tabulation Examination of the responses to one question relative to responses to one or more other questions.

There are a number of considerations regarding the set-up and percentaging of cross-tabulation tables. Some of the more important ones are as follows:

- The previous discussion regarding the selection of the appropriate base for percentages and the appropriate base for the percentaging of tables with multiple responses apply to cross-tabulation tables as well.
- Three different percentages may be calculated for each cell in a cross-tabulation table: column, row, and total percentages. Column percentages are computed on the basis of the column total, row percentages are based on the row total, and total percentages are based on the total for the table. Table 13.5 on page 404 shows a cross-tabulation table with frequencies and all three of the percentages shown for each cell in the table.

Table 13.4

Sample of Cross-tabulation

Q.30 If you or a member of your family were to require hospitalization in the future, and the procedure could be performed in Fort Worth or Dallas, where would you choose to go?

		Age			
	Total	**18–34**	**35–54**	**55–64**	**65 or Over**
Total	300 100%	65 100%	83 100%	51 100%	100 100%
To a hospital in Fort Worth	144 48.0%	21 32.3%	40 48.2%	25 49.0%	57 57.0%
To a hospital in Dallas	146 48.7%	43 66.2%	40 48.2%	23 45.1%	40 40.0%
Don't know/no response	10 3.3%	1 1.5%	3 3.6%	3 5.9%	3 3.0%

Table 13.5

Cross-tabulation Table with Row, Column, and Total Percentages*

Q.34 To which of the following towns and cities would you consider going for hospitalization?

	Total	Male	Female
Total	300 100% 100% 100%	67 100% 22.3% 22.3%	233 100% 77.7% 77.7%
Fort Worth	265 88.3% 100% 88.3%	63 94.0% 23.6% 21.0%	202 86.7% 76.2% 67.3%
Dallas	240 80.0% 100% 80.0%	53 79.1% 22.1% 17.7%	187 80.3% 77.9% 62.3%
Waco	112 37.3% 100% 37.3%	22 32.8% 19.6% 7.3%	90 38.6% 80.4% 30.0%

*Percentages listed are column, row, and total percentages, respectively.

- A common way of setting up cross-tabulation tables is to create a table where the columns represent various factors, such as demographics and lifestyle characteristics, that are expected to be predictors of the state of mind, behavior, or intentions data that are shown as rows of the table. In such tables, percentages are normally calculated on the basis of column totals. This approach permits easy comparisons of the relationship between the state of mind, behavior, or intentions data and the expected predictors, such as sex or age. The question might be: How do people in different age groups differ in regard to the particular factor under examination? An example of this type of table is shown in Table 13.4.

Cross-tabulations provide a powerful and easily understood approach to the summarization and analysis of survey research results. However, it is easy to become swamped by the sheer volume of computer printouts if a careful tabulation plan has not been developed. The cross-tabulation plan should be developed with the research objectives and hypotheses in mind. The results to a particular survey could be cross-tabulated in an almost endless number of ways. This is why it is important for the analyst to exercise some judgment and select from all possibilities those cross-tabulations that are truly responsive to the research objectives of the project.

Most statistical packages can generate cross-tabulations. Later in this chapter we will discuss the chi-square test. This test can be used to determine whether the results in a particular cross-tabulation table are significantly different from what is expected. For example, are the response patterns of men significantly different from those of women? This statistical procedure enables the analyst to determine whether the differences between two groups probably occurred due to chance or probably reflect real differences between the groups.

A more complex cross-tabulation is shown in Table 13.6 on page 406. It was generated using the UNCLE software package. UNCLE was designed with the special needs of marketing researchers in mind and is widely used in the marketing research industry. As indicated, this more complex table is sometimes referred to as a *stub and banner table*. The column headings are referred to as the *banner* and the row titles are referred to as the *stub*. In this table, the relationship between marital status and seven other variables is explored.

Graphic Presentations of Data

"A picture is worth a thousand words." Graphic presentations involve the use of "pictures" rather than tables to present research results. Results, particularly key results, can be presented more powerfully and efficiently by means of graphs. Cross-tabulations and statistical analyses help to identify important findings. Graphs are the best way to present those findings to the users of research.

Graphic representations of your findings can help you effectively communicate your results.

Marketing researchers have probably always known that results could best be presented graphically. However, until recent years the preparation of graphs was tedious, difficult, and time-consuming. The advent of personal computers, coupled with graphics software and laser printers, has changed all of this. The major spreadsheet programs (Lotus 1-2-3 and Excel) have extensive graphics capabilities, particularly in their Windows versions. In addition, programs designed for creating presentations (PowerPoint and Freelance) permit the researcher to create a wide variety of high-quality graphics with ease. With these programs, it is possible to

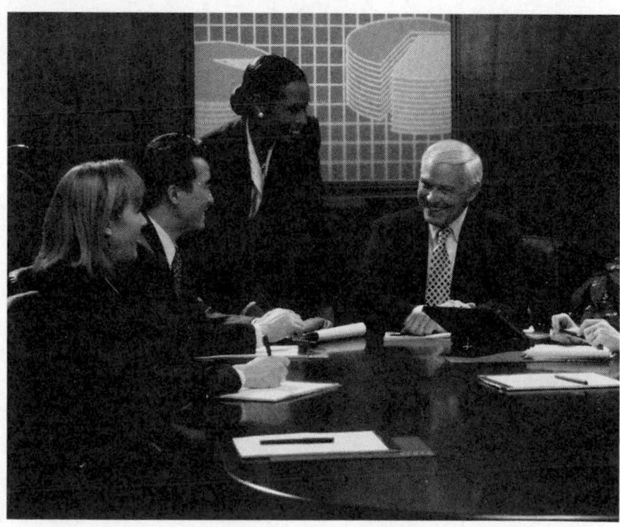

- quickly produce graphs
- display those graphs on the computer screen
- make desired changes and redisplay
- print final copies on a laser printer.

All the graphs shown in this section were produced using a personal computer, a laser printer, and a graphics software package.[3]

Table 13.6

A More Complex Cross-tabulation Table (Sometimes Referred to as a Stub and Banner Table)

North Community College—Anywhere, USA

Q. 1c. Are you single, married, or formerly married?

		Zones			Gender		Age			Race			Family Profiles		Vote History		Registered Voter	
	Total	1	2	3	M	F	18–34	35–54	55 & Over	White	Black	Other	Child <18	Child >18	2–3x	4x or more	Yes	No
Total	300 100%	142 100%	103 100%	55 100%	169 100%	131 100%	48 100%	122 100%	130 100%	268 100%	28 100%	4 100%	101 100%	53 100%	104 100%	196 100%	72 100%	228 100%
Married	228 76%	105 74%	87 84%	36 65%	131 78%	97 74%	36 75%	97 80%	95 73%	207 77%	18 64%	3 75%	82 81%	39 74%	80 77%	148 76%	58 81%	170 75%
Single	5 2%	1 1%	2 2%	2 4%	4 2%	1 1%	2 4%	1 1%	2 2%	5 2%	- -	- -	- -	- -	2 2%	3 2%	1 1%	4 2%
Formerly married	24 8%	11 8%	10 10%	3 5%	12 7%	12 9%	3 6%	9 7%	12 9%	18 7%	6 21%	- -	5 5%	6 11%	10 10%	14 7%	3 4%	21 9%
Refused to answer	43 14%	25 18%	4 4%	14 25%	22 13%	21 16%	7 15%	15 12%	21 16%	38 14%	4 14%	1 25%	14 14%	8 15%	12 12%	31 16%	10 14%	33 14%

Line Charts

Line charts are perhaps the simplest form of graphs. They are particularly useful for presenting a measurement taken at a number of points over time. Monthly sales data for Just Add Water, a retailer of women's swimwear, are shown in Figure 13.7. The data are taken from Just Add Water's 1998 and 1999 sales records.

The results in Figure 13.7 show a similar sales pattern for the two years, with peaks in June and generally low sales in January through March and September through December. Just Add Water is evaluating the sales data to identify product lines that it might add to improve sales in the slower winter and fall periods.

Pie Charts

Pie charts are another frequently used type of graph. They are appropriate for displaying marketing research results in a wide range of situations. Results from a survey of residents of several Gulf Coast metropolitan areas in Louisiana, Mississippi, and Alabama regarding radio music preferences are displayed in Figure 13.8. Note the three-dimensional effect produced by the software.

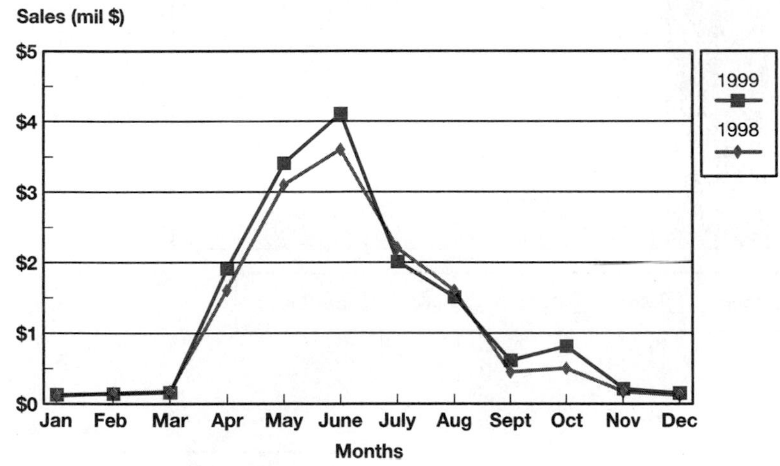

Figure 13.7

1998 and 1999 Sales for Just Add Water (Line Chart)

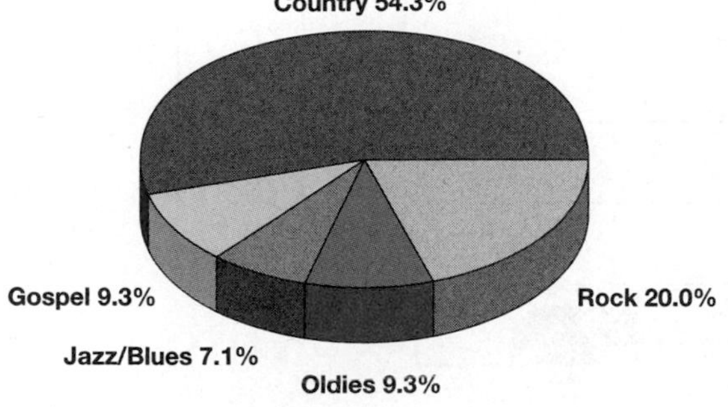

Figure 13.8

Type of Music Listened to Most Often (3-D Pie Chart)

Bar Charts

Bar charts are the most flexible of the three types of graphs discussed in this section. Anything that can be shown in a line graph or a pie chart can also be shown in a bar chart. In addition, many things that cannot be shown, or effectively shown, with other types of graphs can readily be shown with bar charts. Four types of bar charts are discussed here.

1. *Plain bar charts.* As the name suggests, plain bar charts are the simplest form of bar chart. The same information displayed in the previous section in a pie chart is shown in a bar chart in Figure 13.9. Draw your own conclusions about whether the pie chart or the bar chart is the most effective way to present this information. Figure 13.9 is shown as a traditional two-dimensional chart. Many of the software packages available today can take the same information and present it with a three-dimensional effect. The same information is shown with this effect in Figure 13.10. Again, decide which approach is visually most appealing and interesting.

Figure 13.9

Type of Music Listened to Most Often (Plain 2-D Bar Chart)

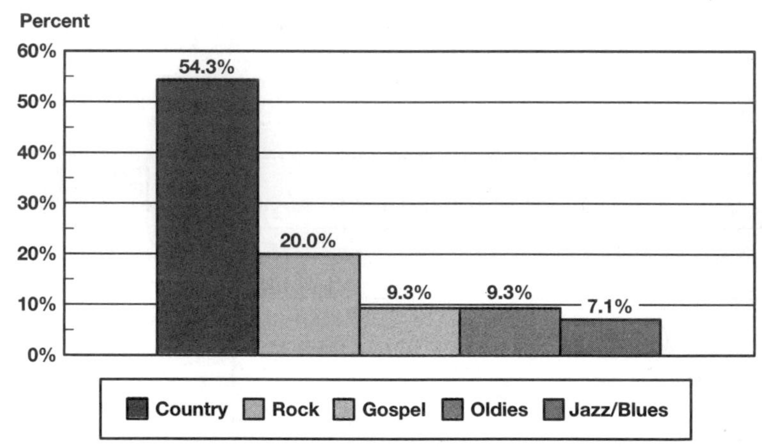

Figure 13.10

Type of Music Listened to Most Often (Plain 3-D Bar Chart)

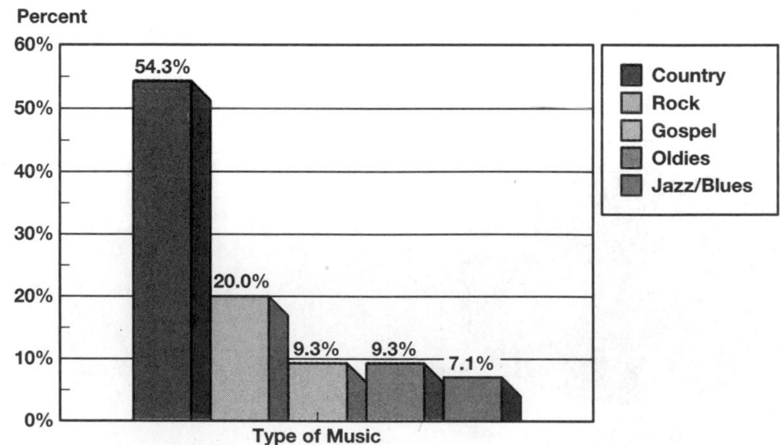

2. *Clustered bar charts.* Clustered bar charts represent the first of three types of bar charts that are useful for showing the results of cross-tabulations. The music preference results cross-tabulated by age are shown in Figure 13.11. The graph shows that country is mentioned most often as the preferred radio music format by those over 35 and those 35 or under. However, the graph also shows that rock is a close second for those 35 or under and least frequently mentioned by both those over 35. The results suggest that if the target audience is those in the 35 or under age group, then a mix of country and rock stations would be appropriate. A focus on country stations would probably be the most efficient approach for those over 35.
3. *Stacked bar charts.* The same information presented in Figure 13.11 is presented in the form of a stacked bar chart in Figure 13.12.
4. *Multiple row, three-dimensional bar charts.* This approach provides what we believe to be the most visually appealing way of presenting cross-tabulation information. The same information displayed in Figures 13.11 and 13.12 is presented in a multiple row, three-dimensional bar chart in Figure 13.13.

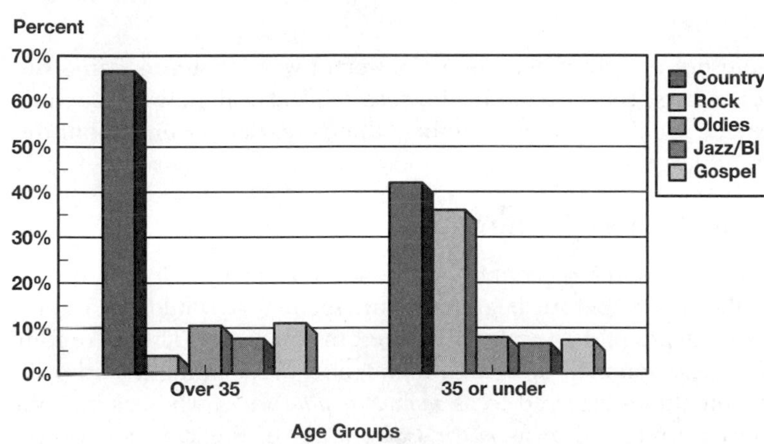

Figure 13.11

Type of Music Listened to Most Often by Age (Clustered Bar Chart)

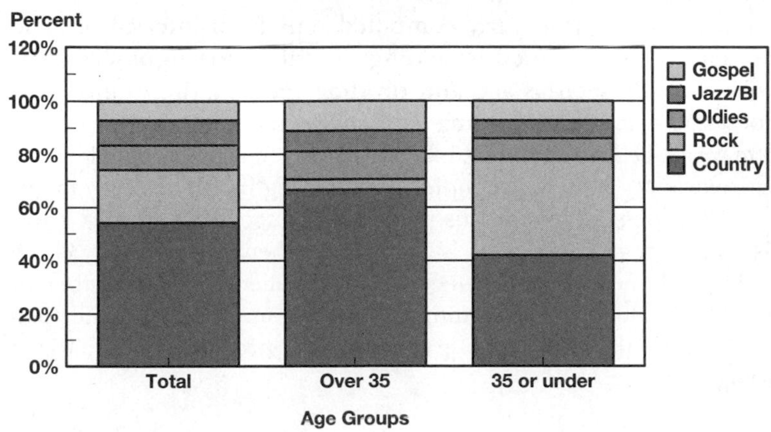

Figure 13.12

Type of Music Listened to Most Often by Age (Stacked Bar Chart)

Figure 13.13

Type of Music Listened to Most Often by Age (Multiple Row, 3-D Bar Chart)

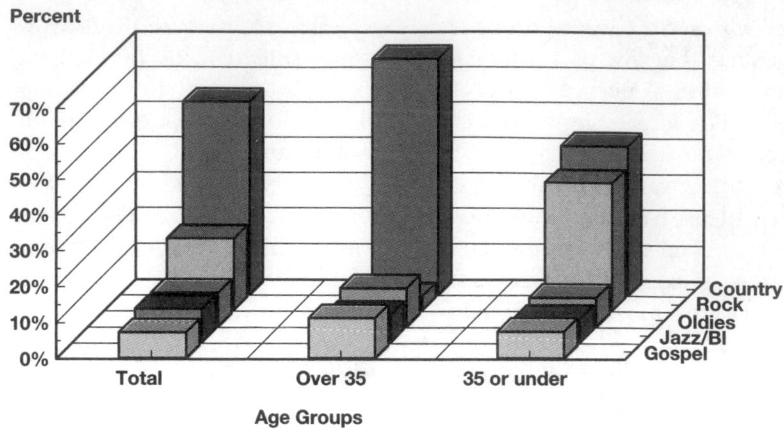

Descriptive Statistics

Descriptive statistics represent even more powerful ways of summarizing the characteristics of large sets of data. In the case of statistical analysis, the analyst calculates one number or a few numbers that reveal something about the characteristics of large sets of data.

Measures of Central Tendency

There are three measures of central tendency: the arithmetic mean, the median, and the mode. Before beginning this section, it would be a good idea to review the types of data scales presented in Chapter 9. There are four basic types of scales: nominal, ordinal, interval, and ratio. Nominal and ordinal scales are sometimes referred to as *nonmetric data scales,* whereas interval and ratio scales are referred to as *metric scales.* Many of the statistical procedures discussed in this section and in following sections require metric data, and others are designed for nonmetric data.

Mean The sum of the values for all observations of a variable divided by the number of observations.

The arithmetic **mean** is properly computed only from interval or ratio scale (metric) data. It is computed by adding the values for all observations for a particular variable such as age and dividing the resulting sum by the number of observations. When working with survey data, the exact value of the variable may not be known, but it may be known that the particular case falls in a particular category. For example, an age category on a survey might be 18–34 years. If a person falls in this particular category, we do not know the person's exact age—only that it is somewhere between 18 and 34. In group data, the midpoint of each category is multiplied by the number of observations in that category, the resulting totals are summed, and the total is divided by the total number of observations. This process is summarized in the following formula:

$$\overline{X} = \frac{\sum_{i=1}^{h} f_i X_i}{n}$$

where

f_i = the frequency of the ith class
X_i = the midpoint of that class
h = the number of classes
n = the total number of observations

The **median** can be computed for all types of data except nominal data. It is calculated by finding the value below which 50 percent of the observations fall. If all of the values for a particular variable were put in an array in either ascending or descending order, the median would be the middle value in that array. The median is often used for variables such as income, where the researcher is concerned that the arithmetic mean will be affected by a few extreme values and not accurately reflect the predominant central tendency for the variable for that group. The **mode** can be computed with any type of data (nominal, ordinal, interval, ratio). It is determined by finding the value that occurs most frequently. In a frequency distribution, the mode is the value of the variable that has the highest frequency. One problem with the mode is that a particular data set may have more than one mode. If three different values occur with the same level of frequency and that frequency is higher than for any other value, then that data set has three modes. The mean, median, and mode for sample data on beer consumption are shown in Table 13.7.

Median The observation below which 50 percent of the observations fall.

Mode The value that occurs most frequently.

Table 13.7

Mean, Median, and Mode

A total of 10 beer drinkers (who drink one or more cans, bottles, or glasses of beer per day on the average) were interviewed in a mall-intercept study. They were asked how many cans, bottles, or glasses of beer they drink in an average day. Their responses are summarized.

Respondent	Number of Cans/Bottles/Glasses Per Day
1	2
2	2
3	3
4	2
5	5
6	1
7	2
8	2
9	10
10	1

Mode = 2 cans/bottles/glasses   Median = 2 cans/bottles/glasses   Mean = 3 cans/bottles/glasses

Measures of Dispersion

Frequently used measures of dispersion include the standard deviation, variance, and range. Whereas measures of central tendency indicate typical values for a particular variable, measures of dispersion indicate how "spread out" the data are. The dangers associated with relying only on measures of central tendency are suggested by the example shown in Table 13.8.

Standard deviation The square root of the sum of the squared deviations from the mean divided by the number of observations minus 1.

The formula for computing the **standard deviation** for a sample of observations is as follows:

$$S = \sqrt{\frac{\sum_{i=1}^{n}(X_i - \overline{X})^2}{n-1}}$$

where

S = sample standard deviation
X_i = the value of the ith observation
$\overline{X}$ = the sample mean
n = the sample size

Variance The sums of the squared deviations from the mean divided by the number of observations minus 1.

Range The maximum value for a variable minus the minimum value for that variable.

The **variance** is calculated by using the same formula as for the standard deviation, with the exception that the square-root sign is removed. Finally, the **range** is equal to the maximum value for a particular variable minus the minimum value for that variable.

Means, Percentages, and Statistical Tests

In terms of basic data analysis, the research analyst is faced with the decision of whether to use measures of central tendency (mean, median) or percentages (one-way frequency tables, cross-tabulations). Responses to questions are either categorical or take the form of continuous variables. Occupation (coded 1 for professional/managerial, 2 for white collar, 3 for blue collar, and 4 for other) is an example of a categorical variable. The only thing that can be done with a variable of this type is to report the frequency and relative percentage with which each category was encountered. Variables such as age can be continuous or categorical, depending on how the information was obtained. For example, we can ask people their actual age or we can ask them which category (under 35, or 35 or older) includes their age. If actual age data are available, mean age can be readily computed. If categories are used, one-way frequency distributions and cross-tabulations are the most obvious choices. However, continuous data can be put into categories, and means can be estimated for categorical data using the formula presented earlier for computing a mean for grouped data.

Finally, statistical tests are available that can tell us whether two means or two percentages differ to a greater extent than would be expected by chance (sampling error)—for example, average expenditures by men and average

Table 13.8

Measures of Dispersion and Measures of Central Tendency

Consider the beer drinker example presented in Table 13.7. Assume that interviewing was conducted in two markets. The results for both markets are shown.

Respondent	Number of Cans Bottles/Glasses Market One	Number of Cans/ Bottles/Glasses Market Two
1	2	1
2	2	1
3	3	1
4	2	1
5	5	1
6	1	1
7	2	1
8	2	3
9	10	10
10	1	10
Mean	3	3
Standard deviation	2.7	3.7

Note: Average beer consumption is the same in both markets—3 cans/bottles/glasses. However, the standard deviation is larger in Market Two, indicating more dispersion in the data. Whereas the mean suggests the two markets are the same, the added information provided by the standard deviation tells us they are different.

expenditures by women at fast-food restaurants—or whether there is a significant relationship between two variables in a cross-tabulation table. These tests are discussed next.

Statistical Significance

The basic motive for making statistical inferences is to be able to generalize from sample results to population characteristics. A basic tenet of statistical inference is that it is possible for numbers to be different in a mathematical sense but not significantly different in a statistical sense. For example, a sample of cola drinkers is asked to try two cola drinks in a blind-taste test and indicate which they prefer. The results show that 51 percent prefer one test product and 49 percent prefer the other. There is a mathematical difference in the results, but the difference would appear to be minor and unimportant. The difference is probably well within the range of accuracy of our ability to measure taste preferences, and the difference is probably not significant in a statistical sense. Three different concepts can be applied to the notion of differences.

- *Mathematical differences.* By definition, if numbers are not exactly the same, they are different. This does not, however, suggest that the difference is either important or statistically significant.
- *Statistical significance.* If a particular difference is large enough to be unlikely to have occurred due to chance or sampling error, then the difference is statistically significant.
- *Managerially important differences.* If results or numbers are different to the extent that the difference would matter from a managerial perspective, then the difference might be important. For example, the difference in consumer response to two different packages in a test market might be statistically significant but yet so small as to have little practical or managerial significance.[4]

Different approaches for testing whether results are statistically significant are discussed below.

Hypothesis Testing

Hypothesis Assumption or theory that a researcher or manager makes about some characteristic of the population under study.

A **hypothesis** can be defined as an assumption or guess that a researcher or manager makes about some characteristic of the population being investigated. The marketing researcher is often faced with the question of whether research results are different enough from the norm to conclude that some element of the firm's marketing strategy should be changed. Consider the following situations:

- The results of a tracking survey show that awareness of the product is lower than it was in a similar survey conducted six months ago. Is the result significantly lower? Is the result sufficiently lower to call for a change in advertising strategy?
- A product manager believes that the average purchaser of his product is 35 years of age. A survey is conducted to test this hypothesis, and the survey shows that the average purchaser of the product is 38.5 years of age. Is the survey result enough different from the product manager's belief to conclude that the belief is incorrect?
- The marketing director of a fast-food chain believes that 60 percent of her customers are female and 40 percent are male. She does a survey to test this hypothesis and finds that, according to the survey, 55 percent are female and 45 percent are male. Is this result sufficiently different from her original theory to permit her to conclude that her original theory was incorrect?

All these questions can be evaluated with some kind of statistical test. In hypothesis testing, the researcher determines whether a hypothesis concerning some characteristic of the population is likely, given the evidence. A statistical hypothesis test allows us to calculate the probability of observing a particular result if the stated hypothesis is actually true.

There are two basic explanations for observing a difference between a hypothesized value and a particular research result: Either the hypothesis is true and the observed difference is quite likely due to sampling error, or the hypothesis is most likely false and the true value is some other value.

Steps in Hypothesis Testing

Five basic steps are involved in testing a hypothesis:

1. Specify the hypothesis.
2. Select an appropriate statistical technique to test the hypothesis.
3. Specify a decision rule as the basis for determining whether to reject or fail to reject (FTR) the null hypothesis H_0. Please note that we did not say "reject H_0 or accept H_0." Although a seemingly small distinction, it is an important one. The distinction will be discussed in greater detail later on.
4. Calculate the value of the test statistic and perform the test.
5. State the conclusion from the perspective of the original research problem or question.

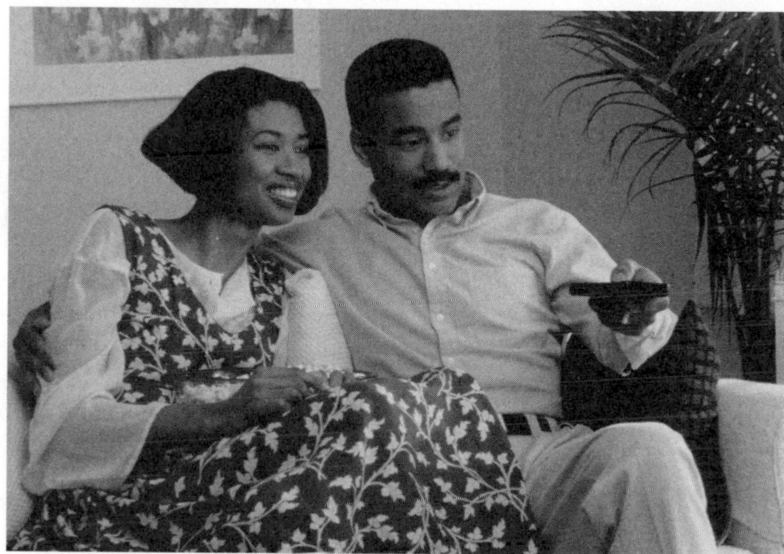

If cable TV viewers in San Francisco generally have higher average satisfaction scores than those in Minneapolis, are customers in San Francisco really more satisfied? Why?

Stating the Hypothesis

Hypotheses are stated using two basic forms: the null hypothesis H_0 and the alternative hypothesis H_a. The null hypothesis H_0 (sometimes called the *hypothesis of the status quo*) is the hypothesis that is tested against its complement, the alternative hypothesis, H_a (sometimes called the *research hypothesis of interest*). For example, the manager of Burger City believes that his operational procedures will guarantee that the average customer will have to wait two minutes in the drive-in window line. He conducts research based on the observation of 1,000 customers at randomly selected stores at randomly selected times. The average customer observed in this study spent 2.4 minutes in the drive-in window line. The null hypothesis and the alternative hypothesis might be stated as follows:

Null hypothesis H_0: Mean waiting time $=$ 2 minutes
Alternative hypothesis H_a: Mean waiting time $\neq$ 2 minutes

Note that the null hypothesis and the alternative hypothesis must be stated in such a way that both cannot be true. The idea is to use the available evidence to ascertain which hypothesis is more likely to be true.

Choosing the Appropriate Test Statistic As you will see in the following sections of this chapter, the analyst must choose the appropriate statistical test, given the characteristics of the situation under investigation. A number of different statistical tests and the situations in which they are appropriate are discussed in this chapter. Table 13.9 provides a guide to selecting the appropriate test for various situations.

Developing a Decision Rule Based on our previous discussions of distributions of sample means, it is very unlikely to get a sample result that is exactly equal to the value of the population parameter. The problem is one of determining whether the difference or deviation between the value of the actual sample mean and its expected value based on the hypothesis could have occurred by chance 5 times out of 100, for example, if the statistical hypothesis is true. A decision rule or standard is needed to determine whether to reject or fail to reject the null hypothesis. Statisticians state such decision rules in terms of significance levels.

The significance level (α) is critical in the process of choosing between the null and alternative hypotheses. The level of significance is the probability that is considered too low—.10, .05 or .01, for example—to justify acceptance of the null hypothesis.

Assume that we want to test a hypothesis at the .05 level of significance. This means that we will reject the null hypothesis if the test indicates that the probability of occurrence of the observed result (such as the difference between the sample mean and its expected value) due to chance or sampling error is less than 5 percent. Rejection of the null hypothesis is equivalent to supporting the alternative hypothesis.

Calculating the Value of the Test Statistic In this step we

- use the appropriate formula to calculate the value of the statistic for the test chosen.
- compare the value calculated (previously) to the critical value of the statistic (from the appropriate table), based on the decision rule chosen.
- state the result, based on your comparison, in terms of either rejecting or failing to reject the null hypothesis (H_0).

Stating the Conclusion A conclusion is a statement that summarizes the results of a test. The conclusion should be stated from the perspective of the original research question.

Hypothesis Tests

Three commonly used statistical hypothesis tests of differences are presented in this section. Many other statistical tests have been developed and are used, but a full discussion of all of them is beyond the scope of this text.

Table 13.9

Statistical Tests and Their Uses

Area of Application	Subgroups or Samples	Level of Scaling	Test	Special Requirements	Example
Hypotheses about frequency distributions	One	Nominal	χ^2	Random sample	Are observed differences in the numbers responding to three different promotions likely/not likely due to chance?
	Two or more	Nominal	χ^2	Random sample, independent samples	Are differences in the numbers of men and women respond ing to a promotion likely/not likely due to chance?
	One	Ordinal	$K - S$	Random sample, natural order in data	Is the observed distribution of women preferring an ordered set of make-up colors (light to dark) likely/not likely due to chance?
Hypotheses about means	One (large sample)	Metric (interval or ratio)	Z-test for one mean	Random sample, $n \geqslant 30$	Is the observed difference between a sample estimate of the mean and some set standard or expected value of the mean likely/not likely due to chance?
	One (small sample)	Metric (interval or ratio)	t-test for one mean	Random sample, $n < 30$	Same as for large sample
	Two (large sample)	Metric (interval or ratio)	Z-test for one means	Random sample, $n \geqslant 30$	Is the observed difference between the means for two subgroups (mean income for men and women) likely/not likely due to chance?
	Two (small sample)	Metric (interval or ratio)	One-way ANOVA	Random sample	Is the observed variation between means for three or more subgroups (mean expenditures on entertainment for high-, moderate-, and low-income people) likely/not likely due to chance?
Hypotheses about proportions	One (large sample)	Metric (interval or ratio)	Z-test for one proportion	Random sample, $n \geqslant 30$	Is the observed difference between a sample estimate of proportion (percentage who say they will buy) and some set standard or expected value likely/not likely due to chance?
	Two (large sample)	Metric (interval or ratio)	Z-test for two proportions	Random sample, $n \geqslant 30$	Is the observed difference between estimated percentages for two subgroups (percentage of men and women who have college degrees) likely/not likely due to chance?

The distributions used in the following section for comparing the computed and tabular values of the statistics are the *Z*-distribution, the *t*-distribution, and the chi-square (χ^2) distribution. The tabular values for these distributions appear in Tables 2, 3, and 4 of the Appendix at the end of the text.

Independent Versus Related Samples

Independent samples Samples in which the measurement of a variable in one population has no effect on the measurement of the variable in the other.

Related samples Samples in which the measurement of a variable in one population may influence the measurement of the variable in the other.

In some cases it may be necessary to test the hypothesis that the value of a variable in one population is equal to the value of that same variable in another population. The selection of the appropriate test statistic requires the researcher to consider whether the samples are independent or related. **Independent samples** involve situations in which measurement of the variable of interest in one sample has no effect on the measurement of the variable in the other sample. It is not necessary that there be two different surveys, only that the measurement of the variable in one population has no effect on the measurement of the variable in the other population. In the case of **related samples**, the measurement of the variable of interest in one sample may influence the measurement of the variable of interest in another sample.

If, for example, men and women were interviewed in a particular survey regarding their frequency of eating out, there is no way that a man's response could affect or change the way a woman would respond to the question in this survey. This would be an example of independent samples. On the other hand, consider a situation in which the researcher needed to determine the effect of a new advertising campaign on consumer awareness of a particular brand. To do this, the researcher might survey a random sample of consumers before introducing the new campaign and survey the same sample of consumers 90 days after the new campaign was introduced. These samples are not independent. The measurement of awareness 90 days after the start of the campaign may be affected by the first measurement.

Degrees of Freedom

Degrees of freedom The number of observations in a statistical problem that are not restricted or are free to vary.

Many statistical tests require the researcher to specify degrees of freedom in order to find the critical value of the test statistic from the table for that statistic. **Degrees of freedom** are the number of observations in a statistical problem that are not restricted or are free to vary.

The number of degrees of freedom (d.f.) is equal to the number of observations minus the number of assumptions or constraints necessary to calculate a statistic. For example, consider the problem of adding five numbers when the mean of the five numbers is known to be 20. In this situation, only four of the five numbers are free to vary because once four of the numbers are known, the last value is also known (can be calculated) because the mean value must be 20. If we knew that four of the five numbers were 14, 23, 24, and 18, then the fifth number must be 21 to produce a mean of 20. We would say that the sample has $n - 1$ degrees of freedom. It is as if the sample had one less observation. The inclusion of degrees of freedom in this calculation adjusts for this fact.

Goodness of Fit

Chi-Square

Data collected in surveys, as noted earlier in the text, are often analyzed by means of one-way frequency counts and cross-tabulations. The purpose of cross-tabulation is to study relationships among variables. The question is: Does the number of responses that fall into different categories differ from what one would expect? This could involve partitioning users into groups, such as gender (male, female), age (under 18, 18–35, over 35), or income level (low, middle, high), and cross-tabulating by the results to questions such as preferred brand or level of use. The **chi-square** (χ^2) **test** enables the research analyst to determine whether an observed pattern of frequencies corresponds to or fits an "expected" pattern. It tests the "goodness of fit" of the observed distribution in relation to an expected distribution.[5]

Chi-square test Test of the goodness of fit between the observed distribution and the expected distribution of a variable.

Chi-Square Test of a Single Sample

Consider a situation in which the marketing manager of a retail electronics chain needs to test the effectiveness of three special deals (Deal 1, Deal 2, and Deal 3). Each deal will be offered for a month. The manager wants to measure the effect of each deal on the number of customers visiting a test store during the time the deal is on. The number of customers visiting the store under each deal was as follows:

Deal	Month	Customers per Month
1	April	11,700
2	May	12,100
3	June	11,780
Total		35,580

The marketing manager needs to know whether there is a significant difference between the number of customers visiting the store during one time period covered by each deal. The chi-square (χ^2) one-sample test is the appropriate way to answer this question. This test would be applied as follows:

1. Specify the null and alternative hypotheses.
   - Null hypothesis H_0: The number of customers visiting the store under the various deals is equal.
   - Alternative hypothesis H_a: There is a significant difference in the number of customers visiting the store under the various deals.
2. Determine the number of visitors that would be expected in each category if the null hypotheses were correct (E_i). In the example, the null hypothesis states that there is no difference in the number of customers

attracted by the different deals. Therefore, an equal number of customers would be expected under each deal. Of course, this assumes that no other factors influenced the number of visits to the store. Under the null (no difference) hypothesis, the expected number of customers visiting the store in each deal period would be 11,860, computed as follows:

$$E = \frac{TV}{N}$$

where

TV = total number of visits
N = number of months

$$E = \frac{35{,}580}{3}$$

$$E = 11{,}860$$

The researcher should check for cells in which small expected frequencies occur because they can distort χ^2 results. No more than 20 percent of the categories should have expected frequencies less than 5, and none should have an expected frequency less than 1. That is not a problem in this case.

3. Calculate the χ^2 value using the formula:

$$\chi^2 = \sum_{i=1}^{k} \frac{(O_i - E_i)^2}{E_i}$$

where

O_i = observed number in ith category
E_i = expected number in ith category
k = number of categories

For our example,

$$\chi^2 = \frac{(11{,}700 - 11{,}860)^2}{11{,}860} + \frac{(12{,}100 - 11{,}860)^2}{11{,}860} + \frac{(11{,}780 - 11{,}860)^2}{11{,}860}$$

$$= 7.55$$

4. Select the level of significance α. If the .05 (α) level of significance is selected, the tabular χ^2 value with 2 degrees of freedom ($k - 1$) is 5.99. (See Table 4 of the Appendix at the end of the text.)

5. Because the calculated χ^2 value (7.55) is higher than the table value (see Table 4 in the Appendix for $k - 1 = 2$ d.f., $\alpha = .05$), we would *reject the null hypothesis*. Therefore, we conclude with 95 percent confidence that customer response to the deals was significantly different. Unfortunately, this test tells us only that the overall variation among the cell frequencies is greater than would be expected by chance. It does not tell us whether any individual cell is significantly different from the others.

Chi-Square Test of Two Independent Samples

Marketing researchers often need to determine whether there is any association between two or more variables. Questions such as, "Are men and women equally divided into heavy-, medium-, and light-user categories?" or "Are purchasers and nonpurchasers equally divided into low-, middle-, and high-income groups?" may need to be answered prior to formulating a marketing strategy. The chi-square (χ^2) test for two independent samples is the appropriate test in this situation.

This technique is illustrated using the data from Table 13.10 on page 422. A convenience store chain wants to determine the nature of the relationship, if any, between gender of customer and the frequency of visiting stores in the chain. Frequency of visits has been divided into three categories: 1 to 5 visits per month (light user), 6 to 14 visits per month (medium user), and 15 and above visits per month (heavy user). Here are the steps necessary for conducting this test:

1. State the null and alternative hypotheses.
   - Null hypothesis H_0: There is no relationship between gender and frequency of visit.
   - Alternative hypothesis H_a: There is a significant relationship between gender and frequency of visit.
2. Place the observed (sample) frequencies in a $k \times r$ table (cross-tabulation or contingency table), using the k columns for the sample groups and the r rows for the conditions or treatments. Calculate the sum of each row and each column. Record those totals at the margins of the table (they are called *marginal totals*). Also, calculate the total for the entire table (N).

Frequency of Visits	Male	Female	Totals
1–5	14	26	40
6–14	16	34	50
15 and above	15	11	26
Totals	45	71	116

3. Determine the expected frequency for each cell in the contingency table by calculating the product of the two marginal totals common to that cell and dividing that value by N.

Frequency of visits	Male	Female
1–5	$\frac{45 \times 40}{116} = 15.52$	$\frac{71 \times 40}{116} = 24.48$
6–14	$\frac{45 \times 50}{116} = 19.40$	$\frac{71 \times 50}{116} = 30.60$
15 and above	$\frac{45 \times 26}{116} = 10.09$	$\frac{71 \times 26}{116} = 15.91$

The χ^2 value will be distorted if more than 20 percent of the cells have an expected frequency of less than 5 or if any cell has an expected frequency of less than 1. The test should not be used under these conditions.

Table 13.10

Data Test

Visits to Conventience Stores by Males				Visit to Convenience Stores by Females			
Number X_m	Frequency f_m	%	Cumulative %	Number X_1	Frequency f_1	%	Cumulative %
2	2	4.4	4.4	2	5	7.0	7.0
3	5	11.1	15.6	3	4	5.6	12.7
5	7	15.6	31.1	4	7	9.9	22.5
6	2	4.4	35.6	5	10	14.1	36.6
7	1	2.2	37.8	6	6	8.5	45.1
8	2	4.4	42.2	7	3	4.2	49.3
9	1	2.2	44.4	8	6	8.5	57.7
10	7	15.6	60.0	9	2	2.8	60.6
12	3	6.7	66.7	10	13	18.3	78.9
15	5	11.1	77.8	12	4	5.6	84.5
20	6	13.3	91.1	15	3	4.2	88.7
23	1	2.2	93.3	16	2	2.8	91.5
25	1	2.2	95.6	20	4	5.6	97.2
30	1	2.2	97.8	21	1	1.4	98.6
40	1	2.2	100.0	25	1	1.4	100.0

Total $n_m = 45$ $n_f = 71$

$$\text{Mean number of visits by males, } \overline{X}_m = \frac{\sum X_m f_m}{45} = 11.49$$

$$\text{Mean number of visits by females, } \overline{X}_f = \frac{\sum X_f f_f}{71} = 8.51$$

4. Calculate the value of χ^2 using

$$\chi^2 = \sum_{i=1}^{r}\sum_{j=1}^{k}\frac{(O_{ij} - E_{ij})^2}{E_{ij}}$$

where

O_{ij} = observed number in the ith row of the jth column
E_{ij} = expected number in the ith row of the jth column

For our example,

$$\chi^2 = \frac{(14 - 15.52)^2}{15.52} + \frac{(26 - 24.48)^2}{24.48} + \frac{(16 - 19.4)^2}{19.4} + \frac{(34 - 30.6)^2}{30.6} + \frac{(15 - 10.09)^2}{10.09} + \frac{(11 - 15.91)^2}{15.91}$$

$\chi^2 = 5.12$

5. The tabular χ^2 value at a .05 level of significance, and $(r - 1)(k - 1) = 2$ degrees of freedom is 5.99 (see Table 4 of the Appendix). Because the calculated $\chi^2 = 5.12$ is less than the tabular value, *we fail to reject the null (FTR) hypothesis* and conclude that there is no significant difference between males and females in terms of the frequency of their visits to the various chain stores tested.

Hypotheses About Proportions

In many situations researchers are concerned with phenomena that are expressed as percentages.[6] For example, marketers might be interested in testing for the proportion of respondents who "prefer brand A" versus those who "prefer brand B" or who are "brand loyal" versus those who are not.

Test of a Proportion, One Sample

A survey of 500 customers conducted by a major bank indicated that slightly more than 74 percent had family incomes of more than $50,000 per year. If this is true, the firm will develop a special package of services for this group. The management wants to determine whether the true percentage is greater than 60 percent before developing and introducing the new package of services. The survey results show that 74.29 percent of the bank's customers surveyed reported family incomes of $50,000 or more per year. The procedure for the **hypothesis test of proportions** follows:

Hypothesis test of proportions Test to determine whether the difference between proportions is greater than would be expected because of sampling error.

1. Specify the null and alternative hypotheses.
   - Null hypotheses $H_0 : P \leqslant .60$.
   - Alternative hypothesis $H_a : P > .60$, where $P =$ the proportion of customers with family incomes of $50,000 or more per year.
2. Specify the level of sampling error (α) allowed. For $\alpha = .05$, table value of Z (critical) $= 1.64$. (See Table 3 in the Appendix for d.f. $= \infty$, .05 significance, one-tail. The table for t is used because $t = Z$ for samples greater than 30.)
3. Calculate the estimated standard error using the P-value specified in the null hypothesis:

$$S_p = \sqrt{\frac{P(1 - P)}{n - 1}}$$

where

$P =$ proportion specified in the null hypothesis
$n =$ sample size

Therefore

$$S_p = \sqrt{\frac{.6(1 - .6)}{35 - 1}}$$
$$= .084$$

4. Calculate the test statistic as follows:

$$Z = \frac{(\text{observed proportion} - \text{proportion under null hypothesis})}{\text{estimated standard error } (S_p)}$$
$$= \frac{(0.7429 - 0.60)}{.084}$$
$$= 1.7$$

5. The *null hypothesis is rejected* because the calculated Z-value is larger than the critical Z-value. The bank can conclude with 95 percent confidence ($1 - \alpha = .95$) that more than 60 percent of its customers have family incomes of $50,000 or more. Management can introduce the new package of services targeted at this group.

Test of Differences Between Two Proportions, Independent Samples

In many instances management is interested in the difference between the proportions of people in two different groups that engage in a certain activity or have a certain characteristic. For example, the management of a convenience store chain had reason to believe, on the basis of a research study, that the percentage of men who visit convenience stores nine or more times per month (heavy users) was larger than the percentage of women. The specifications required and the procedure for testing this hypothesis are as follows:

1. The null and alternative hypotheses are formally stated as follows:
   - Null hypothesis H_0: $P_m - P_f \leq 0$, the proportion of men (P_m) reporting nine or more visits per month is the same or less than the proportion of women (P_f) reporting nine or more visits per month.
   - Alternative hypothesis H_a: $P_m - P_f > 0$, the proportion of men (P_m) reporting nine or more visits per month is greater than the proportion of women (P_f) reporting nine or more visits per month.

   The sample proportions and the difference can be calculated from Table 13.10 as follows:

$$P_m = \frac{26}{45} = .58$$

$$P_f = \frac{30}{71} = .42$$

$$P_m - P_f = .58 - .42$$
$$= .16$$

2. Set the level of sampling error α at .10 (management decision). For α = .10, the table value of Z (critical) = 1.28. (See Table 3 in the Appendix—d.f. = ∞, .10 significance, one-tail. The table for t is used because $t = Z$ for samples greater than 30.)
3. The estimated standard error of the differences between the two proportions is calculated as follows:

$$S_{Pm-f} = \sqrt{P(1 - P)\left(\frac{1}{n_m} + \frac{1}{n_f}\right)}$$

where

$$P = \frac{n_m P_m + n_f P_f}{n_m + n_f}$$

P_m = proportion in sample m (men)
P_f = proportion in sample f (women)
n_m = size of sample m
n_f = size of sample f

Therefore,

$$P = \frac{45(.58) + 71(.41)}{45 + 71}$$

$$= .48$$

and

$$P_{Pm-f} = \sqrt{.48(1 - .48)\left[\frac{1}{45} + \frac{1}{71}\right]}$$

$$= .10$$

4. Calculate the test statistic.

$$Z = \frac{\begin{pmatrix}\text{difference between}\\\text{observed proportions}\end{pmatrix} - \begin{pmatrix}\text{difference between proportions}\\\text{under the null hypothesis}\end{pmatrix}}{\begin{matrix}\text{estimated standard error of the differences}\\\text{between the two means}\end{matrix}}$$

$$Z\,(\text{calculated}) = \frac{(.58 - .42) - (0)}{.10}$$

$$Z = 1.60$$

5. The *null hypothesis is rejected* because the calculated *Z*-value (1.60) is larger than the critical *Z*-value (1.28 for $\alpha = .10$). Management can conclude with 90 percent confidence ($1 - \alpha = .90$) that the proportion of men that visit convenience stores nine or more times per month is larger than the proportion of women.

It should be noted that if the level of sampling error α had been set at .05, the critical *Z*-value would equal 1.64. In this case, we would fail to reject (FTR) the null hypothesis because *Z* (calculated) is smaller than *Z* (critical).

p-Values and Significance Testing

In the various tests discussed in this chapter, we established a standard—the level of significance and the associated critical value of the statistic—and then calculated the value of the statistic to see whether it beat that standard. If the calculated value of the statistic exceeded the critical value, then the result being tested was said to be statistically significant at that level.

However, this approach did not tell us the exact probability of getting a computed test statistic that was largely due to chance. The calculations necessary to compute this probability are tedious. Fortunately, they are easy for computers. This probability is commonly referred to as the ***p*-value.** The *p*-value is the most demanding level of statistical (not managerial) significance that can be met based on the calculated value of the statistic. You may see one of the following in output from various computer statistical packages:

p-value The exact probability of getting a computed test statistic that was largely due to chance. The smaller the *p*-value, the smaller the probability that the observed result occurred by chance.

- *p*-value
- ≤ PROB
- PROB =

These labels are used by various computer programs to identify the probability that such a large distance between the hypothesized population parameter and the observed test statistic could have occurred due to chance. The smaller the *p*-value, the smaller the probability that the observed result occurred due to chance (sampling error).

Figure 13.14 is an example of computer output showing a *p*-value calculation. This analysis shows the results of a *t*-test of the differences between means for two independent samples. In this case, the null hypothesis (H_0) shows that there is no difference between what men and women would be willing to pay for a new communications service. (The variable name is GENDER with the numeric codes of 0 for males and 1 for females. They were asked how much they would be willing to pay per month for a new wireless communications service that was described to them via a videotape. Variable ADDED PAY is their response to the question.) The results show that women were willing to pay an average of $16.82 for the new service and men were willing to pay $20.04. Is this a significant difference? The calculated value of t of -1.328 indicates, via associated *p*-value of .185, that there is an 18.5 percent chance that the difference may be due to sampling. If, for example, the standard for the test had been set at .10 (willing to accept a 10 percent chance of incorrectly rejecting H_0), then the analyst would *fail to reject* H_0 in this case.

Figure 13.14

Sample STATISTICA® *t*-Test Output

Stat. Basic Stats	Grouping: GENDER (pcs. sta) Group 1: G_1:1 Group 2: G_2:0						
Variable	Mean G_1:1	Mean G_2:0	t-value	df	P	Valid N G_1:1	Valid N G_2:0
ADDED PAY	16.82292	20.04717	−1.32878	200	.185434	96	106

Going ON-LINE

Statistics on the Internet

CURRENTLY, IT IS BEST TO LEARN AND WORK WITH ONE of the popular commercially available statistical packages such as SPSS or STATISTICA.® A number of special purpose statistical programs can now be found on the Internet. Some popular software sites are listed in Table 13.11. However, special purpose programs found on the Internet may not offer the comprehensiveness, integration, data management and manipulation features, or widespread use and familiarity offered by the well-known packages. All of this will probably change and Web-accessible statistical software offering all the important features will be available on a per-usage basis.

There is a tremendous amount of statistical information and advice available over the Internet. The Web is becoming a very useful source of information for the selection of appropriate statistical techniques for a particular problem, the proper use of different statistical techniques, and emerging statistical techniques that have not yet found their way into mainstream statistical packages. In addition, news and special-interest groups can be an excellent source of information and advice regarding the proper use of statistical procedures. Your Web browser can be used to access news groups if you have set up this feature with your Internet service provider. News groups are typically accessed through the e-mail menu. Figure 13.15 shows a list of statistics resources on the Internet. ■

Table 13.11

Statistical Software Sites on the Web

Organization	Location	Description
Math Soft	www.mathsoft.com	Features Mathcad 6.0—can use real math notation to solve problems and get instant feedback. It also lets you analyze data, build models, and test different scenarios.
STATA	www.stata.com	Develops and distributes STATA software for statistical analysis. It is available for Windows, DOS, Macintosh, and UNIX computers.
UNISTAT	www.unistat.com	A comprehensive statistical package that can also work as an Excel add-in. UNISTAT provides a one-stop solution for data handling, data analysis, and presentation-quality scientific graphics.
SPSS	www.spss.com	Comprehensive statistical analysis system. Provides links to other sites and sample data sets.
StatSoft	www.statsoft.com	Information on the range of STATISTICA® products, including the student version available with this text. A powerful but easy to use statistical analysis system that has consistently received excellent reviews in various PC and professional publications.

Rainer's Web Site for Statisticians

 Visit my private home page ___ Contact me by e-mail

Table of contents:

- Welcome ...
- WWW Resources for Statisticians
- Mailing Lists and Newsgroups
- Statistical Associations and Organizations
- Statistical Departments and Institutes
- Statistical Software
- Miscellaneous for Statisticians
- Statistical Quotes
- Contacts to Statisticians
- Deutsche WWW-Seiten für Statistiker
- References to Rainer's Web Site for Statisticians
- Feedback on my Web Site for Statisticians
- Symbols of links

Page 1 of 3

 **Welcome to my Web Site for Statisticians ...**

Thank you very much for your interest in my WWW pages. My name is *Rainer Würländer* and I'm working as a *statistical consultant* and IT manager with W.L.Gore & Associates near Munich, Germany.

The intention of this **"Web Site for Statisticians"** is to offer information and mainly links on topics like WWW servers in Statistics, mailing lists and newsgroups, statistical associations and departments, statistical software, miscellaneous, statistical quotes, and a directory of professional statisticians worldwide. In addition German related information is offered to all statisticians with German language skills on a separate page Deutsche WWW-Seiten für Statistiker.

http://ourworld.compuserve.com/homepages/Rainer_Wuerlaender/

Figure 13.15

Internet Statistics Resources

Source: http://www.ourworld.compuserve.com/homepages/Rainer_Wuerlaender/ ©1995–1999 Rainer Würländer.

Summary

Once the questionnaires have been returned from the field, a five-step process takes place. These steps are (1) quality control checks, (2) coding, (3) data entry, (4) machine cleaning of data, and (5) tabulation and statistical analysis. The first step in the process is critical. It is important to make sure that the data have integrity; otherwise, the age-old adage is true, "garbage in, garbage out." Within the quality control process, the first step is called *validation*: determining as closely as possible that each questionnaire is, in fact, a valid interview. A valid interview in this sense is one that was conducted in an appropriate manner. The objective of validation is to detect interviewer fraud or failure to follow key instructions. Validation is accomplished by recontacting a certain percentage of the respondents surveyed by each interviewer.

After the validation process is completed, editing begins. Editing involves checking for interviewer mistakes. This entails making certain that all questions that should be answered were, that skip patterns were followed properly, and that open-ended questions were recorded properly. Upon completion of editing, the next step is to code the data. Most questions on surveys are closed-ended and precoded. This means that numeric codes have already been assigned to the various responses on the questionnaire. With open-ended questions, the researcher has no idea in advance what the responses will be. Therefore, the coder must go back and establish numeric codes for response categories.

After validation, editing, and coding, the next step is data entry. Today, most data entry is done by means of intelligent entry systems that check the internal logic of the data. The data are typically entered directly from questionnaires. New developments in optical scanning have made automated data entry cost-effective for smaller projects.

The final step in the process is tabulation of the data. The most basic tabulation is a one-way frequency table. A one-way frequency table indicates the number of responses to each answer on a survey question. The next step in the analysis is often cross-tabulation: examination of the responses to one question in relation to the responses to one or more other questions. Cross-tabulations are a powerful and easily understood approach to the summarization and analysis of survey results.

Statistical measures are an even more powerful way to analyze data sets. Perhaps the most common statistical measures are those of central tendency: the arithmetic mean, the median, and the mode. The arithmetic mean is computed only from interval or ratio data by adding the values for all observations for a particular variable and dividing the resulting sum by the number of observations. The median can be computed for all types of data except nominal data by finding the value below which 50 percent of the observations fall. The mode can be computed with any type of data by simply finding the value that occurs most frequently. The arithmetic mean is, by far, the most commonly used measure of central tendency.

In addition to central tendency, researchers often want to have an indication of the dispersion of the data. Measures of dispersion include the standard deviation, variance, and range. The range is equal to the maximum value for a particular variable minus the minimum value for that variable.

The purpose of making statistical inferences is to generalize from sample results to population characteristics. Three important concepts relate to the notion of differences: mathematical differences, managerially important differences, and statistical significance.

A hypothesis is an assumption or belief that a researcher or manager has about some characteristic of the population being investigated. By testing, the researcher determines whether a hypothesis concerning some characteristic of the population is valid. A statistical hypothesis test permits the researcher to calculate the probability of observing the particular result if the stated hypothesis was actually true. In hypothesis testing, the first step is to specify the hypothesis. Next, an appropriate statistical technique should be selected to test the hypothesis. Finally, a decision rule must be specified as the basis for determining whether to accept or reject the hypothesis.

Marketing researchers often develop cross-tabulations to uncover interrelationships among variables. Usually the researchers need to determine whether the number of subjects, objects, or responses that fall into some set of categories differ from chance. Thus, a test of "goodness of fit" of the observed distribution in relation to an expected distribution is appropriate. A common test of goodness of fit is chi-square.

When marketing researchers are examining differences between groups, tests of a proportion can be used. Researchers can test a proportion with one sample or test the differences between two proportions when dealing with independent samples.

Key Terms & Definitions

Validation The process of ascertaining that interviews actually were conducted as specified.

Editing The process of checking for interviewer mistakes.

Skip pattern Requirement to pass over certain questions if a respondent gives a particular answer to a previous question.

Coding The process of grouping and assigning numeric codes to the various responses to a question.

Intelligent data entry The logical checking of information being entered into a data-entry device by that machine or one connected to it.

Optical scanner A data-processing device that can "read" responses on questionnaires.

Machine cleaning of data A final computerized error check of data.

Error-checking routines Computer programs that accept instructions from the user to check for logical errors in the data.

Marginal report A computer-generated table of the frequencies of the responses to each question to monitor entry of valid codes and correct use of skip patterns.

One-way frequency table A table showing the number of responses to each answer of a survey question.

Cross-tabulation Examination of the responses to one question relative to responses to one or more other questions.

Mean The sum of the values for all observations of a variable divided by the number of observations.

Median The observation below which 50 percent of the observations fall.

Mode The value that occurs most frequently.

Standard deviation The square root of the sum of the squared deviations from the mean divided by the number of observations minus 1.

Variance The sums of the squared deviations from the mean divided by the number of observations minus 1.

Range The maximum value for a variable minus the minimum value for that variable.

Hypothesis Assumption or theory that a researcher or manager makes about some characteristic of the population under study.

Independent samples Samples in which the measurement of a variable in one population has no effect on the measurement of the variable in the other.

Related samples Samples in which the measurement of a variable in one population may influence the measurement of the variable in the other.

Degrees of freedom The number of observations in a statistical problem that are not restricted or are free to vary.

Chi-square test Test of the goodness of fit between the observed distribution and the expected distribution of a variable.

Hypothesis test of proportions Test to determine whether the difference between proportions is greater than would be expected because of sampling error.

***p*-value** The exact probability of getting a computed test statistic that was largely due to chance. The smaller the *p*-value, the smaller the probability that the observed result occurred by chance.

Questions for Review & Critical Thinking

1. Assume that Sally Smith, an interviewer, completed 50 questionnaires. Ten of the questionnaires were validated by calling the respondents and asking them one opinion question and two demographic questions over again. On one questionnaire, the respondent claimed that his age category was 30–40, and the age category marked on the questionnaire was 20–30. On a second questionnaire, the respondent was asked, "What is the most important problem facing our city government?" and the interviewer had written down, "The city council is too eager to raise taxes." When the interview was validated, the respondent said, "The city tax rate is too high." As a validator, would you assume that these were honest mistakes and accept the entire lot of 50 interviews as valid? If not, what would you do?
2. Give an example of a skip pattern on a questionnaire. Why is it important to always follow the skip patterns correctly?
3. What is the purpose of machine cleaning the data? Give some examples of how data can be machine cleaned. Do you think that machine cleaning is an expensive and unnecessary step in the data tabulation process? Why or why not?
4. It has been said that a cross-tabulation of two variables gives the researcher much richer information than simply two one-way frequency tables. Why is this true? Give an example.
5. Calculate the mean, median, mode, and standard deviation from the data set below.

Respondent	Times Visited Whitehall Mall in Past Six Months	Times Visited Northpart Mall in Past Six Months	Times Visited Sampson Mall in Past Six Months
A	4	7	2
B	5	11	16
C	13	21	3
D	6	0	1
E	9	18	14
F	3	6	8
G	2	0	1
H	21	3	7
I	4	11	9
J	14	13	5
K	7	7	12
L	8	3	25
M	8	3	9

6. Using data from a newspaper or magazine article, create the following types of graphs:
   a. line graph
   b. pie chart
   c. bar chart.

7. Explain the notions of mathematical differences, managerially important differences, and statistical significance. Can results be statistically significant and yet lack managerial importance? Explain your answer.

8. Describe the procedure for testing hypotheses. Discuss the difference between a null hypothesis and an alternative hypothesis.

9. A market researcher has completed a study of pain relievers. The following table depicts the brand purchased most often broken down by men versus women. Perform a chi-square test on the data and determine what can be said regarding the cross-tabulation.

Pain Relievers	Men	Women
Anacin	40	55
Bayer	60	28
Bufferin	70	97
Cope	14	21
Empirin	82	107
Excedrin	72	84
Excedrin PM	15	11
Vanquish	20	26

Real-Life Research

I Can't Believe It's Yogurt

Phil Jackson, research manager for I Can't Believe It's Yogurt (ICBIY), is trying to develop a more rational basis for evaluating alternative store locations. ICBIY has been growing rapidly, and, historically, the issue of store location has not been critical. It didn't seem to matter where it located its stores—all were successful. However, the yogurt craze has faded and some of its new stores and a few of its old ones are experiencing difficulties in the form of declining sales.

ICBIY wants to continue expanding, but it recognizes that it must be more careful in selecting locations than it was in the past. It has determined that the percentage of individuals in an area who have visited a frozen yogurt store in the past 30 days is the best predictor of the potential for one of its stores—the higher that percentage, the better.

ICBIY wants to locate a store in Denver and has identified two locations that, on the basis of the other criteria, look good. It has conducted a survey of households in the areas that would be served from each location. The results of that survey are below.

Results of Surveys in the Two Areas

Yogurt Store Patronage	Both Areas	Area A	Area B
Have patronized in past 30 days	465	220	245
Have not patronized	535	280	255

Questions

1. Determine whether there is a significant difference at the .05 level between the two areas.
2. What would you recommend to ICBIY regarding which of the two areas it should choose for the new store based on this analysis? Explain your recommendation.

CHAPTER *fourteen*

Correlation and Regression Analysis

Learning Objectives

1 *To understand bivariate regression analysis*

2 *To become aware of the coefficient of determination* R^2

3 *To comprehend the nature of correlation analysis*

Lee Chen is the marketing director for the First Mart Supermarket chain. He is trying to convince the president of the chain, Brit Hawrylak, to decrease the overall price level of the chain, but Hawrylak is skeptical about reducing prices. He indicated in a recent meeting with Chen that he does not believe reducing prices will increase sales for the chain.

Chen presented his problem to Amanda Henson, marketing research manager for First Mart, and asked her to analyze past sales and pricing data to determine whether there is a relationship between price level and sales, and if there is, to measure the nature and extent of that relationship. Henson is currently considering the job that has been assigned to her. She is in the process of listing the options, so that she can choose a statistical procedure that is appropriate to the problem.

Techniques to address what Lee Chen is confronting are presented in this chapter. After you finish the chapter, you will know how to analyze the relationship between price and sales in a powerful way. Reconsider the problem after completing the chapter. ■

Find out more about generating revenue through good marketing at http://www.reveries.com

Bivariate Analysis of Association

Bivariate Analysis Defined

Bivariate techniques Statistical methods of determining the relationship between two variables.

In many marketing research studies, the interests of the researcher and manager go beyond issues that can be addressed by the statistical testing of differences discussed in the previous chapter. They may be interested in the degree of association between two variables. Statistical techniques appropriate for this type of analysis are referred to as **bivariate techniques.** When more than two variables are involved, the techniques employed are known as *multivariate techniques.* Multivariate techniques are discussed later in the chapter.

When analyzing the degree of association between two variables, the variables are classified as the independent (predictor) variable or the dependent (criterion) variable. **Independent variables** are those that we believe affect the value of the **dependent variable.** Independent variables such as price, advertising expenditures, or number of retail outlets are often used to predict and explain sales or market share of a brand—the dependent variable. Bivariate analysis can help provide answers to questions such as: How does the price of our product affect sales? and What is the relationship between household income and expenditures on entertainment?

Independent variable The variable believed to affect the value of the dependent variable.

Dependent variable The variable whose value is believed to change in response to the independent variable.

Note that none of the techniques we will present can be used to prove that one variable caused some change in one or more variable. They can be used only to describe the nature of the statistical relationships among variables.

Types of Bivariate Procedures

The analyst has a large number of bivariate techniques from which to choose. In this chapter we discuss three procedures that are appropriate for metric (ratio or interval) data, bivariate regression, Pearson's product moment correlation, and multivariate regression. Other statistical procedures that can be used for analyzing the statistical relationship between two variables include the

- two group *t*-test
- chi-square analysis of cross-tabulation or contingency tables
- ANOVA (analysis of variance) for two groups.

Bivariate Regression

Bivariate Regression Defined

Bivariate regression analysis is a statistical procedure appropriate for analyzing the relationship between two variables when one is considered the dependent variable and the other the independent variable. For example, we might be interested in analyzing the relationship between sales (dependent variable) and advertising (independent variable). If the relationship between advertising expenditures and sales can be estimated by regression analysis, the researcher can predict sales for different levels of advertising. When the problem involves using two or more independent variables (such as advertising and price) to predict the dependent variable of interest, multiple regression analysis is appropriate.

Bivariate regression analysis An analysis of the strength of the linear relationship between two variables when one is considered the independent variable and the other the dependent variable.

Nature of the Relationship

To study the nature of the relationship between the dependent and the independent variables, the data can be plotted in a scatter diagram. The dependent variable Y is plotted on the vertical axis, while the independent variable

X is plotted on the horizontal axis. By examining the scatter diagram, we can determine whether the relationship between the two variables, if any, is linear or curvilinear. If the relationship appears to be linear or close to linear, linear regression is appropriate. If a nonlinear relationship is shown in the scatter diagram, curve-fitting nonlinear regression techniques are appropriate. These techniques are beyond the scope of this discussion.[1]

Figure 14.1 depicts several kinds of underlying relationships between the *X* and *Y* variables. Scatter diagrams A and B suggest a positive linear relationship between *X* and *Y*. However, the linear relationship shown in B is not as strong as that portrayed in A; there is more scatter in the data shown in B. Diagram C shows a perfect negative or inverse relationship between variables *X* and *Y*. Diagrams D and E show nonlinear relationships between the variables, and appropriate curve-fitting techniques should be used to mathematically describe these relationships. The scatter diagram in F shows no relationship between *X* and *Y*.

Figure 14.1

Types of Relationships Found in Scatter Diagrams

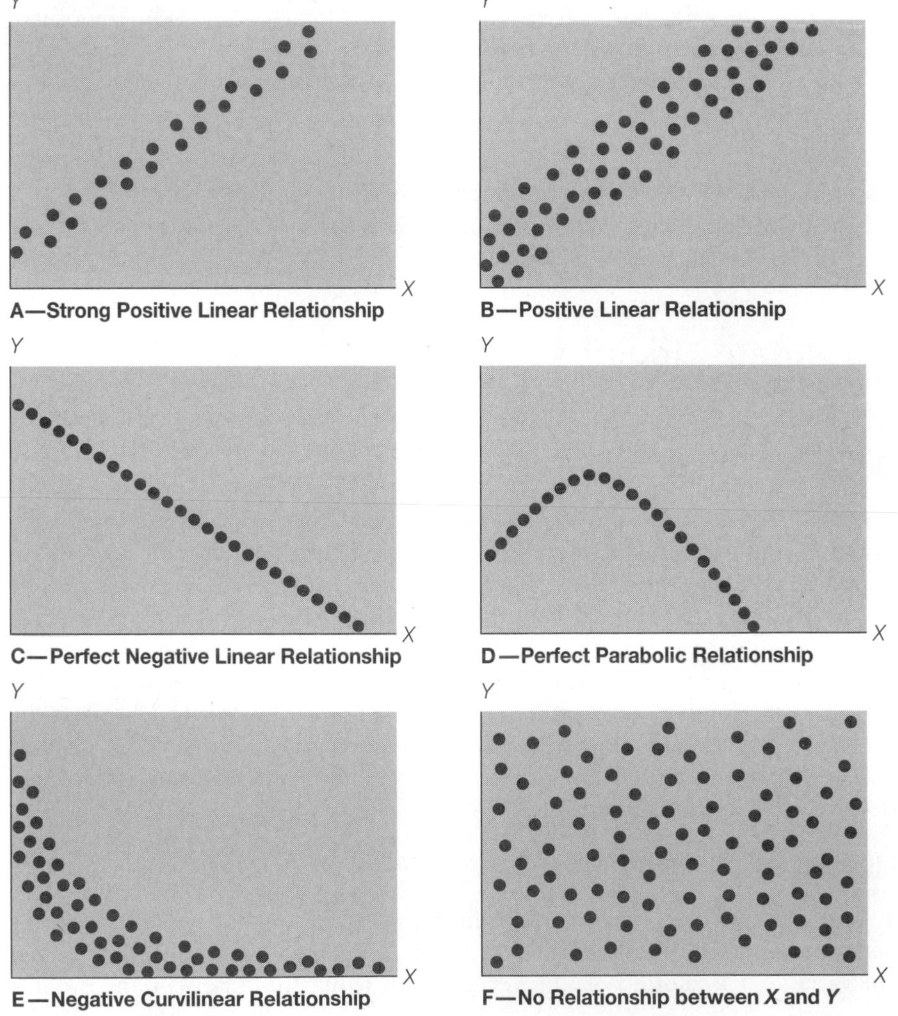

Bivariate Regression Example

Stop 'N Go recently conducted a research effort designed to measure the effect of vehicular traffic by a particular store location on annual sales at that location. To do this properly, it identified 20 stores that were virtually identical on all other variables known to have a significant effect on store sales (square footage, amount of parking, demographics of the surrounding neighborhood, and so on). This analysis is part of an overall effort by Stop 'N Go to identify and quantify the effects of various factors that impact store sales. Its ultimate goal is to develop a model that can be used to evaluate potential sites for store locations and select the ones that will produce the highest level of sales for actual purchase and store construction.

After identifying the 20 sites, Stop 'N Go took daily traffic counts for each site over a 30-day period. In addition, from its own internal records, it obtained total sales data for each of the 20 test stores for the preceding 12 months (see Table 14.1).

A scatter plot of the resulting data is shown in Figure 14.2 on page 440. Visual inspection of the scatter plot suggests that total sales increase as the average daily vehicular traffic increases. The question now is how to characterize this relationship in a more explicit, quantitative manner.

Table 14.1

Annual Sales and Average Daily Vehicular Traffic

Store Number (i)	Average Daily Vehicular Count (in Thousands) (X_i)	Annual Sales (in Thousands of Dollars) (Y_i)
1	62	$1,121
2	35	766
3	36	701
4	72	1,304
5	41	832
6	39	782
7	49	977
8	25	503
9	41	773
10	39	839
11	35	893
12	27	588
13	55	957
14	38	703
15	24	497
16	28	657
17	53	1,209
18	55	997
19	33	844
20	29	883

Figure 14.2

Scatter Plot of Annual Sales by Traffic

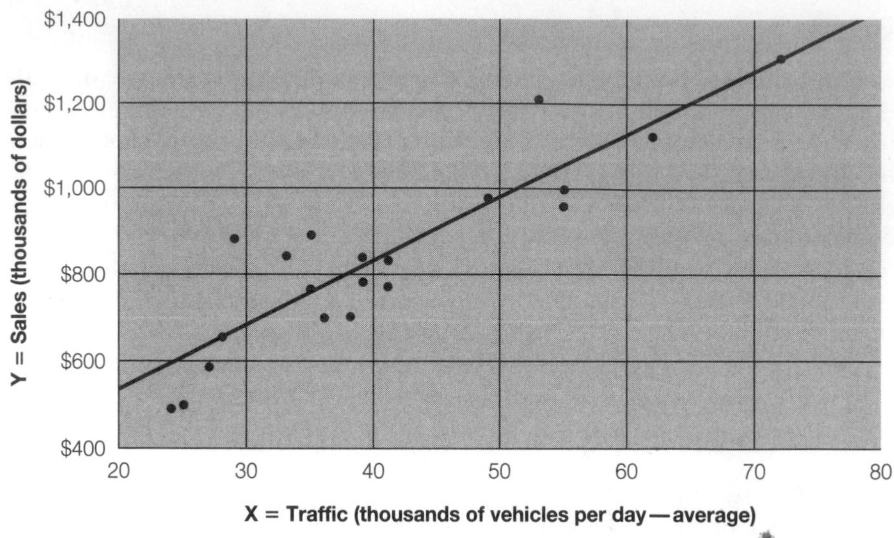

Least Squares Estimation Procedure

The least squares procedure is a fairly simple mathematical technique that can be used to fit a line to data for X and Y (see Figure 14.2) that best represents the relationship between the two variables. No straight line can perfectly represent every observation in the scatter plot. This is reflected in discrepancies between the actual values (dots on scatter diagram) and predicted values (value indicated by the line). Any straight line fitted to the data in the scatter plot will be subject to error. A number of lines could be drawn that would seem to fit the observations in Figure 14.2.

The least squares procedure results in a straight line that fits the actual observations (dots) better than any other line that could be fitted to the observations. Put another way, the sum of the squared deviations from this line (squared differences between dots and the line) is less than for any other line that can be fitted to the observations.

The general equation for the line is $Y = a + bX$. The estimating equation for regression analysis is

$$Y = \hat{a} + \hat{b}X + e$$

where

Y = dependent variable—number of pennants sold
$\hat{a}$ = estimated Y intercept for regression line
$\hat{b}$ = estimated slope of the regression line—regression coefficient
X = independent variable—average daily vehicular traffic in thousands of vehicles
e = error—difference between actual value and value predicted by regression line

Values for $\hat{a}$ and $\hat{b}$ can be calculated as follows:

$$\hat{b} = \frac{\sum X_i Y_i - n\overline{X}\,\overline{Y}}{\sum X_i^2 - n(\overline{X})^2}$$

$$\hat{a} = \overline{Y} - \hat{b}\overline{X}$$

where

$\overline{X}$ = mean value of X
$\overline{Y}$ = mean value of Y
n = sample size (number of units in the sample)

Using the data from Table 14.2, $\hat{b}$ is calculated as follows:

$$\hat{b} = \frac{734{,}083 - 20(40.8)(841.3)}{36{,}526 - 20(40.8)^2}$$

$$= 14.72$$

Table 14.2

Least Squares Computation

Store	X	Y	X^2	Y^2	XY
1	62	1,121	3,844	1,256,641	69,502
2	35	766	1,225	586,756	26,810
3	36	701	1,296	491,401	25,236
4	72	1,304	5,184	1,700,416	93,888
5	41	832	1,681	692,224	34,112
6	39	782	1,521	611,524	30,498
7	49	977	2,401	954,529	47,873
8	25	503	625	253,009	12,575
9	41	773	1,681	597,529	31,693
10	39	839	1,521	703,921	32,721
11	35	893	1,225	797,449	31,255
12	27	588	729	345,744	15,876
13	55	957	3,025	915,849	52,635
14	38	703	1,444	494,209	26,714
15	24	497	576	247,009	11,928
16	28	657	784	431,649	18,396
17	53	1,209	2,809	1,461,681	64,077
18	55	997	3,025	994,009	54,835
19	33	844	1,089	712,336	27,852
20	29	883	841	779,689	25,607
Sum	816	16,826	36,526	15,027,574	734,083
Mean	40.8	841.3			

The value of $\hat{a}$ is calculated as follows:

$$\begin{aligned}\hat{a} &= \overline{Y} - \hat{b}\overline{X} \\ &= 841.3 - 14.72(40.8) \\ &= 240.86\end{aligned}$$

Thus, the estimated regression function is given by

$$\begin{aligned}\hat{Y} &= \hat{a} + \hat{b}X \\ &= 240.86 + 14.72(X)\end{aligned}$$

where $\hat{Y}$ (Y hat) is the value of the estimated regression function for a given value of X.

According to the estimated regression function, for every additional 1,000 vehicles per day in traffic (X), total annual sales will increase by \$14.72 (estimated value of b). The value of a is 240.86. Technically, a hat is the estimated value of the dependent variable (Y or annual sales) when the value of the independent variable (X or average daily vehicular traffic) is zero.

The Regression Line

Predicted values for Y, based on calculated values for $\hat{a}$ and $\hat{b}$, are shown in Table 14.3. In addition, errors for each observation ($Y - \hat{Y}$) are shown. The regression line resulting from the $\hat{Y}$ values is shown in Figure 14.3.

Convenience store chains use regression analysis to predict sales for current and future sales.

Table 14.3

Predicted Values and Errors for Each Observation

Store	X	Y	$\hat{Y}$	$Y - \hat{Y}$	$(Y - \hat{Y})^2$	$(Y - \bar{Y})^2$
1	62	1,121	1,153.3	−32.2951	1,043	78,232
2	35	766	755.9	10.05716	101	5,670
3	36	701	770.7	−69.6596	4,852	19,684
4	72	1,304	1,300.5	3.537362	13	214,091
5	41	832	844.2	−12.2434	150	86
6	39	782	814.8	−32.8098	1,076	3,516
7	49	977	962.0	15.02264	226	18,414
8	25	503	608.8	−105.775	11,188	114,447
9	41	773	844.2	−71.2434	5,076	4,665
10	39	839	814.8	24.19015	585	5
11	35	893	755.9	137.0572	18,785	2,673
12	27	588	638.2	−50.2088	2,521	64,161
13	55	957	1,050.3	−93.2779	8,701	13,386
14	38	703	800.1	−97.0931	9,427	19,127
15	24	497	594.1	−97.0586	9,420	118,542
16	28	657	652.9	4.074415	17	33,966
17	53	1,209	1,020.8	188.1556	35,403	135,203
18	55	997	1,050.3	−53.2779	2,839	24,242
19	33	844	726.5	117.4907	13,804	7
20	29	883	667.6	215.3577	46,379	1,739
Sum	816	16,826	16,826.0		171,604.8	871,860.2
Mean	40.8	841.3				

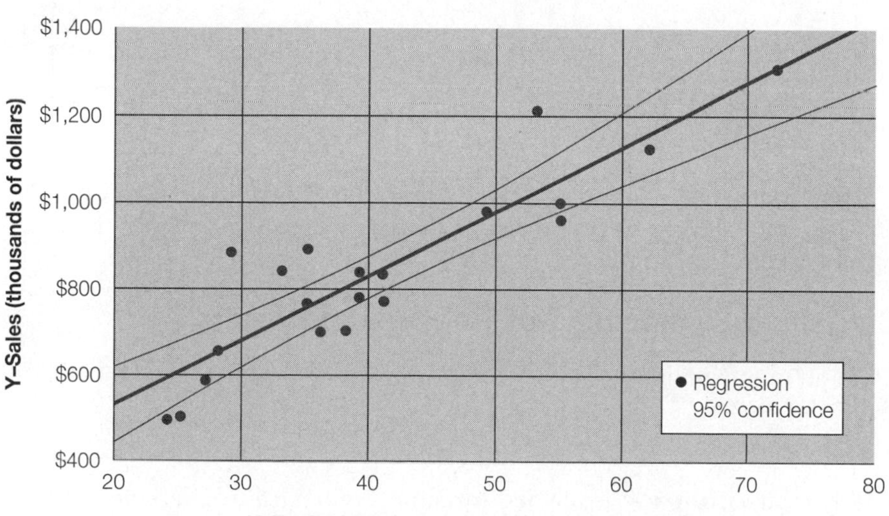

Figure 14.3

Least Squares Regression Line Fitted to Sample Data

Strength of Association—R^2

Coefficient of determination (R^2) The percentage of the total variation in the dependent variable explained by the independent variable.

The estimated regression function describes the nature of the relationship between X and Y. In addition, we are interested in the strength of the relationship between the variables. How widely do the actual values of Y differ from the values predicted by our model?

The **coefficient of determination,** denoted by R^2, is the measure of the strength of the linear relationship between X and Y. The coefficient of determination measures the percent of the total variation in Y that is "explained" by the variation in X. The R statistic ranges from 0 to 1. If there is a perfect linear relationship between X and Y, that is, all the variation in Y is explained by the variation in X, then R^2 equals 1. At the other extreme, if there is no relationship between X and Y, then none of the variation in Y is explained by the variation in X, and R equals 0.

The coefficient of determination for our example would be computed as follows—see Table 14.3 for calculation of $(Y - \hat{Y})^2$ and $(Y - \overline{Y})^2$:

$$R^2 = \frac{\text{explained variance}}{\text{total variance}}$$

$$\text{explained variance} = \text{total variance} - \text{unexplained variance}$$

$$R^2 = \frac{\text{total variance} - \text{unexplained variance}}{\text{total variance}}$$

$$R^2 = 1 - \frac{\text{unexplained variance}}{\text{total variance}}$$

$$R^2 = 1 - \frac{\sum_{i=1}^{n} (Y_i - \hat{Y}_i)^2}{\sum_{i=1}^{n} (Y_i - \overline{Y})^2}$$

$$R^2 = 1 - \frac{171{,}604.8}{871{,}860.2} = .803$$

Of the variation of Y (annual sales), 80 percent is explained by the variation in X (average daily vehicular traffic). There is a very strong linear relationship between X and Y.

Statistical Significance of Regression Results

In computing R^2, the total variation in Y was partitioned into two component sums of squares:

$$\text{total variation} = \text{explained variation} + \text{unexplained variation}$$

The total variation is a measure of variation of the observed Y values around their mean $\overline{Y}$. It measures the variation in the Y values without any consideration of the X values.

Total variation, known as the *total sum of squares* (SST), is given by

$$\text{SST} = \sum_{i=1}^{n}(Y_i - \overline{Y})^2 = \sum_{i=1}^{n}Y_i^2 - \left(\frac{\sum_{i=1}^{n}Y_i^2}{n}\right)$$

The explained variation or the **sum of squares due to regression** (SSR) is given by

Sum of squares due to regression (SSR) The variation explained by the regression.

$$\text{SSR} = \sum_{i=1}^{n}(\hat{Y}_i - \overline{Y})^2 = a\sum_{i=1}^{n}Y_i + b\sum_{i=1}^{n}X_iY_i - \left(\frac{\sum_{i=1}^{n}Y_i}{n}\right)^2$$

Figure 14.4 shows the various measures of variation (sum of squares) in a regression. SSR represents the differences between the $\hat{Y}_i$ (the values of Y predicted by the estimated regression equation) and $\overline{Y}$ (the average value of Y). In a well-fitting regression equation, the variation explained by regression (SSR) represents a large portion of the total variation (SST). If Y_i is

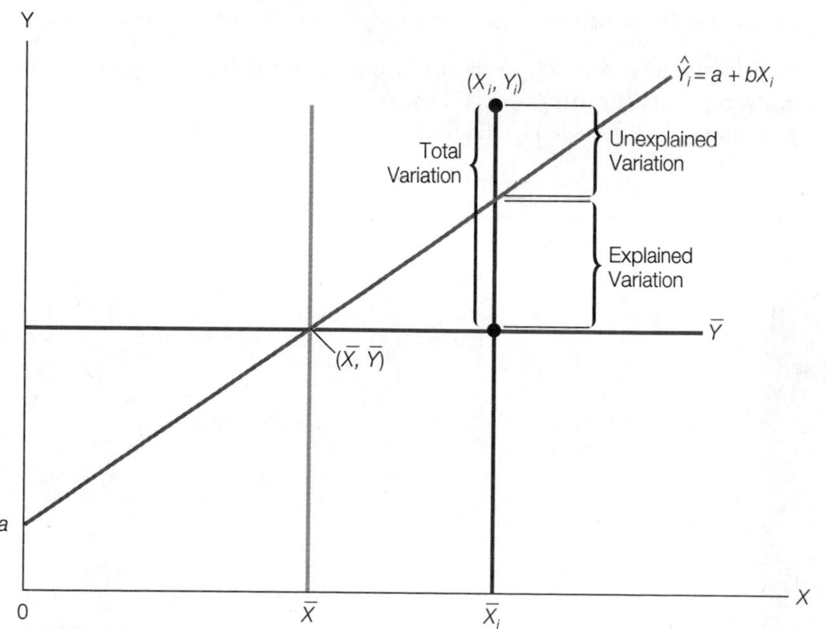

Figure 14.4

Measures of Variation in a Regression

defined as Y_i at each value of X_i, then a perfect fit has been achieved. All the observed values of Y would then be on the computed regression line. In that case SSR is defined as SST.

Error sum of squares (SSE) The variation not explained by the regression.

The unexplained variation or **error sum of squares (SSE)** is obtained from

$$SSE = \sum_{i=1}^{n}(Y_i - \hat{Y}_i)^2 = \sum_{i=1}^{n} Y_i^2 - a\sum_{i=1}^{n} Y_i - b\sum_{i=1}^{n} X_i Y_i$$

From Figure 14.4 note that SSE represents the residual difference (error) between the observed and predicted Y values. Therefore, the unexplained variation is a measure of scatter around the regression line. If the fit was perfect, there would be no scatter around the regression line, and SSE would be zero.

Hypotheses Concerning the Overall Regression

Here we are interested in hypotheses regarding the computed R^2 value for our problem. Is the amount of variance explained in our result (by our model) significantly greater than we would expect due to chance or, as in the various statistical tests discussed in Chapter 13, to what extent can we rule out sampling error as an explanation of our results? Analysis of variance (F-test) is used to test the significance of the results.

The analysis of variance table is set up as shown in Table 14.4. The computer output for our example is shown in Figure 14.5. The breakdowns of the total sum of squares and associated degrees of freedom are displayed in the form of an analysis of variance table. We use the information in this table to test the significance of the linear relationship between Y and X. As noted previously, an F-test will be used for this purpose. Our hypotheses are

- null hypothesis H_0: There is no linear relationship between X (average daily vehicular traffic) and Y (annual sales).
- alternative hypothesis H_a: There is a linear relationship between X and Y.

Table 14.4

Analysis of Variance

Source of Variation	Degrees of Freedom	Sum of Squares	Mean Square	F-Statistic
Due to regression (explained)	1	SSR	$MSR = \frac{SSR}{1}$	$F = \frac{MSR}{MSE}$
Residual (unexplained)	$n - 2$	SSE	$MSE = \frac{SSE}{n-2}$	
Total	$n - 1$	SST		

As in other statistical tests, we must choose alpha, α. This is the likelihood that the observed result occurred due to chance or the probability of incorrectly rejecting the null hypothesis. In this case we decided on a rather standard level of significance or $\alpha = .05$. This means that if the calculated value of F exceeds the tabular value, we are willing to accept a 5 percent chance of incorrectly rejecting the null hypothesis. The value of F or the F-ratio is computed as follows (see Table 14.4):

$$F = \frac{\text{MSR}}{\text{MSE}}$$
$$= \frac{700{,}2553.4}{9{,}533.6}$$
$$= 73.45$$

We will reject the null hypothesis if the calculated F-statistic is greater than or equal to the table or critical F-value. The numerator and denominator degrees of freedom for this F-ratio are 1 and 18, respectively. As noted earlier, it was decided that an alpha level of 5 percent ($\alpha = .05$) should be used.

The table or critical value of F with 1 (numerator) and 18 (denominator) degrees of freedom at $\alpha = .05$ is 4.49 (see Table 5 in the Appendix at the end of the text). Because the calculated value of F is greater than the critical value, we can reject the null hypothesis and conclude that there is a significant linear relationship between the average daily vehicular traffic (X) and annual sales (Y). This result is consistent with the high coefficient of determination R^2 discussed earlier.

Hypotheses about the Regression Coefficient (*b*)

Finally, we may be interested in making hypotheses about b, the regression coefficient. As you may recall, b is the estimate of the effect of a one-unit change in X on Y. The hypotheses are

- null hypothesis H_0: $b = 0$
- alternative hypothesis H_a: $b \neq 0$

The appropriate test is a t-test, and as you can see from the last line of Figure 14.5, the computer program calculates the t-value (8.57) and the p-value

Figure 14.5

STATISTICA® Regression Analysis Output

STAT. MULTIPLE REGRESS.	Regression Summary for Dependent Variable: Y R=.89619973 R²=.80317395 Adjusted R²=.79223917 F(1,18)=73.4.51 p<.00000 Std. Error of estimate: 97.640					
N=20	BETA	St. Err. of BETA	B	St. Err. of B	t(10)	p-level
Intercept			240.8566	73.38347	3.282164	.004141
X	.896200	.104570	14.7168	1.71717	8.570374	.000000

(probability of incorrectly rejecting the null hypotheses of .0000). See Chapter 13 for a more detailed discussion of *p*-values. Given our α criterion of .05, we would reject the null hypothesis in this case.

Correlation Analysis

Correlation for Metric Data: Pearson's Product Moment Correlation

Correlation analysis
Analysis of the degree to which changes in one variable are associated with changes in another.

Pearson's product moment
A correlation analysis technique for use with metric data.

Correlation is the measurement of the degree to which changes in one variable (the dependent variable) are associated with changes in another. If we are analyzing the relationship between two variables, the analysis is called simple or bivariate **correlation analysis.** The **Pearson's product moment** approach is used if metric data are involved.

In bivariate regression, we discussed the coefficient of determination R^2 as a measure of the strength of the linear relationship between X and Y. Another descriptive measure, called the *coefficient of correlation* (R), is a measure of the degree of association between X and Y. It is the square root of the coefficient of determination with the appropriate sign (+ or −):

$$R = \pm\sqrt{R^2}$$

The value of R can range from −1 (perfect negative correlation) to +1 (perfect positive correlation). The closer R is to ±1, the stronger the degree of association between X and Y. If R is equal to zero, then there is no association between X and Y.

If we are not interested in estimating the regression function, R can be computed directly, with the data from our convenience store example, using this formula:

$$R = \frac{n\Sigma XY - (\Sigma X)(\Sigma Y)}{\sqrt{[n\Sigma X^2 - (\Sigma X)^2][n\Sigma Y^2 - (\Sigma Y)^2]}}$$

The correlation coefficient

$$R = \frac{20(734{,}083) - (816)(16{,}826)}{\sqrt{[20(36{,}526) - (816)^2][20(15{,}027{,}574) - (16{,}826)^2]}}$$

$$R = .896$$

This value of R indicates a positive correlation between the average daily vehicular traffic and annual sales. In other words, successively higher levels of sales are associated with successively higher levels of traffic.

Correlation Using Ordinal Data: Spearman's Rank-Order Correlation

Researchers often need to analyze the degree of association between two ordinally scaled variables. The authors recently worked with an ad agency that wanted to determine whether there was a correlation between a company's ranking on product quality and its market share rank. The agency did a small pilot study with users of the product category to obtain quality ranks for the 12 companies in the industry. Market share data for the 12 companies were estimated, and because the agency did not feel they were very accurate, the companies were ranked based on relative market shares. Please note that in the case of both quality rank and market share rank, a smaller number (higher rank) indicates a higher result. The resulting data are provided in Table 14.5 on page 451. Three different conclusions are possible regarding the rankings:

1. They are positively correlated.
2. They are negatively correlated.
3. They are independent.

The **Spearman rank-order correlation** coefficient R_s is the appropriate procedure for analyzing these data. Spearman's rank correlation coefficient is defined by

Spearman rank-order correlation Correlation analysis technique for use with ordinal data.

$$R_s = 1 - \left(\frac{6\sum_{i=1}^{n} d_i^2}{n^3 - n} \right)$$

where

d_i = difference in ranks of the two variables
n = number of items ranked

Using the data from Table 14.5, R_s would be calculated as follows:

$$R_s = 1 - \left(\frac{6(44)}{(12)^3 - 12} \right)$$

$$R_s = .85$$

Based on this analysis, the two rankings are positively correlated. Higher rankings on one are associated with higher rankings on the other.

The value of the coefficient of rank correlation ($R_s = .85$) can be tested against the null hypothesis using a t-distribution for a given sample size ($n = 12$) as follows:

In PRACTICE

The Notion of Spurious Correlation

When two variables are correlated solely because they are both affected by the same cause, a spurious correlation is said to have occurred. Once the effects of the common cause are controlled or removed from the two variables (resulting in a partial correlation coefficient), the correlation between them is no longer evident. Examples of such spurious correlations are the relationship between ownership of a gold watch and a long life (affluence influences both), foot size and performance on achievement tests for individuals (age influences both), and consumption of bottled water and the likelihood of a normal pregnancy (affluence again).

Some correlations are simply hard to explain. The common cause is not evident or doesn't exist—the correlation results from chance occurrence. One example is the outcome of the Super Bowl and the performance of the Dow Jones Industrial Average of the New York Stock Exchange. The almost stupefying occurrence of the Dow Jones Average being higher at the end of the year than at the beginning of the year if the team from the National Football League's National Conference wins the Super Bowl has been noticed and discussed by many observers of the stock market. While the correlation of these two occurrences is high, the importance of this observed relationship is not. ■

Spurious correlation cannot explain the relationship between the outcome of the Super Bowl and the performance of the Dow. Even though the correlation is high, the importance of the observed relationship is not.

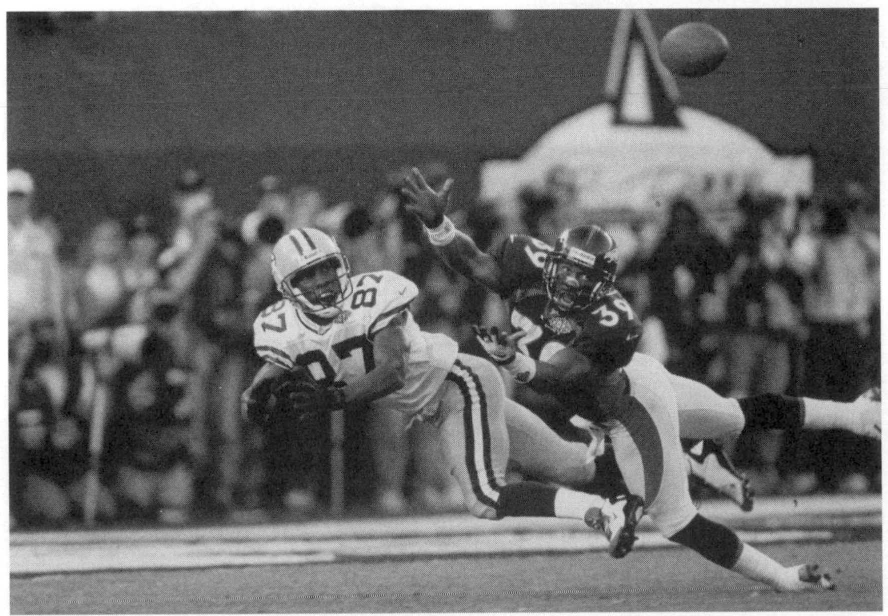

$$t = R_s\sqrt{\frac{n-2}{1-R_s^2}}$$

$$= .85\sqrt{\frac{12-2}{1-.85^2}}$$

$$= 5.1$$

The agency believes that there is a positive relationship between a company's quality image and its market share. The null and alternative hypotheses were formulated as:

- null hypothesis $H_0{:}R_s = 0$
- alternative hypothesis $H_a{:}R_s > 0$

The table value for t with 10 ($n - 2$) degrees of freedom is 2.23 (at α = .05). Because the calculated t-value (5.1) is higher than the table or critical value (2.23), we reject the null hypothesis and conclude that there is a positive association between a company's quality image and it market share rank.

Spearman's coefficient of rank correlation (R_s), like the coefficient of correlation (R), has a lower limit of −1 and an upper limit of +1; that is, the range of R_s is between −1 and +1 ($-1 \leq R_s \leq 1$).

Table 14.5

Quality Image Rank versus Market Share Rank

Company	Quality Rank X	Ranks Market Share Rank Y	d_i	d
A	4	3	1	1
B	6	7	−1	1
C	9	5	4	16
D	7	6	1	1
E	1	2	−1	1
F	3	4	−1	1
G	11	12	−1	1
H	5	9	−4	16
I	8	8	0	0
J	12	10	2	4
K	10	11	−1	1
L	2	1	1	1

$$R_s = 1 - \frac{6(44)}{(12)^2 - 12} = 0.85 \qquad \sum_{i=1}^{n} d_i^2 = 44$$

In PRACTICE

Using the Right Measure of Correlation

The Spearman rank-order correlation coefficient is the correct procedure for estimating the degree of association between ranked objects. But what would the difference be if Pearson's product moment correlation was inappropriately used for gauging the association between ranked objects? Such a case might occur if a marketing researcher mistook the rankings for metric ratings.

In order to examine this question, a data set of 12 ranked objects was first analyzed with the correct Spearman rank-order correlation, and then subsequently with the incorrect Pearson's product moment correlation. The rankings were made by 436 patrons of the Georgia Shakespeare Festival during the summer season in Atlanta, Georgia. The ranked objects were 12 live-entertainment events that were then competing in the local market. Some of these events were the Shakespeare Festival's presentation of *Cyrano de Bergerac* and *Henry V;* a touring Broadway musical, *42nd St.;* a folk music concert featuring Peter, Paul, and Mary; a pop music concert featuring Kenny Loggins; and a professional baseball game between the Atlanta Braves and the San Francisco Giants. The two tables of 66 unique coefficients were then compared.[2]

The comparison revealed that the inappropriately applied Pearson product moment correlations were sometimes inflated and at other times deflated. In all, decisions on about 8 out of 66 coefficients would have been made incorrect at $p = .05$. This is 12 percent of the decisions. In summary, this comparison of correct and incorrect correlation coefficients suggests that using the appropriate rank-order correlation does indeed matter. With this data set, the error was three times the 5 percent error a mistaken marketing researcher would have expected. ■

Summary

This chapter discusses the relationship between variables taken two at a time. The techniques used for this analysis are called bivariate analyses. Bivariate regression analysis is used so that a single dependent variable can be predicted from the knowledge about a single independent variable. One way to examine the underlying relationship between a dependent and an independent variable is to plot them on a scatter diagram. If the relationship appears to be linear, then linear regression analysis may be used. If it is curvilinear, then curve-fitting techniques should be applied. The general equation for a straight line fitted to two variables is given by the equation

$$Y = a + bX$$

where

Y = the dependent variable

X = the independent variable
a = Y intercept
b = the amount Y increases with each unit increase in X

Both a and b are unknown and must be estimated. This is known as *simple linear regression analysis.* Bivariate least squares regression analysis is a mathematical technique for fitting a line to measurements of the two variables X and Y. The line is fitted so that the algebraic sum of deviations of the actual observations from the line is zero and the sum of the squared deviations is less than it would be for any other line that might be fitted to the data.

The estimated regression function describes the nature of the relationship between X and Y. In addition, researchers want to know the strength of the relationship between the variables. This is measured by the coefficient of determination, denoted by R^2. The coefficient of determination measures the percent of the total variation in Y that is "explained" by the variation in X. The R^2 statistic ranges from 0 to 1.

Correlation analysis is the measurement of the degree to which changes in one variable are associated with changes in another. Correlation analysis tells the researcher whether the variables are positively correlated, negatively correlated, or independent.

Key Terms & Definitions

Bivariate techniques Statistical methods of determining the relationship between two variables.

Independent variable The variable believed to affect the value of the dependent variable.

Dependent variable The variable whose value is believed to change in response to the independent variable.

Bivariate regression analysis An analysis of the strength of the linear relationship between two variables when one is considered the independent variable and the other the dependent variable.

Coefficient of determination (R^2) The percentage of the total variation in the dependent variable explained by the independent variable.

Sum of squares due to regression (SSR) The variation explained by the regression.

Error sum of squares (SSE) The variation not explained by the regression.

Correlation analysis Analysis of the degree to which changes in one variable are associated with changes in another.

Pearson's product moment A correlation analysis technique for use with metric data.

Spearman rank-order correlation Correlation analysis technique for use with ordinal data.

Questions for Review & Critical Thinking

1. What are the primary differences between simple regression and correlation analysis?
2. A sales manager administered a standard multiple-item job satisfaction scale to a random sample of the firm's sales force. The manager then correlated the satisfaction scores with the years of school the salespeople had completed. The Pearson correlation between satisfaction and years of school turned out to be .15. On the basis of this evidence, the sales manager came to the following conclusions: "A salesperson's level of education has little to do with his or her job satisfaction. Furthermore, as education level rises, they continue to have the same average levels of job satisfaction." Would you agree or disagree with the sales manager's conclusions? Explain your answer.
3. What is the purpose of a scatter diagram?
4. Explain how a marketing researcher can use the coefficient of determination.
5. Comment on the following: "When the AFC team has won the Super Bowl, the stock market has always risen in the first quarter of the year in every case except one; when the NFC has won the Super Bowl, the stock market has fallen in the first quarter in all cases except two."
6. The following table gives data collected for a convenience store chain for 20 of its stores. The data are

   - Column 1: ID number for each store
   - Column 2: Annual sales for the store for the previous year in thousands of dollars
   - Column 3: Average daily numbers of vehicles that pass the store each day, based on actual traffic counts for one month
   - Column 4: Total population that lives within a two-mile radius of the store, based on 1990 census data
   - Column 5: Median family income for households within a 2-mile radius of the store, based on 1990 census data.

Store ID#	Annual Sales ($000)	Average Daily Traffic	Population in Two-Mile Radius	Average Income in Area
1	$1,121	61,655	17,880	$28,991
2	$ 766	35,236	13,742	$14,731
3	$ 595	35,403	19,741	$ 8,114
4	$ 899	52,832	23,246	$15,324
5	$ 915	40,809	24,485	$11,438
6	$ 782	40,820	20,410	$11,730
7	$ 833	49,147	28,997	$10,589
8	$ 571	24,953	9,981	$10,706
9	$ 692	40,828	8,982	$23,591
10	$1,005	39,195	18,814	$15,703
11	$ 589	34,574	16,941	$ 9,015
12	$ 671	26,639	13,319	$10,065
13	$ 903	55,083	21,482	$17,365

Store ID#	Annual Sales ($000)	Average Daily Traffic	Population in Two-Mile Radius	Average Income in Area
14	$ 703	37,892	26,524	$ 7,532
15	$ 556	24,019	14,412	$ 6,950
16	$ 657	27,791	13,896	$ 9,855
17	$1,209	53,438	22,444	$21,589
18	$ 997	54,835	18,096	$22,659
19	$ 844	32,916	16,458	$12,660
20	$ 883	29,139	16,609	$11,618

Answer the following:

a. Which of the other three variables is the best predictor of sales? Compute correlation coefficients to answer the question.

b. Do the following regressions:
   (1) sales as a function of average daily traffic
   (2) sales as a function of population in a 2-mile radius.

c. Interpret the results of the two regressions.

7. Interpret the following:

a. $Y = .11 + .009X$, where Y is the likelihood of sending children to college and X is family income in thousands of dollars. Remember, it is family income in thousands.
   (1) According to our model, how likely is a family with an income of $30,000 to send its children to college?
   (2) What is the likelihood for a family with an income of $50,000?
   (3) What is the likelihood for a family with an income of $17,500?
   (4) Is there some logic to the estimates? Explain.

b. $Y = .25 - .0039X$, where Y is the likelihood of going to a skateboard park and X is age.
   (1) According to our model, how likely is a 10-year-old to go to a skateboard park?
   (2) What is the likelihood for a 60-year-old?
   (3) What is the likelihood for a 40-year-old?
   (4) Is there some logic to the estimates? Explain.

8. What is the difference between the Pearson correlation coefficient and the Spearman rank-order correlation coefficient?

9. The following ANOVA summary data are the result of a regression with sales per year (dependent variable) as a function of promotion expenditures per year (independent variable) for a toy company.

$$F = \frac{MSR}{MSE} = \frac{34{,}276}{4721}$$

The degrees of freedom are 1 for the numerator and 19 for the denominator. Is the relationship statistically significant at $\alpha = .05$? Comment.

Working the Net

1. What is the correlation between the U.S. unemployment rate and import prices for 1995 to 1997?

   Go to the Bureau of Labor Statistics at http://stats.bls.gov.

   Select Unemployment Rate and U.S. Import Index for 1999 to 2000. Load both series of data into a spreadsheet or statistical analysis program and compute the correlation.
2. How can an individual become more familiar with statistical software program capabilities?

   For STATISTICA®, go to: http://www.statsoftinc.com

   For SPSS, go to: http://www.spss.com

   For SAS, go to: http://www.sas.com

   For Minitab, go to: http://www.minitab.com

Real-Life Research

Style and Quality in Athletic Shoes

Bill Sexton is the new product development manager for Road Runner Athletic Shoe Company. He recently completed consumer testing of 12 new shoe models. As part of this test, a panel of consumers was asked to rank the 12 shoe concepts on two attributes: overall quality and style. The panel of 20 met as a group and came up with the rankings as a group. Bill believes that there is a relationship between the style rankings and the overall quality rankings. He believes that shoes receiving higher rankings on style will also tend to receive higher rankings on overall quality. The ranking results for the 12 shoe concepts are shown in the table below:

Shoe Model	Style Rank	Quality Rank
1	3	4
2	5	2
3	9	10
4	2	1
5	4	3
6	1	8
7	6	11
8	8	5
9	7	7
10	11	2
11	10	9
12	12	6

1. Which of the statistical procedures covered in this chapter is appropriate for addressing Bill's theory? Why would you choose that technique over the others?
2. Use the technique that you choose to determine whether Bill's theory is supported by the statistical evidence. State the appropriate null and alternative hypotheses. Is Bill's theory supported by the statistical evidence? Why or why not?

CD Opportunity

1. Your CD contains a comprehensive case and data set on Rockingham Bank Visa Card. You now have the skills to analyze the data and understand the research design.
2. Ethical Dilemmas for this part can be found on your CD. They will help you understand the responsibilities involved in analyzing and using data.

PART *five*

Marketing Research in Action

Check it out!

Remember to visit http://mcdaniel.swcollege.com for information to help you with the material in Part Five. MR Online in the Resource Center of http://marketing.swcollege.com can also help you review for your final exam!

Communicating the Research Results

Learning Objectives

1

To become aware of the primary roles of a research report

2

To learn how to organize and prepare a research report

3

To review pitfalls in marketing research reports

4

To learn about personal presentations

5

To understand the effective use and communication of marketing research information

CHAPTER *fifteen*

John Speilberg, a New York-based researcher, likes to tell of his carefully prepared 250-page report (including tables and statistical analysis) prepared for one of America's largest candy manufacturers. The report and presentation to three top executives culminated approximately six months of difficult research. John felt that he had several significant findings to report, including new market segments to explore and several product concept ideas.

Organizing volumes of data into a clear and concise marketing research report is a critical part of the decision-making process. Without clear communication of results, decision makers will not be able to act effectively.

After a laborious hour presentation with many facts, figures, and tables, the president of the candy company suddenly rose and said, "Damn it, John, I've been listening to this mumbo-jumbo for over an hour and I'm thoroughly confused. I know I won't be much better off trying to read through a report that's thicker than most dictionaries. I want a five-page summary on my desk tomorrow by 8:00." With that pronouncement, he left the room. John learned a lesson that has helped him throughout his career.

What is the role of the research report? How can marketing researchers communicate more effectively? What constitutes a "good" report? What pitfalls should be avoided in writing a research report? What are the key factors in deciding whether or not to use a research report? We will address these questions in this chapter.

It should almost go without saying that no matter how appropriate the research design, how proper the statistical analyses, how representative the sample, how carefully worded the questionnaire, how stringent the quality control checks for field collection of the data, or how well matched the research was to the original research objectives, everything will be for naught if the researcher cannot communicate with the decision makers. Chapter 15 begins with a discussion of the communication process. Next, the roles of the research report are presented. From here, the chapter delves into the organization of the report and points out how findings are interpreted into conclusions and how conclusions are then formulated into recommendations. Next, the chapter turns to the actual writing of the report. Because personal presentations are common in marketing research, the chapter includes discussion of this aspect of reporting the results. We conclude with suggestions for getting managers to use the research recommendations. ■

Find out more about effective business communication at

http://www.westwords.com/guffey/students.html

Designed specifically for students, this site offers an abundance of resources.

The Research Report

Now that all the data have been collected and analyzed, it is time for the researcher to package the information related to the project for the research users. The marketing research report serves as this package and should satisfy the following objectives:

- *Explain why the research was done.* A brief statement of the motivations for doing the research is often helpful to users in terms of putting the information in context. This is particularly true when a decision maker is reviewing a report done some time ago and may not be familiar with the reasons for doing the research.
- *State the specific research objectives.* Every marketing research project should have a detailed list of research objectives that guided the design and execution of the research and the analysis of the results.
- *Explain how the research was done.* Users need to know how the research was done so they can make a determination of how much weight they are going to put on the results in arriving at the decisions they need to make. Issues such as how the data were collected, the sampling procedures used, the analytical procedures used, and other details regarding the methodology should be clearly specified.
- *Present the findings of the research.* The basic findings of the research should be clearly enumerated. This section provides the basis for supporting the conclusions and recommendations that the researcher drew from those findings.
- *Provide conclusions and recommendations.* The report, to be actionable, must provide clear statements of the conclusions and recommendations that flow from the research findings. It is important in preparing the report that there is a clear linkage between the research findings and the conclusions and recommendations. The users of the information need to understand that the conclusions and recommendations made are supported by the findings of the research and are not merely the opinions of the researcher.

Organization of the Report

In some cases, corporate policy may dictate the exact format of the research report. The most common organization for marketing research reports today is outlined below:

1. *Table of contents.* Lists major sections.
2. *Background and objectives.* Approximately one page for each. This information normally comes from RFP and discussions with the client.
3. *Executive summary.* This is a two- to four-page summary of findings, conclusions, and recommendations.
4. *Methodology.* A two- to five-page description of how the research was conducted. The brief summary here may be supported by more detailed and technical material in appendices.

5. *Findings.* This is the largest section of most reports, which provides a detailed presentation of the research findings.
6. *Appendices.* A number of items are found in most appendices:

   - *Copy of the questionnaire.* This enables users to see exactly how certain questions were asked so that they can properly interpret key findings if they wish to do so.
   - *Cross-tabulations.* Cross-tabulated results for every question in the survey are provided in this appendix. This enables the user to look at specific issues that are not addressed in the findings.
   - *Other supporting material.* Appendices may be used to present detailed technical discussions of procedures and techniques used in the research.

Means of Presentation

The approach to preparing marketing research reports has changed dramatically in recent years. In the quest to find more efficient ways to convey research results, marketing researchers have gravitated to the use of **presentation software.** A number of presentation software packages are available, but Microsoft PowerPoint dominates the market.

Presentation software Personal computer software that provides easy-to-use platforms for creating effective reports and presentations.

We have always known that information can be presented more efficiently and in a more compelling manner in graphs than in words or tables. However, until recently we lacked the tools for the efficient and speedy creation of graphs. The marketing research report of today has become graphics-dominated. It is fairly typical today for clients to specify that they want graphics-based reports in their request for proposals. Research reports that would have included 50 or more pages of text in the past are presented in 10 to 12 pages of text and 20 to 30 pages of graphs today. This permits busy executives to quickly grasp key findings and more ahead to conclusions and recommendations. This trend has been expanded by the common use of color to further enhance efficient communication and make reports more exciting.

Presentation packages available today make it easy for the analyst to:

- create bulleted charts using various font styles and sizes with bold, italicized, and underlined text.
- easily create dozens of different types of graphs and, with a few mouse clicks, experiment with different types of graphs (pie, bar, line, 3-D effects, etc.) that might be used to display a particular research finding.
- apply various special effects, full-motion video, and sound when moving from page to page in an electronic presentation. It is becoming increasingly common for presentations to be presented using a personal computer attached to a color projection panel or a large multisync monitor. The presenter controls the presentation using a mouse, and the software can be programmed to use various fades between slides in the presentation and to include video (such as focus group comments) and sound clips at various points in the presentation.

In summary, the common reporting style in marketing research today has the following characteristics:

- minimizes the use of words
- feeds information to clients in what might be termed "sound bites."
- makes extensive use of bulleted charts
- makes extensive use of graphic presentations of results.

Examples of pages from reports prepared using presentation software are provided in Figures 15.1 through 15.9.

Interpreting the Findings and Formulating Recommendations

Executive summary The portion of a research report that explains why the research was done, what was found and what those findings mean, and what action, if any, management should undertake.

The greatest difficulties faced by individuals who are writing a research report for the first time occur in the interpretation of the findings to arrive at conclusions and using these conclusions to formulate recommendations. The **executive summary** is the portion of the report that explains why the research was done, what the research found and what it means, and what action should be taken based on the research, if any. The difficulties of this process are completely understandable, given that the marketing researcher is often inundated with mounds of computer printouts, stacks of questionnaires, bundles of respondent contact and recontact sheets, and a scratch pad full of notes on the project. There is, however, a systematic method that the researcher can follow to draw conclusions. The overall guide comes from the research objectives stated early in the marketing research process. These research objectives should have been stated as specifically as possible, perhaps even with an explicit priority rank for each objective. Also, the questionnaire was designed to touch facets of the objectives, but the specific bits of information for any one objective were spread across the questionnaire. The computer printouts often contain information in a statistical order rather than in the order in which managers will use the data. Consequently, the researcher's first task is to pull together all the printouts and results pertaining to each of the various objectives. By focusing attention on the objectives one at a time, a system will evolve.

For example, assume that Burger King is considering its breakfast menu. An objective of its breakfast research study is "to determine the feasibility of

Figure 15.1

Bulleted Chart

Executive Summary

- Visit Information:
  - **Overall.** 45.9% say they have visited a casino in the last 6 months.
  - **By market.** Visit rate is highest from Tampa (23.2%) and lowest from Panama City (4.1%).
  - **By demographics.** Those 54 and younger more likely to have visited than those 55+. Positive relationship with income. Those in $71K+ bracket most likely to have visited.
  - **Number of visits.** The average is just over 1.1 times across markets. Frequency highest for Miami (6.1) and lowest for Saint Petersburg (.39).

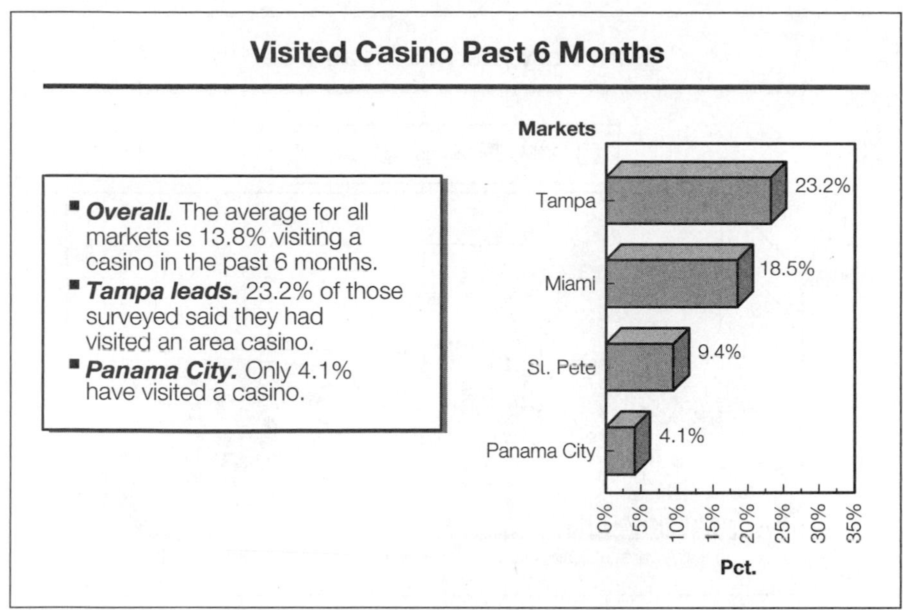

Figure 15.2

Text and 3-D Horizontal Bar Chart

adding (a) bagels and cream cheese, (b) a western omelette, or (c) French toast." All cross-tabulations and one-dimensional tables referring to these food items should be brought together. Generally, the researcher first examines the one-dimensional tables to get the overall picture, that is, which of the three breakfast items was most preferred. Next, cross-tabulations are analyzed to obtain a better understanding of the overall data, that is, which age group was most likely to prefer French toast.

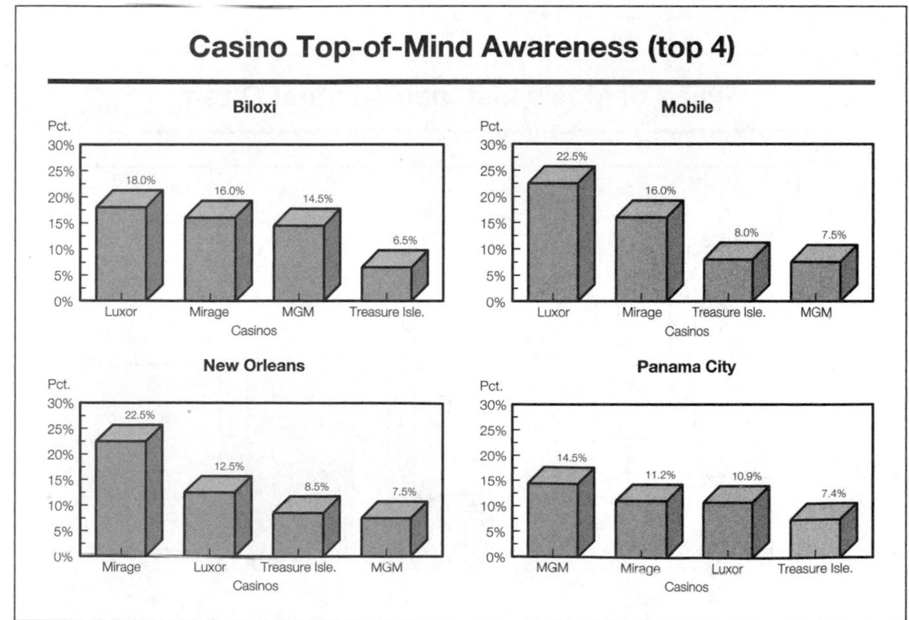

Figure 15.3

Multiple 3-D Bar Charts on Single Pages

Figure 15.4

Area Chart for Summary Measures

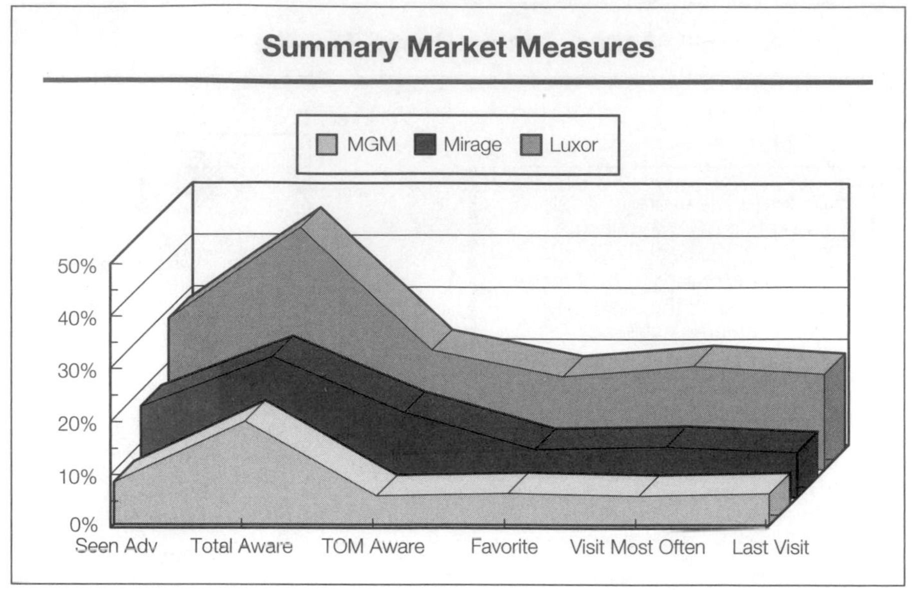

Conclusions Generalizations that answer the questions raised by the research objectives or that otherwise satisfy the objectives.

Conclusions are generalizations that answer the questions raised by the research objectives or otherwise satisfy the objectives. These conclusions are derived through the process of induction, which is the process of generalizing from small pieces of information. The researcher should try to combine the information and to paraphrase it in a few descriptive statements that generalize the results. In short, the conclusion or generalization is a statement or series of statements that communicate the results of the study to the reader but do not necessarily indicate the numbers derived from the statistical analysis.

Figure 15.5

Stacked Bar Chart with 3-D Effect

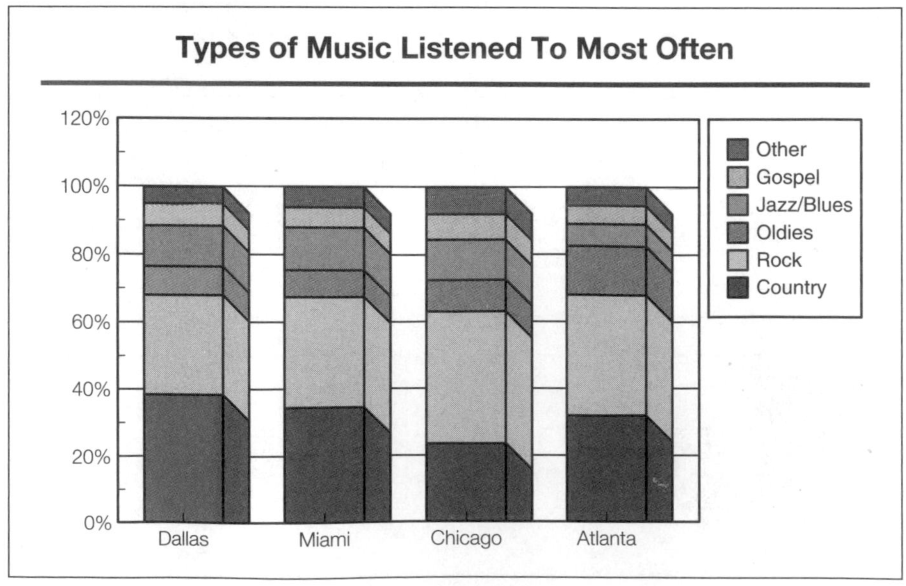

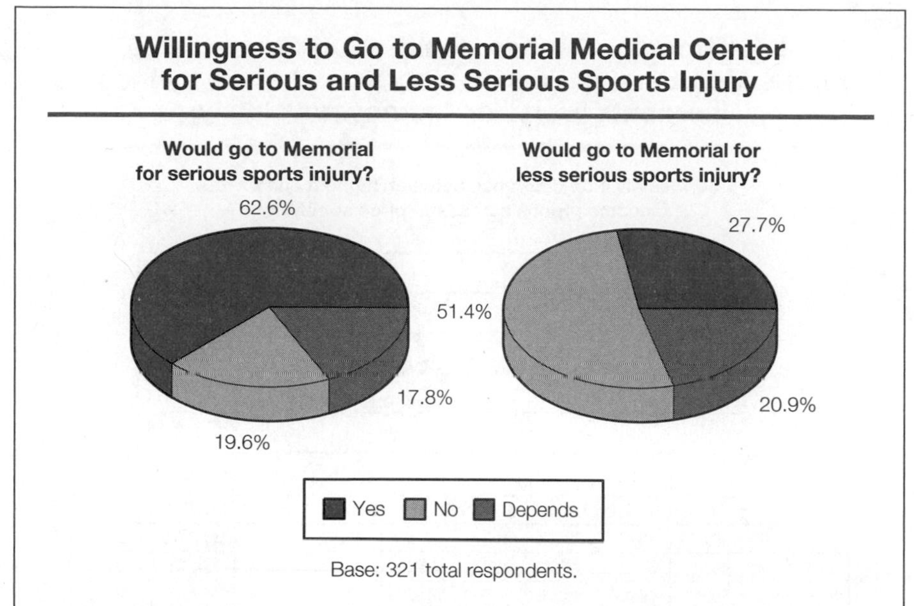

Figure 15.6

Pie Charts with 3-D Effect

Recommendations are gained from the process of deduction. The marketing researcher takes the conclusions to specific areas of application for marketing strategies or tactics. A recommendation normally should focus on how the client can gain a differential advantage. A *differential advantage* is the

Recommendations Conclusions applied to marketing strategies or tactics that focus on a client's achievement of differential advantage.

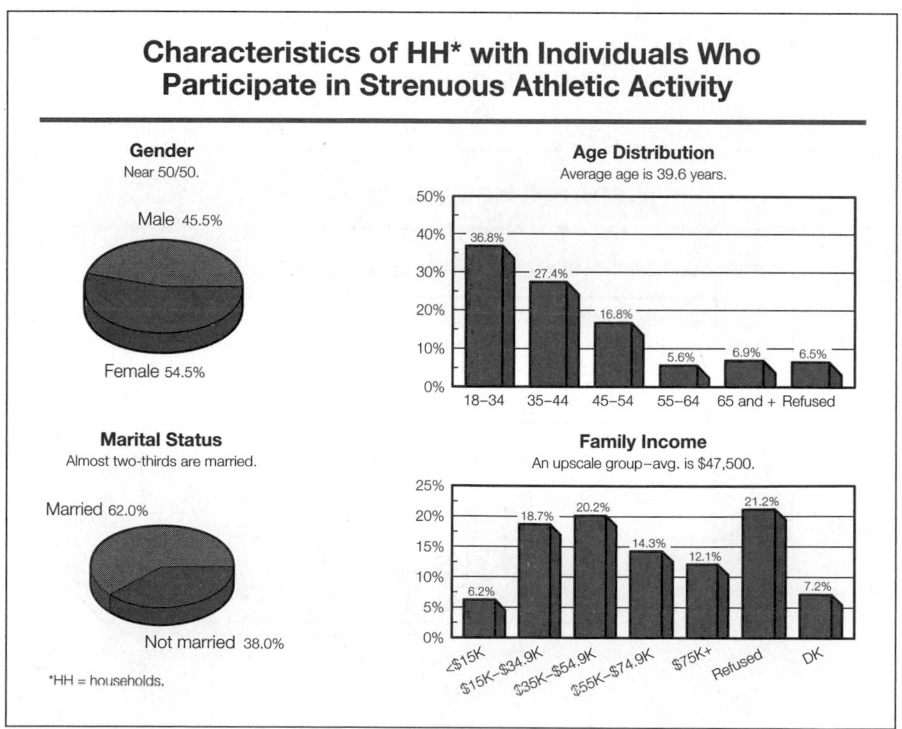

Figure 15.7

Mixing Pie and Bar Charts

Figure 15.8

Line Chart with Table Underneath

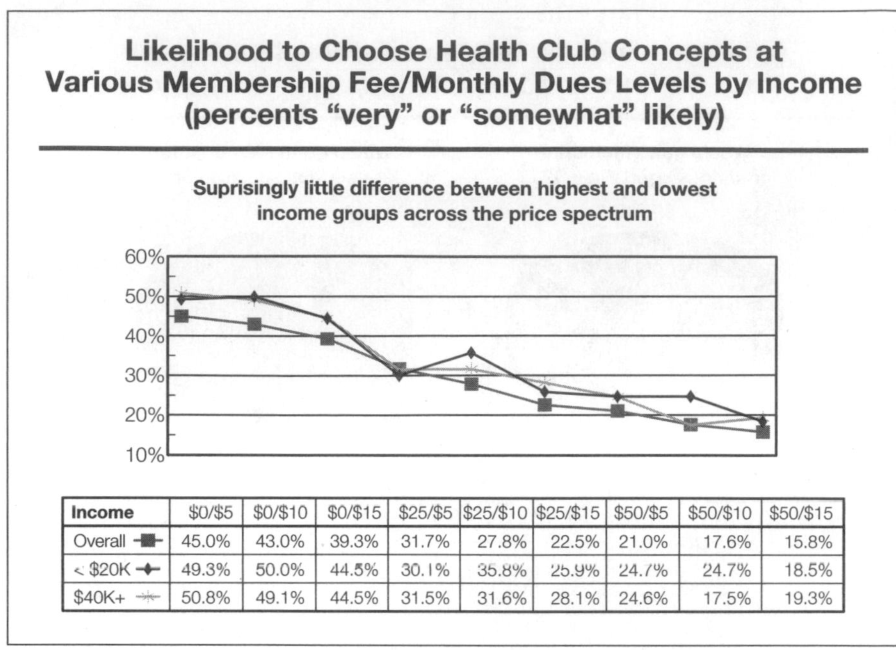

Income	$0/$5	$0/$10	$0/$15	$25/$5	$25/$10	$25/$15	$50/$5	$50/$10	$50/$15
Overall	45.0%	43.0%	39.3%	31.7%	27.8%	22.5%	21.0%	17.6%	15.8%
< $20K	49.3%	50.0%	44.5%	30.1%	35.8%	25.9%	24.7%	24.7%	18.5%
$40K+	50.8%	49.1%	44.5%	31.5%	31.6%	28.1%	24.6%	17.5%	19.3%

true benefit offered by a potential marketing mix that the target market cannot obtain anywhere else, such as United Airlines having exclusive U.S. carrier landing rights at a foreign airport.

Sometimes a marketing researcher must refrain from making specific recommendations and fall back on general ones. These are cases in which the marketing researcher does not have sufficient information about the resource and experience base of the company or decision maker to whom the report

Figure 15.9

XYZ Bar Chart with 3-D Effect

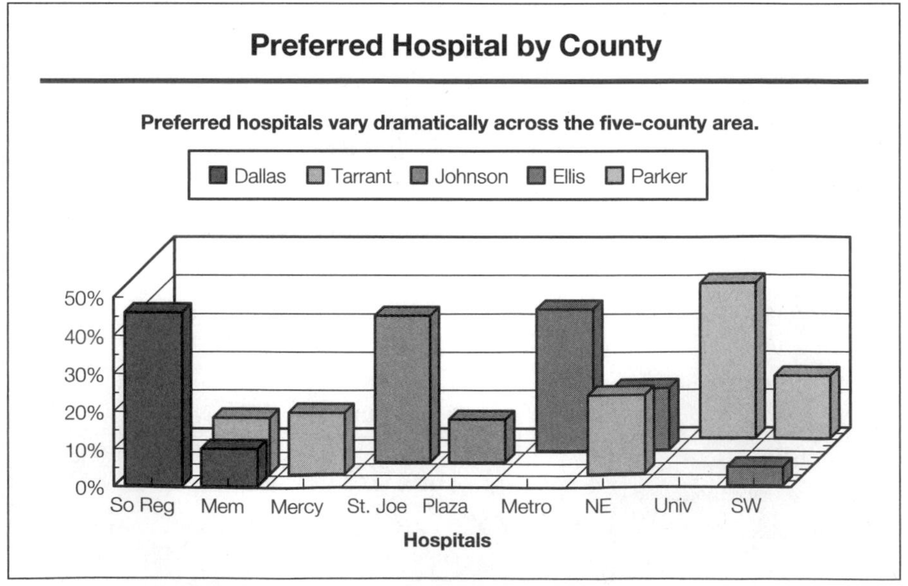

is being directed, or the researcher has been notified that the recommendations will be determined by the decision maker. Under these circumstances, the researcher offers conclusions and stops at that point.

Preparing the Report

The final report, whether written, personal, or both, represents the culmination of the research effort. The quality of the report and its recommendations often determine whether a research user will return to a supplier. Within a corporation, an internal report prepared by a research department may have a smaller impact. If you want to think selfishly, a history of excellent reports prepared by a research staff member may lead to merit salary increases and ultimately promotion.

The Personal Presentation

Clients may expect a personal presentation of the research results. This activity serves many purposes. It assembles the several interested parties together. It reacquaints them with the research objectives and method. Also, a personal presentation brings to light any unexpected events or findings. Most of all, it highlights the research conclusions. In fact, it is safe to say that for some decision makers in the company, the personal presentation will be their *only* exposure to the findings; they will never read the report. Other managers may only skim the written report, using it as a memory-recall trigger for points made in the personal presentation. In short, effective communication in the personal presentation is absolutely critical.

Materials for the Personal Presentation

We recommend the use of four aids in the personal presentation.

1. *Presentation outline.* Every audience member should be supplied with a presentation outline that briefly details the presentation flow (major parts) and significant findings. The outline should not contain statistics or tables, but it should have ample "white space" for the person to jot down notes or comments.
2. *Visuals.* The most commonly used visual devices were either a slide projector or an overhead projector. Today, most researchers use laptop personal computers, presentation software, and a projector that permits them to display their presentation on a screen of almost any size. Not only can traditional charts be shown, but spreadsheets as well. The researcher can display "what if?" situations as questions arise from the audience. Summaries, conclusions, and recommendations should also be made with visuals.
3. *Executive summary.* Each audience member should have a copy of the executive summary (preferably several days in advance). This allows for

Going ON-LINE

Publishing Reports on the Internet

MANY CORPORATIONS AND RESEARCH suppliers are publishing marketing research reports on the Internet. All the researchers we know of are currently publishing to secure sites that require passwords for access.

Publishing reports on the Internet has become extremely easy because all the latest versions of the major word processing, presentation graphics, and spreadsheet packages (Microsoft Office, Lotus Smart Suite, and others) are easy to use. Steps involved in publishing material on the Internet are summarized later in this section.

Publishing reports on the Internet provides qualified users instant access to these documents on a worldwide basis. This can be useful for large, multidivisional, multinational corporations. Users can view the marketing research reports on screen and also have full access to supporting audio, video, and animation features. They can save the reports on their computers for future reference or for more careful analysis. Complete reports or portions of reports can be printed out in hard copy, if desired.

Large organizations are likely to operate their own internal intranets over local or wide-area networks (LANs/WANs). These networks are accessible to internal users and to external users only by means of secure gateways. Some organizations, such as Texas Instruments, have taken the forward-thinking step of cataloging all of their marketing research reports on their intranet sites. This permits authorized users to search for information on topics of interest. Often one group in a large organization finds that another group has done work on the same or a similar problem. The ability of one group to leverage the information already collected by another group in the same organization saves time and money overall.

The Texas Instruments site provides authorized users with a brief description of each report indexed on the site. If users are interested in getting more information or the complete report, then they can send e-mail to the owner of the report (the person who paid for it), and that individual can grant or deny access to the full report. In a few years, intranet sites similar to the one just described will be commonplace and will permit organizations to more efficiently manage and use the marketing research data they collect.

HTML: The Language for Publishing on the Internet

The basic language for publishing documents on the Internet is hypertext markup language (HTML). HTML is an evolving set of standard codes and conventions that make it possible for any Web browser to open a document and view its contents and design style without regard to what operating system or computer software they use.

HTML codes can be manually inserted into an ASCII text document, using only a text editor or a word processor that can save documents as "text only." However, coding can become very tedious because every stylistic change (bold, italics, heading size, new paragraph, etc.) requires a beginning and ending code. For example, to place the word "publish" in bold italic print, you must have the following codes:

<b><i>publish</i></b>

The items in brackets indicate HTML formatting codes (<b> = turn bold on; </b> = turn bold off; <i> = turn italics on; </i> = turn italics off.)

The easiest way to create HTML documents for the Web is to use a word processor like Microsoft Word, which can save any document in HTML format, or obtain an add-in tool (available for most of the other word processors) that also allows you to save documents in HTML format. If you are familiar with a particular word processor, you can easily create a document, add formatting options, and save it as an HTML file.

Unfortunately, word processors were not originally designed to create HTML documents, so they have some shortcomings. Today, however, several programs are designed specifically for creating and maintaining documents on the Web. One of the most popular programs is Microsoft FrontPage. With this program, and others like it, you type in text like you would on any word processor. The real advantages come when you start to use some of the other HTML conventions, such as frames, tables, forms, and scripting. These tools allow you to create many common documents like feedback forms (where visitors can leave you comments concerning your Web site) with little or no knowledge of how to write computer programs. They also make it easy to link to other documents on your site or on any site on the Internet. FrontPage will also help you post your documents onto your Web server with little effort.

Steps for Publishing on the Internet

The three basic steps to Web publishing are:

1. *Create an HTML document.* Convert an existing document to HTML or create a document from scratch and save it as HTML (using any of the options mentioned above).
2. *View your document in a browser.* To see exactly how a document will look when published on the Internet, you should view it from as many different browsers as possible (at least the latest versions of Microsoft Internet Explorer and Netscape Navigator). Each browser renders some things differently from the others.
3. *Upload your document to a Web server.* There are three methods for uploading your documents to your Web server: FTP, Telnet, and remote communications. FTP, or file transfer protocol, is a method for transferring any information between two computers on the Internet. Your Web server has to be set up specifically to allow anonymous file transfers to a particular area on the server. Otherwise, you need a user name and password to access your Web server directly through a protocol known as Telnet, which allows you to execute commands on the server as if you were sitting in front of it. A variation of Telnet involves using remote communications like Symantec's PCAnywhere. Once installed on the Web server, these programs allow you to dial into your computer using an ordinary telephone line (or using TCP/IP over the

continued

Internet). Once connected, your screen will look exactly like the screen that appears on your server when you are sitting in front of it. You can copy, rename, and delete files as needed. Copying files to appropriate places on the Web server will make them available for viewing by any Web surfer. ■

a more fruitful discussion. It also enables managers to contemplate questions to ask in advance of the presentation.

4. *Copies of the final report.* The report serves as physical evidence of the research and should make clear that much detail has been omitted in the personal presentation. It should be made available to interested parties at the end of the presentation.

Making a Personal Presentation

An effective personal presentation is tailored to the nature of the audience. It takes into account the receivers' frame of reference, attitudes, prejudices, educational background, and time constraints. The speaker must select words, concepts, and illustrative figures to which the audience can relate. A good presentation also leaves time at the end for questions and discussion.

Perhaps one reason for inadequate personal presentations is a lack of understanding of the barriers to effective communication. A second factor is the failure to recognize or admit that the purpose of many research reports is persuasion. This does not mean stretching or bending the truth, but rather using research findings to reinforce the researcher's conclusions and recommendations. In preparing a personal presentation, the researcher should keep the following questions in mind:

- What do the data really mean?
- What impact do they have?
- What have we learned from the data?
- What do we need to do, given the information we now have?
- How can future studies of this nature be enhanced?
- What can make information such as this more useful?

Getting Managers to Use the Research Information

Marketing managers today are faced with the significant task of making more effective use of marketing research information. Effective use of research information can enhance productivity and reduce the time it takes to get a new product to market. All companies can make more effective use of marketing research information. Even firms that currently use research information very effectively, such as AMOCO, Citicorp, Kraft General Foods, and Eastman Kodak, still feel they can do a better job. The task is complicated by the fact that marketing managers use research information differently and value information differently.

A research study was conducted recently of Fortune 500 companies in the chemical, consumer packaged goods, and telecommunications industries, along with 40 executives of large and medium-sized companies, all of whom are members of The Strategic Planning Institute, an international business think tank. The purpose of the research was to identify the key factors in the effective use of marketing research. Those factors are:

1. *The perceived credibility and usefulness of the report to the users.* A good study "has data of recommendations that can be used to formulate a strategy." It "redirects activities, accentuates the positive, and corrects weaknesses." A good study also has a clearly defined scope, shows how the quantitative analysis meshes with the qualitative information, and contains no "big surprises" or radical recommendations. At the least, a good study "provides an understanding that wasn't there before."
2. *The degree of client/researcher interaction.* Managers often assess a study's credibility or value even before the final presentation of findings. And

The Texas Instruments Intranet provides authorized users access to information and reports on a variety of topics

this assessment often is based on their involvement (or lack thereof) with the study design and its conduct. "If involvement is low . . . then the lack of communication can cause surprises and the quality of the study becomes a moot point . . . because the study is likely to be shelved."

3. *The organizational climate for research.* Managers have to receive top management's approval for the use of research studies and consultants. One manager noted, "It's crucial to have signals from the top that encourage the use of outside help and openness to new ideas."
4. *The personality and job tenure of key users.* Some managers have a pro-innovation bias and are willing to try almost anything. Other managers view outside information as threatening to their decision-making authority. Also, other research has shown that senior (longer-tenured) managers valued more sources of marketing research information and tended to use more "soft information" than did younger managers. Senior managers also tended to make more conservative decisions. When managers have been in the same business for a long time, they naturally believe they "know the markets and customers in depth" and that marketing researchers are unlikely to offer any new information.[1]

Jeannine Bergers Everett is director of marketing research for the Boston Consulting Group's worldwide Consumer and Retail Practice Group. In the In Practice box she discusses the importance of creating value-added research to increase usage of marketing research information.

The Role of Trust

Instead of distributing lengthy reports, gather keyplayers together to discuss the results, ask questions, and determine a course of action.

Another study focused upon the importance of trust between the researcher and the decision makers. Trust, in this case, simply means relying on one another. A survey of 779 researchers and research users found that trust was more a function of interpersonal factors than individual factors. The most important interpersonal factor was the perceived integrity of the researcher. This was followed by the perceived willingness of the researcher to reduce research uncertainty for the users. This meant that researchers would use fewer data analysis skills and more data interpretation skills. In other words, "Yes, the relationship is significant at the .05 level, but what does this mean in the marketplace?"[2]

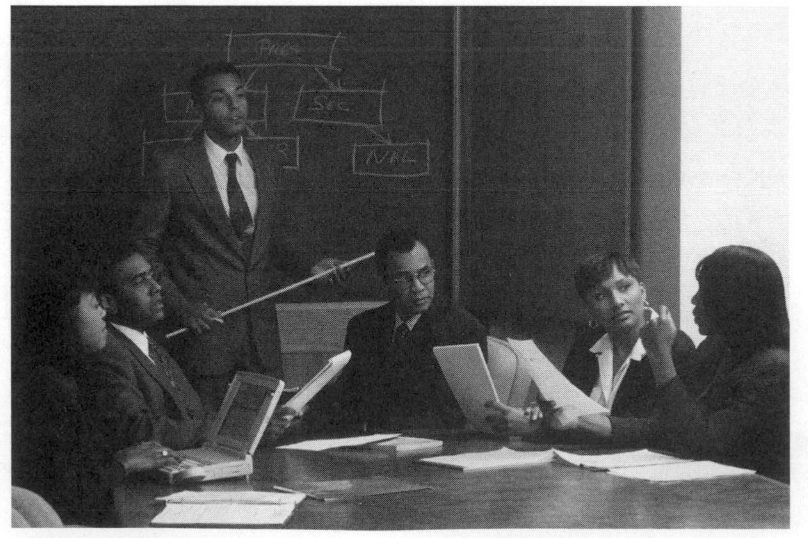

The researcher is called upon to use a broad understanding of the marketplace and research insights to construct explanations about research findings. Other important determinants of trust were researcher confidentiality, level of expertise, and congeniality.[3]

In PRACTICE

"Managers Require Value-Added Strategic Information"

Most marketing managers truly believe that marketing research can be valuable. But they also claim that most of what they see isn't delivering the kind of information they need in order to make business decisions.

Transforming a traditional marketing research organization into a value-added strategic research team takes time, commitment, and something researchers are particularly good at: research. The first question to explore is what the company really needs from its research team. Finding the answer begins with a decision audit.

Before they can change the status quo, researchers need to understand the impact of their past projects on the business. What business decision was being considered with each report and what costs were involved? Which recommendations were made, which ones taken? Answers to these questions will how the organization operates and the importance it assigns to research.

Action statements. Every research proposal should state why the research is being done, beyond such vague terms as "to explore," "to understand," or "to determine." In customer-advocate organizations, the research objective is to "decide." Researchers also delineate the standards for the decision, and every item in the study directly relates to those measures. This brings the research department and management together to discuss the range of possible actions and the decision criteria for each action.

Recommendations for action. Every report should include recommendations. In exploratory organizations, there's lots of data but few recommendations. In fact, the first section of exploratory reports usually deals with methodology, the least relevant topic to the client. Silent-advisor and order-taker organizations tend to bury researchers' recommendations. The report might say what customers think and feel, but shies away from the bottom line—what needs to be done.

The recommendation is the first sentence of the report, followed by a clear rationale that relates to the action statement and criteria set forth in the proposal. Not surprisingly, the recommendations leave less room for debate regarding the value of the research investment, or the implications of the results.

Study debriefs. Executive summaries on top of 40-page reports are a poor way to influence decision makers. Instead of sending a bulky report through interoffice mail, gather the key players together and give management a bullet-point run-down of the results. This presents the opportunity for asking questions, as well as for discussing next steps.

Full backroom principle. Involve senior management in the research. Too often, the closest they get to the customers is a written report or a formal presentation. Having managers meet customers face-to-face creates the opportunity for real-time idea building and strategy discussion.[4] ■

Building Trust Through Feedback

Perhaps one of the most practical ways to build trust and therefore to get managers to use the research information is to use customer satisfaction research. AT&T marketing research, for example, put in a customer satisfaction tracking system to monitor its internal clients' perceptions on an ongoing basis. The system consists of two separate questionnaires. One is a very general, short, high-level view and is completed periodically by marketing directors and other high-level executives. The executives rate the research department on five separate attributes, as well as overall support. The questionnaire is deliberately short because of the respondents' limited exposure to research and the tremendous demands on their time. The second questionnaire is more detailed and aimed at the specific client who requested the study. The surveys provide AT&T researchers a good way to monitor how they are doing, build trust and confidence in the department, and provide useful, decision-making information for the corporation.[5]

Doing "good research" per se does not guarantee that the findings will be used. The researcher must understand how managers think and must work with them to remove potential bias against using the research findings. Remember, marketing research has value only when it is considered and acted upon by management.

Summary

The six primary sections of a contemporary marketing research report, in order, are the table of contents, background and objectives, an executive summary, methodology, findings, and appendices with supporting information.

The primary objectives of the marketing research report are to explain why the research was done, state the specific research objectives, explain how the research was done, present the findings of the research, and provide conclusions and recommendations. All these elements are contained in the executive summary. The conclusions do not necessarily contain statistical numbers derived from the research, but rather generalize the results in relation to the stated objectives. Nor do conclusions recommend a course of action. This is left to the recommendations, which direct the conclusions to specific marketing strategies or tactics that would place a client in the most positive position in the market.

The marketing research report of today makes heavy use of graphics to present key findings. For over three-fourths of researchers, PowerPoint is the software of choice to create their reports. In terms of mechanics, reports today minimize the use of words, feed information to clients in "minibites," make extensive use of bulleted charts, and heavily employ the use of graphics. In addition to the written report, a personal presentation of research results is often required. For this, the researcher needs four aids: the presentation outline, a system to project graphic results on a screen, an executive summary, and copies of the final report to give to the audience after completion of the presentation. It is common for research reports to be published on the Internet by the client or by the researcher at the client's request. This has the advantage of making the results available to other individuals in the client organization worldwide. The Internet can also be used to support the simultaneous worldwide presentation of research results in multiple locations.

Marketing researchers obviously want marketing managers to use the information they provide and to use it appropriately. The marketing researcher needs to understand how managers think and the potential barriers to the use of research information. This task is complicated by the fact that the different marketing managers use research information differently and put varying levels of value on marketing research results. The key determinants of whether marketing research data are used are the perceived credibility and usefulness of the information to users, the degree of client/researcher interaction, the organizational climate for research, and the personalities of key users. Trust also plays an important role in determining whether or not research managers use marketing research information. Trust is derived from the perceived integrity and willingness of the researcher to help reduce uncertainty for users. Other determinants of trust are researcher confidentiality, level of expertise, and congeniality.

Key Terms & Definitions

Presentation software Personal computer software that provides easy-to-use platforms for creating effective reports and presentations.

Executive summary The portion of a research report that explains why the research was done, what was found and what those findings mean, and what action, if any, management should undertake.

Conclusions Generalizations that answer the questions raised by the research objectives or that otherwise satisfy the objectives.

Recommendations Conclusions applied to marketing strategies or tactics that focus on a client's achievement of differential advantage.

Questions for Review & Critical Thinking

1. What are the roles of the research report? Give examples.
2. Distinguish among findings, conclusions, and recommendations.
3. Should research reports contain executive summaries? Why or why not? If so, what should be contained in an executive summary?
4. Discuss the basic components of the research report. List several criteria that may be used to evaluate a research report and give examples of each.
5. How can presentation software impact presentations and reports?
6. What should be done to ensure the success of a personal presentation? Critique the following two paragraphs from a research report:

   The trouble began when the Department of Agriculture published the hot dog ingredients—everything that may legally qualify—because it was asked by the poultry industry to relax the conditions under which the ingredients might also include chicken. In other words, can a chickenfurter find happiness in the land of the frank?

Judging by the 1,066 mainly hostile answers that the department got when it sent out a questionnaire on this point, the very thought is unthinkable. The public mood was most felicitously caught by the woman who replied, "I don't eat feather meat of no kind."

7. What are the advantages of publishing reports on the Internet?
8. Develop one or more visual aids to present the following data. Indicate why you chose your particular form of visual aid.

Candidate	Local # Employees	Revenue (in millions of dollars)	Target as Charter or Affiliate Member	Potential Membership Fee
Mary Kay Cosmetics	958	$360	Charter	$50,000
Arrow Industries	950	50	Charter	20,000
NCH Corp.	800	427	Charter	50,000
Stratoflex, Inc.	622	81	Charter	25,000
BEI Defense Sys.	150	47	Affiliate	7,500
Atlas Match Corp.	150	82	Affiliate	7,500
Mangren R&D	143	20	Affiliate	7,500
Jet Research Ctr.	157	350	Affiliate	7,500

Working the Net

1. Go to http://www.gallup.com and examine some of the special reports on American opinions such as the *Social Audit on Black/White Relations in the United States*. Do these reports meet the criteria discussed in the text for good marketing research reports? Why or why not?
2. Go to http://www.presentersuniversity.com. Describe the different ways this organization can help you become a more effective speaker.

Real-Life Research

The United Way

The United Way was concerned about attitudes toward the organization by nondonors. Specifically, management was interested in why certain people did not give to the United Way. It also was interested in determining what factors might convert nondonors to donors. An executive summary of the research is presented here.

Executive Summary Objectives and Methodology

- The general purposes of this study were to determine the attitudes of noncontributors toward the United Way, to assess the reasons for not contributing, and to ascertain factors that may influence nonparticipants to contribute.
- The study used primary data gathered through a self-administered questionnaire.
- Descriptive research design methods were used to examine the survey results for numerical comparison.
- The study employed nonprobability samples (e.g., convenience samples and judgment samples).
- Primary data were collected through a newly developed self administered questionnaire administered to 134 respondents consisting of co-workers, friends, and students.

Findings

- The percentage of the respondents having positive perceptions of the United Way was greater than those having negative perceptions; however, the majority of the respondents had no opinions concerning the United Way.
- Only 5.2 percent rated the United Way fair or poor in providing benefits to those in need.
- The United Way actually spends 9 percent to 10 percent of contributions on administrative costs, although 80.6 percent believed that the United Way used more than 10 percent of its contributions on administrative costs.
- Primary reasons for not contributing were contribution to other charities or religious organizations, personal financial circumstances, lack of knowledge of how donated funds are used, personal beliefs, absence of favorite charities, pressure to contribute, and preference to donate time rather than money.
- Of those who were asked to contribute, pressure seemed somewhat important in influencing their decision not to contribute.
- Of those respondents who indicated that personal financial reasons influenced their decision not to give, 35.6 percent indicated they would give to the United Way if asked.
- Other charities and religious denominations appear to be in competition with the United Way for donated dollars.
- Many respondents indicated that they would contribute if they could specify the charity to receive their contribution, had more knowledge about the United Way and the charities it supports, were asked to give, had less pressure to give, had availability of payroll deduction, and had the option of spreading contributions over time.
- Of the respondents whose place of employment participated in the United Way campaign, 79.6 percent had been asked to give but did not.
- Workplace campaigns reach a large number of executives and professional and administrative personnel in the higher-income brackets but do not reach a significant number of service personnel or lower-income households.

Conclusions

- Negative perceptions do not appear to be a major factor affecting reasons for not contributing; however, a positive perception does not necessarily translate into a contribution.
- Noncontributors lack sufficient information regarding the United Way to form a perception of the organization.
- There is a lack of knowledge concerning the United Way and the organizations to which it allocates contributions.
- Respondents believe that the United Way uses more for administrative costs than it actually does.
- The United Way is in competition for a limited number of charity dollars.

Recommendations

- Conduct additional research to determine noncontributors' level of knowledge of the United Way and the purpose that the United Way serves.
- Increase education for potential contributors regarding the United Way's purpose, the organizations it supports, and the United Way's reasonable administrative costs.
- Expand the frequency of campaigns in the workplace and develop ways to increase awareness of the methods of contributing.
- Develop appropriate competitive marketing strategy to address the United Way's competitors.

Questions

1. Do you think that the executive summary provides guidance for decision-making information?
2. Are all elements present that should be included within an executive summary?
3. Based on the objectives, do the findings, conclusions, and recommendations logically follow? Why or why not?

CD Opportunity

1. The Rockingham Bank Visa Card case on your CD can be used as the basis for compiling a final research report. Submit a report of your findings to your professor, using the concepts presented in Chapter 15.
2. Review the video and accompanying case about Burke Marketing Research found on your CD. Now that you have completed the course, you will be able to see the video in a different light.
3. Don't forget that your CD contains a PowerPoint presentation that can help you review for the final exam.

APPENDIX

Statistical Tables

1

Random Digits

2

Standard Normal Distribution-Z-values

3

t-*Distribution*

4

Chi-Square Distribution

5

F-*Distribution*

Table 1

Random Digits

63271	59986	71744	51102	15141	80714	58683	93108	13554	79945
88547	09896	95436	79115	08303	01041	20030	63754	08459	28364
55957	57243	83865	09911	19761	66535	40102	26646	60147	15702
46276	87453	44790	64122	45573	84358	21625	16999	13385	22782
55363	07449	34835	15290	76616	67191	12777	21861	68689	03263
69393	92785	49902	58447	42048	30378	87618	26933	40640	16281
13186	29431	88190	04588	38733	81290	89541	70290	40113	08243
17726	28652	56836	78351	47327	18518	92222	55201	27340	10493
36520	64465	05550	30157	82242	29520	69753	72602	23756	54935
81628	36100	39254	56835	37636	02421	98063	89641	64953	99337
84649	48968	75215	75498	49539	74240	03466	49292	36401	45525
63291	11618	12613	75055	43915	26488	41116	64531	56827	30825
70502	53225	03655	05915	37140	57051	48393	91322	25653	06543
06426	24771	59935	49801	11082	66762	94477	02494	88215	27191
20711	55609	29430	70165	45406	78484	31639	52009	18873	96927
41990	70538	77191	25860	55204	73417	83920	69468	74972	38712
72452	36618	76298	26678	89334	33938	95567	29380	75906	91807
37042	40318	57099	10528	09925	89773	41335	96244	29002	46453
53766	52875	15987	46962	67342	77592	57651	95508	80033	69828
90585	58955	53122	16025	84299	53310	67380	84249	25348	04332
32001	96293	37203	64516	51530	37069	40261	61374	05815	06714
62606	64324	46354	72157	67248	20135	49804	09226	64419	29457
10078	28073	85389	50324	14500	15562	64165	06125	71353	77669
91561	46145	24177	15294	10061	98124	75732	00815	83452	97355
13091	98112	53959	79607	52244	63303	10413	63839	74762	50289
73864	83014	72457	22682	03033	61714	88173	90835	00634	85169
66668	25467	48894	51043	02365	91726	09365	63167	95264	45643
84745	41042	29493	01836	09044	51926	43630	63470	76508	14194
48068	26805	94595	47907	13357	38412	33318	26098	82782	42851
54310	96175	97594	88616	42035	38093	36745	56702	40644	83514
14877	33095	10924	58013	61439	21882	42059	24177	58739	60170
78295	23179	02771	43464	59061	71411	05697	67194	30495	21157
67524	02865	39593	54278	04237	92441	26602	63835	38032	94770
58268	57219	68124	73455	83236	08710	04284	55005	84171	42596
97158	28672	50685	01181	24262	19427	52106	34308	73685	74246
04230	16831	69085	30802	65559	09205	71829	06489	85650	38707
94879	56606	30401	02602	57658	70091	54986	41394	60437	03195
71446	15232	66715	26385	91518	70566	02888	79941	39684	54315
32886	05644	79316	09819	00813	88407	17461	73925	53037	91904
62048	33711	25290	21526	02223	75947	66466	06332	10913	75336
84534	42351	21628	53669	81352	95152	08107	98814	72743	12849
84707	15885	84710	35866	06446	86311	32648	88141	73902	69981
19409	40868	64220	80861	13860	68493	52908	26374	63297	45052
57978	48015	25973	66777	45924	56144	24742	96702	88200	66162
57295	98298	11199	96510	75228	41600	47192	43267	35973	23152
94044	83785	93388	07833	38216	31413	70555	03023	54147	06647
30014	25879	71763	96679	90603	99396	74557	74224	18211	91637
07265	69563	64268	88802	72264	66540	01782	08396	19251	83613
84404	88642	30263	80310	11522	57810	27627	78376	36240	48952
21778	02085	27762	46097	43324	34354	09369	14966	10158	76089

Reprinted from page 44 of *A Million Random Digits with 100,000 Normal Deviates* by the Rand Corporation. Copyright 1955 and 1983 by the Rand Corporation. Used by permission.

Table 2

Standard Normal Distribution-*Z*-values

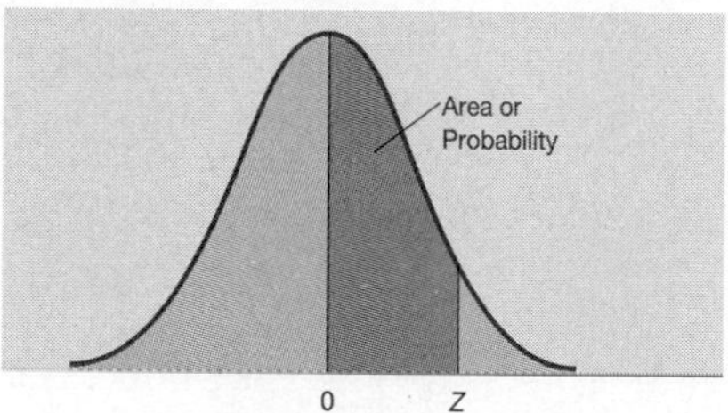

Entries in the table give the area under the curve between the mean and Z standard deviations above the mean. For example, for $Z = 1.25$, the area under the curve between the mean and Z is .3944.

Z	.00	.01	.02	.03	.04	.05	.06	.07	.08	.09
.0	.0000	.0040	.0080	.0120	.0160	.0199	.0239	.0279	.0319	.0359
.1	.0398	.0438	.0478	.0517	.0557	.0596	.0636	.0675	.0714	.0753
.2	.0793	.0832	.0871	.0910	.0948	.0987	.1026	.1064	.1103	.1141
.3	.1179	.1217	.1255	.1293	.1331	.1368	.1406	.1443	.1480	.1517
.4	.1554	.1591	.1628	.1664	.1700	.1736	.1772	.1808	.1844	.1879
.5	.1915	.1950	.1985	.2019	.2054	.2088	.2123	.2157	.2190	.2224
.6	.2257	.2291	.2324	.2357	.2389	.2422	.2454	.2486	.2518	.2549
.7	.2580	.2612	.2642	.2673	.2704	.2734	.2764	.2794	.2823	.2852
.8	.2881	.2910	.2939	.2967	.2995	.3023	.3051	.3078	.3106	.3133
.9	.3159	.3186	.3212	.3238	.3264	.3289	.3315	.3340	.3365	.3389
1.0	.3413	.3438	.3461	.3485	.3508	.3531	.3554	.3577	.3599	.3621
1.1	.3643	.3665	.3686	.3708	.3729	.3749	.3770	.3790	.3810	.3830
1.2	.3849	.3869	.3888	.3907	.3925	.3944	.3962	.3980	.3997	.4015
1.3	.4032	.4049	.4066	.4082	.4099	.4115	.4131	.4147	.4162	.4177
1.4	.4192	.4207	.4222	.4236	.4251	.4265	.4279	.4292	.4306	.4319
1.5	.4332	.4345	.4357	.4370	.4382	.4394	.4406	.4418	.4429	.4441
1.6	.4452	.4463	.4474	.4484	.4495	.4505	.4515	.4525	.4535	.4545
1.7	.4554	.4564	.4573	.4582	.4591	.4599	.4608	.4616	.4625	.4633
1.8	.4641	.4649	.4656	.4664	.4671	.4678	.4686	.4693	.4699	.4706
1.9	.4713	.4719	.4726	.4732	.4738	.4744	.4750	.4756	.4761	.4767
2.0	.4772	.4778	.4783	.4788	.4793	.4798	.4803	.4808	.4812	.4817
2.1	.4821	.4826	.4830	.4834	.4838	.4842	.4846	.4850	.4854	.4857
2.2	.4861	.4864	.4868	.4871	.4875	.4878	.4881	.4884	.4887	.4890
2.3	.4893	.4896	.4898	.4901	.4904	.4906	.4909	.4911	.4913	.4916
2.4	.4918	.4920	.4922	.4925	.4927	.4929	.4931	.4932	.4934	.4936
2.5	.4938	.4940	.4941	.4943	.4945	.4946	.4948	.4949	.4951	.4952
2.6	.4953	.4955	.4956	.4957	.4959	.4960	.4961	.4962	.4963	.4964
2.7	.4965	.4966	.4967	.4968	.4969	.4970	.4971	.4972	.4973	.4974
2.8	.4974	.4975	.4976	.4977	.4977	.4978	.4979	.4979	.4980	.4981
2.9	.4981	.4982	.4982	.4983	.4984	.4984	.4985	.4985	.4986	.4986
3.0	.4986	.4987	.4987	.4988	.4988	.4989	.4989	.4989	.4990	.4990

Table 3

t-Distribution

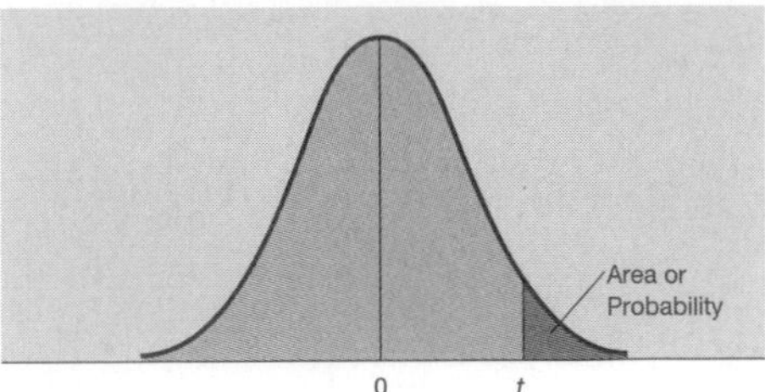

Entries in this table give *t*-values for an area or probability in the upper tail of the *t*-distribution. For example, with 10 degrees of freedom and a .05 area in the upper tail, $t_{.05} = 1.812$.

	Area in Upper Tail				
Degrees of Freedom	**.10**	**.05**	**.025**	**.01**	**.005**
1	3.078	6.314	12.706	31.821	63.657
2	1.886	2.920	4.303	6.965	9.925
3	1.638	2.353	3.182	4.541	5.841
4	1.533	2.132	2.776	3.747	4.604
5	1.476	2.015	2.571	3.365	4.032
6	1.440	1.943	2.447	3.143	3.707
7	1.415	1.895	2.365	2.998	3.499
8	1.397	1.860	2.306	2.896	3.355
9	1.383	1.833	2.262	2.821	3.250
10	1.372	1.812	2.228	2.764	3.169
11	1.363	1.796	2.201	2.718	3.106
12	1.356	1.782	2.179	2.681	3.055
13	1.350	1.771	2.160	2.650	3.012
14	1.345	1.761	2.145	2.624	2.977
15	1.341	1.753	2.131	2.602	2.947
16	1.337	1.746	2.120	2.583	2.921
17	1.333	1.740	2.110	2.567	2.898
18	1.330	1.734	2.101	2.552	2.878
19	1.328	1.729	2.093	2.539	2.861
20	1.325	1.725	2.086	2.528	2.845
21	1.323	1.721	2.080	2.518	2.831
22	1.321	1.717	2.074	2.508	2.819
23	1.319	1.714	2.069	2.500	2.807
24	1.318	1.711	2.064	2.492	2.797
25	1.316	1.708	2.060	2.485	2.787
26	1.315	1.706	2.056	2.479	2.779
27	1.314	1.703	2.052	2.473	2.771
28	1.313	1.701	2.048	2.467	2.763
29	1.311	1.699	2.045	2.462	2.756
30	1.310	1.697	2.042	2.457	2.750
40	1.303	1.684	2.021	2.423	2.704
60	1.296	1.671	2.000	2.390	2.660
120	1.289	1.658	1.980	2.358	2.617
∞	1.282	1.645	1.960	2.326	2.576

Reprinted by permission of Biometrika Trustees from Table 12, Percentage Points of the *t*-Distribution, by E.S. Pearson and H.O. Hartley, *Biometrika Tables for Statisticians,* Vol. 1, 3d. Edition, 1966.

Table 4

Chi-Square Distribution

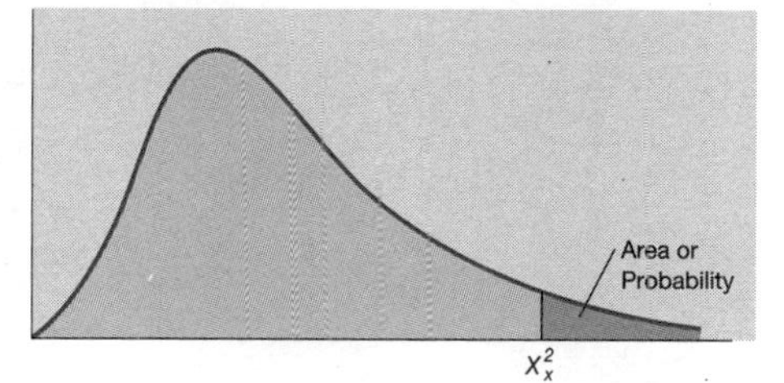

Entries in the table give X^2_a values, where α is the area or probability in the upper tail of the chi-square distribution. For example, with 10 degrees of freedom and a .01 area in the upper tail, $X^2_a = 23.2093$.

Degrees of freedom	Area in Upper Tail .995	.99	.975	.95	.90	.10	.05	.025	.01	.005
1	$392{,}704 \times 10^{-19}$	$157{,}088 \times 10^{-9}$	$982{,}069 \times 10^{-9}$	$393{,}214 \times 10^{-8}$	.01570908	2.70554	3.84146	5.02389	6.63490	7.87944
2	.0100251	.0201007	.0506356	.102587	.210720	4.60517	5.99147	7.37776	9.21034	10.5966
3	.0717212	.114832	2.15795	.351846	.584375	6.25139	7.81473	9.34840	11.3449	12.8381
4	.206990	.297110	.484419	.710721	1.063623	7.77944	9.48773	11.1433	13.2767	14.8602
5	.411740	.554300	.831211	1.145476	1.61031	9.23635	11.0705	12.8325	15.0863	16.7496
6	.675727	.872085	1.237347	1.63539	2.20413	10.6446	12.5916	14.4494	16.8119	18.5476
7	.989265	1.239043	1.68987	2.16735	2.83311	12.0170	14.0671	16.0128	18.4753	20.2777
8	1.344419	1.646482	2.17973	2.73264	3.48954	13.3616	15.5073	17.5346	20.0902	21.9550
9	1.734926	2.087912	2.70039	3.32511	4.16816	14.6837	16.9190	19.0228	21.6660	23.5893
10	2.15585	2.55821	3.24697	3.94030	4.86518	15.9871	18.3070	20.4831	23.2093	25.1882
11	2.60321	3.05347	3.81575	4.57481	5.57779	17.2750	19.6751	21.9200	24.7250	26.7569
12	3.07382	3.57056	4.40379	5.22603	6.30380	18.5494	21.0261	23.3367	26.2170	28.2995
13	3.56503	4.10691	5.00874	5.89186	7.04150	19.8119	22.3621	24.7356	27.6883	29.8194
14	4.07468	4.66043	5.62872	6.57063	7.78953	21.0642	23.6848	26.1190	29.1413	31.3193
15	4.60094	5.22935	6.26214	7.26094	8.54675	22.3072	24.9958	27.4884	30.5779	32.8013
16	5.14224	5.81221	6.90766	7.96164	9.31223	23.5418	26.2962	28.8454	31.9999	34.2672
17	5.69724	6.40776	7.56418	8.67176	10.0852	24.7690	27.5871	30.1910	33.4087	35.7185
18	6.26481	7.01491	8.23075	9.39046	10.8649	25.9894	28.8693	31.5264	34.8053	37.1564
19	6.84398	7.63273	8.90655	10.1170	11.6509	27.2036	30.1435	32.8523	36.1908	38.5822

continued

Table 4

Chi-Square Distribution, (*continued*)

Degrees of freedom	Area in Upper Tail .995	.99	.975	.95	.90	.10	.05	.025	.01	.005
20	7.43386	8.26040	9.59083	10.8508	12.4426	28.4120	31.4104	34.1696	37.5662	39.9968
21	8.03366	8.89720	10.28293	11.5913	13.2396	29.6151	32.6705	35.4789	38.9321	41.4010
22	8.64272	9.54249	10.9823	12.3380	14.0415	30.8133	33.9244	36.7807	40.2894	42.7958
23	9.26042	10.19567	11.6885	13.0905	14.8479	32.0069	35.1725	38.0757	41.6384	44.1813
24	9.88623	10.8564	12.4011	13.8484	15.6587	33.1963	36.4151	39.3641	42.9798	45.5585
25	10.5197	11.5240	13.1197	14.6114	16.4734	34.3816	37.6525	40.6465	44.3141	46.9278
26	11.1603	12.1981	13.8439	15.3791	17.2919	35.5631	38.8852	41.9232	45.6417	48.2899
27	11.8076	12.8786	14.5733	16.1513	18.1138	36.7412	40.1133	43.1944	46.9630	49.6449
28	12.4613	13.5648	15.3079	16.9279	18.9392	37.9159	41.3372	44.4607	48.2782	50.9933
29	13.1211	14.2565	16.0471	17.7083	19.7677	39.0875	42.5569	45.7222	49.5879	52.3356
30	13.7867	14.9535	16.7908	18.4926	20.5992	40.2560	43.7729	46.9792	50.8922	53.6720
40	20.765	22.1643	24.4331	26.5093	29.0505	51.8050	55.7585	59.3417	63.6907	66.7659
50	27.9907	29.7067	32.3574	34.7642	37.6886	63.1671	67.5048	71.4202	76.1539	79.4900
60	35.5346	37.4848	40.4817	43.1879	46.4589	74.3970	79.0819	83.2976	88.3794	91.9517
70	43.2752	45.4418	48.7576	51.7393	55.3290	85.5271	90.5312	95.0231	100.425	104.215
80	51.1720	53.5400	57.1532	60.3915	64.2778	96.5782	101.879	106.629	112.329	116.321
90	59.1963	61.7541	65.6466	69.1260	73.2912	107.565	113.145	118.136	124.116	128.299
100	67.3276	70.0648	74.2219	77.9295	82.3581	118.498	124.342	129.561	135.807	140.169

F-Distribution

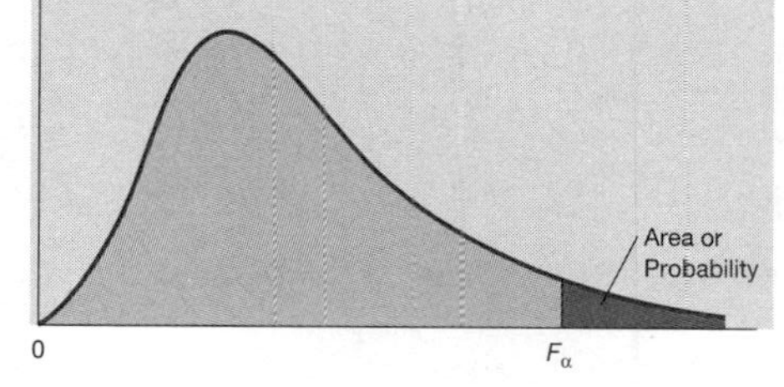

Entries in the table give F_α values, where α is the area or probability in the upper tail of the *F*-distribution. For example, with 12 numerator degrees of freedom, 15 denominator degrees of freedom, and a .05 area in the upper tail, $F_{.05} = 2.48$.

Table of $F_{.05}$ Values

Denominator Degrees of Freedom	Numerator Degrees of Freedom																		
	1	2	3	4	5	6	7	8	9	10	12	15	20	24	30	40	60	120	∞
1	161.4	199.5	215.7	224.6	230.2	234.0	236.8	238.9	240.5	241.9	243.9	245.9	248.0	249.1	250.1	251.1	252.2	253.3	254.3
2	18.51	19.00	19.16	19.25	19.30	19.33	19.35	19.37	19.38	19.40	19.41	19.43	19.45	19.45	19.46	19.47	19.48	19.49	19.50
3	10.13	9.55	9.28	9.12	9.01	8.94	8.89	8.85	8.81	8.79	8.74	8.70	8.66	8.64	8.62	8.59	8.57	8.55	8.53
4	7.71	6.94	6.59	6.39	6.26	6.16	6.09	6.04	6.00	5.96	5.91	5.86	5.80	5.77	5.75	5.72	5.69	5.66	5.63
5	6.61	5.79	5.41	5.19	5.05	4.95	4.88	4.82	4.77	4.74	4.68	4.62	4.56	4.53	4.50	4.46	4.43	4.40	4.36
6	5.99	5.14	4.76	4.53	4.39	4.28	4.21	4.15	4.10	4.06	4.00	3.94	3.87	3.84	3.81	3.77	3.74	3.70	3.67
7	5.59	4.74	4.35	4.12	3.97	3.87	3.79	3.73	3.68	3.64	3.57	3.51	3.44	3.41	3.38	3.34	3.30	3.27	3.23
8	5.32	4.46	4.07	3.84	3.69	3.58	3.50	3.44	3.39	3.35	3.28	3.22	3.15	3.12	3.08	3.04	3.01	2.97	2.93
9	5.12	4.26	3.86	3.63	3.48	3.37	3.29	3.23	3.18	3.14	3.07	3.01	2.94	2.90	2.86	2.83	2.79	2.75	2.71
10	4.96	4.10	3.71	3.48	3.33	3.22	3.14	3.07	3.02	2.98	2.91	2.85	2.77	2.74	2.70	2.66	2.62	2.58	2.54
11	4.84	3.98	3.59	3.36	3.20	3.09	3.01	2.95	2.90	2.85	2.79	2.72	2.65	2.61	2.57	2.53	2.49	2.45	2.40
12	4.75	3.89	3.49	3.26	3.11	3.00	2.91	2.85	2.80	2.75	2.69	2.62	2.54	2.51	2.47	2.43	2.38	2.34	2.30
13	4.67	3.81	3.41	3.18	3.03	2.92	2.83	2.77	2.71	2.67	2.60	2.53	2.46	2.42	2.38	2.34	2.30	2.25	2.21
14	4.60	3.74	3.34	3.11	2.96	2.85	2.76	2.70	2.65	2.60	2.53	2.46	2.39	2.35	2.31	2.27	2.22	2.18	2.13
15	4.54	3.68	3.29	3.06	2.90	2.79	2.71	2.64	2.59	2.54	2.48	2.40	2.33	2.29	2.25	2.20	2.16	2.11	2.07
16	4.49	3.63	3.42	3.01	2.85	2.74	2.66	2.59	2.54	2.49	2.42	2.35	2.28	2.24	2.19	2.15	2.11	2.06	2.01
17	4.45	3.59	3.20	2.96	2.81	2.70	2.61	2.55	2.49	2.45	2.33	2.31	2.23	2.19	2.15	2.10	2.06	2.01	1.96
18	4.41	3.55	3.16	2.93	2.77	2.66	2.58	2.51	2.46	2.41	2.34	2.27	2.19	2.15	2.11	2.06	2.02	1.97	1.92
19	4.38	3.52	3.13	2.90	2.74	2.63	2.54	2.48	2.42	2.38	2.31	2.23	2.16	2.11	2.07	2.03	1.98	1.93	1.88

continued

Table 5

F-Distribution, (*continued*)

Table of $F_{.05}$ Values

Denominator Degrees of Freedom	Numerator Degrees of Freedom 1	2	3	4	5	6	7	8	9	10	12	15	20	24	30	40	60	120	∞
20	4.35	3.49	3.10	2.87	2.71	2.60	2.51	2.45	2.39	2.35	2.28	2.20	2.12	2.08	2.04	1.99	1.95	1.90	1.84
21	4.32	3.47	3.07	2.84	2.68	2.57	2.49	2.42	2.37	2.32	2.25	2.18	2.10	2.05	2.01	1.96	1.92	1.87	1.81
29	4.18	3.33	2.93	2.70	2.55	2.43	2.35	2.28	2.22	2.18	2.10	2.03	1.94	1.90	1.85	1.81	1.75	1.70	1.64
30	4.17	3.32	2.92	2.69	2.53	2.42	2.33	2.27	2.21	2.16	2.09	2.01	1.93	1.89	1.84	1.79	1.74	1.68	1.62
40	4.08	3.23	2.84	2.61	2.45	2.34	2.25	2.18	2.12	2.08	2.00	1.92	1.84	1.79	1.74	1.69	1.64	1.58	1.51
60	4.00	3.15	2.76	2.53	2.37	2.25	2.17	2.10	2.04	1.99	1.92	1.84	1.75	1.70	1.65	1.59	1.53	1.47	1.39
120	3.92	3.07	2.68	2.45	2.29	2.17	2.09	2.02	1.96	1.91	1.83	1.75	1.66	1.61	1.55	1.50	1.43	1.35	1.25
∞	3.84	3.00	2.60	2.37	2.21	2.10	2.01	1.94	1.88	1.83	1.75	1.67	1.57	1.52	1.46	1.39	1.32	1.22	1.00

Table of $F_{.01}$ Values

Denominator Degrees of Freedom	Numerator Degrees of Freedom 1	2	3	4	5	6	7	8	9	10	12	15	20	24	30	40	60	120	∞
1	4,052	4,999.5	5,403	5,625	5,764	5,859	5,928	5,982	6,022	6,056	6,106	6,157	6,209	6,235	6,261	6,287	6,313	6,339	6,366
2	98.50	99.00	99.17	99.25	99.30	99.33	99.36	99.37	99.39	99.40	99.42	99.43	99.45	99.46	99.47	99.47	99.48	99.49	99.50
3	34.12	30.82	29.46	28.71	28.24	27.91	27.67	27.49	27.35	27.23	27.05	26.87	26.69	26.60	26.50	26.41	26.32	26.22	26.13
4	21.20	18.00	16.69	15.98	15.52	51.21	14.98	14.80	14.66	14.55	14.37	14.20	14.02	13.93	13.84	13.75	13.65	13.56	13.46
5	16.26	13.27	12.06	11.39	10.97	10.67	10.46	10.29	10.16	10.05	9.89	9.72	9.55	9.47	9.38	9.29	9.20	9.11	9.06
6	13.75	10.92	9.78	9.15	8.75	8.47	8.26	8.10	7.98	7.87	7.72	7.56	7.40	7.31	7.23	7.14	7.06	6.97	6.88
7	12.25	9.55	8.45	7.85	7.46	7.19	6.99	6.84	6.72	6.62	6.47	6.31	6.16	6.07	5.99	5.91	5.82	5.74	5.65
8	11.26	8.65	7.59	7.01	6.63	6.37	6.18	6.03	5.91	5.81	5.67	5.52	5.36	5.28	5.20	5.12	5.03	4.95	4.86
9	10.56	8.02	6.99	6.42	6.06	5.80	5.61	5.47	5.35	5.26	5.11	4.96	4.81	4.73	4.65	4.57	4.48	4.40	4.31
10	10.04	7.56	6.55	5.99	5.64	5.39	5.20	5.06	4.94	4.85	4.71	4.56	4.41	4.33	4.25	4.17	4.08	4.00	3.91
11	9.65	7.21	6.22	5.67	5.32	5.07	4.89	4.74	4.63	4.54	4.40	4.25	4.10	4.02	3.94	3.86	3.78	3.69	3.60
12	9.33	6.93	5.95	5.41	5.06	4.82	4.64	4.50	4.39	4.30	4.16	4.01	3.86	3.78	3.70	3.62	3.54	3.45	3.36
13	9.07	6.70	5.74	5.21	4.86	4.62	4.44	4.30	4.19	4.10	3.96	3.82	3.66	3.59	3.51	3.43	3.34	3.25	3.17
14	8.86	6.51	5.56	5.04	4.69	4.46	4.28	4.14	4.03	3.94	3.80	3.66	3.51	3.43	3.35	3.27	3.18	3.09	3.00

continued

Table 5

F-Distribution, (*continued*)

Table of $F_{.01}$ Values

Denominator Degrees of Freedom	Numerator Degrees of Freedom 1	2	3	4	5	6	7	8	9	10	12	15	20	24	30	40	60	120	∞
15	8.68	6.36	5.42	4.89	4.56	4.32	4.14	4.00	3.89	3.80	3.67	3.52	3.37	3.29	3.21	3.13	3.05	2.96	2.87
16	8.53	6.23	5.29	4.77	4.44	4.20	4.03	3.89	3.78	3.69	3.55	3.41	3.26	3.18	3.10	3.02	2.93	2.84	2.75
17	8.40	6.11	5.18	4.67	4.34	4.10	3.93	3.79	3.68	3.59	3.46	3.31	3.16	3.08	3.00	2.92	2.83	2.75	2.65
18	8.29	6.01	5.09	4.58	4.25	4.01	3.84	3.71	3.60	3.51	3.37	3.23	3.08	3.00	2.92	2.84	2.75	2.66	2.57
19	8.18	5.93	5.01	4.50	4.17	3.94	3.77	3.63	3.52	3.43	3.30	3.15	3.00	2.92	2.84	2.76	2.67	2.58	2.49
20	8.10	5.85	4.94	4.43	4.10	3.87	3.70	3.56	3.46	3.37	3.23	3.09	2.94	2.86	2.78	2.69	2.61	2.52	2.42
21	8.02	5.78	4.87	4.37	4.04	3.81	3.64	3.51	3.40	3.31	3.17	3.03	2.88	2.80	2.72	2.64	2.55	2.46	2.36
22	7.95	5.72	4.82	4.31	3.99	3.76	3.59	3.45	3.35	3.26	3.12	2.98	2.83	2.75	2.67	2.58	2.50	2.40	2.31
23	7.88	5.66	4.76	4.26	3.94	3.71	3.54	3.41	3.30	3.21	3.07	2.93	2.78	2.70	2.62	2.54	2.45	2.35	2.26
24	7.82	5.61	4.72	4.22	3.90	3.67	3.50	3.36	3.26	3.17	3.03	2.89	2.74	2.66	2.58	2.49	2.40	2.31	2.21
22	4.30	3.44	3.05	2.82	2.66	2.55	2.46	2.40	2.34	2.30	2.23	2.15	2.07	2.03	1.98	1.94	1.89	1.84	1.78
23	4.28	3.42	3.03	2.80	2.64	2.53	2.44	2.37	2.32	2.27	2.20	2.13	2.05	2.01	1.96	1.91	1.86	1.81	1.76
24	4.26	3.40	3.01	2.78	2.62	2.51	2.42	2.36	2.30	2.25	2.18	2.11	2.03	1.98	1.94	1.89	1.84	1.79	1.73
25	4.24	3.39	2.99	2.76	2.60	2.49	2.40	2.34	2.28	2.24	2.16	2.09	2.01	1.96	1.92	1.87	1.82	1.77	1.71
26	4.23	3.37	2.98	2.74	2.59	2.47	2.39	2.32	2.27	2.22	2.15	2.07	1.99	1.95	1.90	1.85	1.80	1.75	1.69
27	4.21	3.35	2.96	2.73	2.57	2.46	2.37	2.31	2.25	2.20	2.13	2.06	1.97	1.93	1.88	1.84	1.79	1.73	1.67
28	4.20	3.34	2.95	2.71	2.56	2.45	2.36	2.29	2.24	2.19	2.12	2.04	1.96	1.91	1.87	1.82	1.77	1.71	1.65
25	7.77	5.57	4.68	4.18	3.85	3.63	3.46	3.32	3.22	3.13	2.99	2.85	2.70	2.62	2.54	2.45	2.36	2.27	2.17
26	7.72	5.53	4.64	4.14	3.82	3.59	3.42	3.29	3.18	3.09	2.96	2.81	2.66	2.58	2.50	2.42	2.33	2.23	2.13
27	7.68	5.49	4.60	4.11	3.78	3.56	3.39	3.26	3.15	3.06	2.93	2.78	2.63	2.55	2.47	2.38	2.29	2.20	2.10
28	7.64	5.45	4.57	4.07	3.75	3.53	3.36	3.23	3.12	3.03	2.90	2.75	2.60	2.52	2.44	2.35	2.26	2.17	2.06
29	7.60	5.42	4.54	4.04	3.73	3.50	3.33	3.20	3.09	3.00	2.87	2.73	2.57	2.49	2.41	2.33	2.23	2.14	2.03
30	7.56	5.39	4.51	4.02	3.70	3.47	3.30	3.17	3.07	2.98	2.84	2.70	2.55	2.47	2.39	2.30	2.21	2.11	2.01
40	7.31	5.18	4.31	3.83	3.51	3.29	3.12	2.99	2.89	2.80	2.66	2.52	2.37	2.29	2.20	2.11	2.02	1.92	1.80
60	7.08	4.98	4.13	3.65	3.34	3.12	2.95	2.82	2.72	2.63	2.50	2.35	2.20	2.12	2.03	1.94	1.84	1.73	1.60
120	6.85	4.79	3.95	3.48	3.17	2.96	2.79	2.66	2.56	2.47	2.34	2.19	2.03	1.95	1.86	1.76	1.66	1.53	1.38
∞	6.63	4.61	3.78	3.32	3.02	2.80	2.64	2.51	2.41	2.32	2.18	2.04	1.88	1.79	1.70	1.59	1.47	1.32	1.00

Reprinted by permission of the Biometrika Trustees from Table 18, Percentage Points of the *F*-Distribution, by E.S. Pearson and H.O. Hartley, *Biometrika Tables for Statisticians,* Vol. 1, 3d. Edition, 1966.

ENDNOTES

Chapter 1

1. Adapted from Gail Gaboda, "For Business Travelers, There's No Place Like Home," *Marketing News* (September 15, 1997), pp. 19-20. Reprinted with permission from *Marketing News,* published by the American Marketing Association.
2. "Three Firms Show that Good Research Makes Good Ads," *Marketing News* (March 13, 1995), p. 18.
3. "New Marketing Research Definition Approved," *Marketing News* (January 2, 1987), pp. 1, 14.
4. "Quality: How to Make It Pay," *Business Week* (August 8, 1994), pp. 54–59.
5. "Quality: How to Make It Pay."
6. "Why Some Customers Are More Equal than Others," *Fortune* (September 19, 1994), pp. 215–224.
7. Why Some Customer Are More Equal than Others.
8. Adapted from Norihiko Shirouzu, "Japan's High-School Girls Excel in Art of Setting Trends," *The Wall Street Journal* (April 24, 1998), pp. B1, B7. Reprinted by permission of *The Wall Street Journal,* © 1998 Dow Jones & Company, Inc. All Right Reserved Worldwide; permission conveyed through Copyright Clearance Center, Inc.
9. Adapted from Yumiko Ono, "Marketers Seek the Naked Truth In Consumers' Psyches," *The Wall Street Journal* (May 30, 1997), pp. B1, B13. Reprinted by permission of *The Wall Street Journal,* © 1997 Dow Jones & Company, Inc. All Right Reserved Worldwide; permission conveyed through Copyright Clearance Center, Inc.

Chapter 2

1. Adapted from "Vegetarianism Can Wait: Meat Is Back," *Roper Reports* (March 1999, 99-1), p. 7. Roper Starch Inc., New York City.
2. "Hey Kid, Buy This," *Business Week* (June 30, 1997), pp. 63–66.
3. Adapted from Paul Conner, "Defining the Decision Purpose of Research," *Marketing News* (June 9, 1997), p. H15. Reprinted with permission from *Marketing News,* published by the American Marketing Association.
4. "Hey Kid, Buy This," p. 67.
5. Joseph Rydholm, "What Do Clients Want from a Research Firm?" *Quirk's Marketing Research Review,* (October 1996), p. 80.
6. Fred Luthans and Janet K. Larsen, "How Managers Really Communicate," *Human Relations* 39 (1986), pp. 161–178; and Harry E. Penley and Brian Hawkins, "Studying Interpersonal Communication in Organizations: A Leadership Application," *Academy of Management Journal* 28 (1985), pp. 309–326.
7. Rohit Deshpande and Scott Jeffries, "Attitudes Affecting the Use of Marketing Research in Decision Making: An Empirical Investigation," in *Educators' Conference Proceedings,* Series 47. Edited by Kenneth L. Bernhardt, et al. (Chicago: American Marketing Association, 1981), pp. 1–4.
8. Rohit Deshpande, "A Comparison of Factors Affecting Researcher and Manager Perceptions of Market Research Use," *Journal of Marketing Research* 21 (February 1989), pp. 32–38; Hanjoon Lee, Frank Acito, and Ralph Day, "Evaluation and Use of Marketing Research by Decision Makers: A Behavioral Simulation," *Journal of Marketing Research* 24 (May 1987), pp. 187–196; and Michael Hu, "An Experimental Study of Managers' and Researchers' Use of Consumer Market Research," *Journal of the Academy of Marketing Science* 14 (Fall 1986), pp. 44–51; Rohit Deshpande and Gerald Zaltman, "Factors Affecting the Use of Market Research Information: A Path Analysis," *Journal of Marketing Research* 19 (February 1982), pp. 14–31.
9. Rohit Deshpande and Gerald Zaltman, "A Comparison of Factors Affecting Use of Marketing Information in Consumer and Industrial Firms," *Journal of Marketing Research* 24 (February 1987), pp. 114–118.
10. Adapted from "Twentysomething Women Declare Themselves Primary Purchasers," *Quirk's Marketing Research Review* (May 1997), p. 43. Reprinted by permission of *Quirk's Marketing Research Review.*

Chapter 3

1. Rachel X. Weissman, "The Green Flag Is Up," *American Demographics* (April 1999), pp. 33–36. Reprinted from American Demographics Magazine, courtesy of Intertec Publishing Corp., Stamford, Connecticut. All Rights Reserved.
2. Speech given by Philip Barnard, CEO of the Kantar Group, at The University of Texas at Arlington, April 9, 1999.
3. "Acquisitions No Hindrance to Growth," *Marketing News* (June 7, 1999), p. H6.
4. Jack Honomichl, "Firm's Play Name Game as Acquisitions Ruled '98," *Marketing News* (June 7, 1999), p. H2.

5. Honomichl, "Firms Play Name Game as Acquisitions Ruled '98."
6. Jay Roth, "The Marketing Research Industry Monitor," *CASRO Journal* (1993), pp. 21–27.
7. Roth, "The Marketing Research Industry Monitor."
8. William Cook and Theodore Dunn, "The Changing Face of Advertising Research in the Information Age: An ARF Copy Research Council Survey," *Journal of Advertising Research* (January 1996), pp. 55–71.
9. "Kraft's Miracle Whip Targets Core Consumers with '97 Ads," *Advertising Age* (February 3, 1997), p. 12.
10. "Kraft's Miracle Whip Targets Core Consumers with '97 Ads."
11. Richard Gibson, "A Cereal Maker's Quest for the Next Grapenuts," *The Wall Street Journal* (January 23, 1997), pp. B1, B7.
12. Data provided by Mary Klupp, Futures Research Manager, Ford Motor Company, 1998.
13. "Strategy Planning," *Business Week* (August 26, 1996), pp. 46–51.
14. "Strategy Planning."
15. "Kendall-Jackson Loses Suit Against Gallo Over Turning Leaf Wines," *Wine Spectator* (May 31, 1997), p. 10.
16. Scott Hume, "Research Partnerships Here to Stay," *Advertising Age* (October 14, 1991), p. 33.
17. Hume, "Research Partnerships Here to Stay."
18. Paul Boughton, "Marketing Research Partnerships: A Strategy for the '90s," *Marketing Research* (December 1992), pp. 8–12; *see also* "Maximizing the Client–Researcher Partnership," *Marketing News* (September 13, 1993), p. 38; and "Partnering with Clients: The External Researcher as Internal Resource," *Marketing Research* (Spring 1997), pp. 49–50.
19. Excerpts from a speech entitled, "Global Research Trends," given by Philip Barnard at The University of Texas at Arlington, September 26, 1996. Reprinted by permission of the author.
20. Diane Bowers, "Tackling a Tacky Technique," *Marketing Research* (Fall 1996), p. 56.
21. Diane Bowers, "Promoting a Positive Image," *Marketing Research* (Winter 1993), pp. 40–42.
22. Robert Lusch and Mathew O'Brien, "Fostering Professionalism," *Marketing Research* (Spring 1997), pp. 25–31.
23. Diane Bowers, "CMOR's First Four Years," *Marketing Research* (Spring 1997), pp. 44–45.
24. Joseph Rydholm, "Can We Meet These Challenges?" *Quirk's Marketing Research Review* (March 1997), pp. 65–66.
25. Bowers, "CMOR's First Four Years," p. 45.
26. Terri Rittenburg and Gene Murdock, "The Pros and Cons of Certifying Marketing Researchers," *Marketing Research* (Spring 1994), pp. 5–9; *see also* Stephen McDaniel and Roberto Solano-Mendez, "Should Marketing Researchers Be Certified?" *Journal of Advertising Research* 33 (July–August 1993), p. 20–31.
27. Diane Bowers, "Saga of a Sugger: Part I," *Marketing Research* (March 1990), pp. 68–72. Reprinted with permission from *Marketing Research* published by the American Marketing Association. Diane Bowers, "Saga of a Sugger: Part II," *Marketing Research* (June 1990), pp. 64–67. Reprinted with permission from *Marketing Research* published by the American Marketing Association. See also Diane Bowers, "Another Victory Against Sugging," *Marketing Research* (September 1992), pp. 44–45.
28. Cyndee Miller, "Research Firms Go Global to Make Revenue Grow," *Marketing News* (January 6, 1997), pp. 1, 22. Reprinted with permission from *Marketing News* published by the American Marketing Association.

Chapter 4

1. Adapted from Emily Nelson, "Why Wal-Mart Sings, 'Yes, We Have Bananas!'" *Wall Street Journal* (October 6, 1998), pp. B1, B4; and from Emily Nelson, "Logistics Whiz Rises at Wal-Mart," *Wall Street Journal* (March 11, 1999), pp. B1, B8; permission conveyed through Copyright Clearance Center, Inc.
2. Adapted from Joe Schwartz, "Databases Deliver the Goods," *American Demographics* (September 1989), p. 24. Reprinted from American Demographics Magazine, courtesy of Intertec Publishing Corp., Stamford, Connecticut. All Rights Reserved.
3. "A Potent New Tool for Selling Database Marketing," *Business Week* (September 5, 1994), pp. 56–62.
4. "KGF Taps Data Base to Target Consumers," *Advertising Age* (October 8, 1990), pp. 3, 83.
5. "Coupon Clippers, Save Your Scissors," *Business Week* (June 20, 1994), pp. 164–166.
6. Adapted from an interview with Mike Foytik, DSS Research, conducted by Roger Gates (November 29, 1994). Reprinted by permission.
7. "Nuggets of Data from Taped Phone Calls," *Business Week* (March 8, 1999), p. 113.
8. Nick Wingfield, "A Marketer's Dream," *Wall Street Journal* (December 7, 1998), p. R20.
9. Wingfield, "A Marketer's Dream."
10. Wingfield, "A Marketer's Dream."
11. "Data Warehouse Generates Surprises, Leads for Camelot," *Advertising Age* (January 4, 1999), p. 20.
12. "What've You Done for Us Lately?" *Business Week* (April 23, 1999), pp. 29–34.
13. The four applications are from Peter Peacock, "Data Mining in Marketing: Part I," *Marketing Management* (Winter 1998), pp. 9–18.
14. For a rebuttal to some of the limitations of secondary data, see Tim Powell, "Despite Myths, Secondary

Research Is a Valuable Tool, *Marketing News* (September 21, 1991), pp. 28, 33.

15. *See* David Steward, *Secondary Research Information Sources and Methods* (Beverly Hills, Calif.: Sage Publications, 1984), pp. 23–33; *see also* "Prospecting for Marketing Treasures in Your Customer's Database," *Banker's Monthly* (June 1989), pp. 44–48.
16. This section was adapted from: Daniel Melmik, "Federal Statistics at Your Fingertips," *American Demographics* (September 1998), pp. 25–30. Reprinted from American Demographics Magazine, courtesy of Intertec Publishing Corp., Stamford, Connecticut. All Rights Reserved.
17. "How to Get Wired," *Business Week* (October 17, 1994), pp. 242–244.
18. Undated brochure from InfoUSA: 5711 South 86th Circle, Omaha, Neb. 68127.
19. "Mapping for Dollars," *Fortune* (October 18, 1993), pp. 91–96.
20. Adapted from Shelly Reese, "Bad Mufflers Make Good Data," *American Demographics* (November 1998), pp. 42–44. Reprinted from American Demographics Magazine, courtesy of Intertec Publishing Corp., Stamford, Connecticut. All Rights Reserved.
21. Adapted from Max Hopper, "Rattling SABRE—New Ways to Compete on Information," *Harvard Business Review* (May–June 1990), p. 125.
22. Hopper, "Rattling SABRE—New Ways to Compete on Information."
23. Interview with Bill Boswell, Central Corporation, _______ conducted by ______ (______).
24. Adapted from "Hand-Held Computers Help Field Staff Cut Paper Work and Harvest More Data," *Wall Street Journal* (January 30, 1990), p. B1; permission conveyed through Copyright Clearance Center, Inc. and from "How Software Is Making Food Sales a Piece of Cake," *Business Week* (July 2, 1990), pp. 54–56.

Chapter 5

1. Kelly Shermach, "What Consumers Wish Brand Managers Knew," *Marketing News* (June 9, 1997), pp. 9, 17. Reprinted with permission from *Marketing News,* published by the American Marketing Association.
2. "Focus Groups Illuminate Quantitative Research," *Marketing News* (September 23, 1996), p. 41.
3. Sid Shapiro, "Focus Groups: The First Step in Package Design," *Marketing News* (September 3, 1990), pp. 15, 17. Reprinted with permission from *Marketing News,* published by the American Marketing Association.
4. "Motives Are as Important as Words When Group Describes a Product," *Marketing News* (August 28, 1987), p. 49. Reprinted with permission from *Marketing News,* published by the American Marketing Association.
5. Peter Tuckel, Elaine Leppo, and Barbara Kaplan, "Focus Groups Under Scrutiny," *Marketing Research* (June 1992), pp. 12–17.
6. Marilyn Rausch, "Qualities of a Beginning Moderator," *Quirk's Marketing Research Review* (December 1996), p. 24. Reprinted by permission of *Quirk's Marketing Research Review.*
7. Yvonne Martin Kidd, "A Look at Focus Group Moderators Through the Client's Eyes," *Quirk's Marketing Research Review* (May 1997), pp. 22–26. Reprinted by permission of *Quirk's Marketing Research Review.*
8. Tom Greenbaum, "Making It Work for You Behind the One-Way Mirror," *Quirk's Marketing Research Review* (December 1996), pp. 22, 50. Reprinted by permission of *Quirk's Marketing Research Review.*
9. B. G. Yovovich, "Focusing on Consumers' Needs and Motivations," *Business Marketing* (March 1991), pp. 41–43. Reprinted with permission from *Business Marketing,* Copyright, Crain Communications Inc. 1991.
10. Yovovich, "Focusing on Consumers' Needs and Motivations."
11. Yovovich, "Focusing on Consumers' Needs and Motivations."
12. "More Better Faster," *Quirk's Marketing Research Review* (March 1996), pp. 10–11, 50–52.
13. Walter S. Brown, "Toto, I Don't Think We're in Kansas Anymore," *Quirk's Marketing Research Review* (December 1995), pp. 12–13, 58. Reprinted by permission of *Quirk's Marketing Research Review.*
14. "The Next Best Thing to Being There," *Quirk's Marketing Research Review* (December 1995), pp. 10–11, 15.
15. Kate Maddox, "Virtual Panels Add Real Insights for Marketers," *Advertising Age* (June 29, 1998), pp. 34, 40.
16. Maddox, "Virtual Panels Add Real Insights for Marketers."
17. Mary Beth Solomon, "Is 'Internet Focus Group' an Oxymoron?" *Quirk's Marketing Research Review* (December 1998), pp. 36–38.
18. Solomon, "Is 'Internet Focus Group' an Oxymoron?"
19. Solomon, "Is 'Internet Focus Group' an Oxymoron?"
20. "Virtual Research Room Adds Banner Rates," *Advertising Age* (May 3, 1999), p. S26.
21. Tom Greenbaum, "Internet Focus Groups Are Not Focus Groups—So Don't Call Them That," *Quirk's Marketing Research Review* (July 1998), pp. 62–63. Adapted by permission of *Quirk's Marketing Research Review.*
22. Hal Sokolow, "In-Depth Interviews Increasing in Importance," *Marketing News* (September 13, 1985), pp. 26, 31; Pamela Rogers, "One-on-Ones Don't Get the Credit They Deserve," *Marketing News* (January 2, 1989), pp. 9–10; Hazel Kahan, "One-on-One Should Sparkle Like the Gems They Are," *Marketing News* (September 3, 1990), pp. 8–9; Thomas Greenbaum, "Focus Groups vs. One-on-Ones: The Controversy Continues," *Marketing News* (September 2, 1991), p. 16; Judith Langer, "Telephone Time: In-Depth Interviews Via Phone Gain Greater Acceptance," *Marketing Research* (Summer 1996), pp. 6–8.

23. "Projective Profiting Helps Reveal Buying Habits of Power Segments," *Marketing News* (August 28, 1987), p. 10.
24. Rebecca Piirto, "Measuring Minds in the 1990s," *American Demographics* (October 1990), pp. 31–35; *see also* Doreen Mole, "Projective Technique to Uncover Consumers' Attitudes," *Quirk's Marketing Research Review* (March 1992), pp. 26–28.
25. "Putting a Face on the Big Brands," *Fortune* (September 19, 1994), p. 80.
26. Piirto, "Beyond Mind Games," p. 52.
27. Ronald Lieber, "Storytelling: A New Way to Get Closer to Your Customer," *Fortune* (February 3, 1997), pp. 102-110; *see also* "Marketers Seek the Naked Truth in Consumers' Psyches," *Wall Street Journal* (May 30, 1997), pp. B1, B13.
28. Paul E. Green and Donald S. Tull, *Research for Marketing Decisions,* 5th ed. (Englewood Cliffs, N.J.: Prentice Hall, 1998), pp. 156–157.

Chapter 6

1. Excerpted from Joseph Rydholm, "Extending Excellence—Mystery Shops Help Bose Make Sure Its Customer Service Matches Its Reputation for Quality," *Quirk's Marketing Research Review* (January 1998), pp. 10–11, 51–52. Reprinted by permission of *Quirk's Marketing Research Review.*
2. E. W. Webb, D. T. Campbell, K. D. Schwarts, and L. Sechrest, *Unobstrusive Measures: Nonreaction Research in the Social Sciences* (Chicago: Rand McNally, 1966), pp. 113–114.
3. Al Goldsmith, "Mystery Shopping 101," *Quirk's Marketing Research Review* (January 1997), pp. 33–34. Reprinted by permission of *Quirk's Marketing Research Review.*
4. Barry Leeds, "Mystery Shopping for the Financial Service Industry—Then and Now," *Quirk's Marketing Research Review* (January 1996), pp. 12–13, 24–26; Tom Quirk, "Mystery Shopping Develops New Image," *Quirk's Marketing Research Review* (January 1996), pp. 42, 72.
5. Dan Prince, "How to Ensure an Objective Mystery Shop," *Quirk's Marketing Research Review* (January 1996), pp. 22, 32–34; and "Patterns Revealed: The Evolution of a Mystery Shopping Program," *Quirk's Marketing Research Review* (January 1997), pp. 12–13, 42.
6. "Taking the Mystery Out of Mystery Shopping," *Quirk's Marketing Research Review* (January 1997), pp. 14, 44–45.
7. Calvin Woodward, "Watch and Learn," as appeared in the *Fort Worth Star Telegram* (June 21, 1997), pp. C1–C2. Adapted by permission of The Associated Press.
8. "Marketers Seek Out Today's Coolest Kids to Plug into Tomorrow's Mall Trends," *Wall Street Journal* (July 11, 1996), pp. B1, B2.
9. Harold Kassarjian, "Content Analysis in Consumer Research," *Journal of Consumer Research* 4 (June 1977), pp. 8–18. An excellent summary article on content analysis is Richard Kolbe and Melissa Burnet, "Content-Analysis Research: An Examination of Applications with Directives for Improving Research Reliability and Objectivity," *Journal of Consumer Research* 18 (September 1991), pp. 243–250. Other examples of content analysis are Mary Zimmer and Linda Golden, "Impressions of Retail Stores: A Content Analysis of Consumer Images," *Journal of Retailing* 64 (Fall 1988), pp. 265–293; and Terence Shimp, Joel Urbany, and Sakeh Camlin, "The Use of Framing and Characterization for Magazine Advertising of Mass-Marketed Products," *Journal of Advertising* (January 1988), pp. 23–30. Several good reference articles on content analysis are Hans Kepplinger, "Content Analysis and Reception Analysis," *American Behavioral Scientist* (November/December 1989), pp. 21–38; Bradley Greenberg, "On Other Perspectives Toward Message Analysis," *American Behavioral Scientist* (November/December 1989), pp. 39–51; Sonia Livingstone, "Audience Reception and the Analysis of Program Meaning," *American Behavioral Scientist* (November/December 1989), pp. 187–190; and Carl Roberts, "Other than Counting Words: A Linguistic Approach to Content Analysis," *Social Forces* (September 1989), pp. 147–177.
10. John Healy and Harold Kassarjian, "Advertising Substantiation and Advertiser Response: A Content Analysis of Magazine Advertisements," *Journal of Marketing* 47 (Winter 1983), pp. 107–117.
11. Anthony Ursic, "A Longitudinal Study of the Use of the Elderly in Magazine Advertising," *Journal of Consumer Research* 13 (June 1986), pp. 131–133.
12. Elizabeth Hirshman, "Humanistic Inquiry in Marketing Research: Philosophy, Method and Criteria," *Journal of Marketing Research* 23 (August 1986), pp. 237–249. Adapted by permission of *Journal of Marketing Research 23,* published by the American Marketing Association. For more detailed information, *see* Yvonna Lincoln and Edward Guba, *Naturalistic Inquiry* (Beverly Hills, Calif.: Sage Publications, 1985); *see also* John Schouten and James McAlexander, "Subcultures of Consumption: An Ethnography of the New Bikers," *Journal of Consumer Research* (June 1995), pp. 43–61.
13. Donal Dinoon and Thomas Garavan, "Ireland: The Emerald Isle," *International Studies of Management and Organization* (Spring/Summer 1995), pp. 137–164. Reprinted by permission from M. E. Sharp, Inc., Armonk, Publisher, NY 10504.
14. Werner Kroeber–Riel, "Activation Research: Psychological Approaches in Consumer Research," *Journal of Consumer Research* 6 (March 1979), pp. 240–250.
15. S. Weinstein, C. Weinstein, and R. Drozdenko, "Brain Wave Analysis

in Advertising Research: Validation from Basic Research and Independent Replications," *Psychology and Marketing* (Fall 1984), pp. 17–42.

16. *See* John Cacioppo and Richard Petty, "Physiological Responses and Advertising Effects," *Psychology and Marketing* (Summer 1985), pp. 115–126.
17. Cacioppo and Petty, "Physiological Responses and Advertising Effects."
18. Michael Eysenek, "Arousal, Learning, and Memory," *Psychological Bulletin* 83 (1976), pp. 389–404.
19. James Grant and Dean Allman, "Voice Stress Analyzer Is a Marketing Research Tool," *Marketing News* (January 4, 1988), p. 22.
20. Glen Brickman, "Uses of Voice-Pitch Analysis," *Journal of Advertising Research* 20 (April 1980), pp. 69–73.
21. Ronald Nelson and David Schwartz, "Voice-Pitch Analysis," *Journal of Advertising Research* 19 (October 1979), pp. 55–59.
22. Nancy Nighswonger and Claude Martin, Jr., "On Using Voice Analysis in Marketing Research," *Journal of Marketing Research* 18 (August 1981), pp. 350–355.
23. "Real-World Device Sheds New Light on Ad Readership Tests," *Marketing News* (June 5, 1987), pp. 1, 18.
24. "RAMS Helps Best Western Tout Worldwide Positioning," *Marketing News* (January 6, 1997), p. 25.
25. "Networks Blast Nielsen, Blame Faulty Ratings for Drop in Viewership," *Wall Street Journal* (November 22, 1996), pp. A1, A8.
26. "Nielsen May Face SMART Competitor," *Marketing News* (September 15, 1997), pp. 1, 12–13; "TVB, Nielsen Examining TV Sweeps Alternatives," *Advertising Age* (May 12, 1997), pp. 10–87; "Nielsen, Lucent to Offer Data on TV Ad Viewership," *Advertising Age* (June 30, 1997), p. 2; "Nielsen Tests Rating Services for TV Commercials," *Marketing News* (May 12, 1997), p. 22; "Reuters Explores Offering Ratings Rival to Nielsens," *Advertising Age* (March 17, 1997), pp. 1, 46. For an interesting look at a "Nielsen Household," *see* James Raymondo, "Confessions of a Nielsen Household," *American Demographics* (March 1997), pp. 24–32.
27. Laurence Gold, "The Coming of Age of Scanner Data," *Marketing Research* (Winter 1993), pp. 20–23.
28. J. Walker Smith, "The Promise of Single Source—When, Where, and How," *Marketing Research* (December 1990), pp. 3–5. Reprinted by permission from *Marketing Research*, published by the American Marketing Association. Another good article on the future of scanning is Laurence Gold, "High Technology Data Collection for Measurement and Testing," *Marketing Research* (March 1992), pp. 29–38.
29. The material on IRI is from information supplied by Kevin Bender, Information Resources, Inc., April, 2000.
30. *See*, for example, William Moult, "Will Anybody Ever Link Survey Data to Scanner Data?," a paper delivered before the 1992 AMA Behavioral Research Conference, Scottsdale, Arizona.
31. Laurence Gold, vice president of marketing, ACNielsen Company, in an undated speech entitled "New Technology Contributions to New Product and Advertising Strategy Testing: The ERIM Testsight System."
32. Joseph Rydholm, "Right on Cue," *Quirk's Marketing Research Review* (January 1997), pp. 10–11, 41. Reprinted by permission of *Quirk's Marketing Research Review.*

Chapter 7

1. "Investing in the Internet," *Quirk's Marketing Research Review* (June/July 1997), pp. 10–11, 64–65. Reprinted by permission of *Quirk's Marketing Research Review.*
2. Patricia E. Moberg, "Biases in Unlisted Phone Numbers," *Journal of Advertising Research 22* (August/September 1982), p. 55.
3. Thomas S. Gruca and Charles D. Schewe, "Researching Older Consumers," *Marketing Research* (September 1992), pp. 18–23. Reprinted by permission of *Marketing Research.*
4. Douglas Berdie, "Reassessing the Value of High Response Rates to Mail Surveys," *Marketing Research* (September 1989), pp. 52–63.
5. Thomas Danbury, "Current Issues in Survey Sampling," *CASRO Journal* (1991), p. 37.
6. *Walker 1990 Industry Image Study,* p. 3.
7. Cynthia Webster, "Consumer's Attitudes Toward Data Collection Methods," in Robert King, ed., *1991 Southern Marketing Association Proceedings* (Richmond, Va.: University of Richmond Press, 1991), pp. 220–223.
8. Beth Schneider, "Using Interactive Kiosks for Retail Research," *Marketing News* (January 2, 1995), p. 5; Kelly Shermach, "Great Strides Made in P-O-P Technology," *Marketing News* (January 2, 1995)), pp. 8–9; and Joseph Rydholm, "Keeping the Kids Interested," *Quirk's Marketing Research Review* (February 1993), pp. 6–7, 37.
9. John P. Dickson and Douglas L. Maclachlan, "Fax Surveys?" *Marketing Research* (September 1992), pp. 26–30; Gary S. Vazzana and Duane Bachmann, "Fax Attracts," *Marketing Research* (Spring 1994); and "Fax-based Surveys Give PC World Magazine Flexibility and Quick Turnaround at a Low Cost," *Quirk's Marketing Research Review* (February 1994), pp. 7, 26–27.
10. "Stay Plugged In to New Opportunities," *Marketing Research* (Spring 1996), pp. 13–16; and "More, Better, Faster," *Quirk's Marketing Research Review* (March 1996), pp. 10–11, 50.
11. Excerpted from Jerry Rosenkranz, "Don't Knock Door-to-Door Interviewing," *CASRO Journal* (1991), p. 45. Reprinted by permission of the Council of American Survey Research Organization (CASRO).
12. Cecil Phillips, "A View from All Sides," *Alert* 17 (September 1978), pp. 6–7.

13. A. B. Blakenship and George Edward Breen, "Format Follows Function," *Marketing Tools* (June 1997), pp. 18–20.
14. Lewis Winters, "What's New in Telephone Sampling Technology," *Marketing Research: A Magazine of Management and Applications* (March 1990), pp. 80–82.
15. Todd Remington, "Rising Refusal Rates: The Impact of Telemarketing," *Quirk's Marketing Research Review* (May 1992), pp. 8–15.
16. Charles D. Parker and Kevin F. McCrohan, "Increasing Mail Survey Response Rates: A Discussion of Methods and Induced Bias," in John Summey, R. Viswanathan, Ronald Taylor, and Karen Glynn, eds., *Marketing: Theories and Concepts for Era of Change* (Atlanta: Southern Marketing Association, 1983), pp. 254–256.
17. Douglas Berdie, "Reassessing the Value of High Response Rates to Mail Surveys," *Marketing Research* (September 1989), pp. 52–63; Jean Charles Chebat and Ayala Cohen, "Response Speed in Mail Surveys: Beware of Shortcuts," *Marketing Research* (Spring 1993), pp. 20–25; and Robert J. Sutton and Linda L. Zeits, "Multiple Prior Notifications, Personalization, and Reminder Surveys," *Marketing Research* (December 1992), pp. 14–21.
18. "Is a Web Political Poll Reliable? Yes? No? Maybe?" *The Wall Street Journal* (April 13, 1999), pp. B1, B4; Bill MacElroy, "Comparing Seven Forms of On-Line Surveying," *Quirk's Marketing Research Review* (July 1999), p. 40; and Beth Clarkson, "Research and the Internet: A Winning Combination," *Quirk's Marketing Research Review* (July 1999), p. 46.
19. Tibbett Speer, "Nickelodeon Puts Kids Online," *American Demographics* (the 1994 Directory), pp. 16–17; and Bill MacElroy and Bill Geissler, "Interactive Surveys Can Be More Fun than the Traditional," *Marketing News* (October 24, 1994), pp. 4–5.
20. Cyber Dialogue website, http://www.cyberdialogue.com, April 16, 1997; and Sharon Weissbach, "Internet Research: Still a Few Hurdles to Clear," *Quirk's Marketing Research Review* (June/July 1997), pp. 22–26.
21. "Is a Web Political Poll Reliable? Yes? No? Maybe?"; Joseph Rydholm, "Are We Getting Ahead of Ourselves?" *Quirk's Marketing Research Review* (July 1999), p. 18; and Weissbach, "Internet Research: Still a Few Hurdles to Clear."
22. Bill Eaton, "Internet Surveys: Does WWW Stand for 'Why Waste the Work?'" *Quirk's Marketing Research Review* (June/July 1997), pp. 28–30; *also see* Robert Peterson, Sridhar Balasubramanian, and Bart Bronnenberg, "Exploring the Implications of the Internet for Consumer Marketing," *Journal of the Academy of Marketing Science* (Fall 1997), pp. 329–346.
23. This section is adapted from Watt, "Using the Internet for Quantitative Survey Research," pp. 67–71, Adapted by permission of *Quirk's Marketing Research Review.*
24. A. B. Blankenship and George Edward Breen, "Format Follows Function," *Marketing Tools* (June 1997), p. 18.
25. Joseph Rydholm, "Keeping the Kids Interested," *Quirk's Marketing Research Review* (February 1993). Reprinted by permission of *Quirk's Marketing Research Review.*
26. The Professional Interviewer Marketing Research Association, 1996.
27. Betsy Peterson, "Interviewers: The Vital Link to Consumer Cooperation," *Marketing Research* (Winter 1994), pp. 48–49.

Chapter 8

1. Gary Ford, Manjo Hastak, Anustree Mitra, and Debra Jones Ringold, "Can Consumers Interpret Nutritional Information in the Presence of a Health Claim? A Laboratory Investigation," *Journal of Public Policy in Marketing* (Spring 1996), pp. 16–27. Reprinted with permission from *Journal of Public Policy in Marketing,* published by the American Marketing Association.
2. Jerome Williams, William Qualls, Sonya Grier, "Racially Exclusive Real Estate Advertising, Public Policy Implications for Fair Housing Practices," *Journal of Public Policy in Marketing* (Fall 1995), pp. 225–244. Reprinted with permission from *Journal of Public Policy in Marketing,* published by the American Marketing Association.
3. For a more detailed discussion of this and other experimental issues, *see* Thomas D. Cook and Donald T. Campbell, "The Design and Conduct of Quasi-experiments and True Experiments in Field Settings," in M. Dunnette, ed., *Handbook of Industrial and Organizational Psychology* (Skokie, Ill.: Rand McNally, 1978).
4. For a more detailed discussion of this and other experimental issues, *see* Cook and Campbell, "The Design and Conduct of Quasi-experiments and True Experiments in Field Study."
5. For a discussion of the characteristics of various types of experimental designs, see Donald T. Campbell and Julian C. Stanley, *Experimental and Quasi-experimental Design for Research* (Chicago: Rand McNally, 1966); *see also* Richard Bagozzi and Youjar Yi, "On the Use of Structural Equation Models in Experimental Design," *Journal of Marketing Research* 26 (August 1989), pp. 271–284.
6. Thomas D. Cook and Donald T. Campbell, *Quasi-experimentation: Design and Analysis Issues for Field Settings* (Boston: Houghton–Mifflin, 1979), p. 56.
7. Adapted from Raymond R. Burke, "Virtual Shopping: Breakthrough in Marketing Research," *Harvard Business Review* (March–April 1996), pp. 120–131. Copyright © 1996 by the President and fellows of Harvard College; all rights reserved.

8. Burke, "Virtual Shopping: Breakthrough in Marketing Research." Reprinted by permission of *Harvard Business Review.*
9. Joseph Rydholm, "To Test or Not to Test," *Quirk's Marketing Research Review* (February 1992), pp. 61–62.
10. Benjamin Lipstein, "The Design of Test Market Experiments," *Journal of Advertising Research* (December 1965), pp. 2–7; and Jeffery D. Zbar, "Blockbuster's CD-ROM Crash Course," *Advertising Age* (May 23, 1994), p. 18.
11. For a discussion of typical American cities and metropolitan areas, see Jane Rippeteau, "Where's Fort Wayne When You Need It?" *The Marketer* (July–August 1990), pp. 46–49; and Judith Waldrop, "All American Markets," *American Demographics* (January 1992), pp. 24–30.
12. Melvin Prince, "Choosing Simulated Test Marketing Systems," *Marketing Research* (September 1992), pp. 14–16.
13. G. L. Urban and G. M. Katz, "Pretest Market Models: Validation and Managerial Implications," *Journal of Marketing Research* (August 1983), pp. 221–234; Stanford Odesky and Richard Kerger, "Using Focus Groups for a Simulated Trial Process," *Quirk's Marketing Research Review* (April 1994), pp. 38–40; Frank Toboloski, "Package Design Requires Research," *Marketing News* (June 6, 1994), p. 4.
14. Adapted from "Test Marketing Is Valuable, But It's Often Abused," *Marketing News* (January 2, 1987), p. 40. Reprinted with permission from *Marketing News,* published by the American Marketing Association.

Chapter 9

1. Joseph Rydholm, "Readdressing the Ball," *Quirk's Marketing Research Review* (May 1997), pp. 10–11, 62, 64. Reprinted by permission of *Quirk's Marketing Research Review.*
2. F. N. Kerlinger, *Foundations of Behavioral Research,* 3rd ed. (New York: Holt, Rinehart and Winston, 1986), p. 403; *see also* Mel Crask and R. J. Fox, "An Exploration of the Internal Properties of Three Commonly Used Research Scales," *Journal of the Marketing Research Society* (October 1987), pp. 317–319.
3. The eight types of scores are excerpted from Claire Selltiz, Laurence Wrightsman, and Stuart Cook, *Research Methods in Social Relations,* 3rd ed. pp. 164–168, copyright © 1976 by Holt, Rinehart and Winston, adapted by permission of the publisher.
4. Martin Weinberger, "Seven Perspectives on Consumer Research," *Marketing Research* (December 1989), pp. 9–17. Reprinted with permission from *Marketing Research,* published by the American Marketing Association.
5. For an excellent discussion of the semantic differential, see Charles E. Osgood, George Suci, and Percy Tannenbaum, *The Measurement of Meaning* (Urbana: University of Illinois Press, 1957).
6. Osgood, Suci, and Tannenbaum, *The Measurement of Meaning,* pp. 140–153, 192, 193; and William D. Barclay, "The Semantic Differential as an Index of Brand Attitude," *Journal of Advertising Research* 4 (March 1964), pp. 30–33.
7. Theodore Clevenger, Jr., and Gilbert A. Lazier, "Measurement of Corporate Images by the Semantic Differential," *Journal of Marketing Research* 2 (February 1965), pp. 80–82.
8. Michael J. Etzel, et al. "The Comparability of Three Stapel Forms in a Marketing Setting," in Ronald F. Bush and Shelby D. Hunt, eds., *Marketing Theory: Philosophy of Science Perspectives* (Chicago: American Marketing Association, 1982), pp. 303–306.
9. Sabra Brock, "Marketing Research in Asia: Problems, Opportunities, and Lessons," *Marketing Research* (September 1989), pp. 44–51. Reprinted with permission from *Marketing Research,* published by the American Marketing Association.
10. *See* Terry Grapentine, "Dimensions of an Attribute," *Marketing Research* (Summer 1995), pp. 19–27.
11. M. V. Kalwani and A. J. Silk, "On the Reliability and Prediction Validity of Purchase Intention Measures," *Marketing Science* 1 (Summer 1982), pp. 243–287.
12. Glen Urban, John Hauser, and Nikhilesh Dholakia, *Essentials of New Product Management* (Englewood Cliffs, N.J.: Prentice Hall, 1987), p. 145; *see also* Tony Siciliano, "Purchase Intent: Separating Fact from Fiction," *Marketing Research* 21 (Spring 1993), p. 56.
13. M. M. Givon and Z. Shapira, "Response to Rating Scalings," *Journal of Marketing Research* (November 1984), pp. 410–419; and D. E. Stem, Jr. and S. Noazin, "The Effects of Number of Objects and Scale Positions on Graphic Position Scale Reliability," in R. F. Lusch et al., *1985 AMA Educators' Proceedings* (Chicago: American Marketing Association, 1985), pp. 370–372.
14. Joseph Duket, "Comment Cards and Rating Scales: Who Are We Fooling?" *Quirk's Marketing Research Review* (May 1997), pp. 30, 32. Reprinted by permission of *Quirk's Marketing Research Review.*

Chapter 10

1. Jennifer Lach, "Intelligence Agents—Upper Crust," *American Demographics* (March 1999), p. 58. Reprinted from American Demographics magazine, courtesy of Intertec Publishing Corp., Stamford Conn. All Rights Reserved
2. Andrew Bean and Michael Roezkowski, "The Long and Short of It," *Marketing Research* (Winter 1995), pp. 21–26.
3. Lewis Winters, "Innovations in Open-Ended Questions," *Marketing Research* (June 1991), pp. 69–70. Reprinted with permission from *Marketing Research,* published by the American Marketing Association.

4. Kevin Walters, "Designing Screening Questionnaires to Minimize Dishonest Answers," *Applied Marketing Research* (Spring/Summer 1991), pp. 51–53.
5. Joseph Marinelli and Anastasia Schleck, "Collecting, Processing Data for Marketing Research Worldwide," *Marketing News* (August 18, 1997), pp. 12, 14. Reprinted with permission from *Marketing News*, published by the American Marketing Association.
6. Pam Bruns, "Field Management: A Better Mousetrap," *Quirk's Marketing Research Review* (June/July 1992), pp. 36–39. Adapted by permission of *Quirk's Marketing Research Review*.
7. Steven Struhl and Chris Kuever, "High Tech Surveys Have Arrived," *Quirk's Marketing Research Review* (July 1998), pp. 16, 72–83. Adapted by permission of *Quirk's Marketing Research Review*.
8. Data about WebSurveyor are from http://www.WebSurveyor.com.
9. Internal company documents were supplied to the authors by The MARC Group, January 1999.
10. Documents supplied by The MARC Group, January 1999.

Chapter 11

1. For excellent discussions of sampling, see Seymour Sudman, *Applied Sampling* (New York: Academic Press, 1976); and L. J. Kish, *Survey Sampling* (New York: John Wiley and Sons, 1965).
2. For a discussion of the debate surrounding the 1990 census, see Eugene Carlson, "Backers of an Adjusted Census Won't Take No for an Answer" *The Wall Street Journal* (November 3, 1987), p. 35.
3. "George Gallup's Nation of Numbers," *Esquire* (December 1983), pp. 91–92. Reprinted by permission of *Esquire*.
4. J. A. Brunner and G. A. Brunner, "Are Voluntary Unlisted Telephone Subscribers Really Different?" *Journal of Marketing Research* 8 (February 1971), pp. 121–124; pp. 395–399.
5. G. J. Glasser and G. D. Metzger, "Random-Digit Dialing as a Method of Telephone Sampling," *Journal of Marketing Research* 9 (February 1972), pp. 59–64.
6. S. Roslow and L. Roslow, "Unlisted Phone Subscribers Are Different," *Journal of Advertising* 12 (August 1972), pp. 25–38.
7. Charles D. Cowan, "Using Multiple Sample Frames to Improve Survey Coverage, Quality, and Costs," *Marketing Research* (December 1991), pp. 66–69.
8. James McClove and P. George Benson, *Statistics for Business and Economics* (San Francisco: Dellen Publishing Co., 1988), pp. 184–185; and "Probability Sampling in the Real World," *CATI News* (Summer 1993), pp. 1, 4–6.
9. J. Jaeger, *Sampling in Education and the Social Sciences* (New York: Longman, 1984), pp. 28–35.
10. Newton Frank, *CASRO Journal* (January 1991), pp. 113–115.
11. Lewis C. Winters, "What's New in Telephone Sampling Technology? *Marketing Research* (March 1990), pp. 80–82; and "A Survey Researcher's Handbook of Industry Terminology and Definitions," *Survey Sampling, Inc.* (1992), pp. 3–20.
12. For discussions of related issues, *see* John E. Swan, Stephen J. O'Connor, and Seuug Doug Lee, "A Framework for Testing Sampling Bias and Methods of Bias Reduction in a Telephone Survey," *Marketing Research* (December 1991), pp. 23–34; and Charles D. Cowan, "Coverage Issues in Sample Surveys: A Component of Measurement Error," *Marketing Research* (June 1991), pp. 65–68.
13. For an excellent discussion of stratified sampling, see William G. Cochran, *Sampling Techniques*, 2d ed. (New York: John Wiley and Sons, 1963).
14. Sudman, *Applied Sampling*, pp. 110–121.
15. Sudman, *Applied Sampling*, pp. 110–112.
16. Earl R. Babbie, *The Practice of Social Research*, 2d. ed. (Belmont, Calif.: Wadsworth Publishing, 1979), p. 167.
17. L. J. Kish, *Survey Sampling* (New York: John Wiley and Sons, 1965).
18. "Convenience Sampling Outpacing Probability Sampling," *Survey Sampling, Inc.* (March 1994), p. 4. Excerpted by permission of *Survey Sampling, Inc.*
19. Leo A. Goodman, "Snowball Sampling," *Annals of Mathematical Statistics* 32 (1961), pp. 148–170.
20. Chuck Martin, *Net Future* (New York: McGraw-Hill Publishing, 1999), p. 16.
21. "Is a Web Political Poll Reliable? Yes? No? Maybe?," *The Wall Street Journal* (April 13, 1999), p. B4.
22. "Is a Web Political Poll Reliable? Yes? No? Maybe?"

Chapter 12

1. For excellent discussions of the various issues discussed in this chapter, see Seymour Sudman, *Applied Sampling* (New York: Academic Press, 1976); Morris Slonim, *Sampling in a Nutshell* (New York: Simon and Schuster, 1960); and Gerald Keller, Brian Warrach, and Henry Bartle, *Statistics for Management and Economics* (Belmont, Calif.: Wadsworth Publishing Co., 1990), p. 455.
2. Thomas T. Semon, "Save a Few Bucks on Sample Size, Risk Millions in Opportunity Loss," *Marketing News* (January 3, 1994), p. 19. Reprinted by permission of *Marketing News*, published by the American Marketing Association.
3. For discussions of these techniques, see Bill Williams, A *Sampler on Sampling* (New York: John Wiley and Sons, 1978), and Richard Jaeger, *Sampling in Education and the Social Sciences* (New York: Longmans, 1984).

4. David Anderson, Dennis Sweeney, and Thomas Williams, *Statistics for Business and Economics,* 4th ed. (Saint Paul: West Publishing, 1990), pp. 355–357.

Chapter 13

1. For recent trends, *see* Raymond Rand and Michael A. Fallig, "Automating the Coding Process with Neutral Networks," *Quirk's Marketing Research Review* (May 1993), pp. 14–16, 40–47; and Eric DeRosia, "Data Processing Made Easy," *Quirk's Marketing Research Review* (February 1993), pp. 18, 34.
2. Joseph Rydholm, "Scanning the Seas: Scannable Questionnaires Give Princess Cruises Accuracy and Quick Turnaround," *Quirk's Marketing Research Review* (May 1993), pp. 6–7, 26–27; and Norma Frendberg, "Scanning Questionnaires Efficiently," *Marketing Research* (Spring 1993), pp. 38–42.
3. For an excellent discussion on creating graphics presentations, see Gus Venditto, "Twelve Tips for Better Presentations," *PC Magazine* (January 28, 1992), pp. 253–260.
4. Michael Baumgardner and Ron Tatham, "Statistical Significance Testing May Hinder Proper Decision Making," *Quirk's Marketing Research Review* (May 1987), pp. 16–19; Hank Zucker, "What Is Significance?" *Quirk's Marketing Research Review* (March 1994), pp. 12, 14; Gordon A. Wyner, "How High Is Up?" *Marketing Research* (Winter 1993), pp. 43–45; Patrick M. Baldasare and Vikas Mittel, "The Use, Misuse, and Abuse of Significance," *Quirk's Marketing Research Review* (November 1994), pp. 16, 32.
5. W. G. Cochran, "The χ^2 Test of Goodness of Fit," *Annals of Mathematical Statistics* 23 (1952), pp. 315–345; Tony Babinee, "How to Think About Your Tables," *Quirk's Marketing Research Review* (January 1991), pp. 10–12. For another discussion of these issues, *see* Gopal K. Kanji, 100 *Statistical Tests* (London: Sage Publications, 1993), p. 75.
6. Gary M. Mullet, "Correctly Estimating the Variances of Proportions," *Marketing Research* (June 1991), pp. 47–51.

Chapter 14

1. Robert Pindyck and Daniel Rubinfield, *Econometric Models and Economic Forecasts,* 2d ed. (New York: McGraw-Hill, 1981), pp. 273–312; Doug Grisaffe, "Appropriate Use of Regression in Customer Satisfaction Analyses: A Response to William McLauchlan," *Quirk's Marketing Research Review* (February 1993), pp. 10–17; Terry Clark; "Managing Outliers: Qualitative Issues in the Handling of Extreme Observations in Marketing Research," *Marketing Research* (June 1989), pp. 31–45.
2. Mark Peterson, "The Motivation-Emotion-Matching (MEM) Model of Television Advertising Effects." Dissertation written at Georgia Institute of Technology, 1994. Excerpted by permission of the author.

Chapter 15

1. Anil Menon, "Are We Squandering Our Intellectual Capital?" *Marketing Research* (Summer 1994), pp. 18–22. Excerpted with permission from *Marketing Research,* published by the American Marketing Association.
2. Christine Moorman, Rohit Deshpande, and Gerald Zaltman, "Factors Affecting Trust in Market Research Relationships," *Journal of Marketing* 57 (January 1993), pp. 81–101.
3. Moorman, "Factors Affecting Trust in Market Research Relationships."
4. Jeannine Bergers Everett, "The Missing Link," *Marketing Research* (Spring 1997), pp. 33–36. Reprinted with permission from *Marketing Research,* published by the American Marketing Association.
5. Richard Kitaeff, "How Am I Doing?" *Marketing Research* (June 1992), pp. 38–39.

GLOSSARY

A

Ad hoc mail surveys Questionnaires for a particular project sent to selected names and addresses with no prior contact by the researcher.

After-only with control group design True experimental design that involves random assignment of subjects or test units to experimental and control groups, but no premeasurement of the dependent variable.

Allowable sampling error The amount of sampling error a researcher is willing to accept.

Applied research Research aimed at solving a specific pragmatic problem—a better understanding of the marketplace, a determination of why a strategy or tactic failed, a reduction of uncertainty in management decision making.

Appropriate time order of occurrence To be considered a likely cause of a dependent variable, a change in an independent variable must occur before a change is observed in the dependent variable.

Audits The examination and verification of the sale of a product.

Balanced scale A scale with the same number of positive and negative categories.

Basic or pure research Research aimed at expanding the frontiers of knowledge rather than solving a specific pragmatic problem.

Before and after with control group design A true experimental design that includes the random assignment of subjects or test units to experimental and control groups and the premeasurement of both groups.

BehaviorScan A scanner-based research system that maintains a panel of approximately 3,000 households to record consumer purchases based on manipulation of the marketing mix.

Bivariate regression analysis An analysis of the strength of the linear relationship between two variables when one is considered the independent variable and the other the dependent variable.

Bivariate techniques Statistical methods of determining the relationship between two variables.

Call record sheets Interviewers' logs listing the number and results of a contact.

Cannibalization rate The extent to which a new product takes business away from a company's existing products.

Cartoon tests Tests in which respondents fill in the dialogue of one character in a cartoon.

Causal research Research designed to determine whether a change in one variable most likely caused an observed change in another.

Causal studies These studies examine whether one variable causes or determines the value of another variable.

Census Data obtained from or about every member of the population of interest.

Central limit theorem A distribution of a large number of sample means or sample proportions that approximate a normal distribution, regardless of the actual distribution of the population from which they were drawn.

Central-location telephone interviews Interviews conducted by calls to respondents from a centrally located marketing research facility.

Chi-square test Test of the goodness of fit between the observed distribution and the expected distribution of a variable.

Closed-ended questions Questions that ask respondents to choose between two or more answers.

Cluster sample A probability sample drawn from a sample of geographic areas.

Coding The process of grouping and assigning numeric codes to the various responses to a question.

Coefficient of determination (R^2) The percentage of the total variation in the dependent variable explained by the independent variable.

Comparative scale A scale that compares another object, concept, or person; rank-order scales are comparative.

Computer-assisted telephone interviews (CATI) Central-location telephone interviews in which interviewers enter answers directly into a computer.

Conclusions Generalizations that answer the questions raised by the research objectives or that otherwise satisfy the objectives.

Concomitant variation The degree to which a presumed cause and presumed effect occur or vary together.

Concurrent validity The degree to which a variable, measured at the same point in time as the variable of interest, can be predicted by the measurement instrument.

Confidence level The probability that a particular confidence interval will include the true population value.

Constant sum scale A scale on which a set number of points is distributed among two or more attributes.

Construct validity The degree to which a measurement instrument represents and logically connects observed phenomena to a construct via an underlying theory.

Consumer drawings Respondents draw what they are feeling or how they perceive an object.

Consumer orientation Identifying and focusing on the people or firms most likely to buy a product and producing a good or service that will meet their needs more effectively.

Contamination The inclusion in a test of a group of respondents who are not normally there; for example, outside buyers who see an advertisement intended only for those in the test area and enter the area to purchase the product being tested.

Content analysis A technique used to analyze written material (usually advertising copy) by breaking it into meaningful units using carefully applied rules.

Content validity The degree to which the instrument items represent the universe of the concept under study.

Convenience sample A nonprobability sample used primarily because data are easy to collect.

Convergent validity A high degree of correlation among different measurement instruments that purport to measure the same concept.

Cookie A text file placed on a user's computer in order to identify the user when he or she revisits the website.

Correlation analysis Analysis of the degree to which changes in one variable are associated with changes in another.

Criterion-related validity The degree to which a measurement instrument can predict a variable that is designated as a criterion.

Cross-tabulation Examination of the responses to one question relative to responses to one or more other questions.

Custom, or ad hoc, marketing research firms Research companies that carry out customized marketing research to address specific projects for corporate clients.

Data mining The use of statistical and other advanced software to discover nonobvious patterns hidden in a database.

Decision support system (DSS) An interactive, personalized mapping information system, designed to be initiated and controlled by individual decision makers.

Degrees of freedom The number of observations in a statistical problem that are not restricted or are free to vary.

Dependent variable A symbol or concept that is expected to be explained or caused by the independent variable.

Depth interviews One-on-one interviews that probe and elicit detailed answers to questions, often using nondirective techniques to uncover hidden motivations.

Descriptive function Gathering and presenting statements of fact.

Descriptive studies Studies that answer the questions who, what, when, where, and how.

Design control Use of an experimental design to control extraneous causal factors.

Diagnostic function Explaining data or actions.

Dichotomous questions Questions that ask respondents to choose between two answers.

Discriminant validity A low degree of correlation among constructs that are supposed to be different.

Discussion guide A written outline of topics to cover during a focus group discussion.

Disguised observation The process of monitoring people who do not know they are being watched.

Disproportional or optimal allocation A sampling in which the number of elements taken from a given stratum is proportional to the relative size of the stratum and the standard deviation of the characteristic under consideration.

Door-to-door interviews Interviews conducted face-to-face with consumers in their homes.

Editing The process of checking for interviewer mistakes.

Electroencephalogram (EEG) A machine that measures rhythmic fluctuations in the electrical potential of the brain.

Equivalent form reliability The ability to produce similar results using two instruments as similar as possible to measure the same thing.

Error sum of squares (SSE) The variation not explained by the regression.

Error-checking routines Computer programs that accept instructions from the user to check for logical errors in the data.

Evaluative research Research to determine the effectiveness and efficiency of specific programs.

Executive interviews The industrial equivalent of door-to-door interviewing.

Executive summary The portion of a research report that explains why the research was done, what was found and what those findings mean, and what action, if any, management should undertake.

Experiment A research approach where one variable is manipulated and the effect on another variable is observed.

Experimental design A test in which the researcher has control over one or more independent variables and manipulates them.

Experimental effect The effect of the treatment variable(s) on the dependent variable.

Exploratory research Preliminary research to clarify the exact nature of the problem to be solved.

External validity The extent to which the causal relationships measured in an experiment can be generalized to outside people, settings, and times.

Face validity A measurement that seems to measure what it is supposed to measure.

Field experiments Tests conducted outside the laboratory in an actual market environment.

Field management companies Firms that provide support services such as formatting questionnaires, writing screeners, and collecting data to full-service research companies.

Field service firms Companies that only collect survey data for corporate clients or research firms.

Finite population correction factor (FPC) An adjustment to the required sample size that is made in those cases in which the sample is expected to be equal to 5 percent or more of the total population.

Focus group A group of 8 to 12 participants who are led by a moderator in an in-depth discussion on one particular topic or concept.

Focus group facility A facility consisting of a conference-room or living-room setting and a separate observation room. The facility also has audiovisual recording equipment.

Focus group moderator The person hired by the client to lead the focus group. This person may need a background in psychology or sociology or, at least, marketing.

Frame error Error resulting from an inaccurate or incomplete sample frame.

Galvanic skin response (GSR) The measurement of changes in the electric resistance of the skin associated with activation responses.

Geographic information system (GIS) Computer-based system that takes secondary or primary data to generate maps that visually display answers to research questions.

Goal orientation Focusing on the accomplishment of corporate goals with a limit set on consumer orientation.

Graphic rating scale A scale showing a graphic continuum that is typically anchored by two extremes.

Group dynamics The interaction among people in a group.

History Things that happen or outside variables that change between the beginning and end of an experiment.

Humanistic inquiry A research method in which the researcher is immersed in the system or group under study.

Hypothesis A conjectural statement about a relationship between two or more variables that can be tested with empirical data.

Hypothesis test of proportions Test to determine whether the difference between proportions is greater than would be expected because of sampling error.

Incidence rate Percentage of people or households in the general population that fit the qualifications to be sampled.

Independent samples Samples in which the measurement of a variable in one population has no effect on the measurement of the variable in the other.

Independent variable A symbol or concept over which the researcher has some control or can manipulate to some extent and that is hypothesized to cause or influence the dependent variable.

Indirect observation Making a record of past behavior.

InfoScan A scanner-based tracking service for consumer packaged goods.

Instrument variation Differences or changes in measurement instruments (such as interviewers or observers) that explain differences in measurements.

Intelligent data entry The logical checking of information being entered into a data-entry device by that machine or one connected to it.

Internal consistency reliability Ability to produce similar results using different samples to measure a phenomenon during the same time period.

Internal database A database developed from data within an organization.

Internal validity The extent to which competing explanations for experimental results can be avoided.

Interrupted time-series design Research in which the treatment "interrupts" ongoing repeated measurements.

Interval estimate Inference regarding the likelihood that a population value will fall within a certain range.

Interval scale An ordinal scale with equal intervals between points to show relative amounts, which may include an arbitrary zero point.

Interviewer error or bias Error that results from the interviewer consciously or unconsciously influencing the respondent.

Interviewer's instructions Written directions to the interviewer on how to conduct an interview.

Itemized rating scale A scale showing a limited number of ordered categories.

Judgment sample A nonprobability sample in which the selection criteria are based on personal judgment that the element is representative of the population under study.

Laboratory experiments Experiments conducted in a controlled setting.

Likert scale A scale that shows a series of attitudes toward an object, which are given numerical values ranging from favorable to unfavorable.

Longitudinal study Study in which the same respondents are resampled over time.

Machine cleaning of data A final computerized error check of data.

Mail panels Precontacted and screened participants who are periodically sent questionnaires.

Mall-intercept interviews Interviews conducted in public areas of malls by intercepting shoppers and interviewing them face to face.

Management decision problem The managerial action required to solve a marketing research problem.

Marginal report A computer-generated table of the frequencies of the responses to each question to monitor entry of valid codes and correct use of skip patterns.

Marketing The process of planning and executing the conception, pricing, promotion, and distribution of ideas, goods, and services to create exchanges that satisfy individual and organizational objectives.

Marketing concept A business philosophy based on consumer orientation, goal orientation, and systems orientation.

Marketing mix The unique blend of product/service, pricing, promotion, offerings, and distribution designed to meet the needs of a specific group of consumers.

Marketing research The planning, collection, and analysis of data relevant to marketing decision making and the communication of the results of this analysis to management.

Marketing research objective The specific information needed to solve a marketing research problem.

Marketing research problem A statement of the specific information needed by a decision maker to help solve a management decision problem.

Marketing strategy Guiding the long-term use of a firm's resources based on its existing and projected capabilities and on projected changes in the external environment.

Maturation Changes in subjects that take place during an experiment that are not related to the experiment but may affect their responses to the experimental factor.

Mean The sum of the values for all observations of a variable divided by the number of observations.

Measurement error Error that results from a variation between the information being sought and what is actually obtained by the measurement process.

Measurement instrument bias Error that results from the design of the questionnaire or measurement instrument.

Measurement The process of assigning numbers or labels to people or things in accordance with specific rules to represent quantities or qualities of attributes.

Median The observation below which 50 percent of the observations fall.

Methodological log A journal of detailed and time-sequenced notes on the investigative techniques used during a humanistic inquiry, with special attention to biases or distortions a given technique may have introduced.

Mode The value that occurs most frequently.

Mortality Loss of test units or subjects during the course of an experiment. The problem is that those who leave may be systematically different from those who stay.

Multidimensional scale A scale that measures more than one attribute.

Multiple time-series design An interrupted time-series design with a control group.

Multiple-choice questions Questions that ask respondents to choose among a list of more than two answers.

Mystery shoppers People employed to pose as consumers and shop at an employer's competitors or their own stores to compare prices, displays, and the like.

Neural network A computer program that mimics the processes of the human brain that are capable of learning from examples to find patterns in data.

Newsgroups Internet sites devoted to a specific topic where people can read and post messages.

Nominal scale A scale that partitions data into mutually exclusive and collectively exhaustive categories.

Nonbalanced scale A scale with an uneven number of positive and negative categories.

Noncomparative scale A scale that does not compare objects, concepts, or person, such as graphic rating and itemized rating scales.

Nonprobability sample A sample that includes elements from the population that are selected in a nonrandom manner.

Nonresponse bias Error that results from a systematic difference between those who do and do not respond to a measurement instrument.

Normal distribution A continuous distribution that is bell-shaped and symmetrical about the mean—mean, median, and mode being equal. Sixty-eight percent of the observations fall within plus or minus one standard deviation of the mean, approximately 95 percent fall within plus or minus two standard deviations, and approximately 99.5 percent fall within plus or minus three standard deviations.

Observation research Descriptive research that monitors respondents' actions without direct interaction.

One-group pretest/posttest design A preexperimental design with pre- and postmeasurements but no control group.

One-shot case study design A preexperimental design with no control group and an after-measurement only.

One-way frequency table A table showing the number of responses to each answer of a survey question.

One-way mirror observation The practice of watching unseen from behind a one-way mirror.

Open observation The process of monitoring people who know they are being watched.

Open-ended questions Questions that ask respondents to reply in their own words.

Optical scanner A data-processing device that can "read" responses on questionnaires.

Ordinal scale A nominal scale that can order data.

***p*-value** The exact probability of getting a computed test statistic that was largely due to chance. The smaller the *p*-value, the smaller the probability that the observed result occurred by chance.

Paired comparison scale A scale showing a series of only two objects as choices.

Pearson's product moment A correlation analysis technique for use with metric data.

People meter A microwave computerized rating system that transmits demographic information overnight to measure national TV audiences.

People Reader A machine that simultaneously records the respondent's reading material and eye reactions.

Photo sorts Respondents sort photos of different types of people, identifying those photos they feel would use the specified product or service.

Physical control Holding the value or level of extraneous variables constant throughout the course of an experiment.

Point estimate Inference regarding the sampling error associated with a particular estimate of a population value.

Population distribution A frequency distribution of all the elements of a population.

Population or universe The total group of people from whom information is needed.

Population parameter A value that defines a true characteristic of a total population.

Population specification error Error that results from incorrectly defining the population or universe from which a sample is chosen.

Population standard deviation The standard deviation of a variable for an entire population.

Predictive function Specifying how to use descriptive and diagnostic research to predict the results of a planned marketing decision.

Predictive validity The degree to which the future level of a criterion can be forecast by a current measurement scale.

Preexperimental design A design that offers little or no control over extraneous factors.

Presentation software Personal computer software that provides easy-to-use platforms for creating effective reports and presentations.

Pretest A trial run of a questionnaire.

Primary data New data gathered to help solve the problem at hand.

Probability sample A sample in which every element of the population has a known, nonzero probability of selection.

Processing error Error that results from the incorrect transfer of information from a document to the computer.

Programmatic research Research done to develop marketing options through market segmentation, market opportunity analysis, or consumer attitude and product usage studies.

Projective techniques Ways of tapping respondents' deepest feelings by having them "project" those feelings into an unstructured situation.

Proportional allocation A sampling in which the number of elements selected from a stratum is directly proportional to the size of the stratum relative to the population.

Pupilometer A machine that measures changes in pupil dilation.

Purchase intent scale A scale that rates the purchase intentions of consumers.

Push polling A style of research gathering in which zealous political supporters deride one candidate to lead voters to support the other candidate.

Q-sorting Distributing a set of objects into piles according to specified rating categories.

Qualitative research Research data not subject to quantification or quantitative analysis.

Quantitative research Studies that use mathematical analysis.

Quasi-experimental design A study in which the researcher lacks complete control over the scheduling of the treatment or must assign respondents to treatment in a nonrandom manner.

Questionnaire A set of questions designed to generate the data necessary for accomplishing the objectives of the research project.

Quota sample A nonprobability sample in which a population subgroup is classified on the basis of researcher judgment.

Random error Error that affects measurement in a transient, inconsistent manner.

Random error or random sampling error Error that results from chance variation.

Random-digit dialing Method of generating lists of telephone numbers at random.

Randomization The random assignment of group subjects to treatment conditions to ensure equal representation of characteristics in all groups.

Range The maximum value for a variable minus the minimum value for that variable.

Rank-order scale A scale that ranks an object, concept, or person in a certain order.

Rapid Analysis Measurement System (RAMS) A machine that allows respondents to record how they are feeling by turning a dial.

Ratio scale An interval scale with a meaningful zero point so that magnitudes can be compared arithmetically.

Recommendations Conclusions applied to marketing strategies or tactics that focus on a client's achievement of differential advantage.

Recruited Internet sample A controlled survey set up on the Internet that is used for target populations.

Regression to the mean The tendency for people's behavior to move toward the average for that behavior during the course of an experiment.

Related samples Samples in which the measurement of a variable in one population may influence the measurement of the variable in the other.

Reliability Measures that are consistent from one administration to the next.

Research design The plan to be followed to answer the marketing research objectives; the structure or framework to solve a specific problem.

Research request A document that describes a potential research project, its benefits to the organization, and estimated costs. In many organizations, a project cannot begin until the research request has been formally approved.

Response bias Error that results from the tendency of people to answer a question incorrectly, through deliberate misrepresentation or unconscious falsification.

Return on quality A management objective based on the principles that the quality being delivered is the quality desired by the target market and that quality must have a positive impact on profitability.

Rule A guide, a method, or a command that tells a researcher what to do.

Sample A subset of the population of interest.

Sample distribution A frequency distribution of all the elements of an individual sample.

Sampling distribution of the proportion A frequency distribution of the proportions of many samples drawn from a particular population which has a normal distribution.

Sampling distribution of the sample mean A frequency distribution of the means of many samples drawn from a particular population, which has a normal distribution.

Sampling error The difference between the sample value and the true value of the population mean.

Sampling frame List of population elements from which to select units to be sampled.

Scale A set of symbols or numbers so constructed that they can be assigned by a rule to individuals or their behaviors or attitudes.

Scaled-response questions Multiple-choice questions in which the choices are designed to capture the intensity of respondents' answers.

Scaling Procedures for attempting to determine quantitative measures for subjective or abstract concepts.

Scanners Devices that read the UPC codes on products and produce instantaneous information on sales.

Screened Internet sample A survey set up on the Internet that restricts respondents by imposing quotas based on some desired sample characteristics.

Screeners Questions used to screen for appropriate respondents.

Secondary data Data that have previously been gathered.

Selection bias Systematic differences between the test group and the control group due to a biased selection process.

Selection error Error that results from following incomplete or improper sampling procedures or not following proper ones.

Selective research Research to choose among several viable alternatives identified by programmatic research.

Self-administered questionnaires Questionnaires filled out by respondents with no interviewer present.

Semantic differential scale A scale that rates opposite pairs of words or phrases on a continuum, which are then plotted as a profile or image.

Sentence and story completion tests Tests in which respondents complete sentences or stories in their own words.

Shopper behavior research A study involving observing, either in person or on videotape, shoppers or consumers in a variety of shopping settings.

Shopper patterns Drawings that record the footsteps of a shopper through a store.

Simple random sample A probability sampling in which the sample is selected in such a way that every element of the population has a known and equal probability of inclusion in the sample.

Simulated test market (STM) or pretest market As an alternative to traditional test market, survey data and mathematical models are used to simulate test market results for a much lower cost.

Skip pattern Requirement to pass over certain questions if a respondent gives a particular answer to a previous question.

Snowball sample A nonprobability sample in which the selection of additional respondents is based on referrals from the initial respondents.

Solomon four-group design Research using two experimental groups and two control groups to control for all extraneous variable threats.

Spearman rank-order correlation Correlation analysis technique for use with ordinal data.

Split-half technique A method of assessing the reliability of a scale by dividing into two the total set of measurement items and correlating the results.

Spurious association A relationship between a presumed cause and a presumed effect that occurs as a result of an unexamined variable or set of variables.

SSL (secure socket layer) technology A computer encryption system that secures sensitive information.

Stability Lack of change in results from test to retest.

Standard deviation A measure of dispersion calculated by subtracting the mean of a series from each value in a series, squaring each result, summing them, dividing the sum by the number of items minus 1, and taking the square root of this value.

Standard error of the mean The standard deviation of a distribution of sample means.

Standard normal distribution A normal distribution with a mean of zero and a standard deviation of one.

Stapel scale A scale that provides a single description in the center, which is usually measured by plus or minus 5 points.

Static-group comparison design A preexperimental design that utilizes an experimental and a control group. However, subjects or test units are not randomly assigned to the two groups and no premeasurements are taken.

Statistical control Adjusting for the effects of confounding variables by statistically adjusting the value of the dependent variable for each treatment condition.

Statistical power The probability of not making a Type II error.

Story telling Respondents tell stories to describe their experiences.

Strategic partnering Two or more marketing research firms with unique skills and resources form an alliance to offer a new service for clients, provide strategic support for each firm, or in some other manner create mutual benefits.

Stratified sample A probability sample that selects elements from relevant population subsets to be more representative of an entire population.

Structured observation A study in which the observer fills out a questionnairelike form or counts the number of times an activity occurs.

Sum of squares due to regression (SSR) The variation explained by the regression.

Supervisor's instructions Written directions to the field service on how to conduct a survey.

Surrogate information error Error that results from a discrepancy between the information needed to solve a problem and that sought by the researcher.

Survey or information objectives The decision-making information sought through the questionnaire.

Survey research Research in which an interviewer interacts with respondents to obtain facts, opinions, and attitudes.

Syndicated service research firms Companies that collect, package, and sell the same general market research data to many firms.

Systematic error Error that results in a constant bias in the measurements.

Systematic error or bias Error that results from research design or execution.

Systematic sample A probability sampling in which the entire population is numbered, and elements are drawn using a skip interval.

Systems orientation Creating systems to monitor the external environment and deliver the marketing mix to the target market.

Temporal sequence Appropriate causal order of events.

Test market Testing a new product or some element of the marketing mix using experimental or quasi-experimental designs.

Test-retest reliability The ability of the same instrument to produce consistent results when used a second time under conditions as nearly the same as possible.

Testing effect An effect that is a by-product of the research process and not the experimental variable.

Theory-construction diary A journal that documents in detail the thoughts, premises, hypotheses, and revisions in thinking of a humanistic researcher.

Third-person technique Way of learning respondents' feelings by asking them to answer for a third party, such as "your neighbor" or "most people."

Traffic counters Machines used to measure vehicular flow over a particular stretch of roadway.

Treatment The independent variable that is manipulated in an experiment.

True experimental design Research using an experimental group and a control group, with randomized assignment of test units to both groups.

Unidimensional scale A scale that measures only one attribute.

Unrestricted internet sample A survey set up on the Internet and accessible to anyone who desires to complete it.

Unstructured observation A study in which the observer simply makes notes on the behavior being observed.

Validation The process of ascertaining that interviews actually were conducted as specified.

Validity Whether what we tried to measure was actually measured.

Variable A symbol or concept that can assume any one of a set of values.

Variance The sums of the squared deviations from the mean divided by the number of observations minus 1.

Voice pitch analysis The study of changes in the relative vibration frequency of the human voice to measure emotion.

Word association tests Tests in which the interviewer says a word and respondents must mention the first thing that comes to mind.

INDEX

D

E

N

Q

R

S